For

CHANGING
CHINA

Mason

May, 1977

J. Mason Gentzler has taught at Columbia and Duke Universities and at Sarah Lawrence College, where he is currently professor of Far Eastern Studies. He received his Ph.D. degree from Columbia in 1966. He is author of *A Syllabus of Chinese Civilization* (Second edition, 1972) and of the chapters on modern China in *The Columbia History of the World* (1972).

CHANGING CHINA

Readings in the History of China from the Opium War to the Present

Edited by
J. Mason Gentzler
Sarah Lawrence College

Praeger Publishers
New York

COPYRIGHT ACKNOWLEDGMENTS

From Nora Waln, *The House of Exile* (Boston: Little, Brown and Company, 1933), pp. 25–28. Copyright 1933 by Nora Waln. Reprinted by permission of the publisher.
From Wm. T. de Bary, et al., eds., *Sources of Chinese Tradition* (New York: Columbia University Press, 1960), pp. 733–35, 744–49, 750–53, 815–18. Reprinted by permission of the publisher.
From James Bertram, *Unconquered* (New York: The John Day Company, 1939), pp. 138–39, Copyright 1939 by James Bertram. Reprinted by permission of Thomas Y. Crowell Company, Inc.
From Li Chien-nung, *The Political History of China*, ed. and trans. by Ssu-yü Teng and Jeremy Ingalls (New York: Van Nostrand Reinhold Company, 1956). Reprinted by permission of the author and publisher.
From Ssu-yü Teng and John K. Fairbank, ed., *China's Response to the West* (Cambridge, Mass.: Harvard University Press, 1954). Copyright 1954 by the President and Fellows of Harvard College. Reprinted by permission of the Harvard University Press.
From Franz Michael, ed., *The Taiping Rebellion,* Vol. 2 (Seattle: University of Washington Press, 1971), pp. 144–49, 312–20, 370–73, 376–77, 388–89, 389–90, 390–91. Reprinted by permission of the publisher.

Published in the United States of America in 1977
by Praeger Publishers,
200 Park Avenue, New York, N. Y. 10017

© 1977 by Praeger Publishers
A Division of Holt, Rinehart and Winston

Library of Congress Cataloging in Publication Data
Main entry under title:

Changing China.

Bibliography: p. 403
1. China—History—19th century—Addresses, essays, lectures. 2. China—History—1900-   —Addresses, essays, lectures. I. Gentzler, J. Mason.
DS757.5.c464   951   76-48175
ISBN 0-275-33880-0
ISBN 0-275-64890-7 pbk.

Printed in the United States of America

789 074 987654321

Preface

This reader focuses on the changes that have taken place in China since the Opium War. Attention has been given to forces both conducive to and impeding change, and to influences both Chinese and foreign on the changes that have occurred. Particular attention has been given to the perspectives of Chinese writers and statesmen on change and continuity in Chinese society and the problems each created, in the belief that the Chinese definitions of national problems influenced the course of that change.

Some alterations have been made in the romanization of Chinese names in nineteenth-century European and American works to make them conform to the Wade-Giles system, and some minor changes have been made in the translations used in Part III for the sake of consistency. In the few cases in which more substantive changes have been made, the original texts have been consulted.

I would like to express my appreciation to the staffs of the East Asian Library of Columbia University, the centre for Asian Studies of the University of Hong Kong, and the Universities Service Centre, Hong Kong, and to Mr. Richard Sorich, for all the assistance they have given me in locating and copying materials. I would also like to thank all those who helped me to formulate my ideas and to improve my translations, especially Professor Hiroshi Yokoyama of Osaka Woman's University, and above all my wife, Bernadette, without whose encouragement and cheerful assistance this work would never have been completed. Any errors that remain are entirely due to my own stubbornness and ignorance.

—J. M. G.

Contents

Preface   v

Introduction   1

PART I   DISINTEGRATION   15

Chapter One   The Opening of China   21

    1. *Two Edicts from the Ch'ien-Lung Emperor to King George III of England 23*

    2. *The Treaty of Nanking, between England and China 29*

    3. *Important Additional Privileges Granted to Foreigners in Subsequent Treaties 32*

    4. *Chinese Attitudes toward Foreigners 33*

    5. *Lin Tse-Hsü's Recognition of Western Military Superiority 35*

    6. *Rutherford Alcock on the Untenability of China's Traditional Policies toward Foreign Nations 35*

    7. *The Position of the British Government on British Aims and Chinese Rights 36*

    8. *Bowring's Argument for the Necessity of Using Force to Overcome Chinese Resistance to Foreign Aims 41*

Chapter Two   The Taiping Rebellion   43

    9. *An Anti-Manchu Proclamation 46*

    10. *The Taiping Version of Their Historical Roots and Mission 49*

11. The Taiping Plan for Reorganizing Chinese Society 54
12. The Persistence of Traditional Values, and Other Problems 60
13. Christianity and Confucianism in Taiping Ideology 62
14. Tseng Kuo-Fan's Ideological Counterattack 65

Chapter Three   The Self-Strengthening Movement   68

15. The Practical Benefits of Western Knowledge 70
16. Practical Self-Strengthening 71
17. The Need for Foreign Language Training 74
18. The Need to Learn Manufacturing 75
19. The Need to Send Students Abroad to Study 75
20. The Inevitability of Change 76

Chapter Four   Radical Reform   80

21. The Social Sources of National Power 84
22. Institutional Reform from Above 86
23. The Vested Interests of the Opponents of Reform 87
24. The Examination System as an Obstruction to Reform 88
25. Modern Bureaucracy and National Strength 90
26. Some Reasons for the Absence of Loyalty to Ruler and Nation in China 91
27. A Conservative Objection to Parliamentary Government 92
28. The Incompatibility of Western Democracy and Chinese Customs 93
29. The Immorality of Inequality 94
30. The Proper Role of Women in National Life 97
31. Moderate Reform within a Traditional Context 100

Chapter Five   Chinese Society in the Late Ch'ing   104

32. The Exalted Status of Officials 106
33. Status and Work 108
34. Corruption as a Way of Life 108
35. Corruption as an Impediment to the Development of Modern Enterprise 113
36. Indifference of the Common People toward National Affairs 114
37. A Foreign Commentary on the Absence of Nationalism in China 115
38. The Self-Perpetuating Inefficiency of Poverty 115

39. *Family and Individual* 117
40. *The Primacy of Family and Other Personal Ties over Economic Efficiency* 120
41. *The Status of Women* 121
42. *The Formalism of Social Roles* 123

Chapter Six   Toward Revolution   125

43. *Commitment to Revolution* 129
44. *Provincial Revolution as a Catalyst* 130
45. *Revolutionary Nationalism and Republicanism* 132
46. *Sun Yat-Sen's Early Revolutionary Program* 134
47. *Literacy and Nationalism* 137
48. *Moral Values and National Strength* 138
49. *The Influence of Fiction on Social Values and National Strength* 142

PART II   DISUNION   145

Chapter Seven   Warlord China   151

50. *Portrait of a Warlord* 152
51. *Soldiers and Civilians in Rural China* 155
52. *Life as a Soldier* 157
53. *Bandits, Soldiers, and Society* 159
54. *Changing Customs among the Westernized Elite in Shanghai, circa 1916* 160
55. *Working Conditions in Shanghai Factories, circa 1916* 162

Chapter Eight   The New Culture Movement   164

56. *New Ethics for a New China* 168
57. *The Incompatibility of Confucianism and the Values of Modern Society* 172
58. *The High Ideals and High Hopes of the Early New Culture Movement* 175
59. *The Pragmatic Approach to Defining and Solving China's Problems* 177
60. *Traditional Educational Methods* 180
61. *The Limits of Freedom* 182
62. *Educational Priorities* 183
63. *The Political Significance of May Fourth* 185
64. *Lu Hsün Explains How He Became a Writer* 185
65. *The Self in a World in Transition* 187

66. *One Kind of Western Education* 189
67. *Leaving Home* 190

Chapter Nine   Change and Tradition under the Kuomintang 193

68. *The Kuomintang National Revolution* 196
69. *The Conflict between New Principles of Organization and Old Patterns of Behavior* 202
70. *Ideology as the Foundation of Party Unity* 204
71. *Problems of Local Government* 205
72. *Problems of Industrializing* 208
73. *Chinese Social Structure and Its Values* 210

Chapter Ten   The Rise of the Communist Party 215

74. *The Peasants as a Revolutionary Force* 217
75. *Maintaining Party Ideals* 223
76. *The Red Army Code of Discipline* 229
77. *The Red Army and the People* 230
78. *A Communist Art and Literature* 230

PART III   TRANSFORMATION 235

Chapter Eleven   The Political Context 240

79. *Ground Rules for the New China* 242
80. *Resolving Conflicts* 247
81. *Freedom and Authority* 256
82. *Party Problems and Party Ideals* 260

Chapter Twelve   Social Revolution 264

83. *Equal Rights in the Family* 268
84. *Land Reform* 272
85. *A Village Revolution* 274
86. *The Benefits of Cooperative Agriculture* 277
87. *The Role of Political Leadership* 283
88. *Problems in the Cooperatives* 284
89. *Communes and Communism* 288
90. *Revolutionizing Wages and Production* 290
91. *New Ways of Supplying Goods and Services* 291
92. *Communal Mess Halls* 293
93. *Equality through Homogeneity* 294
94. *A Mass Campaign* 296
95. *Theory of the Mass Campaign* 300

Chapter Thirteen   Adjustments   303

96. Realism and Results 306
97. The Benefits of Mutual Cooperation 310
98. Profit and Production 313
99. Two Kinds of Cooperation 315
100. Harmony or Struggle? 317
101. A Model Youth 318
102. Cadre Corruption 320
103. The Meaning of Happiness 321
104. Selections on Red and Expert 326
105. The Meaning of Work 330
106. Roles for Women 332

Chapter Fourteen   The Cultural Revolution   334

107. Public and Private in Socialist Society 337
108. Breaking down the Division of Labor 340
109. New Schooling for a New Society 341
110. The Program for the Cultural Revolution 343
111. Red Guards Attack the "Four Olds" 351
112. Revolutionaries Seize Power 352
113. The Revolutionary Committees 354
114. The Two Lines 357
115. Re-educating Cadres 360
116. Reforms in Rural Education 362
117. The Reliability of the Masses 364
118. The Creative Spirit of the Masses 366
119. Two Kinds of Motivation 367

Chapter Fifteen   Reconstruction and Discord   369

120. Rebuilding the Party 371
121. Material Incentives or Rewards for Labor? 374
122. The New Literature 375
123. Revolutionizing Higher Education 379
124. Higher Education and the Needs of Society 382
125. Two Definitions of the Problems of Chinese Society 385
126. Outline for a New Future 387

Sources   397
Selected Bibliography   403

Introduction

A century ago, China was viewed by most Westerners as a perplexing, decaying hulk of what once had been a great civilization; still quaint in its own way, perhaps, but out of touch with the times, a hopeless case whose eventual demise was all but certain, no matter how long its leaders might stubbornly persist in their misguided attempts to preserve their antiquated ways. Today, the image is dramatically reversed. For many people, in the developing nations as well as in industrially more advanced countries, China is a model of the future—intensely purposeful, dynamic, inventive, a vigorous and youthful nation that somehow has avoided, or solved, many of the problems plaguing other countries.

The contrast can easily be overdrawn. Yet no one would deny that immense changes have taken place in China since the Western impact began in the midnineteenth century. Change is inevitably the underlying theme of any history of modern China, and it is the theme of this book. First destructive change—the disintegration of the proud and ancient civilization of imperial China. Then constructive change—the numerous attempts to create a new and modern China in its place, culminating in the most momentous social experiment of the twentieth century, perhaps of all human history, the People's Republic of China.

An understanding of the course of these changes requires some knowledge of the civilization from which they emanated, of the forces that had given that civilization such unparalleled duration, and which continued to give it the internal cohesion that resisted the inevitable so tenaciously, and of those aspects of the tradition that were conducive to the changes that ultimately occurred. The purpose of this introduction is to provide such an analysis, to give a background that will serve to make the documents in this anthology more comprehensible.

Since premodern China has frequently, with some justification, been called Confucian China, and since Confucian ideas and mores both hindered and facilitated change in the nineteenth and twentieth centuries, some general idea of Confucianism and Confucian aspects of Chinese society is essential to any understanding of modern China.

In the Confucian view, man was a social creature. Moreover, man was by nature moral; in some ultimate, fundamental sense, human nature was good. Confucians did not deny that human behavior all too frequently was less than good. After all, Confucius and his earlist disciples had lived in a time of constant warfare, of destruction, chaos, and suffering. Yet, Confucians believed that such conditions were an aberration, caused primarily by a failure of moral leadership, not by men's nature. Everyone, or almost everyone, was potentially good. Man was perfectable; in the words of Mencius, the greatest Confucian after the Master himself, anyone could be a Yao or a Shun, a model sage.[1] The problem was how to put an end to strife and suffering and enable men to live in accordance with their natural potential for good. Since man was by nature good, he had the capacity to achieve this goal, and since he was by nature a social creature, striving to do so was his highest calling. The ultimate purpose of the most important human institutions, the family, education, and above all government, was the creation of an orderly and just society.

Both in theory and in practice the family was crucial, for it was the center of the lives of the vast majority of the people of China. The family was society in small scale, and family relationships set the pattern for other social relationships. In the family each individual learned the mores and the higher ethical values of Chinese society. One learned the desirability of harmony and order. One learned that these were achieved through subordination of oneself to the family group. One learned that one was therefore first and foremost not an individual, but a member of the family, and that one's obligations and behavior were determined by one's status in the family hierarchy. The father was expected to behave the way a father should behave, an elder son the way an elder son should behave, a wife as a wife, and so on. Each family member had a fixed role to play, and harmony and order were achieved by all playing their roles properly.

All family relationships, and most social relationships, were hierarchical. The Three Bonds (between ruler and minister, between father and son, and between husband and wife) and four of the Five Human Relationships (between ruler and minister, father and son, husband and wife, elder and younger brothers, and between friends) were relationships between superiors and inferiors. This was the natural order, and it was natural that elders and other superiors should be obeyed. On their side, superiors were supposed to love and care for those below them; though not a believer in equality, Confucius placed much emphasis on reciprocity in all relationships. The way superiors expressed their love and care was to be determined by their superior wisdom, not by the wishes of inferiors. If superiors behaved wrongly, and Confucius acknowl-

---

[1] Even Hsü Tzu, who thought that human nature was evil, believed that the undesirable effects of this evil nature could be overcome by reason and social convention.

edged that they sometimes did, they might be gently admonished. But Confucian theory provided no guarantees to protect the young, women, or the lowly from the arbitrary whims or the self-indulgence of family elders, husbands, or superiors in general. If after repeated pleas or admonitions, superiors still did not live up to their moral obligations, silence and patient suffering were the proper courses. Harmony and order were to be achieved by each person living up to the obligations entailed in his or her family or social role, and obedience was an unconditional obligation of inferiors. A famous passage in the *Analects* explicitly drew a connection between habits of obedience learned in the family and order in society at large: "There have been few who were filial and loved their elder brothers who nevertheless were fond of offending their superiors. And no one who disliked offending his superiors has ever been fond of disrupting social order." (*Analects,* I: 2) In theory, moral principles inculcated in the home made a major contribution toward peace and stability in society.

In actual practice, imperial law gave the father virtual life and death power over his children, while they had few rights of their own. During the Ch'ing dynasty (1644–1912), making a false accusation against one's father was a crime punishable by death; even a true accusation was a punishable crime, except in the case of treason. A father could not arbitrarily slay his son, but the slightest excuse of disobedience was all that was necessary to make a father's Wrath justifiable motivation for beating a son to death. And even for an unjustified slaying the penalties were light. On the other hand, if a son struck his father, or even raised his hand against him, the penalties were severe. Death by slicing was prescribed for a son who actually killed his father, whether intentionally or not.

Still, sons were not entirely at the mercy of their fathers. Self-interest dictated some moderation on the part of elders. Parents were aware that they would have to rely on the support of their sons when they were too old to support themselves, and it was scarcely prudent to sow seeds of enmity that might be harvested in a defenseless old age. Sternness rather than cruelty tended to be the norm in father-son relationships. The hardships of these inequalities were perhaps made tolerable for boys and young men by the knowledge that they would enjoy the same authority and privileges when they in turn became fathers. Youth was nevertheless a potentially disaffected group, kept in place by the authority the system invested in elders. When the system disintegrated in the twentieth century, youth and women, who were in a similar position through most if not all of their lives, no longer were willing to accept their traditional helpless subordination.

The family was the primary agent of socialization, but it was not expected to guarantee social order or to produce the good society. Those tasks were the responsibility of government, at the top of the social hierarchy. It was therefore of vital importance that the best men in society serve in the government. And hence virtue and ability, not birth or wealth, were in Confucian theory the essential qualifications for government office. Men who proved capable of developing their own innate propensities for good, who in their daily lives adhered to the Confucian moral code, were to become officials. These men were the gentlemen *(chün-tzu),* who strove to do what was right, in contrast to the small men, who were motivated by base self-interest. Confucian theory tended to assume that the public interest and individual self-interest, at least short-sighted self-interest, were antithetical, and that devotion to the public or common interest (in Chinese, *kung*) was moral, while devotion to self-interest, or selfishness (in Chinese, *ssu*) was immoral.[2] Because everyone possessed the innate propensity for good, the narrow selfishness of small men could be overcome by the influence of the gentlemen's virtue. Confucius had an almost mystical belief in the inspirational and suasive force of goodness: "If you truly desire good, the people will be good. The virtue of the gentleman is like the wind, while the virtue of the small man is like the grass. When the wind blows across the grass, the grass will bend." (*Analects*, XII: 19) Mencius, somewhat more practical and more specific than the Master, added that the government should make sure that the common people had the means, primarily land, to provide for their own basic material needs. Human nature being good, people were not by nature inordinately greedy. If the common people felt assured of a constant means of supporting themselves, Mencius wrote, they would have constant hearts; without a constant means of supporting themselves, however, they might do anything. (*Mencius*, IA: 7 and IIIA: 33) The goal of government economic policy was the prevention of an inequitable distribution of the limited available resources, not increasing production to satisfy ever-increasing consumer demands. Like other governmental problems, economics was basically ethical. This was another reason why Confucian gentlemen were uniquely qualified to be officials, for they would put the public interest before their own self-interest, and would not use their authority for their own private benefit.

Since good government depended so much upon good men, finding such men was obviously crucial. Hence the importance of education, for it was through education that innate capacity could be developed and observed. Since innate capacity was not determined by one's social class, there should in principle be equal educational opportunity for all, and those who, whatever their social background, learned to be Confucian gentlemen, would be prepared for government service. And because its principal task was to prepare men for public life, education was necessarily primarily ethical in content.

Education was thus seen as a dividing line in society. As Mencius explained, educated men, "those who worked with their minds," were the rulers, while the rest, "those who worked with their hands," were the ruled. (*Mencius*, IIIA: 4) This division implied that the ruled were to play no active role in government. Only the gentlemen were qualified to do that. Confucius placed even more severe restrictions on political activity. Each official was to confine himself to the specific duties of his own office. As he put it, "Do not make plans for a post you do not hold." (*Analects*, VIII: 14 and XIV: 26) In the hierarchical order of society, superiors were better qualified to decide what was right for everyone, and hence inferiors, in the family or in the state at large, had no legitimate role to play in decision making.

[2]For a brief discussion of the history of these two important terms, which will frequently recur in the following documents, see John R. Watt, *The District Magistrate in Late Imperial China* (New York: Columbia University Press, 1972), pp. 161–68.

Within the government, only the ruler owed his position to birth. True, according to the Confucian version of history, in the most ancient past, two of the three great sage rulers, Yao and Shun, had transmitted the rulership to the most virtuous man in the empire rather than to a relative. However, the third, Yü, had established hereditary succession, and Confucians did not challenge the practice. Nevertheless, although the ruler had a hereditary right to his position, this right was not, like a father's, inalienable. Virtue was required of the ruler not merely because a true ruler was by definition necessarily virtuous, but also because it was in his interest and the interest of his dynasty. For, as Mencius explained, if the ruler was motivated by personal profit rather than by right principle, others would follow his example, selfishness would become pervasive, and this would lead to contention, conflict, disorder, and ultimately the overthrow of the ruling house. A self-centered ruler was his own worst enemy, because the people, though normally docile, would rise up in righteous anger against the suffering caused by his selfish behavior. Mencius said that such a revolt was justified, on the grounds that an immoral ruler was no longer truly a ruler, and hence people were no longer obligated to be loyal to him. By his immoral behavior, he had lost the Mandate of Heaven, and hence his deposition was not an act of insubordination, but a fulfillment, by the people, of Heaven's Will. Thus, to preserve the throne for himself and his descendants, the ruler was obliged to be a good ruler.

And thus morality and order were as directly related as selfishness and disorder. A government of virtuous men was not only desirable on ethical grounds, but also as the only means of ensuring lasting peace and stability. Confucian moral principles were the social cement that gave cohesion and order to society. Moral unity was the surest source of strength, and selfishness, being divisive, was a source of weakness. Morality, the common interest, and long-range self-interest all ultimately coalesced. Indeed, it is sometimes difficult to determine, particularly in the writings of later Confucians, whether the aim of government was the good society or social order, whether Confucian moral principles were ends in themselves or means to the end of peace and dynastic stability. The twin goals of government were inextricably intertwined, and so in actuality too, Confucian principles were inextricably intertwined with the existing social order.

When in modern times that order was disrupted, it was natural that Confucian principles should be called into doubt. Yet, although as we shall see, many Confucian ideas, especially the hierarchical distribution of authority, and the division between mental and physical labor, have repeatedly been attacked, many underlying Confucian assumptions have proven resilient. Among the ideas we shall see reappearing in various forms in spite of recurring challenges are 1) the distinction between public or common interest (*kung*) and private interest or selfishness (*ssu*), and the notion that the pursuit of individual self-interest is immoral and anti-social; the ideas 2) that man is, through education, perfectible, 3) that the most important aspect of education is ethics, 4) that moral character is the principal qualification for political leadership, 5) that the goal of government is the creation of the good society, and 6) that governmental jurisdiction naturally extends to the economic and moral realms.

Confucianism was not the only school of Chinese philosophy that influenced social and political behavior. Taoism, though it was strikingly different from Confucianism, had the similar goal of order and harmony, or perhaps better, tranquillity. Taoists, too, believed that man's nature was good, not in the sense of possessing the roots of social morality, but in the sense of being capable of living in harmony with the natural order of the universe. Moral behavior was not the way to achieve this harmony, however, because good and evil were artificial human fabrications, useless as guides to natural conduct. Worse than useless, actually harmful. For good and evil were mutually dependent concepts; the idea "good" logically entailed the contrasting idea "evil." If nothing contrasted with "good," what need would there be for the concept in the first place? So, in a sense, the very notion of good created evil. Furthermore, morality was inevitably relative and subjective. Each person defined good in terms of himself, and just as each person's views differed, so did his concept of what was good. Hence, moral principles tended to give high-sounding justification to self-centered actions, and therefore morality intensified, even created, quarrels, contention, and strife. And so the Confucians were all wrong: morality did not create peace and harmony; on the contrary, the very notion was responsible for many of the evils that beset society, and was the source of the strife that disrupted the natural harmonious order. Men would be better off if they unlearned moral values, avoided becoming enmeshed in the allurements of society, and turned instead to what the Taoists described in mystical terms as a union with the underlying principle of the universe, the Tao, the ineffable natural order of things. To strive toward the goals of society, or to try to improve society, was all too likely to lead away from the Tao, toward tension and aggravation, strife, or even chaos.

Thus, although more of an individual than a social philosophy, Taoism did have political implications. The ideal society was small in scale, perhaps village size, and the ideal ruler was barely known, if known at all, to his subjects. In the succinct metaphor of Lao Tzu, good government is like frying a small fish —it can, in other words, easily be overdone. This extreme laissez-faire attitude, though not the official doctrine of the imperial state, was not without its influence in imperial times. And the idea that problems were unnatural, that actively attempting to solve them might only make them worse, and perhaps create more, deeply influenced Chinese social and political behavior. The bureaucratic empire was much more passive than we, accustomed as we are to modern bureaucracies intervening in so many areas of social and economic life, might readily conceive. In personal life, too, Taoist ideals were held by members of the Confucian elite. Officials felt the attraction of freedom from the cares and entanglements of bureaucratic life, and built retreats remote from human habitation in order to absorb themselves in the calm beauty of nature. The ideal of the carefree life did not dominate, but it was pervasive, and conspicuous leisure was one sign of success. These attitudes were not without importance in maintaining the status quo. In modern times, they were to prove incompatible with the kind of activist mentality necessary for radical change.

A third school of philosophy, Legalism, was sharply different from both Confucianism and Taoism, and has for Westerners called to mind names like Machiavelli and Hobbes. The Legalists were more concerned about the ruler than the people; for them, the central problem of political life was the ruler's power. How could he keep and increase his power? This was a problem because he was constantly threatened by ambitious domestic and foreign rivals. And those not out to get him were out to get something from him. Fortunately, the cause of these threats also provided the key to the solution: human nature was evil, but that evilness could be manipulated. Evil meant only selfishness, not instinctive malevolence. No amount of moral exhortation or favorable social environment could alter men's selfishness. Indeed, somewhat like the Taoists, the Legalist philosophers thought of morality as, at best, relative. The virtues praised by Confucius might have been appropriate in the ancient past, though this was by no means certain, but they definitely were not suited to the harsh realities of the present. Morality was not the means to preserve the ruler's power in a world composed of selfish men. The solution was not to attempt the impossible task of altering men's selfish nature, but to accept it and work with it, to channel it to serve the true interests, the wealth and power, of the ruler and of the state. With devastatingly consistent logic, the Legalists presented a simple system designed to accomplish this. Activities that enhanced the wealth and power of the state, above all tilling the soil and fighting in the army, would be generously rewarded, and actions detrimental to the state would be severely punished. Written laws were to make clear and explicit which activities would be rewarded and which punished. In this way, selfish men would be compelled to do what was best for the state, for it would be best for them, too. Since morality was based on a distinction between right and profit and on the idea that right not profit should guide behavior, morality was divisive and subversive. The preaching of moral principles would therefore be forbidden, and punished, as harmful to the state. Uniformity of belief was necessary for an orderly society and a secure and powerful state. Thus, paradoxically, the best interests of the ruler were also the true interests of the people, although in their short-sighted selfishness they would never be able to realize it. For by providing for the security of the ruler through a wealthy and powerful state, peace and order were also created.

Legalism was discredited as a political philosophy when the first dynasty to adopt its principles as official state doctrine, the Ch'in (221 B.C.–207 B.C.) fell only fourteen years after it was established. Yet Legalist ideas did not disappear. Throughout the later centuries of the empire, it was acknowledged that the benevolent example of Confucian gentlemen was not sufficient to ensure virtuous behavior among the rest of the populace. Legal codes prescribed harsh punishments for infractions of the law, and thus, as previously mentioned, imperial law upheld Confucian principles.

The differences between these three schools of thought are obvious. There were also similarities, several of which were to be of the utmost significance for China's entrance into the modern world. All focused on life in this world, not on preparation for some after-life. Order was a central concern. All agreed, too, that government should play a crucial role in creating order and in making society as good as each thought it could be. And both Confucians and Legalists agreed that the jurisdiction of the state necessarily extended to the economic and moral realms. It was not surprising, then, that in the modern era the government was expected to play a central role in solving China's problems.

The ideas of these philosophical schools were expressed in ancient texts that only the literate minority could read, but they were nevertheless familiar among the vast illiterate masses in the villages and towns of China. Other beliefs were also widespread. Ancestor worship existed on all levels of society. Awe and veneration for the dead ancestors served to reinforce similar feelings toward their living representatives, the family or clan elders, and thus ancestor worship was an important support for Confucian values. There were universal religions too, Buddhism, and various forms of popular Taoism, with gods, magic formulae, solemn ceremonies, and promises of future rewards for proper behavior in the present life. There were also innumerable local religions, with their own shrines, customs, and beliefs. They differed in many ways, but in general promised what popular religions have promised in most parts of the world—help against pain and suffering, and promises of good fortune and a better life, if not in this world, then in the world beyond.

It would be misleading to think that popular religions taught only acceptance of the status quo. To be sure, the behavior that was to earn the reward of a better life tended to conform with values that supported the existing social order—harmony, respect for authority, acceptance of one's lot, and other virtues with a recognizable Confucian tinge. But some sects taught heretical doctrines: this world was corrupt, bad men held sway and exploited the good but powerless masses. Sects that propagated such ideas were inherently subversive. The government pronounced them illegal, and continually tried to suppress them. But it never succeeded, and these sects were frequently connected with rebellions, especially in times of economic crisis. They were evidence that there were latent dissatisfactions among the normally quiescent peasant masses, and that these dissatisfactions could erupt with powerful force.

Order and stability, so important in Chinese political philosophy, were also the very practical goals of the imperial government. This was especially true in Ch'ing times. The Manchu people who had conquered China in the seventeenth century and established the Ch'ing dynasty comprised at most two percent of the total population. How was this tiny minority to maintain its power and rule the gigantic empire? The Manchus' answer was to rule as Chinese monarchs had ruled, using existing political institutions, with some small but significant alterations.

There were three important levels of government: central, provincial, and district. At the head of the central administration in Peking was the Manchu emperor, a descendant of the men who had conquered China. He was advised by a body of senior counselors, drawn from the highest organs of the central government. The Grand Council, created in 1729, handled urgent matters, while the Grand Secretariat dealt with more routine affairs. Members of the Grand Council were the emperor's closest advisors, and in consultation with them, he made policy decisions. Normally, half the Grand Councilors were Manchus and half Chinese. The staff of the Grand Council was also equally divided between Manchus and Chinese. Under the Grand Council came the Six Boards, in charge of implementing policies. The Boards were functionally divided: Civil Office (or Personnel), Revenue, Rites, Military, Punishments (or Justice), and Public Works. Each Board was headed by two Presidents, one Manchu and one Chinese, with two Manchu and two Chinese Vice-Presidents. High offices were thus open to Chinese, but high Chinese officials were under the surveillance of their Manchu peers. And conversely, powerful Manchu officials, who might on occasion be hostile to the ruling emperor, were under the surveillance of Chinese. In addition to these offices, there were of course numerous other offices and bureaus in the capital.

Outside the capital, there were basically two levels of local administration, the province and the district. China proper was divided into eighteen provinces, under the supervision of Governors-General (usually with responsibility over two adjacent provinces) and Governors (each in charge of one province). The overlapping jurisdictions and the practice of intermingling Manchus and Chinese in the two posts were designed as checks against these powerful officials developing a dangerous degree of autonomy. The most important officials under each Governor, the Financial Commissioner, Judicial Commissioner, and Educational Commissioner, were all appointed by the emperor, and could report directly to the central government, thus providing another check on the autonomy of the Governors and Governors-General. The system sometimes stifled initiative, but it was well designed for its basic purpose, the maintenance of the status quo.

The lowest level of governmental administration under an official directly appointed by the central government was the district (*hsien*), of which there were somewhere between 1,200 and 1,300 in the empire. This was the level of closest contact with the people of China. The two chief responsibilities of the District Magistrate were collecting taxes and maintaining peace and order.

District Magistrates, known as "father and mother officials," were supposed to look after the welfare of the common people with the same care and consideration parents were supposed to give their children. And in practice some officials were indeed wise and benevolent. But not all, and perhaps very few. A post was commonly looked upon as a source of income, not from the small official salary, but from the assessment and collection of all sorts of fees, which up to a certain point were customary and legal. Beyond that point, there were more lucrative forms of extortion: illegal "contributions," heavy assessments of taxes, and various kinds of bribes. Corruption of this sort, while by no means ubiquitous, was common enough to be a generally expected, though generally bemoaned, way of life. It was so widespread that even honest and well-intentioned officials had a difficult time not participating, in order to afford the "gifts" and "contributions" their superiors expected of them. In the view of some Confucian critics, and later, of many foreign observers, such corruption was endemic. Whether it was more widespread than in other countries, and if so, to what degree, is another question, one to which there is as yet no clear answer. It should also be kept in mind that even incorrupt officials were to be held in awe, even feared. They might be kind and benevolent, but in their own terms and in their own way. The gap between officials and the common people was vast.

A district could be quite large, with a population as large as a million or more, and even the average had a population of about 200,000. The District Magistrate obviously needed assistance to accomplish his tasks. In his *yamen,* the combination office-residence, he had a large staff, a few men brought with him from his home area, the rest natives of the district.[3] The magistrate also depended upon the local elite, the gentry, who like the *yamen* staff helped bridge the gap between the magistrate and the local populace, though frequently more for their own benefit than for the people's.

Although the gentry were not officials, they performed many important functions associated with local government in other countries. They raised funds for and supervised the construction and repair of public works, such as roads, bridges, dikes, dams, and irrigation systems; they helped maintain local schools, temples, and shrines; and they frequently were active in philanthropic work, especially when natural disasters occurred. They also acted as mediators in local civil disputes, settling them through arbitration so as to keep them out of the magistrate's court, which could be costly to all involved. If government troops proved incapable of safeguarding the district from marauding bandits or rebels, the gentry might organize and arm local militia for self-protection. The gentry were thus a vital part of the whole system. Numbers tell the story. At any one time there were some 25,000 to 30,000 civil officials in the empire, but well over a million gentry members. Without the assistance and cooperation of the gentry, the government would have been crippled.

Gentry status was acquired by passing the government civil service examinations, or by purchase. The examination route was by far the more prestigious, and virtually a prerequisite for anyone aspiring to a successful official career. Something like two million men took the first level of the examinations each time they were given, which was twice every three years. The 30,000 or so who passed became members of the lower gentry, and were qualified to take the second level, the provincial examinations given once every three years, for which the government set an empire-wide quota of only 1,400. Those who passed received the *chü-jen* ("recommended man") degree, and were eligible to participate in the metropolitan examination, held in the capital soon after the provincial exams. The final step was a shorter examination held in the imperial palace under the supervision of the emperor several weeks later. On the average, less than 250 candidates passed this triennial examination. These fortunate men were awarded the *chin-shih* ("presented scholar") degree, a source of enormous prestige throughout the empire, and the single most important formal qualification for rising to a position of eminence in the government.

The basic texts for the questions and answers on the exams were the Confucian classics. These were the repositories of the ethical precepts upon which

[3]For examples of the power of some of these underlings, see Documents 32a and 34c.

state and society supposedly rested, and of the values which officials supposedly embodied. Intimate knowledge of these works was necessary to pass the exams, though of course mere memorization was no guarantee of genuine belief or of adherence to the doctrines in personal behavior. Equally crucial to passing the exams was the ability to write in the standard mode. Long before the nineteenth century, a highly stylized form, the so-called eight-legged essay, became prescribed for examination essays. There were complicated and rigid rules for each of the eight "legs," or sections, rules that governed length, phraseology, organization, and thematic development. These rules obviously had nothing to do with the moral character of the candidate, and many objected to the "eight-legged essay" for this reason. But their objections never overcame the convenience of evaluation, or the vested interests of all those who had devoted long years to mastering the "eight-legged" form.

The "eight-legged essay" was difficult to master. So were the classics, which were long and written in the classical style, different enough from colloquial speech to justify calling them two separate languages. Preparation for the examinations required a long period of study. And so, although with few exceptions all males were eligible to participate in the examinations, in practice candidates whose families or clans could afford to allow them the necessary time to study, or better yet, could hire a tutor, had a great advantage over the less well-to-do. It was less difficult for a family in the elite to perpetuate its status than for someone from a commoner family to rise into the elite. Less difficult, but not easy. Means were provided to help equalize opportunity, such as government schools, stipends for students on the basis of proven merit, subsidies for travel expenses to and from the examinations, and inexpensive editions of the classics, of model "eight-legged essays," and of successful examination essays. The available evidence demonstrates quite clearly that there was considerable social mobility, both upward and downward. New families did rise into the gentry elite, and older gentry families whose sons failed to pass the exams dropped back into relative obscurity.

Social mobility did not generate structural modifications in Chinese society. On the contrary, those who entered the gentry through the examination system were disinclined toward change. The arduous efforts required to pass the exams had more likely than not been motivated by a desire to enjoy the long-established privileges of the elite. (A few critics thought this was the only motivation.) And the long years of studying the classics in many cases provided a kind of ideological indoctrination in the Confucian principles that justified the existing social order. Few who rose through this process identified themselves with the underprivileged commoners from whose ranks they and their families had come. Thus the social mobility created by the examination system was a source of structural stability, for although the names of the elite might change, each generation had the same education, held similar beliefs, and had identical interests in preserving society the way it was. Moreover, the competitive exams eliminated most of the less able scions of the reigning upper class, and infused new blood into the system. As a result, there was sufficient congruity between ability, interest, and power for the gentry elite to be devoted to the status quo and to be able to preserve it. Even among the rest of the population, the exam system conferred some sense of legitimacy on the gentry and on the social structure they headed. The knowledge that it was possible to rise from obscurity to eminence through the examinations assured many who never passed, or never even had the opportunity to take the exams, that the system was fair, and that the gentry merited its privileges and its authority. Many too must have dreamt that a son, or grandson, or great-grandson would eventually pass and elevate the family's fortunes. Thus, although the civil service examination system did not attain its theoretical goal of bringing men of virtue into government service, it was a central source of social stability.

It was a major obstacle to change in another way too, which became apparent in the nineteenth century. Because being an official was almost universally considered the most desirable career, education was geared toward preparing students for the examinations. The exam system was thus a key institutional link between Confucian learning and the social structure of the imperial state. The principal asset of officials, and of millions who aspired to become officials, was their Confucian education. This made it extremely difficult to make significant changes in the content of education, changes that became necessary when China was threatened by the superior power of the modern West, a power derived from an entirely different kind of knowledge, scientific and philosophical. Only after more than 60 years of humiliating defeats did the imperial government abolish the examination system in order to encourage young students to study this new knowledge. Even after its abolition the exam system left a legacy; the ideas that education confers social status, and that the purpose of education is to improve one's life chances are still widespread in China today.

From the preceding analysis it should be clear that the gentry elite shared many interests with the government, even though the ruling dynasty was non-Chinese. The high degree of integration of state and society made for strong internal cohesion, perhaps the chief reason why the system had lasted so long without undergoing fundamental change. When, in the nineteenth century, changes became imperative, this social structure showed its cohesive strength by resisting the changes forced upon China by the modern world. Its very success through previous centuries helped render it incapable of responding rapidly to the new and unprecedented situation. And so, what seemed to contemporary Western observers to be perverse obstinacy was actually quite understandable, even rational, behavior. Rational in the sense of conforming to the values and the self-interest of those who resisted change. The problem for China, then, was how to move from a social system in which the rational self-interest of the social and political elite was increasingly incompatible with the national interest of China, to a new system in which the ideals and interests of the leaders and the people of China would be more in accord with the interest of China.

The military power of the modern West and the accompanying expansion of modern Western civilization into East Asia thrust China into an entirely new context, in which old answers to old questions no longer applied. As this became increasingly apparent, Chinese thinkers, statesmen, and revolutionaries gradually reinterpreted and redefined the problems China faced, and proposed new solutions. We shall follow this process through three stages. First, the disintegration and destruction of traditional Chinese civilization as it failed to cope with the Western threat. Then, the various social, political, and cultural alternatives proposed and practiced after the collapse of the empire in 1911. And finally, the establishment of the People's Republic of China, and the struggle to build a new society and to make China strong enough to take her rightful place among the great nations of the world.

PART I
Disintegration

Modern Chinese history begins with the Opium War (1840–42). Other events and other dates have been used to demarcate the beginning of China's modern age, but there are compelling reasons for the wide acceptance of this first major clash between the Ch'ing empire and Great Britain. For it was this war that opened China to the modern West. In the brief and intermittent fighting between British and Chinese forces, the superior military strength of the West was first displayed, and this military superiority, demonstrated again and again in later years, was the single most potent stimulant for the changes that eventually came. Moreover, in the treaties that concluded the war, foreigners gained a number of special rights, the first of a long series of restrictions on Chinese sovereignty. The limitations on Chinese sovereignty brought about by what came to be called the Unequal Treaties in turn impelled Chinese statesmen and thinkers to search for effective means to protect China and regain her lost rights. Thus, foreign pressures and foreign presence in China generated dissatisfaction with the status quo, and ultimately to its rejection. Disintegration of the traditional Chinese polity is the underlying theme of Chinese history from the Opium War to the Revolution of 1911, and this disintegration began with China's defeat in the Opium War.

Men of the time could hardly have foreseen the eventual collapse of the Manchu monarchy and the imperial system. The political and intellectual leaders of China were the heirs of a long and justly proud tradition, which for centuries had dominated East Asia, culturally as well as politically. They had no doubts about the superiority of Chinese civilization. China had never been totally isolated from the rest of the world, but there was little interest in learning about distant and exotic lands. Foreigners might come to China in quest of the abundant riches China had to offer, but there was no reason for Chinese to seek for anything abroad. This is not to say that complacency was ubiquitous; Chinese civilization had never lacked its own critics. But they operated within a familiar framework, and criticisms took the form of complaints and lamentations that current political and social practice did not live up to the philosophical ideals of the great sages of the past. Thus, even expressions of dissatisfaction had a ring of normality about them.

This was little altered by the first clashes with the West. Confidence in traditional ways persisted for decades. The statesmen who sought to respond to the new challenge strove to brace the defenses of the empire and to preserve the way of life to which they and their ancestors had been accustomed for centuries. But gradually the dimensions of the problem became apparent. In Part I, we shall follow this growing awareness of the scope and intensity of the foreign threat and of the need for change, starting from proud confidence in China's self-sufficiency and ending with the revolutionary overthrow of the discredited imperial system and its replacement by a republic.

A brief survey of the principal events of the 70 years from the Opium War to the end of the empire shows how events compelled Chinese thinkers to change their perceptions of the issues facing China.

The special rights won by Westerners in the first part of the Opium War laid the foundations for the foreign penetration of China. These rights were supplemented and extended as a result of further skirmishes and wars in subsequent decades. By the end of the nineteenth century China had been forced to open European-style diplomatic relations with many nations, to permit the existence on Chinese soil, mainly in port cities, of enclaves where foreigners governed themselves according to rules they themselves established, and of foreign-owned and foreign-operated businesses and factories. Another, more powerful, civilization thus made its presence felt, forcing China to seek ways to stem the tide of Western incursion.

Powerful internal forces also erupted, in the Taiping and other rebellions of the 1850s and 1860s. New and old were blended in the Taiping Heavenly Kingdom, one of the greatest upheavals in Chinese history. Although it and other rebellions were eventually crushed, and their immediate effects were largely destructive, the rebellions were a portent of future possibilities. Eventually, China would have to face a second problem: the role of the hitherto inchoate masses in the task of strengthening and defending China.

The first attempt to solve these two problems was made by defenders of the traditional order. Their success in suppressing the rebellions appeared to confirm their status as guardians of the true interests of China. Even before the rebellions had ended, these men launched a program of limited reforms to meet the Western threat, the so-called Self-Strengthening movement. The question the Self-Strengtheners posed themselves was—what changes were absolutely necessary to save the Chinese way of life? Their answer was that traditional values and institutions could be preserved through the selective adoption of Western technology. From the 1860s to the 1880s, they built arsenals, shipyards, language schools, machine factories, textile mills, railroads, telegraph lines, and other Western-inspired innovations to achieve this goal.

The accomplishments of the Self-Strengtheners were proven inadequate by China's humiliating defeat in the Sino-Japanese War of 1894–95. China's obvious weakness and vulnerability led many to fear that the empire could no longer defend itself and that it would soon be partitioned among the great powers. This fear added a sense of urgency to the feeling that something more radical had to be done to save China. In 1898, under the auspices of a reform-minded emperor, a group of young reformers attempted to implement a program of Western-influenced institutional reforms. Resistance to change was still strong, however, and the radical reform was quashed in less than four months. But the young reformers, by their words and actions, had raised a new and momentous issue. Their answer to the question of how to save China had implied that much of what was commonly assumed to be essential could actually be discarded; it implied the possibility of redefining what could and should be preserved. And so their answer raised a new question: what, after all, was China? The land? The people? The dynasty? A way of life? (Whose?) A set of values? (Which ones?)

To this question conservatives and radical reformers had very different answers, and their disagreements were intense. But both came from the traditional elite, both wanted reform not revolution, and both sought to preserve the imperial system. The pace of change was becoming so rapid that both groups were soon superannuated. As the situation continued to deteriorate, the feeling that the tradition-bound gentry could not save China began to spread. This was the implication of the government's abolition of the civil service examination system in 1905. It was the key tenet of a new group on the scene, the revolutionaries. These men and women, at first small in number, had a new answer: China must be saved by the Chinese people—not by the alien Manchus, or by the old gentry elite—but by the whole Chinese people. The Manchus, it was argued, wanted only to retain their own position, not to protect China, and they had no compunctions about being subservient to the powers if that would save them. The traditional elite was too weak, corrupt, and decadent, and its interests too tied to the status quo, for it to save China. The system that earlier generations of Chinese leaders had striven to defend was now perceived as an obstacle. It did not conform to eternally valid moral principles or to the interests of China, but merely to the vested interests of a selfish and immoral elite. Hence, the old system had to be abolished.

China was no longer to be a monarchy ruled by Manchus and servile Confucian officials; it would be a republic, ruled by the people of China. How a new China would be built, and what form it would take, was now the central problem.

Thus, each proposed solution to China's problems implied a new conception of what those problems were. Although actual implementation of proposed solutions lagged far behind the changing definitions of the problems, the realization that previous conceptions of the issues and previous solutions were inadequate continued to grow. Each new definition of the problems entailed an erosion of long-held assumptions, until the proud confidence in China's self-sufficiency was replaced by a search for new and better foreign ways. The realization of the extent of the problems was confined to the literate elite, and the implementation of solutions was largely confined to the cities. Still, the ease with which the ancient monarchy collapsed indicates how much had already changed. By the standards of the great European revolutions, the Revolution of 1911 was a trivial affair. There was little violence, no great dramatic event. And yet it brought to an end not only the Ch'ing dynasty, but the 2,100-year-old imperial state. By the time the last emperor was forced to abdicate in 1912, the Manchu house, the monarchy, and the imperial polity had astonishingly few friends or supporters, persuasive evidence of the degree to which faith in traditional Chinese civilization had disintegrated.

From this overview, we now turn to the first stage of the process, the Opium War.

CHAPTER ONE
The Opening of China

It was Western force that impelled China into the modern world, and so we begin with the first clashes between China and the West. The many differences between these two proud civilizations are too complex to be analyzed or illustrated in one short chapter, but some notion of their scope and intensity is essential to understanding modern Chinese history.

Perhaps the most fundamental incompatibility was each civilization's deeply ingrained self-assurance, even self-righteousness. The Chinese attitude toward the outside world can be seen in the first two documents in this chapter, edicts from the supreme authority in the Chinese state, the emperor himself. (Selection 1) Their author, the Ch'ien-lung Emperor (reigned 1736–95), was one of the greatest of all the many rulers of China. His edicts to King George III of England were issued in response to the request, brought in 1793 by a special British emissary, Lord George Macartney, for improving and expanding trade. Foreign trade had always been carefully controlled by the Chinese government, and after 1759 it had been confined to Canton under severe restrictions. The emperor's explanations of these conditions are a classic statement of a number of fundamental and long-standing beliefs. The confident sense of self-sufficiency, the assumption that the emperor had sole jurisdiction over all questions concerning China's domestic and international affairs, and the underlying attitude of superiority were all centuries old.

The rejections of the requests for changes made by Lord Macartney and by later missions from the British crown were disappointing to the foreign merchants engaged in the China trade. But the trade was profitable, and so the numerous restrictions and harassments were tolerated. Profits leapt with the rapid growth of illegal trade in opium, brought to China from

India on foreign ships and then delivered to Chinese smugglers. As the demand for this poisonous and addictive narcotic grew, and the amount imported into China increased, the Ch'ing government became alarmed at the spread of the drug, at its debilitating effects, and at the outflow of silver to pay for it. After many unsuccessful attempts to suppress the illegal traffic, Peking decided to make an all-out effort, and sent a Special Commissioner to Canton to bring it to a halt. The man assigned this task, Lin Tse-hsü (1785–1850), was an official of great ability, keen intelligence, and unquestioned personal integrity.

The difficulties of suppressing illegal drug traffic are today well known. When Lin Tse-hsü arrived in Canton in March 1839, he faced even more formidable problems than modern governments, for British nationalism and the gospel of free trade were at their height. Lin's tough measures, which included confining uncooperative foreign merchants and confiscating their opium holdings, were taken as an affront and a provocation. As tension mounted, the two sides drifted into open hositlities. A British naval force had been dispatched to Chinese waters for just such an eventuality. The British defeated the Chinese with little difficulty in a series of relatively brief skirmishes, which began near Canton in 1840 and ended with a British squadron poised to attack Nanking, more than 200 miles upstream on the Yangtze River, in 1842.

The Ch'ing government was forced to sign a treaty with Great Britain, which, along with the French and American treaties signed in the following two years, set the pattern for the settlement of later conflicts. Foreigners were granted special privileges in China, privileges which defined the conditions of the Western presence in China for a century. Especially important in the sections of these first treaties that are included in this chapter are the provision for indemnities, the loss of tariff autonomy, the most-favored-nation clause, which meant that all countries that came to have similar treaties with China possessed the same special privileges, and the special legal rights granted to foreigners residing in China, rights that later were vastly expanded, and were known as extraterritoriality. (Selections 2 and 3)

Traditional attitudes were too deep to be shaken by defeat in one short war. Within Ch'ing officialdom, the treaties were not seen as the beginnings of a new order, but as undesirable and temporary concessions exacted under duress. The persistence and pervasiveness of the traditional feeling of superiority are revealed in Thomas Meadows's observations on the mentality of the Chinese he knew, written several years after the Opium War. (Selection 4) Meadows, whose acquaintance with Chinese life preceded the war, had a good understanding of China and its people. His own certainty on the superiority of Western ways, which pervades his comments, was typical of most Westerners in China at this time. Note that Meadows believed the Chinese were receptive to new things if their merits could be clearly demonstrated. This was certainly true of Lin Tse-hsü, who was blamed for China's humiliating defeat, dismissed from office, and sent into exile. In letters to friends, Lin told of Western military superiority. But, as is indicated by his plea for silence at the end of the letter included here, Lin was an exception, and there was great hostility to any suggestion of Chinese backwardness or of the need for even limited innovations. (Selection 5) There was much resistance to complying with some of the provisions of the new treaties.

The Western view of the situation, as succinctly expressed by Rutherford Alcock, British Consul at Shanghai, was that foreigners had inviolable rights of access to and trade with China. (Selection 6) It followed that the use of force was justifiable if necessary to uphold the newly won means of guaranteeing these rights. Not only to uphold, but to extend, for the American treaty provided for negotiations to revise the treaties after twelve years, and the Western powers, dissatisfied with Chinese compliance with the provisions of the initial treaties, believed that certain revisions were necessary to rectify the situation. The British position on the negotiations can be seen in the correspondence between the British Foreign Secretary, Lord Clarendon, and the British representative in China, John Bowring. (Selections 7 and 8) Bowring's insistence that force would be required to overcome Chinese stubbornness reflects an unyielding and self-righteous attitude that was to be common among foreigners for many decades. Yet the general point cannot easily be dismissed, and in the twentieth century many Chinese, too, were to argue that violence was necessary to eradicate old habits of thought and to ensure the success of radical change.

It was decades before the long-range consequences of the special privileges won by Westerners in the "Unequal Treaties" began to become apparent. The opening of five ports to trade by the Treaty of Nanking was only the first step. Eventually the number of treaty ports exceeded 80, and the interior of China was opened to foreigners as well. In Shanghai and other concession areas, foreigners lived under their own laws, with their own governments, their own police forces and armies, their own postal and telegraph services, and their own life-style. The Opium War treaties thus laid the groundwork for the penetration and suffusion of Western influences, influences that were to corrode the sense of superiority and self-sufficiency so proudly manifested in the Ch'ien-lung edicts.

1. TWO EDICTS FROM THE CH'IEN-LUNG EMPEROR TO KING GEORGE III OF ENGLAND
[September 1793, on the Occasion of Lord Macartney's Mission to China]

(a)

   You, O King, live beyond the confines of many seas, nevertheless, impelled by your humble desire to partake of the benefits of our civilization, you have dispatched a mission respectfully bearing your memorial. Your Envoy has crossed the seas and paid his respects at my Court on the anniversary of my birthday. To show your devotion, you have also sent offerings of your country's produce.

I have perused your memorial: the earnest terms in which it is couched reveal a respectful humility on your part, which is highly praiseworthy. In consideration of the fact that your Ambassador and his deputy have come a long way with your memorial and tribute, I have shown them high favour and have allowed them to be introduced into my presence. To manifest my indulgence, I have entertained them at a banquet and made them numerous gifts. I have also caused presents to be forwarded to the Naval Commander and six hundred of his officers and men, although they did not come to Peking, so that they too may share in my all-embracing kindness.

As to your entreaty to send one of your nationals to be accredited to my Celestial Court and to be in control of your country's trade with China, this request is contrary to all usage of my dynasty and cannot possibly be entertained. It is true that Europeans, in the service of the dynasty, have been permitted to live at Peking, but they are compelled to adopt Chinese dress, they are strictly confined to their own precincts and are never permitted to return home. You are presumably familiar with our dynastic regulations. Your proposed Envoy to my Court could not be placed in a position similar to that of European officials in Peking who are forbidden to leave China, nor could he, on the other hand, be allowed liberty of movement and the privilege of corresponding with his own country; so that you would gain nothing by his residence in our midst.

Moreover, Our Celestial dynasty possesses vast territories, and tribute missions from the dependencies are provided for by the Department for Tributary States, which ministers to their wants and exercises strict control over their movements. It would be quite impossible to leave them to their own devices. Supposing that your Envoy should come to our Court, his language and national dress differ from that of our people, and there would be no place in which he might reside. It may be suggested that he might imitate the Europeans permanently resident in Peking and adopt the dress and customs of China, but, it has never been our dynasty's wish to force people to do things unseemly and inconvenient. Besides, supposing I sent an Ambassador to reside in your country, how could you possibly make for him the requisite arrangements? Europe consists of many other nations besides your own: if each and all demanded to be represented at our Court, how could we possibly consent? The thing is utterly impracticable. How can our dynasty alter its whole procedure and regulations, established for more than a century, in order to meet your individual views? If it be said that your object is to exercise control over your country's trade, your nationals have had full liberty to trade at Canton for many a year, and have received the greatest consideration at our hands. Missions have been sent by Portugal and Italy, preferring similar requests. The Throne appreciated their sincerity and loaded them with favours, besides authorising measures to facilitate their trade with China. You are no doubt aware that, when my Canton merchant, Wu Chao-p'ing, was in debt to the foreign ships, I made the Viceroy advance the monies due, out of the provincial treasury, and ordered him to punish the culprit severely. Why then should foreign nations advance this utterly unreasonable request to be represented at my Court? Peking is nearly 10,000 *li* from Canton, and at such a distance what possible control could any British representative exercise?

If you assert that your reverence for Our Celestial dynasty fills you with a desire to acquire our civilisation, our ceremonies and code of laws differ so completely from your own that, even if your Envoy were able to acquire the rudiments of our civilisation, you could not possibly transplant our manners and customs to your alien soil. Therefore, however adept the Envoy might become, nothing would be gained thereby.

Swaying the wide world, I have but one aim in view, namely, to maintain a perfect governance and to fulfil the duties of the State; strange and costly objects do not interest me. If I have commanded that the tribute offerings sent by you, O King, are to be accepted, this was solely in consideration for the spirit which prompted you to dispatch them from afar. Our dynasty's majestic virtue has penetrated unto every country under Heaven, and Kings of all nations have offered their costly tribute by land and sea. As your Ambassador can see for himself, we possess all things. I set no value on objects strange or ingenious, and have no use for your country's manufactures. This then is my answer to your request to appoint a representative at my Court, a request contrary to our dynastic usage, which would only result in inconvenience to yourself. I have expounded my wishes in detail and have commanded your tribute Envoys to leave in peace on their homeward journey. It behoves you, O King, to respect my sentiments and to display even greater devotion and loyalty in the future, so that, by perpetual submission to our Throne, you may secure peace and prosperity for your country hereafter. Besides making gifts (of which I enclose a list) to each member of your Mission, I confer upon you, O King, valuable presents in excess of the number usually bestowed on such occasions, including silks and curios—a list of which is likewise enclosed. Do you reverently receive them and take note of my tender goodwill towards you! A special mandate.

(b)

You, O King from afar, have yearned after the blessings of our civilisation, and in your eagerness to come into touch with our converting influence have sent an Embassy across the sea bearing a memorial. I have already taken note of your respectful spirit of submission, have treated your mission with extreme favour and loaded it with gifts, besides issuing a mandate to you, O King, and honouring you with the bestowal of valuable presents. Thus has my indulgence been manifested.

Yesterday your Ambassador petitioned my Ministers to memorialize me regarding your trade with China, but his proposal is not consistent with our dynastic usage and cannot be entertained. Hitherto, all European nations, including your own country's barbarian merchants, have carried on their trade with Our Celestial Empire at Canton. Such has been the procedure for many years, although Our Celestial Empire possesses all things in prolific abundance and lacks no product within it own borders. There was therefore no need to import the manufactures of outside barbarians in exchange for our own produce. But as the tea, silk, and porcelain which the Celestial Empire produces are absolute necessities to European nations and to yourselves, we have permitted, as a signal mark of favour, that foreign *hongs* should be established at Canton, so that your wants might be supplied and your country thus participate in our beneficence. But your Ambassador has now put forward new requests which completely fail to recognise the Throne's principle to "treat strangers from afar with indulgence," and to exercise a pacifying control over barbarian tribes, the world over. Moreover, our dynasty, swaying the myriad races of the globe, extends the same benevolence towards all. Your England is not the only nation trading at Canton. If other nations, following your bad example, wrongfully importune my ear with further impossible requests, how will it be possible for me to treat them with easy indulgence? Nevertheless, I do not forget the lonely remoteness of your island, cut off from the world by intervening wastes of sea, nor do I overlook your excusable ignorance of the usages of Our Celestial Empire. I have consequently commanded my Ministers to enlighten your Ambassador on the subject, and have ordered the departure of the mission. But I have doubts that, after your Envoy's return he may fail to acquaint you with my view in detail or that he may be lacking in lucidity, so that I shall now proceed to take your requests *seriatim* and to issue my mandate on each question separately. In this way you will, I trust, comprehend my meaning.

1. Your Ambassador requests facilities for ships of your nation to call at Ningpo, Chusan, Tientsin and other places for purposes of trade. Until now trade with European nations has always been conducted at Macao, where the foreign *hongs* are established to store and sell foreign merchandise. Your nation has obediently complied with this regulation for years past without raising any objection. In none of the other ports named have *hongs* been established, so that even if your vessels were to proceed thither, they would have no means of disposing of their cargoes. Furthermore, no interpreters are available, so you would have no means of explaining your wants, and nothing but general inconvenience would result. For the future, as in the past, I decree that your request is refused and that the trade shall be limited to Macao.

2. The request that your merchants may establish a repository in the capital of my Empire for the storing and sale of your produce, in accordance with the precedent granted to Russia, is even more impracticable than the last. My capital is the hub and centre about which all quarters of the globe revolve. Its ordinances are most august and its laws are strict in the extreme. The subjects of our dependencies have never been allowed to open places of business in Peking. Foreign trade has hitherto been conducted at Macao, because it is conveniently near to the sea, and therefore an important gathering place for the ships of all nations sailing to and fro. If warehouses were established in Peking, the remoteness of your country lying far to the northwest of my capital, would render transport extremely difficult. Before Kiakhta was opened, the Russians were permitted to trade at Peking, but the accommoda-

tion furnished them was only temporary. As soon as Kiakhta was available, they were compelled to withdraw from Peking, which has been closed to their trade these many years. Their frontier trade at Kiakhta is on all fours with your trade at Macao. Possessing facilities at the latter place, you now ask for further privileges at Peking, although our dynasty observes the severest restrictions respecting the admission of foreigners within its boundaries, and has never permitted the subjects of dependencies to cross the Empire's barriers and settle at will amongst the Chinese people. This request is also refused.

3. Your request for a small island near Chusan, where your merchants may reside and goods be warehoused, arises from your desire to develop trade. As there are neither foreign *hongs* nor interpreters in or near Chusan, where none of your ships have ever called, such an island would be utterly useless for your purposes. Every inch of the territory of our Empire is marked on the map and the strictest vigilance is exercised over it all: even tiny islets and far-lying sandbanks are clearly defined as part of the provinces to which they belong. Consider, moreover, that England is not the only barbarian land which wishes to establish relations with our civilisation and trade with our Empire: supposing that other nations were all to imitate your evil example and beseech me to present them each and all with a site for trading purposes, how could I possibly comply. This also is a flagrant infringement of the usage of my Empire and cannot possibly be entertained.

4. The next request, for a small site in the vicinity of Canton city, where your barbarian merchants may lodge or, alternatively, that there be no longer any restrictions over their movements at Macao, has arisen from the following causes. Hitherto, the barbarian merchants of Europe have had a definite locality assigned to them at Macao for residence and trade, and have been forbidden to encroach an inch beyond the limits assigned to that locality. Barbarian merchants having business with the *hongs* have never been allowed to enter the city of Canton; by these measures, disputes between Chinese and barbarians are prevented, and a firm barrier is raised between my subjects and those of other nations. The present request is quite contrary to precedent; furthermore, European nations have been trading with Canton for a number of years and, as they make large profits, the number of traders is constantly increasing. How could it be possible to grant such a site to each country? The merchants of the foreign *hongs* are responsible to the local officials for the proceedings of barbarian merchants and they carry out periodical inspections. If these restrictions were withdrawn, friction would inevitably occur between the Chinese and your barbarian subjects, and the results would militate against the benevolent regard that I feel towards you. From every point of view, therefore, it is best that the regulations now in force should continue unchanged.

5. Regarding your request for remission or reduction of duties on merchandise discharged by your British barbarian merchants at Macao and distributed throughout the interior, there is a regular tariff in force for barbarian merchant's goods, which applies equally to all European nations. It would be as wrong to increase the duty imposed on your nation's merchandise on the ground that the bulk of foreign trade is in your hands, as to make an exception

in your case in the shape of specially reduced duties. In the future, duties shall be levied equitably without discrimination between your nation and any other, and, in order to manifest my regard, your barbarian merchants shall continue to be shown every consideration at Macao.

6. As to your request that your ships shall pay the duties leviable by tariff, there are regular rules in force at the Canton Custom house respecting the amounts payable, and since I have refused your request to be allowed to trade at other ports, this duty will naturally continue to be paid at Canton as heretofore.

7. Regarding your nation's worship of the Lord of Heaven, it is the same religion as that of other European nations. Ever since the beginning of history, sage Emperors and wise rulers have bestowed on China a moral system and inculcated a code, which from time immemorial has been religiously observed by the myriads of my subjects. There has been no hankering after heterodox doctrines. Even the European (missionary) officials in my capital are forbidden to hold intercourse with Chinese subjects; they are restricted within the limits of their appointed residences, and may not go about propagating their religion. The distinction between Chinese and barbarian is most strict, and your Ambassador's request that barbarians shall be given full liberty to disseminate their religion is utterly unreasonable.

It may be, O King, that the above proposals have been wantonly made by your Ambassador on his own responsibility, or peradventure you yourself are ignorant of our dynastic regulations and had no intention of transgressing them when you expressed these wild ideas and hopes. I have ever shown the greatest condescension to the tribute missions of all States which sincerely yearn after the blessings of civilisation, so as to manifest my kindly indulgence. I have even gone out of my way to grant any requests which were in any way consistent with Chinese usage. Above all, upon you, who live in a remote and inaccessible region, far across the spaces of ocean, but who have shown your submissive loyalty by sending this tribute mission, I have heaped benefits far in excess of those accorded to other nations. But the demands presented by your Embassy are not only a contravention of dynastic tradition, but would be utterly unproductive of good result to yourself, besides being quite impracticable. I have accordingly stated the facts to you in detail, and it is your bounden duty reverently to appreciate my feelings and to obey these instructions henceforward for all time, so that you may enjoy the blessings of perpetual peace. If, after the receipt of this explicit decree, you lightly give ear to the representations of your subordinates and allow your barbarian merchants to proceed to Chekiang and Tientsin, with the object of landing and trading there, the ordinances of my Celestial Empire are strict in the extreme, and the local officials, both civil and military, are bound reverently to obey the law of the land. Should your vessels touch shore, your merchants will assuredly never be permitted to land or to reside there, but will be subject to instant expulsion. In that event your barbarian merchants will have had a long journey for nothing. Do not say that you were not warned in due time! Tremblingly obey and show no negligence! A special mandate!

2. THE TREATY OF NANKING, BETWEEN ENGLAND AND CHINA
[Signed August 29, 1842]

Article I

There shall henceforth be Peace and Friendship between . . . [England and China] and between their respective Subjects, who shall enjoy full security and protection for their persons and property within the Dominions of the other.

Article II

His Majesty the Emperor of China agrees that British Subjects, with their families and establishments, shall be allowed to reside, for the purpose of carrying on their Mercantile pursuits, without molestation or restraint at the Cities and Towns of Canton, Amoy, Foochow-fu, Ningpo, and Shanghai, and Her Majesty the Queen of Great Britain, etc., will appoint Superintendents or Consular Officers, to reside at each of the above-named Cities or Towns, to be the medium of communication between the Chinese Authorities and the said Merchants, and to see that the just Duties and other Dues of the Chinese Government as hereafter provided for, are duly discharged by Her Britannic Majesty's Subjects.

Article III

It being obviously necessary and desirable, that British Subjects should have some Port whereat they may careen and refit their Ships, when required, and keep Stores for that purpose, His Majesty the Emperor of China cedes to Her Majesty the Queen of Great Britain, etc., the Island of Hong-kong, to be possessed in perpetuity by Her Britannic Majesty, Her Heirs and Successors, and to be governed by such Laws and Regulations as Her Majesty the Queen of Great Britain, etc., shall see fit to direct.

Article IV

The Emperor of China agrees to pay the sum of Six Millions of Dollars as the value of Opium which was delivered up at Canton in the month of March, 1839, as a Ransom for the lives of Her Britannic Majesty's Superintendent and Subjects, who had been imprisoned and threatened with death by the Chinese High Officers.

Article V

The Government of China having compelled the British Merchants trading at Canton to deal exclusively with certain Chinese Merchants called Hong

Merchants (or Cohong) who had been licensed by the Chinese Government for that purpose, the Emperor of China agrees to abolish that practice in future at all Ports where British Merchants may reside, and to permit them to carry on their mercantile transactions with whatever persons they please, and His Imperial Majesty further agrees to pay to the British Government the sum of Three Millions of Dollars, on account of Debts due to British Subjects by some of the said Hong Merchants (or Cohong), who have become insolvent, and who owe very large sums of money to Subjects of Her Britannic Majesty.

Article VI

The Government of Her Britannic Majesty having been obliged to send out an Expedition to demand and obtain redress for the violent and unjust Proceedings of the Chinese High Authorities towards Her Britannic Majesty's Officer and Subjects, the Emperor of China agrees to pay the sum of Twelve Millions of Dollars on account of the Expenses incurred, and Her Britannic Majesty's Plenipotentiary voluntarily agrees, on behalf of Her Majesty, to deduct from the said amount of Twelve Millions of Dollars, any sums which may have been received by Her Majesty's combined Forces as Ransom for Cities and Towns in China, subsequent to the 1st day of August 1841.

Article VII

It is agreed that the Total amount of Twenty-one Millons of Dollars, described in the three preceding Articles, shall be paid as follows:
Six Millions immediately.
Six Millions in 1843....
Five Millions in 1844....
Four Millions in 1845....

Article VIII

The Emperor of China agrees to release unconditionally all Subjects of Her Britannic Majesty (whether Natives of Europe or India) who may be in confinement at this moment, in any part of the Chinese Empire.

Article IX

The Emperor of China agrees to publish and promulgate, under his Imperial Sign Manual and Seal, a full and entire amnesty and act of indemnity, to all Subjects of China on account of their having resided under, or having had dealings and intercourse with, or having entered the Service of Her Britannic Majesty, or of Her Majesty's Officers, and His Imperial Majesty further engages to release all Chinese Subjects who may be at this moment in confinement for similar reasons.

Article X

His Majesty the Emperor of China agrees to establish at all the Ports which are by the 2nd Article of this Treaty to be thrown open for the resort of British Merchants, a fair and regular Tariff of Export and Import Customs and other Dues, which Tariff shall be publicly notified and promulgated for general information, and the Emperor further engages, that when British Merchandise shall have once paid at any of the said Ports the regulated Customs and Dues agreeable to the Tariff, to be hereafter fixed, such Merchandise may be conveyed by Chinese Merchants, to any Province or City in the interior of the Empire of China on paying further amount as Transit Duties which shall not exceed——per cent on the tariff value of such goods.[1]

Article XI

It is agreed that Her Britannic Majesty's Chief High Officer in China shall correspond with the Chinese High Officers, both at the Capital and in the Provinces, under the term "Communication" *chao-hui.* The Subordinate British Officers and Chinese High Officers in the Provinces under the terms "Statement" *shen-ch'en* on the part of the former, and on the part of the latter "Declaration" *cha-hsing,* and the Subordinates of both countries on a footing of perfect equality, Merchants and others not holding official situations and, therefore, not included in the above, on both sides, to use the term "Representation" *ping-ming* in all Papers addressed to, or intended for the notice of the respective governments.[2]

Article XII

On the assent of the Emperor of China to this Treaty being received and the discharge of the first instalment of money, Her Britannic Majesty's Forces will retire from Nanking and the Grand Canal, and will no longer molest or stop the Trade of China. The Military Post at Chinhai will also be withdrawn, but the islands of Koolangsoo and that of Chusan will continue to be held by Her Majesty's Forces until the money payments, and the arrangements for opening the Ports to British Merchants be completed. [Article XIII, on ratification, omitted.]

[1]Tariff schedules were not settled at this time. The tariff rates on various goods were fixed after further discussions; they averaged about five percent.

[2]In Chinese official correspondence different terms of address were used for different official ranks. The Ch'ing government had previously required foreigners to use terms which implied inferior status. This Article was designed to ensure that British officials and their Ch'ing counterparts would address one another as equals.

3. IMPORTANT ADDITIONAL PRIVILEGES GRANTED TO FOREIGNERS IN SUBSEQUENT TREATIES

(a) Most Favored Nation Status

[Article VIII of the Supplementary Treaty of the Bogue, between China and Great Britain, signed October 8, 1843]

The Emperor of China having been graciously pleased to grant to all foreign Countries whose Subjects, or Citizens, have hitherto traded at Canton the privilege of resorting for purposes of Trade to the other four Ports of Fuchow, Amoy, Ningpo, and Shanghai, on the same terms as the English, it is further agreed, that should the Emperor hereafter, from any cause whatever, be pleased to grant additional privileges or immunities to any of the Subjects or Citizens of such Foreign Countries, the same privileges and immunities will be extended to and enjoyed by British Subjects; but it is to be understood that demands or requests are not, on this plea, to be unnecessarily brought forward.

(b) Extraterritoriality

[Articles XXI and XXV of the Treaty of Wanghia, between China and the United States of America, signed July 3, 1844]

Article XXI

Subjects of China who may be guilty of any criminal act toward citizens of the United States shall be arrested and punished by the Chinese authorities according to the laws of China, and citizens of the United States who may commit any crime in China shall be subject to be tried and punished only by the Consul or other public functionary of the United States thereto authorized according to the laws of the United States. And in order to prevent all controversy and disaffection, justice shall be equitably and impartially administered by both sides. . . .

Article XXV

All questions in regard to rights, whether of property or person, arising between citizens of the United States in China shall be subject to the jurisdiction of and regulated by the authorities of their own Government; and all controversies occurring in China between the citizens of the United States and the subjects of any other Government shall be regulated by the Treaties existing between the United States and such Governments, respectively, without interference on the part of China.

4. CHINESE ATTITUDES TOWARD FOREIGNERS
[From Thomas Taylor Meadows, *Desultory Notes on the Government and People of China,* 1847]

There seems to be an idea now somewhat prevalent in England, that the Chinese generally have, in consequence of the late war, attained a much more correct knowledge of foreigners and the power and state of their countries than formerly. This is, however, very far from being the case. Those who saw and felt us, though sufficient in number to populate a first-rate European kingdom, form but a very small portion of the Chinese people; and the great body of the nation, inhabiting districts and provinces that we have never yet reached, can only look on the late war as a rebellious irruption of a tribe of barbarians; who, secure in their strong ships, attacked and took some places along the coast; and even managed to get into their possession an important point of the grand canal, whereby they forced the Emperor to make them certain concessions. Nearly all they know of the fighting and of the character of the invading forces they must have learned from the mandarins' reports to the Emperor, and his answers to them, published in the "Pekin Gazette," and from copies of local proclamations which may have reached them. We may easily imagine, from the tone of these papers, that the Chinese, who from want of experience, would be unable to form sound judgments on such matters from *correct* data, must entertain opinions on the subject as erroneous as the accounts in these documents are distorted.[1]

It will be difficult for the Englishman, who is in the habit of obtaining speedy and correct information through the newspapers of all unusual occurrences, not only in his own, but in nearly every other country in the world, to comprehend this fully; but he must remember that the Chinese have (with the single exception of the "Pekin Gazette," containing nothing but official documents full of misrepresentations) no newspaper, and that the great body of the nation have no means of learning what passes at a distance from their own township. . . .

The apathy with respect to foreign things generally, even of the higher and, in the Chinese sense of the word, educated classes, and . . . when they meet a foreigner who understands their own language, is to an European quite astonishing. They very seldom ask questions, still more seldom is the information they seek after of a kind that tends to enlighten their minds on the state of foreign nations. . . . Their exclusion of foreigners and confinement to their own country has, by depriving them of all opportunities of making comparisons, sadly circumscribed their ideas; they are thus totally unable to free themselves from the dominion of association, and judge every thing by rules of purely Chinese convention. . . .

[1]The people in and around Canton *now confidently believe* that, although we beat the regular soldiers during the war, their own volunteer corps could expel us from the country.

"It is in the great size and wealth and the numerous population of our country; still more in its excellent institutions, which may contain some imperfections, but which after all are immeasurably superior to the odd confused rules by which these barbarians are governed; but, above all, in its glorious literature, which contains every noble, elegant, and in particular, every profound idea; every thing, in short, from which true civilization can spring, that we found our claim to national superiority." So thinks even the educated Chinese; and so the whole nation will continue to think until we have proved to them—no easy nor short task—our mental as well as our physical superiority. When some good works shall have been compiled in Chinese on natural law, on the principles of political economy, and on European national and international policy, then (after such works shall have obtained a wide circulation) when they perceive how much more deeply metaphysics have been explored by us than by them, and how studiously the best established principles of the sciences included under that term have been brought into practical operation by us, then, but not till then, will the Chinese bow before the *moral* power of the civilized west.

At present they take the tone of superiors quite unaffectedly, simply because they really believe themselves to be superior. I do not remember meeting among educated Chinese with a single instance of any want of candour in regard to this subject; whenever their minds once acknowledge anything foreign as superior to the Chinese article of the like sort, they at once admit it to be so. . . .

All Chinese who have seen them, are perfectly ready to allow, that our ships, guns, watches, cloths, etc., are much superior to their own articles of the like sort; and most of them would frankly admit us to be superior to them in all respects, if they thought so. But as above said, they do not. They are quite unable to draw conclusions as to the state of foreign countries, from an inspection of the articles produced or manufactured in them. They cannot see that a country where such an enormous, yet beautiful fabric as a large English ship is constructed—an operation requiring at once the united efforts of numbers, and a high degree of skill—*must* be inhabited by a people, not only energetic, but rich and free to enjoy the fruits of its own labour; that such a country *must*, in short, have a powerful government, good laws, and be altogether in a high state of civilization. All this the Chinaman, having never compared the various states of different nations, is not only quite unable to perceive of himself, but often not even when it is pointed out to him at great length. We have, it is true, the power to do some great and extraordinary things, but so have the elephants and other wild animals he occasionally sees and hears of; in his eyes, therefore, we are all barbarians, possessing perhaps some good qualities, congregated perhaps together in some sort of societies, but without regular government, untutored, coarse, and wild.

5. LIN TSE-HSÜ'S RECOGNITION OF WESTERN MILITARY SUPERIORITY
[From a Letter to a Friend, 1842]

[Lin describes to his friend how impossible it proved to control the barbarians.] The rebels' ships on the open sea came and went as they pleased, now in the south and now suddenly in the north, changing successively between morning and evening. If we tried to put up a defense everywhere, not only would we toil and expend ourselves without limit, but also how could we recruit and transport so many troops, militia, artillery, and ammunition, and come to their support quickly? . . .

When I was in office in Kwangtung and Kwangsi, I had made plans regarding the problems of ships and cannon and a water force. Afraid that there was not enough time to build ships, I at first rented them. Afraid that there was not enough time to cast cannon and that it would not be done according to the regulations, I at first bought foreign ones. The most painful thing was that when the Hu-men [the Bogue or "Tiger's mouth," the entrance to the Canton River] was broken into, a large number of good cannon fell into the hands of the rebellious barbarians. I recall that after I had been punished two years ago, I still took the risk of calling the Emperor's attention to two things: ships and guns. At that time, if these things could have been made and prepared, they still could have been used with effect to fight against the enemy in Chekiang last fall [1841]. Now it is even more difficult to check the wildfire. After all, ships, guns, and a water force are absolutely indispensable. Even if the rebellious barbarians had fled and returned beyond the seas, these things would still have to be urgently planned for, in order to work out the permanent defense of our sea frontiers. Moreover, unless we have weapons, what other help can we get now to drive away the crocodile and to get rid of the whales? . . .

But at this time I must strictly observe the advice to seal my lips as one corks the mouth of a bottle. However, toward those with identical aims and interests, I suddenly spit out the truth and am unable to control myself. I extremely regret my foolishness and carelessness. Nevertheless, when I turn my thoughts to the depth of your attention to me, then I cannot conceal these things from myself. I only beg you to keep them confidential. By all means, please do not tell other persons.

6. RUTHERFORD ALCOCK ON THE UNTENABILITY OF CHINA'S TRADITIONAL POLICIES TOWARD FOREIGN NATIONS
[From "Note on Our Present Position and the State of Our Present Relations with China," 1849]

If it be the traditional policy of the Tartar dynasty to keep foreigners at the outer confines of the empire and in a degrading position, it may with better justice be the policy of Great Britain to obtain direct action upon their centre, and freedom from idle and vexatious restrictions. The right of a nation to interdict intercourse and commerce, and therefore to determine upon what conditions it shall exist, is but an imperfect right, and subject to such modifications as the rights of other nations to the use of innocent objects of utility dictate; and the refusal of a common right is an abuse of the sovereign power, and an injury to be resisted.

China, however disposed its rulers may be to deny the fact, is one of a community of nations with common rights and obligations, and any claim to exemption from the recognized terms of national intercourse is inadmissible in the interest of all other countries. To admit such a right of exemption would be to allow the arrogated superiority in power and civilisation, and to pamper the hostile conceit of her people.

So long as the sovereign States of Europe will permit so obvious an inference it cannot be matter of surprise, and scarcely subject of reproach, to the Chinese, that they should be so ready to assert and so pertinacious in acting upon it.

But even if exclusion from the territories, from all trade and intercourse, were an absolute right in the first instance, the Chinese have forfeited all claim to its exercise—first, by voluntarily entering into relations political and commercial in ages past with other States and people, by exchange of embassies, by opening their ports and territories and encouraging trade; and secondly, by aggressive wars and invasion of the territory of Europe by the Tartar and Mongolian races who have ruled the country.

China preserves her undoubted right of self-preservation as a political society and an empire, but this does not involve the incidental right of interdicting intercourse, because her own histor shows that danger does not necessarily follow unlimited access, since as late as the seventeenth century such free communication existed with foreigners; and secondly, because the right of decision must be shared by the interdicted party.

7. THE POSITION OF THE BRITISH GOVERNMENT ON BRITISH AIMS AND CHINESE RIGHTS

[Instructions of the Foreign Secretary Lord Clarendon to Sir John Bowring, dated February 13, 1854]

Sir,

The Queen having been pleased to appoint you to be Her Majesty's Plenipotentiary and Chief Superintendent of British Trade in China, it is my duty to furnish you with such information as to the views of Her Majesty's Government with regard to China, as may serve to guide you in the execution of the duties which you are called upon to discharge.

If we have not as yet reaped all the advantages which were anticipated at the conclusion of our Treaties with China, from the extended intercourse with that Country for which it was the object of those Treaties to provide, it is nevertheless unquestionable that the Commerce of Her Majesty's Subjects in that Quarter has made rapid progress under the protection of those Treaties, and there is therefore good reason to expect that by prudent management commerce may be still further developed, and our intercourse with the Chinese Authorities and People set free from those obstacles which have hitherto beset it. So far indeed from its being a matter of surprise that more has not been done, it is a subject for congratulation that such results have already been secured notwithstanding the difficulties of no ordinary character with which we have had to contend. It is not to be expected that the notions of superiority over other Governments, which the isolated position in which the Government of China had so long entrenched itself had served to foster, should at once give way to a conviction that its claims in that respect were unfounded; or that the arrogance of the Authorities and the prejudices of the people should be altogether exchanged for feelings of cordiality and goodwill towards those who by force of arms had acquired a right to be treated with consideration and respect.

Neither was it to be expected that Trade should immediately receive the full development of which, judging from the vast population of the Country and from the productiveness of the soil and industry of the inhabitants, it might be supposed susceptible. There were habits of long-standing to be overcome, prejudices deeply rooted to be softened down, new Marts for Trade to be established, new arrangements to be made for meeting the increased demands of the Foreign Merchants for the produce of the soil. And it cannot be doubted that much of the disappointment which has been felt at the limited expansion of our intercourse with China since the conclusion of the Treaties, has originated in a disregard of these considerations.

We have now however arrived at a stage in our intercourse with China in which we may hope to turn to account the experience which during the last few years we have acquired. On the 29th of August of this year the period will have arrived at which, in conformity with the stipulations contained in the French and American Treaties with China, admitted by Keying (in his note of the 13th of January 1845, inclosed in Sir John Davis's despatch No. 5 of the 7th of February of that year) to be applicable to ourselves in virtue of the eighth article of the Supplementary Treaty of Humanchai [The Bogue], we are entitled to claim a revision of the British Treaties with China. It will accordingly be advisable at an early period after you enter upon the active exercise of your duties, to apprize the Chinese Authorities of your being instructed to require such a revision at the appointed time. I should observe however that there is a difference between the stipulations of the French and American Treaties on this point, the period of twelve years dating by the former from the exchange of ratifications, by the latter from the date of the Convention.

The Chinese Authorities may perhaps with some degree of plausibility object that the circumstances of the time are unsuitable for the commencement of so important a work; that the Imperial Government, harassed by the insurrection which convulses so many of the provinces,[1] cannot be expected to give its immediate attention to the subject. You will best be able to judge of the validity of this excuse; but you will under any circumstances obtain a recognition of our right to claim the revision on the 29th of August next, and a formal admission that if out of consideration for the embarrassments of the Imperial Government we are willing not to insist immediately upon our right, we are not to be precluded by our forbearance from urging our claim at a later period.

Some advantage may indeed arise from the postponement of the revision for a moderate time. In the first place, we shall have better means of judging of the probable result of the insurrection and be enabled to shape our negotiations accordingly.

It is impossible moreover that the barriers which have hitherto opposed the extension of foreign intercourse can be maintained under the state of anarchy which now prevails in some of the provinces; and we cannot fail, as a consequence of the civil war, to obtain greater insight into the character of the Authorities and the people of China, and in regard to the points to which our commercial energies may be directed with greater prospect of success; while on the other hand, the Chinese Authorities themselves will be induced to take a more correct view of foreign nations by the conviction which has been forced upon them, and of which they have given proof in the anxiety shown at Shanghai to enlist them in the Imperial cause, that their own boasted superiority has no real existence.

A moderate delay in the revision of the British Treaties may not also be without advantage by causing that operation to be effected more closely in point of time with that of the French and American Treaties, for it may be expected that the combined endeavours of the British, French and American Negotiators will be more likely to carry weight with the Chinese Government, than any exertions which may be made by either of those Powers singly to effect an improvement in the present state of things. But whether acting singly or in conjunction with one or both of your colleagues, you will never fail to bear in mind that Her Majesty's Government have no exclusive or selfish views as regards China. They desire that all the nations of the civilized world should share equally with them in whatever benefits, commercial or political, circumstances may enable them to secure for the British Nation in the Chinese Empire. They have nothing to conceal as regards their policy, and therefore you will be at liberty to communicate to your colleagues with the most unreserved freedom all matters to which in the course of your negotiations with the Chinese Authorities your attention may be directed. And in the full assurance that the feelings of Her Majesty's Government in this respect are shared by the Governments of France and the United States, I shall not hesitate to direct Her Majesty's Representatives in those countries to communicate to the respective Governments the Instructions contained in this dispatch.

In all your dealings with the Chinese Government you will always bear in mind that nothing is likely to be more fatal to our influence in China than the

[1] The Taiping Rebellion.

adoption of an authoritative tone in advancing points or urging concessions on which we are not prepared to insist. Such a course of proceeding would infallibly have the effect of encouraging resistance even to our best founded demands, and we might find ourselves on very inadequate grounds, and at a very inopportune moment reduced to the necessity of choosing between one of two alternatives, either of retracting our pretensions with loss of consideration and dignity, or of insisting on them at the risk of interruption of our commerce, and even of resort to force in support of our demands. There are unquestionably points which it would be desirable to secure, and to which we have even a right by Treaty; and among those I would mention free and unrestricted intercourse with the Chinese Authorities, and free admission into some of the cities of China, especially Canton.[2] The treatment of these questions however requires much caution; for if we should press them in menacing language, and yet fail in carrying them, our national honour would require us to have recourse to force; and in order to obtain results the practical advantage of which is not clearly demonstrable, we might place in peril the vast commercial interests which have already grown up in China, and which with good and temperate management will daily acquire greater extension.

But whenever we negotiate for the revision of our Treaties we may make proposals and recede from them without dishonour, if found unpalatable to the Chinese Government; and I do not therefore feel any hesitation in pointing out to you several matters which Her Majesty's Government conceive may very properly be urged on the Chinese Government.

The points are stated at length in a despatch which I addressed to Sir George Bonham on the 7th of May last, and as you will have the means of referring to that despatch, it is unnecessary for me to do more than enumerate them. They are:

1. To obtain access generally to the whole interior of the Chinese Empire as well as to the cities on the Coast: or failing this,
2. To obtain free navigation of the Yangtze Kiang [River] and access to the cities on its banks up to Nanking inclusive, and also to the large and populous cities within the seaboard of the Chekiang Province.

But I must observe that in the improved prospects of the Port of Foochow-foo, Her Majesty's Government would not be prepared, as they were in May last, to barter without further consideration that Port for concessions in any other quarter.

3. To effect the legalization of the Opium Trade.
4. To provide against the imposition of internal or transit duties on goods imported from foreign Countries, or purchased for exportation to foreign Countries.

[2]Although the Ch'ing government had acknowledged the British had the right of access to the walled city of Canton, the Chinese authorities had successfully prevented the British from exercising this right; this issue was a major source of contention between the two governments.

5. To provide for the effectual suppression of piracy on the coast of China.

6. To regulate, if possible, the emigration of Chinese Labourers.

7. To secure the permanent and honourable residence at the Court of Peking of a Representative of the British Crown; and if that cannot be obtained,

8. To provide for habitual correspondence between Her Majesty's Representative and the Chinese Chief Authority at the seat of Government, accompanied with sufficient security for the passage of the correspondence without interruption on the part of local authorities.

9. To provide for ready personal intercourse at the desire of either party, between Her Majesty's Representative and the Governor of the Province in which for the time being he may be residing.

10. To provide that, in the construction of the Treaty to be concluded, all doubts are to be solved by reference to the English version and that alone.

Your long experience in Chinese affairs may suggest to you other points for which it may be desirable to provide, and in regard to such, you may use your own discretion, taking care that whatever you urge be distinctly expressed, and in a manner not to admit of dispute or question hereafter, if the Chinese should agree to your proposals at the present time.

Much advantage would probably result from the negotiation for the revision of the Treaty being carried on at Peking, and you will accordingly propose to repair to that capital for the purpose. But as in the case of the permission given in 1850 to your predecessor to proceed to Peking for the purpose of having personal communication with the proper officers of the Imperial Government on matters of complaint which we had at that time against the Authorities at Canton, you will in the event of your going to the Chinese Capital for the negotiation of the new Treaty be careful not to give to your visit the character of a Mission to the Emperor involving questions of etiquette.

I need scarcely caution you against taking any part in the Civil contest which now rages in China. Justice and good policy equally prescribe to us the observance of the strictest neutrality between the contending parties. But you will at the same time take care that no injury is done to British Subjects by either party, as long as they keep aloof from the contest. If any ill-judging Individuals should be tempted by prospects of gain to favour the cause of either party, notwithstanding the declared determination of their Government to remain neutral, they will forfeit all claim to your protection, whatever prejudice they may suffer either in their persons or in their property from their wanton disregard of their obvious duty.

But as regards the rest of Her Majesty's subjects it will be your duty in communication with Her Majesty's Naval Authorities to afford them the most ample protection on all occasions and at all places where they stand in need of it.

I have only to add in conclusion that, in cultivating the most friendly relations with the Representatives of others Powers in China, you will act in the manner most consistent with the wishes of Her Majesty's Government.

—Clarendon

8. BOWRING'S ARGUMENT FOR THE NECESSITY OF USING FORCE TO OVERCOME CHINESE RESISTANCE TO FOREIGN AIMS

[Sir John Bowring to Lord Clarendon, dated Hong Kong, July 1, 1856]

My Lord,

I have the honour to forward to Your Lordship copy of a letter I have received from the United States' Commissioner announcing his intention of proceeding to the Northern Ports of China, and thence to the Gulf of Pecheli [Pei Chih-li], with a view of opening negotiations for the revision of the Treaty of Wanghia. I also enclose copy of my reply.

Even had the British Admiral received instructions to place the fleet, or any portion thereof, at my disposal, for the purpose of actively cooperating with the American Minister, I should have thought two ships of war an utterly inadequate contingent on the part of the United States for the purpose of effecting any important object. I am told by the French Chargé d'Affaires that he can do nothing whatever, as he has not a single ship at his service. Sir Michael Seymour[1] informs me he has no orders which enable him to offer any naval force to myself. I therefore have declined at present to enter into any engagement to accompany Dr. Parker[2] to the Gulf of Pecheli. I anticipate his utter failure, and fear the step he proposes to take will in no respect forward the common object. I consider Mr. McLane[3] and myself to have exhausted amicable representation in 1854, as I then reported to Your Lordship. A weak demonstration will confirm the obstinacy of the Court, and the Mandarins, whose scornful contempt has of late been more than ever exhibited in the non-acknowledgment by the Imperial Commissioner of the most important communications. To say nothing of ordinary business, to which I cannot obtain any, the slightest, attention, from His Excellency Yeh,[4] he has not condescended to give any reply whatever to either of the communications of the Representatives of the Treaty Powers demanding the revision of Treaties, nor to the despatch I sent on the 17th April, as reported in mine to Your Lordship No. 134 of 19 April on the subject of the Inspectorships. This neglectful and insulting silence is in itself a grievance of an intolerable character. The succession of Imperial honours which have been showered down on the Imperial Commissioner since his successes over the rebels appear to have made him wild with pride and vanity, and I am by no means sure that the simplest and safest policy would not be to humble that pride by *insisting* on

[1]Commander of British Naval Forces.

[2]Dr. Peter Parker, U.S. Commissioner in China, 1855–57.

[3]Robert M. McLane, U.S. Commissioner in China, 1854–55.

[4]Yeh Ming-ch'en, Governor General at Canton and Imperial High Commissioner in charge of foreign affairs, who was antiforeign and an obdurate opponent of granting concessions to the foreign powers.

an official reception at Canton, a reception which I believe he would not dare to refuse if he were informed that it would be *enforced* by us, if it should be denied by him. In such case I do not anticipate any refusal or denial, nor do I think an entrance into the City would be accompanied with risk or danger to myself or suite.

I wait with natural anxiety the views of Her Majesty's Government in reference to the many grave topics which have been from time to time pressed on Your Lordship's attention. In my present isolation I am able to accomplish nothing. If the settlement of Japanese matters be expected from me, a respectable fleet is a *sine qua non* for success; if any serious efforts are to be made to extend and improve our relations with China, ships of war are absolutely necessary; and if Cochin China is to be opened, I must have the means of proceeding to Hue, so as to compel attention from the Annamites. But I am in no condition to undertake anything at present, and I am informed by Sir Michael Seymour that if other instructions do not reach him it is his intention to proceed to India on the breaking up of the South West monsoon.

Meanwhile, we are losing time and influence in China, and I am wholly unable to avail myself of advantages which the present condition of the country might offer, keeping constantly in view that neutrality between contending parties which it is our duty and policy to observe.

—John Bowring

CHAPTER TWO
The Taiping Rebellion

Throughout Chinese history there has been a symbiotic relationship between foreign invasion and domestic rebellion, particularly during the declining years of a dynasty. That the Ch'ing government was faced with tumultuous rebellions at the time of the Western assault was thus not an unprecedented situation. Nor was it surprising that the imperial government responded with traditional methods.

Yet the Taiping Rebellion, the greatest of the internal threats to the dynasty, was not a replica of a familiar pattern, for the Taipings were not merely peasant rebels, but social and cultural revolutionaries as well.

Hung Hsiu-ch'üan (1814–64), the leader of the Taipings, was the third son of a poor peasant family of the Hakka minority people of southeastern China. As a young man Hung had enough ambition and ability to aspire to an official career, and his family was able to scrape together sufficient resources to enable him to study for the civil service examinations. He failed in each of four efforts to pass the exams for the lowest degree. During visits to Canton to study for and participate in the examinations, Hung came into contact with Protestant missionary tracts, and, briefly, with missionaries themselves. Through some complex psychological process, as yet not fully understood, he had a series of visionary experiences and came to believe that he was the younger brother of Jesus Christ, whose mission on earth was to extirpate the evils that infested Chinese society and to establish a Heavenly Kingdom in China. The quasi-Christian "Society of Good Worshippers" which Hung and a friend organized in 1846–47 soon came into conflict with the local gentry, and eventually with the government, partly because of the God Worshippers' iconoclasm, and partly because of the long-standing hostility between the Hakka minority and the non-Hakka majority of the population. In this hostile environment, Hung's religious organization increasingly took on political overtones, and by 1850 he and his followers were in open revolt against the Manchu dynasty. The rebellion spread rapidly over southeastern China, and then moved northward. In 1853 Nanking was captured and made the capital of the T'ai-p'ing T'ien-kuo, or Heavenly Kingdom of Great Peace. Here, Hung ruled as T'ien Wang [Heavenly King] until the city fell to Ch'ing armies in 1864.

In its growth as well as in its inception the Taiping Rebellion resembled previous peasant uprisings in a number of ways. Impoverishment of the peasantry due to population growth and pressure on the land, a militant religious ideology with a messianic tinge, nationalistic hatred of alien rulers, ineffective government armies grown stale after decades of relative inactivity and widespread corruption, had all contributed to previous rebellions. But there were also new forces at work. The foreign presence in China after the Opium War treaties had already begun to have an economic impact. Taiping ranks were swollen by inland transportation workers who had lost their jobs as trade shifted from Canton to the newly opened ports, especially Shanghai. And, as the documents in the following pages reveal, foreign ideas—some new, some reinforcing ideas previously associated with rebellions—played an important role in Taiping ideology.

Like later revolutionaries, Taiping leaders were not immune to the allurements of success. The Heavenly King and some of his closest associates lived in extravagant luxury in the Heavenly Capital. And as in later revolutionary movements, factional strife took a heavy toll within the highest levels of leadership. The Tung Wang [Eastern King], Yang Hsiu-ch'ing, second only to Hung Hsiu-ch'üan among the leaders, became increasingly ambitious, and was eliminated along with many others in a series of assassinations and massacres in 1856. The Heavenly Kingdom survived this crisis, but continuing weaknesses in leadership and the growing strength of new regional armies loyal to the Ch'ing ultimately led to the defeat of the rebellion. Nanking was overrun by government troops in 1864, and remnant Taiping forces were subdued within a few years.

Thus, although at one time or another Taiping armies penetrated sixteen of the eighteen provinces of China proper, the Heavenly Kingdom of Great Peace was never truly established. The ideals of the Taipings were put into effect only to a very limited extent and for a very short time. Nevertheless, the ideals are of immense significance as indicators of the kind of social order that so many among the usually inarticulate masses could find attractive. The documents in this chapter are relevant not only for what they tell us about actuality, but for what they reveal about latent forces, about potentialities.

Nationalism, as expressed in a virulent hatred of the alien Manchu rulers and the desire for a China ruled by Chinese, is one conspicuous example of a latent force to which the Taipings appealed and that later reappeared, in the revolutionary movement in the early twentieth century. The hostility toward Chinese officials who served the Manchus, which can be detected in Selection 9, became more pronounced among the later revolutionaries. The combination of political nationalism and foreign ideological influences also links the Taipings to the future. The influence of the Bible is immediately apparent in the Taiping version of history, in which Taoism, Buddhism, and the gods of Chinese folk religion are denounced as agents of evil. (Selection 10) Here, the past is used to serve a present political purpose, for like later revolutionaries, the Taipings reinterpreted history to prove the legitimacy of their claim to power, to designate the evils that were to be extirpated, and to show that the most powerful force in human affairs was on the revolutionary side. In the Taiping Christian-inspired history of the world, Chinese history is one part of an integral whole, and the great events of past and present, in China and elsewhere, are described as being the result of God's intervention in human affairs.

Although religion played an important role in their ideology, the Taipings were also concerned with more mundane matters. The elaborate system of land distribution and social organization detailed in *The Land System of the Heavenly Dynasty* (Selection 11) was the Taiping plan for a revolutionary alteration of Chinese society. It was not the first bureaucratic utopia in Chinese history, and resemblances to the People's Republic of China can also be seen, for example, the combination of egalitarianism (including equality of the sexes) and a hierarchically organized political and social order under the disciplined leadership of an ideological elite.

From these documents it may be inferred that the Chinese masses were not always and not uniformly instinctively conservative. Other documents, however, reveal the persistence of traditional values, even where they were logically inconsistent with new revolutionary doctrines. In Selection 12 we can discern a conflict between the Christian concept that all men and women are equally children of the one God and Confucian family relations, as well as hints of other tensions created by newly defined social relationships. The idea that private interest should be subordinated to the public interest links the Taipings to both the Confucian tradition and the Communist future. Also noteworthy is the appeal to the traditional ideals of harmony and propriety, both of which are again stressed in the *Ode for Youth*, where we find the Confucian theory that harmony is achieved by each individual fulfilling the obligations of his or her role in family and society. (Selection 13) Thoughtful readers will undoubtedly spot other interesting mixtures of the new and the old, of Chinese and foreign ideas.

Such doctrinal inconsistencies may reveal which traditional values were most deeply rooted. They also make it difficult to assess exactly how revolutionary the Taipings actually were, and historians still disagree over the degree to which the Heavenly Kingdom was a threat to traditional Chinese civilization. But it is clear from the final document in our selection that Tseng Kuo-fan (18ll–72), the leader of the campaign against the Taipings, perceived them as quite different from previous rebels, and that he saw their antagonism to traditional ways as their most distinctive and reprehensible trait. In his *Proclamation* (Selection 14), Tseng nevertheless follows the time-tested strategy of attempting to divide the rebel masses from their leaders by offering amnesty to the followers and vowing death

to those who refuse the offer. By referring to the Taipings as the Kwangtung and Kwangsi bandits, Tseng calls attention to their regional origins,
thereby attempting to arouse men from other provinces to resist these
"outsiders." In addition, he tries to demonstrate that the rebels are a threat
to the Chinese way of life, not merely to the Manchu dynasty. Tseng, who
throughout his career showed himself to be a model Confucian official and
loyal minister of the Ch'ing, was not the last conservative in modern China
to accuse revolutionaries of being un-Chinese, and to assume that the
people of China were basically content with the existing social and political
structure. It is significant that through such appeals, and other means,
Tseng succeeded in recruiting an army powerful enough to defeat the
Taipings. But it is also significant that the normally docile Chinese peasantry had demonstrated a revolutionary potential, which was to be more
effectively mobilized by later revolutionary leaders.

9. AN ANTI-MANCHU PROCLAMATION
[1852]

We, Yang, Assistant on the Left, the Chief of Staff, the Tung Wang, and
Hsiao, Assistant on the Right, the Chief of Staff, the Hsi Wang, of the true
Heavenly-mandated T'ai-p'ing T'ien-kuo, upholding Heaven's will to destroy
the Manchus, declare to the four directions, proclaiming:

O you masses, listen to our words. It is our belief that the empire is China's
empire, not the Manchu barbarians' empire; food and clothing are China's
food and clothing, not the Manchu barbarians' food and clothing; sons, daughters, and citizens are China's sons, daughters, and citizens, not the Manchu
barbarians' sons, daughters, and citizens. Alas! since the Ming's misrule, the
Manchus availed themselves of the opportunity to throw China into confusion;
they stole China's empire, appropriated China's food and clothing, and ravished China's sons, daughters, and citizens. Yet China, with the vastness of its
six combines and the multitudes of its nine divisions, permitted the Manchus
to act barbarously without considering it improper. Can the Chinese still deem
themselves men? Ever since the Manchus spread their poisonous influences
throughout China, the flames of oppression have risen up to heaven, the vapors
of corruption have defiled the celestial throne, the filthy odors have spread over
the four seas, and their devilishness exceeds that of the Five Barbarians. Yet
the Chinese with bowed heads and dejected spirits willingly became their
servants. Alas! there are no men in China. China is the head and Tartary the
feet; China is the land of spirits and Tartary the land of demons. Why is China
called the land of spirits? Because the Heavenly Father, the Great God, is the
true Spirit; heaven and earth, mountains and seas are his creations, therefore
from of old China has been named the land of spirits. Why are the barbarians
considered demons? Because the devilish serpent, the demon of Hades, is a
perverse demon; the Tartar demons worship only him, therefore we should
now consider the barbarians as demons. But alas! the feet have assumed the

place of the head; the demons have usurped the land of spirits and have forced us Chinese to become demons. Even using all the bamboo of the southern hills would not be sufficient to record the licentiousness that pervades the land; all the waves of the Eastern Sea would not be sufficient to wash away the sins which fill the heavens. We shall enumerate the facts which are known to all men, and discuss them briefly.

The Chinese have Chinese characteristics; but now the Manchus have ordered us to shave the hair around the head, leaving a long tail behind, thus making the Chinese appear to be brute animals. The Chinese have Chinese dress; but now the Manchus have adopted buttons on the hat, introduced barbarian clothes and monkey caps, and discarded the robes and headdresses of former dynasties, in order to make the Chinese forget their origins. The Chinese have Chinese family relationships; but the former false demon, K'ang-hsi, secretly ordered the Tartars each to control ten families and to defile the Chinese women, hoping thereby that the Chinese would all become barbarians. The Chinese have Chinese spouses; but now the Manchu demons have taken all of China's beautiful girls to be their slaves and concubines. Thus three thousand beautiful women[1] have been ravished by the barbarian dogs, one million pretty girls have slept with the odorous foxes; to speak of it distresses the heart, to talk of it pollutes the tongue. Thus Chinese womanhood has been humiliated. The Chinese have Chinese institutions; but now the Manchus have created devilish regulations and laws so that we Chinese cannot escape their nets, nor can we move our hands and feet. Thus all the men of China are in their bondage. The Chinese have the Chinese language; but now the Manchus have introduced slang of the capital and changed the Chinese tones, desiring to delude China with barbarian speech and barbarian expressions.

Whenever floods and droughts occur, there is not the slightest compassion; they sit idly by and watch the starving wander about until the bleached bones grow like wild weeds, for they desire to reduce China's population. Moreover, the Manchus have let loose covetous officials and corrupt lesser officials throughout the empire to strip the people of their fat until men and women weep by the roadsides, for they desire to impoverish us Chinese. Offices are to be obtained by bribes, and punishments to be bought off with money; the rich hold authority and heroes despair, for they seek to drive our Chinese heroes to a despairing death. Should any seek to launch a righteous uprising and revive China, the Manchus would as a rule charge him with plotting a rebellion and execute his nine relations,[2] for they desire to put an end to the plans of China's heroes. The Manchus in deluding China and abusing China have not failed to employ every extreme. What schemers they are! Formerly, Yao I-chung,[3] of barbarian origin, advised his son Hsiang to swear allegiance to China. Fu Yung,[4] also of barbarian origin, repeatedly advised his elder brother

[1]The palace concubines and slaves.

[2]Blood relations and members of the wife's family.

[3]Yao I-chung was a chieftain of the Ch'iang tribe who led an invasion of China during the Chin dynasty.

[4]Fu Yung was a general of one of the states during the Chin dynasty.

Chien against attacking China. Now the Manchus, having forgotten the meanness and baseness of their origin, have taken advantage of Wu San-kuei's[5] invitation, occupied China by force, and carried their villainy and viciousness to the extreme. We have carefully investigated the Manchu Tartar's origins and have found that their first ancestor was a crossbreed of a white fox and a red dog, from whom sprang this race of demons. They daily multiplied and contracted marriages among themselves, there being no proper human relationships nor civilization. Availing themselves of China's lack of heroes, they seized China. They established their own imperial throne and the wild fox ascended to occupy it; in the court the monkeys are bathed and dressed. We Chinese could not plow up their caves or dig up their dens; instead we fell into their treacherous plots, bore their insults, and obeyed their commands. Moreover, our civil and military officials, coveting their emoluments, bowed and knelt in the midst of these herds of foxes and dogs. Now, a child but three feet tall is extremely ignorant, but point out a pig or a dog for him to bow down to and he would redden with anger. The Manchu barbarians are not more than dogs and swine. Some of you, sirs, have read books and know your history; yet you do not know the slightest shame. Formerly, Wen T'ien-hsiang and Hsieh Fang-te[6] swore to die rather than serve the Yüan; Shih K'o-fa and Ch'ü Shih-ssu[7] swore to die rather than to serve the Ch'ing. This you gentlemen all know well. According to our calculations, the Manchu multitudes do not exceed a hundred and several tens of thousands, while we Chinese number no less than some fifty millions; for some fifty millions to come under the yoke of one hundred thousand is the greatest humiliation.

Now fortunately Providence is retributive and China will have every reason to revive; as men's minds are bent on order, there is evidence that the Manchu barbarians shall soon be destroyed. The demon's fortune of three by seven[8] has come to an end, and the true sovereign of nine by five[9] has already appeared. The Manchu's crimes having reached their full, August Heaven thunders with anger and commands our T'ien Wang sternly to display Heaven's majesty, to erect the standard of righteousness, to sweep away the barbarians, to pacify China, and respectfully to carry out Heaven's punishments. He says to all, whether far or near, that there is none without the willingness to support Him; whether official or citizen, all have the determination to hurry to unfurl the standard. Our arms and armor amidst righteous shouts are full of color; husbands and wives, men and women, prompted by public indignation, press to the fore, determined to slaughter the eight banners in order to pacify the nine provinces.

[5]Wu San-kuei was a Ming general who went over to the Manchus.

[6]The former refused to submit to the Mongols and was killed; the latter, when captured, starved himself to death.

[7]The former committed suicide at the close of the Ming dynasty; the latter was killed in the service of the last Ming emperor.

[8]Wen Shu, a Han astrologist, predicted the end of the Han dynasty in three by seven decades, or two hundred and ten years, from the beginning of the dynasty.

[9]From the *Book of Changes*; signifies a great ruler.

We hereby call upon the brave and noble of the four directions immediately to submit to God, in order to comply with God's will. Let us again capture a Shou Hsü[10] at Ts'ai-chou and seize a T'o Huan[11] at Ying-ch'ang; let us recover the long-lost territory and raise up God's principles. Any person who captures the Tartar dog, Hsien-feng, and brings him before us, anyone who can cut off his head and present it to us, or anyone who can seize or behead any of the Manchu barbarian chieftains shall be invested with high office; this promise shall not be broken.

Our Chinese empire has now received the great favor of the Great God who has ordered our Sovereign, the T'ien Wang, to rule; how can the occupation and prolonged misrule of the Manchu barbarians be permitted to continue? You gentlemen have for generations resided in China; who among you is not a child of God? If you can uphold Heaven in destroying the demons, seize the standard and be the first to mount the battlements and warn yourselves of Fan Feng's[12] late arrival, you shall be a hero without compare in the mortal world, and in Heaven you shall receive glory without bounds. If instead you cling to your delusions, protect the false and reject the true, in life you will be a barbarian and in death a barbarian demon. Between obedience and disobedience there is a great principle; Chinese and barbarians are clearly distinguished. Let each obey Heaven and free himself from the demons that he may be a man. You gentlemen have suffered under the Manchu oppression long enough; if you still do not know how to change your attitude and with united hearts and concerted efforts to sweep clean the barbarian dust, how are you to answer to God in high Heaven? We have raised our righteous army; for God above we shall avenge those who have deceived Heaven, and for China below we shall free the common people from their miseries. We are determined to sweep away every vestige of barbarian influence and to enjoy in union the happiness of T'ai-p'ing. Those who obey Heaven shall be richly rewarded; those who disobey Heaven shall be publicly executed. Publicize this throughout the empire; let all hear and know it.

10. THE TAIPING VERSION OF THEIR HISTORICAL ROOTS AND MISSION

[From *The Book on the Principles of the Heavenly Nature,* 1854]

With regard to the world of the ancients, there was only the true Way, and everyone, whether sovereign, minister, scholar, or commoner, worshipped the Great God. The *Book of History* says, "Thereafter, he sacrificed specially, but

---

[10]A Mongol Khan who committed suicide at Ts'ai-chou.

[11]The last emperor of the Yüan dynasty, who died at Ying-ch'ang.

[12]Yü of the Hsia dynasty summoned a meeting of the nobles; Fan Feng arrived late and was executed.

with the ordinary forms, to God." It also says, "The Ways of God are not invariable; on the good-doer He sends down blessings, and on the evil-doer He sends down all miseries." The *Book of Odes* says, "...with entire intelligence served God." It also says, "[Its kings] were the assessors of God." Mencius says, "Though a man may be wicked, yet if he adjust his thoughts, fast, and bathe, he may sacrifice to God." From these it may be known that God must be revered. The old records still exist, clear and evident, and can be examined. Moreover, since the creation of heaven and earth, only God, the true God, has been master of all; there have been no idols of clay, wood, and stone to confuse the people. Coming down to later generations, lost in the distant years, worldly ways daily entered the realm of heterodoxy; men's minds daily turned ever more to the frivolous. When they were men of slightly superior ambition and intelligence, and they showed some slight kindness for the people, then clay was molded and wood was carved in their images. These images were enshrined and all men reverently worshipped them, and generation after generation imitated them. Evil doctrines, therefore, arose from this, and strange acts were born from this. They did not know that the soul of man was given birth by the great power and the great virtue of the Heavenly Father. Occasionally there were men of superior ambition and intelligence who displayed a kindness for the people, yet these men were also given birth and nourished by the Heavenly Father, and blessed by the Heavenly Father. It is only that their ambition was great, and that they passed on the kindness of the Heavenly Father to the people. How could they falsely receive sacrifices and usurp the Heavenly Father's merits?

However, worldly customs daily degenerated. There were even those who likened themselves to rulers, and, being deluded in heart and nature, arrogant yet at fault, and falsely self-exalted, forbade the prime minister and those below to sacrifice to Heaven. Then [these men] competed in establishing false gods and in worshipping them, thus opening up the ways of the devilish demons. The people of the world all followed in like fashion, and this became firmly fixed in their minds. Thereupon, after a considerable time, they did not know their own errors. Hence the Heavenly Father, the Great God, in view of mortal man's serious crimes of disobedience, at his first anger, sent down forty days and forty nights of heavy rain, the vast waters spreading in all directions and drowning mortal men. Only Noah and his family had unceasingly worshipped the Heavenly Father, the Supreme Lord and Great God; therefore, relying on the Heavenly grace, they were fortunate and they alone were preserved. In this, the first instance of the Heavenly Father's great anger, was the great proof of his great powers displayed.

After the Flood, the devilish king of Egypt, whose ambition was mediocrity and who was possessed by demons, envied the Israelites in their worship of God and bitterly persecuted them. Therefore, the Heavenly Father in his great anger led the Israelites out of Egypt. In this, the second instance of the Heavenly Father's great anger, was the great proof of his great powers displayed.

However, the rulers and people of that time still had not completely forgotten the heavenly grace. But since the emergence of Taoism in the Ch'in [dynasty] and the welcoming of Buddhism in the Han [dynasty], the delusion of man by the demons has day by day increased, and all men have forgotten the grace and virtue of the Heavenly Father. The Heavenly Father's merits were falsely recognized as the merits of the demons. Therefore, the Heavenly Father, observing this from above, saw that the people of the mortal world followed the demons and were being transformed into demons; strange and peculiar, they were no longer men. The Heavenly Father once again became greatly angered; yet if he were to annihilate them completely, he could not bear it in his heart; if he were to tolerate them, it would not be consonant with righteousness. At that time, the elder son of the Heavenly Father, the Heavenly Elder Brother, Jesus, shouldered the great burden and willingly offered to sacrifice his life to redeem the sins of the men of the world. The Heavenly Father, the Supreme Lord and Great God, sincere in his pity for the world and profound in his love for man, spared not his eldest son, but sent him down to be born in Judea, and to redeem our sins in order to propagate the true Way. At the time of his redemption of our sins, he was falsely accused and nailed upon the cross, so that mortal man could rely upon his precious blood and be cleansed of all sin. Thereby did he make complete the grace of the Heavenly Father, who had sent him down to be sacrificed for the world. Thus, in the Heavenly Elder Brother's salvation of the world, how bitterly did the Heavenly Elder Brother suffer. Three days after his death he was resurrected, and as before he preached to his disciples on the Heavenly Way for forty days, after which he returned to Heaven. Moreover, he ordered his disciples to spread the gospel widely throughout the nations so that believers could turn to Heaven and non-believers be punished. Therefore, that the true Way has been transmitted everlastingly is largely due to the Heavenly Elder Brother's propitiation. Were it not for the Heavenly Elder Brother's merit in sacrificing his life, how could we younger brothers and sisters be as we are today? In this, the third instance of the Heavenly Father's great anger, was the great proof of his great powers displayed.

After the devilish barbarians seized and occupied China, they induced man to believe in demons even more profoundly. The devilish demons conducted strange practices to an even greater extreme; they deceived, seduced, and ensnared the souls of men under Heaven, causing them to sink into Hell where they could not turn to Heaven. The men of the world fell for their schemes and were thoroughly poisoned by them, due to their excessive belief in strange and abnormal things; thus they sank unknowingly. Moreover, the men of the world even mistook the things created by the Heavenly Father, God, to be the demons' things; therefore, they blindly failed to recognize the Great God, and were bold enough not to fear the Great God. Deluded and confused as they were, to hope that they would not be deceived by the demons would be of little avail.

Let us ask you elder and younger brothers: formerly the people sacrificed only to the demons; they worshipped the demons and appealed to the demons only because they desired the demons to protect them; how could they think that the demons could really protect them? Let us consider one example. During a drought, no man failed to worship the demons and to pray for rain. Certainly they did not understand that when the Heavenly Father decrees a drought, a drought follows; when he decrees rain, rain follows. If the Heavenly Father did not decree sweet rain, then even though they worshipped the demons of the mortal world, one and all, still the drought would continue as before. A popular saying has it, "If beating a drum can bring rain, then high mountains can be opened to cultivation; if the burning of incense can bring protection, then a smoking kiln can satisfy opium smokers; if a vegetarian diet can bring immortality, then bulls can ascend to Heaven; if taking opium can satiate hunger, then a fart can fertilize a field." Another popular saying goes, "The bean curd is only water; the king of Hell is only a demon." In view of this, it can be seen that the demons are not responsive and are unable to protect man. The people pray for rain, yet they cannot send down rain. To worship them is of no avail. However, the men of the world sank even deeper, not knowing how to awaken themselves. Therefore, the Heavenly Father again became angry.

In the *ting-yu* year [1837], our Heavenly Father displayed the heavenly grace and dispatched angels to summon the T'ien Wang up to Heaven. There He clearly pointed out the demons' perversities and their deluding of the world. He also invested the T'ien Wang with a seal and a sword; He ordered the Saviour, the Heavenly Elder Brother, Jesus, to take command of the heavenly soldiers and heavenly generals and to aid the T'ien Wang, and to attack and conquer from Heaven earthward, layer by layer, the innumerable demons. After their victory they returned to Heaven and the Heavenly Father, greatly pleased, sent the T'ien Wang down upon the earth to become the true Taiping Sovereign of the ten thousand nations of the world, and to save the people of the world. He also bade him not to be fearful and to effect these matters courageously, for whenever difficulties appeared, the Heavenly Father would shoulder the burden. In this, the fourth instance of the Heavenly Father's great anger, is seen the great evidence of his great powers in showing mercy and saving man. . . .

In the *jen-tzu* year [1852], at Yung-an *chou*, our food supplies were almost exhausted, nor was there any red powder [gunpowder]. The demons, several hundred thousand in number, rank upon rank, encircled the city from all directions. There was no avenue of escape. By this time the devilish demons knew of our situation and became unusually fierce, all believing their plan would succeed. In the third month the Heavenly Father greatly displayed His powers and ordered us younger brothers and sisters, one and all, to uphold the true Sovereign and attack Kuei-lin. We then moved the camps and broke through the encirclement; and because the Heavenly Father had changed our hearts, we one and all, with utmost energy and disregard for our persons struck through the iron passes and copper barriers, killing innumerable devilish demons, and directly arrived at the Kwangsi provincial capital. Thereupon Kwei-lin was encircled. Later, because the people of the city came out and spoke to the Tung Wang, reporting that the city granaries were empty and that provisions were deficient, the Tung Wang, seeing that their strength was exhausted, showed great mercy and immediately ordered a temporary lifting of the siege until another good plan of attack could be contrived. You all should know of the Heavenly Father's power, his omniscience, omnipotence, and omnipresence. Was it that the one city of Kuei-lin alone could not be attacked and secured? This was because our Heavenly Father secretly made it so; this is not easily understood by man.

Thereafter, from Kuei-lin we moved on to capture Hsing-an, Ch'üan-chou, Tao-chou, Ch'en-chou, and other moated cities. Wherever the Heavenly Army went, battles were won and objectives taken; wherever it went, the enemy scattered, our strength being like the splitting of bamboos. We moved from Ch'ien-chou to Ch'ang-sha; the latter city was attacked several times, and again we rushed by the city; this also was the result of the Heavenly Father's having secretly willed it so. If the army had entered Ch'ang-sha and had been stationed there long, then the boatmen at I-yang and other places along the river, being unable to avoid the trickery and intimidation of the demons, would have had to flee to distant localities. How then could we have obtained boats for a million brave soldiers, that we might float downstream to capture Wu-ch'ang? From this we can see that our Heavenly Father's power secretly made it so.

From Wu-ch'ang to Chin-ling [Nanking] the land extends as far as a thousand li; how strategic and important are the passes and river crossings, and how strong and firm are the cities and moats! To attack and capture the cities seemed difficult; even if victory could have been secured, it appeared that it would take a very long time. Yet in not more than one month's time, we had followed the stream eastward from Wu-ch'ang, passing Kiangsi, crossing An-hwei, and pushing directly up to Chin-ling, without the least resistance. After reaching this provincial capital, we found the height and thickness of the city walls and the vastness of the land to be indeed twice that of other provincial cities; to attack it seemed comparatively difficult. Who would have known that within ten days one single effort would bring success? Chin-ling was captured with our hands hanging at our sides. Had it not been for our Heavenly Father's power, how could things have been so quick and easy? From this we can again see the Heavenly Father's power to predetermine things. From this we can see that today our Heavenly Father and Heavenly Elder Brother are at work; if they desire to make the devilish demons live, they will live; if they desire to make the devilish demons die, they will die. The slightest manifestation of their power will sweep clean the devilish atmosphere, and the four seas will be at peace. The T'ien Wang has proclaimed: "Let the devilish demons plot for thousands and thousands of years; it will be difficult for them to escape the Heavenly Father's true measures. As rivers and mountains were created in six days, so must each of you believe in the Spiritual Father and be brave men." It can be known that the Heavenly Father's power and ability are indeed omnipresent. However, the fact that our Heavenly Father refrains from immediately exterminating the remaining demons is perhaps due to his desire to make our younger brothers and sisters determined at heart, to make them double their efforts in purification that they may enjoy the Heavenly Father's great blessings.

11. THE TAIPING PLAN FOR REORGANIZING CHINESE SOCIETY

[From *The Land System of the Heavenly Dynasty*, 1853]

Every army must have attached to it two persons in charge of land division, two in charge of law, two in charge of money and grain, two in charge of receipts, and two in charge of disbursement; in each case one is the chief and one the assistant, which positions are held by a colonel and a captain respectively, concurrently with their regular position. Those who are in office shall administer the affairs, while those who are not in office shall also assist. In each army, with regard to all births, deaths, promotions, demotions, and other such matters, the corps general shall report to the corps superintendent, the corps superintendent shall report to the royally-appointed corps commandant, the royally-appointed corps commandant shall next report to the general, then to the imperial guard, the commander, the senior secretary, and the chancellor. The chancellor shall report to the chief of staff, and the chief of staff shall report to the T'ien Wang. When the T'ien Wang hands down his edict, the chief of staff will respectfully carry it out.

Those meritorious officials of the original following shall through successive generations enjoy heavenly emoluments; as for those who have since joined the cause, under each army every family shall provide for one man to serve as a private. In case of alarm, the headman shall lead them as soldiers to fight the enemy and capture the bandits. In peacetime the headman shall supervise them as farmers in cultivating the fields and offering up the produce to the superiors.

All fields are to be divided into nine grades: every *mou* of land, which during the two seasons, both early and late [i.e., a two-crop harvest], can produce 1,200 catties [of grain] shall be ranked as a superior field of the first class; every *mou* that produces 1,100 catties as a superior field of the second class; and every *mou* that produces 1,000 catties as a superior field of the third class. Every *mou* that produces 900 catties shall be considered as a medium field of the first class; every *mou* that produces 800 catties as a medium field of the second class; and every *mou* that produces 700 catties as a medium field of the third class. Every *mou* that produces 600 catties shall be considered as an inferior field of the first class; every *mou* that produces 500 catties as an inferior field of the second class; and every *mou* that produces 400 catties as an inferior field of the third class. One *mou* of superior field of the first class shall be considered equal to a *mou* and one-tenth of a superior field of the second class, and to a *mou* and two-tenths of a superior field of the third class; also to a *mou* and three-and-a-half tenths of a medium field of the first class, to a *mou* and five-tenths of a medium field of the second class, and to a *mou* and seven-and-a-half tenths of a medium field of the third class; also to two *mou* of an inferior field of the first class, to two *mou* and four-tenths of an inferior field of the second class, and to three *mou* of an inferior field of the third class.

The division of land must be according to the number of individuals, whether male or female; calculating upon the number of individuals in a household, if they be numerous, then the amount of land will be larger, and if few smaller; and it shall be a mixture of the nine classes. If there are six persons in a family, then for three there shall be good land and for three poorer land, and of good and poor each shall have half. All the fields in the empire are to be cultivated by all the people alike. If the land is deficient in one place, then the people must be removed to another, and if the land is deficient in another, then the people must be removed to this place. All the fields throughout the empire, whether of abundant or deficient harvest, shall be taken as a whole; if this place is deficient, then the harvest of that abundant place must be removed to relieve it, and if that place is deficient, then the harvest of this abundant place must be removed in order to relieve the deficient place; thus, all the people in the empire may together enjoy the abundant happiness of the Heavenly Father, Supreme Lord and Great God. There being fields, let all cultivate them; there being food, let all eat; there being clothes, let all be dressed; there being money, let all use it, so that nowhere does inequality exist, and no man is not well fed and clothed.

All men and women, every individual of sixteen years and upwards, shall receive land, twice as much as those of fifteen years of age and under. Thus, those sixteen years of age and above shall receive a *mou* of superior land of the first class, and those of fifteen years and under shall receive half that amount, five-tenths of a *mou* of superior land of the first class; again, if those of sixteen years and above receive three *mou* of inferior land of the third class, then those of fifteen years and below shall receive half that amount, one and one-half *mou* of inferior land of the third class.

Throughout the empire the mulberry tree is to be planted close to every wall, so that all women may engage in rearing silkworms, spinning the silk, and making garments. Throughout the empire every family should keep five hens and two sows, which must not be allowed to miss their proper season. At the time of the harvest, every sergeant shall direct the corporals to see to it that of the twenty-five families under his charge each individual has a sufficient supply of food, and aside from the new grain each may receive, the remainder must be deposited in the public granary. Of wheat, pulse, hemp, flax, cloth, silk, fowls, dogs, etc., and money, the same is true; for the whole empire is the universal family of our Heavenly Father, the Supreme Lord and Great God. When all the people in the empire will not take anything as their own but submit all things to the Supreme Lord, then the Lord will make use of them, and in the universal family of the empire, every place will be equal and every individual well fed and clothed. This is the intent of our Heavenly Father, the Supreme Lord and Great God, in specially commanding the true Sovereign of T'ai-p'ing to save the world.

However, the sergeant must keep an account of money and grain figures in a record book, which he must present to those in charge of money and grain, and those in charge of receipts and disbursements. For every twenty-five families there must be established one public granary, and one church where the sergeant must reside. Whenever there are marriages, or births, or funerals, all may go to the public granary; but a limit must be observed, and not a cash be used beyond what is necessary. Thus, every family which celebrates a marriage or a birth will be given one thousand cash and a hundred catties of grain. This one rule is applicable throughout the empire. In the use of all things let there be economy, to provide against war and famine. As for marriages in the empire, wealth should not be a consideration.

In every circle of twenty-five families, the work of the potter, the blacksmith, the carpenter, the mason, and other artisans must all be performed by the corporal and privates; when free from husbandry they are to attend to these matters. Every sergeant, in superintending marriages and funeral events in the twenty-five families, should in every case offer a eucharistic sacrifice to our Heavenly Father, the Supreme Lord and Great God; all corrupt ceremonies of former times are abolished.

In every circle of twenty-five families, all young boys must go to church every day, where the sergeant is to teach them to read the Old Testament and the New Testament, as well as the book of proclamations of the true ordained Sovereign. Every Sabbath the corporals must lead the men and women to the church, where the males and females are to sit in separate rows. There they will listen to sermons, sing praises, and offer sacrifices to our Heavenly Father, the Supreme Lord and Great God.

In every circle of twenty-five families, the diligent husbandmen will be rewarded and the idle husbandmen punished; should disputes arise among the families, both parties must go to the sergeant. The sergeant will hear the case; if it is not settled, the sergeant must bring both parties before the lieutenant. The lieutenant will hear the case; if it is not settled, the lieutenant will report the case successively to the captain, the colonel, the provost marshal, and the corps general. The corps general, in consultation with the provost marshal, must try to decide the case. Having come to a decision, the corps general must send up a report of the case to the corps superintendent, the corps superintendent must next report it to the corps commandant, the general, the imperial guard, the commander, the senior secretary, and the chancellor. The chancellor must report to the chief of staff, and the chief of staff must memorialize the T'ien Wang. The T'ien Wang will then issue an edict instructing the chief of staff, the chancellor, the senior secretary, the provost marshal, and others, to examine the case carefully; and if there is no discrepancy, then the chief of staff, the chancellor, the senior secretary, the provost marshal, and others shall report the case directly to the T'ien Wang for his final decision. The T'ien Wang will then issue an edict giving his verdict; and whether it be for life or for death, for giving or for taking, the chief of staff shall, in obedience to the edict, carry out the judgment.

Among all officials and subjects throughout the empire, those who universally keep and obey the Ten Commandments of Heaven and who obey orders and faithfully serve the state shall thus be considered loyal subjects, and shall be raised from a low to a high station, their descendants inheriting their official title. Those officials who break the Ten Commandments of Heaven, disobey orders, receive bribes, or engage in corrupt practices shall thus be considered traitors, and shall be degraded from a high to a low station and reduced to mere husbandry. Those subjects who obey the Commandments and orders and exert themselves in husbandry shall be considered honest and faithful, and either elevated or rewarded; but those subjects who disobey the Commandments and orders and neglect the duties of husbandry shall be considered as evil and vicious, to be either put to death or punished.

Throughout the empire there shall be annual recommendations to fill the various official vacancies; if those recommended prove satisfactory, the recommenders shall receive rewards, but if the recommended prove unsatisfactory, the recommenders shall receive punishment. As for those privates and subjects who obey the Commandments and orders and are diligent in husbandry, the sergeant shall enumerate their virtues, record their names and surnames together with his own name and surname as the recommender, and present it to the lieutenant; the lieutenant, having examined the individual within his jurisdiction of 100 families and found the accounts correct, shall report the man, together with the name of his recommender, to the captain; the captain shall carefully examine the individual within his jurisdiction of 500 families, and if he finds the accounts correct, he shall report the man, together with the name of his recommender, to the colonel; the colonel shall examine the individual within his jurisdiction of 2,500 families, and if he finds the account correct, he shall report the man, together with the name of his recommender, to the corps general; the corps general shall examine the individual within his jurisdiction of the army, and if he finds the account correct, he shall report the man, together with the name of his recommender, to the corps superintendent; the corps superintendent shall next report to the corps commandant, the corps commandant shall next report to the general, the imperial guard, the commander, the senior secretary, and the chancellor; the chancellor shall then report to the chief of staff and the chief of staff shall report to the T'ien Wang; the T'ien Wang will then issue an edict transferring and selecting persons from the various armies throughout the empire who are recommended to serve under such and such a flag, as colonel, captain, lieutenant, sergeant, or corporal. Should any persons improperly recommend others, they shall be reduced to husbandmen.

All the various officials throughout the empire shall be promoted or demoted once every three years, in order to display the justice of the Heavenly Court. All those who improperly recommend others, as well as those who improperly accuse others, shall be reduced to husbandmen. When the year for promotion or demotion arrives, every headman shall recommend promotion or demotion for those under his command. Each lieutenant shall carefully examine the sergeants and the corporals under his command; if such and such a person indeed has a virtuous record, then record his virtuous acts, and if such and such a person indeed has a bad record, then record his bad deeds. He shall record the name of the individual, together with his own name as the person recommending promotion or demotion, and send both to the corps general. If it appears that a person can neither be recommended for promotion nor demotion, then retain him in his position and do not report it. Each captain shall also carefully examine the lieutenants, sergeants, and corporals under his command; and if such and such a person indeed has a virtuous record, then record his virtuous acts, and if such and such a person indeed has a bad record, then record his bad deeds. He shall report the name of the individual, together with his own name as the person recommending promotion or demotion, and send both up to the colonel. Each colonel shall carefully examine the captains and subordinate officers under his command; and if such and such a person indeed has a virtuous record, then record his virtuous acts, and if such and such a person indeed has a bad record, then record his bad deeds. He shall record the name of the individual, together with his own name as the person recommending promotion or demotion, and send both to the corps general. The corps general shall submit the names of those recommended for promotion or demotion by the colonels and subordinate officers, together with the names of those officers he himself has recommended for promotion or demotion, to the corps superintendent. The corps superintendent shall carefully examine those corps generals under his command; and if such and such a person indeed has a virtuous record, then record his virtuous acts, and if such and such a person indeed has a bad record, then record his bad deeds. He shall record the name of the individual, together with his own name as the person recommending promotion or demotion, and send both up to the royally appointed corps commandant. The royally appointed corps commandant shall carefully examine those corps superintendents under his command; and if such and such a person indeed has a virtuous record, then record his virtuous acts, and if such and such a person indeed has a bad record, then record his bad deeds. He shall record the name of the individual and his own name as the person recommending promotion or demotion and submit them together to the comptroller general and the commanding general. The comptroller general and the commanding general shall submit them to the commandants of the six boards and the chief of staff. The chief of staff shall directly report to the T'ien Wang for his final decision. The T'ien Wang will thereupon issue an edict on his final decisions, promoting the various corps superintendents who have been recommended for promotion by the various royally appointed corps commandants to either royally appointed corps commandants or imperial guards, and demoting the various corps superintendents who have been recommended for demotion by the various royally appointed corps commandants to either corps generals or colonels; promoting the various corps generals who have been recommended by the various corps superintendents to either corps superintendents or imperial guards, and demoting the various corps generals who have been recommended for demotion by the various corps superintendents to either colonels, captains, or lieutenants; promoting the various officers who have been recommended for promotion by the various corps generals to either one or two grades higher, or to corps generals, and demoting the various officers who have been recommended for demotion by the various corps generals to either one or two grades lower, or to husbandmen. When the T'ien Wang issues an edict, the chief of staff shall proclaim it to the Lieh Wangs, and the Lieh Wangs shall proclaim it to the commandants and subordinate officials, who shall put it into execution.

Those officials below the rank of corps superintendent shall all be recommended for promotion by their superiors, and recommended for demotion by their inferiors; however, as for the office of the royally appointed corps commandants, the T'ien Wang permits the various corps superintendents subordinate to this office to recommend these royally appointed corps commandants for promotion or demotion. As for chancellors, senior secretaries, commanders, generals, imperial guardsmen, and various officials within the Heavenly Court, the T'ien Wang permits their superiors to recommend one another for promotion or demotion, in order to preclude the malpractice of superiors and inferiors protecting one another. Moreover, with respect to the various officials within and without, if there are cases of great merit and accomplishment or great misconduct and malpractice, the T'ien Wang permits superiors and inferiors from time to time to recommend others for promotion or demotion, without the necessity of holding to the year for promotion or demotion. Whenever a superior's recommendation of an inferior for promotion or demotion is found to be false, he shall be reduced to a husbandman. Whenever an inferior's recommendation of a superior for promotion or demotion is found to be false, he shall be doubly punished. In recommending others for promotion or demotion, the detail of virtuous acts and bad deeds must contain substantial proof in order to verify their statements.

In the creation of an army, for each 13,156 families there must first be a corps general; next there must be five colonels under the command of the corps general; next there must be five captains under the command of each colonel, altogether twenty-five captains; next each of the twenty-five captains must have under his command five lieutenants, altogether 125 lieutenants; next each of the 125 lieutenants must have under his command four sergeants, altogether 500 sergeants; next each of the 500 sergeants must have under his command five corporals, altogether 2,500 corporals; next each of the 2,500 corporals must have under his command four privates, altogether 10,000 privates, the entire army numbering altogether 13,156 men.

After the creation of an army, should the number of families increase, with the increase of five families there shall be an additional corporal; with the increase of twenty-six families there shall be an additional sergeant; with the increase of 105 families there shall be an additional lieutenant; with the increase of 526 families there shall be an additional captain; with the increase of 2,631 families there shall be an additional colonel; with the total increase of 13,156 families there shall be an additional corps general. Before a new corps general is appointed, the colonel and subordinate officers shall remain under the command of the old corps general; with the appointment of a corps general they must be handed over to the command of the new corps general.

Within [the court] and without, all the various officials and people must go every Sabbath to hear the expounding of the Holy Bible, reverently offer their sacrifices, and worship and praise the Heavenly Father, the Supreme Lord and Great God. On every seventh seven, the forty-ninth day, the Sabbath, the colonel, captains, and lieutenants shall go in turn to the churches in which reside the sergeants under their command and expound the Holy books, instruct the people, examine whether they obey the Commandments and orders or disobey the Commandments and orders, and whether they are diligent or slothful. On the first seventh seven, the forty-ninth day, the Sabbath, the colonel shall go to a certain sergeant's church, on the second seventh seven, the forty-ninth day, the Sabbath, the colonel shall then go to another sergeant's church, visiting them all in order, and after having gone the round he must begin again. The captains and lieutenants shall do the same.

Each man throughout the empire who has a wife, sons, and daughters amounting to three or four mouths, or five, six, seven, eight, or nine mouths, must give up one to be a soldier. With regard to the others, the widowers, widows, orphaned, and childless, the disabled and sick, they shall all be exempted from military service and issued provisions from the public granaries for their sustenance.

Throughout the empire all officials must every Sabbath, according to rank and position reverently present sacrificial animals and offerings, sacrifice and worship, and praise the Heavenly Father, the Supreme Lord and Great God. They must also expound the Holy books; should any dare to neglect this duty, they shall be reduced to husbandmen. Respect this.

12. THE PERSISTENCE OF TRADITIONAL VALUES, AND OTHER PROBLEMS
[From *The Book on the Principles of the Heavenly Nature,* 1854]

Speaking of worldly feelings, it is true that each has his own parents and there must be distinction in family names; it is also true that as each has his own family, there must be a distinction between this boundary and that boundary. Yet we must know that the ten thousand names derive from the one name, and the one name from one ancestor. Thus our origins are not different. Since our Heavenly Father gave us birth and nourishment, we are of one form though of separate bodies, and we breathe the same air though in different places. This is why we say all are brothers within the four seas. Now, basking in the profound mercy of Heaven, we are of one family. Brothers and sisters are all of the same parentage; as all are born of one Spiritual Father, why should there be the distinction of "you and I," or "others and ourselves"? When there is clothing, let all wear it; when there is food, let all eat of it. When someone is ill, others should ask a doctor to treat him .and take care of his medicine. We must treat parentless boys and girls and persons of advanced age with more care, bathing them and washing and changing their clothes. Thus we will not lose the idea of sharing joys and sorrows, as well as mutual concern over pain and illness. Safety for the old, sympathy for the young, and compassion for the orphaned, all emerge from the Tung Wang's understanding of our Heavenly Father's love for the living and from the T'ien Wang's treating all as brothers and fellow beings. It is for this reason that [the Tung Wang's] mercy reaches the lowest of people in their minutest trouble. The edict says, "Help others when they are in distress, and Heaven will help you when you are in distress. Regard others' calamity and sickness as your own sickness; regard others' hunger and cold as your own hunger." In this it can be seen that since ancient times the vastness of mercy and the virtue of kindness of the Heavenly Kingdom have been unsurpassable.

As for [maintaining] our brothers' peace in the camps, everyone must be kind, industrious, and careful. When the skies are clear the soldiers should be drilled, and when it rains the heavenly books should be read, clearly expounded, and mutually discussed, so that everybody will know the nature of Heaven and forever abide by the true Way. If the demons advance, at the first beat of the signal drums, everyone must hurriedly arm himself with gun, sword, or spear, and hasten to the palace to receive orders. In charging forward, each must strive to be in the front, fearing to be left behind, and none must shirk responsibilities. Thus will we be of one virtue and of one heart. Even if there are a million demons, they will not be hard to exterminate instantly.. . . .We brothers, our minds having been awakened by our Heavenly Father, joined the camp in the early days to support our Sovereign, many bringing parents, wives, uncles, brothers, and whole families. It is a matter of course that we should attend to our parents and look after our wives and children, but when a new rule is first created, the state must come first and the family last, public interests first and private interests last.

Moreover, as it is advisable to avoid suspicion [of improper conduct] between the inner [female] and the outer [male] and to distinguish between male and female, so men must have male quarters and women must have female quarters; only thus can we be dignified and avoid confusion. There must be no common mixing of the male and female groups, which would cause debauchery and violation of Heaven's commandments. Although to pay respects to parents and to visit wives and children occasionally are in keeping with human nature and not prohibited, yet it is only proper to converse before the door, stand a few steps apart, and speak in a loud voice; one must not enter the sisters' camp or permit the mixing of men and women. Only thus, by complying with rules and commands, can we become sons and daughters of Heaven. . . .

We brothers and sisters should each know how to exert our efforts and be correct. There is one special warning for our brothers. We often see people who rely on force and the favor of their superiors, who neglect the line between superior and inferior. But we must know that the practice of propriety lies chiefly in harmony; those above must not oppress the inferiors because of their superiority, nor oppress the small because they are great; those below must not humiliate their elders because of their youth, nor, because of their inferiority, usurp their preeminent position. Each must control himself with propriety and meet others in harmony. In this manner we shall not lose our chance of becoming good citizens of the Heavenly Kingdom. The T'ien Wang's edict says, "High Heaven and the ten thousand people are of one heart; each must strive for harmony in order to promote mutual discussion." It also says, "To all who are given birth and nourished by Heaven, harmony is precious; everyone must be at peace with others in order to enjoy the great tranquillity." This clearly indicates that harmony is worth cherishing. In the streets especially one must not resort to force and become self-indulgent, nor act wildly and without restraint. One must be humble and submissive in order to maintain dignity; one must not take advantage of the kindness and liberality of the Tung Wang and the tolerance of the other Wangs to oppress the small and humiliate the great. The Tung Wang regards everyone under Heaven as of the same flesh, and his love and hatred are based on justice; therefore, if one resorts to force, misbehaves, and forgets humility, he will incur the righteous anger of the Tung Wang, who, upholding and exercising Heaven's law, will judge him justly, with a judgment not biased by personal feelings. Furthermore, the Tung Wang has published edicts and proclamations and has taught tirelessly. He has repeatedly warned you because he wants us younger brothers and sisters to be harmonious with each other. How then could any person be arrogant and act recklessly without fear?

13. CHRISTIANITY AND CONFUCIANISM IN TAIPING IDEOLOGY

[From *Ode for Youth*, 1851]

On Reverence for God

1

Let the true Spirit, the Great God,
Be honored and adored by all nations;
Let the many men and women of the world,
Morning and evening worship him alike.

2

Above and below, look where you may,
All things are imbued with God's favor.
At the beginning, in six days,
All things were created, perfect and complete.

On Reverence for Jesus

1

Jesus, His first-born son,
Was in former times sent by God;
To redeem us from sin he willingly gave his life,
Truly must we acknowledge his merits.

2

His cross was hard to bear;
The sorrowing clouds obscured the sun.
Heaven honors its noble Son,
Who died for you, the men of the world.

3

After his resurrection he ascended to heaven;
Resplendent in glory, he wields authority supreme.
To him we know that we may trust,
To secure salvation and ascend to high heaven.

On Reverence for Parents

1

As grain is stored against a day of need,
So men bring up children to tend their old age.
A filial son begets filial children;
The recompense here is truly wonderful.

2

Ask yourself how this, your body,
Is to attain maturity?
Obey the Fifth Heavenly Commandment,
And honor and emolument will descend from heaven.

On the Sovereign's Way

When one man heads an upright government,
All nations become settled and tranquillized.
When the sovereign alone holds majestic power,
Calumny and evil sink into the abyss.

On the Ministers' Way

When the ruler is upright, ministers are upright;
When the sovereign is intelligent, ministers will be virtuous.
I and Chou[1] are models worthy of imitation;
They grasped the upright and upheld governmental principles.

On the Households' Way

The family members related by bone and flesh
Should in joy and harmony unite.
When the feeling of concord unites the whole,
Blessings will descend upon them from heaven.

[1]I-yin of the Shang dynasty, and Chou Kung of the Chou dynasty, both noted as virtuous ministers.

On the Fathers' Way

When the ridgepole is straight, nothing will be irregular below;
When the father is strict, the Way will be formed.
Let him not provoke his children to wrath,
And the whole dwelling will be filled with harmony.

On the Sons' Way

Sons, be patterns to your wives;
Obedience to parents is your natural duty.
To the tattle of women never listen,
And you will not be estranged from your own flesh.

On the Daughters-in-Law's Way

You who are espoused into other families,
Be gentle and yielding, and your duty will be fulfilled.
Do not quarrel with your sisters-in-law
Or quarrel and vex the father-in-law and mother-in-law.

On the Elder Brothers' Way

Elder brothers, instruct your younger brothers;
Remember always your common parentage.
Should the younger brother commit some trifling fault,
Bear with it and be indulgent.

On the Younger Brothers' Way

That there should be old and young is ordered by Heaven;
The way to follow elder brothers lies in respect.
When younger brothers understand Heaven's manifest principles,
Happiness and honor will be their portion.

On the Husbands' Way

The husband's way is based on firmness;
Love for a wife should be qualified by prudence.
And should the lioness east of the river roar,[2]
Let not the heart be filled with terror.

---

[2]"Lioness east of the river" is an idiom for "domineering wife."

On the Wives' Way

The wife's way lies in the three obediences;[3]
Do not disobey your husband.
If hens crow in the morning,
There will be self-sought misery for the family.

Heaven

Honor and vulgarity come from the self;
Manliness depends on self-strengthening.
Keep the Ten Heavenly Commandments,
And enjoy bliss in heaven.

14. TSENG KUO-FAN'S IDEOLOGICAL COUNTERATTACK
["Proclamation against the Bandits of Kwangtung and Kwangsi," 1854]

It has been five years since the rebels Hung Hsiu-ch'üan and Yang Hsiu-ch'ing started their rebellion. They have inflicted bitter sorrow upon millions of people and devastated more than 5000 *li* of *chou* and *hsien*. Wherever they pass, boats of all sizes, and people, rich and poor alike, have all been plundered and stripped bare; not one inch of grass has been left standing. The clothing has been stripped from the bodies of those captured by these bandits, and their money has been seized. Anyone with five taels or more of silver who does not contribute it to the bandits is forthwith decapitated. Men are given one *ho* [1/10th pint] of rice per day, and forced to march in the forefront in battle, to construct city walls, and dredge moats. Women are also given one *ho* of rice per day, and forced to stand guard on the parapets at night, and to haul rice and carry coal. The feet of women who refuse to unbind them are cut off and shown to other women as a warning. The corpses of boatmen who secretly conspired to flee were hung upside down to show other boatmen as a warning. The Yüeh [Kwangtung and Kwangsi] bandits indulge themselves in luxury and high position, while the people in our own Yangtze provinces living under their coercion are treated worse than animals. This cruelty and brutality appalls anyone with blood in his veins.

Ever since the times of Yao, Shun, and the Three Dynasties, sages, generation after generation, have upheld the Confucian teachings, stressing proper human relationships, between ruler and minister, father and son, superiors and subordinates, the high and the low, all in their proper place, just as hats and shoes are not interchangeable. The Yüeh bandits have stolen a few scraps from

---

[3]Obedience to father, husband, and sons.

the foreign barbarians and worship the Christian religion. From their bogus ruler and bogus chief ministers down to their soldiers and menial underlings, all are called brothers. They say that only heaven can be called father; aside from him, all fathers among the people are called brothers, and all mothers are called sisters. Peasants are not allowed to till the land for themselves and pay taxes, for they say that the fields all belong to the T'ien Wang. Merchants are not allowed to trade for profit, for they say that all goods belong to the T'ien Wang. Scholars may not read the Confucian classics, for they have their so-called teachings of Jesus and the New Testament. In a single day several thousand years of Chinese ethical principles and proper human relationships, classical books, social institutions and statutes have all been completely swept away. This is not just a crisis for our Ch'ing dynasty, but the most extraordinary crisis of all time for the Confucian teachings, which is why our Confucius and Mencius are weeping bitterly in the nether world. How can any educated person sit idly by without thinking of doing something?

Since ancient times, those with meritorious accomplishments during their lifetimes have become spirits after death; the Kingly Way governs the living and the Way of the Spirits governs among the dead. Even rebellious ministers and wicked sons of the most vicious and vile sort show respect and awe toward the spirits. When Li Tzu-ch'eng reached Ch'ü-fu [Confucius' birthplace], he did not molest the Temple of the Sage.[1] When Chang Hsien-chung reached Tzu-t'ung, he sacrificed to Wen Ch'ang.[2] But the Yüeh bandits burned the school at Shen-chou, destroyed the wooden tablet of Confucius, and wildly scattered the tablets of the Ten Paragons in the two corridors all over the ground.[3] Afterwards, wherever they have passed, in every district, the first thing they have done is to burn down the temples, defiling the shrines and maiming the statues even of loyal ministers and righteous heroes such as the awesome Kuan Yü and Yüen Fei.[4] Even Buddhist and Taoist temples, shrines of guardian dieties and altars to local gods have all been burned, and every statue destroyed. The ghosts and spirits in the world of darkness are enraged at this, and want to avenge their resentment.

I, the Governor-General, having received His Imperial Majesty's command, leading 20,000 men advancing together on land and water, vow that I shall sleep on nettles and sip gall [to strengthen my determination] to exterminate these vicious traitors, to rescue our captured boats, and to deliver the persecuted people, not only in order to relieve the Emperor of his strenuous and conscientious labors from dawn to dusk, but also to comfort Confucius and Mencius for their silent sufferings over the proper human relationships; not

[1]Li Tzu-ch'eng was a major rebel leader at the end of the Ming dynasty.

[2]Chang Hsien-chung was another important rebel leader at the end of the Ming. Wen Ch'ang was the God of Literature, closely associated with the literati, and with the civil service examination system.

[3]The Ten Paragons were ten famous Confucians, whose tablets were arranged along two corridors, East and West, in Confucian temples.

[4]Two famous generals and loyal officials. Kuan Yü was deified as the God of War.

only to avenge the millions who have died unjust deaths, but also to avenge the insults to all the spirits.

Therefore, let this proclamation be disseminated far and near so that all may know the following: Any red-blooded hero who assembles a company of righteous troops to assist in our extermination campaign will be taken in as my personal friend, and the troops given rations. Any Confucian gentleman who cherishes the Way, is pained at Christianity running rampant over the land, and who, in a towering rage, wants to defend our Way, will be made a member of the Governor-General's personal staff and treated as a guest teacher. Any benevolent person, stirred by moral indignation, who contributes silver or assists with provisions, will be given a treasury receipt and a commission from the Board of Civil Appointments for a donation of 1000 *chin* or less, and a special memorial will be composed requesting a liberal reward for a donation of over 1000 *chin*. If anyone voluntarily returns after a long stay among the bandits, and kills one of their leaders or leads a city to surrender, he will be taken into the army of the Governor-General, and, upon the request of the Governor-General to the Emperor, will be given an official title. Anyone who has lived under the bandits' coercion for some years, whose hair has grown several inches long, but who discards his weapon when the fighting is about to commence and returns to the fold barehanded, will receive an amnesty from the death sentence, and will be given travel expenses to return home.

In the past, at the end of the Han, T'ang, Yuan, and Ming, bands of rebels were innumerable, all because of foolish rulers and misgovernment, so that none of these rebellions could be stamped out. But today the Son of Heaven is deeply concerned and examines his character in order to reform himself, worships Heaven, and is sympathetic to the people. He has not increased the land tax, nor has he conscripted soldiers from households. With the profound benevolence of the sages, he is suppressing the cruel and worthless bandits. It does not require any great wisdom to see that sooner or later they will all be destroyed.

Those of you who have been coerced into joining the rebels, or who willingly follow the traitors, and oppose the Imperial Crusade [are warned that] when the Imperial forces sweep down it will no longer be possible to discriminate between the good and the evil—every person will be crushed.

I, the Governor-General, am scant in virtue and of meager ability. I rely solely on two words, trust and loyalty, as the foundation for running the army. Above are the sun and the moon, below the ghosts and spirits; in this world, the vast waters of the Yangtze, and in the other world, the souls of loyal ministers and stalwart heroes who gave their lives in battle against previous rebellions. Let all peer into my heart and listen to my words.

Upon arrival, this proclamation immediately has the force of law. Do not disregard it!

CHAPTER THREE
The Self-Strengthening Movement

With the suppression of the Taiping and other rebellions, the governance of the empire reverted to defenders of the traditional order. The men who had organized and led the pro-Ch'ing forces to victory took the lead in attempting to solve the problems of restoring order, reviving the economy, and stemming the foreign threat. These men had a better understanding of the dimensions of the Western challenge than their predecessors had had in the 1840s and 1850s, and they realized that some changes would be necessary to deal with the unprecedented situation.

Their response was a program of reforms that came to be known as Self-Strengthening. A limited number of Western techniques were to be adopted and accommodated within the framework of revitalized traditional institutions. Though progressive for their time, the Self-Strengtheners were essentially conservatives, willing to make necessary adjustments, but opposed to fundamental alterations. Western technology was to be used to preserve the Chinese way of life, not to erode it.

The first section of this chapter contains brief statements of some of the most important themes of the Self-Strengthening movement, drawn from the writings of several of the best-known proponents of limited reform. Feng Kuei-fen (1809–74) was one of the earliest and most important theoreticians of the Self-Strengthening movement. Although a *chin-shih* graduate, Feng never rose to high office; his influence was exerted through his writings and his serving as an advisor to senior statesmen such as Tseng Kuo-fan and Li Hung-chang. Feng's essay on Western learning is a succinct presentation of the basic program of the Self-Strengtheners, which Feng summarizes in the last sentence of this excerpt. (Selection 15) In his essay on Western technology (Selection 16), Feng makes three important points, linked together in a logical sequence. To be militarily strong, China must have ships and guns as good as those of the Westerners. In order to be certain of possessing these weapons when they are needed, China must be able to manufacture them independently, and hence must encourage the development of the requisite skills, both manufacturing techniques and underlying scientific principles. Finally, adequate rewards must be offered to encourage men to acquire these difficult new skills. Like other Self-Strengtheners, Feng assumes that these innovations can grow alongside existing insititutions without subverting them.

Foreign humiliation of China is cited by Feng as a reason for self-strengthening. Feelings of shame and humiliation, so central a part of the traditional scheme of values, were frequently to be mentioned by reformers, and later by revolutionaries, as a compelling motive for making changes. In such ways, this and other traditional values were instrumental in justifying the alteration, or rejection, of some traditional ways.

Tseng Kuo-fan, the chief strategist and organizer of the victory over the Taipings, was the most eminent leader of the Self-Strengthening movement in its early years. Li Hung-chang (1823–1901), who rose to prominence as a protégé of Tseng, became the most vigorous promoter of Self-Strengthening projects, and was a leading statesman from Tseng's death till the end of the century. In the short excerpts from two writings by Li in 1863 and 1864, Feng's influence is apparent. Li's main recommendations are simply stated: 1) in order to counter the foreign threat, China must first of all have qualified foreign language experts, so as to be able to communicate with the foreigners on their own terms, and to learn their technology; (Selection 17) 2) China must learn how to manufacture the weapons that are the source of the foreigners' power. (Selection 18) Li does not conceive of these measures as requiring large investments or major alterations of existing institutions. The 1871 joint memorial of Tseng and Li proposes a further innovation. To fully understand Western technology, they argue, Chinese must receive the best Western training, and this can only be done by studying in the West. (Selection 19) The next year, thirty teenage students were sent to the United States. All together 120 students were sent to the United States and thirty to Britain and France before the project was terminated in 1881 because of alarms raised by conservatives over the subversive influences of Western life on the young men. Not until the early twentieth century did large numbers of Chinese go abroad to study.

Like Feng Kuei-fen, Hsüeh Fu-ch'eng (1838–94) achieved fame and influence as a writer and as a secretary and advisor to Tseng and Li. But unlike Tseng, Li, and Feng, Hsueh was not a *chin-shih*, never took the higher civil service examinations, and was a harsh critic of the exam system. Hsueh advocated more extensive reforms than earlier writers had done. His essay on reform (Selection 20) shows that he believed the adoption of Western machinery and technology would not be sufficient to solve China's problems, that a major change was not only necessary but inevitable. Yet because of the high level of abstraction, and the absence of any definition of such a key term as *fa*, which can mean "method," "law," and/or "institutions," he does not convey a clear idea of how far he proposed to go, or indeed whether he had any precise notion himself. Hsüeh can therefore be seen as a transitional figure, still aiming to preserve the essence of traditional ways, but willing to make greater changes than earlier Self-Strengtheners.

Compared to reformers and revolutionaries in following generations, these men had a limited conception of China's problems. Yet they were the most progressive leaders of their time, and the strength of the opposition to even their modest goals can be seen in the defensive tone of their writings and the amount of space they devoted to answering possible objections to their proposals. The widespread hostility to reform and reformers also helps to explain why Feng Kuei-fen's essays, though written around 1860 and privately circulated after 1861, were not published until much later.

15. THE PRACTICAL BENEFITS OF WESTERN KNOWLEDGE

[From Feng Kuei-fen, "On the Adoption of Western Learning," ca. 1860]

... Today the world is 90,000 *li* around. There is no place boats and vehicles do not travel or human power does not reach. ... According to Westerners' maps, there are at least one hundred countries in the world. Of the books of these hundred countries, only those from Italy from the time of the end of the Ming and from present-day England, numbering in all several tens, have been translated. Among them, those about Christianity are trivial and vulgar, not worthy of mention. In addition to these, books on mathematics, mechanics, optics, light, chemistry, and others all contain the ultimate principles of understanding things. The books on geography thoroughly list the mountains, rivers, strategic points, customs, and products of the hundred countries. Most of this information is unavailable to people in China. ...

If we wish to adopt Western knowledge, we should establish an official translation bureau at Canton and Shanghai. Young students, fifteen years of age or younger, who are quick at understanding, should be selected from nearby areas and given double stipends to live at these schools and learn this profession. Westerners should be appointed to teach the spoken and written languages of the various countries, and famous teachers from within China should teach the classics, history, and other subjects. The students should concurrently learn mathematics. (Note: All Western learning derives from mathematics. Westerners above the age of ten all study mathematics. Hence, if we wish to adopt Western learning, we must study mathematics. It can be taught either by Westerners or by Chinese who understand the subject.) . . .

I have heard that with their new methods the Westerners have found that the movements of the earth conform closely to those of the heavens. This can be of assistance in fixing the calendar. . . . I have heard that the Westerners' method of clearing sand from harbors is very effective. . . . This can be of assistance to keep the water flowing. Also, for agricultural and sericultural tools, and things required for the various crafts, they mostly use mechanical wheels, which require little energy but accomplish much. These can assist the people to earn their living. Other things beneficial to the national economy and the livelihood of the people should also be used. We need not bother about rare skills or cunning arts.

After three years, all those students who can readily recite the foreign books should be granted the licentiate degree. And if there are any who are especially bright and adept, who have acquired the ability to apply their knowledge, the Superintendent of Trade should recommend that they be granted the *chü-jen* degree as a reward, as I previously proposed. There are many intelligent people in China. Surely there are some who, having learned from the barbarians, can surpass them. . . .

The principles of government are derived from learning. In discussing good government, Ssu-ma Ch'ien (Note: following Hsün Tzu) said, "Take the later kings as models," because they were closer to his own time, and customs, having changed, were more alike, so that their ideas were easy to implement because they were plain and simple. In my humble opinion, at the present time it is also appropriate to say "Learn from the various nations," for they exist at the same time and in the same world as we do. They themselves have been able to achieve wealth and power. Is it not evident that they are similar to us and hence their ways are easy to implement? What could be better than to take Chinese ethical principles of human relations and Confucian teachings as the foundation, and supplement them with the techniques of wealth and power of the various nations? . . .

16. PRACTICAL SELF-STRENGTHENING
[From Feng Kuei-fen, "On Manufacturing Western Machines," ca. 1860]

An extraordinary rage, unprecedented since the beginning of the world, is alarming every thoughtful person who has blood in his veins. For the largest country in the entire world is under the control of small barbarians. . . . According to a geography compiled by an Englishman, the territory of our China is eight times larger than Russia, ten times larger than America, a hundred times larger than France, and two hundred times larger than England. (Note: This refers only to the home countries and does not include dependencies.) In the five continents, only China is this large, self-sufficient in daily necessities and needing nothing from other countries. Our land is thus so good that, even in their geography books, China must be given first place. This is not because they fear us, or respect us, but only because our country is the largest in the entire world, unequaled in climate, soil, or resources.

Our shameful humiliation by these four countries is not because our climate, soil, or resources are not as good as theirs, but because our people cannot be compared with them. Their people are not physically extraordinary, nor are ours weak dwarfs. Why then cannot we be compared with them? . . . This is not due to natural endowments, but rather to human causes. It would be shameful if we were inferior because of natural endowments, but there would be nothing we could do about that. Being inferior because of our own faults is even more shameful, but we can do something about that. If we are ashamed, the best thing is self-strengthening. . . . The way to do this is to truly realize the reasons for our inferiority, why they are strong though small and why we are weak though large. We must find how to be as good as they are, and this also lies solely in human beings.

There are several main points to be made about the current situation: the barbarians are better than we are in not wasting human abilities, in making maximum use of the earth, in having no gap between ruler and people, and in assuring that name and reality conform. In all four of these, the proper way [of solving the problems] is to be found within ourselves. If the Emperor would only cleanse and invigorate the basic legal and political structure, this could be accomplished immediately. For this we need not depend upon the barbarians.

As for military matters, the strong ships and effective guns of the barbarians are better than ours, and they are better than us in advancing and not retreating. (Note: In training soldiers, the barbarians give prime emphasis to marching in ranks. . . . When the army moves, the soldiers march in step. Even if arrows fly among them, piercing them, the neat order of the formation is not affected. In this they truly surpass us, but is this something we cannot do? . . .) They are not necessarily superior to us in ability or physical strength. . . . Only in the single matter of their strong ships and effective guns need we depend upon the barbarians. . . .

The way lies in giving importance to this matter, and showing esteem for those selected [to accomplish these tasks]. A special examination should be established to attract the able, and funds allotted to establish shipyards and arsenals in all treaty ports. Some barbarians should be appointed [as instructors] and Chinese who are good at using their minds should be recruited to learn their methods, in order to pass them along to artisans. Anyone whose work is indistinguishable from barbarian manufactures should be awarded the *chü-jen* degree, and permitted to participate in the metropolitan examinations on the same basis as other candidates. Anyone whose work is superior to barbarian manufactures should be awarded the *chin-shih* degree, and permitted to participate in the Palace Examinations on the same basis as other candidates. Artisans should receive from double to fivefold salaries so as to prevent them from leaving. Our country has given importance to the civil service examinations, so that they have long occupied people's minds. Intelligent and astute scholars have exhausted their time and energies till old age, wearing themselves out on useless matters such as eight-legged essays, examination papers, and fine script. Even though the quality of performance, and success or failure, are not predetermined, no one is willing to leave these studies for other occupations because those above give importance to the examinations. Now we should order one half of them to engage in manufacturing weapons and machines modelled on those of the foreigners. Those who do well should be rewarded and those who do poorly should lose. With things so clearly demarcated and fixed, and the rewards for eight-legged essays, examination essays, and fine script still attainable, who would not be happy to hear this? . . . Chinese are more intelligent and clever than barbarians, but previously their intelligence and cleverness have not been utilized. Whatever those above like, those below like even more. . . . There must be some exceptionally clever Chinese who can devise new ideas beyond any devised by the Westerners. At first they must study with the barbarians and follow their ways, then they may become their equals, and finally they will overtake and surpass them. This is the way to self-strengthening. . . .

Some may ask, "Kuan Chung repelled the barbarians, and Confucius praised him as benevolent; the state of Chu adopted barbarian ways of life, and [Confucius in] *The Spring and Autumn Annals* condemned it. Does not this present proposal run contrary to the way of the sages?" This is not so. When talking about repelling the barbarians, one must have concrete means to repel them, not mere arrogant bluster. May I ask those among my contemporaries who speak of repelling the barbarians what means they intend to use?

Times change. What was once substantial becomes merely decorative, what was oafish becomes clever. This is due to the force of circumstances. The calendar, clocks, watches, rifles and cannon are all Western devices. Can we live in the present and fix the dates on the lunar calendar according to the six calendars of the ancient past, use the clepsydra to tell time, and go off to fight barbarians with bows and arrows, saying, "I will not adopt foreign ways of life"? Moreover, we are using their instruments, not their way of life. We use them in order to repel them.

Some may ask, "Why not buy their ships and guns and hire their people?" The answer is that we cannot do this. Weapons and machines which we can manufacture, repair, and operate, are ours. If we cannot manufacture, repair, and operate them, then they are still others' weapons and machines. If these weapons and machines are in others' hands and are used to transport grain, then one day they can cause us to starve; if they are used to transport salt, then one day they can make our food bland; if they are used to cross the rivers and seas, then they can capsize and drown us. . . . Borrowing troops and hiring ships are temporary measures, not permanent ones. Since at present there are no disagreements [between China and the West], we can temporarily do this; but since we cannot be certain there will be no disagreements in the future,

such measures cannot be permanent. Ultimately, the best thing is to manufacture, repair, and operate the weapons and machines ourselves. . . .
The way of the sages is not militaristic. To imitate the Westerners in their wrongdoings should really not be necessary. But if we possess latent might, when war comes we shall win, and when there is no war we can also make others submit. Only in this way can China be independent among the nations of the world. Otherwise, if there is a way to strengthen ourselves but we disregard it without regrets, if there is a way to wipe out our shame but we bear our sufferings patiently, too ignorant to make plans, then not only Russia, England, France, and America will cause disaster—our China will become meat for every country in the world. How could we bear that? . . .

17. THE NEED FOR FOREIGN LANGUAGE TRAINING
[From a Memorial by Li Hung-chang, 1863]

In China's contacts with foreigners, we must first of all comprehend their ambitions, be aware of their desires, and have a thorough knowledge of their strengths and weaknesses, of where they are sincere and where they dissemble, before we can expect to be treated equitably. During the past twenty years of trade relations, quite a few of their leaders have learned our language, . . . but among our officials and gentry only a very small number understand foreign languages. All the foreign countries have one or two interpreters at Shanghai, and whenever there are discussions between Chinese and foreign high officials, we depend upon these foreign interpreters to transmit the discussions. It is difficult to guarantee that there are no biases or misinterpretations. . . .

Your Minister requests that, following the example of the T'ung-wen Kuan,[1] we establish an additional foreign language school at Shanghai, select bright, upright, and quiet youngsters fourteen years of age or under from the vicinity, invite Westerners to teach them [foreign languages] and *chü-jen* and licentiates of superior character and learning to teach them the classics, history, and literature. After completing their studies, they should be sent to the Governor-General and Governor of their home provinces and examined to be made supplementary district licentiates.[2] . . . In three to five years, after we have these educated men skilled in foreign languages, an interpreter should be added to the yamens of all Governors and Governors-General who deal with foreign trade and to the Superintendent of Maritime Customs to handle foreign affairs. . . . Chinese wisdom and intelligence are hardly inferior to those of the Westerners. If we attain mastery of Western languages, and then teach them to one another, a thorough understanding of all their clever techniques of steamships and firearms can gradually be attained in China.[3]

[1] The first Chinese school for foreign languages, established in Peking in 1862, and later expanded into an institute for foreign studies.

[2] The lowest-ranking licentiates.

[3] The Shanghai foreign studies school was established in 1863.

18. THE NEED TO LEARN MANUFACTURING
[From a Letter by Li Hung-chang, 1864]

I believe that when events reach the extreme limit, a change takes place, and once change occurs, things go smoothly.[1] Chinese scholars and officials have been emersed in the inveterate habit of learning commentaries [on the classics] and writing fine script, while most military men are coarse, stupid, and careless, so that what scholars and officials use is not what they have studied, and what they study is not what they use. When there are no troubles, they deride the sharp weapons of the foreigners as some strange and indecent craft, which they do not deem necessary to study. When troubles arise, they are amazed that these sharp weapons are so strange and marvelous, and believe that Chinese can never learn about them. . . . China's civil and military institutions are in every way superior to those of the Westerners. Only in weapons are the Westerners unsurpassed. Why is this so? Because in China the way of manufacturing machines is for the scholars to learn the principles while the artisans learn how to run the machines, so that there is no coordination of their expertise. Hence their achievements are not combined.

The most skillful craftsman, who develops his capacities to the fullest, can advance no further than becoming a chief artisan. The foreigners are different. Whoever builds a machine that is useful to the nation can become a prominent official, and for generations his family can live from his attainments and inherit his position. . . . "If the emperor wants fish, the ministers will dry up the valleys [to catch them]." Wherever honor and profit are to be gained, men will exert themselves in study, exhausting their energies day and might, with the hope of achieving mastery. . . .

I believe that if China wishes to self-strengthen, the best thing to do is to learn about the foreign weapons, and that to learn about the foreign weapons, the best thing to do is to find out about the machines which manufacture these weapons—to learn their methods so as not to [need to] employ their people. If we want to seek the machines which manufacture these weapons, and men to make them, we might establish a special examination to recruit scholars. Seeing this as a means of attaining wealth, high position, and fame, scholars will occupy themselves with it throughout their lives. Then the profession can be established, there will be skill in the craft, and talents can be assembled. . . .

19. THE NEED TO SEND STUDENTS ABROAD TO STUDY
[From a Memorial by Tseng Kuo-fan and Li Hung-chang, 1871]

[Those who object to sending students abroad] do not understand that the establishment of arsenals for manufacturing and the opening of schools for

[1]A well-known concept from the *Book of Changes*, frequently cited by Self-Strengtheners.

instruction have [only] laid the foundation for our revival. To travel abroad to study, to collect ideas, and to obtain the benefits of broader knowledge, will have long-lasting and great results. Westerners study for practical use. Scholars, artisans, and soldiers without exception all go to school to study to understand the principles, to practice on the machines, and to become personally familiar with the work. . . . If we Chinese want to adopt their strong points, and try to buy their machines all at once, not only will our resources be inadequate, but without broad observation and extended familiarity with their inner workings, neither the basic principles nor the intricate details can be understood. The ancients had a saying: "He who wants to learn the language of Ch'i must place himself in the midst of Chiang and Yü [names of streets in an ancient city of Ch'i], and, as another saying goes, "Seeing once is better than hearing a hundred times."

20. THE INEVITABILITY OF CHANGE
[Hsüeh Fu-ch'eng, "On Reform," 1879]

In my opinion, there have been no more than ten thousand years from the beginnings of humankind to the present day. How can this be shown? By the rapidity of changes in the world. It is the Way of Heaven that there is a minor change every several hundred years and a major change every several thousand years. In the primeval world of early times, there was no difference between men and other creatures. From the period when Sui-jen, Yu-chao, Fu-hsi, Shen-nung, and the Yellow Emperor successively ruled the world, teaching the people how to use fire, how to build shelter, how to fish with nets and till the soil, how to make boats, bow and arrows, clothing, and written records, to the time of Yao and Shun was several thousand years. With the accumulation of the sages' industrious enterprises, All-under-Heaven changed from primitive to civilized. From Yao and Shun to the Hsia, Shang, and Chou dynasties was a time of peaceful rule. By the time Ch'in Shih-huang annexed the six states, abolished the feudal lords, and destroyed the well-field system, obliterating the institutions [fa] of the former kings, two thousand years had passed since Yao and Shun. All-under-Heaven changed from the feudal system to the imperial system. Since the Ch'in, although prosperity and decline, unity and division, have occurred with no fixed regularity, nevertheless external troubles have come only from the tribes of the northwest beyond the passes, such as the Hsiung-nu, the T'u-ch'üeh, the Uighurs and Turfan, the Khitan and Mongols. But now, because of their knowledge of machinery and mathematics, the nations of the West thrive beyond the seas, reaching the farthest limits of the earth as easily as strolling in their own yards, harnessing the wind and thunder as easily as they move their own fingers and arms. Over the 90,000 li of the globe, there is no place where they do not trade or send envoys. Confronted with this, even Yao and Shun would not be able to close the gates and rule in isolation. And now once again it has been two thousand years since the

Ch'in and the Han. All-under-Heaven has changed from China and the barbarians being separated to China and the barbarians having contacts and connections. It was several thousand years from the time of the industrious enterprises of the sages to Yao and Shun, two thousand years from Yao and Shun to Ch'in Shih-huang, and two thousand years from then till now. Hence I say, no more than ten thousand years, and such have been the changes in the world.

When minor changes occur, minor changes accordingly take place in the methods [*fa*] of ruling the world; and when major changes occur, major changes accordingly take place in the methods [*fa*] of ruling the world. . . . After a few hundred years, defects reach the extreme, and then change occurs; sometimes within only a few decades the methods [*fa*] of rule cannot remain the same. Hence, sometimes when one sage succeeds another, the outer forms must be changed, and sometimes during the reign of one sage, a whole series of changes must be made. Hence, only a sage can model [*fa*] himself on another sage, and only a sage can change the model [*fa*] used by another sage. He makes changes not because he likes to, but because of the circumstances of the time.

Today, the world is rapidly changing. In my opinion, with regard to the immutable Way [*tao*], the present should be changed so as to restore the past, and with regard to the changeable laws [*fa*], the past should be changed to bring it up to date. Alas, if we do not examine into the circumstances of the past and present and do not give careful consideration to what is appropriate, how will we be able to remedy the defects?

Our state has accumulated the laws [*fa*] of a hundred rulers. Those without defects need not be altered, even in ten thousand generations. But the meagerness of official salaries, the multiplicity of regulations, the corruption in the Green Banner Forces, and the shortcomings in recruiting officials with practical learning are the end result of the accumulated defects of several hundred years, and these institutions [*fa*] long ago ceased to fulfill the original intentions for which they were established. If slight changes are made, the defects will be removed and the institutions [*fa*] will remain intact; but without changes the defects will remain and the institutions [*fa*] will be nullified. Even if enemy nations were not all around us, watching and waiting, we should hasten to remedy these defects. If we do not change, there will be an abundance of elaborate trimmings, but little substantial government, and the severe restrictions will hamper getting anything done.

The nations of the West rely on intelligence and energy to compete with one another. So that our China can stand up to them, we should make plans for commerce and mining; unless we change, they will be rich and we poor. Skills in crafts and manufacturing should be perfected; unless we change, they will be skillful and we clumsy. Steamships, trains, and the telegraph should be promoted; unless we change, they will be swift and we slow. The advantages and faults of treaties, the qualities of envoys, and changes in military systems and organization should all be studied; unless we change, they will cooperate with each other and we shall be isolated, they will be strong and we frail.

In ancient times, when Ch'ih-yu made weapons and inflicted violence upon the feudal lords, the Yellow Emperor invented the bow and arrow and the compass to vanquish him. . . . The Yellow Emperor was a sage. In ruling All-under-Heaven and the state, how could he have been concerned only for wealth and power? Since he found himself in the midst of enemies there was something in the art of acquiring wealth and power which could not be disregarded.

Some may say, "If our great country imitates the Westerners, is this not using barbarian ways to change China?" This is not so. In clothing, language, and customs, Chinese and foreigners differ, but in making use of the forces of nature and in benefiting the people, Chinese and foreigners are alike. The Westerners happen to have been the first to catch the winds of change. But are the Westerners to monopolize the secrets nature discloses? How do we know that within several decades or a century China will not overtake them? There is profound meaning in the examples of King Wu-ling of Chao learning horseback riding and mounted archery [from barbarian tribes], in Han Wu-ti learning how to build towering ships [to campaign against southern barbarians], and in T'ang T'ai-tsung handling his foreign generals and his civilian ministers in the same manner. If today we adopt the machinery and mathematics of the Westerners to protect the Way of Yao, Shun, Yü, T'ang, Kings Wen and Wu, the Duke of Chou, and Confucius, the Westerners will not dare despise China. I think that even if these sages were to be reborn, they would certainly attend to this task, and surely their Way would gradually suffuse the far corners of the earth. This would be using Chinese ways to change the barbarians.

Some may also say, "In making reforms [*pien fa*], we should strive to surpass the Westerners, not [merely] to pursue them. Today, Western methods [*fa*] excel; if we imitate them slavishly, how will we ever surpass them?" This too is not so. In order to surpass others, we must first have a thorough knowledge of their methods [*fa*] before we can change, and only after changing can we surpass them. We cannot surpass them by sitting upright and immobile. If now, seeing that others are ahead of us, we scornfully say that we will not condescend to follow them, we shall not be able to budge half a step. Moreover, they brought together the talents and energies of millions of people and expended vast sums of money over a long period of time before acquiring this knowledge. Now we want to surpass them in a single day. Can this really be done? Mighty rivers begin from a trickle; a basketful of earth is the foundation of vaulting mountains. Buddhism came from India, and yet it flourished in the East. Mathematics originated in China, and yet it has been perfected in Western lands. If we compare the talent and intelligence of Chinese and Westerners, can we find any reason why we should not be able to surpass them? The answer lies in urging ourselves on.

Alas! The world's changes are endless, and so, the sages' ways of handling these changes are also endless. To live in the world of today and still cling stubbornly to the methods [*fa*] of the past, is like living during the time of Shen-nung [who according to legend invented cooking] and eating raw meat and drinking blood, or like living during the time of the Yellow Emperor and trying to resist the violence of Ch'ih-yu with bare hands, saying, "I am adhering to the ways [*fa*] of the ancient sages." Who would not become exhausted and collapse? And is there any reason why the essence of the ways [*fa*] of the ancient sages cannot be retained in the ways [*fa*] that should be changed today?

CHAPTER FOUR
Radical Reform

Given the strength of the opposition and the inherent limitations of their own program, the Self-Strengtheners made some impressive innovations: foreign language schools and translation bureaus, arsenals, shipyards, modern factories and communications, and an embryonic foreign office were all established. Nevertheless, these were few in number, and moreover on the periphery of Chinese life. Beyond the treaty ports, the vast interior of the empire was little affected, if at all. Change was coming, but slowly.

The tempo of reform was quickened by China's disastrous defeat in the Sino-Japanese War of 1894–95. As so often happened, it was not so much the compelling force of rational arguments as a new demonstration of foreign military superiority and a humiliating defeat that convinced tradition-bound gentry and officials of the need for further change. Both conservatives and reformers saw the quick Japanese victory as a sign that the Self-Strengthening movement had not been a success. And the demands from European powers for new and wide-ranging concessions precipitated a crisis; some feared the very existence of the Chinese state was now imperiled.

By this time, increasing knowledge about the West had led a small number of the literate elite to the conclusion that the roots of Western strength went deeper than the technological and scientific knowledge the Self-Strengtheners had been willing to borrow. These new intellectual leaders saw Western social and political institutions as the source of the drive for scientific and material progress, as well as of the social cohesion and strong sense of national loyalty they discerned in Western countries but found lacking in China. From this new conception of the situation, they concluded that, in order to match the strength of the West, China (like Japan) would not only have to learn how to manufacture ships and guns, but also to alter her basic political institutions along Western lines.

This is the argument of Yen Fu (1853–1921), who introduced such Western thinkers as Charles Darwin, Herbert Spencer, Adam Smith, John Stuart Mill, and Montesquieu to the Chinese literati through his elegant translations into classical Chinese. In his long essay "On Power," Yen analyzed the relationship between Western social and political institutions and Western power. (Selection 21) The influence of Darwin and Spencer is immediately apparent in Yen's use of the concepts of the struggle for existence, natural selection, and the survival of the fittest at the beginning of his essay. Yen proceeds to argue that Western strength derives from institutions that provide the necessary freedom for the most talented individuals to manifest their abilities, thereby bringing forth those strong enough to enable their nation to survive in the international struggle for existence. Yen uses the familiar terms *kung* [public, public spirit, common interest] and *ssu* [private, self-interest, selfish] as the analytical framework for his central thesis that Western nations are powerful because they effectively link individual self-interest to the national interest, and that China's weakness is due to the absence of such a link. Like his Western mentors, Yen conceives of equality as equality of opportunity, and assumes that this equality can be provided by legal institutions and will not require radical socio-economic change. It was not until much later that the complexities of the notion of equality were to become manifest.

Darwinian doctrines seemed so pertinent to China's situation that they became increasingly accepted by later generations of Chinese intellectuals, and Darwinian terms were absorbed into the Chinese language. Struggle, not harmony, came to be perceived by many as the rule of life.

Although Yen Fu was considered a dangerous radical by many conservatives, he was not a political activist, and he served the Ch'ing government as Superintendent of the Tientsin Naval Academy. Other intellectual leaders, however, sought greater power in order to implement their ideas. These radical reformers thought of themselves as good Confucians and they were loyal to the Ch'ing dynasty. They believed that sweeping reforms were imperative, and they felt that the recent accomplishments of Meiji Japan confirmed their belief that extensive reforms could be made from above, through the support of the emperor, within the framework of the imperial state. In 1898, a group of these men, led by K'ang Yu-wei (1858–1927), won the approval of the young Kuang-hsü Emperor for a program of broad institutional reform. Among the most important measures in their program were the replacement of the stylized eight-legged essay in the civil service examinations by essays on current events, the encouragement of commerce, the modernization of the imperial bureaucracy, and the elimination of sinecure posts.

It is not the details of K'ang Yu-wei's plan to create a constitutional monarchy but fundamental assumptions that are the subject of one of

K'ang's most important memorials to the emperor, written just a few months before he and his party came to power. (Selection 22) K'ang's main point is that means and ends must be clearly distinguished. A standard conservative objection to institutional reform was that altering dynastic institutions implied disrespect for the imperial ancestors who had established them, something no filial son, especially the emperor, would want to do. K'ang's reply is that institutions are not ends in themselves; if they no longer serve the purposes for which they were designed, they should be replaced by new ones that can. And since existing institutions are not fulfilling their function of protecting the territory of China, change is not only justified but necessary. K'ang's second main point is that opposition to reform is so strongly entrenched that no reform program can be implemented without the determined and wholehearted support of the emperor.

K'ang's conservative opponents, who included most high officials, were quick to discern the theoretical and practical implications of his reasoning. If institutions were merely means, what institutions, what principles, could not be discarded on grounds of expediency? K'ang had clearly implied that the preservation of China, not the preservation of the Ch'ing dynasty, was the basic problem. High Manchu officials in particular were apprehensive at what they took to be incipient Chinese nationalism. Many scholars, both inside and outside the government, were also antagonized by K'ang's bold self-assurance, and by his reinterpretations of the classical past, in which he portrayed Confucius not as a guardian of time-honored tradition, but as a reformer, much like K'ang himself. More practically, K'ang's insistence on the full support of the emperor implied great power for K'ang and his followers. Thus, as one of K'ang's leading disciples, Liang Ch'i-ch'ao (1873–1929), points out in Selection 23, opposition to the reforms can readily be explained in terms of the self-interest of superannuated officials.

Whatever the motives of the conservatives, they were fortunate enough to have a powerful person to back them. The empress dowager, Tz'u-hsi (1835–1908), had been the real power behind the throne for several decades. Because of her domineering character and the position she had created for herself, she was far more powerful than the young emperor. Her presence made it possible for conservatives to oppose the emperor without risking accusations of disloyalty or jeopardizing their lives or careers. When opponents of reform convinced her that she should intervene, the reforms were doomed. She forced the emperor to withdraw from active political life. K'ang and Liang escaped to Japan, but six of their colleagues were summarily executed, becoming martyrs to the cause of reform.

Although K'ang Yu-wei and his followers were in power less than four months, their failure did not end their influence, for the issues they and others like them had raised were too basic to be easily dismissed. It is those issues, not the aborted program of 1898, that require our attention here.

For centuries, the civil service examination system had been a central issue for reformers. In the late nineteenth century it was seen as one of the most serious impediments to change. The arguments against the exams in the editorial from the reform journal *China and Foreign News* (Selection 24) are typical of the many attacks made at this time, which contributed to the decision to abolish the exam system in 1905.

Far more fundamental, however, were the philosophical issues raised by the radicals. The relationship between self-interest and the common interest, between the individual and the nation, so cogently analyzed by Yen Fu, was seen as a basic issue by both reformers and conservatives. Both realized that the kind of changes envisioned by the radicals entailed expanding the sphere of activity of the government and greater government intrusion into the lives of the people. Mai Meng-hua (1874–1915), a disciple of K'ang Yu-wei, lists some of the ways government authority should be extended, and argues that these innovations will increase the ruler's power. (Selection 25) Another of K'ang's disciples, Ou Chü-chia (1858–1912), who later drifted toward the revolutionary camp, sees a parliamentary system as the solution to a classic Confucian problem—how to unite the ruler and the people. (Selection 26) On the conservative side we see the standard Confucian objection, astutely illustrated by an example drawn from contemporary Europe: the free expression of self-interest is divisive, and hence representative political institutions will weaken, not strengthen the country. (Selection 27) The relation between public [*kung*] and private [*ssu*] is analyzed in a quite different fashion by Wang Hsien-ch'ien (1842–1918), an eminent classical scholar and a leading conservative. (Selection 28) Wang argues for the continuation of what he views as the traditional policy of laissez-faire, the ruler and the common people each taking care of their own clearly demarcated interests and not demanding too much of one another. Wang holds the typically conservative belief that institutions are the products of long evolutionary development in specific historical settings, and that it is therefore dangerous to tamper with them.

Thus, the question of how best to unite the government and the people, the rulers and the ruled, a fundamental issue in Chinese political philosophy since Confucius, remained relevant, but now began to be viewed from a different perspective. Was this unity to come from above, through moral leadership, as advocated by the traditionalists? Or could it be brought about by narrowing the gap between the government and the people through the creation of new institutions that would give the people a share in the political life of the nation? The latter implied an equality not allowed by Confucian theory or actual practice, and thus introduced the issue of equality vs. hierarchy, so central to modern societies and to China's future.

One of the earliest and most forceful advocates of equality was T'an Ssu-t'ung (1865–98), a disciple of K'ang Yu-wei, who was executed in 1898 after the empress dowager's coup against the reformers. T'an was persuaded by K'ang that equality was compatible with Confucianism as it had originally been conceived. In Selection 29, taken from his major philosophical work, *The Study of Humanity*, T'an stresses the intrinsic moral truth of equality rather than its social or political utility.

The subordination of women to men was one of the most pervasive inequalities in Chinese society. By the end of the century, however, the movement for the emancipation of women, partly inspired by missionaries and other Westerners and partly stemming from native roots, had begun. In Selection 30, K'ang Yu-wei's daughter, T'ung-wei, argues that improving the status of women will strengthen China. Unlike later critics of Confucianism, she assumes that women can play a significant role in national life by following Confucian principles. This line of reasoning was not to prevail; improvements in women's status were to be connected with the rejection of Confucianism.

From the writings of these late-nineteenth-century reformers we can see that belief in at least some fundamental traditional values had begun to erode. The concluding selection in this chapter, taken from *Exhortation to Learn* by Chang Chih-tung (1837–1909), should serve as a reminder that this erosion was still limited. Chang, a leading statesman and moderate reformer, identifies the hierarchical organization of society as the essence of Chinese civilization, and he insists that it is possible to preserve this and the rest of the tradition while mastering Western learning. (Selection 31) *Exhortation to Learn* was widely read, and in its time extremely influential. Intellectual leaders of the next generation were to agree that inequality was the essence of the traditional social order; but they were to reject both.

21. THE SOCIAL SOURCES OF NATIONAL POWER
[From Yen Fu, "On Power," 1895]

[The term] "struggle for existence" means that living things struggle to survive; "natural selection" means that the fittest species survive. The idea is that people and other living things are intermingled in the world, all feeding themselves from the environment and the benefits of nature. When they come into contact, they contend with one another, struggling with each other in order to survive. At first, species struggle with species, but after some further development, groups struggle with groups. The weak are consumed by the strong, and the ignorant are made subservient to the intelligent. Species which succeed in surviving must be tenacious and hardy, agile and sharp-witted, the best-fitted to the climate, the geographical conditions, and the human affairs of the time. . . .

[Yen goes on to argue that in order to survive in the present competitive world, a nation must be wealthy and powerful. He then discusses the sources of wealth and power.] To be specific, wealth and power are nothing more than benefitting the people. If the government wants to benefit the people, it must begin by enabling each person to benefit himself, and the beginning of each person being able to benefit himself is freedom for everyone. If all are to be allowed to have freedom, each must first be able to govern himself. Otherwise, there will be chaos. Indeed, for a people to be capable of governing themselves and of being free, their energies, their intelligence, and their morality must be truly superior. For this reason, the policies urgently needed at present consist of three fundamentals: 1) encourage the people's energies; 2) enlarge their intelligence; 3) renovate their morality. . . .

[After discussing each of these three points, Yen explains the sources of China's weaknesses.] Ever since the Ch'in dynasty, rulers of China have for the most part treated our people as slaves, though some have been lenient and others harsh. . . . And since those above treated the people like slaves, the people treated themselves like slaves. By the nature of the situation, slaves' relationship to their master is shaped by coercion and prohibitions. There is nothing they can do about it. They do not join in preserving this relationship gladly and willingly, out of love for their country or their master. Hence, as long as the situation persists and the country's laws continue to be enforced, the slaves will mindlessly grovel and mortify themselves, hoisting those above to the highest level, and abasing themselves to the lowest because they are told to. But if one day the situation changes and the laws are no longer enforced, they will know only about their own interests. It would scarcely be strange if they rose up in rebellion. . . .

The doctrine of the West is equality. Hence, the common good [*kung*] is used to govern the masses. And so freedom is esteemed, and because freedom is esteemed, trust and achievement are valued. The doctrine of the East is the principle of human bonds [of hierarchical personal relationships]. Hence, filial piety is used to rule the empire, and primacy is given to respect for parents. And because parents are respected, trust and achievement are slighted. At the worst, this can lead to fraudulent practices, such as mutual deception and evasion of responsibility by superiors and inferiors. Hence, the actual results of [valuing] trust and achievement are greater than those of [valuing] loyalty and filial piety. There is a good reason why Western nations can use their people, why the people have a deep personal feeling [*ssu*] and great love for their country and their ruler, and so go off to public [*kung*] wars as though going to take personal [*ssu*] revenge. The laws originate from the lower legislature, and thus the people abide by agreements they themselves have voluntarily concluded, which are not regulations imposed upon them from above. From the Prime Minister on down, all officials are selected by the entire nation. Hence, officials are established by the people in order to supervise all kinds of work, not merely to be shown respect, waited upon, and looked up to with admiration [as in China]. . . . Paying taxes to provide for public works is no different from managing one's own lands and house. Rushing toward death to kill the enemy is no different from defending one's own home. Whenever I hear Englishmen talk about England, Frenchmen talk about France, or anyone mention the land of his birth, they say the name in the same tone of voice [as when] we utter our parents' names, with sincerity and solidarity, with what seems to be unbounded love. And what is the reason? There is only one answer: They think of their country as their own [*ssu*] because they believe it belongs to them.

Hence, dwelling in the present, if we desire to advance our people's morality to get them to work together for common goals, to unite in one spirit to resist the foreign enemy, we must have a way to make each think of China as his own [ssu]. Ku Yen-wu[1] once said that for the people to be without private interests [ssu] is impossible, and hence, in establishing governmental institutions a sage combines each person's individual private interests [ssu] to make the public interest [kung]. But how are we to make each person think of China as his own? By establishing a legislature in the capital, and ordering the provinces and districts of the empire to publicly select local officials.

22. INSTITUTIONAL REFORM FROM ABOVE

[From a Memorial by K'ang Yu-wei to the Kuang-hsü Emperor, Submitted January 29, 1898]

A survey of all states in the world will show that those states which undertook reforms became strong while those states which clung to the past perished. The consequences of clinging to the past and the effects of opening up new ways are thus obvious. If Your Majesty, with your discerning brilliance, observes the trends in other countries, you will see that if we can change, we can preserve ourselves; but if we cannot change, we shall perish. Indeed, if we can make a complete change, we shall become strong, but if we only make limited changes, we shall still perish. If Your Majesty and his ministers investigate the source of the disease, you will know that this is the right prescription.

Our present trouble lies in our clinging to old institutions without knowing how to change. In an age of competition between states, to put into effect methods appropriate to an era of universal unification and laissez-faire is like wearing heavy furs in summer or riding a high carriage across a river. This can only result in having a fever or getting oneself drowned.

It is a principle of things that the new is strong but the old weak; that new things are fresh but old things rotten; that new things are active but old things static. If the institutions are old, defects will develop. Therefore there are no institutions that should remain unchanged for a hundred years. Moreover, our present institutions are but unworthy vestiges of the Han, T'ang, Yüan, and Ming dynasties; they are not even the institutions of the [Manchu] ancestors. In fact, they are the products of the fancy writing and corrupt dealing of the petty officials rather than the original ideas of the ancestors. To say that they are the ancestral institutions is an insult to the ancestors. Furthermore, institutions are for the purpose of preserving one's territories. Now that the ancestral territory cannot be preserved, what good is it to maintain the ancestral institutions? . . .

Although there is a desire for reform, yet if the national policy is not fixed and public opinion not united, it will be impossible for us to give up the old

[1]A famous early Ch'ing scholar. The citation is from the fifth of his well-known essays on the prefectural system.

and adopt the new. The national policy is to the state just as the rudder is to the boat or the pointer is to the compass. It determines the direction of the state and shapes the public opinion of the country.

Nowadays the court has been undertaking some reforms, but the action of the emperor is obstructed by the ministers, and the recommendations of the able scholars are attacked by old-fashioned bureaucrats. If the charge is not "using barbarian ways to change China," then it is "upsetting the ancestral institutions." Rumors and scandals are rampant, and people fight each other like fire and water. A reform in this way is as ineffective as attempting a forward march by walking backward. It will inevitably result in failure. Your Majesty knows that under the present circumstances reforms are imperative and old institutions must be abolished. I beg Your Majesty to make up your mind and to decide on the national policy. After the fundamental policy is determined, the methods of implementation must vary according to what is primary and what is secondary, what is important and what is insignificant, what is strong and what is weak, what is urgent and what can wait. . . . If anything goes wrong, no success can be achieved.

After studying ancient and modern institutions, Chinese and foreign, I have found that the institutions of the sage-kings and Three Dynasties [of Hsia, Shang, and Chou] were excellent, but that ancient times were different from today. I hope Your Majesty will daily read Mencius and follow his example of loving the people. The development of the Han, T'ang, Sung, and Ming dynasties may be learned, but it should be remembered that the age of universal unification is different from that of sovereign nations. I wish Your Majesty would study *Kuan Tzu*[2] and follow his idea of managing the country. As to the republican governments of the United States and France and the constitutional governments of Britain and Germany, these countries are far away and their customs are different from ours. Their changes occurred a long time ago and can no longer be traced. Consequently I beg Your Majesty to adopt the purpose of Peter the Great of Russia as our purpose and to take the Meiji Reform of Japan as the model of our reform. The time and place of Japan's reform are not remote and her religion and customs are somewhat similar to ours. Her success is manifest; her example can easily be followed.

23. THE VESTED INTERESTS OF THE OPPONENTS OF REFORM

[From Liang Ch'i-ch'ao, *A General Discussion of Reform*, 1896–97]

The reason why the conservative party obstructs institutional reform is not really because they see any harm to the state or the people in the new laws. If the eight-legged essay is the means by which I passed the civil service examinations, but now suddenly practical studies are be pursued, then my road

[2]Early book on political and economic institutions which foreshadows Legalist doctrines.

to personal advancement is going to be cut off. If I have depended upon conventional credentials to attain high office, but now suddenly appointments are to be based on ability, then the things that brought me vainglory will vanish. If I rely on embezzlement to fill my pockets, and now suddenly accounts are to be audited, then my plans for my descendants are going to be disrupted. And this is not all. My present ministerial post and my fief were obtained only after many long years of savings from salaries and hectic scurrying [for office].

If everything goes along the way it always has, then there is nothing I have to get done, and I can leisurely enjoy wealth and high position, have my fill of pleasure and everything I desire. Perhaps I may become a high ranking official, and after dying be given the posthumous title of *Wen-tuan* [cultivated and upright]; my family wealth will exceed a million and my sons and grandsons will have the hereditary right to first rank. If suddenly one day there is institutional reform, all those holding office will be required to manage affairs. Will I obey the order and manage affairs? Since I lack both learning and ability, and energy besides, how can I do so? Will I not manage? But how can I resolutely resign to make way for the talented, and willingly abandon the high office I attained through thousands of hardships and decades of [saving from] salaries and hectic scurrying? And so, after thinking it over again and again, the only thing for me to do is to obstruct with every last bit of strength. And so, tens of thousands of men in the conservative party all over the nation are one in heart without conferring, different mouths all utter the same words, and they disregard everything else to obstruct the new laws. [Liang goes on to recommend that conservatives be permitted to retain their titles and positions, but not to manage affairs, and also that supplemental salaries be increased in order to prevent corruption.]

24. THE EXAMINATION SYSTEM AS AN OBSTRUCTION TO REFORM
[From an Editorial in *China and Foreign News*, August 23, 1898]

The dynasty's examination system is extremely annoying and cumbersome. From the district examinations to the two Palace Examinations, there is not a single year without exams of some sort, and not one exam without a preliminary test, in order to prevent cheating and to stress recruiting men of talent. In the district and prefectural examinations there are at least four or five sessions, and as many as six or seven. And in addition, there are three or four sessions of examinations supervised by the Provincial Commissioner of Education. Students go through innumerable hardships before they can obtain the right to wear the robes designating them as officially authorized students. Hence, year after year they persist in their studies until their hair turns white.

One half of each year is taken up with examinations, and the other half is burdened with wife, children, home and family. Any spare time is spent trying to master the eight-legged essay style. And yet, it still is very difficult to attain satisfactory competence in the eight-legged style, even though it is considered so vital, and pursued month after month and year after year. What then, if in addition, one wants to read useful books and study useful subjects?

The Palace Examinations rely solely upon ability in fine script [*hsiao-k'ai*], poetry, and rhyme-prose, not at all what the candidates are used to studying. [Even] members of the Han-lin Academy do not dare to discard the eight-legged style, poetry, rhyme-prose, and fine script before attaining the Third Rank, because they want to pass the test for Supervisor of Imperial Instruction. This is all because the difference between passing and failing the examinations depends on abilities in these areas. Hence, though after entering officialdom and becoming officials in the provinces for five or ten years scholars may gain some experience and some knowledge and understanding, it is easy to be infected by the heavy-laden atmosphere of officialdom, and the desire for personal gain is apt to affect the mind. As for Han-lin and other metropolitan officials, they are busily occupied with writing poetry, rhyme-prose, and fine script. And what is even more ridiculous, they spend their days going to the residences of fellow graduates of the same year, with a volume in hand, earnestly encouraging each other at their group study, just like in their *hsiu-ts'ai* days. Alas, are they this vulgar? Nevertheless, since those above recruit and select this way, those below respond accordingly. This is a circumstance about which aspiring scholars can do nothing. . . .

For the court to use poetry, rhyme-prose, and fine script as the criteria for passing or failing the examinations for men of ability is truly vulgar and ridiculous. Now, if peace reigned throughout the empire, and the court had no problems on its hands, then it would be proper for officials in the Han-lin Academy to serve His Majesty by lauding peace and plentitude through these means. But the multitude of problems on the coast has steadily weakened the nation. Poetry and rhyme-prose are not adequate to cope with this changing situation, and fine script is not adequate to withstand the enemy. How are we to devise a policy to bring peace and to emulate the wealth and power [of Western nations]? Every meaningless and extravagant custom should be reformed, one after another—the strings must be changed, and then tightened up. Only then will officials of the court and members of the Han-lin Academy, as well as scholars outside officialdom, be able to devote themselves to useful studies. Their ambitions will no longer be diverted by eight-legged essays, poetry, rhyme-prose, and fine script, nor will their minds be disturbed by all the various examinations. Who but a sagacious sovereign could thus respond to the times with the appropriate measures, and reform anachronistic laws? Nevertheless, scholars fortunate enough to have been born in an age when men of ability are sought out and rewarded, and incentives are given for practical learning, but who still fail to exert themselves to be of use and to respond to the generous intentions of the court, should feel ashamed of themselves, should they not?

25. MODERN BUREAUCRACY AND NATIONAL STRENGTH

[From Mai Meng-hua, "China Should Venerate the Power of the Ruler and Restrain the Power of the People," 1898]

Nowadays, men of broad learning all say China is weak because the power of the ruler is mighty while the power of the people is slight. Those who like to map out plans for the nation say that the Western nations are strong because their way is exactly the opposite of this. Mai Meng-hua says: This is not so. China's misfortunes arise not because the people have no power but because the ruler has no power. Hence, over all five continents and throughout all past ages, no ruler has had less power than in present-day China, and no rulers have had more power than in present-day European nations. There are far too many points for me to compare them all here, but permit me to say something about a few.

In Western countries, the age, birth, and death of every person in every household is reported to the officials, who record and investigate it. An omission in a report is punished as a criminal offense. In China, birth, death, and taking care of oneself are all personal matters, beyond state intervention. In Western countries, when property is inherited by descendants, the amount of the property and its location must be reported and registered with the authorities. An inheritance tax must be paid before the property is transmitted to the inheritors. In China, people give and take as they please, and the state is unable to investigate. In Western countries, when children reach the age of eight [*sui*], they all go to elementary school. Doting parents who neglect their children's studies are punished. In China, 70 to 80 per cent of the population is indolent, worthless, uncouth and illiterate, and the state can do nothing to encourage them to improve themselves. In Western countries, one must go through school to become an official, and unless one does adequately, one cannot make his own way. In China, one can be a slave in the market place in the morning, and bedecked in the robes of high office by evening, and this is beyond the capacity of the state to control. In Western countries, the currency system is fixed by the court; one country has the pound, another the ruble, and another the franc, but each currency is uniform throughout the entire country, and no one dares to differ. In China, each of the 18 provinces has a different currency, and the shape of the money is different. The people are satisfied with what they are accustomed to, and the state is unable to enforce uniformity.

In Western countries, only the government may print and distribute paper money within its borders. In China, banks in every province and money-changers in every port make and circulate their own money, and the state is unable to audit and prohibit them. In Western countries, all new buildings are inspected by officials, who examine the quality of the construction materials as a precaution against collapse causing injuries. Older houses are periodically inspected, and ordered demolished or repaired. In China, one can construct as one pleases. Even if there are cracks and flaws, the state cannot supervise and reprove the builder. In Western countries, roads and highways must be broad and spacious, neat and clean. There are legal penalties for discarding trash [on the roads]. Broad roads in Chinese cities are swamped in urine and litter, filled with beggars and corpses, and the state is unable to clean them up. In Western countries, all doctors must be graduates of medical schools and be certified before they can practice medicine. In China, those who fail to do well academically switch to the medical profession; quack doctors, who casually kill patients, are everywhere, and the state is unable to punish them. In Western countries, the postal service is controlled by the government. In China, post offices run by private persons are everywhere, and the government is unable to unify them.

In Western countries, there is an official for commerce. Inferior goods cannot be sold in the market. New inventions are patented, and other merchants are forbidden to manufacture imitations. In China, dishonest merchants are everywhere, devising illicit means to make imitation products, and everything is of inferior quality, and yet the state has no control. In Western countries, wherever railroads pass, homes, temples, huts, or gravestones must be demolished. No one dares obstruct the opening up of new mineral resources in mountains. In China, conservatives raise an outcry and block every major project, and the state is unable to punish them. In Western countries, foresters are appointed to superintend mountains and forests, and there are officials to oversee the fishing industry. Trees are felled only at the proper time, and large numbers of fishing nets are not permitted [in order to protect the stock of fish]. In China, no one is master of the woods and waters; the people can despoil them as they please, and the state has no way to know about it. In Western countries, statutory weights and measures are all fixed by the government; a pound of weight or a pound of money is uniform and circulates everywhere. In China, the Treasury, the Bureau of Tributary Rice, and markets all have their own scales, and the Board of Public Works and markets have their own linear measurements. Every household has its own system, and everyone uses his own private measurements, and the state is unable to regulate them.

26. SOME REASONS FOR THE ABSENCE OF LOYALTY TO RULER AND NATION IN CHINA

[From Ou Chü-chia, "On the Relationship between Institutional Reform and the Preservation of China," 1898]

Westerners say that the Chinese are neither loyal to the ruler nor patriotic, that although the people are numerous there is no need to be afraid of them, and although the country is large there is no cause for worry. How true these words are! And there are several reasons for this:

1. Those above give no kind favors [en-tse] to the people. All they want from them is that they pay their taxes and do not become bandits. With no

"government" and no "education," there is little emotional attachment between those above and those below.

2. The people possess abundant powers of self-government. All they want from those above is that the taxes, which pay officials' salaries, are not a nuisance. They have no notion of progress, nor any ambition to participate in government, and there is little communication between those above and those below.

3. Ever since the Ch'in and the Han, the ruler has been haughty and the ministers sycophantic. Anyone who has a mind to achieve fame and perform meritorious services, or to obtain wealth and high position, has to be obsequious to be used by the world. As for the common people, the ruler's gates are ten thousand *li* away, and some never see his face to the end of their lives.

4. Ever since the Ch'in and the Han, those who have controlled China have all gone along with things the way they were and lived complacently, without great plans or far-sighted ambitions. Their sole aim has been that there be no trouble within the country, that the common people be tame and submissive, so that their descendants could inherit the throne.

5. Since the eight-legged essay has been used to recruit officials, the ruler has given priority to entrapping men of talent, while the ambition of those below has been to snare rank and salary. Those above and those below both think in terms of their own self-interest, and sincere ties [between them] have never really existed. The so-called [bond between] ruler and minister is empty words, a hollow name.

27. A CONSERVATIVE OBJECTION TO PARLIAMENTARY GOVERNMENT

[From Su Yü, *Materials on the Heterodox Teachings*, 1898]

[Quoting Fan Chui, a reformer:] "All within the four seas should be of one mind; each person must have the right to be his own master, then everyone will consider saving the country from destruction the right thing to do. When the extreme limit is reached, change occurs; when frustration reaches the extreme, wisdom is born."

The refutation: The ruler of the empire should not let ultimate authority slip from his hands, much less transfer it downward to the common people. It is certainly proper for there to be open communication between those above and those below, but only of the feelings. Fan Chui says that each person has the right to be his own master, but if each and every person considers his mind to be *the* mind, this would cause our hundreds of millions of people to be scattered and disorganized. Fan Chui says that their minds would be united; I say that there would be hundreds of millions of minds. This would hasten destruction; how could it possibly save the country? Most Western countries are democratic, but in the French parliament factions swarm like hornets, eventually causing misfortune to the country, so that even in the West [demo-cracy] doesn't work. Fan Chui says, "When the extreme limit is reached, change occurs; when frustration reaches the extreme, wisdom is born." I surmise that his intention is to change the empire, over which the monarch has had sole control ever since the time of our sages, into a Western democracy. Is this supposed to be wisdom? Actually, it is the highest treason.

28. THE INCOMPATIBILITY OF WESTERN DEMOCRACY AND CHINESE CUSTOMS
[From Wang Hsien-ch'ien, *Hsü-shou-t'ang shu-cha*, ca. 1898]

So-called self-government came into being because in the past Western countries had no government or education, the common people could not bear their sufferings, and so those below abrasively chided those above.[1] In China, for several thousand years sagacious emperors and enlightened monarchs have exerted their minds and their energies to the utmost, making plans and ar-rangements to be good rulers and teachers. And since planning for [the peo-ple's] comforts was adequate, and precautions and supervision were particularly thorough, the foundation upon which the Chinese state has stood has been unlike that of Western nations. Such is the origin of the vast difference between the public-spirited [*kung*] West and self-centered [*ssu*] China.

In the West, individuals use their right of self-government to assemble together in one great community, and impose restrictions upon one another. The plans they make together are for the public [*kung*] interest; and their deliberations are made public. Government orders, wealth, property, and land are all public. (Note: India was taken by a private company but was turned over to the state.) This situation was the inevitable result of the circumstances, and having grown accustomed to it, those above do not harbor differences of opinion or feel uneasy about it, while the people do not think of shirking their responsibilities or being passive spectators.

Since the times of the Yellow Emperor, Yao, and Shun, the Chinese people have revered the ruler like Heaven, and looked upon him as a god. They delight in his abundant tolerance and find contentment in attending to their own

[1]An allusion to *Han-shu*, Chapter 51. Chia Shan, an official of the early Han dynasty, warned Emperor Wen of the dangers of not heeding the admonitions of officials, no matter how unpleasant they might be. He warned that if the empire were treated as the emperor's own private property, as the first Ch'in emperor had done, the people would overthrow the emperor as they had overthrown the Ch'in emperor. On another occasion, Chia disapproved of a plan of the emperor because it entailed altering the laws of former emperors [*pien hsien-ti fa*]. That Emperor Wen listened to the blunt criticisms of an official can be taken as symbolic of the difference between the Ch'in and Han dynasties, between Legalist rule and Confucian rule, and, Wang implies, between Western and Chinese principles of government.

selfish concerns [*tzu-ssu*], as can be seen in the ancient folk song.[2] In addition, since the Hsia made the empire a family affair [by establishing dynastic rule], the people have come to think of themselves as the ruler's children, so that they share this self-centeredness [*ssu*] with him, which has created the situation in which both ruler and people are self-centered. . . . Under these circumstances, the implementation of Western self-government would certainly be incompatible with the self-centeredness of the Chinese people.

29. THE IMMORALITY OF INEQUALITY
[From T'an Ssu-t'ung, *The Study of Humanity*, 1898]

When Confucius first set forth his teachings, he discarded the ancient learning, reformed existing institutions, rejected monarchism, advocated republicanism, and transformed inequality into equality. He indeed applied himself to many changes. Unfortunately, the scholars who followed Hsün Tzu forgot entirely the true meaning of Confucius' teaching, but clung to its superficial form. They allowed the ruler supreme, unlimited powers, and enabled him to make use of Confucianism in controlling the country. The school of Hsün Tzu insisted that duties based on human relationships were the essence of Confucianism, not knowing that this was a system applicable only to the Age of Disorder.[1] Even for the Age of Disorder, any discussion of the human relationships[2] without reference to Heaven would be prejudicial and incomplete, and the evil consequences would be immeasurable. How much worse, then, for them recklessly to have added the three bonds,[3] thus openly creating a system of inequality with its unnatural distinctions between high and low, and making men, the children of Heaven and earth, suffer a miserable life. . . .

For the past two thousand years the ruler-minister relationship has been especially dark and inhuman, and it has become worse in recent times. The ruler is not physically different or intellectually superior to man: on what does he rely to oppress 400 million people? He relies on the formulation long ago

[2]"Chi-jang ko"—a folk song allegedly from the time of Yao, when peace is said to have prevailed:

> When the sun rises, I go to work;
> When the sun sets, I rest.
> I drill a well to drink,
> And plow the fields to eat.
> What does the emperor's power have to do with me?

[1]The first of the three ages of human history, according to a theory of K'ang Yu-wei, which he derived from ancient Confucian texts.

[2]The relationships between ruler and minister, father and son, husband and wife, elder brother and younger brother, and friends.

[3]Binding the minister to the ruler, the son to the father, the wife to the husband.

of the three bonds and five human relationships, so that, controlling men's bodies, he can also control their minds. As Chuang Tzu said: "He who steals a sickle gets executed; he who steals a state becomes the prince." When T'ien Ch'eng-tzu stole the state of Ch'i, he also stole the [Confucian] system of humanity, righteousness and sage wisdom. When the thieves were Chinese and Confucianists, it was bad enough; but how could we have allowed the unworthy tribes of Mongolia and Manchuria, who knew nothing of China or Confucianism, to steal China by means of their barbarism and brutality! After stealing China, they controlled the Chinese by means of the system they had stolen, and shamelessly made use of Confucianism, with which they had been unfamiliar, to oppress China, to which they had been strangers. But China worshiped them as Heaven, and did not realize their guilt. Instead of burning the books in order to keep the people ignorant [as did the Ch'in], they more cleverly used the books to keep the people under control. Compared with them, the tyrannical emperor of the Ch'in dynasty was but a fool! . . .

At the beginning of the human race, there were no princes and subjects, for all were just people. As the people were unable to govern each other and did not have time to rule, they joined in raising up someone to be the prince. Now "joining in raising up" means, not that the prince selected the people [as for civil service],[4] but that the people selected the prince; it means that the prince was not far above the people, but rather on the same level with them. Again, by "joining in raising up" the prince, it means that there must be people before there can be a prince: the prince is therefore the "branch" [secondary] while the people are the "root" [primary]. Since there is no such thing in the world as sacrificing the root for the branch, how can we sacrifice the people for the prince? When it is said that they "joined in raising up" the prince, it necessarily means that they could also dismiss him. The prince serves the people; the ministers assist the ruler to serve the people. Taxes are levied to provide the means for managing the public affairs of the people. If public affairs are not well managed, it is a universal principle that the ruler should be replaced. . . .

The ruler is also one of the people; in fact, he is of secondary importance as compared to ordinary people. If there is no reason for people to die for one another, there is certainly less reason for those of primary importance to die for one of secondary importance. Then, should those who died for the ruler in ancient times not have done so? Not necessarily. But I can say positively that there is reason only to die for a cause, definitely not reason to die for a prince. . . .

In ancient times loyalty meant actually being loyal. If the subordinate actually serves his superior faithfully, why should not the superior actually wait upon his subordinate also? Loyalty signifies mutuality, the utmost fulfillment of a mutual relationship. How can we maintain that only ministers and subjects should live up to it? Confucius said: "The prince should behave as a prince, the minister as a minister." He also said: "The father should behave

---

[4]The term "raised up" or "recommended" had been applied to candidates selected for office.

as a father, the son as a son, the elder brother as an elder brother, the younger brother as a younger brother, the husband as a husband, the wife as a wife." The founder of Confucianism never preached inequality. . . .

As the evils of the ruler-minister relationship reached their highest development, it was considered natural that the relationships between father and son and between husband and wife should also be brought within the control of categorical morality.[5] This is all damage done by the categorizing of the three bonds. Whenever you have categorical obligations, not only are the mouths of the people sealed so that they are afraid to speak up, but their minds are also shackled so that they are afraid to think. Thus the favorite method for controlling the people is to multiply the categorical obligations. . . .

As to the husband-wife relationship, on what basis does the husband extend his power and oppress the other party? Again it is the theory of the three bonds which is the source of the trouble. When the husband considers himself the master, he will not treat his wife as an equal human being. In ancient China the wife could ask for a divorce, and she therefore did not lose the right to be her own master. Since the inscription of the tyrannical law [against remarriage] on the tablet at K'uai-chi during the Ch'in dynasty, and particularly since its zealous propagation by the Confucianists of the Sung dynasty—who cooked up the absurd statement that "To die in starvation is a minor matter, but to lose one's chastity [by remarrying] is a serious matter"—the cruel system of the Legalists has been applied to the home, and the ladies' chambers have become locked-up prisons. . . .

Among the five human relationships, the one between friends is the most beneficial and least harmful to life. It yields tranquil happiness and causes not a trace of pain—so long as friends are made with the right persons. Why is this? Because the relationship between friends is founded on equality, liberty, and mutual feelings. In short, it is simply because friendship involves no loss of the right to be one's own master. Next comes the relationship between brothers, which is somewhat like the relationship between friends. The rest of the five relationships which have been darkened by the three bonds are like hell. . . .

The world, misled by the conception of blood relations, makes erroneous distinctions between the nearly related and the remotely related, and relegates the relationship between friends to the end of the line. The relationship between friends, however, not only is superior to the other four relationships, but should be the model for them all. When these four relationships have been brought together and infused with the spirit of friendship, they can well be abolished. . . .

People in China and abroad are now talking of reforms, but no fundamental principles and systems can be introduced if the five relationships remain unchanged, let alone the three bonds.

[5]Under the influence of Buddhism and perhaps utilitarianism, T'an viewed the traditional moral values as mere "names" or empty concepts [*ming*] in contrast to reality or actuality [*shih*].

30. THE PROPER ROLE OF WOMEN IN NATIONAL LIFE
[From K'ang T'ung-wei, "On the Advantages and Disadvantages of Educating Women," 1898]

Education is what differentiates civilized people from barbarians. If half of the population of a country are barbarians, and the management of family affairs is shared by barbarians, are not collapse and disorder to be expected? I used to think that there has been a difference between male and female, wise and foolish, since the time Heaven gave birth to the people, that a clever wife was not as good as a stupid husband, that an uncouth fellow was better than a wise consort, and that mankind could do nothing about what had been endowed or withheld by Heaven. But now I realize this is an absurd misconception. What do I mean? Persia and India are ashamed that there are women in their countries, and they do not dare show them to others. In America, people are pleased to see and congratulate those who have many daughters. In both cases, the women are human beings, and yet they are valued so differently. So I have come to realize that there are reasons for the relative status of men and women, and that this is not unrelated to the prosperity or weakness of a nation.

The power of Europe and America is unprecedented. If we examine the excellence of their institutions, the profusion of their human talents, the flourishing of intelligence and wisdom, the sincerity and honesty of their customs, and their overwhelming superiority over the myriad nations, all are due to their schools. Their educational system provides penalties for parents of children over seven years of age who do not send them to school. Boys and girls attend elementary school together, but when they grow up girls are taught in separate girls' schools. The schools are divided into three stages, and promotions follow a regular order. From the higher teachers' colleges down to vocational schools, students specialize in the field which best suits their natural inclinations. This is supplemented by places to learn sewing and embroidery and augmented by women's study societies. Women are taught everything from ethics to crafts. The subjects consist of religion, lady-like behavior, ethics, education, astronomy, geography, law, home economics, medicine, mathematics, physics, music, art, and sewing and embroidery. Each student specializes in one field, and those who succeed in learning it are given diplomas of excellence. Hence, there are American and European women judges, English and American women astronomers, police officers, telegraph operators, record keepers, doctors, lawyers, teachers, and missionaries, none any different from the men.

Japan, which emulates the West, also emphasizes women's education, which is divided into roughly thirteen subjects: ethics, education, Japanese language, classical Chinese, history, geography, mathematics, science, home economics, drawing and calligraphy, music, and physical training. Only a few of these are different from male education. Thus, women's virtue is sufficient for them to take care of themselves, and their abilities are sufficient for them to support themselves. [Within the family, men and women] encourage one another to be honest and frugal, and their mutual trust is based on virtue and rightness, so that no strict prohibitions are needed and suspicions and doubts do not arise. Since their anxiety over family matters is slight, industry grows strong on their energies, and since there are no parasites who live off the nation, the people reap the benefits of economic and industrial development. That is why the West has become so wealthy and powerful, and why, in order to establish the Kingly Way, order at home must precede order outside the home.

Prosperity has its basis, and disorder in a country has its origin. The strength or weakness of a state depends on its human talents, and the quality of these talents depends on elementary education. Primary schools in the West use mostly women teachers, probably because women have specialized training and are modest and careful. But this is not as good as having a good mother. Why? Because a newborn baby is by nature unformed, and only a woman can guide it according to its temperament and predilections. Moreover, young children are close to their mothers but hold their fathers in awe. Few learn from their fathers; most are formed by their mothers. What one learns in childhood becomes behavior in adulthood . . . a nine floor building rests on its initial foundation. [K'ang goes on to argue that since mothers have such a great influence on the character of their children, all mothers, i.e., all women, should receive a good education.]

And, while it is not true that none of the virtuous and modest ladies of China are literate and cultivated, still, the best of them are immersed in poetry, content with brush and ink [rather than useful skills and moral principles]. Words about sighing over old age and lamenting sorrow fill the women's quarters; phrases about spring flowers and the autumn moon abound in ink on paper. And the poorest are buried in stories from fiction and popular rhymes. Their fathers and elder brothers have failed to guide them according to their inclinations. On the contrary, they consider these [literary pursuits] useless and prohibit them. Even if such pursuits are indeed useless, would it not be lamentable if one thought that a good way to do away with short-sightedness was to pluck out the eyes, that lameness could be eliminated by cutting off feet, or if one stopped up one's ears when one heard the burglar alarm?

Even men, not to say women, know that there is no advantage to studying what one does not use, or to use what one has not studied. Pan Ch'ao continued the compilation of the *History of the Han* [after her father's and brother's deaths], Fu Hsi-o's daughter transmitted the *Book of History* [to Ch'ao Ts'o], Wei Ch'eng's mother lectured on the *Rites of Chou* from behind a curtain [so as not to be immodest], and, by insisting that the younger brother should never precede the elder, an Empress taught the two Sung brothers a lesson.[1] Thus can we see that women of wisdom in the past could cite the classics and rely on moral scruples to make decisions in times of crisis and difficulty. If they had not studied, which of them could have accomplished what they did? For

---

[1] Historical examples of women whose education enabled them to do what Confucian ethics stipulated should have been done in the situation.

this reason the countries of the West, deeply understanding the principles of the past, emphasize women's education. Even in small countries like Sweden and Norway only one percent of the women are illiterate. Japan is a recently modernized small country, but in the last ten years there have been over 2,000,000 women students, more than 2000 women teachers, and over 300 [women's] schools. Yet, our civilized country, fountain of the teachings of the Sage, land of descendants of celestial spirits, and of beautiful mountains and rivers, with 20,000 *li* of territory and 200,000,000 women, has never had a single women's school for the education of women. Why should this be? And furthermore, the Westerners have built schools and churches to teach our women in places where they trade with us and in their concession territories. It is disgraceful for us to depend on others for the education of Chinese women! How lacking we are in will! . . .

The women of China worship the Buddha, but have never heard the names of the Supreme Sage and his wise disciples. They practice the Buddhist rituals, but are ignorant of the historical biographies and of the true meanings of the classics. They are miserly in doing good deeds, but lavish in feeding Buddhist monks, foolish about medicine, but wise about prayer. Nothing can compare with the dedication or numbers of women serving the Buddha. Among the 400,000,000 people of China, only 10 to 20 percent have heard the teachings of Confucius, while one-half serve the Buddha. No wonder China is called Buddhist! If we do not start making plans soon, but complacently continue old habits and customs, permitting this oval-headed and dainty-footed group to pass their lives [as they have], I am afraid that those who are not Buddhist will become Christians, and that the adherents of these religions will daily increase while those who adhere to our [Confucian] Way will daily diminish. This is not only an imminent danger to the nation, but before long our Way may also perish. Moreover, everyone knows of the harm of footbinding, suffered by women all over the empire. This was all brought about by women being deluded by belief in fate and not understanding the true Way.

Today, although the disaster of footbinding may be slightly abating, public meetings on the issue are held in only a few urban centers of foreign trade, and are attended by only a few exceptionally enlightened people. China's provinces are immense, and [most people] pay no attention, so that very few understand [about the harm of footbinding]. If we want to spread the desire to save [women from their plight], we must open women's schools everywhere to raise their consciousness. Some may ask, granted that the establishment of women's schools is so crucial and urgent, how can it be done? Given the size of the country, the distance separating the provinces, and the wide diffusion of this custom, it is not easy to reach everywhere. I would answer that the first step is to erect elementary schools everywhere in the villages, to enable females all over the country to acquire a rudimentary knowledge of Confucian ethics and the basics of Chinese writing. We should establish middle schools in the towns, for the study of useful subjects and to wipe out vicious and evil customs, and then morality will be established. In particular, we should establish higher schools in provincial capitals, gather the clever and intelligent, expand their skills and minds, strive for equality between men and women, and not allow energies to go to waste. Then the fundamental framework will be erected and women of virtue and ability will emerge. Let us rescue 200,000,000 prisoners from the dungeons, eradicate the foul and absurd customs of more than 2,000 years, propagate the Way of the Sage, and restore our great utopian commonwealth [*Ta-t'ung*]. Alas, China, do not impoverish yourself by stopping up talents and stifling intelligence!

31. MODERATE REFORM WITHIN A TRADITIONAL CONTEXT
[From Chang Chih-tung, *Exhortation to Learn*, 1898]

The crisis of China today has no parallel either in the Spring and Autumn period [i.e., the time of Confucius] or in all the dynasties from the Ch'in and Han down through the Yüan and Ming. . . . Our imperial court has shown the utmost concern over the problem, living in anxiety and worry. It is ready to make changes and to provide special opportunities for able ministers and generals. New schools are to be established and special examinations are to be held. All over the land men of serious purpose and sincere dedication have responded with enthusiasm and vigor. Those who seek to remedy the present situation talk of new learning; those who fear lest its acceptance should destroy the true Way hold fast to the teachings of the ancients. Both groups are unable to strike the mean. The conservatives resemble those who give up all eating because they have difficulty in swallowing, while the progressives are like a flock of sheep who have arrived at a road of many forks and do not know where to turn. The former do not know how to accommodate to special circumstances; the latter are ignorant of what is fundamental. Not knowing how to accommodate to special circumstances, the conservatives have no way to confront the enemy and deal with the crisis; not knowing the fundamental, the innovators look with contempt upon the teachings of the sages. Thus those who hold fast to the old order of things despise more and more the innovators and the latter in turn violently detest the conservatives. As the two groups are engaged in mutual recriminations, imposters and adventurers who do not hesitate to resort to falsification and distortion pour out their theories to confuse the people. Consequently students are in doubt as to which course to pursue, while perverse opinions spread all over the country. . . .

UNITED HEARTS. I have learned of three things that are necessary for saving China in the present crisis. The first is to maintain the state. The second is to preserve the doctrine of Confucius; and the third is to protect the Chinese race. These three are inseparably related. We must protect the state, the doctrine, and the race with one heart, and this is what we mean by united hearts.

In order to protect the race we must first preserve the doctrine, and before the doctrine can be preserved, we must preserve the state and the race. How is the race to be preserved? If we have knowledge, it will be preserved; and by knowledge we mean the doctrine. How is the doctrine to be maintained? It is to be maintained by strength, and strength lies in armies. Thus, if the empire has no power and prestige, the doctrine will not be followed; and if the empire is not prosperous, the Chinese race will not be respected. . . .

THE THREE BONDS. The subject is bound to the sovereign, the son is bound to the father, and the wife is bound to the husband. . . . What makes a sage a sage, what makes China China, is just this set of bonds. Thus, if we recognize the bond of subject to sovereign, the theory of people's rights cannot stand. If we recognize the bond of son to father, then the theory that father and son are amenable to the same punishment and that funeral and sacrificial ceremonies should be abolished cannot stand. If we recognize the bond of wife to husband, then the theory of equal rights for men and women cannot stand. . . .

Our sage represented the highest ideal of human relationships. He established in detail and with clarity rules of decorum based on human feelings. Although Westerners have such rules only in abbreviated form, still foreigners have never abandoned the idea of decorum. For the norm of Heaven and the nature of man are about the same in China and in foreign countries. Without the rules of decorum no ruler could ever govern a state, and no teacher could ever establish his doctrine. . . .

RECTIFYING POLITICAL RIGHTS. Nowadays scholars who become vexed with the present order of things are angry at the foreigners for cheating and oppressing us, at the generals for being unable to fight, at the ministers for being unwilling to reform, at the educational authorities for not establishing modern schools, and at the various officials for not seeking to promote industry and commerce. They therefore advocate the theory of people's rights in order to get the people to unite and exert themselves. Alas, where did they find those words that would lead to disorder?

The theory of people's rights will bring us not a particle of good but a hundred evils. Are we going to establish a parliament? Among Chinese scholar-officials and among the people there are still many today who are obstinate and uneducated. They understand nothing about the general situation of the world, and they are ignorant of the affairs of state. They have never heard of important developments concerning the schools, political systems, military training, and manufacture of machinery. Suppose the confused and tumultuous people are assembled in one house, with one sensible man there out of a hundred who are witless, babbling aimlessly, and talking as if in a dream—what use would it be? Moreover, in foreign countries the matter of revenue is mainly handled by the lower house, while other matters of legislation are taken care of by the upper house. To be a member of parliament the candidate must possess a fairly good income. Nowadays Chinese merchants rarely have much capital, and the Chinese people are lacking in long range vision. If any important proposal for raising funds comes up for discussion, they will make excuses and keep silent; so their discussion is no different from nondiscussion. . . . This is the first reason why a parliament is of no use. . . .

At present China is indeed not imposing or powerful, but the people still get along well with their daily work, thanks to the dynastic institutions which hold them together. Once the theory of people's rights is adopted, foolish people will certainly be delighted, rebels will strike, order will not be maintained, and great disturbances will arise on all sides. Even those who advocate the theory of people's rights will not be able to live safely themselves. Furthermore, as the towns will be plundered and the Christian churches burned, I am afraid the foreigners, under the pretext of protecting [their nationals and interests], will send troops and warships to penetrate deeply and occupy our territories. The whole country will then be given to others without a fight. Thus the theory of people's rights is just what our enemies would like to hear spread about....

Recently those who have picked up some Western theories have gone as far as to say that everybody has the right to be his own master. This is even more absurd. This phrase is derived from the foreign books on religion. It means that God bestows upon man his nature and soul and that every person has wisdom and intelligence which enable him to do useful work. When the translators interpret it to mean that every person has the right to be his own master, they indeed make a great mistake.

Western countries, whether they are monarchies, republics, or constitutional monarchies, all have a government, and a government has laws. Officials have administrative laws, soldiers have military laws, workers have labor laws, and merchants have commercial laws. The lawyers learn them; the judges administer them. Neither the ruler nor the people can violate the law. What the executive recommends can be debated by the parliament, but what the parliament decides can be vetoed by the throne. Thus it may be said that nobody is his own master....

FOLLOWING THE PROPER ORDER.   If we wish to make China strong and preserve Chinese learning, we must promote Western learning. But unless we first use Chinese learning to consolidate the foundation and to give our purpose a right direction, the strong will become rebellious leaders and the weak, slaves. The consequence will be worse than not being versed in Western learning....

Scholars today should master the Classics in order to understand the purpose of our early sages and teachers in establishing our doctrine. They must study history in order to know the succession of peace and disorder in our history and the customs of the land, read the philosophers and literary collections in order to become familiar with Chinese scholarship and fine writing. After this they can select and utilize that Western learning which can make up for our shortcomings and adopt those Western governmental methods which can cure our illness. In this way, China will derive benefit from Western learning without incurring any danger....

ON REFORM.   It is the human relationships and moral principles that are immutable, but not legal systems; the Way of the sage, not instruments; the discipline of the mind, not technology.

Laws and institutions are what we meet changing situations with; they therefore need not all be the same. The Way is what we establish the foundation upon; it therefore must be uniform. . . . What we call the basis of the Way consists of the Three Bonds and the Four Cardinal Virtues.[1] If these are abandoned, great disorder will occur even before the new laws can be put into effect. But as long as they are preserved, even Confucius and Mencius, if they were to come back to life, could hardly condemn the reforms. . . .

If we do not change our habits, we cannot change our methods; and if we cannot change our methods, we cannot change our instruments. . . . In Chinese learning the inquiry into antiquity is not important; what is important is knowledge of practical use. There are also different branches of Western learning: Western technology is not important, what is important is Western administration. . . .

There are [two] important factors in the administration of the new schools. First, both the old and the new must be studied. By the old we mean the *Four Books,* the five Classics, Chinese history, government, and geography; by the new we mean Western administration, Western technology, and Western history. The old learning is to be the substance; the new learning is to be for application [function]. Neither one should be neglected. Second, both administration and technology should be studied. Education, geography, budgeting, taxes, military preparations, laws and regulations, industry and commerce belong to the category of Western administration. Mathematics, drawing, mining, medicine, acoustics, optics, chemistry, and electricity belong to the category of Western technology.

[1]Decorum, righteousness, integrity, sense of shame.

CHAPTER FIVE

Chinese Society in the Late Ch'ing

The most basic problems China faced can perhaps best be seen where they ultimately existed, in the daily lives of the people, in the habits, the customs, the patterns of behavior that were the Chinese way of life. In this chapter, descriptions of scenes and episodes from everyday life have been assembled to give the reader a more concrete sense of a few of the most important problems, and of the relevance of the generalizations and theories of Chinese statesmen and thinkers. The selections have been taken from the writings of European and American missionaries, scholars, and officials familiar with China through long residence in the country and intimate contact with the people. In addition to informing us about Chinese life, they reveal, sometimes explicitly, sometimes inadvertently, Western attitudes about China, and Western conceptions of China's problems.

In Selection 32, a typical street scene in a Chinese town serves as a vivid metaphor for the gap separating officials and common people, one of the key divisions in Chinese society. The sounds announcing the impending arrival of the mandarin are a signal for everyone to evacuate the area, so as not to obstruct such an exalted personage. The problem of introducing modern enterprises into a society in which status was determined by traditional criteria is briefly analyzed by Edward A. Ross, an American sociology professor. (Selection 33) Officials frequently used their public office for private gain, as we see in Selection 34. Extralegal "gifts" and "fees" were so much taken for granted that their amount was regulated by custom; deviation from imperial law and Confucian standards for official behavior was commonplace enough to be the accepted norm. The story of the land dispute is a graphic illustration of an all too frequent occurrence: Instead of government serving the people, the people are subservient to the interests of an official and his staff. In Selection 35, Professor Ross describes some of the difficulties of introducing modern industry into such a social context.

It is easy to understand why the average subject of the Ch'ing empire should have no sense of identification with the government or its representatives. As we have already seen, late-nineteenth-century reformers attributed the lack of public spirit to the separation between government and people, and between public and private interests. Whatever the reasons, the absence of a sense of common interest shared with the government was apparent, and was frequently remarked by Westerners in China. (Selections 36 and 37)

Another facet of the relation between public and private interests is examined through the division of labor at a ferry crossing, which illustrates how vested interests in existing economic arrangements could be inimical to even the most elementary improvements for the common good. (Selection 38) The author's bias, reflected in such pejoratives as "rascals" and "loafers," does not prevent him from recognizing that the impoverished men he describes have no alternative means of earning a living. As a consequence, in the narrow context of the economic realities of each individual family or village unit, poverty is a conservative force, an impediment to economic efficiency and progress; consideration of a larger community is a luxury the poor cannot afford. This is the kind of situation that had led Mai Meng-hua to argue that modernization would require greatly expanding the powers and responsibilities of the government.

Of course, it was with the family, not with some abstraction such as the common good or the nation, that the individual identified. Selection 39 contains several examples of how profound this identification could be, and how thoroughly the individual was subjugated in the family. The Darwinian argument of Selection 40 is that while family and group solidarity is appropriate under prevailing economic conditions, it is a hindrance to modern economic efficiency. Although the family did indeed provide a kind of economic security, it was not always so considerate of the emotional well-being of its members. For women, conditions could be especially harsh, and Selection 41 surveys some of the more inhuman aspects of women's lives.

The prescribed formalities of the individual's family and social roles could be radically independent of personal feelings. In Selection 42, the writing of a letter illustrates the disjunction between the individual and his family role. Human relations are so ritualized that there is no difference between a standard son-mother letter and a letter from one particular son to his mother. As in the eight-legged essay, style matters more than content. The substitution of form for content was an old problem in Confucian society, and one which was to continue long into the future.

These selections range over a period of half a century, during which much happened. Yet it is evident that although a few members of the literate urban elite had begun to question the viability of some traditional ways, little or nothing had altered in the villages and towns of China. More revolutionary changes were soon to be advocated by new political and intellectual leaders, but the Chinese countryside and much of social life was to remain largely unaffected for some time to come.

32. THE EXALTED STATUS OF OFFICIALS
[From J. Doolittle, *Social Life of the Chinese,* 1865; and J. Macgowan, *Sidelights on Chinese Life,* 1907]

(a)

When high officers appear in the street, it is accounted a misdemeanor for the common people to mix up in the procession. When it is passing by, a civilian in a sedan must cause his sedan to be put down upon the ground, and people bearing loads or walking must stop, and stand still by the side of the street. People on horseback must dismount and stand in a respectful manner. The sign-boards of stores and shops, which usually are placed in front of the stores, must be removed from the street when the high mandarins pass by, as a mark of respect on the part of the shopkeepers. Should they be left standing in their usual positions, it would be considered disrespectful to the mandarins, as though civilians should sit in the presence of high officials. When the mandarin is below the fourth official rank, the common people may mix up in the street with his runners and assistants with impunity. In regard to high mandarins, the lictors are sure to see that the established customs are properly observed, beating unceremoniously and unmercifully any one who does not make haste to comply with their orders as they pass swiftly along.

(b)

In looking at this moving panorama [on an ordinary street in a Chinese city] there is one thing that is strikingly conspicuous, and that is the good-natured, easy, tolerant way with which they treat each other on the street. It would seem as though every man, the moment he got on it, had determined that forbearance shall be the word that should guide his conduct in his treatment of every one that he meets. Just think of it: a roadway of five or six feet wide, along which constant cross currents of people, of all kinds and conditions, are travelling, and yet no collisions, or at least so rarely that they are not enough to be quoted. Business men, clerks, coolies, opium-smokers, thieves and vaga-bonds, country bumpkins and elegant and refined scholars, all with an instinc-tive sense of the rights of others, yield to the necessities of the road, and bear with infinite good nature whatever inconveniences may arise, and treat each other with patience and courtesy.

As we have been watching the motley crowds passing and repassing before us, the man with the [itinerant] kitchen has been doing a roaring business. Customers have come and gone with most pleasing succession, and the heap of cash that he has received in payment for the savoury bowls of rice has grown into a little mound, and as he looks at it his eyes glisten with pleasure. All at once there is a sudden and mysterious change in his attitude. Instead of standing with a benevolent look upon the group sitting on their haunches round his eating-house, he becomes agitated, and hastily bidding his customers to hurry up, he begins to make preparations for an immediate move. The men gulp down their rice, the bowls are hurriedly piled up on the dresser, and before one can hardly realize what is taking place the kitchen has been shouldered, and he has disappeared at a jog-trot amid a stream of people that have engulfed him and his belongings.

Whilst we are wondering what it is that has caused this sudden panic and collapse in a business that was so prosperous, we hear the clang of the slow and measured beatings of gongs. Higher, too, than the voices around us there comes trailing on the air, as though unwilling to leave the locality from which it started, the sound of the word I-O in a crescendo note, but which finally dies away in a decreasing volume till it finally vanishes in silence. There is now an agitated movement amongst the crowds in the street before us. Some seem full of hesitation, as though undecided what to do; others assume a perplexed air and look about for some opening into which they may escape. A sedan chair, that comes lumbering up with the shouts that the bearers usually indulge in to get the people to make way for them, comes up, but no sooner is the sound of I-O heard than the men hastily retrace their steps and disappear in the opposite direction from which they were coming.

The beating of the gongs, and the prolonged wailing sound I-O, in the meanwhile advance rapidly in our direction, when all at once, all indecision on the part of the passers-by vanishes, and every man flattens himself up against the outstanding shop counters, drops his queue that has been twisted round his head, lets fall his hands by his side and assumes a look of humility and respect. The centre of the street is in a moment deserted, and there bursts into view a mandarin with his retinue.

The first members of it who come swaggering down the empty lane are the men that fill the air with the sound of I-O, in order to warn the crowds ahead of the coming of the great man. They are a most villainous-looking set of men, and seem as though they might have been picked up out of the slums and gutters for the special duty of today. At first sight one is inclined to burst into a loud fit of laughter, for to a Westerner they have a most comical and ludicrous appearance. Each one has a tall hat on his head, shaped very much like a fool's cap, but set on awry to meet the contingencies of their tails that are twisted round their heads. This makes them look like clowns that have come on to the street from some neighboring circus to amuse the populace. A closer look at them, however, soon dispels that idea, for in their hands they carry long rattans, which they wield menacingly as though waiting for a chance to let them fall heavily on the shoulders of some unwary one who is transgressing the rules of the road and thus showing disrespect to his Excellency. They have a truculent look as they furtively glance over the silent walls of human beings that line the roadway, and a discontented, sullen frown overcasts their faces as they find no chance to use their despotic power on the person of any unfortunate one.

Immediately behind them comes another set of men, quite as evil-looking, with chains in their hands. These have a proud and haughty mien, as though the supreme authority of the town rested in their hands. Should any one be unwise enough to dispute that for a moment, he would find himself instantly bound and shackled, and bundled off to prison, where ample time would be given him to review his temerity.

Coming closely behind these scamps, the luxurious chair of the madarin, carried by eight bearers, fills the vacant space in the street. He is the mayor of the town, and for all practical purposes the supreme power in it. He is an ideal-looking official, for he is large and massive in appearance, whilst he has that stern and uncompromising look that is supposed to be necessary in any magistrate who would hope to keep his subjects in order. He has a stern and forbidding aspect, as though he were on his way to the execution ground to have some criminal decapitated. This is the kind of air that the mandarins put on when they appear in public. In the course of many years' experience, I have never once seen any one of them, from the highest to the lowest, with a smile on his face or a look of sympathy for the people whilst he was being carried officially through the streets. In a few seconds the procession has passed by, and the human stream again flows along its ancient channel, and the life of the street is once more resumed.

33. STATUS AND WORK
[From Edward A. Ross, *The Changing Chinese,* 1911]

The inefficiency of the management of Chinese undertakings is heartrending in its waste of sweat-won wealth. The superintendent of construction of a railroad will be a worthy mandarin, without technical knowledge or experience, who has to rely wholly on his subordinates. Or the prominent financier chosen president of the company feels himself quite above the vulgar details of management and so delegates the task to someone of less consequence. This gentleman, too, feels above the work, and passes it down to someone else. So the big men become figureheads and little men run the enterprise. Any government undertaking suffers from the conceit and impracticality of the mandarins.

34. CORRUPTION AS A WAY OF LIFE
[From J. Macgowan, *Sidelights on Chinese Life*, 1907; and J. Doolittle, *Social Life of the Chinese,* 1865]

(a)

The mandarins as a class are the privileged men of the Empire. They have large and extensive powers. In the exercise of their functions a wide discretion is allowed them, and in their decisions as magistrates, whilst they have to keep themselves within certain general laws recognized as the statutes of the dynasty, they are left very much to their own wit and common-sense as to how they shall reach the conclusions they may finally come to. In addition to the above, the mandarins have almost unlimited opportunities of making money and of enriching themselves and their families.

This latter has a fascination for the Chinaman, which explains the intense longing that every youth, who has any ambitions for the future, has to some day become a mandarin. I presume there is hardly a son born in this wide Empire, about whom the father does not at once begin to have his dreams. He pictures to himself the time when the little fellow whose cries are awakening new echoes in the home shall have taken his degree and have qualified himself for some Government appointment. His visions widen and he sees him advanced from one post to another, and growing in power and in wealth, until he finally returns to his ancestral home to build a magnificent mansion and to enrich every member of it. . . .

In order to give the reader some practical idea of what are the duties and responsibilities of a mandarin, I propose to select one and describe him as graphically as I can, so that one may have a picture of him before the mind's eye. For this purpose, I shall take the "County Mandarin,"[1] for though there are many others that are superior to him in rank, there is not one whose duties are so multifarious, or who is so responsible for the order and good government of his district as he is. . . .

The mandarin whom I am describing has just received an appointment to the county, say, of "Eternal Spring," for which he has paid the modest sum of [the equivalent of] a thousand pounds to the high official who had the disposal of the office. He is an ambitious man, and his great aim is not only speedily to recoup himself this initial outlay, but also to lay by a considerable sum to carry with him to his ancentral home and enable him to live in easy circumstances for some years to come. As his term of office lasts only three years and his salary is not more than three hundred a year, it would seem that he would require to be a conjuror to accomplish these two objects in the limited time at his command.

That he can do, and in the great majority of cases actually does perform, such remarkable financial legerdemain is a fact that is entirely due to the vicious system on which the whole civil service in China is based. It is perfectly understood by the Government that when a mandarin is appointed to any official position under it, the squeezes he has to pay for it, and the inadequate salary he will receive for his services, are all to be met and supplemented by what he can wring out of the people. This system is as old as the nation, and has become so inwrought and worked into its very fibre, that a new creation of national life would seem to be essential before it could be eradicated from the body politic. When the mandarin arrives at his Yamen, which is his residence and the place where all the official business of the country is transacted, he is met by the whole staff of men who are to assist him in the arduous

[1] I.e., the District Magistrate.

duties that fall to him as the chief magistrate in the large district he has been appointed to rule. These consist of a private secretary, an interpreter, a number of writers who write dispatches and conduct any correspondence that may arise, a large body of policemen, or runners as they are generally called in the East, and a dozen disreputable-looking men who form the retinue of the mandarin, when he is called out to settle disturbances in any part of his large field, or adjudicate on cases that have to be tried on the spot.

(b)

On arriving at the place of his mandarinate, it is customary . . . for clerks and inferior officials connected with his own establishment to make presents to the new mandarin. He expects a present graduated in value according to the comparative lucrativeness of the stations which the officers fill. The amount from each is fixed by custom. Unless they should give it on the arrival of the mandarin, professedly as an expression of their satisfaction and respect, but really in order to ingratiate themselves in his good will, matters would not go smoothly with them. They would be frequently faulted and required to do their work over again, etc. They give the customary present to the mandarin, as soon as he arrives, as a bribe to treat them well.

All of the officers inferior to the new-arrived in the district, prefecture, or province, who are under his supervision, are expected to make him a present. The district magistrate expects a present from all who are beneath him, the prefect from all who are beneath him, and the governor from the officers under his jurisdiction who report to him, and the viceroy from all the principal officers in the two provinces under his control. The value of these presents from the different officials who greet their new superior mandarin in this manner is regulated by custom, and has respect to the comparative rank and profits of the positions occupied by them. Those who do not make the customary token of respect may be sure that they are marked, and that they will suffer the consequences of their violation of custom in the subsequent inattention and ill will of their superior. Some of these presents, given by a single subordinate to his superior of high rank and in a high office, are said to amount to several hundred dollars, especially if he has a great favor which he hopes to gain from him, or if he desires to be promoted through his influence. It is easy to perceive that on the arrival of a viceroy or of a provincial governor at the place where he enters upon office, he ordinarily, before he has performed much work, receives in the aggregate a large sum of ready money, as presents or as bribes, from the large staff of subordinate officers resident in various parts of the province. Mandarins of lower rank receive much smaller, but still a comparatively large amount of money from their subordinate officers.

(c)

Nominally [the District Magistrate] is responsible for all the salaries that this great crowd of men receive, and one wonders how he manages to pay them all out of his three hundred a year. The real fact of the case is, the only man that receives any salary from him is his private secretary. All the rest purchase the privilege of being employed in his service, and give the whole of their time free simply for being permitted to extract out of the people who come to engage in lawsuits, or from those who have fallen within the grip of the law, fees and squeezes and perquisites enough to give them a very good permanent income.

It is very interesting to watch the way in which these gentry carry on their official work, and how as ministers of justice in executing the decisions of the mandarin their one aim seems to be to extract as much out of the pockets of the people they are operating on as it is possible for them to do.

A farmer, for example, comes one day into the Yamen to lay a complaint against a rich neighbour who has taken forcible possession of some of his fields. He produces the deeds of his lands, and shows how they have been in his family for several generations and that they have never been alienated either by sale or by mortgage. The rich man has simply taken forcible possession of them because he belongs to a formidable clan, he declares, and not because he has any right to the fields.

The runners are delighted with this case, for the fact that there is a rich man in it makes it certain that some of his dollars will be transferred to their pockets. The complaint is formally accepted by the mandarin, and the court fees having been paid, a warrant is issued for the arrest of the man who has been accused.

The runners or policemen start out on their journey with light and joyous hearts. The road that leads away from the main thoroughfare takes them through rice fields, and skirts the foothills, and runs through villages, until at last it brings them by a narrow pathway to the house of the rich man they have come to arrest.

The whole village is excited by the arrival of these messengers of the law, for they are always a sign of ill omen, and the only man who can face them without being terrified is the man who knows that he has the means to satisfy their cupidity and to thus avoid being roughly handled by them. A crowd as if by magic silently gathers round the open door through which the runners have entered, and the women from the neighbouring houses collect in excited knots, and with flushed faces discuss the wonderful news of their village life.

The rich man, with as calm and as indifferent a manner as he can assume, though his heart is beating fast, comes out into the courtyard where the runners are standing and politely asks them what is their business with him. They tell him they have a warrant for his arrest for seizing some fields that belong to one of his neighbours, and the mandarin has ordered them to bring him to his court to be tried for the offence.

Whilst the warrant is being read, the accused has had time to collect his wits. He of course denies the accusation, and politely asks the men to be seated. At the same time he calls the cook, and declaring that they must be tired and hungry after their long walk, he orders him to at once get dinner ready for them, and in a whisper he gives him a hint that he does not wish him to spare any expense in providing such a meal as will put them in the best humour possible.

The runners freely protest that they have no time to delay, that their orders are imperative, and that the "Father and Mother of his People" [the District Magistrate] is impatiently awaiting their return. This of course is all put on, for dinner is just the one thing they have been looking forward to; so pretending to yield to the entreaties of their host, they at once make themselves at home. They smoke their pipes and then laugh and chat with the members of the household, just as though they had been invited guests, and not policemen who had come to carry off the head of it to prison.

After a time, when they have got into a comfortable humour with each other, the rich man takes the head runner aside, and after a few minutes of earnest conversation and the slipping of a few dollars into his hand, an air of increased geniality seems to have suddenly sprung up between him and his uninvited guests. They are now most polite and deferential to him, and the swaggering, bullying manner natural to them is replaced by a childlike gentleness that is really most touching. Dinner over, instead of incontinently grabbing him by the tail and hauling him along the road as their instinct would prompt them in the case of any of the common people, they part from him with smiles and bows and high-flown compliments, whilst the culprit actually stands at his door, and ostentatiously, for the benefit of the man who has accused him of stealing his fields, entreats them not to leave him too soon, and assures them that his heart will be desolated if they do not come quickly and pay him another visit.

When they reach the Yamen, the "Man that knows the County" [the District Magistrate] demands of them where their prisoner is. They have their story all ready, and they explain that when they reached his home they could find no trace of him, and that without any explanation to his friends he had disappeared and they could not find him. . . .

The runners have scarcely left the house, when the rich man hastens, as fast as he can hurry, to the city, and enters his reply to the accusation that has been laid against him. He denies that *in toto,* and produces deeds, that have been so deftly manufactured that they have the impress of a hundred years upon them, and which he declares prove decisively that the fields in question belong to him, and have come to him in proper legal succession from his forefathers.

He is careful, however, after he has put in his plea, to find out some relatives of the "Father and Mother of the People" who have followed him from his distant home for occasions like this, with whom he confers. An earnest but not an unduly prolonged conversation takes place, when a certain sum of money changes hands, which is destined to find its way into the pocket of the mandarin, and whose purpose is to give him such a clear and profound grasp of the case that he will have no difficulty in deciding that the accusation against the rich man has been a trumped-up one.

Ten days go by and no further proceedings have been taken. The complainant, well aware of the cause of this, scrapes together as large a sum as he can possibly afford, and by the same underground method sends it to the "Man that knows the County," with the hope that he will be able to see the justice of his case and give him back his fields. At the same time he enters what in legal phraseology is called a hurrying petition, the object of which is to hasten the action of the mandarin so as to finish up the case without delay.

Upon the receipt of this, an order is issued to the runners to go and arrest the accused with all possible dispatch and bring him to the Yamen so that he may be tried. The previous farce such as I have already described is once more gone through. The runners are received with lavish hospitality and a certain number of dollars are transferred to their pockets, that put a smile on their features that lights them all up and that spreads away to the back of their necks, till it finally vanishes down their tails into thin air. On their return to the Yamen they report that the man is still away from home, and though they have made diligent inquiries they have not yet been able to trace his whereabouts.

And so the case goes on, bribes being paid by both sides that go to swell the gains of the "Father and Mother of his People," whilst fees also are squeezed out of them by the runners, who, as in some difficult cases in Chancery in England, grow fat upon the spoils that they extract out of both the complainant and defendant. Finally, after many months of vexatious delays, when the whole hungry tribe in the Yamen see that no more money can be got out of either side, the case is tried, when some compromise is suggested and the parties leave the court fully convinced that there is no such thing as justice in China. . . .

If money could only be eliminated out of the life of a mandarin he would cease to be the despicable character he often is. In their private life they are kind and hospitable and have the courtly manners of gentlemen. In their public capacity, when a bribe is not in view, they have a desire as a rule to do justice in the cases that are brought before them. In some respects they are much to be pitied. As no man may be a higher official in his own province, it follows that he has to live far away from his home and his friends, amongst people strange to him, who often speak a different language from his own. It is true that his wife and children accompany him to his new position, but they never cease to long to be back again at the place where their kindred dwell. To be a mandarin means power and the facility for acquiring a fortune, but it means also exile for the time being from the ancestral home, and constant danger of being involved with the higher authorities should any of his mistakes or his misdeeds be brought to light.

35. CORRUPTION AS AN IMPEDIMENT TO THE DEVELOPMENT OF MODERN ENTERPRISE
[From Edward A. Ross, *The Changing Chinese*, 1911]

[T]he courage of the Chinese capitalist is chilled by the rapacity of officials unchecked by law court or popular suffrage. . . . The case of Fukien shows how irresponsible government paralyzes the spirit of enterprise. For half a century Fukienese have been wandering into the English and Dutch possessions in

Southeastern Asia, where not a few of them prosper as merchants, planters, mine operators, contractors and industrialists. Some of them return with capital, technical knowledge, and experience in managing large undertakings. Yet aside from a saw mill—the only one I saw in China—I hear of not one modern undertaking in the province. The coal seams lie untouched. The mandarin lay it to the difficulty of getting the coal to tidewater. The Fukienese rich from his tin-mining in Perak—there are thirty Chinese millionaires in the Malay States—tells you it is dread of official "squeeze."

The country back of Swatow is rich in minerals. But what probably would happen to a retired Singapore contractor so rash as to embark on a mining venture there? The clan of Hakkas in the neighborhood of the ore deposit would demand something for letting him work it unmolested. The local mandarin would have to be squared. The *likin* officials would sweat him well before letting his imported machinery go up the river. The magistrate of every district his product touched in going down to the coast would hold him up. Finally, at any moment, his operations might be halted by an outbreak of superstitious fear lest they were disturbing the earth dragon and spoiling the luck of the community. Small wonder a high imperial official confessed to me—in confidence—that not one penny of his fortune ever goes into a concern not under foreign protection.

36. INDIFFERENCE OF THE COMMON PEOPLE TOWARD NATIONAL AFFAIRS
[From M. Huc, *The Chinese Empire*, 1855]

In 1851, at the period of the death of the Emperor Tao-kuang, we were travelling on the road from Peking, and one day, when we had been taking tea at an inn in company with some Chinese citizens, we tried to get up a little political discussion.

We spoke of the recent death of the Emperor, an important event which, of course, must have interested everybody. We expressed our anxiety on the subject of the succession to the Imperial throne, the heir to which was not yet publicly declared. "Who knows," said we, "which of the three sons of the Emperor will have been appointed to succeed him? If it should be the eldest, will he pursue the same system of government? If the younger, he is still very young; and it is said there are contrary influences, two opposing parties, at court—to which will he lean?" We put forward, in short, all kinds of hypotheses, in order to stimulate these good citizens to make some observation. But they hardly listened to us. We came back again and again to the charge, in order to elicit some opinion or other, on questions that really appeared to us of great importance. But to all our piquant suggestions, they replied only by shaking their heads, puffing out whiffs of smoke, and taking great gulps of tea.

This apathy was really beginning to provoke us, when one of these worthy Chinese, getting up from his seat, came and laid his two hands on our shoulders in a manner quite paternal, and said, smiling rather ironically,—

"Listen to me, my friend! Why should you trouble your heart and fatique your head by all these vain surmises? The Mandarins have to attend to affairs of State; they are paid for it. Let them earn their money, then. But don't let us torment ourselves about what does not concern us. We should be great fools to want to do political business for nothing."

"That is very conformable to reason," cried the rest of the company; and thereupon they pointed out to us that our tea was getting cold and our pipes were out.

37. A FOREIGN COMMENTARY ON THE ABSENCE OF NATIONALISM IN CHINA
[From Arthur H. Smith, *Chinese Characteristics*, 1894]

When it is remembered that in the attack on Peking, in 1860, the British army was furnished with mules bought of the Chinese in the province of Shantung; that Tientsin and Tungchow made capitulations on their own account, agreeing to provide the British and French with whatever was wanted if these cities were not disturbed; that most indispensable coolie work was done for the foreign allies by Chinese subjects hired for the purpose in Hongkong; and that when these same coolies were captured by the Chinese army they were sent back to the British ranks with their queues[1] cut off—it is not difficult to perceive that patriotism and public spirit, if such things exist in China, do not mean what these words imply to Anglo-Saxons.

38. THE SELF-PERPETUATING INEFFICIENCY OF POVERTY
[From Arthur H. Smith, *Village Life in China*, 1899]

In the northern part of China, although the streams are not so numerous as at the south, they form more of an obstruction to travel, on account of the much greater use made of animals and of wheeled vehicles. The Chinese cart is a peculiarly northern affair, and appears to be of much the same type as in ancient days. The ordinary passenger cart is dragged by one animal in the cities, and by two in the country. The country cart, employed for the hauling of produce and also for all domestic purposes by the great bulk of the population, is a machine of untold weight. We once put the wheel of one of these carts on a platform-scale and ascertained that it weighed 177 pounds, and the axle fifty-seven pounds in addition, giving a total of 411 pounds for this portion of the vehicle. The shafts are stout as they have need to be, and when the cart

[1]The pigtails that the Manchus compelled all Chinese males to wear.

upsets—a not infrequent occurrence—they pin the shaft animal to the earth, effectually preventing his running away. . . .

Under these conditions of travel, a Chinese ferry is one of the most characteristic specimens of the national genius with which we are acquainted. Ferries are numerous, and so are carts to be ferried. . . .

At a low stage of water the ferry-boat is at the base of a sloping bank, down which in a diagonal line runs the track, never wide enough for two carts to pass each other. To get one of these large carts down this steep and shelving incline requires considerable engineering skill, and here accidents are not infrequent. When the edge of the ferry is reached the whole team must be unhitched, and each animal got on the boat as best may be. Some animals make no trouble and will give a mighty bound, landing somewhere or everywhere to the imminent peril of any passengers that may be already on board. None of the animals have any confidence in the narrow, crooked, and irregular gang planks which alone are to be found. The more crooked these planks the better, for a reason which the traveller is not long in discovering. The object is by no means to get the cart and animals on with the minimum of trouble, but with the maximum of difficulty, for this is the way by which hordes of impecunious rascals get such an exiguous living as they have. When an animal absolutely refuses to budge—an occurrence at almost every crossing—its head is bandaged with somebody's girdle, and then it is led around and around for a long time so as to induce it to forget all about the ferryboat. At last it is led to the edge and urged to jump, which it will by no means do. Then they twist its tail —unless it happens to be a mule—put a stick behind it as a lever and get six men at each end of the stick, while six more tug at a series of ropes attached to the horns. . . .

But while we have been busy with the animals, we have neglected the cart, which must be dragged upon the ferryboat by the strength of a small army of men. There may be only one man or a man and a boy on a ferry, but to pull a loaded cart over the rugged edges of the planks, up the steep incline, requires perhaps ten or fifteen men. This is accomplished by the process so familiar at Chinese funerals, the wild yelling of large bands of men as they are directed by the leader.

Every individual who so much as lays a hand upon the cart must be paid, and the only limit is the number who can cluster around it. As in all other Chinese affairs there is no regular tariff of charges, but the rule is that adopted by some Occidental railway managers to "put on all the traffic can bear." Suppose for example that the passenger cart only pays a hundred cash for its transport across the stream; this sum must be divided into three parts, of which the ferry gets but one and the bands of volunteer pullers and pushers on the two banks the other two-thirds. In this way it often happens that all that one of these loafing labourers has to show for his spasmodic toil may be four cash, or in extreme cases only two, or even one.

On the farther bank the scene just described is reversed, but occupies a much shorter time, as almost any animal is glad enough to escape from a ferry. The exit of the carts and animals is impeded by the struggles of those who want to get a passage the other way, and who cannot be content to wait till the boat is unloaded. There is never any superintendent of the boat, any more than of anything else in China, and all is left to chance or fate. . . .

It is not unnatural for the Occidental whose head is always full of ideas as to how things *ought* to be done in the East, to devise a plan by which all this wild welter should be reduced to order. He would, to begin with, have a fixed tariff, and he would have a wide and gently sloped path to the water's edge. He would have a broad and smooth gang-plank, over which both animals and carts could pass with no delay and no inconvenience. He would have a separate place for the human passengers and for beasts, and in general shorten the time, diminish the discomforts and occidentalize the whole proceedings.

Now stop for a moment and reflect *how* any one of these several "reforms" is to be made a fact accomplished. The gently sloping banks will wash away with the first rise of the river; who is to repair them? Not the boatman, for "it is not the business of the corn-cutter to pull off the stockings of his customers." If the ferry is an "official" one, that only means that the local magistrate has a "squeeze" on the receipts, not that there are any corresponding obligations toward facilitating travel. Who is to provide those wide gang-planks over which the passage is to be so easy? Not the boatman. Not the passenger, whose only wish is to get safely over for that single time. Not the swarm of loafers whose interest it is not to have any gang-planks at all, or as nearly as possible none.

And even if the roads were made, and the gang-planks all provided by some benevolent despot, it would not be a week before the planks would be missing, and things going on as they have been since the foundation of the Chinese world.

39. FAMILY AND INDIVIDUAL

[From R. F. Johnston, *Lion and Dragon in Northern China*, 1910]

The units of the village community are not individuals but families. Nothing is more important for an understanding of the wonderfully stable and long-lived social system of China than this fact: that the social and the political unit are one and the same, and that this unit is not the individual but the family. . . .

But the European must not too hastily assume, when he sees individualism largely replacing the old family system in such countries as Japan, that the wiser heads in those countries regard the change as being in all respects beneficial. Some of them are inclined to fear that the new system—though its adoption may possibly be necessary in order to supply their country with a certain brute strength which the old system lacked, and so to enable it to cope with European aggression—tends to the grievous injury of much that they believe to be essential to true civilisation. They do not welcome with enthusiasm the emergence above the social and political horizon of that strange new star—the self-contained individual. They contemplate with something like dismay the weakening or breaking of the old family bonds, which if they were sometimes a hindrance to personal advancement and had a cramping influence on the individual life, at least did much to keep within bounds the primitive instincts of selfishness and greed. . . .

Weihaiwei [where the author was British district officer and magistrate; in Shantung province] has as yet shown but little tendency to modify its semi-patriarchal social system as a consequence of its fifteen years of continuous contact with Western civilisation. The individual is still sunk in the family. He cannot divest himself of the rights any more than of the responsibilities that belong to him through his family membership. The Weihaiwei farmer has indeed so limited a conception of his own existence as a separate and distinct personality that in ordinary speech he continually confuses himself with his ancestors or with living members of his family. Examples of this are of repeated occurrence in the law-courts. "I bought this land and now the Tung family is trying to steal it from me," complains a petitioner. "When did you buy it?" asks the magistrate. "Two hundred years ago," promptly replies the oppressed one. Says another, "My rights to the property of Sung Lien-teng are being contested by my distant cousin. I am the rightful owner. I buried Sung Lien-teng and have charge of his soul-tablet and carry out the ancestral ceremonies." "When did Sung Lien-teng die?" questions the magistrate. "In the fortieth year of K'ang Hsi" is the reply. This means that the deceased whose property is in dispute died childless in 1701, that plaintiff's ancestor in that year defrayed the funeral expenses and acted as chief mourner, that by family agreement he was installed as adopted son to the deceased and heir to his property, and that plaintiff claims to be the adopted son's descendant and heir. Looking upon his family, dead and alive, as one and indivisible, he could not see any practical difference between the statement that certain funeral rites had been carried out by himself and the statement that they had been carried out by a direct ancestor. . . .

But after all, if we wish to assure ourselves that the individual is not regarded as an independent unit we must rely on stronger evidence than strange verbal inaccuracies. Perhaps the best and most convincing proofs will be found in the restrictions placed on the powers of the individual to dispose of real property.

. . . In practice, land is privately owned in China just as it is privately owned in England; but whereas in England a land-owner may (if his land is not "tied up") exercise all the rights of absolute ownership quite regardless of the wishes of his nearest relations, not to mention his distant cousins, in China the individual land-owner cannot disregard the inextinguishable rights of his family.

Be it remembered, moreover, that "family" does not imply merely a father and a mother with their children. It implies also nephews, grand-nephews, cousins of several degrees, and in fact all who come within the description of *wu fu*, or persons on whose decease one must assume one of the five degrees of "mourning." . . . in Weihaiwei, which is a typical Chinese agricultural district, the man who tried to dispose of his landed property without fully discussing the whole matter with all the prominent members and "elders" of his village—or rather with those among them who are of the same surname and come within the *wu fu*—would find himself foiled at the outset, for no one would venture to run the risk of buying land that was being offered for sale in so peculiar and irregular a manner. Even if the purchaser, being a man of wealth and influence, were prepared to run all possible risks, who would be found to draw up the deed of sale? Who would take the place of the numerous relatives who always append their signatures to such documents as proof that all is in order? The would-be seller's title-deeds may be in perfect order; the land may have come down to him from his direct ancestors and his right to sell may be apparently incontestable. But he is not the less bound to satisfy his uncles and brothers and cousins, as well as his own sons, as to the reason for his desire to sell, and even if they agree that a sale is necessary (owing perhaps to the seller's debts) he is by no means permitted to dispose of the property by public auction or offer it to the highest bidder.

All his relatives, more or less in the order of their seniority or proximity, must be given the option of purchase, and if the price offered by an influential relative is considered fair by the general voice of the village or the clan, he must perforce accept it and be thankful or refrain from selling his land. The theory that seems to lie at the root of this custom is not that the land is the common property of the clan but that the individual *per se* is only the limb of a body, and cannot therefore act except in accordance with the will of the organism to which he belongs; and that it is contrary to the interests of the family that a portion of the real property belonging to any of its members should pass into alien hands.

Absolute sales of land are, indeed, not regarded with favour even if conducted according to the "rules." They have grown common in Weihaiwei during the past few years, partly because the great increase in the value of agricultural land has tempted many to take advantage of a condition of the real-estate market which they think may only be temporary; partly because foreign occupation and other recent events have opened out new avenues of employment to large numbers of the people who are willing, therefore, to dispose of the little plots of land that are no longer their all-in-all; partly because many of the smaller land-holders are engaging in commerce or emigrating to Chihli and to Manchuria. For these and other reasons a good deal of land has changed and is changing hands, but the old custom whereby real property can be transferred only from relative to relative is still observed with very slight if any relaxation of its former strictness. . . .

Mortgages in Weihaiwei, as probably in the rest of China, are much commoner than sales. A farmer will generally sell his land only because he must; he will mortgage it on very slender provocation. As a mortgage does not definitely alienate the land from the family, the customary rules regulating this transaction are much more flexible than those relating to sales. Sometimes a piece of land is merely mortgaged as security for a temporary loan, in which case the mortgagor remains on the land; in other cases it is mortgaged because the owner is going abroad or because the opposition on the part of the family

to a definite sale is too strong to be overcome. In such cases the rights of
cultivation are transferred to the mortgagee. In the great majority of cases
mortgaged lands are subsequently redeemed.[1] . . .

If the Chinese restrictions on a man's freedom to dispose of his own property
are regarded from the Western point of view as an intolerable and unjustifiable
interference with the rights of the individual, let it be remembered that the
Chinese system is expressly intended to protect the family rather than the
individual. But even so, does it not safeguard the rights of the individual as
well? If A has complete control over his land and can bequeath it or sell it to
whom he chooses, what about his son B? The average Chinese villager is at
birth a potential landed proprietor. His share in the family inheritance may
be small, but his wants, too, are small. One often hears of an Englishman's
desire to "found a family," by which is generally meant that he aspires to a
position "in the county." The "family" of a Chinese never requires to be
founded; it is there already. He does not require to engage a searcher of records
to find out who his ancestors were so that he may be provided with a pedigree:
he will find all the necessary information in the Ancestral Temple of his clan.

40. THE PRIMACY OF FAMILY AND OTHER PERSONAL TIES OVER ECONOMIC EFFICIENCY
[From Edward A. Ross, *The Changing Chinese,* 1911]

With us the individual early detaches himself from his family and circulates
through society as a free self-moving unit. In China family and clan ties mean
more, and there are few duties more sacred than that of helping your kinsmen
even at other people's expense. You feel it is *right* to provide berths for your
relatives and no scruple as to their compatative fitness tweaks your conscience.
When an expectant is appointed to office (not in his own province, of course),
his relatives even unto the nth degree call upon him with congratulations and
suggest that he find places for them in his new post. . . .

Now, this pestilent nepotism quickly fastens itself upon industrial undertakings. The manager of a government plant on looking into one of the departments, which was going badly, found that thirty-three out of the fifty-five men
in that department were relatives of the foreman. Since two years ago, when
the Peking-Hankow Railway came under Chinese management, the positions
along the line have been filled on the basis of sheer favoritism, with the result
of loading the pay-roll with incompetents. . . . So desperate is the struggle to
live and so ingrained is the spirit of nepotism that whenever capital is laid out
by anyone else than the owner, employees multiply like locusts. . . .

In a press [of poverty] so desperate, if a man stumbles he is not likely to get
up again. . . . In China you should move slowly in getting rid of an incompe-

[1]In Weihaiwei a mortgage is regarded as an out-and-out sale if the right of redemption is not
exercised after a definite number of years.

tent. Ruthless dismissal, such as we tolerate, is bitterly resented and leads to extreme unpopularity. Again, no one attempts to stand alone, seeing the lone man is almost sure to go under. The son of Han dares not cut himself off from his family, his clan, or his guild, for they throw him the life-line by which he can pull himself up if his foot slips. . . . The whole bidding of his experience has been "Conform or starve." Likewise no duty is impressed like that of standing by your kinsmen. The official, the arsenal superintendent, or the business manager of a college, when he divides the jobs within his gift among his poor relations, is obeying the most imperative ethics he knows.

It is an axiom with the Chinese that anything is better than a fight. They urge compromise even upon the wronged man and blame him who contends stubbornly for all his rights.

41. THE STATUS OF WOMEN
[From M. Huc, *The Chinese Empire*, 1855]

The condition of the Chinese women is most pitiable; suffering, privation, contempt, all kinds of misery and degradation, seize on her in the cradle, and accompany her pitilessly to the tomb. Her very birth is commonly regarded as a humiliation and a disgrace to the family—an evident sign of the malediction of Heaven. If she is not immediately suffocated, . . . she is regarded and treated as a creature radically despicable, and scarcely belonging to the human race.

This appears so incontestable a fact, that Pan Hui-pan,[1] celebrated though a woman, among Chinese writers, endeavors, in her works, to humiliate her own sex, by reminding them continually of the inferior rank they occupy in the creation. "When a son is born," she says, "he sleeps upon a bed; he is clothed with robes, and plays with pearls; every one obeys his princely cries. But when a girl is born, she sleeps upon the ground, is merely wrapped up in a cloth, plays with a tile, and is incapable of acting either virtuously or viciously. She has nothing to think of but preparing food, making wine, and not vexing her parents."

. . .The young girl lives shut up in the house where she was born, occupied exclusively with the cares of housekeeping, treated by every body, and especially by her brothers, as a menial, from whom they have a right to demand the lowest and most painful services. The amusements and pleasures of her age are quite unknown to her; her whole education consists in knowing how to use her needle; she neither learns to read nor to write; there exists for her neither school nor house of education; she is condemned to vegetate in the most complete and absolute ignorance, and no one ever thinks of, or troubles himself about her, till the time arrives when she is to be married. Nay, the idea of her

[1] Pan Chao of the later Han dynasty, authoress of a well-known work on the proper behavior of women, from which the following passages are taken.

nullity is carried so far, that even in this, the most important and decisive event in the life of a woman, she passes for nothing; the consulting her in any way, or informing her of so much as the name of her husband, would be considered as most superfluous and absurd.

The young girl is simply an object of traffic, an article of merchandise to be sold to the highest bidder, without her having the right to ask a single question concerning the merit or quality of her purchaser. On the day of her wedding there is great anxiety to adorn and beautify her. She is clad in splendid robes of silk, glittering with gold and jewels; her beautiful plaits of raven hair are ornamented with flowers and precious stones; she is carried away in great pomp, and musicians surround the brilliant palanquin, where she sits in state like a queen on her throne. You think, perhaps, on witnessing all this grandeur and rejoicing, that now, at last, her period of happiness is about to begin. But, alas! a young married woman is but a victim adorned for the sacrifice. She is quitting a home where, however neglected, she was in the society of the relations to whom she had been accustomed from her infancy. She is now thrown, young, feeble, and inexperienced, among total strangers, to suffer privation and contempt, and be altogether at the mercy of her purchaser. In her new family, she is expected to obey every one without exception. According to the expression of an old Chinese writer, "the newly married wife should be but a shadow and an echo in the house." . . .

The state of perpetual humiliation and wretchedness to which the women of China are reduced, does sometimes drive them to frightful extremities; and the judicial annals are full of the most tragical events arising from this cause. The number of women who hang themselves, or commit suicide in various ways, is very considerable. When this catastrophe occurs in a family, the husband shows usually a great deal of emotion, for, in fact, he has suffered a considerable loss, and will be under the necessity of buying another wife. . . .

One day we were witnesses of a terrible scene in a Chinese family we knew intimately. On coming in we found a numerous party assembled round a young woman, who appeared on the point of yielding her last breath. A few days before she had been the very image of health, but now she was scarcely recognisable, her face was so bruised and covered with blood. . . We asked for some explanation of this heart-rending spectacle. "It is her husband," said the bystanders, "who has brought this poor creature to this state." The husband was standing there gloomy, silent, almost stupefied, his eyes fixed upon his unfortunate victim.

"What motive," said we, "could possibly have urged you to such a dreadful excess? What crime has your wife committed to be treated in this way?"

"None, none!" he cried in a voice broken by sobs. "She never deserved any punishment; we have only been married two years, and you know we have always lived in peace. But for some days I have had something on my mind. I thought people were laughing at me, because I had never beaten my wife; and this morning I gave way to a bad thought." And the young man, whom we could never have suspected of such a piece of insanity, abandoned himself to tardy and useless remorse. Two days afterwards the poor woman, who had always been an angel of goodness, expired in terrible convulsions. . . .

As for ordinary infanticides—the suffocation and drowning of infants—they are innumerable. . . . and their principal cause is pauperism. From the information we have collected in various provinces, it appears that persons in embarrassed circumstances kill their new-born female children in the most pitiless manner. The birth of a male child in a family is an honour and a blessing; but the birth of a girl is regarded as a calamity especially with necessitous parents. A boy is soon able to work and help his parents, who count upon his support for their old age; the family is continued also by a boy, and a new link added to the genealogical chain. A girl, on the contrary, is a mere burden. According to Chinese manners, she must remain shut up till the period of her marriage, and she cannot exercise any kind of industry, by which she might make amends to her parents for the expenses she occasions. It is therefore the girls only that are murdered, as they are regarded as causes of indigence. In certain localities, where the culture of cotton, and the breeding of silkworms furnish young girls with suitable occupations, they are allowed to live, and the parents are even unwilling to see them marry and enter another family. . . .

We might quote a great number of proclamations of the first Mandarins of the Empire, which speak in reprobation of the conduct of parents unnatural enough to put their girls to death, and which threaten them with all the rigours of the law.

These proclamations certainly themselves show how frequent infanticides must be in China, but at the same time they afford a proof that Government and public opinion do not favour such crimes. The foundling hospitals alluded to also testify to a certain amount of solicitude in the Chinese administration towards these unfortunate little creatures. We know very well, nevertheless, that these establishments afford a very poor resource, and can by no means remedy so extensive an evil; the Mandarins and officers of the hospital are far too busy in making as much money as they can out of it, to attend much to the treatment of the children.

42. THE FORMALISM OF SOCIAL ROLES
[From M. Huc, *The Chinese Empire*, 1855]

. . .We were staying at the time with a literary man, a native of Pekin, who had left his family eight years before to take the office of schoolmaster in one of the towns of the south. . . . One day we were on the point of sending off a messenger to Pekin, and we asked him whether he would not like to take the opportunity of sending something to his family or friends. After considering for a moment he said, "Oh, yes; I think I should write a letter to my old mother; I have heard nothing of her for four years, and she does not know where I am. Since there is such a good opportunity it would not be amiss if I were to write a few lines."

We thought his filial piety did not seem of a very fervent complexion; but we merely told him that he had better, in that case, write immediately, as the messenger was going off that evening. "Directly, directly," he replied; "you shall have the letter in a few minutes," and he called to one of his pupils, who was singing out his classical lesson in the next room—probably some fine passage out of Confucius upon the love that children owe to their parents. The pupil presented himself with the proper air of demure modesty.

"Interrupt your lesson for a moment," said the master; "take your pencil, and write me a letter to my mother. But don't lose any time, for the courier is going directly. Here, take this sheet of paper;" and the pupil accordingly took the paper, and set about writing to his master's mother. . . .

When the pupil had left the room with his sheet of ornamented paper, we asked the schoolmaster whether this lad knew his mother. "Not in the least," he answered. "I don't think he knew whether she was living or had already 'saluted the world'."

"In that case, how can he write the letter? You did not even tell him what he was to say."

"Doesn't he know quite well what to say? For more than a year he has been studying literary composition, and he is acquainted with a number of elegant formulas. Do you think he does not know perfectly well how a son ought to write to his mother?". . .

The pupil, obedient to his master's orders, lost no time. He returned soon afterwards, with his letter in an elegant envelope, which he had even had the politeness to seal all ready; so that this admirable son did not even give himself the trouble to read the unctuous expressions of tenderness and respect that he had addressed to his mother. No doubt he had known them by heart for a long while, and had himself taught them to the pupil. He wished, however, to write the address with his own hand; which appeared to us rather superfluous, for the letter would have done just as well for any other mother in the Celestial Empire as for the one to whom it was addressed, and any other would doubtless have felt as much satisfaction in the receipt of it.

CHAPTER SIX
Toward Revolution

The years from the reform movement of 1898 to the revolution of 1911 were marked by accelerated change, political, intellectual, social, and economic. After the disaster of the Boxer Rebellion, in which poorly organized bands of peasants attempting to purge China of the foreign presence were crushed by a joint foreign expeditionary force, further concessions were exacted from the Ch'ing court by the powers. China's helplessness intensified domestic pressures for change, and even Tz'u-hsi was forced to recognize the need for major reforms.

But some Chinese were gradually coming to believe that China's problems could not be solved within the framework of existing political institutions, in particular, under the Manchu monarchy. At first few in number, these men and women drew the conclusion that the Manchus and the imperial state would have to be overthrown; revolution from below would succeed where reform from above had failed.

The most prominent revolutionary, Sun Yat-sen (1866–1925), was a new kind of leader. He came from a peasant family, was educated in Westernized schools in Hawaii and Hong Kong, where he graduated from a Western medical college, and was a Christian convert. Although Sun had some training in the Chinese classics, and throughout his life was influenced by traditional values, he was the first major Chinese leader to be Western-educated and to profess belief in a Western creed. Sun's initial attempt at revolt, in 1895, was on a small scale. It failed, but it produced the first sacrifices for the revolution, one of whom, Lu Hao-tung (1868–95), came to be known as the first revolutionary martyr. Lu's statement to his captors just prior to his execution conveys the spirit of conviction and dedication of the revolutionaries. (Selection 43) It was the voice of the future, though many more were to die in unsuccessful uprisings before the Ch'ing dynasty was finally overthrown.

What were the goals of the revolution? And what was the proper strategy to achieve them? Over these questions there were disagreements. Some, like Ou Chü-chia in his *New Kwangtung,* argued that the provinces should take the lead. Like many others at this time, Ou justifies revolution on Confucian grounds: if the ruler fails to fulfill his responsibilities to the people, he no longer is a true, or legitimate, ruler. The Manchus, in other words, have lost the Mandate of Heaven. Ou, who never fully committed himself to the revolutionary camp, is noncommittal about the future form of government; neither monarchy nor republic is mentioned. (Selection 44)

Far more radical was Tsou Jung (1885–1905), whose virulent anti-Manchu pamphlet *The Revolutionary Army,* written at the age of 18, led to his arrest in the Shanghai International Settlement in 1903. After a celebrated trial, Tsou was given a light sentence, and Shanghai authorities refused the Manchu government's repeated demands that he be extradited to stand trial in a Ch'ing court. Tsou died in prison less than three months before his term was to expire. His trial and imprisonment had given him national eminence, and his example and *The Revolutionary Army* inspired many. (Selection 45) For Tsou, the problem is that the Chinese people have grown accustomed to being servile—to autocratic emperors, to the Manchu conquerors, to the foreign imperialists. His solution is violent revolution, the complete destruction of Manchu rule and the monarchical system. How this is to be accomplished is not made clear; his appeal to his countrymen to discard their servility does not seem an adequate response to the problem as he himself defines it. Not logic, but the moral fervor of Tsou's anti-Manchu nationalism and republicanism, engages the reader.

Ideas and enthusiasm, however, were not sufficient to destroy the Ch'ing. The ineffectiveness of their fragmented forces led Sun Yat-sen and the leaders of several other revolutionary groups to join together in 1905 to bring unity to the anti-Manchu movement. In Tokyo, a center of revolutionary activity because of the large numbers of Chinese students in Japan, they founded the T'ung-meng Hui (United League), with Sun as chairman. Within a year, the membership of the new organization grew to almost 1,000. The T'ung-meng Hui Manifesto, which was written in the format of a proclamation to be issued when uprisings took place in the future, was an important statement of common principles, although support for the socialist aspects was far from unanimous. (Selection 46) It contains an early formulation of two of Sun's main doctrines, his Three People's Principles (Nationalism, Democracy, and People's Livelihood) and the three stages of revolution. The concept of the period of government under a provisional constitution is Sun's solution to the problem of how the Chinese people were to make the transition from the old autocracy to the future constitutional government. Sun believed that because China had no hereditary aristocracy, and because long experience with what he took to be village self-government had prepared the Chinese people for democracy, the transition would not be difficult. China's decline into warlordism after the revolution of 1911 diminished his confidence in the people's readiness, and in later versions of the three stages of revolution the length of what he called the period of political tutelage, set at six years in the Manifesto, was left unspecified.

Optimistic perceptions of China's problems were not uncommon among the early revolutionaries. For the "Colloquial Master" (*Pai-hua tao-jen;* Lin Hsieh, 1873–1926), illiteracy was the main impediment to the people becoming involved in national affairs, and hence the primary cause of China's weakness. In the editorial for the inaugural edition of his *Chinese Vernacular Journal,* he argues that the basic problem is communication, and that it can be solved relatively easily by abandoning the difficult classical written language and replacing it with the far simpler colloquial language *[pai-hua].* (Selection 47) Lin's optimism did not prove warranted, nor was his appeal immediately effective. But with the New Culture Movement in the next decade, colloquial Chinese did become the principal written language, and the enormous task of spreading literacy was begun.

As a revolutionary, who advocated the violent expulsion of both Manchus and foreign imperialists, Lin Hsieh had considerable faith in the natural patriotism of the Chinese people. Others, such as Liang Ch'i-ch'ao, thought the problem of mobilizing the masses was much more difficult, and would take longer to solve. Liang was a leader of the constitutional movement, and probably the most influential publicist in the decade prior to the revolution of 1911. Although after 1898 he gradually drifted away from K'ang Yu-wei toward Sun Yat-sen, Liang never became convinced that political revolution was a viable solution. In some ways, however, his ideas were more profoundly revolutionary than those of the culturally conservative Sun. For, according to Liang, it was traditional morality and traditional culture that had made the Chinese people so inert. In order to renovate China, much of the old morality and the old culture would have to be purged. Thus Liang's nationalism, as expressed in his immensely popular *Renovating the People,* led him to subordinate ethical and cultural values to national needs, and to assert that the ideals of the past must be tested according to the criterion of their effectiveness as means to strengthen China in the present. (Selection 48) Literature, too, he saw in utilitarian terms. (Selection 49) As is apparent in these selections, Liang tended to overstate his arguments. He did not actually repudiate as much of the past as his words frequently seem to imply. Although he goes so far as to state that an absolute good can be bad if it is detrimental to the nation, he does not mean to abolish all ethical standards, nor to elevate expediency to the highest principle. And in spite of his advocacy of a new, uplifting fiction, it is unlikely that he would have entirely approved of the quite similar literary policies of the People's Republic a half century later. Yet ideas once expressed are beyond the control of the author; Liang's writings stimulated many young readers to question and reject more of the past than he perhaps intended.

From these documents we can see that change was in the wind. Even the Manchu court realized it could not be resisted. In the first decade of the new century, a large part of the program of the radical reformers of 1898 was implemented by those who had opposed K'ang Yu-wei. The aim of many of the administrative and military reforms was to gather more power into the hands of the eviscerated Manchu central government. But it was too late, and the innovations tended to alienate conservatives without satisfying the reform-minded. Although the reforms did not succeed in reinvigorating the Ch'ing dynasty, some of them had far-ranging historical consequences. In particular, the abolition of the civil service examinations in 1905 not only severed the institutional ties between Confucianism, education, and social status, but also eliminated the government's chief instrument of control over the intellectual elite. This presaged the end of the Confucian gentry, the class that had for so long supported the monarchy. Meanwhile, provincial assemblies, established in 1909, provided platforms for the expression of discontent, and issued demands for more changes than the Manchu government was willing to make.

The end of the Manchu dynasty was the result of a combination of forces. As the years passed, the number of uprisings by various revolutionary groups increased; but all were unsuccessful. It seemed that, without additional support, the revolutionaries had little chance of success. Then, in late 1911 other forces did coalesce to aid the revolutionary cause. Anger at a change in the central government's policy of financing railroad development led to dissatisfaction among investors, most vigorously expressed in the far western province of Szechwan, where in August and September antigovernment demonstrations got out of control. A rather poorly organized revolutionary uprising in the central Yangtze city of Wuchang on October 10 precipitated the collapse of the dynasty, not so much from a revolutionary upsurge as from dissolution of obedience to the Ch'ing court. One after another, provinces declared their independence from the central government. Administrative ties, traditional loyalties and feelings of legitimacy had lost their effectiveness.

Realizing that the threat, or actual use, of military force was their sole hope of retaining power, the Manchus turned to the most powerful military leader in China, Yüan Shih-k'ai (1859–1916). Yüan, the former commandant of the best equipped and best trained of the modern armies, had been forced into retirement soon after the deaths of the empress dowager and the Kuang-hsü emperor in 1908. Now he was recalled, on his own terms. Yüan perceived how fluid the situation was, and instead of supporting the Ch'ing, he negotiated himself into power. He persuaded the emperor to abdicate, and in return won Sun Yat-sen's resignation from the presidency of the newly proclaimed republic. The revolutionaries were not strong enough to risk challenging Yüan's armies. Moreover, most feared that prolonged civil strife would invite foreign intervention.

Thus, the scenario of the end of Manchu rule was far from the one envisioned by the revolutionaries. Their ideas had not yet gained wide acceptance, and by and large the common people of China remained quiescent, unaffected, inert. Nevertheless, the end of the Ch'ing was not merely the end of a dynasty, but the end of the 2,100-year-old imperial monarchy. In 1916 Yüan tried to revive it by making himself a constitutional monarch, but he had to withdraw in the face of strong opposition. An attempt to restore the Ch'ing in 1917 rapidly fizzled out. Too much had been destroyed to rebuild on the old foundations. And yet, before a new China could emerge, still more was to be destroyed, not by the nationalistic intellectuals and leaders represented in this chapter, but by their more radical successors.

43. COMMITMENT TO REVOLUTION
[Verbal Deposition of Lu Hao-tung, 1895]

My surname is Lu, my given-name is Chung-kuei, and my courtesy-name is Hao-tung. I am from Ts'ui-wei *hsiang* in Hsiang-shan district. I am 29 years old *[sui]*. I have been living away from home, and just recently returned to Kwangtung. My fellow villager, Sun Wen [Sun Yat-sen], and I are both outraged over the rotten despotism of the alien nationality, the corruption and cowardice of the officials, and the schemes of the foreigners spying for an opportunity to strike. We are grieved at the troubles all over China, everywhere the eye can see. Every time I think about it, the tears well up from nowhere. Living in Shanghai for many years, all my efforts led to nothing. So I returned to Kwangtung, and just happened to run into Mr. Sun. I visited this old friend I hadn't seen in ages at the inn where he was staying. Comrades in the storm, we talked straight through the night. Because of the ever-pressing foreign troubles, I wanted to correct these peripheral matters [the foreign threat]. But Mr. Sun advocated taking vengeance on the Manchus, to cure [the problem at] the root. After arguing several days, we settled on our goals. This was the origin of our espousing the cause of overthrowing the Manchus. We endeavored to awaken the souls of the Chinese, and to restore China to the Chinese *[Han]* people. But unfortunately the greedy and corrupt officials, the despicable gentry, and the pedantic scholars, unashamed and unabashed, are willing to collaborate with the enemy. If they don't say the present dynasty is benevolent and generous, then they say that the food they eat and the land they live on all come from the Ch'ing. How can they fail to realize that the Manchu-Ch'ing are the descendants of the bandits from Chien-chou[1] who invaded and subjugated china, grabbed our land, killed our ancestors, and took our women and wealth? Just think for a moment—who eats whose food and who lives on whose land? The ten days of slaughter in Yang-chou, the three massacres in Chia-ting, and the entry of the two Princes into Kwangtung[2]— there are plenty of tales of their cruel killing of us Chinese. Does anyone who knows about these massacres call them kind favors [*en-tse*]?

[1]The base area of Nurhachi, the founder of Manchu power.

[2]Incidents during the Ch'ing subjugation of south China in the seventeenth century.

At present, it is essential to realize that unless the Manchu-Ch'ing is destroyed, there is no way to restore China to the Chinese people, and unlesss the Chinese traitors are exterminated, there is no way to destroy the Manchu-Ch'ing. Hence, we very much desired to exterminate a few dog-officials, in order to arouse the Chinese people. Well, even though this attempt didn't succeed, I feel comforted in my heart. I am only one person; you can kill me, but you can never kill all those who will rise up after me.... I have said all I have to say. Please hurry up with the execution.

44. PROVINCIAL REVOLUTION AS A CATALYST
[From Ou Chü-chia, *New Kwangtung,* 1902]

Alas! Ever since the Sino-Japanese War, the whole world knows that the court is not dependable. Men of high purpose know that only by urgently striving for immediate independence can the country and the race be saved from the disaster of extinction. Those who try to gauge which of the provinces can become independent and avoid becoming the dogs, horses, and slaves of the Westerners, and fish and meat on the chopping board, all say, "Kwangtung!" "Kwangtung!". If Kwangtung does not become independent, all of China could very well be destroyed....

Critics say, "It is not that we do not recognize our obligation to resist foreigners, but what about the court accusing us of being rebels and sending troops to exterminate us?" To this I reply, Gentlemen! Gentlemen! The reason we Chinese consented to be obedient people was because the court could protect us. When the court cannot protect us, but, on the contrary, abandons us, then the court is the first to be a rebel. A rebel is one who betrays his obligations and acts in an unprincipled way. What could more obviously be a betrayal of obligations and an unprincipled act than a ruler abandoning his subjects ...?

Mencius said, "When the ruler regards his subjects as weeds and grass, they regard him as an enemy."[1] The proper response to being regarded as weeds and grass is to regard [the ruler] as an enemy. All the more so since [the ruler] cannot protect us, but rather cedes our territory, abandons us, sells us, and furthermore, does not allow us to defend ourselves, but uses others to kill us. What is wrong with regarding him as an enemy? Since the obligations between ruler and subjects have now been sundered, he is not our ruler and we are not his subjects. All intruders should uniformly be regarded as enemies. We should restore domestic order and resist outsiders, and let blood and iron flow freely in exchange for the happiness of the people of our country....

Gentlemen! Gentlemen! You know that today the power of the so-called court has declined, and that our people can protect themselves better than the court can protect itself. Are not the three provinces of Manchuria the land that

[1] *Mencius,* IVA: 3, 1.

brought their ancestors good fortune, the ancestral home of the dynasty, which they have occupied for many generations? After the Sino-Japanese War, anxiety over their imminent peril caused them to send Li Hung-chang on an embassy to Russia, where he secretly signed a treaty voluntarily making Manchuria a Russian dependency. When their ancestors were at the height of their power, they led their iron-shod horses from beyond the passes, and rampaged over China, slaughtering the Chinese people. Wherever they committed their fearsome atrocities, the entire land was intimidated. But now their descendants have given up their possession and sought Russian protection in order to obtain one more night of peace. How weak they have become! Since they are unable to protect themselves, how can they protect us? Since they are selling more land and more people every day to seek security for their own kind, why cannot we seek independence in order to find security for ours? . . .

Independence is a responsibility which must be borne and energetically carried out, for it is the great principle of Heaven and Earth and the birthright of mankind. We daily groan under the despotic form of government, unable to achieve freedom and equality and to embark upon the road of modern civilization. As soon as possible we should raise the flag of independence, lift up the liberty bell, and arouse the spirits of the Chinese people, so as to recover our Heaven-given rights. . . .

Kwangtung is far from the court, which has abandoned us without regret. Hence our territory has been ceded more often than that of any other province. First there was Hong Kong, then Macao, Canton Bay was third, and Hsin-an fourth. And now we hear that the entire district of Hsiang-shan is to be ceded. When Hong Kong and Macao were ceded, the people of Canton Bay and Hsin-an certainly never expected that it could happen to them. And when Hsin-an and Canton Bay were ceded, the people of Hsiang-shan did not think that it could happen to them. If the people of Kwangtung try to speculate over which prefectures and districts will be ceded and which not, I am afraid no one will be able to decide for certain. The current trend is for the entire province of Kwangtung to become the dogs, horses, and slaves of others, and to become fish and meat on a chopping board. Would it not be better for all of Kwangtung to unite and plan for independence? . . .

Gentlemen! Gentlemen! If we are to be independent, we must devise an independent form of government, an independent army and navy, an independent financial administration, an independent foreign policy, and so forth. My discussion of independence has covered only a very few matters; it has been crude and simple, far from complete. However, the form of government and other issues are matters to be settled after independence, not the prior foundation upon which independence is to be built. Hence, we should wait for the initiation of independence and then request some learned authority to compile a book for us on the form of government and other issues. For the time being, this can be deferred. Alas! If the people of Kwangtung do not become independent, how can they face the world, or the mountains and rivers of Kwangtung? And so I ask the people of Kwangtung to join together and hear me: Kwangtung is the Kwangtung of the people of Kwangtung! Through the efforts of the people of Kwangtung, Kwangtung will become independent, set the example for every other province, and become an independent southern nation, on a par with the other nations of the world. . . . Some may ask, "How is this different from partitioning China? The foreign nations desire to partition us, but this way we would partition ourselves." This is not so. I advocate one province becoming independent in order for it to stimulate thoughts of independence in the other provinces, to be the starting point for the other provinces' independence. It is not at all like partitioning. But even looking at it from the standpoint of partitioning, if China partitions herself, it will be an easy matter for China to unite herself.

45. REVOLUTIONARY NATIONALISM AND REPUBLICANISM

[From Tsou Jung, *The Revolutionary Army*, 1903]

The single, supreme goal of revolution is to sweep away thousands of years of autocracy, cast off thousands of years of slavery, eradicate 5,000,000 nomadic barbarian Manchus, and wash away the terrible humiliation of 260 years of cruel oppression, so that the territory of China will be cleansed and the descendants of the Yellow Emperor will all become Washingtons. . . . Revolution! How lofty and magnificent is Revolution!

Revolution is the general law of evolution, the universal principle of the world, the essence of the struggle for survival during a period of transition. Revolution accords with Heaven and responds to the needs of man; it eliminates corruption and retains all that is good. Revolution proceeds from barbarism to civilization; it turns slaves into human beings who are their own masters. . . .

There are citizens, and there are slaves. Citizens are strong; slaves are hopeless. Citizens are independent; slaves are submissive. Under the Yellow Dragon flag of China, there exists a kind of people who are really neither citizens nor slaves, but a multifarious mixture organized into one huge race. Can they be called citizens? I dare to say that these 400,000,000 people all look like slaves and concubines. How can they be called citizens? To do them the honor of calling them "citizens" would besmirch this beautiful word. . . .

The Indians were enslaved by England, not because the English wanted to enslave them, but because the Indians like being slaves. The Annamese were enslaved by France, not because the French wanted to enslave them, but because the Annamese like being slaves. We Chinese were enslaved by the Manchus, the Europeans, and the Americans, not because the Manchus, Europeans, and Americans wanted to enslave us, but because Chinese like being slaves. . . . We Chinese did not commence to like being slaves today. Some say that there were citizens before the Ch'in and Han dynasties,[1] but none thereafter. I say that everyone living contentedly under an autocracy is a slave. The

[1] I.e., the beginning of the imperial system.

two great principles of loyalty and filial piety, interpreted to mean loyalty to the ruler and filial piety toward parents, have been handed on generation after generation by men with noble titles, high officials, teachers, and great Confucians. I do not understand what loyalty to a ruler means. I see that France, America, and other countries have no rulers to be loyal to—do the people of these countries have no place in the human race? I see that although France, America, and other countries have no rulers to be loyal to, the people of these countries spare no pains to fulfill their duties in national affairs, without a day's respite. Certainly, loyalty and filial piety are cardinal human virtues; loyalty to the country is entirely proper—but not loyalty to a ruler. Why? Because without parents, no one would be born, and without a country, no one can survive. Hence, there are duties toward parents and country that must be fulfilled. But these duties should not be twisted, perverted, and perpetuated by one family or by its menials and running dogs.

The Chinese people have no history. The so-called twenty-four dynastic histories are really one long history of slaves. From the end of the Han until the present is more than 1,700 years; during 358 of these years all China was enslaved by alien peoples, and for 759 of these years all the land north of the Yellow River was enslaved by alien peoples. Alas! How can the descendants of the Yellow Emperor bear to allow their own blood-related compatriots to give up the land they inherited and become the slaves of alien peoples? How can this have happened again and again? . . . Loyalty to the ruler! Loyalty to the ruler! . . . That is the reason why the Chinese are slaves. . . .

Being submissive and obedient, knowing one's place, keeping out of trouble, wanting to be an official, wanting to get rich . . . these are the textbooks that have made slaves of the Chinese people. No one in the whole country is not a slave, and no one is not the slave of a slave. Two thousand years ago they were all slaves, and now, 2,000 years later, they are still all slaves. . . .

Let me say a word to arouse my compatriots: Citizens of China! I wish my fellow compatriots will all unite together with one heart, exert all their energies, urge one another on to eradicate your deep-rooted servility, and move forward to become citizens of China. . . . This deep-rooted servility must be eliminated before there can be a revolution. Otherwise, due to evolution, due to the struggle for existence, countries whose people *are* citizens will all come to grab our Chinese land, and my compatriots will be reduced from their present status to multifold slaves, then to apes, wild boars, and clams, and the land will become a wilderness, a desert without a trace of human habitation. . . .

Compatriots of the great Han race, men and women of all ages! Be revolutionary: each and every one of you, look upon this revolution as your duty, as necessary as daily food and drink! Don't deprecate yourselves! Your land occupies two-thirds of the Asian continent, your compatriots comprise one-fifth of the world's population. Your tea is more than enough to supply beverage for all the millions of the people of the world, and your coal can supply the whole world with fuel for 2,000 years. There are forebodings of your being the Yellow Peril, and you do possess the might of the sacred race. You have government; administer it yourselves. You have laws; keep them yourselves. You have industries; run them yourselves. You have armaments; marshal them yourselves. You have land; protect it yourselves. You have inexhaustible natural resources; you should exploit them yourselves. You truly possess all the qualifications for revolutionary independence. Lead your 400,-000,000 compatriots forward, to save their own lives and to save the life of our ancestral land. . . . Amidst the forest of spears and the hail of bullets, attack your hereditary foe, the Manchus, and your public enemy, the Manchu ruling clan. Then wipe out the foreign devils who have infringed upon your sovereignty, so that the stains upon your national history can be washed away, and your country's reputation will spread far and wide. . . .

Long live the revolutionary independence of the great Han people!

Long live the Chinese Republic!

Long live the freedom of 400,000,000 compatriots of the Chinese Republic!

46. SUN YAT-SEN'S EARLY REVOLUTIONARY PROGRAM
[Manifesto of the T'ung-meng Hui, 1905]

By order of the Military Government, on the ––––– day, ––––– month, ––––– year[1] of T'ien-yun, the Commander-in-Chief of the Chinese National Army proclaims the purposes and platform of the Military Government to the people of the nation:

Now the National Army has established the Military Government, which aims to cleanse away two hundred and sixty years of barbarous filth, restore our four-thousand-year-old fatherland, and plan for the welfare of the four hundred million people. Not only is this an unavoidable obligation of the Military Government, but all our fellow-nationals should also take it as their own responsibility. We recall that, since the beginning of our nation the Chinese have always ruled China; although at times alien peoples have usurped the rule, yet our ancestors were able to drive them out and restore Chinese sovereignty so that they could hand down the nation to posterity. Now the men of Han [i.e., the Chinese] have raised a righteous [or patriotic] army to exterminate the northern barbarians. This is a continuation of heroic deeds bequeathed to us by our predecessors, and a great righteous cause lies behind it; there is none among us Chinese who does not understand this. But the revolutions in former generations, such as the Ming dynasty and the Taiping Heavenly Kingdom, were concerned only with the driving out of barbarians and the restoration of Chinese rule. Aside from these they sought no other change. We today are different from people of former times. Besides the driving out of the barbarian dynasty and the restoration of China, it is necessary also to change

––––––––––––––––

[1]The dates were left blank so that they could be filled in when the Manifesto was used as an official proclamation by future local revolutionary regimes.

the national polity and the people's livelihood. And though there are a myriad ways and means to achieve this goal, the essential spirit that runs through them all is freedom, equality, and fraternity. Therefore in former days there were heroes' revolutions, but today we have a national revolution [*Kuo-min ko-ming*, literally, revolution of the people of the country]. "National revolution" means that all people in the nation will have the spirit of freedom, equality, and fraternity; that is, they will all bear the responsibility of revolution. The Military Government is but their agent. From now on the people's responsibility will be the responsibility of the Military Government, and the achievements of the Military Government will be those of the people. With a cooperative mind and concerted effort, the Military Government and the people will thus perform their duty. Therefore we proclaim to the world in utmost sincerity the outline of the present revolution and the fundamental plan for the future administration of the nation.

1. *Drive out the Tartars:* The Manchus of today were originally the eastern barbarians beyond the Great Wall. They frequently caused border troubles during the Ming dynasty; then when China was in a disturbed state they came inside Shanhaikuan, conquered China, and enslaved our Chinese people. Those who opposed them were killed by the hundreds of thousands, and our Chinese have been a people without a nation for two hundred and sixty years. The extreme cruelties and tyrannies of the Manchu government have now reached their limit. With the righteous army poised against them, we will overthrow that government, and restore our sovereign rights. Those Manchu and Chinese military men who have a change of heart and come over to us will be granted amnesty, while those who dare to resist will be slaughtered without mercy. Chinese who act as Chinese traitors in the cause of the Manchus will be treated in the same way.

2. *Restore China:* China is the China of the Chinese. The government of China should be in the nands of the Chinese. After driving out the Tartars we must restore our national state. Those who dare to act like Shih Ching-t'ang or Wu San-kuei [both were traitors] will be attacked by the whole country.

3. *Establish the Republic:* Now our revolution is based on equality, in order to establish a republican government. All our people are equal and all enjoy political rights. the president will be publicly chosen by the people of the country. The parliament will be made up of members publicly chosen by the people of the country. A constitution of the Chinese Republic will be enacted, and every person must abide by it. Whoever dares to make himself a monarch shall be attacked by the whole country.

4. *Equalize land ownership:* The good fortune of civilization is to be shared equally by all the people of the nation. We should improve our social and economic organization, and assess the value of all the land in the country. Its present price shall be received by the owner, but all increases in value resulting from reform and social improvements after the revolution shall belong to the state, to be shared by all the people, in order to create a socialist state, where each family within the empire can be well supported, each person satisfied, and no one fail to secure employment. Those who dare to control the livelihood of the people through monopoly shall be ostracized.

The above four points will be carried out in three steps in due order. The first period is government by military law. When the righteous army has arisen, various places will join the cause. The common people of each locality will escape from the Manchu fetters. Those who come upon the enemy must unite in hatred of him, must join harmoniously with the compatriots within their ranks and suppress the enemy bandits. Both the armies and the people will be under the rule of military law. The armies will do their best in defeating the enemy on behalf of the people, and the people will supply the needs of the armies, and not do harm to their security. The local administration, in areas where the enemy has been either already defeated or not yet defeated, will be controlled in general by the Military Government, so that step by step the accumulated evils can be swept away. Evils like the oppression of the government, the greed and graft of officials, the squeeze of government clerks and runners, the cruelty of tortures and penalties, the tyranny of tax collections, the humiliation of the queue—shall all be exterminated together with the Manchu rule. Evils in social customs, such as the keeping of slaves, the cruelty of foot-binding, the spread of the poison of opium, the obstructions of geomancy (feng-shui), should also all be prohibited. The time limit for each district (hsien) is three years. In those hsien where real results are achieved before the end of three years, the military law shall be lifted and a provisional constitution shall be enacted.

The second period is that of government by a provisional constitution. When military law is lifted in each hsien, the Military Government shall return the right of self-government to the local people. The members of local councils and local officials shall all be elected by the people. All rights and duties of the Military Government toward the people and those of the people toward the government shall be regulated by the provisional constitution, which shall be observed by the Military Government, the local councils, and the people. Those who violate the law shall be held responsible. Six years after the securing of peace in the nation the provisional constitution shall be annulled and the constitution shall be promulgated.

The third period will be government under the constitution. Six years after the provisional constitution has been enforced a constitution shall be made. The military and administrative powers of the Military Government shall be annulled; the people shall elect the president, and elect the members of parliament to organize the parliament. The administrative matters of the nation shall proceed according to the provisions of the constitution.

Of these three periods the first is the period in which the Military Government leads the people in eradicating all traditional evils and abuses; the second is the period in which the Military Government gives the power of local self-government to the people while retaining general control over national affairs; the third is the period in which the Military Government is divested of its powers, and the government will by itself manage the national affairs under the constitution. It is hoped that our people will proceed in due order and cultivate their free and equal status; the foundation of the Chinese Republic will be entirely based on this.

47. LITERACY AND NATIONALISM
[From Lin Hsieh, Editorial in *Chinese Vernacular Journal,* December 1903]

It's turning cold. You can hear the howl of the northeast wind, and in the sky, huge banks of black clouds drift back and forth obscuring the sun. Along about this time of year, people getting on in years put on their fur-lined long gowns and stay at home, closing the windows tightly, sipping their wine, playing mahjong, or puffing their opium, in relaxed comfort. Well, if you have read the reports in *Chung-wai jih-pao* [*China-International Daily*] and *Hsin-wen pao* [*The News*] during the past few days—"Alarming News from Manchuria," "An Important Telegram concerning Russian Affairs"—you know that Fengtien has already fallen and that several tens of warships are now off the mouth of Port Arthur harbor, and you know what an extremely precarious situation our China will be in once Japan and Russia start fighting. When you think about this, I'm afraid you may have no taste for even your very best Shao-hsing wine, or forget to win in mahjong, or you may even find the highest quality Cantonese opium insipid.

We Chinese have always been men of conscience and very patriotic. Why is it that now we don't lift a hand or make the slightest sound? The reason is that so many of us are illiterate. If you're illiterate, you can't read the papers, and if you can't read the papers you don't know what's going on outside, so that even though everyone is patriotic at heart, there's no way for this patriotism to vent itself. Now, at about this point, someone may want to contradict me, saying that, at the present time many daily newspapers of all kinds are published, and those monthlies and semi-monthlies, aren't they run by absolutely first-rate scholars? Well, if there are actually so many people reading these papers, why does such ignorance still prevail, why are there so few enlightened individuals, and why is China still unable to strengthen herself? Now, let me, the Colloquial Master, explain this for all of you to hear.

Scholars are the most hopelessly useless thing we have in China. Leaving aside for the moment those who have no ideas, no talent, and no learning, even those with excellent ideas, talent, and learning only mumble a few empty phrases or write a few empty essays. Besides this, what kind of important matters are they capable of handling? Those monthly and daily newspapers are all written for scholars to read, so regardless how mournfully they are written, it's always like playing a lute in front of a cow—a complete waste of effort. Since scholars are useless, those among us who till the fields, do handicraft work, or engage in trade, as well as our brothers in the army, have all lived tough lives since our youth, lacked money for study, and we've had to spend the whole day running around doing all kinds of decent, honest work; so when we see all that "Yea, verily," "According to the *Book of Odes,*" and "Confucius says . . .," we don't feel like reading those papers. And after a while when we do give a thought to reading them, not only our brothers can't understand all those peculiar essays and terms, even we feel a bit confused.

The foreigners have two kinds of written languages: one is the classical language, i.e., Greek and Latin, and the other is the national language, that is, the written language of each country. Everyone knows the written language of his own country, and, because the written and spoken languages are the same, if you can speak, you know the grammar; and hence everyone can understand any book or newspaper. It's not necessary for each and every person to study the classical languages, so it doesn't make any difference if the average person can't understand them. We Chinese don't have separate classical and national languages, nor do we have an alphabet. A real mess of a written language is, after all, not easy to understand, especially when in addition there are separate spoken and written languages, and you have to study both written grammar and how to speak. No wonder our brothers don't have enough time to study them. And to top it all off, there isn't even a standard spoken language. Hunanese speak Hunan dialect, people from Hupei speak Hupei dialect, and if you open a huge lecture hall in Shanghai and invite men and women from the 18 provinces to attend a lecture, when I, the Colloquial Master, would step out on stage and begin speaking in my Fukien dialect, I'm afraid no one would understand me.

Alas, abstruse grammar you can't read, and you can't understand me when I talk to you. Moreover, if I speak in Shanghai, how can people in the 18 provinces hear me? My voice isn't very loud. I've discussed this fully with friends over the past few weeks, and all said there was only one solution, to put out a colloquial language newspaper. It would be in absolutely first-rate Mandarin, each and every phrase very clear, all interesting and easy to understand. If this newspaper continues to be published, I guarantee that in less than three years each and every tiller in the fields, handicraft worker, business man, and soldier, as well as children and women, will all understand, will increase their learning and their knowledge, and then the prospects for China's self-strengthening will really be good.

48. MORAL VALUES AND NATIONAL STRENGTH
[From Liang Ch'i-ch'ao, *Renovating the People,* 1902–3]

From the time human beings first existed on earth till the present day, there have been hundreds of thousands of countries on the globe. How many of them survive independently today, colored in on maps of the five continents? Some one hundred or so. And among these, how many can stand imposing and strong, with world-swaying might, capable in the future of emerging victorious in the world of natural selection? Only four or five. Yet, all share the same sun and moon, have mountains and rivers, and [the various peoples] all have the same square feet and round heads. Why do some rise and others fall, and why are some weak and others strong? Some say, "Because of geographical advantages." But the America of today is the same America of ancient times; why then do the Anglo-Saxon people there enjoy prosperity? The Rome of ancient times was the same Rome of today; why has the reputation of the Latin peoples declined? Others say, "It is due to great men." But Macedonia had its Alexander; why is it dust and ashes today? Mongolia had its Genghis Khan; why is it virtually at its last gasp today? Ah, I know the reason. A nation is an aggregation of people. The people are to the nation like the four limbs, the five viscera, the tendons and veins and corpuscles to the body. The body cannot survive if the four limbs are broken, the five viscera decay, the tendons and veins are injured, and the corpuscles dry up. And similarly, a country cannot stand if its people are ignorant, faint-hearted, disorganized, and confused. Hence, if one wants the body to remain eternally young, the art of hygiene must be understood, and if one wants the nation to be secure, wealthy, respected, and prosperous, the way of renovating the people must be discussed.

Renovating the people does not mean that our people should completely discard everything old and follow others. New has two meanings: 1) Renovating what originally existed by toughening it, and 2) Adopting what originally was missing as a supplement to renovate it. If either of these two is lacking, the effort will be wasted. . . .

The people of a country capable of standing in the world must have their own particular characteristics. From moral principles and laws, down to customs, habits, literature, and the arts, all possess an independent spirit, which is passed on by grandfathers and fathers and continued by sons and grandsons; and thus the group has cohesion and the nation is formed. This is actually the fundamental source of nationalism. Our countrymen must have their own characteristics to be able to stand on the Asian continent for several thousand years, great, lofty, beautiful, distinctively different from other peoples. We should preserve these and not lose them. But preserving them does not mean letting them live and grow by themselves, casually saying, "I'm preserving them! I'm preserving them!" Like a tree, unless new shoots appear each year, it will soon wither. Or like a well, unless new springs gush forth continually, before long it will dry up. Do these shoots and these springs come from outside? Though they are old, they must be called new. Precisely because they are renewed each day, they complete the old. . . . There are those who consider the words "preserve the old" extremely despicable. But are they? My worry is not about preserving the old, but about not being truly able to preserve the old. For how is the old to be truly preserved? By what I have said, by toughening what has always been there.

But is it enough to toughen what has always been there? No, for today's world is not the world of the past, and the peoples of today are not the peoples of the past. In the past, China had a tribal people, but no citizens. This was not because we were unable to have citizens, but because of the force of circumstances. Formerly, our country dominated East Asia, surrounded by minor barbarian peoples. There was no communication with major countries elsewhere, and hence our people normally regarded the country as All-under-Heaven [t'ien-hsia]. The brain is influenced by what comes into contact with the eyes and ears. The instructions of our sage philosophers, the legacies of our ancestors, all enable us to possess the qualifications for being individuals, or

members of a family, or members of a village or of a clan, or residents of
All-under-Heaven. But they just do not enable us to possess the qualifications
for being citizens of a country.[1] The qualifications for being a citizen are not
necessarily vastly superior, but if they are lacking in this age of many countries
existing side by side, in which the strong devour the weak, the superior are
victorious and the inferior are defeated, there is absolutely no way to survive
in the world. Hence, if today we do not desire to strengthen our country, then
there is nothing more to be said; but if we do want to strengthen it, we must
broadly examine the principles whereby the peoples of the various countries
are capable of standing independently, and select and adopt the superior points
to supplement what we lack. . . .

ON PUBLIC MORALITY.   Our nation's most serious deficiency is public
morality. What *is* public morality? It is the morality which makes a group of
men a group, and a nation a nation. Man is a gregarious animal (these are the
words of the Western philosopher, Aristotle). If men do not gather together
in groups, what distinguishes them from beasts? But this cannot be achieved
merely by uttering empty words and high sounding phrases, "Group them
together! Group them together!" There must be something that brings them
together before they can really become a group. This is what is called public
morality.

The essence of morality is oneness. But when it is expressed in outward
form, the terms public *[kung]* and private *[ssu]* appear. In private morality,
everyone takes care only of himself. In public morality, people in a group take
care of one another. Human life cannot lack either of these. Without private
morality, no one could establish himself. But joining together innumerable vile,
hypocritical, cruel, foolish, and cowardly persons cannot make a nation. And
so without public morality, togetherness would be impossible. Even innumerable self-restrained, modest, and honest men cannot make a nation.

No one can say that China's morality was late in developing. Yet, it is partial
to private morality, while public morality has been somewhat lacking. If you
take a look at such books as the *Analects* and *Mencius,* the guides for our
people and the sources of our morality, you will see that private morality
constitutes 90 per cent and public morality less than 10 per cent of their
teachings. [Liang cites many examples from the Confucian classics.] These
leave little left to be said on the subject of private morality. They are virtually
complete for the nourishing of the private person (private person is used in
contrast to public person, in the sense of one person not in contact with others).
And yet, are the qualifications for a private person by themselves sufficient to
make a whole personality? They certainly are not.

Let us try to compare the old ethics of China with the new ethics of the West.
The categories of the old ethics are ruler and minister [or subject], father and
son, elder and younger brother, husband and wife, and friends. The categories
of the new ethics are family ethics, social (i.e., group) ethics, and national

[1]Elsewhere in this same work, Liang defines these qualifications as nationalism and self-government.

ethics. The old ethics emphasizes matters between one private person and another. . . . The new ethics emphasizes matters between a private person and a group. . . . Needless to say, it is preferable for morality to exist in the personal conduct of a private person and in his dealings with other private persons. Nevertheless, this is only one part of morality, not its entirety. The entirety consists of combining both private and public and paying attention to both. Basically, private morality and public morality go together and are not incompatible. . . .

A person lives in a group, enjoys the rights of his group, and so has obligations toward the group that he should fulfill. If he doesn't, then he is nothing but a parasite on his group. Those who hold to the principle of self-control to minimize making errors think that although they do not benefit the group, neither do they harm it. Don't they realize that not benefiting *is* harming? Why is this so? Because, the group benefits me, and if I do not benefit the group, I have evaded fulfilling my responsibilities to it. If a private person evades fulfilling his responsibilities in his social dealings with another private person, this most certainly would be considered a fault in private morality because of the harm he had done to the other person. How then do those who evade their responsibilities to the group, quite to the contrary, falsely assume the reputation of being good? If everyone in a group follows one another in evading their responsibilities, how much of the hard-earned capital reserves of the group would be left? How could the group grow, with innumerable debtors living off it day and night, dividing it up, consuming without contributing anything? The group would inevitably be dragged down by those who evaded their responsibilities; the result would be the same as overburdening a person. Such would be the inevitable force of circumstances. Can there be any other reason for China's steady decline? . . .

Parents give birth to their children, raise, shelter, protect, and educate them. Hence, children have an obligation to repay their parents' kind favors. If everyone fulfills this obligation, the more children parents have, the better things go for them, and the more prosperous the family becomes. But if the opposite happens, then children are a burden on the family. Hence, children who evade their responsibilities to their parents are called unfilial. This, as everyone knows, is the highest principle of private morality. The kind favors of the group toward the individual, and of the nation toward the people of the nation, are the same as those of parents [toward their children]. For, if there were no group or no nation, there would be no place to which we could entrust our lives and our property, and no channel for our intelligence and abilities. Then there would be no way for us to establish ourselves in this world for one single day. Hence, every red-blooded person has an obligation to repay the kind favors of the group and the nation. Anyone who neglects this responsibility, no matter whether he is good or bad in private morality, is a grain devouring grub on the group and the nation. . . .

Do those who have discussed this issue know the origin of morality? Morality exists to benefit the group. Hence, the appropriate morality for a group differs according to its degree of civilization or barbarism. The main aim is to enable the group to be cohesive, good, and progressive. According to the

English constitution, offending the monarch is treason. (All monarchies are this way.) According to the French constitution, plotting to enthrone a monarch is treason, while the American constitution goes so far as to make the false establishment of titles of nobility treasonable. . . . The external forms of these moral principles are opposite, but the spirit is exactly the same. And what is it that is the same? The common interest of the group. . . . The spirit of all morality arises from the interests of the group. Anything which runs counter to this spirit, even if it is the highest good, can, at times, become the worst evil. (For example, free institutions are perfect for the present, but if they were applied in a primitive, uncivilized group, they would be terrible. Autocratic government was perfect in ancient times, but applied to a civilized group, it would be terrible.) For this reason, public morality is the origin of all morality. Whatever is beneficial to the group is good, and whatever is not, is bad. (That which is harmful and not beneficial is a great evil; that which is neither harmful nor beneficial is a lesser evil.) This principle applies at all times and in all places.

The external form taken by morality varies according to a group's degree of progress. As groups differ in civilization and barbarism, so what is beneficial to them differs, and it naturally follows that their moral principles also differ. Virtue is not something which, once having been formed, does not change. . . . It is not a definitive formula established by the ancients thousands of years ago which encompasses all generations to come throughout the entire world. . . . We at present, who were born and grew up in this group, should take a broad look at the world situation, calmly examine what is appropriate for our people, and create a new morality in order to achieve cohesion, goodness, and progress for our group. We should not draw a line we dare not overstep because it was rarely expounded by former kings and previous sages. Once public morality is made known, a new morality, and a new people, will emerge.

49. THE INFLUENCE OF FICTION ON SOCIAL VALUES AND NATIONAL STRENGTH
[From Liang Ch'i-ch'ao, "On the Relationship between Fiction and Democratic Government," 1902]

If the people of a country are to be renovated, first of all the country's fiction must be renovated. Hence, to renovate morality, fiction must be renovated; to renovate religion, fiction must be renovated; to renovate government, fiction must be renovated; to renovate customs, fiction must be renovated; to renovate learning and the arts, fiction must be renovated; and to renovate men's minds and men's characters, fiction must be renovated. Why? Because fiction has a marvelous power to control human behavior.

If I ask, what is it in the nature of human beings that makes people love fiction more than any other kind of writing, someone will certainly reply, "Because fiction is simple and easy to understand, because it is pleasurable and interesting." This is true, to be sure, but it is not an adequate explanation, for fiction is not the only kind of writing which is simple and easy to understand. . . . For this reason, this first explanation is incomplete.

Although pleasure is the aim of much fiction, fiction of this kind is not highly esteemed. The most enthusiastically received fiction is exciting, startling, sad, and moving, so that when reading it one has boundless nightmares, and one must wipe away an endless flood of tears. If fiction were loved out of a desire for pleasure, why would anyone deliberately make himself suffer by choosing to read something that had the opposite effect? For this reason, this second explanation is incomplete.

I have given this question much deep and searching reflection, and think there are two reasons. First, human beings are not normally able to feel complete satisfaction with the actual world around them. And the world which touches and affects these restless beings is confined, narrow, and very limited. Hence, they frequently want to vicariously come into touch with and be affected by something beyond that which directly touches and affects them, the so-called self beyond the self and the world beyond the world. Not only perceptive sentient beings, but obtuse ones too have this wish. And nothing is more powerful than fiction to abet one's inherent propensity toward becoming more perceptive, or more obtuse, day by day. Fiction frequently leads people into another world, changing the atmosphere that normally touches and affects them.[1]

Second, it is a common human failing for people not to understand their own behavior, and to take the familiar world around them for granted, in what they experience and what they imagine. Whether feeling sorrow, joy, resentment, anger, love, shock, worry, or embarrassment, it often seems that one knows how one feels, but doesn't understand why. One may want to describe the general circumstances, but the mind is unable to explain, the mouth is unable to elucidate, and the brush is unable to communicate. So, when someone else reveals everything, leaving nothing undisclosed, one beats on the table and joyfully exclaims, "Great! Great! That's it! That's it!" . . .

Readers of fiction are as though transformed; they enter into the book themselves, and become the chief character. . . . And since they have been transformed and entered into the book, when reading a book they are different persons, and have distinctly left this world and entered another. . . . Thus, if the hero of the book is [George] Washington, the reader will be transformed into Washington; if the hero is Napoleon, the reader will be transformed into Napoleon; and if the hero is Buddha or Confucius, the reader will be transformed into Buddha or Confucius. . . . If fiction enters people as easily as this, if it has the effect of moving people as easily as this, then there must be a natural psychological function, which human strength cannot change, that makes it normal for human beings to love fiction more than other kinds of writing. This does not merely apply to the people in our country; it is the same for everyone with blood in their veins in all the nations of the world. And since

[1]Liang, who believed that some Buddhist values were conducive to modernizing China, frequently uses Buddhist terms in his analyses, as in this paragraph.

fiction is loved, everywhere, within the whole group it is like the air, or like basic foodstuffs, impossible to avoid or eliminate even if one wanted to. One breathes it every day, eats it every day. And if this air is dirty, or these basic foodstuffs contain poison, then people who breathe this air and eat these foods will be emaciated, debilitated, die miserable deaths, or degenerate. One need not cast divining stalks to be certain of this. This being so, if the air is not purified, if other foodstuffs are not chosen, then even if the members of this group eat fine herbs every day and are daily treated with medicines, no one will be able to save them from their chronic ailments and bitter deaths. If we understand this, then we can realize the underlying cause of everything rotten in government in China. Where do we Chinese get our notions about being at the top of the list of *chin-shih* graduates, or of becoming a Chief Minister? From fiction. Where do we get our notions about romances between talented young men and beautiful maidens? From fiction. Where do we get our notions about adventurers and bandits? From fiction. Where do we get our notions about demons, sorcerors, fox spirits, and ghosts? From fiction. Has anyone ever been taken by the ear and given personal instruction in these things? Were they formally conferred upon people, like a mantle? [Of course not.] And yet these notions are uniformly shared by everyone, from butchers and cooks, pedlars, old women and little boys and girls, on up to eminent men, men of superior talents, and profound scholars. Nothing actually made this happen, though it seems as though something did. This is now deeply the power of the hundreds of varieties of fiction has poisoned people, directly and indirectly. . . .

Tens of thousands of words taught with untiring diligence by great sages and wise philosophers have had little impact, while one or two books by superficial literati or common booksellers are more than enough to do great harm. And the more that refined gentlemen disdain fiction, the more it will be in the hands of superficial literati and common booksellers. Yet the nature and role of fiction is like the atmosphere, like basic foodstuffs, something no society can ignore or do without. So the sovereign power of the nation is under the sway of superficial literati and common booksellers. Alas! If this situation persists, our country's future is unthinkable. Hence, if we want to reform the government of the group, we must begin with a revolution in the world of fiction, and if we want to renovate the people, we must first begin with renovating fiction.

PART II
Disunion

The era from the fall of the empire to the establishment of the People's Republic of China in 1949 is generally known as the Republican Period. As a description, this is not an entirely satisfactory term. Perhaps the Modern Period of Disunion might be a more accurate characterization. For during these years China was divided—geographically, politically, socially, and ideologically—much as it had been during the four centuries from the fall of the Han dynasty in A.D. 220 to the reunification of the empire under the Sui and the T'ang. And, as during those centuries, weak central governments, widespread discontent with the social and political order, and the introduction of new ideas from abroad had a stimulating effect on intellectual life. There was, however, no equivalent of the Buddhist flight from society that had occurred in the earlier period, for thoughtful men and women were deeply concerned with the problems of this world. Although China was in fact divided, the ideal of a united nation under a strong central government persisted. The theme of these decades, already adumbrated at the end of the Ch'ing, is the search for a new unity.

In 1915, the president of the republic, Yüan Shih-k'ai, attempted to unify the country by creating a constitutional monarchy, with himself as monarch. The reasons for his failure were an omen for the future: he was opposed by influential intellectual leaders, who thought any monarchy a step backward; foreign powers, led by Japan, disapproved; provincial governors and other regional authorities openly declared their opposition; and some of his subordinate commanders did not want him to become too self-reliant. Part of the opposition was to Yüan himself, and to his son, his presumptive successor. But part was an indication that there were powerful vested interests preventing the reassertion of central authority.

That this was the situation became more apparent after Yüan's death in 1916. The shift of power from the capital to the provinces and from civilian to military hands, which had begun in the midnineteenth century, now reached its final extremity. China was divided among militarists, called warlords, each dominating a few districts or a province or two, none powerful enough to eliminate his rivals. Warlordism was an unstable but self-perpetuating system. Whenever one or another of the major warlords threatened to become ascendant, others allied long enough to redress the balance and reassert the status quo. The politics of warlordism thus militated against reunification. Even the central government in Peking perpetuated a divided China. It was formed of unstable coalitions of militarist and civilian factions, its composition altered with each shift in the military balance of power in north China, and it had little authority outside the territories held by the armies of the warlords who supported it. Moreover, many of the most important warlords had ties with imperialist powers. These ties, combined with the general weakness of the central government, helped to ensure the continuation of foreign privileges in China. Not surprisingly, few Chinese believed the warlords could solve China's problems.

Meanwhile, a new leadership was being created among the youth of China. For many, if not most of this future elite, the tradition was discredited, and the West seemed to offer viable alternatives. More and more young Chinese men and women went abroad to learn about the science, technology, society, and culture of the modern West. The May Fourth Movement, which began with student demonstrations against the government for its incapacity, or unwillingness, to protect Chinese sovereign territory at the Versailles peace conference, generated further enthusiasm for the new learning, and Western ideas and ideals spread rapidly among the young intellectuals of China in the 1920s and 1930s. Much of the past was rejected, and many, very many, new ideas were fervently proclaimed —too many for there to be any consensus over which were best for China. Yet, in spite of disagreements, in the process of study and debate China's intellectuals became Westernized. Western ideals were to play an important role in the future of China. The question was, which ideals, and how were they to be related to the sordid realities of a divided China.

Sun Yat-sen was the first to find a way to combine the enthusiasm of the new youth and military power. With the assistance of advisors from Soviet Russia, he reorganized his Kuomintang (Nationalist Party) along disciplined Leninist lines, trained an officer corps for a party army, and, with Russian aid, began to build an effective military force. A united front was formed with the infant Chinese Communist Party. By the time Sun unexpectedly died in early 1925, the Kuomintang and its growing army were powerful enough to challenge the warlords. When a sudden upsurge of anti-imperialist sentiment swept over China a few months later, the ranks of the Kuomintang and the Communist Party swelled, and the Kuomintang rode to national power on a revolutionary wave. In 1928, after a rapid and successful military campaign, and after the collapse of the coalition with the Communists, a new Nationalist Government under the Kuomintang was formed, headed by the Commander-in-Chief of the Nationalist armies, Chiang Kai-shek. For many, the prospects for China's future seemed brighter than they had been in a long time.

The new government faced enormous problems. Unification was far from complete. Warlords still retained autonomous control over much of China, though they nominally acknowledged the authority of the Nationalist government. The Communists were suppressed in the cities, but they took to the countryside, and, although their numbers had been severely reduced, in the long run they were a more serious threat than the warlords. The Kuomintang itself was divided by feuding factions, astutely balanced but not fully controlled by Chiang. And once in power, the former revolutionary party became dominated by politically and culturally conservative elements, and developed vested interests of its own. With all these problems, the Kuomintang was not an effective instrument for social change, and, especially in the rural areas, had little impact on Chinese society. Nevertheless, China did not stand still; in the late 1920s and early 1930s some progress was made toward modernizing the country. But Japanese expansion, first into Manchuria, then southward into north China, forced the government to give increasing attention to this new foreign threat. In 1937 full-scale warfare between the two nations began. The long eight-year struggle against Japan enervated the Nationalist Government, and, especially in the postwar period, its leaders and many of its members developed a reputation of serving their own interests far better than those of the nation. Unable to hold China together, possessing neither the vision nor the energy to solve China's problems, the Nationalists lost their mandate.

The Communists offered the only viable alternative to Kuomintang rule. After having been driven from the cities by the Nationalists, they had learned to live in the countryside, where they came face to face with the problems of rural China. Under Mao Tse-tung, Marxism-Leninism was domesticated and applied to Chinese society. According to Mao's analysis, the fundamental problem was the agrarian problem, and it could only be solved by destroying the small but powerful minority with vested interests in the existing unjust and obsolete social system and liberating the disadvantaged majority. The Japanese invasion, the last stage of foreign imperialism's disruption of the old Chinese order, created conditions favorable to the Communists. It penetrated to the villages, and in response villagers were drawn into national political life. The Communists' staunch stand against the Japanese invaders won them widespread support; under the red banner, intellectuals and peasants joined to rid China of the foreign aggressors, and to build a new China. By 1945, the Communist Party had grown to be a well-led and well-disciplined political party of over a million members, with an experienced and effective army almost as large. The Communists' rapid victory in the civil war of 1945–49 brought an end to almost half a century of disunity, and brought to power a new leadership with new conceptions of China's problems, new solutions to them, and an effective political instrument to put their solutions into practice.

CHAPTER SEVEN
Warlord China

Central-government control over the provinces had begun to decline when regional armies had been needed to suppress the Taiping and other rebellions in the midnineteenth century. In the last decades of the empire, central political authority deteriorated at an accelerated pace, culminating in the provinces' withdrawal of allegiance to the Ch'ing during the revolution of 1911. The newly proclaimed republic formally replaced the monarchy, but the new rulers in Peking did not command the automatic assent to their orders that legitimate governments normally require and possess. Yüan Shih-k'ai was able to preserve some semblance of unity, but after his death in 1916, civil government further disintegrated. Force, above all military force, increasingly became the basis of political power, and military men became the new political elite. The warlords came from all kinds of backgrounds. Some had been officers in the Ch'ing armies, others had begun as peasants. One of the most powerful had been a bandit; another was a *chin-shih* graduate and a former Han-lin scholar. What they had in common was command of armed forces, from a few hundred or a thousand men to several hundred thousand. For a decade, until the establishment of the Nationalist Government in 1928, they were the rulers of China.

Raw force was the ultimate basis of the warlords' political power, but they did to some extent serve a real public need and did enjoy some degree of public support. The dissolution of the imperial state left no legitimate authority capable of enforcing public order, and so, it could be and was argued, armed strength was necessary to maintain order in a time of chaos. This notion is the core of Louis Magrath King's portrait of General Ch'en Hsi-ling, a minor Szechwan warlord. (Selection 50) The author, a British consul in the province, presents General Ch'en in a favorable light, but he is fair enough to allow the reader to see another side.

The other side was the one most Chinese associated with the warlords, for though some warlords did make worthy contributions to the public welfare, they were exceptions. The chaos and the threats to peace and order that were cited as justifications for the existence of the warlords were frequently caused by the warlords themselves. For most Chinese, the warlords and their armies were not preservers of the peace, but predators and parasites, not a solution, but a problem. There was much costly and destructive warfare. And the civilian population was helpless against the depredations of warlord troops; incidents such as those described by an American visitor to rural China in Selection 51 were common occurrences.

The impact of militarism on local society is the subject of Shen Ts'ung-wen's recollections of his youthful career as a soldier. Shen (b. 1902), who became one of the major writers of modern China, maintains an ironic distance from the grim life he depicts. That inhuman behavior could be so commonplace, so routine, is finally an indictment of the warlord ethos. (Selection 52) The banditry Shen mentions was widespread, and its symbiotic relationship with warlordism is analyzed by Paul S. Reinsch, United States Ambassador to China during the early warlord years. (Selection 53)

Although warlords contributed little toward solving China's problems, Chinese society was not static. Changes were taking place, most noticeably in the great metropolis of Shanghai, where, as Selection 54 shows, Western clothes, Western attitudes, and Western values were becoming fashionable among the Westernized urban elite. Modern industry too was growing, especially in the treaty ports. Selection 55 describes working conditions in Shanghai, and demonstrates that the gap between the elite and the common people remained vast and unbridged. Neither the Westernized elite nor the industrial workers were of major political significance at this time, but they were to play far greater roles in the future.

50. PORTRAIT OF A WARLORD
[From Louis Magrath King, *China in Turmoil*, 1927]

He recognized no authority superior to his own conscience. And in actual fact, by virtue of the disorganization and disruption that followed the Revolution, he was untrammelled dictator in his own region. He commanded an army of ten thousand men, and ruled a vast district according to his own will, his sense of right and wrong; and the ultimate court of appeal of five millions of people was simply his conscience.

He was a masterful man, with a dominant sense of duty. He had been brought up in a hard school, had joined the army thirty years before, and had been through the mill. Those were the old days before modern ideas of the value of life and the dignity of the individual had permeated the army. The bamboo and the executioner's sword met all exigencies. Discipline, that was the keynote; and when he attained a satrapy of his own he applied it also to civil administration.

If men would not do their duty, in whatever walk of life, of their own volition, they must be made to. He could not supervise everybody, but he could and would make a striking example of offenders who came to his personal notice. Thus he shot a couple of Magistrates—that is, district governors—for abuse of authority. He shot the Governor of a jail because an important prisoner had escaped. He flogged a number of leading merchants for failing to pay their taxes on time, and one of them died of it; a couple of conceited shopboys for ogling the ladies at a public festival. "Women must be protected from this sort of thing," he said to me at the time; soldier and civilian for this or that misfeasance, and so on. He had no sense of privilege: a transgressor was a transgressor whatever his status. He shot his own nephew for due cause.

He exacted unquestioning obedience to his authority, for without it, government, in his eyes, could not go on. But apart from that his spirit was democratic. He made no display himself, and disliked it in others. Men's worth rested not on their wealth or rank, but on their character. He hated the idea that anyone should, by virtue of anything at all, take the subservience of others as their due. Penury and lowliness did not strike him as something to be ashamed of. He had, in fact, a soft spot for the underdog. A private soldier or an artisan could be just as good a man as anybody else. Indeed, many of his best officers were men he had himself raised from the ranks. He liked his officers to dress and live, of their own volition, no better than their men.

. . . On one occasion he had left his capital to face on the border a menacing move on the part of a rival satrap. In his absence a large body of outlaws threatened his capital. He hurried back, a week's journey, to deal with this more urgent matter, and arrived in time. The people, in relief and gratitude, turned out in mass to meet him. And the autocrat, with power of life and death over them all, dismounted from his horse and walked humbly through the crowded streets, so moved he could hardly speak.

On another occasion it was rumoured that he was going to retire. All classes of the people were worried. Even people who were habitually shocked at his severity said that a change of ruler was unlikely to be for the better, and might very easily be for the worse. His people, in fact, appreciated him; he might be severe, but he had their interests at heart. He was their father and mother.

He was beset with difficulties. The province within which his satrapy lay was torn by internal dissensions and constant fighting. It was all the aftermath of revolution. Each satrap had to support himself on his own domains. And most of them had armies so swollen that they could not so support them. If, however, this General or that were to reduce his forces, and cut his coat according to his cloth, he would inevitably be swallowed up by his neighbour acting on the opposite principle of increasing his area to meet his expenses. General disbandment by consent? But who was to make the men in power disband if they did not want to? And the troops themselves were unwilling to be disbanded. Who was to force them to disband and form the underworld which the produce of the province relative to its population demands shall more or less starve? They had rifles in their hands, and if one General did not want them, another would; if nobody wanted them, better be brigands than starve.

It was all so simple in the old days of the Empire. Then there were few weapons of precision in private hands, and law and order were maintained with a relatively inconsiderable number of troops. The great bulk of the population was kept under, constrained to be content with a bare subsistence as the reward of constant toil, and the rabble was constrained to starve. But the Revolution scattered arms throughout the province, and individual and conflicting ambitions recruited troops by the thousands; the able-bodied of the erstwhile underworld were absorbed into the armies, and there they stayed, so that there were now more troops in the province than it could support. Send them off to other provinces? But the other provinces are in like plight. . . .

The immediate concern of our autocrat was, however, the governance of his satrapy. He sternly kept his army within the limits of the economic resources of his domain, and in doing so risked the danger of political extinction. But that could not be helped. His sense of duty precluded him from putting upon his people a burden they could not bear.

His area was well governed; his methods, while drastic, were anyway effective. But, of course, they made him enemies. The latter were wise enough to dissemble their hatred so long as they were in his district. Occasionally, however, he would get a broadside, in the shape of diatribes in newspaper and leaflet, issued from the security of a rival satrapy. Therein they would let themselves go, curse him up hill and down dale, accuse him of every crime they could think of. And his enemies within the gate would read these attacks in silent joy. . . .

How had he got into this state? His conscience was clear. He had done his best to restore the security that used to obtain before the disintegration of recent years. He had kept taxation down to the old time-honoured levels. He had held aloof from the internecine warfare that harassed the rest of the province. He had put down brigandage. Perhaps he had overstepped on occasion the strict letter of the law in his administration of justice. But had he? Surely martial law was the only effective law in the prevalent circumstances? He might, of course, have sheltered himself from the first behind an impersonal system of government. But would that have secured the people the administration they were entitled to, and which it was his duty to give them? It would not have. Clearly there was no help for it. The malice was there. His bed was made. He had enough to do in the present. The future must look after itself.

. . . He would on occasion fly off into ungovernable rages. Why were men so obdurate? Why did they need constant coercion to make them do their duty? "Sack the lot" became with him "bamboo the lot," or "shoot the lot." In one of these outbursts he had two of his body-guards trussed and flung into the river, where they duly drowned. . . .

His immediate entourage, his councillors, and his household, and notably his wife, would do their best to restrain him in this mood. Their interference would, of course, increase his rage, but their object was to play for time and allow his good-nature to assert itself. And they usually succeeded, for his anger was as short-lived as it was intense. And when they failed in some particular case, and after it was all over, he would remorsefully ask them why they had allowed him to do it.

He was always very friendly to the "stranger from afar." He looked upon us in the old-world courtly Chinese way as his guests. I got to know him very well in the course of years. By virtue of our positions I was his only official equal throughout his domain. And I suppose he found it a relief to talk with someone not a subordinate, and he apparently attached some value to my opinion of him, for he would on occasion go out of his way to explain to me this or that unorthodox action of his. We talked of many subjects—politics, religion, horses and dogs, and shooting, and of the future. What did he look forward to? He had an industrial institute for orphans in his home town in a far-away province. He had established it years before, and maintained it at his own expense. He would retire there, he told me more than once, and pass his days helping the poor and the weak. And I thought to myself that his orphans would not be spoilt for lack of the paternal rod. He would assuredly impress upon them all the sense of duty which was his own sheet-anchor, and start each of them off in life with the backbone of a guardsman.

A rival satrap, who hated him, once said to me bluntly that he was mad, that no one in his area could feel personally secure. And he quoted the Chinese proberb: "In the mountains far from Court the monkey rules as King." I disagreed. I parried with our own saying: "The proof of the pudding is in the eating." He maintained order, and the people liked him.

51. SOLDIERS AND CIVILIANS IN RURAL CHINA[1]
[From Nora Waln, *The House of Exile*, 1933]

While we ate [in an inn] a soldier came in. He leaned over Shun-ko's husband and examined our food. He stared at me for what seemed a long time. The others took no notice of him but continued intent on their chopsticks and bowls. I tried to do the same.

Finally he laid his gun, which had a bayonet at one end, across the only other table in the room. The soldier had a stupid heavy face and wore ill-fitting garments of course cotton, but our elegantly gowned inn host carried food to him with his own delicate hands. The servants who waited on us were called away to help please him, and he was even given our dish of jelly without any of the Lins seeming to notice his insolence.

He fed quickly, sucking and hiccuping. Having finished, he rose and slapped down a twenty-dollar paper note (which Shun-ko later told me was worthless because printed by a governor who had since gone out of office). Our inn host bowed so that his skirt swept the floor, and told the soldier with soft cadence that he had been the guest of the house for his meal. The soldier did not return the bow. He drew himself up stiffly. In a harsh rumble of sound he replied that

[1]These incidents occurred in rural Hopei province in December 1920.

he did not accept bribes of food, and wanted his change in silver. Then he thrust the note in the host's face.

Our host took the worthless money. He deducted one dollar as the price of the dinner and gave the soldier nineteen silver dollars. The soldier rang each dollar against his bayonet to test the purity of the coin. All rang true. He dropped them into his purse. Then, picking his teeth as he went, he walked out. As he passed, I saw that his soldier shoes were of cloth like his poor uniform, and badly torn. He had put newspapers in them to keep his feet warm.

A brazier heated the room. When the noise of the soldier's departure had died away, the innkeeper dropped the twenty-dollar bill and the chopsticks that the soldier had used into the fire. . . .

[After having returned to their boat] For a time fields and frozen highway were occupied as before. Then we crossed paths with a sledge boat over-crowded with soldiers and propelled by a frightened boatman. Farther on we saw another boat commandeered by half a dozen young boys and an officer. They pushed an old farmer and his "lily foot" [bound-feet] wife about ruth-lessly, scattering their produce over the ice. One lad speared the old lady's brown rooster with his bayonet and held him high while the others applauded. When she struggled to help the dying bird, the officer clouted her on the head. Half a mile on, we heard a shot and saw a child fall—she had been reluctant to give up the donkey hitched to the mill where she was grinding flour. The soldier who shot her then led the donkey down to the canal for sledge transport to "the war."

. . . The fields we now passed were deserted. We met no one on the way to the hamlet where the uncle of one of the Lin boatmen lives. The boatman went in to borrow a cart to take us overland to the Lin homestead.

He returned weeping. Five boys from the hamlet, one of them his uncle's only son, had been taken to be made soldiers. All five were between the ages of twelve and fourteen years. . . . There had been no soldiers in the district for the previous five months. This foraging raid had come as a surprise in mid-morning, when the gates were open and fold scattered. They had lost carts, animals, food, winter clothing, and all their sons between the ages of twelve and sixteen—excepting those few who had been shrewdly and quickly hidden. One Village Elder had parleyed with the soldiers while three boys had been dropped in a well bucket to a niche in the well wall prepared for such emergen-cies, and the bucket left to swing empty.

"The soldiers passed too quickly," villagers said. "This was but a survey and they will return in larger numbers." So they were busy tightening walls and gates, taking their saddles, sedan chairs, and carts apart to hide the pieces separately, driving their cattle in, and sharpening kitchen knives and farm tools as weapons.

All our party agreed that we were safest to keep off the main canal. We could not walk, as Shun-ko, Mai-da's mother, and the serving matrons had "lily" feet. We sledged devious ways. I saw plentiful supplies of hot food set in cauldrons before each barred village gate. Twice we saw tired-looking soldiers feeding on this "peace rice."

52. LIFE AS A SOLDIER[1]
[From Shen Ts'ung-wen, *Autobiography*, 1946]

... Four months later we were transferred to another place, a small country town called Huai-hua. ... I stayed there about 16 months, and personally observed the executions of about 700 people. I developed a comprehensive understanding of the conditions under which some people would be beaten and the circumstances under which others would be decapitated.

It was just a small town, of about 600 households. The only fairly large building was the ancestral hall of a family named Yang, which we occupied for our quarters immediately upon our arrival.

There was a licensed medicine shop, with a broken pot sitting out in front of the entranceway, half-filled with black ointment plasters. Dried snakes, lizards, centipedes, etc. were pasted on the sides to show that the goods were authentic and the price fair. There usually was a man wearing a stiff blue silk jacket, a blue cloth gown, and a coral-red cap standing in front of the entrance. As soon as he would see us passing by, he would always unfold his hands, bow slightly from the waist, and politely and affably address us: "Sirs, Sirs, please come in and have a seat. Please allow me to present you with some ointment plasters." ...

A woman in her early forties was generally sitting in front of the opium shop, her whole face covered with a thick layer of powder, and her eyebrows finely pencilled. She would intentionally raise her dyed green home-spun trousers very high, revealing pink foreign stockings. When soldiers or cooks passed by, she would turn away, without a glance, to show how chaste and pure she was. But when an army officer or someone wearing a long robe passed, she would give a coy glance, move the corners of her mouth slightly, and deliberately call in a soft feminine voice to one of the men inside, and ask him to do something for her. When I went by with other soldiers, I only saw her back, but when I was with the battalion executive officer, I got to see her from the front. At the time I really enjoyed these workings of human nature, and when I think back over those times, I have never had an ugly feeling; I have only felt that it was a very "human" kind of thing to do. During my life I have become all too familiar with this kind of "human" doings.

Besides executions, our unit didn't have very much to do, and watching executions was about the only activity for our soldiers. Killing people isn't exactly an elegant pastime, but we were so lonesome that there never was a lack of men from the unit scurrying to the execution grounds to apprize these events. Every time I went there would always be several adjutants and a staff colonel standing by the bridge railing watching the spectacle.

When execution time came, our learned Provost Marshall would often casually proclaim the charges against the criminal, and add a vermilion mark on the execution form which had been written out beforehand. As soon as he

[1] In rural Hunan province, ca. 1919.

saw the culprit being ushered out of the large gate by the soldiers, he would
hastily lift up the hem of his long gown, and, holding his shiny brass water-
pipe, dash out the rear door, through the vegetable patch, and race along a
short-cut to get to the fairly high mound of earth not far from the foot of the
bridge. There he could see the blade decapitate the culprit kneeling on the road
by the foot of the bridge.

Some days when there was an execution the person being executed would
do something out of the ordinary before he died. He might be very cheerful
and uninhibited when he proclaimed his crimes to the crowd, or his face might
remain impassive when execution time came, or he might be so petrified that
he didn't realize what was going on, or perhaps his body would not topple over
after his death. Then there were sure to be long discussions about his interesting points at the Adjutant's office, in the guard barracks, in the supply room,
and in the office of the Provost Marshall's secretary. Sometimes the conversation would turn to tales about other executions. If the day of execution happened to fall on a market day, there would be people selling pork and beef in
the marketplace. It was customary for the executioner to set off carrying his
great blade, still dripping with blood, and, followed by two cooks carrying a
bamboo basket on a pole between them, he would slice off two or three *chin*
of meat at each butcher's table. When he finished, the big basket of pork and
beef would be divided up equally, and everyone would go cook the meat over
an open stove and drink as much warmed wine as they liked. When everyone
had got a little high, someone would rise unsteadily to his feet, casually raise
his chopsticks high into the air, and bring them down across the nape of the
neck of another one of the men squatting there eating and drinking. Then some
of the men would bunch together, laughing loudly and raising a commotion
for a while. If anyone got so drunk that he fell down, no one paid any attention.
It was all only a bother for young recruits, who had to stand guard like dogs
watching over their masters, unable to go to bed until the masters wake
up. . . .

Sometimes I would accompany the high officers out of town to gentry homes
at the foot of the mountains to eat steamed goose and drink home-brewed wine.
Other times, I would go with some mechanics from the machine repair shop
to the mountains to pick herbs and flowers and look for mountain fruit. . . .

There were lots of other things you could see in our unit too. Sometimes a
cook would do something wrong and the Officer of the Day would order him
to the hall and give him a bawling out, and then order, "Guard! Give this
bastard a hundred blows." Then the cook, knowing he was going to get a
beating, would pull down his pants, crawl up onto the cold, hard stone steps,
expose his filthy black buttocks, and be beaten with the flat bamboo stick.
When he had received the stipulated number of blows, he would stand up, pull
up his trousers, and leave crying.

In the daytime, when we would go down to the end of the street to fool
around, sometimes you could see a very moving sight: in front, a few soldiers
followed by a 12 or 13 year old kid carrying two human heads on a pole, which
frequently were the heads of the kid's father or uncle; then, in the rear, several
more soldiers, perhaps taking into custody a couple of men with their hands

tied behind their backs, or a clothing trunk, or a plow ox. This line of people was, of course, on the way to our headquarters, and as soon as we saw them we would follow along.

In the evening at beating time you could see them beat some culprit's instep with a stick held in both hands. . . . In about 20 blows, the marrow of the bones of a foot could be beaten out. They also burned incense sticks right under a person's nose, and burned the chest and ribs with them. Or an iron bar would be used to snap a leg in two with one loud crack. The next morning, the person would be dragged out and decapitated. During the beatings of these ignorant villagers, I was supposed to sit at one side and take down what they said, to record in an official document the confessions these peasants heedlessly made while being tortured. When the soldiers finished, they would smear some ink on the palm of the peasant's hand and press it down on the blank space at the bottom of the document, to make a handprint. After all this had been done, it was my job to put everything neatly in order, and then to hand the document to the Provost Marshall for his files.

53. BANDITS, SOLDIERS, AND SOCIETY
[From Paul S. Reinsch, *An American Diplomat in China*, 1922]

Brigandage is an established institution in China, where it has operated so long that people have become accustomed to it and take it for granted as a natural visitation. At this time there was a vicious circle around which brigands and troops and rich citizens and villagers were traveling, one in pursuit of the other. The brigands were recruited from disbanded soldiers—men who had lost connection with their family and clan. Often their families had been wiped out by famine, flood, or disease, or had been killed in the revolution. At other times the individual may have lost touch through a fault of his own causing him to be cast out. It is very difficult for an isolated person, without family and clan connections, to re-establish himself. The easiest way is to enlist in the army. If that cannot be done, he becomes a brigand. Brigands foregather in provinces where the administration is lax or in remote regions difficult to reach. They lie in ambush and seize wealthy persons, who are carried off to the hills and released only when ransom is paid. In this way, a considerable tax is levied on accumulated wealth. This money the brigands spend among the villagers where they happen to be. Meanwhile the Provincial Governor bethinks himself that a certain brigade or division has not been paid for a long time and therefore might cause trouble, so he announces what is called a "country cleansing campaign." The situation is so intolerable that the general sees himself forced to go to extremes, and to send his troops with orders to exterminate the brigands. They proceed to the infested regions; the brigands, having meanwhile got wind of these movements, depart for healthier climes, leaving the troops to quarter themselves on the villagers, who are by them

relieved of the money which they have made out of the brigands. Some brigands may be unfortunate enough to be caught; some will be shot as an example,
and others will be allowed to enlist. When the soldiers have dwelt for a while
among the villagers, they report that the bands have now been fully suppressed
and that the country is cleansed. They are then recalled to headquarters; their
general reports to the governor, and is appropriately rewarded. Meanwhile, the
brigands return from their safer haunts and begin again to catch wealthy
people, whom they relieve of their surplus liquidable property. And so the
circle revolves interminably.

54. CHANGING CUSTOMS AMONG THE
WESTERNIZED ELITE IN SHANGHAI, CIRCA 1916
[From Mary Ninde Gamewell, *The Gateway to China:
Pictures of Shanghai*, 1916]

The ultra-stylish dress of the "fast set" among young women in Shanghai
is tight trousers, short tight jacket with short tight sleeves, and very high
collars. To Western eyes this is neither pretty nor modest, and Chinese from
the interior look upon it askance. Instead of bare heads, girls in winter are
coming to wear, not hats, except those who have adopted foreign dress, but
worsted caps, usually trimmed with coloured ribbon or artificial flowers. There
is a shop on a busy street, called "Love Your Country Shop," which deals
largely in these fancy articles. Foreign shoes are also gradually taking the place
of the cloth-soled, satin-topped Chinese shoes, and it is a wise change if women
are to go much abroad in this city of heavy and frequent rains.

The old-time wedding procession is no longer an every day sight in the
International Settlement, though happily for lovers of the antique, still common about the Chinese City. Carriages have to a large extent superseded the
gorgeous sedan chairs, draped with embroidered crimson satin, and pale pink
silk the orthodox crimson satin wedding gown. Veils are much worn too, and
occasionally a very up-to-date bride is decked out in a gown of white silk or
satin made in the most extreme Western fashion. More often, however, there
is a painfully inartistic combination of Chinese and foreign styles. Little Miss
Y. invited her foreign friends to inspect her trousseau shortly before her
marriage. Garment after garment, evolved from heavy brocaded satin, sheeny
silks, and gauzy web-like stuffs, was unfolded before admiring eyes. . . . But
when a common pink net veil, cheap white imitation flowers and coarse white
cotton gloves bought at a foreign department store and plainly regarded as the
crowning touches to the outfit were laid beside the exquisite Chinese gown,
there were inward groans from the disappointed visitors. Miss Y. wore on the
third finger of her left hand a heavy ring set with diamonds and pearls. On her
wedding day she would have her band of gold like a Western bride. "You are
very fond of the gentleman, of course," some one asked her. The bright eyes
dropped quickly as the low answer came back, "I have seen him only once."

"Were you alone?" "No, my aunt was in the room." Plainly then, notwithstanding her foreign finery, this was not one of the so-called present day
"liberty girls."

The case of Miss W. was quite different. She and her fiance had met and
fallen in love in the good old-fashioned [i.e., Western] way. They were married
by the bride's father, an Episcopal clergyman, who, being tall and well-
favoured, made a rather imposing figure in his priestly robe. After he had
walked in and taken his place inside the chancel, a church warden to the strains
of Lohengrin's Wedding March ushered up the aisle with due ceremony the
groom and best man. That done, they were left standing for fully ten minutes.
The wedding march was played and re-played, the party at the altar shifted
and turned while the audience craned their necks till they were sore in an effort
to catch a glimpse of the incoming bride. What was the matter? Was she sick?
Was she panic-stricken? Had an accident befallen the wedding dress? None of
these calamities had overtaken the girl, who was dressed and ready to follow
her fiance into the church. But ancient marriage customs in China prescribe
that a bride must be sent for again and again by the groom before, with tears
and great reluctance, she is at last persuaded to leave her home. Although this
was a modern wedding, it would not do to disregard wholly the time-honoured
practice, hence a proper interval was allowed to elapse before the bride made
her appearance. . . .

Occasionally a clash occurs between customs past and present which results
in tragedy. A while ago a youth and maiden, both teaching in a government
school in Shanghai, fell deeply in love. The girl's father heard of it but objected
to his daughter's marrying because she was the mainstay of the family, and
he argued that filial duty required her to continue their support although
perfectly competent to shoulder the burden himself. Taking her one day in a
small boat to the middle of a deep stream near their home, he demanded of
the girl that she give up her lover. When she loyally clung to him her inhuman
parent threw her overboard and let her drown before his eyes. A few years ago
a deed like this would have attracted little attention "The girl belonged to her
father and it is nobody's business what he did to her," would have been the
popular verdict. But it is not so in Shanghai today. The papers were full of the
awful crime, the broken-hearted lover carried the case to the Chinese court,
and so great a stir was made that no one will dare to repeat such an act, at
least openly. . . .

One of the hopeful signs of these later days in China is the changing attitude
of the people toward physical exercise, for it means better health and better
morals for the nation. Not long ago, really only a very few years, round
shoulders were by every one highly commended, in the women as indicating
modesty and in the men scholarly habits. A girl who held herself erect, with
well developed chest, would have been set down at once as bold and forward,
and not only that, but any kind of physical exertion was regarded by the upper
classes, young and old alike, as coolie's work and quite beneath their dignity.
Some Chinese girls were watching a game of tennis for the first time, when one
turned to her companion with a puzzled expression and the remark, "Can't
they get coolies to do that work for them?" . . . A couple of foreigners were

crossing Garden Bridge when a troop of Chinese youths went rushing past
with foot-balls tucked under their arms. Said the gentleman laughingly to his
companion, "You wouldn't have seen that a short time ago in Shanghai."
"Why? Because the boys were not playing ball?" "Yes, and neither would they
have done such an unmannerly thing as to run. Just now they were so interested in the coming ball game they forgot all about appearances."

55. WORKING CONDITIONS IN SHANGHAI FACTORIES, CIRCA 1916

[From Mary Ninde Gamewell, *The Gateway to China: Pictures of Shanghai*, 1916]

Wages in all the [cotton] mills are about the same, and are good, as pay goes
in China. Children receive from eleven to fifteen cents a day, women from
fifteen to thirty-five according to their skill, and men fifteen to twenty dollars
a month. This is reckoned in Mexican currency, which would yield less than
one-half that amount in American money. Some of the mill people come from
farms in the suburbs and are in comfortable circumstances. One or two members of a family may work in the mill, not so much from necessity as to be able
to add a little to the general income. But others, and these far outnumber the
more fortunate class, are the poorest of the poor, often unable to pay the
"cash" or two required to ride in a wheelbarrow between the mill and their
home which is frequently miles distant. A single instance may be given. A
young girl supports a widowed mother and little brothers and sisters on two
dollars and a half a month. She starts to the mill each morning at four o'clock,
as it takes her two hours to walk there, and when her day's work is over, at
six in the evening, she is two hours more walking home. Many a time when
the moon is shining the child mistakes its bright light for dawn and sets out
at three or earlier. The walk is not so bad in pleasant weather, lonely only until
she joins crowds of other mill folk moving in the same direction. But what of
the chill days in winter, with a bleak wind blowing, rain falling, and roads
treacherously slippery with mud? It is hardest for the women who have bound
feet, women too poor to pay for a seat on a wheelbarrow with five or six others.
Yonder comes a group uncertainly picking their way along in the blinding
mist. One poor soul at last reaches the gate of the mill and drops all in a heap
on the cold wet ground to wait for the blowing of the whistle. "Have you come
far?" is asked of her pityingly. Half fearfully, half defiantly, as if braced for
a reprimand, she struggles to her feet and answers, "From Honkew," a distance of nearly three miles. A fleeting smile is by and by coaxed into her pale
face, but she is tired, so very tired, and a long twelve hours of unremittent
labour lies before her. Let us hope she is one who works at a loom, for then
she can have a seat on a narrow bench. The women and children who watch
the spindles must stand the long night through.

The employees carry their lunch in a small round basket, all of uniform size. The basket is half filled with cold boiled rice, and set in the midst of it is sure to be a little bowl containing a few mouthfuls of bean curd, salt fish or some other simple relish. Before eating, the food is warmed by pouring boiling water into the basket and allowing the water to filter through the rice and out at the bottom. Hot water is also furnished in the mills for tea. In the new Japanese mill tea itself is given the hands. "Not the best kind," says the superintendent, "but nevertheless, tea." This mill has rough dining halls for its employees, and allows a half hour at noon and the same at midnight for eating. Another mill gives fifteen minutes at noon and at midnight. . . . In most mills no intermission whatever is granted for rest or food, and the people eat whenever they are hungriest, snatching a morsel now and then as they tend their looms or watch their reels and spindles. Formerly mothers brought their nursing babies to the mills, and laid them at their feet while they worked, but this is no longer permitted in the large mills. Some relative, it may be a grandmother, carries the little one to the mother to nurse twice a day, in the middle of the morning and again in the afternoon. Mothers who work at night often draw from the breast before they leave home sufficient milk to last the baby until they return in the morning.

All of the mills run their spinning department through the twenty-four hours, but weaving can not be done as well at night, so the looms shut down. One mill makes its day fourteen hours long. "And these little children must stand and work all those hours?" asked a visitor of the manager. "Yes," and with a slight shrug of the shoulder, "rather hard on them, isn't it?" "But then you know how it is in the Chinese shops," he added, "they keep their apprentices at work often eighteen and twenty hours on a stretch."

CHAPTER EIGHT

The
New Culture
Movement

The New Culture Movement, also known as the May Fourth Movement after student demonstrations in Peking on May 4, 1919, was a turning point in modern Chinese history, for it resulted in nothing less than the reorientation of Chinese education, and hence of the educated elite, away from China's classical past and toward modern Western values. Such a profound transformation does not occur in a day, a year, or even a generation. The process of the Westernization of Chinese intellectuals had begun long before May 4, 1919, and continued long afterward. But the most dramatic changes did take place in the first decade of the republic, when, in the intellectual realm as in the political, the authority of traditional ideals and values was deteriorating at an accelerated pace, Western learning was increasingly taught in the schools, and more and more Chinese students were going abroad to learn about the modern world.

The sordid realities of Chinese political life in the warlord period accentuated disillusionment with the old China and enthusiasm for the West, especially in the great cities of Shanghai and Peking. In Peking the center of the new learning was Peking National University, where the liberal Chancellor Ts'ai Yüan-p'ei (1867–1940) had gathered an outstanding group of scholars representing the full spectrum of ideological views.

Of these, perhaps the most controversial and certainly one of the most influential, was Ch'en Tu-hsiu (1879–1942), who, as Dean of the Faculty of Letters and editor of the most prominent Westernizing journal, *Hsin*

Ch'ing-nien (New Youth), was a leader of the New Culture Movement from its earliest stages. Ch'en's own life indicates how rapidly China was changing: A *chü-jen* graduate of the old civil service examination system, he later became one of the founders of the Chinese Communist Party. Ch'en was an outspoken critic of Confucian China and an ardent partisan of the modern West, especially of democracy and science. In his survey of the previous 300 years of Chinese history, Ch'en arrives at a conclusion similar to the one Liang Ch'i-ch'ao had reached—China must adopt a new morality. (Selection 56) But in Ch'en's writing, one can detect a feeling that this new, imported morality is not merely a means for China to preserve herself in the international struggle for survival, but also intrinsically superior to the old morality.

Ch'en, like most Westernizers of his time, denounced Confucianism as a major cause of China's ills. In "The Way of Confucianism and Modern Life," he attempts to show that the central tenets of Confucianism are antithetical to the principles governing modern life. Significantly, he uses the status of women to illustrate his theme that traditional Chinese social organization is incompatible with the individualism, freedom, and equality required in the modern world. The liberation of women was an important part of the New Culture Movement. Ch'en's arguments are pragmatic, but again, the tone of his article conveys a commitment to Western values that transcends the purely practical. (Selection 57)

Once again, however, it was neither emotional rhetoric nor rational arguments but events that gave credibility to radicals and their ideas. In early May 1919, the great powers at the Versailles Peace Conference decided to award former German rights in the Shantung peninsula to Japan. When this news reached Peking, student demonstrations were held to protest the Peking government's apparent willingness to concede Chinese sovereign rights to Japan. By boldly opposing the government, and by refusing to be intimidated by government attempts to suppress the demonstrations, the students of Peking's modern schools showed themselves to be selflessly patriotic, while their conservative elders appeared unwilling or unable to do anything to save China. The events of May and June 1919 greatly magnified the influence of Westernizing intellecturals by giving them unprecedented national prominence and by conferring on them a degree of legitimacy they had not previously enjoyed. They capitalized on their newly won prestige to publicize their ideas. In the next few years, hundreds of new magazines as well as new books proliferated in the cities of China. In them, much of the past was critically scrutinized and rejected and Western ideas and institutions were extolled. The enthusiasm, idealism, and hope of the time are conveyed in the statement on editorial policy published in the December 1919 issue of *Hsin Ch'ing-nien*. (Selection 58)

Education was the principal instrument for introducing the new ideas and values, and educators played a major role in the Westernization process. One of the best-known and most active proponents of Westernization was Hu Shih (1891–1962), a leading advocate of pragmatism and of the use of colloquial Chinese as the standard literary language. Hu had studied under John Dewey in the United States, and vigorously disseminated his teacher's ideas in China throughout his long and distinguished career as teacher, scholar, and diplomat. In his 1919 article on the new thought, Hu contrasts the new attitude of systematic criticism with the old habit of unquestioning acceptance. (Selection 59) The difference between this new concept and previous practice can be seen in Ts'ai Yüan-p'ei's reminiscences of his own traditional education. (Selection 60)

The West, of course, was not monolithic, and ideological differences soon split the May Fourth intellectuals. Anarchism, liberalism, socialism, materialism, pragmatism, Marxism, and numerous other "isms," as they were called, all found ardent advocates. Educational leaders such as Ts'ai and Hu were criticized by radicals for not giving sufficient attention to the political dimensions of modernization, and for insisting on a piecemeal, evolutionary approach to solving China's problems. Retrospectively, they and many other leaders of the New Culture Movement no longer seem to have made as complete a break with the past as most of their contemporaries believed. As Chancellor of Peking University during the May Fourth era, Ts'ai was a staunch defender of academic freedom against conservative political pressures. More than any other single person, he made Peita (as it was known in short) one of the great universities of the world. But freedom must have limits, and in attempting to define them in his brief discussion of "Freedom and License" (Selection 61), Ts'ai argues that self-restraint is an essential corollary of true freedom. The issue is, of course, extremely complex; yet the reader may ponder whether the self-imposed restrictions described by Ts'ai do not, in the Chinese context, insinuate a Confucian-like subordination of the individual to the existing social order. Similarly, in Hu Shih's gradualist approach to educational reform (Selection 62), are not, as Ch'en Tu-hsiu and others objected at the time, the old elitism and the notion of reform from above by an enlightened minority being reintroduced in a new form? Should knowledge precede action, or did the urgency of the situation mandate that action be given first priority? What, after all, was the prime significance of the May Fourth Movement? Was it the beginning of a long, slow process of creating a new intellectual culture, or the beginning of new political activism? On both these questions, Li Ta-chao (1888–1927), a Peita professor and cofounder of the Communist Party, disagreed with Hu Shih. (Selection 63) A half-century later, opinions were still to be divided over the relative importance of academic study and political activity, over the obligations of the individual to society, over the demarcation line between public and private, and over whether change should be introduced in orderly stages under the careful supervision of a specially qualified elite or through enthusiastic mass movements, potentially erratic though they might be.

The new ideas were not merely abstract theories; they were also personal values. They influenced not only the ways Westernized intellectuals thought about the world around them, but how they conceived of themselves as individuals and how they felt about their own lives. The rejection of the past and the adoption of new ideals, eagerly grasped as solutions to China's problems, not infrequently created other, more personal, problems. The final selections in this chapter illustrate four different responses by men who changed more rapidly than the society around them, and who felt alienated in a society whose values they could not accept.

The disparity between the harsh realities of China and the new ideals could be a source of frustration, or a stimulus to action. In the case of China's greatest modern writer, it was both. In his preface to the first collection of his short stories, Lu Hsün (1881–1936) recalls the incident that made him decide to become a writer. Like Liang Ch'i-ch'ao, Lu Hsün concludes that a new literature is needed to cure China's spiritual ills. Then, in a somber and bleak metaphor, he expresses his sense of frustration at the seeming impossibility of the task. And yet, though reason and imagination despair, hope unexplainably remains. (Selection 64) Throughout his life, Lu Hsün's writings combined an uncompromising depiction of the hypocrisy, cant, and corruption of Chinese society with a moral fervor that implied that, somehow, a better world should be possible.

One of the strongest attractions of Marxism and Communism in China, as in other countries, was precisely its promise of fulfilling hopes for a better future. In his introspective notes in a diary, written while on a journey to Soviet Russia, Ch'ü Ch'iu-pai (1899–1935), a left-wing intellectual who played a leading role in the Communist Party during its early years, defines his own personal problem as an identity crisis. His solution is to identify himself with the future, to dedicate himself to a cause that will give meaning to his life. (Selection 65)

Of course not everyone who conceived of a better life was willing to devote himself to bringing it about. Westernized intellectuals were not immune from selfishness, as Lao She (1898–1966), a major novelist of the 1930s and 1940s, shows in a brief vignette. His American-educated Dr. Mao disparages everything Chinese because he has identified himself completely with everything American, including the prejudices of his American acquaintances. Instead of preparing him to play a role in modernizing China, Dr. Mao's study abroad has made him a misfit, of no use to anyone, including himself. (Selection 66)

Dr. Mao is a fictional character, exaggerated for satiric effect. But the underlying problem was very real. Where did modern-educated Chinese belong? In "Back View," one of the most popular works of modern Chinese literature, Chu Tzu-ch'ing (1898–1948) captures the ambivalence felt by many of his generation. The image of his ineffectual but kind and considerate father in the impersonal modern railroad station is a vivid symbol of an emotional dilemma. Chu realizes that as a young man of his times he had to take the train that carried him away from his disintegrating old home, just as China must abandon its past heritage, but in retrospect his youthful rejection of his unsuccessful father is replaced by sentimental fondness for the human warmth of traditional family relations. (Selection 67)

56. NEW ETHICS FOR A NEW CHINA
[Ch'en Tu-hsiu, "Our Final Awakening," February 1916]

Human life inevitably ends in death, but death is not the purpose of life, nor can we nonchalantly assert the meaning of life to be life itself. Human actions must have goals, and so it is with life too. Our understanding of these goals would truly be our final awakening. The desire to attain this awakening is the origin of all the world's philosophies and religions, but that kind of awakening is not the subject of discussion here. We, having been living in one corner of the world for several decades, must ask ourselves what is the level of our national strength and our civilization. This is the final awakening of which I speak. To put it another way, if we open our eyes and take a hard look at the situation within our country and abroad, what place does our country and our people occupy, and what actions should we take? . . .

Our China is in East Asia, one of the oldest countries in the world. It has been civilized for a long time, and surrounded by minor barbarian peoples. With our gates shut, conditions were created for feeling superior, and Chinese scholarship, government, and education all developed their own styles, unaware of any others.

When Buddhism entered during the Wei and Chin dynasties and thereafter, the literati within and without the court were somewhat receptive to a different view. But India was powerless, and moreover, Buddhism was a religion concerned with other-worldly things, and hence unable to bring about any major change in the Chinese people, to provide any assistance for the necessities of daily existence. And so, was it not the importation of European culture that caused our living conditions to change and daily hastened us down the road to awakening?

The culture imported from Europe was the diametrical opposite of our ancient Chinese culture. Perhaps 80–90 per cent of the confusion and disorder within our country over the past few centuries has been due to clashes between these two cultures. Each time there was a clash, the people learned a lesson. But our lethargy is exceptionally tenacious, and no sooner was there an awakening that it was followed by befuddlement, to the extent that befuddlement increased with each awakening, and we continued to be confused and muddleheaded. If we sum up the stages of transition down to the present day, there have been seven periods.

The first period was the middle of the Ming dynasty, when Western religion and Western technology first entered China. Only an extremely tiny minority knew anything about this, and moreover, in their surprise they thought it was "far-fetched talk." Only one man, Hsü Kuang-ch'i,[1] was a believer.

The second period was the beginning of the Ch'ing, when firearms and the Western calendar were accepted by the Ch'ing court. Old Confucians within

---

[1]A high official at the Ming court who was converted to Christianity by Matteo Ricci.

and without the court rose in swarms to criticize this. This was the beginning of the strife between conservatives and reformers in China.

The third period was the mid-Ch'ing. After the Opium War, Western military might struck fear into the land; the situation deteriorated, and China was compelled to engage in trade [with other nations]. When Tseng [Kuo-fan] and Li [Hung-chang] had charge of state affairs, they successively promoted Western techniques of manufacturing weapons and military training, whereupon the terms "Foreign Affairs" and "Western Learning" appeared within and without the court. At that time, the subject of dispute within the court was whether or not to construct railroads, while without the court the dispute was whether or not the earth was round and whether or not it moved. Today, even small children know the answers to these questions. But at the time, the stubborn literati exerted themselves ceaselessly in writing and talking, appointing themsleves sages and men of wisdom with the task of exterminating heresies and correcting the people's minds. Their slumber was thought at the time to be contemptible, but in later generations it seemed merely pitiful.

The fourth period was the late Ch'ing. In the war with Japan of 1894–95, the army was smashed, and the territory of the country was reduced. The upper and middle levels of society all over the country first awoke from their dreams and anyone with some knowledge recognized that even sages could not have avoided following the policy of strengthening and enriching the country. K'ang [Yu-wei], Liang [Ch'i-ch'ao], and others took advantage of the moment to bring foward the theory of institutional reform, to incite people to action. The conservatives impeded them, and consequently there was the coup d'etat of 1898. But then men fell back into a deep sleep, and dark clouds spread everywhere. The views of the conservatives inclined toward the extreme, and led to the Boxer Rebellion. Thereafter, the state still existed, but only precariously, and the conservative forces abruptly lost their support. The new thought gradually spread, and the issue of the administrative system turned into the fundamental political issue.

The fifth period was the beginning of the Republic. After the Sino-Japanese War, the strife between the conservatives and the reformers had been confined to the issue of whether the administrative system was good or bad, which had been raised by K'ang and Liang. This was still far removed from the fundamental political issue. Things considered novel at that time were actually very superficial. And even these superficial things were suppressed when the stubborn conservatives held power. Consequently, a portion of the best men in the country gradually awoke to the fundamental political issue, and proceeded to discuss republican democracy and constitutional monarchy. The Republic was proclaimed after the Revolution of 1911. The ruler and ministers who had looked with enmity on constitutional government failed in their attempt to preserve their exalted status by slow institutional reforms.

The sixth period is the present war.[2] For the past three years we have suffered from autocratic government under a republican form of state. Having gone through this experiment, love for the republic by men of wisdom in the

[2]The campaign against Yüan Shih-k'ai's monarchical movement.

country has suddenly burst forth, and they have clearly and definitely spurned autocracy.

We can never forget the generosity we have received from those in office. However, henceforth can we feel assured that the republican form of state will be consolidated? Will constitutional government actually be implemented without obstruction? In my view, the resolution of the fundamental political issue still awaits our final awakening. This is the seventh period, the era of the practice of constitutional democracy.

Our task today can be said to be the intense combat between the old and the modern currents of thought. Those with shallow views all expect this to be our final awakening, without understanding how difficult it is to put [constitutional government] into practice. What does this mean? At the present time, the so-called republic and so-called constitutionalism are advocated by small political parites. The vast majority of the people, having no feeling of any personal interest being involved, have no preference. Now, a minority can be the vanguard for awakening the majority, but they cannot take their place. A minority can be the advocates of the great enterprise of republican constitutionalism, but they cannot put it into practice [by themselves]. The evolution of mankind always has discernable tracks. Hence, I do not permit myself to be pessimistic about the present war, no do I adopt a contemptible negative attitude. But neither do I dare entertain a complascent optimism. And so I say, the resolution of this fundamental political issue must await a our final awakening in the seventh period. Please allow me to present my views with great care to the young people of the nation.

Political Awakening

Our country has long had autocratic institutions; officials gave orders, and they were obeyed. Aside from lawsuits and paying taxes, the people had nothing to do with the government; they didn't know anyhing about the nation, or politics. This accumulated to create the nation's present crisis. And yet, the average merchant still thinks that it is not his place to interfere in politics. He chooses a neutral attitude, and leaves national political changes to the government and the political parties, as though he was watching a fire across a river, not realizing that the nation is the common property of all the people, or that man is a political animal. Most Europeans, however, do realize this. That is why no one dares insult them. This is the first step toward our political awakening.

Since we cannot stand apart from the political tide, the initial step is settling the issue of which is the best form of government. In all nations, past and present, there have been various forms of government, some orderly, some chaotic. Those which have transformed chaos into order have all cast aside the old and devised plans for the new, have developed from autocratic government toward free government, from personal government toward government by all the people, and from bureaucratic government toward self-government. This is what is called the tide of constitutional institutions, the track toward a world system. Since our country has not been able to shut its gates and keep to itself, there is no way for us to deviate from this track or go against this tide. The survival of the fittest is the scientific law of evolution. Those unable to adapt to the requirements of their environment and settle in proper surroundings cannot avoid extinction—Japan's treatment of Korea is a historical lesson from the recent past. If our country wants to exist in this world, we must discard the bureaucratic, autocratic, personal government which has been passed down for thousands of years, and change to free, self-government by all the people. This is the second step toward our political awakening.

Whether or not a constitutional form of government, a government by all the people, can actually be put into effert, depends entirely upon one fundamental condition: can the majority of the people consciously realize that they are in the master's seat, that they are the initiators? Since they are in the master's seat, and are the initiators, they should step forward and build a government, obey the legal institutions they themselves have established, and respect the rights they themselves have defined. If the intiative for constitutional government does not belong to the people, but belongs to the government, not only will the constitution be nothing but empty words, but there will be no guarantee of its perpetual and strict enforcement. Moreover, not considering the constitutional rights of freedom to be of any particular importance, the people will not safeguard them with their lives, and then the spirit of constitutional government will be completely lost. If constitutional government is not created through the conscious realization and the voluntary action of the majority of the people, the people merely hope everyday for good government from men of wisdom. The shameful disgrace of this submissiveness is no different from slaves hoping for favors from their masters, from humble people hoping that sage rulers and wise ministers will practice benevolent government. There is no difference between the shameful disgrace of submissiveness of men of ancient times hoping that sage rulers and wise ministers will practice benevolent government and present day men hoping that dignitaries and influential elders will build a constitutional republic. Why should I reject the desires of dignitaries and influential elders, who are after all a part of the people, to build a constitutional republic? Only because a constitutional republic cannot be conferred by the government, cannot be maintained by one party or one group, and certainly cannot be carried on the backs of a few dignitaries and influential elders. A constitutional republic which does not derive from the conscious realization and voluntary action of the majority of the people is a bogus republic and bogus constitutionalism. It is political window-dressing, in no way like the republican constitutionalism of the countries of Europe and America, because there has been no change in the thought or the character of the majority of the people, and the majority of the people have no personal feeling of direct material interest. This is the third step toward our political awakening.

Ethical Awakening

Ethical thought influences politics; this is true in every country, and especially true in our China. The Confucian doctrine of the three bonds is the major source of our political ethics. These bonds are so intimately intertwined that none can be singly abolished. The basic significance of the Three Bonds is the class system. Confucianism is the system which upholds these distinctions between superior and inferior and defines who is high and who low. The polar opposites of the class system are the doctrines of freedom, equality, and independence, which are the source of the political morality of the modern West. This is one of the major watersheds dividing the civilizations of the East and the West.

Should we desire to chose the political system of a constitutional republic, but still preserve the ethical system of bonds and classes so as to enjoy the effects of blending the new and the old, the internal clash would make this absolutely impossible. Republican constitutionalism is based on the principles of independence, equality, and freedom, and absolutely cannot co-exist with the system of bonds and classes. If one is to exist, the other must be abolished. If in politics autocracy is repudiated but in the family and society the old special rights are still preserved, then in law the principle of equal rights, and in economics the principle of independent production, will be completely destroyed. How can they possibly co-exist?

When Western civilization was imported into our country, it was [Western] scholarship which first impelled us to awaken, for it was seen to be superior, as everyone knows. Next came political institutions, for, as the political situation has shown in recent years, circumstances render it impossible to retain the defective [old political institutions]. From now on, it should be the ethical question about which the people raise questions. If there is no awakening to this, then the previous "awakenings" have not been thorough, and we are still lost and confused. I dare assert that ethical awakening is our final, final awakening.

57. THE INCOMPATIBILITY OF CONFUCIANISM AND THE VALUES OF MODERN SOCIETY
[Ch'en Tu-hsiu, "The Way of Confucianism and Modern Life," December 1916]

The pulse of modern life is economic and the fundamental principle of economic production is individual independence. Its effect has penetrated ethics. Consequently the independence of the individual in the ethical field and the independence of property in the economic field bear witness to each other, thus reaffirming the theory [of such interaction]. Because of this [interaction], social mores and material culture have taken a great step forward.

In China, the Confucianists have based their teachings on their ethical norms. Sons and wives possess neither personal individuality nor personal property. Fathers and elder brothers bring up their sons and younger brothers and are in turn supported by them. It is said in chapter thirty of the *Book of*

Rites that "While parents are living, the son dares not regard his person or property as his own." [XXVII:14] This is absolutely not the way to personal independence. . . .

In all modern constitutional states, whether monarchies or republics, there are political parties. Those who engage in party activities all express their spirit of independent conviction. They go their own way and need not agree with their fathers or husbands. When people are bound by the Confucian teachings of filial piety and obedience to the point of the son not deviating from the father's way even three years after his death[1] and the woman obeying not only her father and husband but also her son,[2] how can they form their own political party and make their own choice? The movement of women's participation in politics is also an aspect of women's life in modern civilization. When they are bound by the Confucian teaching that "To be a woman means to submit,"[3] that "The wife's words should not travel beyond her own apartment," and that "A woman does not discuss affairs outside the home,"[4] would it not be unusual if they participated in politics?

In the West some widows choose to remain single because they are strongly attached to their late husbands and sometimes because they prefer a single life; they have nothing to do with what is called the chastity of widowhood. Widows who remarry are not despised by society at all. On the other hand, in the Chinese teaching of decorum, there is the doctrine of "no remarriage after the husband's death."[5] It is considered to be extremely shameful and unchaste for a woman to serve two husbands or a man to serve two rulers. The *Book of Rites* also prohibits widows from wailing at night [XXVII:21] and people from being friends with sons of widows. [IX:21] For the sake of their family reputation, people have forced their daughters-in-law to remain widows. These women have had no freedom and have endured a most miserable life. Year after year these many promising young women have lived a physically and spiritually abnormal life. All this is the result of Confucian teachings of decorum [or rites].

In today's civilized society, social intercourse between men and women is a common practice. Some even say that because women have a tender nature and can temper the crudeness of man, they are necessary in public or private gatherings. It is not considered improper even for strangers to sit or dance together once they have been introduced by the host. In the way of Confucian teaching, however, "Men and women do not sit on the same mat," "Brothers- and sisters-in-law do not exchange inquiries about each other," "Married sisters do not sit on the same mat with brothers or eat from the same dish," "Men and women do not know each other's name except through a match-

[1]Referring to *Analects*, I:11.
[2]*Book of Rites*, IX:24.
[3]*Book of Rites*, IX:24.
[4]*Book of Rites*, I:24.
[5]*Book of Rites*, IX:24.

maker and should [not] have . . . social relations or show affection until after marriage presents have been exchanged,"⁶ "Women must cover their faces when they go out,"⁷ "Boys and girls seven years or older do not sit or eat together," "Men and women have no social relations except through a matchmaker and do not meet until after marriage presents have been exchanged,"⁸ and "Except in religious sacrifices, men and women do not exchange wine cups."⁹ Such rules of decorum are not only inconsistent with the mode of life in Western society; they cannot even be observed in today's China.

Western women make their own living in various professions such as that of lawyer, physician, and store employee. But in the Confucian way, "In giving or receiving anything, a man or woman should not touch the other's hand,"¹⁰ "A man does not talk about affairs inside [the household] and a woman does not talk about affairs outside [the household]," and "They do not exchange cups except in sacrificial rites and funerals."¹¹ "A married woman is to obey" and the husband is the standard of the wife.¹² Thus the wife is naturally supported by the husband and needs no independent livelihood.

A married woman is at first a stranger to her parents-in-law. She has only affection but no obligation toward them. In the West parents and children usually do not live together, and daughters-in-law, particularly, have no obligation to serve parents-in-law. But in the way of Confucius, a woman is to "revere and respect them and never to disobey day or night,"¹³ "A woman obeys, that is, obeys her parents-in-law,"¹⁴ "A woman serves her parents-in-law as she serves her own parents,"¹⁵ she "never should disobey or be lazy in carrying out the orders of parents and parents-in-law." "If a man is very fond of his wife, but his parents do not like her, she should be divorced."¹⁶ (In ancient times there were many such cases, like that of Lu Yü [1125–1210].) "Unless told to retire to her own apartment, a woman does not do so, and if she has an errand to do, she must get permission from her parents-in-law."¹⁷ This is the reason why the tragedy of cruelty to daughers-in-law has never ceased in Chinese society.

According to Western customs, fathers do not discipline grown-up sons but leave them to the law of the country and the control of society. But in the way of Confucius, "When one's parents are angry and not pleased and beat him

⁶*Book of Rites,* I:24
⁷*Book of Rites,* X:12.
⁸*Book of Rites,* X:51.
⁹*Book of Rites,* XXVII:17.
¹⁰*Book of Rites,* XXVII:20.
¹¹*Book of Rites,* X:12.
¹²*Book of Rites,* IX:24.
¹³*I-li,* ch. 2.
¹⁴*Book of Rites,* XLI:6.
¹⁵*Book of Rites,* X:3.
¹⁶*Book of Rites,* X:12.
¹⁷*Book of Rites,* X:13.

until he bleeds, he does not complain but instead arouses in himself the feelings of reverence and filial piety."[18] This is the reason why in China there is the saying, "One has to die if his father wants him to, and the minister has to perish if his ruler wants him to." . . .

Confucius lived in a feudal age. The ethics he promoted is the ethics of the feudal age. The social mores he taught and even his own mode of living were teachings and modes of a feudal age. The objectives, ethics, social norms, mode of living, and political institutions did not go beyond the privilege and prestige of a few rulers and aristocrats and had nothing to do with the happiness of the great masses. How can this be shown? In the teachings of Confucius, the most important element in social ethics and social life is the rules of decorum and the most serious thing in government is punishment. In chapter one of the *Book of Rites,* it is said that "The rules of decorum do not go down to the common people and the penal statutes do not go up to the great officers." [I:35] Is this not solid proof of the [true] spirit of the way of Confucius and the spirit of the feudal age?

58. THE HIGH IDEALS AND HIGH HOPES OF THE EARLY NEW CULTURE MOVEMENT
["Public Declaration of the Policy of *Hsin Ch'ing-nien,*" December 1919]

This magazine has never made fully explicit all of its concrete beliefs. The opinions of members of our magazine do not always agree, which has unavoidably raised doubts among some of our readers, and led to misunderstandings in society. Now, with the beginning of our seventh volume, we would like to clearly proclaim the opinions shared by all members of our magazine. Those who join our magazine in the future will share responsibility for this declaration. Not included, however, is the column "Reader's Opinions," which was created for the [expression of] differing views of persons not members of the magazine.

We believe that all over the world militarism and power politics [*ch'üan-li chu-yi*] have created immeasurable evil, and should now be discarded.

We believe that the conventional political, moral, and economic concepts in every country in the world contain many elements that are unreasonable and impede evolution. If we seek social evolution, we must smash preconceptions such as "eternal moral principles" and "thus has it ever been since ancient times." We must make up our minds to discard old concepts like these, to synthesize the wisdom of good and wise teachers of past and present with our own ideas, to create new political, moral, and economic concepts, and to establish the spirit of a new age, adapted to the new social environment.

The ideal new age and new society we have in mind is honest, progressive, affirmative, free, equal, creative, beautiful, good, peaceful, filled with mutual

[18]*Book of Rites,* X:12.

love and mutual aid, one in which people find enjoyment in their work, and in which the whole of society is happy. We hope that the hypocritical, conservative, negative, restrictive, class, conventional, ugly, warlike, anxiety causing phenomena, along with worrying due to lethargy, and the happiness of [only] a minority will gradually decrease and disappear.

The young people of our new society will of course respect work; but work should accord with individual talents and interests, and should be regarded as free, enjoyable, and beautiful. Such a sacred thing should not be regarded merely as a means of sustaining the necessities of life.

We believe that the progress of human morality should transcend instinct (i.e., aggression and acquisitiveness). Hence we should show feelings of love and assistance to the peoples of the world. But we must treat the aggressive and acquisitive warlords and financial magnates as our enemies.

We advocate the popular movement and social reform, but we completely sever relations with all political parties and factions, past and present.

Although we hold no superstitious belief that government can accomplish everything, we recognize that government is an important aspect of public life. And we believe that a truly democratic government certainly can distribute political power among all the people. Even if limitations are to be set [on the franchise], lack of employment, not lack of property, should be the criterion. This kind of government is a necessary transitional stage to the creation of the new age, a useful instrument for the development of the new society. As for political parties, we recognize too that they are a means which should be utilized in government. But we shall never be able to bring ourselves to join any political party which upholds the selfish advantages of a small minority or the interests of one single class, and which ignores the happiness of all of society.

We believe that the core of politics, morality, science, art, religion, and education should be the real needs of the progress of present and future social life.

Because we desire to create the literary morality needed for the progress of the new age and new social life, we must discard those elements in the old conventional literary morality that are not conducive to this.

We believe that respect for natural science and experimentalist philosophy, and the eradication of superstition and illusion are necessary conditions for the evolution of present day society.

We believe that respect for women's personality and rights has become a real need for the progress of present day social life. And we hope that women will all be fully aware of their responsibilities to society.

Because we want to test our views and strengthen our defenses, we welcome conscious opposition based on conviction, rather than unconscious echoes not based on any conviction. However, until the opposition convinces us, we shall continue to propagate our views boldly and resolutely. We shall not adopt a compromising tone of hypocritical conformity, of confusing right and wrong, of encouraging inertia, impeding evolution, and not standing on our own feet. Nor will we adopt an absolute skepticism, which believes in nothing, lacks conviction, has no opinions, transcends actuality, and leads to no result.

59. THE PRAGMATIC APPROACH TO DEFINING AND SOLVING CHINA'S PROBLEMS
[From Hu Shih, "The Significance of the New Thought," November 1919]

Study the problems. Introduce academic theories. Reorganize our national heritage. Recreate civilization.

Part I. Several articles explaining the "New Thought" have recently appeared in the newspapers. After reading these articles, I feel that their characterization of the New Thought is either too fragmentary or too general, neither an accurate explanation of it nor an indication of its future tendencies.... From my own observation, its basic significance lies merely in a new attitude. We may call this "a critical attitude." The critical attitude is, in short, to distinguish anew the merits and demerits of all things. In more detail, the critical attitude involves several special prerequisites:

1. Of the traditional systems and conventions, we must ask, "Do these systems still possess the value to survive today?"
2. Of the teachings of sages and philosophers handed down from ancient times, we must ask, "Are these words still valid today?"
3. Of all behavior and beliefs receiving the blind approval of society, we must ask, "Is everything that has been approved by the public necessarily correct? Should I do this, just because others are doing it? Is there no other way that is better, more reasonable and more beneficial?"

Nietzsche said that the modern era is "an era of re-evaluation of all values." These words, "re-evaluation of all values," are the best explanation of the critical attitude. In former days people said that the smaller a woman's feet, the more beautiful they were; now we not only deny the "beauty" of bound feet, but say that foot-binding is "inhumanly cruel." Ten years ago opium was offered to guests in homes and stores; now opium has become a prohibited article. Twenty years ago K'ang Yu-wei was a feared and radical reformer, like a big flood or a fierce beast; now he has become an old curio. It is not K'ang Yu-wei who has changed, but his evaluators, and accordingly his value has also changed. That is a "re-evaluation of all values...."

Part II. When expressed in practice, this critical attitude tends to adopt two methods. One is the discussion of various problems, social, political, religious, and literary. The other is the introduction of new thought, new learning, new literature, and new beliefs from the West. The former is "study of the problems"; the latter is "introduction of academic theories." These two things comprise the methods of the New Thought.

These two tendencies can be observed by a casual glance at the contents of new magazines and newspapers of the past two or three years. On the side of studying the problems, we can point to (1) the problem of Confucianism; (2) the problem of the literary revolution; (3) the problem of a unified national language; (4) the problem of the emancipation of women; (5) the problem of chastity; (6) the problem of ethical conventions; (7) the problem of educational reform; (8) the problem of marriage; (9) the problem of the father-son relationship; (10) the problem of the reform of the drama . . . and so on. On the side of the introduction of academic theories, we can point to the special issues "On Ibsen" and "On Marx" of the *Hsin Ch'ing-nien,* the issue "On contemporary thought" of the *Min-to* [The people's tocsin], the issue "On Dewey" of *Hsin Chiao-yü* [The new education], the theory of *ch'üan-min cheng-chih* [total democracy] in *Chien-she* [Reconstruction], and the various new Western theories that have been introduced in such newspapers and magazines as the *Peking Morning Post* [and other papers in Peking, Shanghai, and Canton].

Why must problems be studied? Because our society is now undergoing a period in which its foundations are shaken. Many customs and systems which were not questioned have become difficult issues owing to their failure to meet the needs of circumstance and satisfy the people; therefore we cannot but thoroughly study them, cannot but ask whether or not the old solutions were wrong; if they were wrong, wherein the mistake lies; and when the mistake is discovered, whether there is a better solution, or whether there is any way that will better meet the demands of the present time. For example, the question of Confucianism never arose before. Later, when the civilization of the East came into contact with that of the West, the influence of Confucianism gradually weakened; whereupon a group of Confucianists attempted to restore its dignity by resorting to governmental laws and decrees, not knowing that such high-handed methods would only rouse in people a sort of skeptical reaction. Therefore when the Confucianist Society was the most active, around 1915 and 1916, the anti-Confucianists were also the most numerous. It was at this time that Confucianism became a problem. At present most enlightened people have already broken through these illusions regarding it, and this problem is gradually subsiding, so that when the parliamentary members of the *An-fu* clique passed the resolution defining Confucianism as the basis of moral cultivation, no one in the country even paid it any attention.

Again, take the instance of the literary revolution. Heretofore education has been the special privilege of a small group of "scholars," and has not concerned the majority of the people; therefore the difficulties of the language have not constituted a problem. In recent years education has become a common privilege of all the people, and every man knows that universal education is indispensable; so gradually some people began to realize that the classical style is really not suited to education for all, so then classical versus vernacular style became an issue. Later others felt that writing only textbooks in the vernacular style was not effective because no one in the world would be willing to learn a language that was of no use except in textbooks. . . . If we wish to advocate a vernacular education, then we must first advocate a vernacular literature. The problem of the literary revolution was thus engendered. Now that the National Education Association has unanimously passed a resolution to change the primary school textbooks into the vernacular, moreover, more and more people are writing in the vernacular, and this problem is gradually subsiding.

Why do we have to introduce academic theories? This probably can be explained in several ways. First, some persons are convinced that China lacks not only cannon, warships, telegraphs and railways, but also new ideas and new learning; therefore they introduce as many modern Western theories as possible. Secondly, some persons deeply believe in certain theories themselves, and wish to spread and develop them; therefore they exert themselves to advocate them. Thirdly, some persons are unable to do actual research work themselves, and feel that it is easier to translate ready-made theories; therefore they are glad to engage in this kind of middleman's business. Fourthly, while studying concrete social or political problems one has to do destructive work on the one hand, and on the other hand to make out a prescription to fit the malady. This is not only difficult in itself, but also can easily offend others and cause trouble; therefore one may prefer to embark upon the introduction of academic theories and, under the beautiful phrase "study of academic theories," one can avoid being accused of being an "extremist" or radical, as well as succeed in sowing a few seeds of revolution. Fifthly, those who study a problem cannot limit their discussion to the problem itself; they have to approach it by considering its meaning in the context; and when one extends the study of a problem to the realm of this sort of significance, it is necessary to rely on various theories as material for reference and comparison. Therefore the introduction of academic theories usually aids in the study of problems.

Although the above five motives differ from one another, they all embody the "critical attitude" to a greater or lesser degree; they all express a dissatisfaction with old learning and thought, and a new awakening to the spiritual aspect of Western civilization. . . .

Part III. In the above we have mentioned the two practical expressions of the "critical spirit" of the New Thought. Now we must ask, "What is to be the attitude of the New Thought movement toward the old learning and thought of China?" My answer is, "It should also be a critical attitude."

Under analysis, our attitude toward the old learning and thought should be threefold: first, opposition to blind obedience; second, opposition to compromise; third, advocacy of a reorganization of our national heritage.

Blind obedience is the opposite of critical-mindedness. Since we advocate a "re-evaluation of all values," we naturally must oppose blind obedience. This need not be elaborated.

Why must we oppose compromise? Because the critical attitude recognizes only one right and one wrong, one good and one evil, one suitability and one unsuitability—it does not recognize any compromise of the ancient and modern, or of the foreign and the Chinese. . . . Compromise is the natural tendency of human indolence; it does not require our advocacy. The majority of people can probably, with effort, walk only thirty or forty *li* while we go a hundred *li*. Now if we start talking of compromise and only go fifty *li*, then they will not move even one step. Therefore the duty of the reformer is to set his goal in the right direction and go forward, not to turn back and talk of compromise. There will inevitably be numerous laggards and cowards in society to come out for compromise.

In its positive aspect we make only one proposition regarding our attitude toward the old learning and thought, that is: "to reorganize the national heritage." To reorganize the national heritage means finding order out of chaos, finding the relations of cause and effect out of confusion, finding a real significance out of absurdities and fantasies, and finding true value out of dogmatism and superstition....

Part IV.   ... From my personal observation, the future tendency of the New Thought should be to lay emphasis on the study of problems important to life and society, and to carry out the task of introducing academic theories through studies of these problems.... What is the sole aim of the New Thought? It is to re-create civilization. Civilization was not created *in toto*, but by inches and drops. Evolution was not accomplished overnight, but by inches and drops. People nowadays indulge in talk about "liberation and reform," but they should know that there is no liberation *in toto*, or reform *in toto*. Liberation means the liberation of this or that system, of this or that idea, of this or that individual; it is liberation by inches and drops. Reform means the reform of this or that system, of this or that idea, of this or that individual; it is reform by inches and drops. The first step in the re-creation of civilization is the study of this or that problem. Progress in the re-creation of civilization lies in the solution of this or that problem. (November 1, 1919, 3 A.M.)

60. TRADITIONAL EDUCATIONAL METHODS
[Ts'ai Yüan-p'ei, "Recollections of My Old-Fashioned Education," 1934]

When I was six years old (according to the lunar calendar; using the new way, I was only slightly over four), I entered the family school, and read the *Book of the Hundred Surnames*, the *Thousand Character Primer*, and *Poems by Precocious Children*. Some beginning students read the *Three Character Classic*, or *Poems by a Thousand Authors*, or even started with the *Book of Songs*, but I didn't read these. After finishing these three "Little Books," I read the Four Books, and after that, the Five Classics. When I was reading the Little Books and the Four Books, the teacher didn't explain them, but he did start to explain a little when I got to the Five Classics. However, I had to memorize them and recite them aloud; regardless of whether or not I understood the books I read, after reading them over numerous times, I was able to recite them by heart.

Besides reading, there was studying characters, calligraphy, and pairing phrases, the beginning of my understanding of the meanings of words. The study of characters was taught with characters printed on small, square paper. We had to be able not only to pronounce each character correctly, but to tell its meaning as well. This method is still used in elementary schools, but now pictures have been added—progress over the old way. . . .

Pairing phrases is a way of constructing phrases, starting with one character and going on to four. . . . In this method, not only do nouns, verbs, and adjectives have to be precisely paired, but moreover, among nouns, animal, vegetable and mineral, as well as implements, buildings, and so forth, must all be paired according to the same kind. The same is true for adjectives, such as colors, characteristics, numbers, and so forth. For example, if the teacher gives "white horse," and the students pair it with "yellow ox," "gray fox," and so forth, that is good; but if they pair it with "yellow gold," or "sly fox," then that would not be so good.If the teacher gives "climb up the high mountain," and the students pair it with "gaze at the distant sea," "look at the still water," and so forth, that is good; but it would not be so good to pair it with "till the green field," or "reach the four seas," because a color or number should not be paired with a characteristic. You can surmise the rest from these few examples. One more point: when pairing phrases, we also practiced the differences in the four tones. For example, although it is not absolutely impermissible to pair level tone characters with other level tone characters, or deflected tones with other deflected tones, the normal way is to pair level tones with deflected tones. And furthermore, when we were practicing, the teacher not only made us learn the level and deflected tones, but from time to time also reminded us of the difference between the third, fourth, and entering tones among the deflected tones.

After I had attained a certain degree of proficiency in pairing phrases, the teacher taught me how to write eight-legged essays. . . . Although they are usually called "eight-legged," by the time I was studying them, the six-legged form had become the most common. Before the six legs is the first part, the "leading into the topic," meaning "opening section," which cites the topic; and after the six legs is the conclusion. So you can see that from leading into the topic to conclusion makes one whole piece. But preceding "leading into the topic" there is the "introductory discourse" (sometimes called "minor discourse"), about ten phrases or so, a hundred or more characters in length. And before that comes the "taking up the topic" of four or five phrases, twenty or more characters in length. Before the "taking up the topic" comes "broaching the topic," merely two phrases, ten or more characters. Now what is this if not repetition on top of repetition? I never could quite understand it, but now I finally do. It's a kind of excercise: first you break one phrase of the topic into two phrases (you can also shorten several phrases of the topic into two phrases, but this is done only by those who can write a complete piece); then you go a step further and extend it into four phrases, then another step, extending it to ten or more phrases, until finally you extend it into a complete piece. If you go by the basic meaning of the terms, if there is a "taking up the topic," then there is no further need for a "broaching the topic"; if there is an "introductory discourse," then there is no further need for a "broaching the topic" and "taking up the topic." And if you have a complete piece, then there is no further need for broaching, taking up, and introductory discourse. I don't know when it happened that some eight-legged gentleman [first] piled one thing on top of another, placing this excercise procedure on the very top, but I have not hesitated to write it all out in bothersome detail for the information of those who have never composed eight-legged essays.

From the time I was 17 [*sui*], I began to read books on textual research [*k'ao-chü*], fancy literary style, and such things on my own, and stopped practicing eight-legged essays.

61. THE LIMITS OF FREEDOM
[Ts'ai Yüan-p'ei, "Freedom and License," 1916]

Freedom is a beautiful virtue. Thought, body, speech, residence, occupation, and assembly all have degrees of freedom. If due to external constraints this degree of freedom is not attained, men will struggle with all their might, disregarding even the flowing of blood. This is what has been called "Better dead than not free." Yet, if the [proper] degree is exceeded, causing one to feel ashamed of oneself, and to inflict harm upon others, this no longer is freedom; it is license. License is the enemy of freedom!

If man's thought is not confined by religion, and not hampered by social mores, but consistently takes good conscience as its standard, this is true freedom. But, if on occasion evil thoughts occur, which, though forbidden by conscience, are licentiously tolerated, so that they gradually grow stronger than conscience, this is licentious thought.

To eat when hungry, drink when thristy, and sleep when tired is freedom of health. But if one eats without restraint, gets up and goes to sleep at irregular hours, fostering bad habits, this freedom has become license, and is harmful to health.

To sing when happy and cry when sad is freedom of emotion. But, "When someone is mourning in the neighborhood there should be no singing in the alleys" and "A widow does not cry at night [and disturb others],"[1] because they do not dare permit their emotions to be licentious.

There is freedom of speech, but sometimes there is telling of others' secrets, or directing others to do bad deeds. There is freedom of residence, but some people manufacture dangerous things, or make loud noises all night long. There is freedom of occupation, but some people make counterfeit goods and deal in drugs. There is freedom of assembly, but some spread superstitions and commit wild and wicked acts. All such outrageous acts are manifestations of an extreme one-sided freedom, which disregards other people's freedom; they are errors of license.

[1]Both quotations are from the *Book of Rites.*

The French Revolution was a struggle for freedom, and as such is worthy of our esteem. But because men like Robespierre and Danton were excessive in their fervor, they slaughtered nobles and instigated the reign of terror, degenerating from license to cruelty. English women's recent struggle for the right to vote is also a struggle for freedom, and we should not presume to demean it. Yet their coercive tactics toward the government, even burning mail and destroying works of art, have degenerated from license to vulgarity.

Freedom is a beautiful virtue, but we must take care not to indulge unconsciously in license, and then, unawares, further degenerate to vulgarity or cruelty.

62. EDUCATIONAL PRIORITIES
[Hu Shih, "Elevating and Diffusing," 1920]

During the summer recess, I lectured at the summer session of Nanking Higher Normal College. The seven or eight hundred people who attended my lectures came from 17 provinces, and might be considered the most up-to-date teachers. So I frequently was glad to chat with them. Upon meeting, they would first compliment me by calling me the leader of the "New Culture Movement." Whenever I heard that, I felt extremely ashamed and nervous. For I have never, at any place, dared say that what I have been engaged in is a new culture movement. They also frequently asked me about the future of the new culture, a question to which I really had no reply. For I believe that we have no culture to speak of. Doesn't everyone say that our Peking University is the center of the new culture movement? But, in the most recent issue of *Hsüeh-yi Magazine,* there is an article "New Requests to the Academic World," which contains some earnest words of admonition for our university. It quotes Mr. Ch'en Hsing-nung's public notification about the editing of *Peking University Monthly*. In two years, the more than 400 teachers and 3000 students of our university, working together on a monthly magazine, have put out only five issues. By the time Mr. Ch'en became editor, no manuscripts were coming in at all, so that he was forced to write many pieces himself in order to keep the magazine going. Our University Collectiana started two years ago, and yet so far only five large volumes have been published. Later we thought that even though there might not be any writers, we should at least be able to locate a few translators. So the first half of this year we worked on a World Library Series, never expecting the result of five months' experience would be that we have so far found only one manuscript worth publishing from among the over one hundred we have received. With this kind of bankruptcy in the academic world, who has the nerve to talk about a cultural movement? So my answer to that question is "There's no culture at present; and there's even less of a new culture." Now for the second question. We do have to acknowledge that there is a new phenomenon in the scholarly world outside the university. We may call this a new motive, new needs, but not the new cultural movement about which I was asked. However, since it is in motion, according to the laws of physics it definitely cannot be brought to a standstill. So the only method is to guide the tendencies of this new movement onto a useful road, one that will bring results.

There are two tendencies in this movement.

1. Widespread Diffusion [*p'u-chi*]. To be quite frank, at present the so-called new culture movement is a new terminology movement. A few half-cooked terms, like liberation, reconstruction, sacrifice, vigorous struggle, free love, anarchism. . . . I hand them to you, you hand them to me—this is what is meant by "widespread diffusion." Outside the university there are a lot of people engaged in this task. Well, let them. I swear that I won't engage in it, and I hope that Peita students won't join in either.

2. Elevate [Standards] Higher [*t'i-kao*]. This means—we have no culture, so we should create culture; we have no scholarship, so we should create scholarship; we have no ideas, so we should create ideas. We should create everything, as though bringing it forth from nothing. I hope that everyone will join in and cooperate wholeheartedly with all their energies in this direction. Only when there are higher standards can there be real widespread diffusion; the higher the elevation, the more widespread the diffusion. Just think, a table lamp doesn't shine as far as a ceiling light, and a ceiling light doesn't shine as far as the sun high above. This is my reasoning.

Since at present there are new needs and new aspirations, we should prepare something substantial to satisfy them. If we slovenly use a few half-cooked terms to relieve the hunger for knowledge, wouldn't that be like what Jesus said: "People ask me for bread, but I give them stones"?

In the last several years our Peking University has, I think we may say, been hoisting up signs as the "vanguard of the new tide of thought" and the "center of the new culture." But, as I have just finished saying, if our own knowledge and learning is so impoverished, is it not shameful, really shameful, for us to hoist these gold-lettered signs! So I hope that all of us at Peita, teachers and students alike, will turn away from the current superficial enterprise of "dissemination" and turn back to doing research on "elevating [standards] higher." If we hope to create a new culture for China, we must commence by seeking higher learning. And if we want to seek higher learning, we must first seek the necessary tools. Foreign languages, the Chinese language, the rudiments of science—these are the indispensable tools of learning. We should replace the new terminology movement with these practical tools, use them to seek true learning earnestly, and elevate our own level of scholarship a bit higher. If we can do this, then, in ten or twenty years, perhaps we might just barely be qualified to do some work for a "cultural movement." . . .

Let me sum up what I have said:

"If people curse Peita for being inactive, don't pay any attention; if they curse Peita for having no enthusiasm, don't pay any attention. But, if people say that Peita's level is not high, that the scholarship of the students is poor, that the atmosphere at the university is poor, *that* would really be humiliating! I hope that you will clear us of those charges." "I hope that Peita won't engage in any superficial 'widespread diffusion' movement; I hope that all of us at Peita will work together to exert all our strength in the direction of 'elevating higher.' To create culture, scholarship, and ideas, only after genuine higher elevation can there be genuine widespread diffusion."

63. THE POLITICAL SIGNIFICANCE OF MAY FOURTH
[An Address by Li Ta-chao to the Student Assembly of Peking University, May 4, 1923]

Today is the anniversary of "May Fourth," the anniversary of students' entrance into politics, and also the anniversary of students rectifying political life. Because politics isn't clean, we have no alternative but to involve ourselves in politics at the sacrifice of our scholarly pursuit of learning. The Republic has been in existence for more than a decade, and yet the revolution has not yet been accomplished. We are the ones who must carry on the revolution. However, in this task, we must hold firmly to our goals and principles. At present there are two things students should do: 1) organize the masses of the people as a means to achieve the great revolution; 2) take a denunciatory stance against the existing government. Merely to organize the masses of the people is not enough, because the government can destroy our organizing work. I hope that students will strive to do these two things, for then they are bound to achieve great results in the future.

64. LU HSÜN EXPLAINS HOW HE BECAME A WRITER
[From Lu Hsün, "Preface to *A Call to Arms*," December 1922]

When I was young I, too, had many dreams. Most of them came to be forgotten, but I see nothing in this to regret. For although recalling the past may make you happy, it may sometimes also make you lonely, and there is no point in clinging in spirit to lonely bygone days. However, my trouble is that I cannot forget completely, and these stories have resulted from what I have been unable to erase from my memory.

For more than four years I used to go, almost daily, to a pawnbroker's and a medicine shop. I cannot remember how old I was then, but the counter in the medicine shop was the same height as I, and that in the pawnbroker's twice my height. I used to hand clothes and trinkets up to the counter twice my height, take the money proffered with contempt, then go to the counter the same height as I to buy medicine for my father, who had long been ill. On my return home I had other things to keep me busy, for since the physician who made out the prescriptions was very well-known, he used unusual drugs: aloe root dug up in winter, sugar-cane that had been three years exposed to frost, twin crickets, and Ardisia . . . all of which were difficult to procure. But my father's illness went from bad to worse until he died.

I believe those who sink from prosperity to poverty will probably come, in the process, to understand what the world is really like. I wanted to go to K——school in N——,[1] perhaps because I was in search of a change of scene and faces. There was nothing for my mother to do but to raise eight dollars for my travelling expenses, and say I might do as I pleased. That she cried was only natural, for at that time the proper thing was to study the classics and take the official examinations. Anyone who studied "foreign subjects" was looked down upon as a good for nothing fellow, who had been forced to sell his soul to foreign devils out of desperation. Besides, she was sorry to part with me. But in spite of that, I went to N—— and entered K—— school; and it was there I heard for the first time the names of such subjects as natural science, arithmetic, geography, history, drawing and physical training. They had no physiology course, but we saw woodblock editions of such works as *A New Course on the Human Body* and *Essays on Chemistry and Hygiene*. Recalling the talk and prescriptions of physicians I had known and comparing them with what I now knew, I came to the conclusion those physicians must be either unwitting or deliberate charlatans; and I began to sympathize with the invalids and families who suffered at their hands. From translated histories I also learned that the Japanese [Meiji] Restoration had originated, to a great extent, with the introduction of Western medical science to Japan.

These inklings took me to a provincial medical college in Japan. I dreamed a beautiful dream that on my return to China I would cure patients like my father, who had been wrongly treated, while if war broke out I would serve as an army doctor, at the same time strengthening my fellow countrymen's faith in reform.

I do not know what advanced methods are now used to teach microbiology, but at that time lantern slides were used to show the microbes, and if the lecture ended early, the instructor might show slides of natural scenery or news to fill up the time. This was during the Russo-Japanese War, so there were many war films, and I had to join in the clapping and cheering in the lecture hall along with the other students. It had been a long time since I had seen any compatriots, but one day I saw a film showing some Chinese, one of whom was bound, while many others stood around him. They were all strong fellows but appeared completely apathetic. According to the commentary, the one with his hands bound was a spy working for the Russians, who was to have his head cut off by the Japanese military as a warning to others, while the Chinese beside him had come to enjoy the spectacle.

Before the term was over I had left for Tokyo, because after this film I felt that medical science was not so important after all. The people of a weak and backward country, however strong and healthy they may be, can only serve to be made examples of, or to witness such futile spectacles; and it doesn't

[1]The Kiangnan Naval Academy in Nanking.

really matter how many of them die of illness. The most important thing, therefore, was to change their spirit, and since at that time I felt that literature was the best means to this end, I determined to promote a literary movement. There were many Chinese students in Tokyo studying law, political science, physics and chemistry, even police work and engineering, but not one studying literature or art. However, even in this uncongenial atmosphere I was fortunate enough to find some kindred spirits. We gathered the few others we needed, and after discussion our first step, of course, was to publish a magazine, the title of which denoted that this was a new birth. As we were then rather classically inclined, we called it *Hsin Sheng* [*New Life*].

When the time for publication drew near, some of our contributors dropped out, and then our funds were withdrawn, until finally there were only three of us left, and we were penniless. Since we had started our magazine at an unlucky hour, there was naturally no one to whom we could complain when we failed; but later even we three were destined to part, and our discussions of a dream future had to cease. So ended this abortive "New Life."

[Lu Hsün next tells how, after returning to China, he tried to forget about the present, until one night a friend asked him to write something for *Hsin Ch'ing-nien*. At first he refused, saying:] "Imagine an iron house without windows, absolutely indestructible, with many people fast asleep who will soon die of suffocation. But you know that since they will die in their sleep, they will not feel any of the pain of death. Now if you cry out to wake a few of the lighter sleepers, making those unfortuante few suffer the agony of irrevocable death, do you think you are doing them a good turn?"

"But if a few awake, you can't say there is no hope of destroying the iron house."

True, in spite of my own conviction, I could not blot out hope, for hope lies in the future. I could not use my own evidence to refute his assertion that it might exist. So I agreed to write, and the result was my first story, "A Madman's Diary." From that time onwards, I could not stop writing.

65. THE SELF IN A WORLD IN TRANSITION
[From Ch'ü Ch'iu-pai, *History of the Heart in the Red Capital*, 1921]

The "self" [*wo*] of Ch'iu-pai is not the filial son and obedient grandson of the old era, and should not be contaminated by contemporary "civilization." To be sure, the influence of Western European culture, like a rising tide, has smashed the "Great Wall" of China, and penetrated Chinese life, but, from childhood, this young man's life has been intermingled with the styles of several world cultures, so that he can no longer definitely prove his own pure "Chinese nature." Still, the cultivation of an "identity" requires a clear and accurate compass. And moreover, no one preserves his intrinsic individuality in the abstract—the environment (perhaps this is what is called "society") always exerts an influence.

Nevertheless, the problem of individuality does have a profoundly intrinsic nature. Some persons, in developing their own self-individuality, can also strive forward, sweeping aside all *subjective* environmental obstructions, being flexible, relaxed and self-possessed. Others, who *want* to develop their own individuality, fight the obstacles, exploding in violent anger and turning red in the face, eventually exhausting their creative energies for striving forward as they lose all their strength in defensive struggle. And others, who don't know how to develop their individuality, are completely *swallowed up* by "society," and haven't the slightest capacity for expressing their individuality. These are three different types. To be concrete: among those who live during a time when different cultures of various peoples are intermingling, or in conflict, some can exert their energies in this process of human progress, and at the same time *realize their own self-individuality*; and this advances human culture. Others aren't good at being accommodating and adapting, and blindly hold fast to a single people's cultural character; they wear out their individuality, becoming the victims of a moribund old era. And finally, some blatantly expose their "ignorance," knowing only, like flies, to go where the stench is, *obliterating the individuality of a people, and maiming their individual selves* in order to affiliate themselves with the so-called "progressives." From among these three, which is the one to choose?

In such a situation, my duty is clear. "What am I to become?" I hope that "I" shall become an embryo of the new culture of mankind. The foundation of this new culture should unite the two cultures which have historically stood in opposition, but which, with the beginning of the present era, complement one another: the East and the West. At present, in both cultures, the representatives of the past are manifesting dangerous symptoms: one disease, the philistinism of the bourgeoisie; the other, "oriental" death-like stillness.

"I" am not the filial son and obedient grandson of the old era, but a sprightly child of the "new period."

Of course, to be sure, I naturally can only serve as one tiny, insignificant soldier; but I shall always be an active fighter.

Although I am only one small soldier, nevertheless I am enlisted in the ranks of the vanguard of the world cultural movement, which will open up a new road for the culture of all mankind, and thereby restore China's splendid 4,000-year-old culture.

The meaning of "myself": with respect to society, I am individuality; with respect to the world, the people are individuality.

Without "me" there is no society, and without an *active* "me" there is even less of a society. If there is no national character, there is no world, and without an *active* national character, there is even less of a world. No society and no world, no intermingling and cooperating, no collective and complete society and world—then there is no so-called "me," no so-called people, no so-called culture.

66. ONE KIND OF WESTERN EDUCATION
[From Lao She, "Sacrifice,"[1] 1934]

He wasn't very tall, and though he wasn't exactly stout you couldn't say he was thin either. His body was just about right to dutifully bear his suit of Western clothes. On top of his neck was set that ingot-like head, and on top of the head was a pile of dutiful black hair, dutifully combed slick and shiny.

He was moving back and forth looking at himself in the mirror, as though he really appreciated his own good looks. But I felt he was strange indeed. His back was to the sunlight, so that the middle part of his face, which was quite indented, was rather dark. As soon as I saw that dark indentation, I hastily looked out the window to see whether the sky had suddenly gone dark. Dr. Mao made you have doubts about even such bright sunny weather. This guy gave you the creeps.

He didn't seem to have been listening to what we were saying, but he didn't want to leave either. He was bored, and because he was bored he was paying so much attention to himself. I realized that this guy's Western clothing and his life were a kind of duty.

I forget exactly what we were talking about; but anyway he suddenly turned his head around, with his sunken eyes momentarily closed, as though he was searching for something in his heart. When he opened them, his mouth was just about to break into a smile when it changed its plan and let out a light sigh, probably a sign that he hadn't found anything in his heart after all. Maybe his heart was a complete blank.

"What? Dr.?" Old Mei's tone of voice revealed a certain lack of respect for this Ph.D.

Dr. Mao didn't appear to sense this. Availing himself of his sigh, he spat out a wad, "p'u," as though the weather was very hot. "This is too great a sacrifice," he said, and set himself down into a chair, stretching his legs way out in front of him.

"You mean a Harvard Ph.D. shouldn't suffer this kind of punishment," Old Mei was making fun of the Dr.

"Really!" Dr. Mao's voice was almost trembling. "Really! No one should suffer this kind of punishment. No girl friends . . . , no movies. . . ." he stopped for a moment as though he couldn't think what else it was he needed. That made me feel uncomfortable, but then out came a phrase that summed it all up: "Absolutely nothing!" Fortunately his eyes were so sunken, otherwise he would have started to cry. He really and truly felt bad.

"But, if you were in America?" Old Mei helped him by adding a sentence.

"Really! Even in Shanghai, good movies, plenty of girl friends," then he stopped again.

[1]"Hsi-sheng," which means both "sacrifice" and "victim."

Probably the only things in his mind were girls and movies. I thought I'd try to feel him out, "Dr. Mao, Peking opera is pretty good, really worth going to see."

He looked dumbfounded for some time before he answered, "My foreign friends say Chinese opera is barbarous."

That ended that. I couldn't sit still any more, so after a while I suggested we all go out for a bath. There was a new public bath house in town which was supposed to have pretty good equipment. I had originally intended to ask Old Mei to go, but I couldn't very well leave without inviting Dr. Mao, since he was right there, and so lonely.

The Dr. shook his head from side to side. "They're dangerous, you know."

I got all confused again—I'd always gone to public baths, and never once had I drowned.

"Those massage women! And those filthy bath tubs!" He seemed really afraid.

I understood—in his mind the only decent places were America and Shanghai.

"It's not like Shanghai here," I offered in explanation.

"But is there any place in China as civilized as Shanghai?" This time he actually smiled, but it wasn't a pleasant smile to look at: his mouth almost touched his forehead and his nose sank into his face.

"But Shanghai can't compare with America, can it?" Old Mei was deliberately putting him on.

"Really!" The Dr. got serious again. "In America every family has a bath tub, every hotel room has a bath tub. If you want to wash, *whoosh*—you turn on the water: hot or cold, whichever you want. If you want to change the water, *whoosh*—you let out the dirty water, and refill the tub with clean water, *whoosh*—" He said it all in one breath, and each "*whoosh*" was accompanied by a spray of saliva, as if his mouth was an American faucet. Then he added a short phrase: "Chinese are absolutely filthy!"

While the Dr. was "whooshing" Old Mei had put on his coat and shoes. The Dr. went out first, with a "See you." The way he said it made you feel very uncomfortable, as though his heart was filled with tears. He couldn't bear to leave us, he was so lonely; but he just couldn't go to a "Chinese" bath house, no matter how clean it might be.

67. LEAVING HOME
[Chu Tzu-ch'ing, "Back View," 1925]

It's been two years since I last saw my father, and what I most remember about him is a view of his back. In the winter of that year, grandmother had died, and father had left his job. Truly, those were days when calamities didn't come one at a time. I left Peking for Hsü-chou to join father and hurry home for the funeral. When I arrived in Hsü-chou and met father, I saw that the courtyard was all in a mess, and, at the thought of my grandmother, I couldn't stop the tears from streaming down. Father said, "It's already happened, don't feel so bad. Fortunately, Heaven always leaves a way out."

We returned home and father sold and pawned some things. He paid off the debts and then borrowed some money to take care of the funeral. Those days the atmosphere around the house was rather dismal, partly because of the funeral, and partly because father was out of a job. When the funeral was over, father was to go to Nanking to look for work, and I was to return to my studies in Peking, so we left together.

When we reached Nanking, a friend had made arrangements to go sightseeing, so I stayed over for a day. The next morning I was to cross the Yangtze to Pu-k'ou and take the afternoon train north. Because he was busy, father had originally said he wouldn't be able to see me off, and he had asked a waiter from our hotel whom he knew well to accompany me to the station. He went over his instructions to the waiter several times, in great detail, but in the end he couldn't stop worrying that he might not handle everything just right. And so he hesitated for a while. Actually, I was already twenty [sui], and had been to Peking two or three times, so there was no need for so much fuss. Still after hesitating awhile, father decided that he had better see me off himself. I told him several times that he didn't have to, but he only said, "Never mind. I'd better go myself."

We crossed the river and entered the station. While I went to buy my ticket, he busily watched over the luggage. I had too many bags, so we had to give a porter a tip before we could pass. And father busily argued over the tip. In those days, I really was terribly smart, and I felt that his language wasn't very elegant, so I had to put in a few words myself. But he finally settled on an amount, and accompanied me to the train. He picked out a seat for me next to the car door, and I spread the dark wool overcoat he had had made for me over the seat. He told me to be on the alert while travelling, to sleep lightly at night, and not to catch a chill. And he asked the waiter to look after me. I smiled to myself at how simple-minded he was; those kind of people only understand money, so it was a waste of time to ask them to do anything. And besides, I was grown up. Couldn't I take care of myself? When I think about it now, in those days I really was terribly smart.

I said, "Father, you'd better go." He looked outside the train and said, "I'll go buy you some tangerines. You stay here. Don't wander off." I saw that beyond the platform railing there were several vendors waiting for customers. To get to that platform you had to jump down onto the tracks, cross over, and then climb up the other side. Father was rather stout, and it wasn't easy for him to get across. I wanted to go myself, but he wouldn't let me, so I had to let him go himself. He was wearing his small black hat, and his loose black jacket over his dark blue cotton-padded long gown; I watched him waddle over toward the track and slowly lower himself down. That part wasn't too difficult. But after he had crossed the tracks and had to climb up onto the platform on the other side, that wasn't so easy. He reached up and clutched the platform with both hands, and pulled up his legs; his heavy body tilted slightly to the left, showing what an effort it was for him. As I looked at this view of him from the back, the tears flowed rapidly down. I hastily wiped them away, afraid that he or someone else might see. When I looked outside again, he was on his way back, carrying some bright tangerines. When he had to cross the track, he set them down on the platform, slowly lowered himself down, and then picked them back up again. When he reached the platform on my side, I hastened to give him a hand, and we walked back to the train together. He plumped the tangerines down on my wool overcoat. Then he dusted himself off, as though he could finally relax. After a while, he said, "I'll be going now. Don't forget to write after you get there!" I watched him leave. After a few steps, he turned around and said, "You'd better get back inside; there's no one to watch your things." After his back blended into the crowd of people coming and going and I couldn't make him out any more, I went back inside and sat down, and the tears came again.

Lately, father and I have been scurrying around in different directions, and times haven't been so good for our family. When he was young, father left home to make a living, to support himself on his own, and he did some great things. Who would have expected that he could have such bad luck in his old age. Wherever he turns there's something to make him feel bad. And of course he can't keep his feelings to himself. Inner depression will naturally find a way to vent itself. Little household details frequently touch him off. He gradually began to treat me differently than he had in the past. But after not having seen me during these past two years, he has forgotten my faults, and has only fond thoughts of me and my son. After I came north, he wrote me a letter, in which he said, "My health is fine, except that my arm hurts quite a bit, and I find using chopsticks and writing with a brush rather difficult. Probably the time for the final departure isn't far off." When I read this, through the crystal tears I once again saw that view of his stout back, with the black cloth jacket over the deep blue padded long gown. Alas. I don't know when I'll see him again.

CHAPTER NINE
Change and Tradition under the Kuomintang

The students and young intellectuals of the 1920s were acutely conscious of the discrepancies between the bright new ideas from the West and the grim realities of warlord China. The frustration of which Lu Hsun wrote was a common theme in the new colloquial fiction that burgeoned in the May Fourth period. To many it seemed that in a world dominated by the gun, ideas, no matter how true, were in themselves inadequate to transform reality.

Sun Yat-sen understood this as much as anyone. In the years after he had relinquished the presidency of the Republic to Yuan Shih-k'ai, Sun had sought military and financial support from many sources, with no substantial success. But Sun believed in his destiny, and in 1923 his persistence was rewarded. After two years of discussions with emissaries from Moscow, he concluded an alliance with Soviet Russia. Under the guidance of Russian advisors, and with Russian financial and material aid, Sun's party, the Kuomintang was reorganized along Leninist lines, and a party army was built up. A military academy was established in Whampoa, near Canton. There, under the young commandant Chiang Kai-shek (1887–1975), an officer corps was trained to lead the new army. In January 1924, the first National Congress of the reorganized Kuomintang (KMT) was convened in Canton. It ratified the reorganization, gave approval to Sun's policies of cooperating with the Russians and forming a united front with the small Chinese Party (CCP), and issued a manifesto stating the party's aims.

The Kuomintang Manifesto of 1924 presents the Nationalists' explanation of China's problems and their proposed solutions. (Selection 68) As in most pre-1911 writings of the revolutionaries, the analysis is largely political. Warlords and capitalists have replaced Manchus and their Chinese collaborators as the chief culprits, but the essential point remains that the political leaders of China conspire with foreigners to hinder Chinese political and economic development. In the revisions of Sun's Three Principles of the People, more attention is given to the harmful effects of imperialism, and it is stated that the struggle for the liberation of the Chinese people is an anti-imperialist struggle. The solution, also familiar in pre-1911 writings, is a national coalition of all those suffering from these conditions to bring to power a government committed to eliminating the barriers to national reconstruction. The Kuomintang is said to be best qualified to unify China because it alone represents the common interests of the people, rather than any special interest. How these common interests are to be determined is not made clear, but since democratic rights are subordinated to "the needs of the Chinese revolution," and moreover are bestowed by the government and, by implication, neither inherent nor inalienable, the determination of the common interest would seem to reside in the KMT.

Sun Yat-sen's sudden death in March 1925 came only a few months before an upsurge of antiforeign feeling after foreign police killed strikers and other demonstrators protesting conditions in foreign-owned factories in Shanghai. Much of the anger was channeled into the Nationalist and Communist parties. Between early 1925 and mid-1927, the CCP grew from roughly 950 members to almost 58,000. By mid-1926 the KMT had something like 200,000 members, and the National Revolutionary Army numbered about 100,000. Under the command of Chiang Kai-shek, and with the support of workers' and peasants' movements organized and led by the CCP and the left wing of the KMT, the Nationalist armies undertook a Northern Expedition to reunify China and eliminate foreign privilege. As Chiang's forces moved northward, tensions within the coalition increased. In April 1927 Chiang struck against the Communists and allied himself with more conservative elements within the KMT and the Chinese bourgeoisie. The worker and peasant movements were suppressed, the CCP was driven underground, and the Russian advisors left China. Within a year, the Northern Expedition came to a conclusion with the official capitulation of the northern warlords. A provisional constitution for the new government was promulgated in October 1928 by the KMT, which was to be the ruling party until the country was prepared for constitutional government. Formally, at least, China was unified.

But in fact unification was nominal. Warlords still retained autonomous authority in large areas of the country. The Communists, suppressed in the cities, shifted their activities to the countryside. The land tax, so vital a source of revenue, was largely out of the control of the new central government. And factional rivalries divided the KMT itself. Hampered by limited revenues and limited administrative control, by armed domestic enemies and by power struggles within the top ranks of the party, and menaced by the growing threat of Japanese expansion in the north, the Nationalist Government was handicapped in its attempts to deal with the basic problems of China. Nevertheless, it was not ineffectual. One after another, warlords were subdued. In foreign affairs, tariff autonomy, lost in the Opium War treaties, was regained, though the "unequal treaties" were not completely abolished until 1943, during World War II. Significant accomplishments could be seen in education, finance, public health, industry, transportation, and other areas. But progress was uneven, due partly to the morass of domestic and foreign political difficulties, partly to the conservatism of top party leaders and of officials with vested interests in the status quo, and partly to the persistence of traditional modes of thought and behavior, both within the KMT and in Chinese society at large. It is these latter problems that are the subject of the remaining selections in this chapter.

One of the first to point out the debilitating effects of certain traditional values on the KMT was Tai Chi-t'ao (1891–1949), a leading party theoretician. Unlike May Fourth intellectuals, Tai did not blame Confucianism, whose high ideals of social service he believed could provide the needed selfless motivation to deal with China's modern problems. Rather, he attributed much of the divisiveness that weakened the party to the influence of Taoist ideas, in particular to what he called "individualism." This individualism, he thought, led to an excessive reliance on interpersonal relations, which undermined "democratic centralism," the fundamental Leninist concept that had been adopted as the organizational principle of the Kuomintang. (Selection 69) Tai's solution was party unity through the shared values of a common ideology, the Three People's Principles. This common ideology he saw as the common faith necessary for mutual trust. (Selection 70) Tai thus saw the problems of modern political organization within a Confucian-like context: Self-interest was divisive, and unity brought about by common values was the ultimate source of strength. In spite of Tai's warnings, however, lack of trust and reliance on personal relationships were to continue to infest the KMT in later years.

Similar conflicts between modern organizational exigencies and traditional cultural values can be seen in the next two selections. The description of local officials in 1936 (Selection 71), eight years after the KMT had come to power on a revolutionary platform, is remarkably like the characterizations of late Ch'ing officials, and shows that the problems Tai had perceived had not been solved. Selection 72 gives a broader list of factors inhibiting industrial growth, but also shows examples of continuity with late Ch'ing conditions. But from another perspective, these two selections indicate how much attitudes had actually changed, for by the mid-1930s, the validity of such criticisms of traditional values was becoming widely accepted, as more and more Chinese received the kind of specialized Western education these two authors utilize in their analyses. And many such Western-trained experts believed that the West provided models for the solution of China's problems that could be implemented within the framework of the existing government. Whether this might somehow have been possible can never be known for certain, for the long war against Japan, the deterioration of the KMT during and after the war, and the Communist victory in the civil war of 1946–49 deprived the Nationalists of any further opportunity to attempt to solve China's problems in their way.

The final selection in this chapter is an explanation of the persistence of many of the traditional traits we have seen in this and previous chapters, by Fei Hsiao-t'ung (b. 1901), one of modern China's foremost social scientists. Using the familiar concepts of *kung* and *ssu*, Fei analyzes Chinese society in Chinese terms. Here, the main problems of rural China are not so much economic as social and psychological attitudes that preclude the effective organization of forces to deal with general problems. Aside from its usefulness for understanding rural society, Fei's theory of moral values as a function of self-interest can be fruitfully applied to Chinese politics as well. Indeed, Fei demonstrates how political ordinary Chinese social life was. And, as we shall see, this theory still retains some relevance to the new society of the People's Republic of China.

68. THE KUOMINTANG NATIONAL REVOLUTION
[Manifesto of the First National Congress of the Kuomintang, January 30, 1924]

Report on the State of the Nation

The revolution in China has been in process since 1895, reached its crest in 1900, and in 1911 swept away the monarchy. Revolution does not come suddenly. Inequality of status and opportunity has oppressed and depressed the peoples of China since the Manchus first occupied China. When restrictions on maritime trade were lifted, China was further overwhelmed, as under raging tides, by the military pressures and economic pressures from foreign imperialists, which deprived China of independence and submerged her to the status of a semicolony. The Manchu government not only lacked means of stemming foreign aggression but, as if further to assist the foreign powers, it increasingly surrendered the powers of government to eunuchs and court favorites. Following our leader Sun Yat-sen, who realized that for the reconstruction of China the Manchus must first be overthrown, the members of our party rose courageously, fighting as the vanguard of the people to hurl down the corrupt Manchu government. The fall of the Manchus in 1911 accomplished only one stage in the whole process of revolution for the reconstruction of China. In the enthusiasm over the fall of the dynasty it appeared that the despotism of one race over other peoples had been wholly abolished and that an equal union of all races had immediately ensued, that the monarchy was disposed of and the nation securely established as a republic, and that old handicraft industries would be immediately transformed to machine production supported by large capital investments.

The actual social and political conditions of the early days of the Republic were not so far advanced as our first enthusiasm led us to believe, but our hopes in those days still represent the direction in which we must work in order to free China from semicolonial status and establish her as an independent nation respected among the major nations of the world.

In liberating the Chinese people from enslavement by the Manchus the revolution appeared to be already successful but the Republic soon suffered from other pressures which forced temporary compromises with dictators and counterrevolutionaries. The several links between the counterrevolutionaries and the foreign imperialists contributed to the pressures which held back the process of revolution. Though Yüan Shih-k'ai, representative of the despotism of the counterrevolutionaries, was not himself very powerful, the Revolutionary Party constrained itself from attacking him directly in the hope, thereby, of avoiding a prolonged civil war. The party was also handicapped in these years by members who lacked discipline and lacked adequate understanding of the party's function and purpose. Had we at that time possessed a thoroughly disciplined party, we could most certainly have outwitted the plots of Yüan Shih-k'ai and prevented his exploitation of members of the party. As it was, during those years the Revolutionary Party yielded power to this man who, as leader of the Peiyang warlords, intrigued with foreign powers and with militarists and politicians who depended on his favors. It goes without saying that the outcome of these compromises was disastrous for the Republic.

Even after the death of Yüan Shih-k'ai the efforts of the revolutionists met repeated failure. The war lords have now become so arrogant and so unprincipled that like knives and swords hacking cattle and fish they hack the people to pieces. No political democracy worth mentioning has as yet existed; the war lords conspired with foreign imperialists; and the so-called republican governments, controlled by the war lords, abuse the authority of government to serve the pleasure of foreign powers. In return, the foreign powers, by lending the war lords funds to finance unremitting civil war in China, obtain special privileges and secure their spheres of influence. Furthermore, by indirectly supporting China's civil wars, the foreign powers secure the services of the war lords in conflicts among foreign powers who themselves have competing spheres of interest in China.

The continuing civil wars not only hinder the development of Chinese industry but fill the Chinese market with foreign goods. Chinese industrial goods cannot compete with foreign goods even in the domestic market. Foreign capitalists control our economic as well as our political life.

Because of our failure thus far to complete the process of revolution, the middle class has undergone many vicissitudes and has become impoverished. Small businessmen have become bankrupt and handicraft workers have become vagrants, soldiers, or bandits. Having no capital with which to work their land, farmers have been forced to sell their best fields at a loss. The cost of living increases daily, rents grow more exorbitant, and the misery of the whole people is everywhere visible.

Since 1911 the national situation, politically and economically, has deteriorated year by year and day by day. The accelerating lawlessness of the war lords and the encroachments by foreign powers have not only reduced China to a semicolony but visited upon the people of China the tortures of hell. With the nation in the throes of death, farsighted people have no choice but to find means of instilling new life in the whole people.

How shall we proceed to discover and establish this new life? Many political parties and many individuals, both Chinese and foreigners residing in China, all offer their own suggestions.

The Constitutionalists, for example, assert that only the lack of a constitution prevents unification and causes chaos. They do not recognize that a constitution can be effective only when it is actively supported by the whole people; a constitution as words on paper cannot defend the rights of the people from the arrogance of the war lords. Furthermore, since 1912 China has had the text of a constitution, but this has not deterred the monarchists, the war lords, or corrupt career politicians from exploiting the text of the constitution as an excuse for visiting further injury upon the people. Ts'ao K'un, for example, recently bribed his way into the presidency, using the text of a so-called constitution to gloss over his usurpation. From experience we must now recognize that the whole people must be prepared to defend the constitution before a constitution can be effective. An unorganized people cannot make a constitution. Furthermore no constitution can be effective until we have first driven out the foreign imperialists and destroyed the war lords.

As for the Federalists, they argue that the present chaos has been created by overconcentration of power in the central government. Concluding that we must allot the power of the central government to the provinces, they argue that with limited power the central government can do no evil. But the Federalists have not sufficiently reflected upon the fact that although the Peking government was not bestowed by law on the big war lords, these war lords control it and utilize it to expand their own military power. Instead of proposing to destroy the military power of the great war lords, the Federalists have been encouraging the small war lords in the provinces to flout the authority of the central government. In practice China has been divided and every self-seeking small war lord not only occupies a province from which he can compete for status with the great war lords of Peking but is also a supporter of this *status quo* which serves his personal interests. Can this be called self-government? Genuine democracy is a prime requisite, but no single province can maintain true freedom and independence so long as the whole nation is not yet free and independent.

As for the Peace Conventioners, they suppose a civil war of which they are desperately weary can be stopped by a conference. But war in China is waged by feuding war lords who are concerned only for personal advantage and wholly indifferent to the welfare of the nation. Competing personal interests among individual war lords make both reconciliation and reunion impossible.

As for business executives, they assume that if China were ruled by capitalists rather than by militarists and politicians the nation could live in peace. These businessmen argue that people hate militarists and career politicans because such men do not represent the people's interests. Would the capitalists represent the people's interests? Militarists and our career politicians notoriously rely upon foreign support. Can the capitalists be independent of foreign capital? We have no basic objection to businessmen in government. We urge, however, that all the people organize a government to represent all interests and not solely the interests of commerce and industry. The government must be independent, must not ask help from special interests, and must represent the principles and interests common to the whole people.

Our Kuomintang has long believed that China's only resource for new life is the nationalist revolution and enforcement of the Three Principles of the People. This present survey of the state of the nation helps us understand that the nationalist revolution is inevitable and imminent. We are therefore proceeding to an explanation of our principles and a declaration of our political platform to the people of the whole nation.

The Principles of the Kuomintang

Sun Yat-sen's doctrine of the Three Principles of the People is accepted as the political doctrine of the Kuomintang. As the only means of saving the people of China, the nationalist revolution must proceed to implement the Three Principles of the People. The recent thorough reorganization of party structure and the discipline established for party members are intended to encourage every member to devote all his energy to the fight for establishment and enforcement of the Three Principles.

Of these three principles the principle of nationalism [*min-tsu chu-i*] supports two aims: the liberation of China by the Chinese people; and establishment of equal rights for all the races living in China.

In support of the first aim of nationalism the Kuomintang proposes to secure the recognition of the freedom and independence of China among the nations of the world. Although before 1911 the Manchus dominated all the other races in China, the foreign imperialists also dominated the Manchus. The nationalist revolution was aimed both at destroying the Manchus and putting a stop to the aggressions by foreign powers who were slicing the empire of China like a melon. Since 1912 Manchu domination has been disposed of but we have not yet driven off the foreign imperialists. Although their former military encroachments are now relinquished in favor of economic oppression, so long as such oppression exists China has neither freedom nor independence. Because Chinese militarists conspire with the imperialists and Chinese capitalists share the profits, the Chinese people are robbed daily of both political and economic independence.

Members of the Kuomintang must exert utmost effort in the fight to emancipate the Chinese people. In this fight they rely on the intelligentsia, on the farmers, and on the merchants for defense and support, because all classes are suffering from imperialist aggression, which the nationalist revolution has set out to destroy. Nationalism is the defense of industry because only release from the economic pressure of foreign powers can make it possible for China to develop as an industrial nation. Nationalism is the support of the industrial workers because only in a nationalist China can they escape exploitation by militarists and by native and foreign capitalists on whom they now depend and who squeeze and choke them and grudge them a living.

In the eyes of the masses the fight for the emancipation of the Chinese people is an anti-imperialist movement. Nationalism is a powerful weapon against imperialism. When imperialism has been beaten down, the people can then enlarge their activities and unify themselves to accomplish the other aims of the revolution. We must assist and encourage the organization of the proletariat to help our people recognize their own powers and abilities. Only a firm alliance between the Kuomintang and the common people can realize China's hope for freedom and independence.

In support of the second aim of nationalism, equality of the Chinese with all the other races living in China, the Kuomintang will work for alliances and organized discussion of problems which concern us all. The Kuomintang solemnly declares that the party will recognize the right of self-determination for all the peoples in China and that following the defeat of the imperialists and the war lords and the establishment of a free and united Republic of China, every people in China shall be allowed freedom of decision in joining the Republic.

Of the Three Principles of the People, the principle of democracy [*min-ch'üan chu-i*] is recognized by the Kuomintang as supporting not only many indirect rights but also the specific rights of election, initiative, referendum, and recall. The exercise of these rights is described in Sun's Five Power Constitution, which provides for the separation of powers: namely the legislative, judicial, administrative, examining, and supervisory powers. This system of government avoids the defects of other modern parliamentary governments and also corrects the weaknesses of the traditional Chinese civil service examination system.

In contrast to most modern democratic governments in which power is monopolized by capitalists who oppress the common people, Kuomintang democracy means government shared by the common people. Kuomintang democracy is, however, different from any system which claims to bestow rights on everyone; Kuomintang democracy must meet the needs of the Chinese revolution and therefore it must be understood that the rights enjoyed by recognized citizens of the Republic are not allowed to enemies of the Republic. Upright individuals and recognized organizations will be permitted freedom and the rights enjoined by the constitution, but those who betray the nation, those who give their loyalty to the imperialists or to the war lords, will be permitted neither freedom nor rights.

As to the third of the Principles of the People, the principle of livelihood for the people [*min-sheng chu-i*] comprises two major aims: equalization of landholdings and regulation of capital. To achieve economic equilibrium we must no longer permit to a minority among our people a monopoly in land ownership. The state must regulate the ownership, use, and purchase of land as well as tax levies on land. Such regulations implement the principle of equality in property rights.

To prevent private captialism from controlling the people's livelihood, the state will manage and control all banks, railroads, and ship lines, and all other large-scale enterprises. With the regulation of landholdings and the regulation of capital we establish socialism on a secure foundation.

Our farmers will understand us when we assert that agriculture is the basic source of China's wealth; and at the same time, of all classes in the nation, farmers have endured the greatest hardships. Under the Kuomintang the state will grant land to all landless and tenant farmers and also issue tools to work the land. Moreover, the state will repair irrigation works, instruct farmers in the rotation of crops, and assist farmers in the cultivation of new lands. By establishing and managing banks for farmers, the state will assist those who lack capital and have now been enslaved by enforced loans at exorbitant rates of interest. Ultimately farmers will enjoy the good life they deserve.

Chinese laborers without security and protection may be assured that it is the express policy of the Kuomintang to protect workers and to find employment for those who are out of work. Since poverty-stricken farmers and laborers exist everywhere in China and share in the common misery, they understand the need of liberation from oppression and should be able to understand the need to drive out the imperialists. Since the success of the nationalist revolution depends on cooperation from farmers and laborers, the Kuomintang must actively assist farmers' and workers' movements and also subsidize such efforts. We must also work untiringly to persuade farmers and workers to become members of the Kuomintang, making clear to them that since the Kuomintang is fighting against the imperialists and the war lords and all privileged classes, the nationalist revolution is also a revolution to emancipate farmers and laborers. Farmers and laborers participating in the work of the Kuomintang will be working for their own best interests.

We are here presenting a definitive interpretation of the Three People's Principles. To maintain the effectiveness of the party as now reorganized, party members will receive education and training under strict discipline to enable them to propagate the party doctrine, rouse the masses of the people, and qualify as experts in revolution and political organization. To maintain our effectiveness we must also develop an active propaganda to draw all the people of the nation into the revolutionary movement, to assist us in seizing political power and vanquishing the enemies of the people. When political power is in our hands and a new government established, the Kuomintang will continue to function as the nerve center of the state, controlling political power to check any subsequent counterrevolutionary effort and to guard against any conspiracy by foreign powers to oppress our victorious people. We must attack and remove whatever hinders the enforcement of Kuomintang principles. Only an efficiently organized and agressive party can adequately protect an aroused people and properly fulfill its duty to the people of the whole nation.

69. THE CONFLICT BETWEEN NEW PRINCIPLES OF ORGANIZATION AND OLD PATTERNS OF BEHAVIOR

[From Tai Chi-t'ao, *The National Revolution and the Chinese Kuomintang*, 1925]

. . . As for interpersonal relations, everyone knows that the old Chinese bad habit of individualism has already reached the point where nothing can get done. In our experience in performing our tasks, we constantly see two major bad habits. One is the "getting in touch [*chieh-t'ou*] disease" and the other is the "smoothing things out [*shu-t'ung*] disease." People in political work are busy all day long just "smoothing things out" and "getting in touch." Just when things are smoothed out here, a snag develops over there. And when people have "gotten in touch" here, some relationship is disrupted over there. And the worst part is that whenever there is a problem between one person and another, those two are the only ones who can get in touch [to talk things over], and if there is a difference of opinion between one person and another, those two are the only ones who can smooth things out. Because of these circumstances all kinds of real work is obstructed and comes to a standstill. Moreoever, we can see that all political evils come from this getting in touch and smoothing things out, or not being able to get in touch and not being able to smooth things out. What is the explanation for this peculiar phenomenon? It is because Chinese have only individualism, so that those in political work know only their own self-interest, what is personally right and wrong for them, and give no thought to the nation or the masses of society. The only remedy for this ideological disease is for everyone to abandon individualism and believe in the Three People's Principles, to make common belief in the same ideology the foundation for mutual trust. Only in this way can these two serious diseases obstructing our work be cured. . . . Today a few men here join together to oppose a few men there, but after a little while a split occurs, and yesterday's enemies become friends again today, and join together to fight those who yesterday were friends but today are enemies, in interminable chaos. And things are this way within the party, too. At any time you can see a group of private individuals uniting, but you never see an ideological group. . . .

Average comrades should know why our party is called a "system of democratic centralism." What is the meaning of the word "democratic"? This system requires that in their intra-party activities members of our party must adopt democratic methods and observe the discipline which is the crystallization of the common will. Discipline is the party's will, and the democratic activities of party members form the basis for the creation of the party's will in accordance with the members' wills. If party members lack the democratic spirit, and their activities do not comply with democratic forms, the true will of the majority of party members cannot be thoroughly manifested. If party discipline is not obeyed, our party will completely lose its organizational effectiveness. Ever since the reorganization [of 1923–24], many old party members, because they are deeply affected by the poisons of liberalism and individualism and have never sincerely studied [the party's] ideology, have lacked correct beliefs. Some have even forgotten the word "people" in the term "people of the nation [*kuo-min*]." Since they have become officials, and are addressed as Your Honor, they act like mandarins. In the recent reorganization, democracy was created in form and method, so that every single party member, no matter what his position, is uniformly equal within the party organization. But how do you expect men who have grown accustomed to thinking of themselves as superior suddenly one day to be willing to stand on the same level as people they are used to regarding as inferior? Another most pitiful situation is that those from the political world of old China have completely lost the desire to try to improve their knowledge. Of those old revolutionaries who have come close to political and military power after the revolution, 70 to 80 percent make absolutely no effort to improve their knowledge. And so, because their knowledge is substandard, they grow terribly afraid of relatively knowledgeable young people. They fear that under a democratic system, they will be suppressed by the knowledge possessed by these young people. For all these various reasons, they are unwilling to create a strict organization, and still hope to restore the permissive ways that used to exist. But they cannot express their opposition in theory, so the only thing for them to do is to resist passively or do things in a perfunctory manner, by not registering or applying for party identification, or by registering but not attending party meetings. This kind of behavior indirectly and directly shakes the foundations of the party and, moreover, causes young people to lose their trust in the old revolutionaries, and even, because of this, to become skeptical about the Three People's Principles. It is a very big shortcoming that many middle-aged party members are unwilling to attend party meetings. The middle-aged are the pillars of the nation, the hard core of society, and the basis of the party's political work. If they abandon their important responsibility of serving the nation and society, and are only concerned about their own self-interests, and think of their own convenience, the nation and society will lose its center, and this, of course, could result in a grotesque change. . . . In intra-party activities, party members should bear in mind the words "fight for a majority decision." Exerting oneself to the utmost in activities, using the right method to fight to win a majority decision, is the only road a party member should follow. If one's proposal is defeated, one must submit to the decision of the majority, and if later one once again wants to put one's ideas into practice, as always, one should use the right method, and once again bring up one's views at the proper meeting, and solicit the agreement of the majority. . . . I can say with certainty that any party member who does not obey democratic principles in his party activities absolutely cannot be a true republican citizen in society and in politics. If this kind of party member leads troops, he will certainly become a war lord; if he is a government official, he will certainly become a bureaucrat; if he does local work, he will certainly become a bad gentry who cheats and oppresses the rural people; and if he works in business, he will certainly become a dishonest merchant who mistreats the workers.

As for the meaning of "centralism," that is very clear. In its programs and activities, our party completely takes the views of the Central Committee as the highest views of the entire party. The reason why we have chosen this centralized concentration of power is that if we want to reform Chinese government and society, we must gather together the views of Chinese revolutionaries, and create a solid and powerful leadership organ, which has tight-knit organization and strict training, and which issues strict orders, in order to put the revolutionary ideology into practice. From the point of view of theory, in today's scientific, advanced industrial world, all social organizations, under the principle of unified motivating power, practice the division of labor and the concentration of tasks. A political party is a society too, and it of course cannot deviate from this principle. Only in this way can the organizational spirit of the division of labor and the concentration of tasks be carried out thoroughly. But let us not talk about that any more. It can be comprehended simply from the history of the past failure of the revolution. A revolutionary party, in which everyone fought his own battles, like a sheet of loose sand, would definitely be incapable of bearing the heavy responsibility of this reform. . . . To begin with, it is extremely difficult for our party in its present condition to complete democratic centralism. Eighty percent of this difficulty is a result of the poor foundation of Chinese society, and the great inadequacy of training for democracy. Too few people both possess the ability to be active in democratic organizations and have studied politics and economics. [Most] don't have a cultivated knowledge of organization and discipline, and, on the most elementary point, don't even know the common rules for holding meetings. These are all deficiencies in Chinese politics and society, and also the reason why it has been impossible to build the foundation for a republic. It has not been easy to implement a democratic system in a short time in a Kuomintang organized with this kind of people as raw material.

70. IDEOLOGY AS THE FOUNDATION OF PARTY UNITY
[From Tai Chi-t'ao, *The Road for Youth*, 1928]

. . . Among the many comrades in our party since the reorganization—old, young, men, women, middle-aged, youthful—there are some who, although they never actually say so, have doubts in their hearts about the ideology of the Director General [Sun Yat-sen], who believe that it contains errors and inadequacies. This doubt is the greatest danger to the party, for we must realize that the cohesion of the party depends upon its ideology. What is ideology? The Director General said, "Ideology is a kind of thought. It must be internally consistent in order to generate belief, and there must be belief in order to generate strength." This strength can only arise through belief. . . . Unity depends solely upon men's hearts [or minds: *hsin*], and unless men's thoughts and beliefs are the same, there can be no unity. Only if there is common thought and belief can there be mutual trust, can we attack our external enemies and assist our comrades within the party. Everyone assembling together in a room cannot be called unity. . . . Just look at our party, which at present has almost a million members. Which of them can know hundreds or thousands, can remember the names of hundreds, thousands, or tens of thousands, and know their personalities too? This is impossible, and all the more so when there are hundreds of thousands, or millions, some as far away as Europe, and even the closer ones are scattered over the various provinces. Hence, it is not a territorial group, nor the political party of an association of people in the same occupation. Especially in a revolutionary party, unity can depend only upon thought and belief. If comrades have doubts about the ideology which forms the core of our party, and towards the basic principles derived from the ideology, no matter how many party members there may be, they are a sheet of loose sand, and the more there are, the more dangerous it is. . . . Why could the Kuomintang be manipulated by the Communist Party, causing trouble? Because within our party there are some members who harbor doubts about the teachings bequeathed by the Director General, and are unable to have common beliefs and mutual trust or join hearts and work together. Long ago I saw two centers of thought appearing in the party. When I saw that many members had never believed the Director General's ideology, I knew that the foundation of our party was already shaky. And among cadre comrades at that time, not only were there some who did not strive to work for the unification of thought, but there were even some who went from bad to worse, thinking of expelling loyal and faithful followers of the Director General from the party. There were a few cadres whose party work was very important, who held high posts, and were quite prominent, and who can be considered loyal to the party and the nation. They were not members of both parties, and they also recognized the importance of the national revolution. When I asked them, "What is your view of the thought and ideology of the Director General?" they answered, "I have doubts." When I said, "Since you have doubts, you shouldn't be a member of the Kuomintang," they said, "I came to work for the revolution. So long as we carry through the revolution, why should everyone have the same beliefs?" Now think a moment. Under such conditions, can we still say that our party has a foundation, an organization, or strength? After the Director General died, I saw this threat, and loudly and boldly stated, "Without a common faith, there will be no mutual trust." If you doubt me and I doubt you, you will be afraid that I am going to attack you, and I will fear that you are going to attack me. And so you will organize a faction, and someone else will organize a faction, and then what party organization or party discipline will there be to speak of?

71. PROBLEMS OF LOCAL GOVERNMENT
[From C. M. Chang, "A New Government for Rural China," 1936]

. . . The prestige of the office of magistracy has in recent years greatly declined. Men of genuine ability are seldom attracted to it. Those who become magistrates are not usually animated by a spirit of service, but are prompted by a desire to become a "mandarin" or, worse still, to get rich quickly. It is true that a majority of the magistrates at present are, according to the statistics of the Ministry of Interior, graduates of universities and law colleges. But it is also true that the reason for their appointment is probably not so much due to their special attainment in any field of work as to their family connections or friends. "Pull" goes farther than merit. The prerequisite for a successful magistrate after appointment is the possession of an ability to ingratiate himself with his superiors by his attentions and a show of deference. Only in very exceptional cases does he find himself promoted merely on the basis of his being a good administrator.

Ever since the establishment of the Republic, civil service examinations have been held from time to time both by the National and Central authorities to select qualified persons to be magistrates. But owing to the absence of real authority of the Central Government to enforce the Civil Service Laws, persons who have passed the examinations wait in vain for appointment. And those who hold the office are not necessarily persons who have passed the examinations.

If the magistrate himself is often ignorant of what is required of him as the chief executive of the *hsien*, how much more are his subordinates! ... The bureau and section chiefs are probably as efficient in their work as we can expect them to be, considering the beggarly salaries they receive. Below them are a host of petty officers who are competent in the sense that they know the mysteries of their work intimately as no section or bureau chief can pretend to know. These petty officers include the scribes, the archive-keepers, the tax collectors, the tax farmers, persons who serve judicial notices to litigants, etc. They learn their work by apprenticeship through years of labor and drudgery. They consider their jobs as "legal commissions" to be handed down from father to son or sold to the highest bidder. They receive no salary from the government. They make a living by manipulating accounts, by other recognized means of "squeezing," and by extortion. In the absence of a body of civil servants in the modern sense, they are indispensable to the government. A magistrate holds his office ... only for a very short time. He is ignorant of the details of administration. He has no idea how taxes are collected or archives are kept. He is content to leave the "dirty job" to these "experts." As long as the routine of his office runs smoothly, he refuses to look into the details. If he is a strong man the best he can do is to keep these fellows in proper check, i.e., to keep their manipulations and extortions within bounds. The voluminous manuals written by experienced administrators from times immemorial for the guidance of magistrates devote considerable space to the means of keeping these petty officers in check. But it never occurred to these eminent writers to devise a new system. The reason is not far to seek. The *ya-yi* or *hsü-li*, as these fellows are collectively called in common parlance, are considered lowly in social standing. No respectful man would think for a moment of associating with them. Thus, the most important work of *hsien* administration is left to a band of rascals, parasites, and ruffians.

The fundamental problem of *hsien* government is, therefore, the creation of an effective administrative system, staffed by persons trained in the modern science of administration. If the Chinese state is to be a reality, it must show the people that government, instead of a burden, can be an organ of effective service. The *hsien* government, among all grades of government, stands closest to the common mass. It is precisely here that concrete results of good government can be demonstrated to best advantage. . . .

. . . [T]he Provincial Government in China does nothing but interfering with the work of *hsien* government. There is no clear line of demarcation between the powers of the province and those of the *hsien*. Anything that the *hsien* undertakes to do must have the express permission of the Provincial Government. There is nothing that the province cannot compel the *hsein* government to do irrespective of the latter's ability and competence. The *hsien* is the final depository of all things. Almost anything can be unloaded on it by means of an order. . . . For instance, the Commissioner of Reconstruction of the Provincial Government may think it an excellent thing, as indeed it is, to reforest the bare mountains of the province. An order is forthwith given to all *hsien* under its jurisdiction to do so within a fixed period of time. It may happen that a particular *hsien* has no mountains within its boundaries. Much time is wasted in convincing the Commissioner of the fact. Now, the Commissioner of Education has the brilliant idea of increasing the number of primary schools. The *hsien* government is called upon to take immediate steps to do so. The magistrate, if he is conscientious, does his best to comply with the wishes of his superior. But he has to find the required money for the project. A certain kind of tax has to be levied or new surcharges have to be added. He petitions the Commissioner of Finance for authorization. Now the Commissioner of Finance refuses, quite legitimately, to sanction the proposal on the ground that the peasants have already been over-taxed and that any attempt to impose additional burdens upon an impoverished peasantry is to be discouraged. The poor magistrate is left in the lurch.

The conflicting and contradictory orders have somewhat been alleviated recently by the consolidation of the various departments of the Provincial Government. But the fundamental problem remains. . . . If the *hsien* government is to function properly it must be given sufficient authority to decide upon things that are eminently local in character. The line of demarcation between what belongs to the sphere of provincial authority and what belongs to the *hsien* must be drawn. Without such a distinction the *hsien* will forever remain an agent of the provincial government. The energy of the magistrate, instead of being used to promote the welfare of the people under his charge, will be dissipated in the drafting of an endless number of replies to provincial orders. Administration degenerates into mere correspondence. The result is that politics too often ends where it should begin, with the assertion of intentions. A clever magistrate is one who engages a good secretary who has at his command an excellent literary style which, like charity, covers a multitude of sins. The provincial orders will then be carried out beautifully on paper and nothing further will be asked of them. An old hand at the game knows that since the orders are so numerous, no one is expected to take them seriously. A well-composed official document goes a long way. . . .

In a very striking manner, the government in China has been a government from without. The *hsien* government has never been a part of the people. It has been regarded more as an instrument of oppression than as an agency of service. It has been responsible in part for the lack of public spirit on the part of the Chinese people. The general mass of the people are apathetic to and suspicious of the process of government. A vivid and creative local life is impossible under the circumstances. A gradual introduction of some degree of local self-government is imperative. . . .

. . . With a highly trained body of officers imbued with the ideals of service and equipped with modern technique of administration, endowed with sufficient powers and subject to little unnecessary interference and obstruction, and supplied with adequate sources of revenue,[1] a more effective local government could be developed. Naturally, there are numerous difficulties in the way. History, tradition, and vested interests hamper reconstruction. But sooner or later the obstacles must be cleared away. In the end, when genuine reconstruction is effected, we shall find ourselves better equipped to meet the needs of the common people.

72. PROBLEMS OF INDUSTRIALIZING

[From H. D. Fong, *Cotton Industry and Trade in China*, 1932]

Among the factors retarding the development of China's cotton industry, the most important is undoubtedly the chaotic political conditions that prevail today. The recurrence of civil war entails an increasing burden of taxation, gives rise to the uncertainty of transport, reduces the area of cotton production, and shuts off the market within the war area. It interrupts normal operation, and saps the vitality of almost every industry. Capital, instead of being invested in profitable channels, is concentrated in a few port cities and deposited in the vaults of a few reliable banks, sometimes actually at a negative rate of interest. Under such circumstances, new mills can be erected only in a few exceptionally favored spots, while old ones are hard pressed from all sides by the increasing burden of taxation, the growing uncertainty of transport, the declining supply of raw cotton, the decreasing size of the market, and above all, the higher rate of interest for running capital.

Other factors, mainly economic, are more or less inherent in the transition of China from a medieval to a modern economic order. . . . In China's cotton industry, the largest factory industry today, the economic factors are at work everywhere. The textile machinery can be imported wholesale from foreign countries, but its efficient operation demands a managing and working staff which is impossible to train overnight. The large scale organization on a share basis can be copied from the writings of the West, but its application as an instrument of prudent investment requires the necessary capitalistic traits which are as yet absent in the Chinese manufacturers. As a result, the native owned mills in China, unlike the foreign owned ones, have not proven to be

---

[1] The author proposed that the land taxes should be given to the *hsien*.

profit-making enterprises except during the abnormal period of the World War. The lack of capital, the corruption of management, and the inefficiency of labor—all these become at once fundamental factors retarding the development of Chinese owned mills.

The lack of capital, applying chiefly to the Chinese owned mills, is the most important of the economic factors. A Chinese owned mill is handicapped at the very beginning by the insufficiency of capital. The mill, after having its plan for a certain size in respect of building and machinery made out on the basis of the subscribed capital and approved by the board of directors, starts to place orders with the building contractors and foreign importers of textile machinery. But before the arrival of machinery or the completion of building, it is confronted with the practical difficulty of having to collect the full share of the subscribed capital, because in the cotton as in many other industries, the subscribed capital is seldom paid up to the full amount. This difficulty is enhanced by a second practice, that of heavy investment in fixed assests. . . . "The big sums of money [mills] made in . . . golden times," according to a leading millowner in Shanghai who has himself been the victim of insufficient capital, "were used up in extending existing plants. Only a very small percentage was set aside for reserve. So when hard times come, their financial conditions are just as tight as ever, although their assets may be larger, i.e., they may have more spindles than before. But this fact, as can readily be seen, makes it still harder for them to finance." . . .

Poor management is another economic factor retarding the development of China's cotton industry. The whole system of management among Chinese owned mills is usually polluted by ignorance, favoritism and squeeze. In particular, the mills established by inexperienced men who were attracted solely by the magnetism of huge profits during the war period are utterly inefficient. The whole plant, worth millions of dollars, may be entrusted to a manager who knows nothing about spinning. The latter, usually the trusted appointee of the most influential stockholder, has frequently neither a grasp of the technical complexity of spinning and weaving, nor a knowledge of cost accounting, financing and marketing. Instead, he delegates his duties to subordinates, and relies upon the good turn of luck for the mill's profits. In such a mill, the head of the spinning and weaving department, oftentimes a close friend or relative of the manager or the stockholder, considers his job as the source of squeeze, and delegates in turn his duties to one of the foremen, who, although skilled in mechanics, lacks scientific training. Consequently, machinery is not well kept, and is not running in an efficient order. Laborers are not well selected and trained, but recruited under the notorious contract system. The finished products deteriorate in quality, while their cost mounts higher and higher. In time of short supply like during the war, profits are easily made, and these deficiencies ignored. But once "normalcy" returns with the end of the war, these mills are immediately confronted with foreign competitors who have not only a superior command of capital and technique, but also a better marketing organization.

Labor inefficiency constitutes a third economic factor retarding the rapid development of Chinese mills. In the past, too much has been written about the cheapness of Chinese labor because of wretchedly low wages. But labor is not cheap because wages are low. On the contrary, low wages in China are partly if not wholly responsible for the high cost of labor [because of the low efficiency of the cheap, unskilled and semiskilled labor].

73. CHINESE SOCIAL STRUCTURE AND ITS VALUES
[From Fei Hsiao-t'ung, *Rural China*, 1948]

... [T]he greatest fault of rural China has always been self-centeredness [*ssu*]. At the mention of self-centeredness, we may immediately think of the common saying, "Everyone sweeps away the snow in front of his own gate, but pays no attention to the frost on other people's roofs." No one would dare deny that this saying is to some extent the creed of the Chinese people. Actually, not only the rural people hold this attitude; the so-called city people are just the same. Those who do sweep the snow from their own gates can actually be considered terribly public-spirited—most people dump their garbage on the street in front of their gates and forget about it. In Suchow, the rear doors of the houses frequently open upon a stream. One always hears about Suchow's unsurpassed beauty—in the writings of the literati it is the Venice of China. But I think that no canals in the world are filthier than those in Suchow. Anything may be dumped into these small waterways, which do not flow very freely in the first place. Not a few families need no toilets at all. Everyone knows perfectly well that people wash clothes and rinse vegetables in these streams, but they don't feel it necessary to restrain themselves in any way. And why? Because these streams are public [*kung-chia-te*].

As soon as you say they are public, it's almost the same as saying everyone can take advantage of it, that they have rights without responsibilities. Even in so small a matter as two or three families living in the same courtyard, the common passageways are normally dirty and the yard is overgrown with wild grass and weeds, which no one thinks of clearing away. And of course it is more difficult to find a place to put your feet down in the outhouse. No family wants to butt into "others' business"; whoever can't stand the sight can perform this service [of cleaning up the mess] free of charge for the rest—without getting half a word of thanks. And so, like Gresham's Law that bad money drives out good money, civic virtue is driven out by selfishness.

From these examples, one can see that in China the fault of self-centeredness is far more widespread than ignorance or disease. It seems that everyone on every level of society suffers from this fault. It has become a handy weapon which foreign opinion uses to attack us. So-called corruption and incompetence are certainly not a question of the innate ability of every individual. Rather, they are relative, referring to the individual's duties and responsibilities to the public. Chinese are not bad at managing businesses—just look at the business achievements of overseas Chinese in Southeast Asia. Don't all Westerners look at them with envy? And Chinese are not incompetent; in matters concerning themselves and their families, in money-grabbing and flattery, they are the most capable people in the world. Consequently, the problem of what I have been calling "self-centeredness" is a question of how to draw the demarcation line between the group and the self [*chi*], between "them" and "me." Our traditional way of drawing this line obviously differs from the Western way. Consequently, in order to discuss the problem of self-centeredness, we must take into consideration the entire configuration of the social structure.

In some ways Western society bears a resemblance to the way we bundle kindling wood in the fields. A few rice stalks are bound together to make a handful, several handfuls are bound together to make a small bundle, several small bundles are bound together to make a larger bundle, and several larger bundles are bound together to make a stack to carry on a pole. Every single stalk in the entire stack belongs to one specific large bundle, one specific small bundle, and one specific handful. Similar stalks are assembled together, clearly classified, and then bound together. In a society, these units are groups. I say that Western social organization resembles a bundle of kindling wood in order to make clear that Westerners frequently form separate groups from numbers of people. The group has a definite demarcation line. There is no ambiguity over who is and who is not a member of the group; it is quite clearly defined. Members of the group are partners, all sharing the same relation to the group. If there are subdivisions or ranks within the group, these are stipulated in advance. My analogy to a bundle of kindling wood is not quite accurate in one point; that is, one person can participate in many groups, but it is of course impossible for one particular stalk to be in many bundles of kindling wood. This is the difference between men and kindling wood. I have used this analogy so as to enable us to see more concretely a kind of configuration of personal relations in social life, which may be called a "group configuration."

In the West, the family is a group with clearly demarcated boundaries. If a friend writes you a letter saying that he is going to "bring his family" to visit you, you know very well who will be coming with him. In China, this phrase is extremely vague. In England and America, the family comprises the man, his wife, and their children not yet of age. If he were only bringing his wife, he would not use the word "family." In China, although we frequently see the phrase "Your entire family is invited," very few people could say exactly which persons really should be included under "family." . . . Why are our terms for this most basic social unit so lacking in clarity? In my view, this shows that our social structure differs from the Western configuration. Our configuration is not like a bundle of firewood neatly bound together, but rather like the rings of successive ripples that are propelled outward on the surface when you throw a stone into water. Each individual is the center of the rings emanating from his social influence. Wherever the ripples reach, affiliations occur. The rings used by each person at any given time or place are not necessarily the same.

The most important kinship relations in our society have the characteristics of these ripples of concentric circles formed by throwing a stone. Kinship relations are social relationships based on the facts of birth and marriage. The network formed by birth and marriage can emanate outward to include an infinite number of persons, past, present, and future. . . . This network, like a spider's web, has a center, which is oneself. Every one of us has such a web of kinship relations, but no web covers the same people as another. The people in a society [of this kind] can use the same system to identify their kin relations, but they share only this system. A system is an abstract configuration, a conceptual category. When we apply this system to identify actual relatives, those recognized by each person are different. Within the kinship system we all have parents, but my parents are not your parents. To go one step further, it is impossible for any two people in the world to have the exact same relatives. Brothers of course have the same parents, but each has his own wife and children. Consequently, the network of social relations formed by the affiliations of kinship relations is particularistic. Every network has a "self" as center, and the center of each and every network is different.

In our rural society, not only are kinship relations of this sort, but territorial relations as well. . . . In the traditional structure, each family takes its position as the center, and draws a ring around it. This ring is the "neighborhood." When there is a wedding, you have to invite the neighbors to a banquet; when a child is born you must give them red eggs; and when there is a funeral you have to help out and carry the coffin. This is an organization for mutual assistance in life. But there is no fixed group; instead, there is a sphere. The size of the sphere is determined by the amount of influence of the center. The neighborhood of an influential family can extend throughout the entire village, while the neighborhood of a poor family is only two or three next-door neighbors. This resembles our ring of kinship relations. Like the Ta Kuan Yuan of the Chia family [in *Dream of the Red Chamber*], . . . anyone who is related in any way can be included. But as soon as there is a reversal of fortune, it shrinks into a small group—when the tree falls the monkeys scatter. At the extreme, it can be like Su Ch'in [an impoverished itinerant scholar of the Warring States period] returning home a failure: "His wife did not consider him her husband and his elder brother's wife did not consider him her brother-in-law." Such is the elasticity of the differentially ordered configuration[1] of China's traditional structure. In rural areas, the family can be very small, but when it comes to wealthy landlord and bureaucratic strata, it can be as large as a small state. Chinese are particularly sensitive to the fickleness of the world precisely because this highly elastic social ring can alter in size due to changes in the influence of the center.

In Western society, where grown-up children who live with their parents have to contribute toward their room and board, everyone recognizes the group's boundaries. Those within the group have definite qualifications. Those who lose these qualifications must leave the group. For them this is not a question of their feelings running hot and cold, but a question of rights. In Western society the object of struggle is rights, while for us it is to make good connections and doing things for the sake of friendship.

[1] *Ch'a-hsü ko-chü;* I can find no satisfactory translation for this key term, but its meaning should be clear from the context and from the analogy of concentric rings of waves on the water.

Social relations formed by affiliations with others, with the "self " as center like a stone thrown into water, differ from elements in a group where everyone stands more or less on the same plane. They resemble the ripples on water propelled outward one after another—the more they are propelled the further they go, and the further they go, the more faint they become. And here we have located the basic characteristic of the Chinese social structure. Our Confucians are most fastidious about human relationships *[jen-lun]*. And just what are these relationships? In my view, they are the differentially ordered rings of ripples emanating outward from oneself and produced by the persons with whom one has formed social relationships. . . . Indeed, the most basic concept in our traditional social structure, this order of the network formed by associations between individuals, is just this differential order, which is human relationships. . . .

Within this highly flexible network, there is always a "self" as center. This is *not* individualism *[ko-jen chu-i]*, but rather egoism *[tzu-wo-chu-i]*. The term individual is used in contrast to group, an element to the whole. In individualism there is, on the one hand, the concept of equality, that within the same group each constituent element's position is equal, that no individual can violate others' rights; on the other hand there is the constitutional concept, that the group may not obliterate the individual, but only control individuals according to the portion of their rights which they have willingly entrusted to the group. These concepts necessarily presuppose the existence of a group. No such thing exists in our traditional Chinese thought, because what we have is egoism, the ideology whereby the "self" is the center of all value. . . .

Once we comprehend this social sphere capable of extending or withdrawing, of stretching or contracting, we can understand the problem of self-centeredness in Chinese society. I often think "Chinese can sacrifice the family for themselves, their party for their family, their country for their party, or the world for their country." . . . Sacrificing the family for oneself, sacrificing the clan for the family—this formula is an actual fact. Under such a formula, what would someone say if you called him self-centered? He would not be able to see it that way, because when he sacrificed his clan, he might have done it for his family, and the way he looks at it, his family is the common interest *[kung]*. When he sacrificed the nation for the benefit of his small group in the struggle for power, he was also doing it for the common interest—for the common interest of his small group. Within a differentially ordered configuration, common interest and selfishness *[ssu]* are relative terms; anything within the circle in which one is standing can be called common [or public: *kung*]. . . .

In a differentially ordered configuration, our social relationships are extended gradually outward from each individual person, the accumulation of personal affiliations. The sphere of society is the network interwoven, thread by thread, by these personal affiliations. Consequently, what social morality we do possess takes on significance only within these personal affiliations. . . .

In a differentially ordered configuration, there are no moral concepts which transcend personal relationships. This kind of concept must occur in a group configuration. Filial piety, brotherly love, loyalty, and trustworthiness are all moral components of a system of personal relationships.[2] [Fei next argues that even the key Confucian concept of *jen,* benevolence, was also particularistic, and as such entirely different from the Christian concept of universal love.]

A society with a differentially ordered configuration is a network interwoven of innumerable personal relationships. To each knot in the network is affixed a moral component. Accordingly, within traditional morality one cannot additionally find a moral concept of a universal nature. No criterion of value can transcend the differentially ordered human relationships.

Consequently, Chinese morality and law depend on the relationship between oneself and the object to which they apply, plus the degree of elasticity. I have seen many friends who castigate corruption, but who, when they discovered their fathers were corrupt, not only did not castigate them, but covered up for them. And furthermore, they might also ask their fathers for some of the money obtained through corruption, while at the same time castigating other people's corruption. And when they themselves became corrupt, they can rationalize it as "being able to get things done." In a differentially ordered society, this is not necessarily felt to be a contradiction, because in this kind of society, no universal norm has any effect. One must find out exactly who one is dealing with and his relation to oneself before one can decide which standard to use [in dealing with him].

[2]Fei gives the following explanation of what he means by moral concepts: "Moral concepts are beliefs which people living in society feel they should observe as rules of social behavior. They include rules of action, beliefs of the actors, and social constraints. Their contents are the rules of behavior in interpersonal relations, which are determined in accordance with the configuration of society. From the viewpoint of society, morality is the social force constraining individual actions to make them abide by the prescribed forms, which function to preserve the society's existence and continuity."

CHAPTER TEN
The Rise
of the
Communist Party

The founding of the Chinese Communist Party in 1921 was part of the New Culture Movement. The cofounders were Ch'en Tu-hsiu and Li Ta-chao, and most of the other early members were also urban intellectuals who saw Marxism as the answer to China's problems. In 1924, under the guidance of Comintern advisors, the small party joined together with the KMT in a united front, and many Communists played important roles in the reunification drive of 1925–27.

One of these was Mao Tse-tung (1893–1976), who was active in the movement to mobilize the peasants in his native province of Hunan. "Report on an Investigation of the Peasant Movement in Hunan," based on his experiences there, is an early statement of his faith in the revolutionary potential of the peasantry. (Selection 74) Mao's main point is disarmingly simple: those with the least vested interest in the existing social order are most eager to overthrow it. In his analysis, the revolutionary impulse is more moral than economic, aimed at destroying all forms of subjugation, familial and religious as well as economic and political, and the moral rightness of this goal justifies the excesses he sees as an inevitable part of the revolutionary process.

Chiang Kai-shek's expulsion of the Communists from the united front and the suppression of the worker and peasant movements brought an end to the revolutionary wave. In the following years, the center of Communist activities gradually shifted from the cities to the countryside, and

Mao's position in the party rose. By the mid-1930s, after the Long March, the CCP was established in Yenan, in the northwestern province of Shensi, and Mao had become its leader.

The Japanese threat brought about a second united front between the KMT and the CCP. During the war against Japan, the CCP attracted large numbers of peasants and young patriotic intellectuals, many of whom joined the party to help in the fight against the foreign invaders. The rapid influx of so many new members not necessarily committed to all the party's policies made discipline an important issue, and elicited several works on the subject, of which "How to Be a Good Communist," by Liu Shao-ch'i (1898?–1973) was to become the best known. (Selection 75) Originally a speech in 1939, in its printed form it was a principal text in the party rectification campaign several years later, and was much more widely read after the establishment of the People's Republic, when Liu rose to a position second only to Mao.

On the assumption that the party is the instrument of history, Liu argues that it must maintain its purity so that it will not be diverted from its course. All party members must therefore subordinate themselves to the party. Liu's references to Confucius and Mencius, as well as to European Marxist leaders, show that this self-discipline in the public interest was not a new, alien idea. Also significant are the kinds of ideological deviations Liu ascribes to erring party members, some of which should not be unfamiliar, and many of which were to continue to trouble the party in later years. As in Tai Chi-t'ao's analysis of the KMT, ideology is the source of party unity. The two ideologies were of course different, and, as Liu points out, the relationship between theory and practice was a crucial matter. While members of the KMT developed a reputation for putting their own interests first, the Communists were better able to maintain discipline as their party grew.

Discipline was also central to the conception of the Red Army as an army of the people. Its famous code was simple, direct, and easy to learn. (Selection 76) Numerous observers, of whom the New Zealand journalist James Bertram was typical, commented on the excellent relations between Communist troops and the people. (Selection 77)

Service to the people for the revolution is also the theme of Mao's "Talks at the Yenan Forum on Art and Literature." These lectures, originally part of the party rectification campaign of 1941–44, became the standard work on Communist policy toward the arts. (Selection 78) Mao's repeated references to petit bourgeois intellectuals reflect a major concern of the leadership, for at this time many educated party members were dissatisfied with what they felt to be the party's dogmatism on a number of issues. Mao's response is the same as Liu's. The views of the party are correct because it is the vanguard of the class destined by history to forge the future. Other views serve the interests of other classes, and hence have no place in the party of the proletariat. Mao argues that since literature and art derive from social life, they have political implications and effects, and therefore fall within the sphere of party supervision. Like

Lenin, and like Liang Ch'i-ch'ao, Mao judges art by its political utility at a given historical time. This relativistic standard is directly related to his egalitarianism. Since all culture comes from social life, and since the new culture is for the people, it cannot be created by an elite isolated from the lives of the people, but only through a process in which creation, elevation, and dissemination occur simultaneously and in conjunction. There are no logical grounds for any aesthetic criticism of the new culture, since the only nonpolitical standards by which it can be judged are immanent in its own development. Mao's position is thus the opposite of Hu Shih's. These ideas were to have immense consequences for culture and education in the People's Republic.

In the meantime, the rectification campaign helped to prepare the CCP for the postwar period. In the civil war between the CCP and the KMT following the Japanese surrender, the relative superiority of the Communists' organization, discipline, and morale contributed greatly to their victory over the Nationalists.

74. THE PEASANTS AS A REVOLUTIONARY FORCE

[From Mao Tse-tung, "Report on an Investigation of the Peasant Movement in Hunan," 1927]

The Importance of the Peasant Problem

During my recent visit to Hunan I made a first-hand investigation of conditions in the five districts of Hsiangtan, Hsianghsiang, Hengshan, Liling and Changsha. In the thirty-two days from January 4 to February 5, I called together fact-finding conferences in villages and district seats, which were attended by experienced peasants and by comrades working in the peasant movement, and I listened attentively to their reports and collected a great deal of material. Many of the hows and whys of the peasant movement were the exact opposite of what the gentry in Hankow and Changsha are saying. I saw and heard of many strange things of which I had hitherto been unaware. I believe the same is true of many other places, too. All talk directed against the peasant movement must be speedily corrected. Only thus can the future of the revolution be benefited. For the present upsurge of the peasant movement is a colossal event. In a very short time, in China's central, southern and northern provinces, several hundred million peasants will rise like a mighty storm, like a hurricane, a force so swift and violent that no power, however great, will be able to hold it back. They will smash all the shackles that bind them and rush forward along the road to liberation. They will sweep all the imperialists, warlords, corrupt officials, local tyrants and evil gentry into their graves. Every revolutionary party and every revolutionary comrade will be put to the test,

to be accepted or rejected as they decide. There are three alternatives. To
march at their head and lead them? To trail behind them gesticulating and
criticizing? Or to stand in their way and oppose them? Every Chinese is free
to choose, but events will force you to make the choice quickly. . . .

Down with the Local Tyrants and Evil Gentry! All Power to the Peasant Associations!

The main targets of attack by the peasants are the local tyrants, the evil
gentry and the lawless landlords, but in passing they also hit out against
patriarchal ideas and institutions, against the corrupt officials in the cities and
against bad practices and customs in the rural areas. In force and momentum
the attack is tempestuous; those who bow before it survive and those who resist
perish. As a result, the privileges which the feudal landlords enjoyed for
thousands of years are being shattered to pieces. Every bit of the dignity and
prestige built up by the landlords is being swept into the dust. With the collapse
of the power of the landlords, the peasant associations have now become the
sole organs of authority and the popular slogan "All power to the peasant
associations" has become a reality. Even trifles such as a quarrel between
husband and wife are brought to the peasant association. Nothing can be
settled unless someone from the association is present. The association actually
dictates all rural affairs, and, quite literally, "whatever it says, goes". Those
who are outside the associations can only speak well of them and cannot say
anything against them. The local tyrants, evil gentry and lawless landlords
have been deprived of all right to speak, and none of them dares even mutter
dissent. In the face of the peasant associations' power and pressure, the top
local tyrants and evil gentry have fled to Shanghai, those of the second rank
to Hankow, those of the third to Changsha and those of the fourth to the
district seats, while the fifth rank and the still lesser fry surrender to the
peasant associations in the villages.

"Here's ten yuan. Please let me join the peasant association," one of the
smaller evil gentry will say.

"Ugh! Who wants your filthy money?" the peasants reply. . . .

"It's Terrible!" or "It's Fine!"

The peasants' revolt disturbed the gentry's sweet dreams. When the news
from the countryside reached the cities, it caused an immediate uproar among
the gentry. Soon after my arrival in Changsha, I met all sorts of people and
picked up a good deal of gossip. From the middle social strata upwards to the
Kuomintang right-wingers, there was not a single person who did not sum up
the whole business in the phrase, "It's terrible!" Under the impact of the views
of the "It's terrible!" school then flooding the city, even quite revolutionary-
minded people became down-hearted as they pictured the events in the countryside in their mind's eye; and they were unable to deny the word "terrible".
Even quite progressive people said, "Though terrible, it is inevitable in a
revolution." In short, nobody could altogether deny the word "terrible". But,

as already mentioned, the fact is that the great peasant masses have risen to fulfill their historic mission and that the forces of rural democracy have risen to overthrow the forces of rural feudalism. The patriarchal-feudal class of local tyrants, evil gentry and lawless landlords has formed the basis of autocratic government for thousands of years and is the cornerstone of imperialism, warlordism and corrupt officialdom. To overthrow these feudal forces is the real objective of the national revolution. In a few months the peasants have accomplished what Dr. Sun Yat-sen wanted, but failed, to accomplish in the forty years he devoted to the national revolution. This is a marvelous feat never before achieved, not just in forty, but in thousands of years. It's fine. It is not "terrible" at all. . . . What the peasants are doing is absolutely right; what they are doing is fine! "It's fine!" is the theory of the peasants and of all other revolutionaries. Every revolutionary comrade should know that the national revolution requires a great change in the countryside. The Revolution of 1911 did not bring about this change, hence its failure. This change is now taking place, and it is an important factor for the completion of the revolution. Every revolutionary comrade must support it, or he will be taking the stand of counter-revolution.

The Question of "Going Too Far"

Then there is another section of people who say, "Yes, peasant associations are necessary, but they are going rather too far." This is the opinion of the middle-of-the-roaders. But what is the actual situation? True, the peasants are in a sense "unruly" in the countryside. . . . At the slightest provocation they make arrests, crown the arrested with tall paper hats, and parade them through the villages, saying, "You dirty landlords, now you know who we are!" Doing whatever they like and turning everything upside down, they have created a kind of terror in the countryside. This is what some people call "going too far", or "exceeding the proper limits in righting a wrong", or "really too much". Such talk may seem plausible, but in fact it is wrong. First, the local tyrants, evil gentry and lawless landlords have themselves driven the peasants to do this. For ages they have used their power to tyrannize over the peasants and trample them underfoot; that is why the peasants have reacted so strongly. The most violent revolts and the most serious disorders have invariably occurred in places where the local tyrants, evil gentry and lawless landlords perpetrated the worst outrages. The peasants are clear-sighted. Who is bad and who is not, who is not quite so vicious, who deserves to be let off lightly—the peasants keep clear accounts, and very seldom has the punishment exceeded the crime. Secondly, a revolution is not a dinner party, or writing an essay, or painting a picture, or doing embroidery; it cannot be so refined, so leisurely and gentle, so temperate, kind, courteous, restrained and magnanimous.[1] A revolution is an insurrection, an act of violence by which one class overthrows another. A rural revolution is a revolution by which the peasantry overthrows the power of the feudal landlord class. Without using the greatest force, the peasants

---

[1] These were the virtues of Confucius, as described by one of his disciples.

cannot possibly overthrow the deep-rooted authority of the landlords which has lasted for thousands of years. The rural areas need a mighty revolutionary upsurge, for it alone can rouse the people in their millions to become a powerful force. All the actions mentioned here which have been labelled as "going too far" flow from the power of the peasants, which has been called forth by the mighty revolutionary upsurge in the countryside. . . . To put it bluntly, it is necessary to create terror for a while in every rural area, or otherwise it would be impossible to suppress the activities of the counter-revolutionaries in the countryside or overthrow the authority of the gentry. Proper limits have to be exceeded in order to right a wrong, or else the wrong cannot be righted. . . .

Vanguards of the Revolution

We said above that the peasants have accomplished a revolutionary task which had been left unaccomplished for many years and have done an important job for the national revolution. But has this great revolutionary task, this important revolutionary work, been performed by all the peasants? No. There are three kinds of peasants, the rich, the middle, and the poor peasants. The three live in different circumstances and so have different views about the revolution. [When] an official of the township peasant association . . . would walk into the house of a rich peasant, register in hand, and say, "Will you please join the peasant association?" how would the rich peasant answer? A tolerably well-behaved one would say, "Peasant association? I have lived here for decades, tilling my land. I never heard of such a thing before, yet I've managed to live all right. I advise you to give it up!" A really vicious rich peasant would say, "Peasant association! Nonsense! Association for getting your head chopped off! Don't get people into trouble!" . . .

How about the middle peasants? Theirs is a vacillating attitude. They think that the revolution will not bring them much good. They have rice cooking in their pots and no creditors knocking on their doors at midnight. They, too, judging a thing by whether it ever existed before, knit their brows and think to themselves, "Can the peasant association really last?" "Can the Three People's Principles prevail?" Their conclusion is, "Afraid not!" They imagine it all depends on the will of Heaven and think, "A peasant association? Who knows if Heaven wills it or not?" In the first period, people from the association would call on a middle peasant, register in hand, and say, "Will you please join the peasant association?" The middle peasant would reply, "There's no hurry!" It was not until the second period, when the peasant associations were already exercising great power, that the middle peasants came in. They show up better in the associations than the rich peasants but are not as yet enthusiastic; they still want to wait and see. It is essential for the peasant associations to get the middle peasants to join and to do a good deal more explanatory work among them.

The poor peasants have always been the main force in the bitter fight in the countryside. They have fought militantly through the two periods of underground work and of open activity. They are the most responsive to Communist

Party leadership. They are deadly enemies of the camp of the local tyrants and evil gentry and attack it without the slightest hesitation. . . . This great mass of poor peasants, or all together 70 percent of the rural population, are the backbone of the peasant associations, the vanguard in the overthrow of the feudal forces and the heroes who have performed the great revolutionary task which for long years was left undone. Without the poor peasant class (the "rifraff", as the gentry call them), it would have been impossible to bring about the present revolutionary situation in the countryside, or to overthrow the local tyrants and evil gentry and complete the democratic revolution. The poor peasants, being the most revolutionary group, have gained the leadership of the peasant associations. . . . Leadership by the poor peasants is absolutely necessary. Without the poor peasants there would be no revolution. To deny their role is to deny the revolution. To attack them is to attack the revolution. They have never been wrong on the general direction of the revolution. They have discredited the local tyrants and evil gentry. They have beaten down the local tyrants and evil gentry, big and small, and kept them underfoot. Many of their deeds in the period of revolutionary action, which were labelled as "going too far", were in fact the very things the revolution required. . . .

Overthrow the Clan Authority of the Ancestral Temples and Clan Elders, the Religious Authority of Town and Village Gods, and the Masculine Authority of Husbands.

A man in China is usually subjected to the domination of three systems of authority: (1) the state system (political authority), ranging from the national, provincial and district government down to that of the township; (2) the clan system (clan authority), ranging from the central ancestral temple and its branch temples down to the head of the household; and (3) the supernatural system (religious authority), ranging from the King of Hell down to the town and village gods belonging to the nether world, and from the Emperor of Heaven down to all the various gods and spirits belonging to the celestial world. As for women, in addition to being dominated by these three systems of authority, they are also dominated by the men (the authority of the husband). These four authorities—political, clan, religious and masculine—are the embodiment of the whole feudal-patriarchal system and ideology, and are the four thick ropes binding the Chinese people, particularly the peasants. How the peasants have overthrown the political authority of the landlords in the countryside has been described above. The political authority of the landlords is the backbone of all the other systems of authority. With that overturned, the clan authority, the religious authority and the authority of the husband all begin to totter. Where the peasant association is powerful, the clan elders and administrators of temple funds no longer dare oppress those lower in the clan hierarchy or embezzle clan funds. The worst clan elders and administrators, being local tyrants, have been thrown out. No one any longer dares to practise the cruel corporal and capital punishments that used to be inflicted in the ancestral temples, such as flogging, drowning and burying alive. The old rule barring women and poor people from the banquets in the ancestral temples has also been broken. . . . Everywhere religious authority totters as the peasant movement develops. In many places the peasant associations have taken over the temples of the gods as their offices. . . . In places where the power of the peasants is predominant, only the older peasants and the women still believe in the gods, the younger peasants no longer doing so. Since the latter control the associations, the overthrow of religious authority and the eradication of superstition are going on everywhere. As to the authority of the husband, this has always been weaker among the poor peasants because, out of economic necessity, their womenfolk have to do more manual labor than the women of the richer classes and therefore have more to say and greater power of decision in family matters. With the increasing bankruptcy of the rural economy in recent years, the basis for men's domination over women has already been weakened. With the rise of the peasant movement, the women in many places have now begun to organize rural women's associations; the opportunity has come for them to lift up their heads, and the authority of the husband is getting shakier every day. In a word, the whole feudal-patriarchal system and ideology is tottering with the growth of the peasants' power. At the present time, however, the peasants are concentrating on destroying the landlords' political authority. Wherever it has been wholly destroyed, they are beginning to press their attack in the three other spheres of the clan, the gods and male domination. But such attacks have only just begun, and there can be no thorough overthrow of all three until the peasants have won complete victory in the economic struggle. Therefore, our present task is to lead the peasants to put their greatest efforts into the political struggle, so that the landlords' authority is entirely overthrown. The economic struggle should follow immediately so that the land problem and the other economic problems of the poor peasants may be fundamentally solved. As for the clan system, superstition, and inequality between men and women, their abolition will follow as a natural consequence of victory in the political and economic struggles. If too much of an effort is made, arbitrarily and prematurely to abolish these things, the local tyrants and evil gentry will seize the pretext to put about such counter-revolutionary propaganda as "the peasant association has no piety towards ancestors", "the peasant association is blasphemous and is destroying religion" and "the peasant association stands for the communization of wives." . . .

The Cooperative Movement

The peasants really need cooperatives, and especially consumers', marketing and credit cooperatives. When they buy goods, the merchants exploit them; when they sell their farm produce, the merchants cheat them; when they borrow money or rice, they are fleeced by the usurers; and they are eager to find a solution to these three problems. . . . A major problem is the absence of detailed, standard rules of organization. . . . Given proper guidance, the cooperative movement can spread everywhere along with the growth of the peasant associations.

75. MAINTAINING PARTY IDEALS
[From Liu Shao-ch'i, "How to Be a Good Communist," 1939]

Comrades, why must Communist Party members undertake self-cultivation?

Ever since man came into the world, in order to be able to live, he has had to struggle against nature to produce the material values essential to his existence.

However, men carry on a struggle against nature and utilise nature for the production of material values not in isolation from each other, not as separate individuals, but in common, in groups, in societies. Production, therefore, is at all times and under all conditions *social* production. In the production of material values men enter into mutual relations of one kind or another within production, into relations of production of one kind or another. *(The History of the Communist Party of the Soviet Union (B), Short Course)*

Thus, the struggle carried on by men against nature is social in character. It is a struggle of men as social beings against nature. It is in this ceaseless struggle against nature that human beings have been continuously changing nature and simultaneously themselves and have changed their relations with one another. . . .

In other words, men change themselves not only in their struggle against nature but also in constant social struggle. The proletariat will also have to consciously go through a long period of social struggle to change society and itself.

Thus, men should regard themselves as being in need of, and capable of, being changed. They should not look upon themselves as something unchanging, perfect, holy and beyond reform. It is no disgrace to regard this as necessary because it conforms to the inevitable laws of natural and social evolution; otherwise, men cannot make progress.

We Communist Party members are the most advanced revolutionaries in modern history and are the contemporary fighting and driving force in changing society and the world. Revolutionaries exist because counter-revolutionaries still exist. Therefore, to conduct a ceaseless struggle against the counter-revolutionaries constitutes an essential condition for the existence and development of the revolutionaries. If they fail to carry on such a struggle, they cannot be called revolutionaries and still less can they advance and develop. It is in the course of this ceaseless struggle against the counter-revolutionaries that Communist Party members change society, change the world and at the same time change themselves. . . .

. . . [A]ll those who have succeeded in becoming very good and experienced revolutionaries must certainly have gone through long years of steeling and self-cultivation in the revolutionary struggle. Hence, our Party members can make themselves politically inflexible revolutionaries of high quality only by steeling themselves, strengthening their self-cultivation, not losing their sense

of the new and by improving their thinking ability in the course of the revolutionary struggle of the broad masses under all difficulties and hardships.
Confucius said:

At fifteen, I had my mind bent on learning. At thirty, I stood firm. At forty, I had no doubts. At fifty, I knew the decree of Heaven. At sixty, my ear was an obedient organ for the reception of truth. At seventy, I could follow my heart's desire, without transgressing what was right.

Here Confucius was relating the process of his steeling and self-cultivation. He did not regard himself as a born "sage."
Mencius said:

When Heaven is about to confer a great office on any man, it first exercises his mind with suffering, and his sinews and bones with toil. It exposes his body to hunger, and subjects him to extreme poverty. It confounds his undertakings. By all these methods it stimulates his mind, hardens his nature, and remedies his incompetencies.

What Mencius said also refers to the process of steeling and self-cultivation that a great man must undergo. As Communist Party members have to shoulder the unprecedentedly "great office" of changing the world, it is all the more necessary for them to go through such steeling and self-cultivation. . . .
Steeling and cultivation are important for every Party member, whether he be a new member of non-proletarian origin or even a veteran member of proletarian origin. This is because our Communist Party did not drop from the heavens but was born out of Chinese society and because every member of our Party came from this squalid old society of China and is still living in this society today. Hence, our Party members have more or less brought with them remnants of the ideology and habits of the old society and they remain in constant association with all the squalid things of the old society. We are still in need of steeling and cultivation in every respect for the sake of enhancing and preserving our purity as the proletarian vanguard and for the sake of raising our social qualities and revolutionary technique.
That is the reason why Communist Party members must undertake self-cultivation. . . .
First of all, we must oppose and resolutely eliminate one of the biggest evils bequeathed to us by the education and learning in the old society—the separation of theory and practice. In the course of education and study in the old society many people thought that it was unnecessary or even impossible to act upon what they had learned. Despite the fact that they read over and over again books by ancient sages they did things the sages would have been loath to do. Despite the fact that in everything they wrote or said they preached righteousness and morality they acted like out-and-out robbers and harlots in everything they did. Some "high-ranking officials" issued orders for the reading of the *Four Books* and the *Five Classics,* yet in their everyday administra-

tive work they ruthlessly levied exorbitant taxes, ran amuck with corruption and killing, and did everything against righteousness and morality. Some people read the *Three People's Principles* over and over again and could recite the *Will of Dr. Sun Yat-sen,* yet they oppressed the people, opposed the nations who treated us on an equal footing, and went so far as to compromise with or surrender to the national enemy. . . . Then why did they still want to carry on educational work and study the teachings of the sages? Apart from utilising them for window-dressing purposes, their objects were: (1) to make use of these teachings to oppress the exploited and to make use of righteousness and morality for the purpose of hoodwinking and suppressing the culturally backward people, (2) to attempt thereby to secure better government jobs, make money and achieve fame and reflect credit on their parents. Apart from these objects, their actions were not restricted to the sages' teachings. This was the attitude and return of the "men of letters" and "scholars" of the old society to the sages they "worshipped". Of course we Communist Party members cannot adopt such an attitude in studying Marxism-Leninism and the excellent and useful teachings bequeathed to us by our ancient sages. We must live up to what we say. We are honest and pure and we cannot deceive ourselves, the people or our forefathers. This is an outstanding characteristic as well as a great merit of us Communist Party members. . . .

What is the most fundamental and common duty of us Communist Party members? As everybody knows, it is to establish Communism, to transform the present world into a Communist world. Is a Communist world good or not? We all know that it is very good. In such a world there will be no exploiters, oppressors, landlords, capitalists, imperialists or fascists. There will be no oppressed and exploited people, no darkness, ignorance, backwardness, etc. In such a society all human beings will become unselfish and intelligent Communists with a high level of culture and technique. The spirit of mutual assistance and mutual love will prevail among mankind. There will be no such irrational things as mutual deception, mutual antagonism, mutual slaughter and war, etc. Such a society will, of course, be the best, the most beautiful and the most advanced society in the history of mankind. Who will say that such a society is not good? Here the question arises: Can Communist society be brought about? Our answer is "yes". About this the whole theory of Marxism-Leninism offers a scientific explanation that leaves no room for doubt. It further explains that as the ultimate result of the class struggle of mankind, such a society will inevitably be brought about. The victory of Socialism in the U.S.S.R. has also given us factual proof. Our duty is, therefore, to bring about at an early date this Communist society, the realization of which is inevitable in the history of mankind.

This is one aspect. This is our ideal.

But we should understand the other aspect, that is, in spite of the fact that Communism can and must be realized it is still confronted by powerful enemies that must be thoroughly and finally defeated in every respect before Communism can be realized. Thus, the cause of Communism is a long, bitter, arduous but victorious process of struggle. Without such a struggle there can be no Communism. . . .

Apart from clearly establishing his Communist outlook on life and his Communist world outlook, a Communist must also clearly define the correct relationship between his personal interests and the interests of the Party. The Marxist-Leninist principle is that personal interests must be subordinated to the Party's interests, partial interests to total interests, temporary interests to long-range interests, and the interests of one nation to the interests of the world as a whole.

The Communist Party is the political party representing the proletariat. Apart from the interests of the emancipation of the proletariat, the Party has no other interests and aims of its own. The ultimate emancipation of the proletariat, however, must needs be the ultimate emancipation of mankind as a whole, because the proletariat cannot emancipate itself if it fails to emancipate all the working people and all nations, in other words, if it fails to emancipate mankind as a whole. . . .

Whether or not a Communist Party member can absolutely and unconditionally subordinate his personal interests to the Party's interests under all circumstances is the criterion with which to test his loyalty to the Party, to the revolution and to the Communist cause. Since the realization of Communism must depend upon the proletariat and the Communist Party, Communism will never be brought about if the interests of the proletariat and the Communist Party are impaired.

At all times and on all questions, a Communist Party member should take into account the interests of the Party as a whole, and place the Party's interests above his personal problems and interests. It is the highest principle of our Party members that the Party's interests are supreme. . . .

Of course, a Party member has his personal interests and personal development. At certain times such personal interests may come in conflict with, or become antagonistic to, the Party's interests. Should this happen, a Party member is required to sacrifice his personal interests unconditionally and should not sacrifice the Party's interests to meet his personal interests (no matter under what cloak or pretext). Since the personal interests and development of the Party member are included in the interests and development of the Party, the success and victory of the Party and class also mean the success and victory of a Party member. Therefore, only in the struggle for the development, success and victory of the Party can a Party member hope to develop himself. He cannot divorce himself from the development of the Party in order to strive for his personal development. In short, only in the course of the struggle for the development, success and victory of the Party can a Party member develop himself; without this, he cannot develop himself at all. Therefore, the personal interests of a Party member must and can be made completely identical with the Party's interests and development. . . .

What are the basically incorrect ideologies among comrades in the Party? They can be listed roughly as follows:

Firstly, those who have joined our Party not only come from different social strata, but bring with them different aims and motives. . . . At the present time quite a few people have joined the Party chiefly because of the Communists' determined resistance to Japan and because of the anti-Japanese national united front. Certain other people have joined the Party as a way out because they could not find a way out in society—they had no trade, no job, no school to attend, or they wanted to escape from their families, or from forced marriages, etc. Some came because they looked up to the prestige of the Party, or because they recognized, though only in a vague way, that the Communist Party can save China. And finally there were even some individuals who came because they counted on the Communists for tax reduction, or because they hoped to become influential in the future, or because their relatives and friends brought them in, etc. It is very natural that such comrades should lack a clear and definite Communist outlook on life and world outlook, should fail to understand the greatness and difficulties of the Communist cause, and should be unable to take a firm proletarian stand. Therefore, it is also very natural that at certain turning points, under certain conditions, some of them should have wavered or changed. They have brought with them all kinds and shades of ideologies into the Party. Consequently, their education, steeling and self-cultivation are an extremely important matter. Otherwise, they simply will not be able to become vanguard fighters of the proletariat. . . . Although such persons still do not thoroughly understand Communism they can become active fighters in the course of the present Communist movement and the present revolutionary movement. Moreover, in the long course of the revolutionary struggle, they can become excellent and conscious Communists through intensive studies and cultivation. Besides, our Party Constitution further stipulates that Communist Party members shall have the freedom to withdraw from the Party (there is no freedom to join the Party). If any member lacks a profound belief in Communism, cannot endure strict inner-Party life, or for any other reason, he is free to withdraw from the Party. . . . In this way the purity of our Party can be preserved.

Secondly, certain Party members still have an ideology marked by relatively strong individualism and self-interest.

This kind of individualism finds expression in the following ways: certain persons, when solving all kinds of concrete problems, place their personal interests above the Party's interests; or they are always worrying about their personal gains and losses, weighing their personal interests; or they manage public affairs to benefit themselves [*chia-kung ying-ssu*], taking advantage of Party work to achieve certain personal aims; or they attempt to pay off their personal grudges against other comrades on the pretext of a question of principle, or of Party interests.

When it comes to questions of salaries, amenities and other matters concerning private life, they always want to surpass others, and to compare and compete with the very highest cadres and "use any means to achieve this end" and will brag about such things. But when it comes to work, they want to compare with those who are less capable. When there are hardships, they try to avoid them; in times of danger, they attempt to run away. As to orderlies, they always want more. As to living quarters, they always want the best. They want to show off and share the honors bestowed on the Party. They try to monopolize all the good things, but will have no part in anything that is in something of a mess. . . .

As to departmentalism [*pen-wei chu-i*] in the Party, it is different from such individualism. Departmentalism comes out chiefly because a comrade sees only partial interests, sees only his part of the work, does not see the situation as a whole and does not see the work of others. Therefore, he commits the mistake of only looking after the interests of his part of the work, does not see the situation as a whole and does not see the work of others. Therefore, he commits the mistake of only looking after the interests of his part of the work to such an extent that he obstructs others. . . . This of course cannot be compared with individualism. Nevertheless, persons with an individualistic outlook often commit the mistake of departmentalism.

Thirdly, self-conceit, individual heroism, showing off [*feng-t'ou chu-i*] etc., still exist to a greater or lesser extent in the ideology of quite a few comrades in the Party.

The first consideration of people with such ideas is their position in the Party. They like to show off, and want others to flatter them and admire them. They have a personal ambition to become leaders. They take advantage of their abilities and like to claim credit, to show off themselves, to keep everything in their hands and they are intolerant. They are full of vanity, do not want to bury their heads in hard work and are unwilling to do technical work. They are haughty. . . . They have not yet got rid of their deep-rooted "desire for fame" and they try to build themselves up into "great men" and "heroes" in the Communist cause, and even have no scruples in employing any means for the gratification of such desires. . . .

Fourthly, there are a small number of comrades in the Party who strongly reflect the ideology of the exploiting classes. . . . Persons with such an ideology seek to elevate and develop themselves in the Party, but they achieve this purpose by holding others down and obstructing their development. They want to jump over the heads of others and are jealous of those who are more capable. . . . In the Party they also take advantage of the weaknesses in the Party's organization and work to serve their ulterior purposes, to garner certain personal benefits by means of exacerbating such weaknesses. In the Party they are fond of spreading rumors, speaking ill of others behind their backs, and scheming to drive a wedge in the relations between comrades. . . .

Fifthly, bureaucracy still exists in our Party and in various organizations. . . . Among some comrades, there still exist such weaknesses as narrow-mindedness and the minding of small matters without taking into consideration the overall situation. They do not have the great courage or the far-sightedness of a Communist. Blind to the bigger issues, they are very much interested in small matters under their noses. . . . They can also be easily bribed by others with small favors or gifts. They have all the characteristics of narrow-mindedness of the small producer in rural society. . . .

The reason why inner-Party struggle is necessary is that differences over principles inside the Party are brought about in the course of the development of the Party and the struggle of the proletariat; at such times, differences can be overcome and contradictions solved "only by a fight for one or the other principle, for one or the other goal of the struggle, for one or the other method in the struggle leading to that goal." No compromise will be of any avail. . . .

It is necessary to prod, publicly criticize or even mete out organizational penalties to certain comrades in the Party who, having committed mistakes in principle and displayed opportunist ideology, turn a deaf ear to persuasion, ignore Party criticism, and furthermore persist in their errors and become so headstrong and obstinate as to struggle against the policy of the Party or adopt a double-faced attitude. But we should not attack or punish comrades who have committed mistakes if they do not persist in their mistakes and after discussion and persuasion, are willing to correct their mistakes and give up their former points of view, or when they are calmly thinking over their mistakes or are dispassionately discussing them with other comrades. In carrying on self-criticism and inner-Party struggle we do not mean that the grimmer the face the better nor do we mean that the more comrades we punish the better. The highest aim of self-criticism and inner-Party struggle is to effectively educate the Party, to educate the comrades who have committed mistakes, to correct errors and to consolidate the Party. . . .

76. THE RED ARMY CODE OF DISCIPLINE

[Unified Codification of Rules First Drawn up by Mao Tse-tung in 1928; Revised and Issued by General Headquarters, People's Liberation Army, 1947]

The Three Main Rules of Discipline:

1. Obey orders in all your actions.
2. Don't take a single needle or piece of thread from the masses.
3. Turn in everything captured.

The Eight Points for Attention:

1. Speak politely.
2. Pay fairly for what you buy.
3. Return everything you borrow.
4. Pay for anything you damage.
5. Don't hit or swear at people.
6. Don't damage crops.
7. Don't take liberties with women.
8. Don't ill-treat captives.

77. THE RED ARMY AND THE PEOPLE
[From James Bertram, *Unconquered,* 1939]

The first night out we spent in such a village [of cave homes in North Shensi], and I had the chance to see what the communists meant by their slogan of "non-violation of the interests of the people." Though this was within the Special District [under communist control], where a military party might easily have demanded a billet, rooms (or rather caves) were rented with the consent of their owners, and paid for in national currency. That evening scene was typical. Though they had covered a day's march that would have pros- trated regular troops of most countries, with no food since early morning, as soon as our quarters were decided upon it was the soldiers themselves who set to work, sweeping out the rooms, cooking the evening meal, cutting chaff for the horses—all with invincible good humor. As soon as the word of their arrival got around, half the village gathered in the courtyard—some of them come to gaze with unconcealed dismay at the first foreigner they had ever seen; but more to mingle with the soldiers, talk with them about the war, and pass the time of day. And always someone came with gifts; old men would bring tobacco, and offer a communal pipe; or small boys would shyly offer fruit. In the morning, cave and court were scrupulously swept out, and the reckoning —not without traditional bargaining—paid in full.

What it means from a purely military point of view to have a countryside solidly behind your armies, only those who have learned to depend upon the support of the masses really know. I had seen the fatal effects of a lack of co-operation between the peasants and the Chinese armies in Hopei, when the Japanese in their first occupation of the north ran open lines of communication across a densely populated country without the slightest interference. They would have met with a different reception here.

78. A COMMUNIST ART AND LITERATURE
[From Mao Tse-tung, "Talks at the Yenan Forum on Literature and Art," May 23, 1942]

The first problem is: For whom are our art and literature intended?

This problem, as a matter of fact, was solved long ago by Marxists, and especially by Lenin. As far back as 1905 Lenin emphatically pointed out that our art and literature should "serve the millions upon millions of working people." . . .

Who, then, are the people? The overwhelming majority constituting more than 90 percent of our total population are the workers, peasants, soldiers and the urban petty bourgeoisie. . . . Our art and literature should be intended for these four kinds of people. To serve them we must take the standpoint of the proletariat instead of that of the petty-bourgeoisie. Today writers and artists who cling to their individualistic petty-bourgeois standpoint cannot truly serve the mass of revolutionary workers, peasants and soldiers, but will be interested mainly in the small number of petty-bourgeois intellectuals. . . . Many comrades are concerned with studying the petty-bourgeois intellectuals, analysing their psychology, giving effective expression to their life and excusing or even defending their shortcomings, rather than guiding the intellectuals to get closer, together with themselves, to the workers, peasants and soldiers, join in their actual struggles, give expression to their life and educate them. Many comrades who are petty-bourgeois in origin and intellectuals themselves, seek friends only in the ranks of the intellectuals and concentrate their attention on studying and describing them. . . . The feet of these comrades are still planted squarely on the side of the petty-bourgeois intellectuals, or, to put it more elegantly, their innermost soul is still the domain of the petty-bourgeois intelligentsia. . . .

A complete solution of this problem will require a long time, maybe eight or ten years. But, no matter how long it takes, we must find the solution, and it must be unequivocal and complete. Our artists and writers must fulfill this task; they must gradually shift their standpoint over to the side of the workers, peasants and soldiers, to the side of the proletariat, by going into their midst and plunging into the actual struggle and by studying Marxism and society. Only in this way can we have art and literature that are genuinely for the workers, peasants and soldiers, and genuinely proletarian. . . .

Having solved the problem of whom to serve, we come now to the problem of how to serve. As our comrades put it: Should we devote ourselves to elevation [*t'i-kao*] or to popularization [*p'u-chi*]?

In the past some comrades to some extent or even very much despised and neglected popularization and unduly stressed elevation. It is right to stress elevation, but it is wrong to stress it exclusively in disregard of any other factor and to excess. . . . Since our art and literature are primarily intended for the workers, peasants and soldiers, popularization means diffusion of art and literature among them, while elevation means the raising of their artistic and literary standards. What should we popularize among them? The stuff needed and readily accepted by the feudal landlord class? By the bourgeoisie? Or by the petty-bourgeois intelligentsia? No, none of these will do. We must popularize what is needed and can be readily accepted by the workers, peasants and soldiers themselves. Consequently the duty of learning from the workers, peasants and soldiers precedes the task of educating them. This is even more true of elevation. There must be a level from which to elevate. When we lift a bucket of water, for instance, are we not lifting something that lies on the ground rather than hangs in mid-air? What then is the level from which the standard of our art and literature is to be raised? . . . It can only be raised from the level of the workers, peasants and soldiers. And this means not that we raise the workers, peasants and soldiers to the level of the feudal class, the bourgeoisie or the petty-bourgeois intelligentsia, but that we raise them up along their own line of ascent, along the line of ascent of the proletariat. . . .

What in the last analysis is the source of all art and literature? Ideological expressions in the form of artistic or literary work are the product of the human brain reflecting the life of a given society. Revolutionary art and literature are the products of the brains of revolutionary artists and writers reflecting the life of the people. In the life of the people there lies a mine of raw material for art and literature, namely, things in their natural state, crude but at the same time the most lively, rich and fundamental; in this sense, they throw all art and literature into the shade and provide for them a unique and inexhaustible source. This is the only source; there can be no other. . . .

Though man's social life is the only source of art and literature and is incomparably richer and more vivid, the people are not satisfied with life alone and demand art and literature. Why? Because, although both are beautiful, life as reflected in artistic and literary works can and ought to be on a higher level and of a greater intensity than real life, in sharper focus and more typical, nearer the ideal, and therefore more universal. Revolutionary art and literature should create all kinds of characters drawn from real life and help the people to make new history. For instance, there are on the one hand the victims of hunger, cold and oppression and on the other those who exploit and oppress their fellow men, and this contrast exists everywhere and seems quite common-place; artists and writers, however, can create art and literature out of such daily occurrences by bringing them into organized form and sharper focus and making the contradictions and struggles typical of life and so awaken and arouse the masses and impel them to unite and struggle to change their environment. Without such art and literature, this task cannot be fulfilled or at least not so effectively and speedily fulfilled. . . .

Is this utilitarianism? Materialists are not opposed to utilitarianism in general, but to the utilitarianism of the feudal, bourgeois and petty-bourgeois classes and to those hypocrites who attack utilitarianism in words but embrace the most selfish and shortsighted utilitarianism in deeds. In this world there is no utilitarianism which transcends classes; in a class society utilitarianism is either of this or of that particular class. We are proletarian, revolutionary utilitarians and we take as our point of departure the uniting of the present and future interests of the great majority, more than 90 percent, of the people of the country; therefore we are revolutionary utilitarians who pursue interests of the broadest scope and the longest range, not narrow utilitarians who are concerned only with what is limited and immediate. . . . A thing is good only when it brings real benefit to the people. . . .

. . . In the world today all culture, all art and literature belong to definite classes and follow definite political lines. There is in fact no such thing as art for art's sake, art which stands above classes or art which runs parallel to or remains independent of politics. Proletarian art and literature are part of the whole cause of the proletarian revolution, in the words of Lenin, "cog and wheel" of a single mechanism. Therefore the Party's artistic and literary activity occupies a definite and assigned position in the Party's total revolutionary work and is subordinated to the prescribed revolutionary task of the Party in a given revolutionary period. . . .

. . . Is there such a thing as human nature? Of course there is. But there is only human nature in the concrete, no human nature in the abstract. In a class society there is only human nature that bears the stamp of a class; human nature that transcends classes does not exist. We uphold the human nature of the proletariat and of the mass of the people, while the landlord and bourgeois classes uphold the human nature of their own classes as if—though they do not say so outright—it were the only kind of human nature. The human nature boosted by certain petty-bourgeois intellectuals is also divorced from or opposed to that of the mass of the people; what they call human nature is in substance nothing but bourgeois individualism, and consequently in their eyes proletarian human nature is contrary to their human nature. This is "the theory of human nature" advocated by some people in Yenan as the so-called basis of their theory of art and literature. It is utterly mistaken.

PART III
Transformation

The official proclamation of the People's Republic of China in Peking on October 1, 1949, signaled not only the Communists' defeat of the Nationalists but also the imminent reunification of China after decades of division. Much of southern China had not yet fallen to the People's Liberation Army, and administrative control over the vast subcontinent was yet to be achieved. Nevertheless, the establishment of the People's Republic did mean that for the first time since the fall of the empire, all of China was to be ruled by one government.

The Communists had won control of an economically underdeveloped country, which had been ravaged by a dozen years of full-scale warfare and had experienced unprecedented upheaval and strife for more than a century. The problems the new rulers of China faced were enormous. But they believed they understood the nature of these problems and had solutions for them. The old China had to be destroyed and a new China created in its place. Unlike the old elite, the new leaders, the vanguard Communist Party, would be the instrument of revolutionary change.

And change—vast, unparalleled, and frequently bewildering—has been the hallmark of the Communist period. In the first decade, the CCP launched a broad attack on existing institutions. The former elite was destroyed or deprived of its power, and guided by the experience of new China's closest ally, the Soviet Union, new forms of social and economic organization, of art and literature, were established. Under Communist leadership, a vast land reform took place in the first years of the new regime. Soon thereafter, the Communists initiated their program for solving the millennia-old land problem: Chinese agriculture was reorganized from small-scale family cultivation to larger-scale, and it was hoped more efficient, collectivized labor and management. Concurrently, industry, banking, and commerce were brought under government control, and the planned industrialization of China began. As the decade progressed, opposition grew; but it was suppressed, and the pace of change accelerated. In the Great Leap Forward of 1958–60, China diverged from the Soviet path and, in an intensely emotional campaign, attempted a complete transformation of man and society, the rapid and simultaneous solution of all fundamental problems.

It soon became apparent that the goals of the Great Leap were unrealistic, that there were limits to the speed of change, and that the huge amount of energy expended in the mass campaign had not produced commensurate results. Not all the changes of the previous decade had been as successful or as welcome as officially proclaimed. Adjustments were necessary, and so in the early 1960s the policy was retrenchment and moderation. Less attention was given to revolutionary ardor and more to immediate calculable results, less to ideology and more to production. During this respite, party and people deliberated over the new society and the future. Some believed that the ultimate transformation of China could not be brought about by disruptive mass movements, but would occur by means of sustained, long-range economic growth within the framework of the newly established institutions. But some saw disturbing evidence of atrophy, within the younger generation and within the party itself as its primary function shifted from fostering social revolution toward routine administration of the state-controlled economy. Within the context of the new institutions many old problems were reappearing. A new hierarchy was developing its own vested interests in the status quo. Foremost among those alarmed by these signs was Chairman Mao, who had withdrawn into a kind of semiretirement after the failures of the Great Leap.

Unable to impose his solution to these problems on the party leadership, Mao turned elsewhere. In alliance with the army and Red Guard youth, he launched the Great Proletarian Cultural Revolution to purge China of the pernicious influences of the past. The CCP was attacked from above by Mao and his inner-party supporters and from below by "revolutionary masses," and many party members, including Liu Shao-ch'i and other top leaders, were demoted or expelled. With the fragmentation of authority, conflicts between various groups increased, and led to violent confrontations and bloodshed. The army restored order, and the power of the Minister of Defense, Lin Piao, steadily grew until he became Mao's new heir apparent.

As in the case of the Great Leap, the intensity of political activity during the mass campaign was great, but many of the more radical changes proved superficial or ephemeral. Red Guard organizations were disbanded and rebellious urban youth were sent to the countryside for practical experience. The CCP was shaken, but not shattered, and it began to rebuild itself as the revolutionary frenzy subsided. The influence of the PLA was circumscribed, especially after an attempted coup against Mao by Lin Piao in 1971. With the return of more normal conditions, many disgraced party leaders reappeared and were restored to office. Many of the tendencies attacked in the Cultural Revolution also began to reassert themselves. Tensions within the party became increasingly pronounced after a radical faction launched an ideological and organizational counterattack in 1975. The power struggle came to a sudden climax shortly after the death of Mao Tse-tung in September 1976. The downfall of the radical leaders in October, subsequent purges of their followers, assertions of the superiority of experience over dogma, and the long-range program to modernize the Chinese economy announced by the new party Chairman, Hua Kuo-feng, were signs that a more systematic, orderly solution to China's problems would now be attempted.

A note on sources. The selections in Part III are all taken from newspapers and magazines published in the People's Republic of China, where the press and other media are government-controlled. They give the official version of the issues and the facts. Like all documents they are partial and, like all government versions of events, best treated with a healthy skepticism. There is a strong tendency to exaggerate the virtues of the winners and the iniquities of the losers, and to ascribe more widespread support and implementation of official policies, and greater successes for them, than the facts merit. Yet, these documents do not exclude hints of other points of view, or of unapproved behavior, and in the very process of defining problems, the gap between ideal and actuality is always implied and frequently expressed. Even the recurrence of "successful" solutions to a problem can be taken as an indication of its persistence. In addition, because policy shifts are often explained in terms of a response to problems arising from past policies, the documents of each successive period help to illuminate events in preceding periods. The problems of the Great Leap Forward, which can be glimpsed even in the documents of the time, are more clearly revealed in the publications of the post-Leap period, and documents from the Cultural Revolution throw new light (of a particular hue) on earlier years. Thus, the accumulated effect of many documents by different kinds of authors from differerent periods is a fuller and more complex picture.

CHAPTER ELEVEN
The Political Context

Victory in the civil war gave the Communists the task that they had insisted they alone could accomplish; the responsibility for solving China's problems was now theirs. In June 1949, even before the formal establishment of the new government, Mao Tse-tung, who was to be its chairman, outlined the party's goals and the political strategy to achieve them. Nationalism is an important element in "On the People's Democratic Dictatorship," and is reflected in the broad coalition of classes whose interests are seen as conforming to the interests of the nation. Only a small fraction of the population, the old elite, is excluded. Consistent with the strategy of maximizing the CCP's base of political support, Mao minimizes the potential conflicts between different groups in the coalition, and envisions a long process of gradual development. He offers no institutional guarantees that this moderate policy will last. Since socialism is the only road for China, the national interest would seem to be comprehended through the party's ideology, and is not contingent upon the views or separate interests of the members of the coalition. The party's authority derives from its unique capacity to meet China's needs. (Selection 79) The reader may well ask, how is the common interest to be determined, and what is to prevent the new elite from developing interests of its own?

This issue is central to Mao's 1957 speech "On the Correct Handling of Contradictions among the People," perhaps his most important post-1949 speech, and certainly one of his major theoretical statements. (Selection 80) The issue of allowing public criticism of the party and the government had been raised by events both within China and abroad. De-Stalinization in Russia and the uprisings against Stalinist regimes in

Poland and Hungary in 1956 were viewed with apprehension by CCP leaders, and some thought special caution was necessary to avoid a similar occurrence in China. The current intensive drive to collectivize agriculture and nationalize industry and commerce, and policies toward artists and intellectuals, had caused much dissatisfaction. Mao's response is based on an optimistic assessment of the Chinese situation. Proceeding from his premise that conflicts of interest still exist and will continue to exist, he argues that these conflicts are "non-antagonistic contradictions" because of the underlying harmony of interests among the "people." Here, Mao's concept of the people seems less class-bound. Attitude is crucial: Those who actively support and work for the goals and policies of the regime, those who put the public interest, as defined by the party, before their own narrowly conceived personal or group interests, all come within the category of the "people." Conflicts between these groups, or between them and the state, can be resolved by discussion because of the underlying mutuality of interests. Under these conditions, open criticism is not only permissible, but even beneficial, for it is a means to overcome difficulties. Mao views conflict and resolution as a continual process, not merely a momentary issue raised by recent events. Instability is permanent, a natural and healthy phenomenon, but also a constant challenge to vigilance because it must be properly handled to be a force for progress. On the basis of his presuppositions that the party and the state represent the true interests of the people, and that freedom and democracy are of subsidiary importance because they are only means, not ends in themselves, Mao establishes broad criteria for the expression of opinion. In effect, only constructive criticisms are to be tolerated. No mention is made of the process for determining whether the effects of any given idea are beneficial or detrimental. Though not explicitly stated, this crucial power presumably remains in the hands of the party.

The new policy of sanctioning open discussion, popularized under the slogan "Let a Hundred Flowers Blossom, Let a Hundred Schools of Thought Contend," brought a flurry of complaints in the late spring of 1957. A number of prominent non-Communist supporters of the regime expressed their criticisms in open forums provided by the government. Of these, one of the most outspoken was Ch'u An-p'ing, a liberal journalist who, as a result of the new policy, had become editor-in-chief of *Kuangming jih-pao*, a newspaper oriented toward intellectuals. Selection 81 is a digest of the course of events of the brief period of "Blossoming and Contending" as illustrated by Ch'u's case, from his speech at a forum for non-Communist intellectuals in early June to his recantation, under intense public pressure—including a denunciation by his eldest son—in July. Ch'u does not question CCP supremacy. But he does assert that the party's monopoly on positions of power (and prestige) is unmerited. The July 10 editorial from the *People's Daily*, the official CCP organ, is one of many official responses to the basic thrust of the various criticisms. It also provides a useful, succinct explanation of the theoretical distinction between party and government. Ch'u's confession of error is typical of the self-repudiation exacted from critics. As the concluding document in this sequence indicates, the public debate was brought to a conclusion with a stepped-up antirightist rectification campaign, in which not only dissent but lack of active support was interpreted as a negative sign. By thus intimidating people who expressed even well-intentioned reservations or misgivings, this campaign reinforced the radical fervor that culminated in the Great Leap Forward.

The Hundred Flowers episode made unmistakably clear that the Communist Party would define the realm of its own affairs and handle them itself. This underscored the importance of internal party discipline, a particularly acute problem due to the rapid expansion of the party during the first decade of the new regime—from approximately 4,500,000 in October 1949 to almost 14,000,000 by mid-1959. Not all the millions of new members were knowledgeable about the principles of the party, nor were all motivated solely by a selfless desire to see those principles put into action. *Questions and Answers on Party Organization Work,* designed to help new members better understand the party, reveals some of the party's internal problems. (Selection 82) Published in 1959, this guidebook shows the influence of the egalitarian ideals of the Great Leap, which stand in sharp contrast to the divisions between mental and physical labor and between officials and common people so salient in imperial China, and obviously still sufficiently prevalent to be a cause of concern. Continuity with the past also appears in the idea, expressed in the same terms used by Confucians for over two millennia, that virtue is the prime qualification for political leadership. A pervading theme is the need to prevent personal interests of members from subverting the general interests of the party. This was not a new problem, and it was to become a key issue in the 1960s.

79. GROUND RULES FOR THE NEW CHINA
[From Mao Tse-tung, "On the People's Democratic Dictatorship," June 30, 1949]

From the time of China's defeat in the Opium War of 1840, Chinese progressives went through untold hardships in their quest for truth from the Western countries. Hung Hsiu-ch'üan, K'ang Yu-wei, Yen Fu, and Sun Yat-sen were representative of those who had looked to the West for truth before the Communist Party of China was born. Chinese who then sought progress would read any book containing the new knowledge from the West. The number of students sent to Japan, Britain, the United States, France and Germany was amazing. At home, the imperial examinations were abolished and modern schools sprang up like bamboo shoots after a spring rain; every effort was made to learn from the West. In my youth, I too engaged in such studies. They represented the culture of Western bourgeois democracy, including the social theories and natural sciences of that period, and they were called "the new learning" in contrast to Chinese feudal culture, which was called "the old learning." For quite a long time, those who had acquired the new learning felt confident that it would save China, and very few of them had any doubts on this score, as the adherents of the old learning had. Only modernization would save China, only learning from foreign countries could modernize China. Among the foreign countries, only the Western capitalist countries were then progressive, as they had successfully built modern bourgeois states. The Japanese had been successful in learning from the West, and the Chinese also wished to learn from the Japanese. The Chinese in those days regarded Russia as backward, and few wanted to learn from her. That was how the Chinese tried to learn from foreign countries in the period from the 1840s to the beginning of the 20th century.

Imperialist aggression shattered the fond dreams of the Chinese about learning from the West. It was very odd—why were the teachers always committing aggression against their pupil? The Chinese learned a good deal from the West, but they could not make it work and were never able to realize their ideals. Their repeated struggles, including such a country-wide movement as the Revolution of 1911, all ended in failure. Day by day, conditions in the country got worse, and life was made impossible. Doubts arose, increased and deepened. World War I shook the whole globe. The Russians made the October Revolution and created the world's first socialist state. Under the leadership of Lenin and Stalin, the revolutionary energy of the great proletariat and laboring people of Russia, hitherto latent and unseen by foreigners, suddenly erupted like a volcano, and the Chinese and all mankind began to see the Russians in a new light. Then, and only then, did the Chinese enter an entirely new era in their thinking and their life. They found Marxism-Leninism, the universally applicable truth, and the face of China began to change.

It was through the Russians that the Chinese found Marxism. Before the October Revolution, the Chinese were not only ignorant of Lenin and Stalin, they did not even know of Marx and Engels. The salvoes of the October Revolution helped progressives in China, as throughout the world, to adopt the proletarian world outlook as the instrument for studying a nation's destiny and considering anew their own problems. Follow the path of the Russians— that was their conclusion. In 1919, the May 4th Movement took place in China. In 1921, the Communist Party of China was founded. Sun Yat-sen, in the depths of despair, came across the October Revolution and the Communist Party of China. He welcomed the October Revolution, welcomed Russian help to the Chinese and welcomed cooperation of the Communist Party of China. Then Sun Yat-sen died and Chiang Kai-shek rose to power. Over a long period of twenty-two years, Chiang Kai-shek dragged China into ever more hopeless straits. In this period, during the anti-fascist Second World War in which the Soviet Union was the main force, three big imperialist powers were knocked out, while two others were weakened. In the whole world only one big imperialist power, the United States of America, remained uninjured. But the United States faced a grave domestic crisis. It wanted to enslave the whole world; it supplied arms to help Chiang Kai-shek slaughter several million Chinese. Under the leadership of the Communist Party of China, the Chinese people, after driving out Japanese imperialism, waged the People's War of Liberation for three years and have basically won victory.

Thus Western bourgeois civilization, bourgeois democracy and the plan for a bourgeois republic have all gone bankrupt in the eyes of the Chinese people. Bourgeois democracy has given way to people's democracy under the leadership of the working class and the bourgeois republic to the people's republic. This has made it possible to achieve socialism and communism through the people's republic, to abolish classes and enter a world of Great Harmony. . . . There are bourgeois republics in foreign lands, but China cannot have a bourgeois republic because she is a country suffering under imperialist oppression. The only way is through a people's republic led by the working class.

All other ways have been tried and failed. Of the people who hankered after those ways, some have fallen, some have awakened and some are changing their ideas. Events are developing so swiftly that many feel the abruptness of the change and the need to learn anew. This state of mind is understandable and we welcome this worthy desire to learn anew. . . .

Twenty-four years have passed since Sun Yat-sen's death, and the Chinese revolution, led by the Communist Party of China, has made tremendous advances both in theory and practice and has radically changed the face of China. Up to now the principal and fundamental experience the Chinese people have gained is twofold:

1. Internally, arouse the masses of the people. That is, unite the working class, the peasantry, the urban petty bourgeoisie and the national bourgeoisie, form a domestic united front under the leadership of the working class, and advance from this to the establishment of a state which is a people's democratic dictatorship under the leadership of the working class and based on the alliance of workers and peasants.

2. Externally, unite in a common struggle with those nations of the world which treat us as equals and unite with the peoples of all countries. That is, ally ourselves with the Soviet Union, with the People's Democracies and with the proletariat and the broad masses of the people in all other countries, and form an international united front.

"You are leaning to one side." Exactly. The forty years' experience of Sun Yat-sen and the twenty-eight years' experience of the Communist Party have taught us to lean to one side, and we are firmly convinced that in order to win victory and consolidate it we must lean to one side. In the light of the experiences accumulated in these forty years and these twenty-eight years, all Chinese without exception must lean either to the side of imperialism or to the side of socialism. Sitting on the fence will not do, nor is there a third road. We oppose the Chiang Kai-shek reactionaries who lean to the side of imperialism, and we also oppose the illusions about a third road.

"Victory is possible even without international help." This is a mistaken idea. In the epoch in which imperialism exists, it is impossible for a genuine people's revolution to win victory in any country without various forms of help from the international revolutionary forces, and even if victory were won, it could not be consolidated. This was the case with the victory and consolidation of the great October Revolution, as Lenin and Stalin told us long ago. This was also the case with the overthrow of the three imperialist powers in World War II and the establishment of the People's Democracies. And this is also the case with the present and the future of People's China. . . .

"You are dictatorial." My dear sirs, you are right, that is just what we are. All the experience the Chinese people have accumulated through several decades teaches us to enforce the people's democratic dictatorship, that is, to deprive the reactionaries of the right to speak and let the people alone have that right.

Who are the people? At the present stage in China, they are the working class, the peasantry, the urban petty bourgeoisie and the national bourgeoisie. These classes, led by the working class and the Communist Party, unite to form their own state and elect their own government; they enforce their dictatorship over the running dogs of imperialism—the landlord class and bureaucrat-bourgeoisie, as well as the representatives of those classes, the Kuomintang reactionaries and their accomplices—suppress them, allow them only to behave themselves and not to be unruly in word or deed. If they speak or act in an unruly way, they will be promptly stopped and punished. Democracy is practiced within the ranks of the people, who enjoy the rights of freedom of speech, assembly, association and so on. The right to vote belongs only to the people, not to the reactionaries. The combination of these two aspects, democracy for the people and dictatorship over the reactionaries, is the people's democratic dictatorship.

Why must things be done this way? The reason is quite clear to everybody. If things were not done this way, the revolution would fail, the people would suffer, the country would be conquered.

"Don't you want to abolish state power?" Yes, we do, but not right now; we cannot do it yet. Why? Because imperialism still exists, because domestic reaction still exists, because classes still exist in our country. Our present task is to strengthen the people's state apparatus—mainly the people's army, the people's police and the people's courts—in order to consolidate national defence and protect the people's interests. Given this condition, China can develop steadily, under the leadership of the working class and the Communist Party, from an agricultural into an industrial country and from a new-democratic into a socialist and communist society, can abolish classes and realize the Great Harmony. . . .

The serious problem is the education of the peasantry. The peasant economy is scattered, and the socialization of agriculture, judging by the Soviet Union's experience, will require a long time and painstaking work. Without socialization of agriculture, there can be no complete, consolidated socialism. The steps to socialize agriculture must be coordinated with the development of a powerful industry having state enterprise as its backbone. The state of the people's democratic dictatorship must systematically solve the problems of industrialization. . . .

The people's democratic dictatorship is based on the alliance of the working class, the peasantry and the urban petty bourgeoisie, and mainly on the alliance of the workers and the peasants, because these two classes comprise 80 to 90 percent of China's population. These two classes are the main force in overthrowing imperialism and the Kuomintang reactionaries. The transition from New Democracy to socialism also depends mainly upon their alliance. . . .

The national bourgeoisie at the present stage is of great importance. . . . To counter imperialist oppression and to raise her backward economy to a higher level, China must utilize all the factors of urban and rural capitalism that are beneficial and not harmful to the national economy and the people's livelihood; and we must unite with the national bourgeoisie in common struggle. Our present policy is to regulate capitalism, not to destroy it. But the national bourgeoisie cannot be the leader of the revolution, nor should it have the chief role in state power. The reason it cannot be the leader of the revolution and should not have the chief role in state power is that the social and economic position of the national bourgeoisie determines its weakness; it lacks foresight and sufficient courage and many of its members are afraid of the masses. . . .

To sum up our experience and concentrate it into one point, it is: the people's democratic dictatorship under the leadership of the working class (through the Communist Party) and based upon the alliance of workers and peasants. This dictatorship must unite as one with the international revolutionary forces. This is our formula, our principal experience, our main program.

Twenty-eight years of our Party are a long period, in which we have accomplished only one thing—we have won basic victory in the revolutionary war. This calls for celebration, because it is the people's victory, because it is a victory in a country as large as China. But we still have much work to do; to use the analogy of a journey, our past work is only the first step in a long march of ten thousand *li*. Remnants of the enemy have yet to be wiped out. The serious task of economic construction lies before us. We shall soon put aside some of the things we know well and be compelled to do things we don't know well. This means difficulties. . . .

We must overcome difficulties, we must learn what we do not know. We must learn to do economic work from all who know how, no matter who they are. We must esteem them as teachers, learning from them respectfully and conscientiously. We must not pretend to know when we do not know. We must not put on bureaucratic airs. If we dig into a subject for several months, for a year or two, for three or five years, we shall eventually master it. . . . The Communist Party of the Soviet Union is our best teacher and we must learn from it. The situation both at home and abroad is in our favor, we can rely fully on the weapon of the people's democratic dictatorship, unite the people throughout the country, the reactionaries excepted, and advance steadily to our goal.

80. RESOLVING CONFLICTS
[From Mao Tse-tung, "On the Correct Handling of Contradictions among the People," February 27, 1957[1]]

Two Different Types of Contradictions

Never before has our country been as united as it is today. The victories of the bourgeois-democratic revolution and the socialist revolution and our achievements in socialist construction have rapidly changed the face of old China. A still brighter future for our motherland lies ahead. The days of national disunity and chaos which the people detested have gone, never to return. Led by the working class and the Communist Party, our six hundred million people, united as one, are engaged in the great task of building socialism. The unification of our country, the unity of our people and the unity of our various nationalities—these are the basic guarantees of the sure triumph of our cause. However, this does not mean that contradictions no longer exist in our society. To image that none exist is a naive idea which is at variance with objective reality. We are confronted by two types of social contradictions —those between ourselves and the enemy and those among the people themselves. The two are totally different in their nature.

To understand these two different types of contradictions correctly, we must first be clear on what is meant by "the people" and what is meant by "the enemy." The concept of "the people" varies in content in different countries and in different periods of history in the same country. Take our own country for example. During the War of Resistance Against Japan, all those classes, strata and social groups opposing Japanese aggression came within the category of the people, while the Japanese imperialists, the Chinese traitors and the pro-Japanese elements were all enemies of the people. During the War of Liberation, the U.S. imperialists and their running dogs—the bureaucrat-capitalists, the landlords and the Kuomintang reactionaries who represented these two classes—were the enemies of the people, while the other classes, strata and social groups, which opposed these enemies, all came within the category of the people. At the present stage, the period of building socialism, the classes, strata and social groups which favor, support and work for the cause of socialist construction all come within the category of the people, while the social forces and groups which resist the socialist revolution and are hostile to or sabotage socialist construction are all enemies of the people.

The contradictions between ourselves and the enemy are antagonistic contradictions. Within the ranks of the people, the contradictions among the

---

[1]Originally a speech made at the Eleventh Session (Enlarged) of the Supreme State Conference; Mao made some alterations prior to its publication in the *People's Daily* on June 19 of the same year.

working people are non-antagonistic, while those between the exploited and the exploiting classes have a non-antagonistic aspect in addition to an antagonistic aspect. There have always been contradictions among the people, but their content differs in each period of the revolution and in the period of socialist construction. In the conditions prevailing in China today, the contradictions among the people comprise the contradictions within the working class, the contradictions within the peasantry, the contradictions within the intelligentsia, the contradictions between the working class and the peasantry, the contradictions between the workers and peasants on the one hand and the intellectuals on the other, the contradictions between the working class and other sections of the working people on the one hand and the national bourgeoisie on the other, the contradictions within the national bourgeoisie, and so on. Our People's Government is one that genuinely represents the people's interests, it is a government that serves the people. Nevertheless, there are still certain contradictions between the government and the people. These include contradictions among the interests of the state, the interests of the collective and the interests of the individual; between democracy and centralism; between the leadership and the led; and the contradictions arising from the bureaucratic style of work of certain government workers in their relations with the masses. All these are also contradictions among the people. Generally speaking, the people's basic identity of interests underlies the contradictions among the people. . . .

Since they are different in nature, the contradictions between ourselves and the enemy and the contradictions among the people must be resolved by different methods. To put it briefly, the former are a matter of drawing a clear distinction between right and wrong. It is, of course, true that the distinction between ourselves and the enemy is also a matter of right and wrong. For example, the question of who is in the right, we or the domestic and foreign reactionaries, the imperialists, the feudalists and bureaucrat-capitalists, is also a matter of right and wrong, but it is in a different category from questions of right and wrong among the people.

Our state is a people's democratic dictatorship led by the working class and based on the worker-peasant alliance. What is this dictatorship for? Its first function is to suppress the reactionary classes and elements and those exploiters in our country who resist the socialist revolution, the suppress those who try to wreck our socialist construction, or in other words, to resolve the internal contradictions between ourselves and the enemy. For instance, to arrest, try and sentence certain counter-revolutionaries, and to deprive landlords and bureaucrat-capitalists of their right to vote and their freedom of speech for a specified period of time—all this comes within the scope of our dictatorship. To maintain public order and safeguard the interests of the people it is likewise necessary to exercise dictatorship over embezzlers, swindlers, arsonists, murderers, criminal gangs and other scoundrels who seriously disrupt public order. The second function of this dictatorship is to protect our country from subversion and possible aggression by external enemies. In that event, it is the task of this dictatorship to resolve the external contradictions between ourselves and the enemy. The aim of this dictatorship is to protect all our people so that they can devote themselves to peaceful labor and build China into a socialist country with a modern industry, agriculture, science and culture. Who is to exercise this dictatorship? Naturally, the working class and the entire people under its leadership. Dictatorship does not apply within the ranks of the people. The people cannot exercise dictatorship over themselves, nor must one section of the people oppress another. Law-breaking elements among the people will be punished according to law, but this is different in principle from the exercise of dictatorship to suppress enemies of the people. What applies among the people is democratic centralism. Our Constitution lays it down that citizens of the People's Republic of China enjoy freedom of speech, of the press, assembly, association, procession, demonstration, religious belief, and so on. Our Constitution also provides that the organs of state must practice democratic centralism, that they must rely on the masses and that their personnel must serve the people. Our socialist democracy is democracy in the broadest sense such as is not to be found in any capitalist country. Our dictatorship is the people's democratic dictatorship led by the working class, and based on the worker-peasant alliance. That is to say, democracy operates within the ranks of the people, while the working class, uniting with all others enjoying civil rights, and in the first place with the peasantry, enforces dictatorship over the reactionary classes and elements and all those who resist socialist transformation and oppose socialist construction. By civil rights, we mean, politically, the rights of freedom and democracy.

But this freedom is freedom with leadership and this democracy is democracy under centralized guidance, not anarchy. Anarchy does not accord with the interests or wishes of the people.

... Democracy sometimes seems to be an end, but it is in fact only a means. Marxism teaches us that democracy is part of the superstructure and belongs to the category of politics. That is to say, in the last analysis, it serves the economic base. The same is true of freedom. Both democracy and freedom are relative, not absolute, and they come into being and develop in specific historical conditions. Within the ranks of the people, democracy is correlative with centralism and freedom with discipline. They are the two opposites of a single entity, contradictory as well as united, and we should not one-sidedly emphasize one to the denial of the other. Within the ranks of the people, we cannot do without freedom, nor can we do without discipline; we cannot do without democracy, nor can we do without centralism. This unity of democracy and centralism, of freedom and discipline, constitutes our democratic centralism. Under this system, the people enjoy extensive democracy and freedom, but at the same time they have to keep within the bounds of socialist discipline. All this is well understood by the broad masses of the people.

In advocating freedom with leadership and democracy under centralized guidance, we in no way mean that coercive measures should be taken to settle ideological questions or questions involving the distinction between right and wrong among the people. All attempts to use administrative orders or coercive measures to settle ideological questions or questions of right and wrong are not only ineffective but harmful. ... The only way to settle questions of an ideological nature or controversial issues among the people is by the democratic method, the method of discussion, of criticism, of persuasion and education, and not by the method of coercion or repression. . . .

This democratic method of resolving contradictions among the people was epitomized in 1942 in the formula "unity, criticism, unity." To elaborate, it means starting from the desire for unity, resolving contradictions through criticism or struggle and arriving at a new unity on a new basis. In our experience this is the correct method of resolving contradictions among the people. . . .

In ordinary circumstances, contradictions among the people are not antagonistic. But if they are not handled properly, or if we relax our vigilance and lower our guard, antagonism may arise. In a socialist country, a development of this kind is usually only a localized and temporary phenomenon. The reason is that the system of exploitation of man by man has been abolished and the interests of the people are basically the same. . . .

Marxist philosophy holds that the law of the unity of opposites is the fundamental law of the universe. This law operates universally, whether in the natural world, in human society, or in man's thinking. Between the opposites in a contradiction there is at once unity and struggle, and it is this that impels things to move and change. Contradictions exist everywhere, but they differ in accordance with the different nature of different things. In any given phenomenon or thing, the unity of opposites is conditional, temporary and transitory, and hence relative, whereas the struggle of opposites is absolute. . . .

Many dare not openly admit that contradictions still exist among the people of our country, although it is these very contradictions that are pushing our society forward. Many do not admit that contradictions continue to exist in a socialist society, with the result that they are handicapped and passive when confronted with social contradictions; they do not understand that socialist society will grow more united and consolidated through the ceaseless process of the correct handling and resolving of contradictions. . . .

. . . To sum up, socialist relations of production have been established and are in harmony with the growth of the productive forces, but they are still far from perfect, and this imperfection stands in contradiction to the growth of the productive forces. Apart from harmony as well as contradiction between the relations of production and the developing productive forces, there is harmony as well as contradiction between the superstructure and the economic base. The superstructure consisting of the state system and laws of the people's democratic dictatorship and the socialist ideology guided by Marxism-Leninism plays a positive role in facilitating the victory of socialist transformation and the establishment of the socialist organization of labor; it is suited to the socialist economic base, that is, to socialist relations of production. But survivals of bourgeois ideology, certain bureaucratic ways of doing things in our state organs and defects in certain links in our state institutions are in contradiction with the socialist economic base. We must continue to resolve all such contradictions in the light of our specific conditions. Of course, new problems will emerge as these contradictions are resolved. And further efforts will be required to resolve the new contradictions. For instance, a constant process of readjustment through state planning is needed to deal with the contradiction between production and the needs of society, which will long remain as an objective reality. Every year our country draws up an economic plan in order to establish a proper ratio between accumulation and consumption and achieve a balance between production and needs. Balance is nothing but a temporary, relative unity of opposites. By the end of each year, this balance, taken as a whole, is upset by the struggle of opposites; the unity undergoes a change, balance becomes imbalance, unity becomes disunity, and once again it is necessary to work out a balance and unity for the next year. Herein lies the superiority of our planned economy. As a matter of fact, this balance, this unity is partially upset every month or every quarter, and partial readjustments are called for. Sometimes, contradictions arise and the balance is upset because our subjective arrangements do not correspond to objective reality; this is what we call making a mistake. The ceaseless emergence and ceaseless resolution of contradictions is the dialectical law of the development of things. . . .

The Question of Agricultural Cooperation

The cooperatives are now in the process of gradual consolidation. Certain contradictions remain to be resolved, such as those between the state and the cooperatives and those among and within the cooperatives themselves.

We must give constant attention to problems of production and distribution as the way to resolve these contradictions. Take the question of production. The cooperative economy must be subject to the unified economic planning of the state, while retaining a certain leeway and independence of action that are not incompatible with the state's unified plan or with its policies, laws and regulations. At the same time, every household in a cooperative must comply with the overall plan of the cooperative or production team to which it belongs, apart from any appropriate plans it makes for itself in regard to land allotted for private use and to other economic undertakings left to private management. On the question of the distribution of income, we must take account of the interests of the state, the collective and the individual. We must properly handle the three-way relationship between the state agricultural tax, the cooperative's accumulation fund and the peasant's personal income, and take constant care to make readjustments so as to resolve contradictions between them. Accumulation is essential both for the state and for the cooperative, but in neither case should it be excessive. We should do everything possible to enable the peasants to raise their personal incomes year by year in normal years on the basis of increased production. . . .

As a matter of fact, with very few exceptions, there has been some improvement in the peasants' life as well as in that of the workers. Since liberation, the peasants have been free from landlord exploitation and their production has increased year by year. Take grain crops. In 1949, the country's output was only something over 210,000 million catties. By 1956, it had risen to something over 360,000 million catties, an increase of nearly 150,000 million catties. The state agricultural tax is not heavy, only amounting to some 30,000 million catties a year. State purchases of grain from the peasants at standard prices only amount to something over 50,000 million catties a year. These two items together total over 80,000 million catties. Furthermore, more than half this grain is sold back to the villages and nearby towns. Obviously no one can say that there has been no improvement in the life of the peasants. We are preparing to stabilize the total annual amount of the grain tax plus the grain purchased by the state at approximately 80,000 million catties in the next few years, so as to help agriculture to develop and the cooperatives to become consolidated. In this way, the small number of grain-deficient households still found in the countryside will cease to go short, and all peasant households, with the exception of some growing industrial crops, will have grain reserves or at least become self-sufficient; there will be no more poor peasants and the standard of living of the entire peasantry will reach or surpass the middle peasant level. It is not right simply to compare a peasant's average annual income with a worker's and draw the conclusion that one is too low and the other too high. The productivity of the workers is much higher than that of the peasants, while the latter's cost of living is much lower than that of workers in the cities, so the workers cannot be said to have received special favors from the state. However, the wages of a small number of workers and some government personnel are a bit too high, and the peasants have reason to be dissatisfied with this, so it is necessary to make certain appropriate readjustments according to specific circumstances. . . .

The Question of the Intellectuals

The contradictions within the ranks of the people in our country also find expression among the intellectuals. The several million intellectuals who worked for the old society have come to serve the new society, and the question that now arises is how they can fit in with the needs of the new society and how we can help them to do so. This, too, is a contradiction among the people.

Most of our intellectuals have made marked progress during the last seven years. They have expressed themselves in favor of the socialist system. Many are diligently studying Marxism, and some have become communists. The latter, though small in number, are steadily growing. Of course, there are still some intellectuals who are sceptical about socialism or who do not approve of it, but they are a minority.

China needs the services of as many intellectuals as possible for the colossal task of socialist construction. We should trust the intellectuals who are really willing to serve the cause of socialism, and should radically improve our relations with them and help them solve any problems requiring solution, so that they can give full play to their talents. Many of our comrades are not good at uniting with intellectuals. They are too crude in dealing with them, lack respect for their work, and interfere in certain matters in scientific and cultural work where interference is unwarranted. We must do away with all such shortcomings. . . .

Recently there has been a falling off in ideological and political work among students and intellectuals, and some unhealthy tendencies have appeared. Some people seem to think that there is no longer any need to concern oneself with politics or with the future of the motherland and the ideals of mankind. It seems as if Marxism was once all the rage but is currently not so much in fashion. To counter these tendencies, we must strengthen our ideological and political work. . . . Not to have a correct political point of view is like having no soul. The ideological remolding carried on in the past was necessary and has yielded positive results. But it was carried on in a somewhat rough and ready fashion and the feelings of some people were hurt—this was not good. We must avoid such shortcomings in the future. All departments and organizations should shoulder their responsibilities in ideological and political work. This applies to the Communist Party, the Youth League, government departments in charge of this work, and especially to heads of educational institutions and teachers. Our educational policy must enable everyone who receives an education to develop morally, intellectually and physically and become a worker with both socialist consciousness and culture. We must spread the idea of building our country through diligence and frugality. We must help all our young people to understand that ours is still a very poor country, that we cannot change this situation radically in a short time, and that only through the united efforts of our younger generation and all our people, working with their own hands, can China be made strong and prosperous within a period of several decades. The establishment of our socialist system has opened the road leading to the ideal society of the future, but to translate this ideal into reality needs hard work. Some of our young people think that everything ought to be perfect once a socialist society is established and that they should be able to enjoy a happy life ready-made, without working for it. This is unrealistic. . . .

On "Let a Hundred Flowers Blossom, Let a Hundred Schools of Thought Contend" and "Long-Term Coexistence and Mutual Supervision"

"Let a hundred flowers blossom, let a hundred schools of thought contend" and "long-term coexistence and mutual supervision"—how did these slogans come to be put forward? They were put forward in the light of China's specific conditions, on the basis of the recognition that various kinds of contradictions still exist in socialist society, and in response to the country's urgent need to speed up its economic and cultural development. Letting a hundred flowers blossom and a hundred schools of thought contend is the policy for promoting the progress of the arts and the sciences and a flourishing scoialist culture in our land. Different forms and styles in art should develop freely and different schools in science should contend freely. We think that it is harmful to the growth of art and science if administrative measures are used to impose one particular style of art or school of thought and to ban another. Questions of right and wrong in the arts and sciences should be settled through free discussion in artistic and scientific circles and through practical work in these fields. They should not be settled in a summary fashion. A period of trial is often needed to determine whether something is right or wrong. . . .

It will take a fairly long period of time to decide the issue in the ideological struggle between socialism and capitalism in our country. The reason is that the influence of the bourgeoisie and of the intellectuals who come from the old society will remain in our country for a long time to come, and so will their class ideology. If this is not sufficiently understood, or is not understood at all, the gravest mistakes will be made and the necessity of waging the struggle in the ideological field will be ignored. Ideological struggle is not like other forms of struggle. The only method to be used in this struggle is that of painstaking reasoning and not crude coercion. . . .

People may ask, since Marxism is accepted as the guiding ideology by the majority of the people in our country, can it be criticized? Certainly it can. Marxism is scientific truth and fears no criticism. If it did, and if it could be overthrown by criticism, it would be worthless. . . . Marxists should not be afraid of criticism from any quarter. Quite the contrary, they need to temper and develop themselves and win new positions in the teeth of criticism and in the storm and stress of struggle. Fighting against wrong ideas is like being vaccinated—a man develops greater immunity from disease as a result of vaccination. Plants raised in hot-houses are unlikely to be sturdy. Carrying out the policy of letting a hundred flowers blossom and a hundred schools of thought contend will not weaken but strengthen the leading position of Marxism in the ideological field.

What should our policy be towards non-Marxist ideas? As far as unmistakable counter-revolutionaries and saboteurs of the socialist cause are concerned, the matter is easy: we simply deprive them of their freedom of speech. But incorrect ideas among the people are quite a different matter. Will it do to ban such ideas and deny them any opportunity for expression? Certainly not. It is not only futile but very harmful to use summary methods in dealing with ideological questions among the people, with questions concerned with man's mental world. You may ban the expression of wrong ideas, but the ideas will still be there. On the other hand, if correct ideas are pampered in hot-houses without being exposed to the elements or immunized from disease, they will not win out against erroneous ones. Therefore, it is only by employing the method of discussion, criticism and reasoning that we can really foster correct ideas and overcome wrong ones, and that we can really settle issues. . . .

At first glance, the two slogans—let a hundred flowers blossom and let a hundred schools of thought contend—have no class character; the proletariat can turn them to account, and so can the bourgeoisie or other people. But different classes, strata and social groups each have their own views on what are fragrant flowers and what are poisonous weeds. What then, from the point of view of the broad masses of the people, should be the criteria today for distinguishing fragrant flowers from poisonous weeds? In the political life of our people, how should right be distinguished from wrong in one's words and actions? On the basis of the principles of our Constitution, the will of the overwhelming majority of our people and the common political positions which have been proclaimed on various occasions by our political parties and groups, we consider that, broadly speaking, the criteria should be as follows:

1. Words and actions should help to unite, and not divide, the people of our various nationalities.
2. They should be beneficial, and not harmful, to socialist transformation and socialist construction.
3. They should help to consolidate, and not undermine or weaken the people's democratic dictatorship.
4. They should help to consolidate, and not undermine or weaken, democratic centralism.
5. They should help to strengthen, and not discard or weaken, the leadership of the Communist Party.
6. They should be beneficial, and not harmful, to international socialist unity and the unity of the peace-loving people of the world.

Of these six criteria, the most important are the socialist path and the leadership of the Party. These criteria are put forward not to hinder but to foster the free discussion of questions among the people. Those who disapprove of these criteria can still put forward their own views and argue their case. However, since the majority of the people have clear-cut criteria to go by, criticism and self-criticism can be conducted along proper lines, and the criteria can be applied to people's words and actions to determine whether they are right or wrong, whether they are fragrant flowers or poisonous weeds. These are political criteria. Naturally, in judging the validity of scientific theories or assessing the aesthetic value of works of art, additional pertinent criteria are needed. But these six political criteria are applicable to all activities in the arts and the sciences. In a socialist country like ours, can there possibly be any useful scientific or artistic activity which runs counter to these political criteria? . . .

On Practicing Economy

Here I wish to speak briefly on practicing economy. We want to carry on large-scale construction, but our country is still very poor—herein lies a contradiction. One way of resolving it is to make a sustained effort to practice strict economy in every field.

. . . The Chinese Communist Party, the democratic parties, the democrats with no Party affiliation, the intellectuals, industrialists and merchants, workers, peasants and handicraftsmen—in short, all the 600 million people of our country—must strive for increased production and economy, and against extravagance and waste. This is of prime importance not only economically, but politically as well. A dangerous tendency has shown itself of late among many of our personnel—an unwillingness to share the joys and hardships of the masses, a concern for personal fame and gain. This is very bad. One way of overcoming it is to simplify our organizations in the course of our campaign to increase production and practice economy, and to transfer cadres to lower levels so that a considerable number will return to productive work. We must see to it that all our cadres and all our people constantly bear in mind that ours is a big socialist country but an economically backward and poor one, and that this is a very great contradiction. To make China rich and strong needs several decades of intense effort, which will include, among other things, the effort to practice strict economy and combat waste, i.e., the policy of building up our country through diligence and frugality. . . .

81. FREEDOM AND AUTHORITY

[From Ch'u An-p'ing, "Allow Me to Offer Some Opinions to Chairman Mao and Premier Chou," *People's Daily*, June 2, 1957]

After the liberation, intellectuals warmly supported the Party and accepted the leadership of the Party. But in the past few years the relations between the Party and the masses have not been good and have become a problem in our political life that urgently needs readjustment. Where is the key to the problem? In my opinion, the key lies in the idea that "the world belongs to the Party." I think a Party leading a nation is not the same thing as a Party owning a nation; the public supports the Party, but members of the public have not forgotten that they are masters of the nation. The aim of a Party in power is to realize its ideals, to promote its policies. To guarantee that its policies will be implemented, to consolidate the regime it has won, it is natural that the Party should want to remain strong and hold the key positions in government. But isn't it too much that . . . there must be a Party man as leader in every unit, big or small . . . or that nothing, big or small, can be done without a nod from a Party man? In the state's major policies, all non-Party people willingly follow the Party. The reason they do this is that the Party's ideals are great, not because these people have no ideas of their own or because they have no respect or sense of responsibility to the nation. For many years, the talents and capabilities of many Party men have not matched their duties. They have bungled their jobs, to the detriment of the state, and have not been able to command the respect of the masses with the result that the relations between the Party and the masses have been tense. . . . Before the liberation, I heard tell that Chairman Mao wanted to organize a coalition government with non-Party members. In 1949 when the new nation began, three of the deputy chairmen of the central government were non-Party persons, and two out of the four deputy premiers were non-Party persons. It looked like a coalition government. Later when the government was reorganized, there was only one deputy chairman of the People's Republic of China, and the seats of the non-Party deputy chairmen were moved to the standing committee of the People's Congress. That is not all. Now there are 12 deputy premiers in the State Council, not one of whom is a non-Party man. Could it be that there is not a single person among the non-Party people who can sit in a deputy premier's chair, or that none of them can be cultivated to hold this chair?

[From a Letter by Ch'u Wang-ying, to Shanghai (Wen-hui Pao), dated June 26, 1957]

I am Ch'u An-p'ing's eldest son. I have recently been demobilized and come home.

Since the publication of his anti-socialist views, Ch'u An-p'ing has met with the stern reproach of the whole nation. I myself, a soldier of the revolutionary army and a socialist youth, resolutely stand on the side of the whole nation in opposition to his fallacies against the Communist Party, socialism and the people's leadership.

Many of his anti-Party and anti-socialist views have been exposed by the press. It has been adequately proved that he has entertained such vicious ideas for a long time, that he has political ambitions and that he exploited the *Kuang-ming Jih-pao* as the basis for launching anti-socialist attacks. I am thus made aware of his anti-Party face.

I wish to offer Mr. Ch'u An-p'ing one word of advice: I hope that you will repent in time; listen to the opinions of the people; uproot your own anti-socialist thought; render a thorough account of yourself; you may thus find grace with the people.

[From "Is the Party Supposed Not to Issue Orders?" *People's Daily* Editorial, July 10, 1957]

In opposing socialism, bourgeous rightists in general are not directly against socialism but against the leadership of the Communist Party—the fundamental condition for translating socialism into reality. And in opposing the leadership of the Communist Party, they say they support the leadership of the Communist Party and that they are only against the "world belongs to the Party" idea, against the leading role of the Communist Party organizations in state organs and against Party "issuance of orders" direct to the people. We wish to devote ourselves here to the question of the so-called issuance of Party orders to the people while leaving other questions to later discussion. . . .

First, if the so-called issuance of orders refers to promulgation of a compulsory order, then this is not the Party's business. The Party is the ideological and political leading core of the masses and not a state organ that necessarily enforces certain compulsion against the masses. The Party not only guards against and resolutely opposes commandism in its mass work but also requires the government organs under its leadership to guard against and oppose commandism. That is to say, while the government is often required to issue compulsory orders to the people, it should not be supposed that it can merely depend upon issuance of orders instead of propaganda and explanation for carrying out its tasks.

Second, if the so-called issuance of orders refers to promulgation of a directive on every-day administrative affairs, then this is not the Party's business either. The Party is the leading force of our government; it takes the lead in formulating the guilding principles and policies of government work and strives to ensure their correct application but it cannot and should not take the place of government organs in their administrative activities. The Party is opposed to the practice of taking the place of any non-Party organs in their activities and is opposed to the tendency towards routinism and departure from its own political tasks.

Third, if the so-called issuance of orders refers to promulgation of the slogans of political tasks to the people and promulgation of directives on the guiding principles and policies of government work, then the promulgation of such slogans and directives is necessary, whether they are promulgated by the Party alone or jointly by the Party and government. This was so in the past, is so at present and will be so in the future (as long as the Party exists).

The Communist Party is an organized detachment of the most conscious part of the working people and is the highest form of the class organization of the working class. . . .

Has this leading position of the Party among the people undergone any change since the founding of the People's Republic of China? It has undergone a change in the sense that the leading position of the Party is more stable and the leading role of the Party has spread penetratingly to all parts of China and has built extensive and close relations with the six hundred million people. And this is the basic guarantee of our unprecedented unity and unification and of our unprecedented and rapid development of all aspects of our state work. The administrative work of our country certainly has to be done by the government organs. But the Party is required not only to take the lead in drawing up the guiding principles and policies of the Central Government's work (in taking the lead in drawing up such guiding principles and policies, the Party primarily relies on studying the experience of the masses while at the same time attaching importance to consultations with non-Party people), but is also required to ensure correct implementation of these guiding principles and policies in conformity with concrete conditions in local areas and at primary strata and to do massive ideological work among the masses so as to transform such guiding principles and policies into their thought and action. . . .

This position and role of the Communist Party are not only the natural results of the historical development of the Chinese revolution but also the necessary condition of a socialist country for realizing the dictatorship of the proletariat and cannot be assumed by any other political parties or any other political organizations.

[From Ch'u An-p'ing's "Surrender to the People," *People's Daily*, July 15, 1957]

I committed serious anti-Party and anti-socialist errors both in my speech at the June 1 forum . . . and in my work for the *Kuang-ming Jih-pao*. Having been criticized by all people of our country, I now come to recognize my errors and sincerely bow my head to all people of our country and admit my guilt.

My allegation is absolutely wrong. To begin with, my view that the Party dominates the world today is completely inconsistent with facts. After liberation, the people led by the Party have risen to the status of owners. The world today is the people's world with tremendous people's power growing everywhere. The Party in a sincere, just and selfless spirit leads the people, educates the people and unites with the people. . . .

Facts tell us that where there is no Party leadership (through Party members), there Party policies cannot be correctly carried out and mistakes are likely to occur in work. Therefore, that Party members take part in the work at each locality and in each department is an extremely normal, reasonable and necessary thing. Not only does the Constitution confirm the leading position of the Party in the political life of the state but all the people of our country in their thoughts and feelings regard the Party as the greatest wealth in our state and as the leading force and core in building socialism and effecting socialist transformation. The existence and might of the Party are strong guarantees to safeguard the gains of victory in the people's democratic revolution, build a powerful socialist new China and guide the people to a happy life. The Chinese people unanimously recognize the countless good things the Party has done for the whole nation. All people of our country are cheering and taking pride in the great accomplishments made under Party leadership and are grateful to the Party from the bottoms of their hearts. It is precisely because of this that the people ask the Party to select and appoint Party members to lead them in their study and work. The responsibility of the Party is identical with the interests of the people. But I represented all such things as signs of "Party domination of the world" and attempted to use this charge to oppose the leadership of the Party. . . .

My mistakes did not come all of a sudden. They had their historical roots. I received many years of British and American bourgeois education and made a blind cult of decadent bourgeois democracy. Before liberation, I stood against the Kuomintang on the one hand and against the Communist Party on the other. Ideologically, I preached bourgeois "liberalism"; politically, I followed the middle-of-the-road line. . . . The severe criticism to which the whole nation has subjected me has brought home to me that, if I don't make up my mind to remold my thinking and change my stand, I shall have no future. In particular, I have come to realize that if I do not follow the Party honestly I will take the wrong way and will commit mistakes in my work. . . . I take my surrender to the people as a hallmark of my determination to reform myself. From now on I will honestly accept Party leadership and wholeheartedly follow the socialist road.

[Decision of the State Council on the Rectification Campaign, July 26, 1957]

The people of our country under the leadership of the Chinese Communist Party are at present engaged in a rectification campaign and serious struggle against bourgeois rightists. This is a struggle to safeguard China's socialist revolution and the basic system of our state. In accordance with the provision of the Constitution of the People's Republic of China that "all servants of the state must be loyal to the people's democratic system, observe the Constitution and the law and strive to serve the people," all personnel of state institutions should regard their participation in this campaign and struggle as their lofty duty and due responsibility. Therefore the State Council decides that in units where rectification is being carried out, all members of the staff should actively take part in this campaign and struggle. In the course of it, they should take a firm standpoint, clearly distinguish between right and wrong, and expose and thoroughly criticize all words and actions of bourgeois rightists, and so increase their own political consciousness and make serious efforts to overcome shortcomings and improve their work so that the socialist revolution and construction of our country will achieve further success.

82. PARTY PROBLEMS AND PARTY IDEALS

[From *Questions and Answers on Party Organization Work*, 1959]

The traditional cadre work line of our Party is to emphasize the selection of excellent worker and peasant elements as well as intellectuals who maintain close liaison with the worker-peasant masses to undertake leadership work in all spheres. . . .

A cadre is someone who can be high or low, who can be an "official" or a citizen, who can come from production, and return to production, who can lead the masses, or accept leadership from the masses. He is a mental laborer as well as a manual laborer; he can forge ahead not only to be "thoroughly red and profoundly expert," but he can also make himself into a versatile man [*to-mien-shou*]. . . .

In our society, cadres of the Party and state comprise advanced elements recruited from the people and the masses to lead the people to undertake revolution and reconstruction and to serve the people. A cadre is not a permanent profession; nor is it a special class. Any difference in the work and duties of a cadre or any difference in status between cadres and the masses constitutes merely a division of labor in society. . . .

During the long and arduous revolutionary wars and mass struggles in the past, we have fostered and steeled a large number of cadres who had close liaison with the masses and were loyal to revolutionary enterprises. These cadres are the reliable pillars of the Party and the nation. However, young cadres who now form the majority of our rank and file of cadres, especially young intellectuals who have joined the work since national liberation, generally have had no experience in revolutionary wars and no steeling through mass struggle and productive labor. Many of them have not been proletarianized, and in the depth of their ideological concepts and living habits sinister bourgeois and petty bourgeois influences are retained. . . .

A common feature of intellectual cadres who have not gone through transformation is that they despise manual labor and manual laborers. Many of their setbacks in ideology and working style are inseparable from this feature.

Consequently, a basic method should be to allow these cadres to participate in manual labor and to work in basic level units in order to transform their ideology. . . . Since 1957, large numbers of cadres throughout the nation have been dispatched downward to undertake labor steeling and to work in basic level units, and salutary results have been achieved. It has been borne out by facts that this method is the most effective in enabling intellectual cadres to more rapidly achieve proletarianization. It is also a basic method for eliminating contradictions between cadres and laboring people as well as fusing them into one.

It is not only essential for intellectual cadres who have not been steeled and transformed to participate in manual labor and to acquire basic level work experience, but it is also essential for leadership personnel on all levels and other cadres. . . .

Leadership cadres are to appear as common laborers when they participate in manual labor. This helps them not only to understand conditions, but also to uncover and resolve problems. It also enables them to improve leadership methods and working style, thus surmounting the "three styles" [bureaucratism, factionalism, and subjectivism in working style] and "five airs" [officiousness, plushness, senility, arrogance, and effeminacy] of leadership cadres and bringing the masses closer with the leadership cadres. In the meantime, there is a greater significance in the participation of cadres in manual labor, that is, coordinating mental labor with manual labor so cadres can become fully developed men, and creating the prerequisites for transition to a Communist society.

The reason why cadres must obtain working experience on the basic level is not only that they can be steeled and transformed in this practical work, but also because it is only after acquiring basic level work experience that cadres will be enabled to assume leadership work. . . . Inasmuch as all basic level units serve as the foundations of our entire state and society, all our tasks are based upon the work of basic level units. If we can learn to do basic level work and if we can acquire basic level working experience, we will have the prerequisites for leadership work. . . .

The selection and use of cadres according to the principle of "virtue with talent" [ts'ai-te chien-pei] has been a firm policy of the Party in its cadres work. "Virtue with talent" serves as a standard of the Party in recruiting cadres; it also serves as the goal of cadre training by the Party.

"Virtue with talent" is not abstract. . . . Both "virtue" and "talent" have concrete contents. From the viewpoint of Marxism-Leninism, "virtue" denotes political quality. It means that cadres should have a firm proletarian stand, be loyal to socialist and Communist enterprises, and wholeheartedly serve the people. "Talent" denotes ability. It means that cadres should have a definite policy level and professional knowledge, that they can undertake certain work. While both "virtue" and "talent" should be present, "virtue" is the basic thing. If a cadre has the "virtue" of serving the people wholeheartedly, it will be possible for him to incessantly enhance his "talent" under the fostering and education of the Party and the state, and through his own efforts. Similarly, it is only with good political quality that a talented cadre will be able to forge his talents to serve the people. Without a proletarian stand, one cannot be loyal to socialism and communism, and even if one has a certain "talent," he will not be able to serve the people, and such "talent" is worthless. . . .

To be "both red and expert" and "thoroughly red and profoundly expert" constitutes the cadre work policy of the Party during the current stage of socialist construction. This cadre work policy and that of "virtue with talent" are basically the same. Today, our requirement for "virtue" is "red" and our requirement for "talent" is "expert." In the new historic stage, the Party's demand on its cadres has become higher. Being "both red and expert" and "thoroughly red and profoundly expert" is richer and more developed in content than "virtue with talent." . . .

The bringing [into the Party] of cadres by private individuals constitutes a kind of "nepotism" which violates the cadre policy of our Party and state, and runs counter to the interests of our Party and state. The cadres thus brought in are often chosen from among relatives or friends who do not work in accordance with work procedures. This is very dangerous because sometimes persons who are not qualified and even counter-revolutionaries and undesirable elements may worm their way into the rank and file of our cadres.

There are also some people who cherish ulterior motives who bring in cadres privately from the standpoint of personal ambitions and deliberately sabotage the organizational principles of the Party and state. . . . With a view to maintaining the purity of the rank and file of our cadres, and preventing persons with ulterior motives from committing sabotage, we must insist that on the question of personnel employment, the principle of screening and approval by the organization be observed. . . .

The following stipulations have been made on duties of Party members in the Party Constitution of the Eighth Congress [1956]: 1) endeavor to study Marxism-Leninism and incessantly enhance one's own degree of awareness; 2) uphold Party solidarity and consolidate Party unity; 3) earnestly execute Party policies and resolutions and actively consummate tasks assigned by the Party; 4) stringently observe the Party Constitution and laws of the state, as well as communist morality, there being no exceptions for any members, whatever their merits or positions; 5) place the interest of the Party and state, that is also the interest of the people and the masses, above personal interest, and in the case of a conflict between the two kinds of interest, resolutely submit to the interest of the Party and state, which is also the interest of the people and the masses; 6) wholeheartedly and single-mindedly serve the people and the masses, maintain close liaison with the people and the masses, learn from the people and the masses, modestly listen to and timely reflect to the Party the demands and opinions of the people and the masses, and interpret the Party's policies and resolutions to the people and the masses; 7) be an exemplar in work and incessantly enhance productive technology and professional ability; 8) carry out criticism and self-criticism, expose defects and mistakes in work and strive to surmount and rectify them; report work defects and mistakes to the leadership organs of the Party, all the way to the Central Committee; struggle against all phenomena both in and out of the Party that are inimical to the interests of the Party and people; 9) be loyal and honest to the Party by not concealing or distorting facts; 10) be vigilant at all times over intrigues and activities of enemies and preserve Party and state secrets. . . .

The general tasks of the basic level organizations of the Party are: undertake propaganda and organizational work among the masses in order to realize the Party's decisions and the various resolutions of superior organizations; pay constant attention to the sentiments and demands of the masses and reflect them to superior organizations; care about and strive to improve the material and cultural life of the masses; accept [new] Party members, collect Party dues, screen and appraise Party members, and exercise Party discipline among members; organize Party members to study Marxism-Leninism and the experiences and policies of the Party in order to enhance the ideological and political levels of Party members; lead the masses to actively participate in the political life of the state; lead the masses to develop their creativeness and positiveness in order to consolidate labor discipline and to insure the consummation of production and work plans; unfold criticism and self-criticism, expose and eliminate all shortcomings and mistakes, and struggle with all phenomena of law violation, corruption and extravagence, and bureaucratism; undertake education of alertness among Party members and the masses, and pay constant attention to struggling against the sabotage of class enemies. . . .

The basic level organization of the Party is established in accordance with production units and work units. This is an organic principle of the Party. The reason why this principle must be enforced by the Party is because production units and work units form the cells of social organization as well as places where people and masses congregate. By setting up the Party's basic level organization in accordance with production units and work units, it enables the organizational basis of the Party to be set up directly in the cells of social organization and among the broad masses of the people.

CHAPTER TWELVE

Social
Revolution

The new leaders of China were dedicated not merely to preserving their newly won power, but to transforming China. Indeed, they believed that the party's commitment to change was a vital source of Communist power. Even before the civil war was over, revolution had begun in areas under Communist control, and in the first year of the new regime, two major measures were promulgated, the new marriage law and the land reform law.

The CCP had supported women's and youth movements since its inception, and so the Marriage Law of 1950 was not an expression of a new policy. But it was basic to creating a new China. Its explicit intent was to eliminate arranged marriages and concubinage, to give wives equal rights (and economic means to support these rights), and to provide certain basic rights for dependent children. (Selection 83) The law did not immediately end centuries-old customs all over China. In spite of a campaign for the implementation of the marriage law that began in 1950, arranged marriages, bridal prices, and other practices could not be completely eliminated in a year or even a generation. But the law did define ideals and provide an instrument for enforcing and spreading the practice of these ideals. And it did give impetus toward extending equality for women and rights for young people. In this sense it was one of the most revolutionary acts of the new regime.

The Agrarian Reform Law of 1950 was a second major revolution. In his speech on the purpose of this reform, Liu Shao-ch'i stresses its intended economic effects. (Selection 84) By taking land from those who have too much to till themselves and giving it to those who do not have enough, the energies of the rural population will be freed to produce more for themselves and for China's industrialization. The principal appeal is to individual initiative and self-interest. Liu foresees a long period of gradual development, but he also states that collectivization will eventually be necessary.

The prospect of economic gain was not the only motive at work in land reform, as we see in the fictional account of the process in one peasant village by Ting Ling (b. 1904), one of modern China's most eminent women writers and, at this time, a member of the CCP. Her novel of land reform, one of many in this genre, is based on her own experiences in a north China village in 1946. The scene she depicts is typical of actual events throughout rural China during the nationwide upheaval in the early 1950s. As she tells it, a passion for justice, for revenge, is the driving force behind the villagers' brutal treatment of the landlord, Schemer Chien. And the result is not merely a seizure of property, but a transformation of attitudes and social relationships. (Selection 85) In this, and in the integral role of violence in breaking down old social barriers, Ting Ling's fiction recalls Mao's 1927 report on the Hunan peasant movement. In the novel, Chien is allowed to live. But as the high tide of agrarian reform swept over the Chinese countryside, many landlords and wealthy peasants were executed. By the end of 1952, more than 100,000,000 acres of land (40–50 percent of the total arable land) had been confiscated and redistributed among 300,000,000 peasants (60–70 percent of the rural population).

In both these revolutionary measures, the creation of greater equality coincided with both the ideological ideals and the political interests of the Communist Party, for in both cases equality subverted the old hierarchy. The weakening of the legal and economic authority of the head of the household was a major step toward replacing the family with the nation (or, as in later years, Chairman Mao) as the focus of individual loyalty. The execution of landlords and wealthy peasants and the confiscation of their lands destroyed the old rural elite, the group most likely to be hostile to Communist programs. And the CCP won the good will of many millions of those who benefited from these changes.

Small, scattered peasant landholdings, however, could not solve the basic problems of rural China, nor did they conform to the Russian model of development, which was the CCP's guide in these early years. Even before the redistribution of land had been completed, initial steps were taken toward collectivization, or as the Chinese version was called, cooperativization. At first, Mutual Aid Teams, of four to ten households, were organized to share resources and labor power. Next was the lower-stage, or "semi-socialist" Agricultural Producers Cooperative (APC), several times larger than the Mutual Aid Team, in which each member was not only remunerated for the labor he or she contributed in collective production, but also received a dividend for the share of the land, tools, and animals contributed at the time of joining. In the lower-stage APC, a small amount of land could also be retained by the individual household for private cultivation. Thus, better-off peasants were not entirely deprived of their larger assets if they decided to join a cooperative. Only in the still larger advanced-stage APC was income to be determined solely by labor.

In his July 1955 speech on agricultural cooperativization, Mao gives a number of reasons for the superiority of cooperatives. (Selection 86) Not only will larger scale bring greater efficiency in the allocation of available resources, but it will facilitate the introduction of modern agricultural technology. The increases in production will benefit the peasants, and are essential for the ever-growing needs of China's expanding urban industries. Mao does not discuss whether the greater centralization of management will also enable the state to extract larger percentages of agricultural production by administrative methods. He gives the impression that the benefits of cooperativization will be equitably distributed, and thus satisfy both the legitimate needs of the peasants and the requirements of the larger national economy. The power of Mao's vision lies in its comprehensiveness: self-interest and national interest, agriculture and industry, politics and economics, are all interrelated. The possible flaws are in his assumptions. Would the peasants be as favorably disposed toward the new cooperatives as Mao asserts? Were party cadres capable of providing the right kind of leadership? And was the alliance between the party and the poor and middle peasants the real basis not only for the party's power but also for increasing production?

As Mao repeatedly indicates, some of his colleagues did not share his enthusiasm, and, citing evidence of peasant resistance, preferred a more cautious approach. In a brief commentary to one of a collection of articles on successful cooperatives, published later in the year, Mao acknowledged that peasant enthusiasm was by no means universal, and that opposition was strong enough to require constant political and ideological struggle. (Selection 87)

Collectivization was completed in two intensive years, 1956 and 1957. By the end of 1957 well over 90 percent of peasant households were enrolled in higher-stage co-ops. In theory, membership was supposed to be voluntary; in practice, many households were pressured or coerced into joining by cadres convinced of the superiority of cooperatives or eager to demonstrate the high calibre of their leadership. In some areas there were disorders and other kinds of resistance, though nothing as formidable as had occurred during collectivization in the Soviet Union.

The formal establishment of cooperatives did not mean they all operated as they ideally should. In discussing the new organizational problems created by the co-ops, Teng Tzu-hui (b. 1895), Director of the CCP's important Rural Work Department, uses Mao's theory of nonantagonistic contradictions to analyze conflicts of interest. His solution is based on the key Maoist concept of the mass line, and he cites Mao's own classic description of the process. Unlike Mao, Teng sees the contradictions more as problems pure and simple than as forces engendering progress. He assumes that no new patterns of motivation have been created by the new forms of organization, and that adjustments must be made to self-interest.

He therefore advocates a conciliatory policy so as to minimize the discontent caused by depriving any individual or group of too much too fast. (Selection 88)

Other leaders believed the way to overcome such resistance was to move still further forward. In spite of some uneasiness, still more radical policies were undertaken with the Great Leap Forward of 1958–60. An editorial from the *People's Daily* in September 1958 reflects the official enthusiasm for the nationwide campaign, and especially for the newly created people's communes. (Selection 89) Once more, the argument is that larger scale improves efficiency, in administration as well as production. Ideological considerations are also highlighted, and, on the basis of an assumption of ever-expanding political consciousness, the rapid attainment of an advanced stage of socialism is predicted. The remainder of the timetable for the transition to communism is vague, but promising. Such attributions of advanced ideological and social development, with their implicit challenge to Russian supremacy, exacerbated the growing tensions between China and the Soviet Union.

The mass campaign brought an almost total politicization of life. On the premise that the good society would be the most productive society, it was repeatedly asserted that total social transformation would skyrocket production. Among the most radical aspects of the Great Leap were new systems of remuneration for labor—both in urban industry (Selection 90) and rural communes (Selection 91)—and communal mess halls (Selection 92). The egalitarian ideals of the Great Leap pervade another article from the *People's Daily.* (Selection 93) Perhaps the most widely publicized phenomenon of the Great Leap was the 600,000 small-scale blast furnaces set up throughout rural China, as part of the effort to eliminate the rural/urban and agriculture/industry divisions. The spirit of this movement is captured in "The Strength of the Masses Is Limitless," a title that accurately sums up not only the theme of this article, but of the whole mass campaign approach. (Selection 94) The author deals exclusively with the positive results of mass zeal, but a reflective reading also discloses several crucial flaws. Concentration on the single task of producing steel tends to disrupt the routine performance of other work. The lack of quality control is also apparent. These and other considerations caused the leaders to slow down and make adjustments. But, as the article by Teng Hsiao-p'ing (b. 1904) makes clear, admonitions for moderation were rejected, and the campaign was reaccelerated. (Selection 95) Teng gives a good explanation of the economic rationale for the mass movement approach, and from his refutations of its critics, some understanding of the objections can also be gained. Although the Great Leap was soon to come to an end, the mass campaign was to remain an important instrument of party policy.

83. EQUAL RIGHTS IN THE FAMILY
[The Marriage Law of the People's Republic of China, May 1, 1950]

Chapter One: General Principles

ARTICLE 1. The feudal marriage system which is based on arbitrary and compulsory arrangement and the superiority of man over woman and ignores the children's interests shall be abolished.

The New-Democratic marriage system, which is based on the free choice of partners, on monogamy, on equal rights for both sexes, and on the protection of the lawful interests of women and children, shall be put into effect.

ARTICLE 2. Bigamy, concubinage, child betrothal, interference with the remarriage of widows, and the exaction of money or gifts in connection with marriages, shall be prohibited.

Chapter Two: The Marriage Contract

ARTICLE 3. Marriage shall be based upon the complete willingness of the two partners. Neither party shall use compulsion and no third party shall be allowed to interfere.

ARTICLE 4. A marriage can be contracted only after the man has reached 20 years of age and the woman 18 years of age.

ARTICLE 5. No man or woman shall be allowed to marry in any of the following instances:

1. Where the man and the woman are lineal relatives by blood or where the man and woman are brother and sister born of the same parents or where the man and woman are half-brother and half-sister. The question of prohibiting marriage between collateral relatives by blood (up to the fifth degree of relationship) is to be determined by customs.
2. Where one party, because of certain physical defects, is sexually impotent.
3. Where one party is suffering from veneral disease, mental disorder, leprosy or any other disease which is regarded by medical science as rendering a person unfit for marriage.

ARTICLE 6. In order to contract a marriage, both the man and the woman shall register in person with the people's government of the district or *hsiang* in which they reside. If the marriage is found to be in conformity with the provisions of this law, the local people's government shall, without delay, issue marriage certificates.

If the marriage is not found to be in conformity with the provisions of this law, registration shall not be granted.

Chapter Three: Rights and Duties of Husband and Wife

ARTICLE 7.   Husband and wife are companions living together and shall enjoy equal status in the home.

ARTICLE 8.   Husband and wife are in duty bound to love, respect, assist and look after each other, to live in harmony, to engage in productive work, to care for the children and to strive jointly for the welfare of the family and for the building up of the new society.

ARTICLE 9.   Both husband and wife shall have the right to free choice of occupation and free participation in work or in social activities.

ARTICLE 10.   Both husband and wife shall have equal rights in the possession and management of family property.

ARTICLE 11.   Both husband and wife shall have the right to use his or her own family name.

ARTICLE 12.   Both husband and wife shall have the right to inherit each other's property.

Chapter Four: Relations between Parents and Children

ARTICLE 13.   Parents have the duty to rear and to educate their children; the children have the duty to support and assist their parents. Neither the parents nor the children shall maltreat or desert one another.
   The foregoing provision also applies to foster-parents and foster-children. Infanticide by drowning and similar criminal acts are strictly prohibited.

ARTICLE 14.   Parents and children shall have the right to inherit one another's property.

ARTICLE 15.   Children born out of wedlock shall enjoy the same rights as children born in lawful wedlock. No person shall be allowed to harm them or discriminate against them.
   Where the paternity of a child born out of wedlock is legally established by the mother of the child or by other witnesses or by other material evidence, the identified father must bear the whole or part of the cost of maintenance and education of the child until the age of 18.
   With the consent of the mother, the natural father may have custody of the child.
   With regard to the maintenance of a child born out of wedlock, in case its mother marries, the provisions of Article 22 shall apply.

ARTICLE 16.   Husband or wife shall not maltreat or discriminate against children born of a previous marriage.

Chapter Five: Divorce

ARTICLE 17.   Divorce shall be granted when husband and wife both desire it. In the event of either the husband or the wife alone insisting upon divorce, it may be granted only when mediation by the district people's government and the judicial organ has failed to bring about a reconciliation.

In cases where divorce is desired by both husband and wife, both parties shall register with the district people's government in order to obtain divorce certificates. The district people's government, after establishing that divorce is desired by both parties and that appropriate measures have been taken for the care of children and property, shall issue the divorce certificates without delay.

When only one party insists on divorce, the district people's government may try to effect a reconciliation. If such mediation fails, it shall, without delay, refer the case to the county or municipal people's court for decision. The district people's government shall not attempt to prevent or to obstruct either party from appealing to the county or municipal people's court. In dealing with a divorce case, the county or municipal people's court must, in the first instance, try to bring about a reconciliation between the parties. In case such mediation fails, the court shall render a verdict without delay.

In the case where, after divorce, both husband and wife desire the resumption of marital relations, they shall apply to the district people's government for a registration of remarriage. The district people's government shall accept such a registration and issue certificates of remarriage.

ARTICLE 18.   The husband shall not apply for a divorce when his wife is with child. He may apply for divorce only one year after the birth of the child. In the case of a woman applying for divorce, this restriction does not apply.

ARTICLE 19.   The consent of a member of the revolutionary army on active service who maintains correspondence with his or her family must first be obtained before his or her spouse can apply for divorce.

Divorce may be granted to the spouse of a member of the revolutionary army who does not correspond with his or her family for a subsequent period of two years from the date of the promulgation of this law. Divorce may also be granted to the spouse of a member of the revolutionary army who had not maintained correspondence with his or her family for over two years prior to the promulgation of this law and who fails to correspond with his or her family for a further period of one year subsequent to the promulgation of the present law.

Chapter Six: Maintenance and Education of Children after Divorce

ARTICLE 20.   The blood ties between parents and children do not end with the divorce of the parents. No matter whether the father or the mother acts as guardian of the children, they still remain the children of both parties.

After divorce, both parents still have the duty to support and educate their children.

After divorce, the guiding principle is to allow the mother to have custody of a baby still being breast-fed. After the weaning of the child, if a dispute arises between the two parties over the guardianship and an agreement cannot be reached, the people's court shall render a decision in accordance with the interests of the child.

ARTICLE 21.   If, after divorce, the mother is given custody of a child, the father shall be responsible for the whole or part of the necessary cost of the maintenance and education of the child. Both parties shall reach an agreement regarding the amount and the duration of such maintenance and education. In the case where the two parties fail to reach an agreement, the people's court shall render a decision.

Payment may be made in cash, in kind or by tilling land allocated to the child.

Such agreement reached between parents or a decision rendered by the people's court in connection with the maintenance and education of a child shall not prevent the child from requesting either parent to increase the amount decided upon by agreement or by judicial decision.

ARTICLE 22.   In the case where a divorced woman remarries and her husband is willing to pay the whole or part of the cost of maintaining and educating the child or children by her former husband, the father of the child or children is entitled to have such cost of maintenance and education reduced or to be exempted from bearing such cost in accordance with the circumstances.

Chapter Seven: Property and Maintenance after Divorce

ARTICLE 23.   In case of divorce, the wife shall retain such property as belonged to her prior to her marriage. The disposal of other family properties shall be subject to agreement between the two parties. In cases where agreement cannot be reached, the people's court shall render a decision after taking into consideration the actual state of the family property, the interests of the wife and the child or children, and the principle of benefiting the development of production.

In cases where the property allocated to the wife and her child or children is sufficient for the maintenance and education of the child or children, the husband may be exempted from bearing further maintenance and education costs.

ARTICLE 24.   After divorce, debts incurred during the period of their married life together shall be paid out of the property jointly acquired by husband and wife during this period. In cases where no such property has been

272

acquired or in cases where such property is insufficient to pay off such debts, the husband shall be held responsible for paying these debts. Debts incurred separately by the husband or wife shall be paid off by the party responsible.

ARTICLE 25. After divorce, if one party has not remarried and has maintenance difficulties, the other party shall render assistance. Both parties shall work out an agreement with regard to the method and duration of such assistance; in case an agreement cannot be reached, the people's court shall render a decision.[1]

84. LAND REFORM
[From Liu Shao-ch'i, "Report on the Question of Land Reform," June 14, 1950]

The essential content of agrarian reform is the confiscation of the land of the landlord class for distribution to the landless or land-poor peasants. Thus the landlords as a class in society are abolished and the land ownership system of feudal exploitation is transformed into a system of peasant land ownership. This is indeed the greatest and most thorough reform in thousands of years of Chinese history.

Why should such a reform be made? In a nutshell, it is because the original land ownership system in China is extremely irrational. In general, the land situation in old China is roughly as follows:

Landlords and rich peasants, who constitute less than 10 percent of the rural population possess approximately from 70 to 80 percent of the land and brutally exploit the peasants by means of their land.

Poor peasants, farm laborers, middle peasants and others, however, who make up 90 percent of the rural population, possess in all only 20 to 30 percent of the land. They toil all the year round but can hardly have a full belly and warm back. . . . In Szechuan and other areas the landlords possess about 70 or 80 percent of the land.

In other areas such as the middle and lower reaches of the Yangtze River, land ownership is somewhat dispersed. According to the data obtained in our recent investigation of a number of villages in East China and Central-South China, the situation is roughly as follows:

Land owned by landlords and public land constitute 30 to 50 percent; rich peasants possess 10 to 15 percent of the land; middle peasants, poor peasants and farm laborers possess 30 to 40 percent of the land.

The total area of land rented out in the rural areas constitutes about 60 to 70 percent of the land. Land rented out by rich peasants represents about 3

[1]Chapter Eight, "By-Laws," omitted.

to 5 percent, while land cultivated by rich peasants themselves constitutes about 10 percent.

In other words, 90 percent of the rural land is cultivated by middle peasants, poor peasants and a section of the farm laborers, who own merely a part of the land, and the greater part does not belong to them. Such a situation is still very serious.

Herein lies the basic reason why our nation has become the object of aggression and oppression and has become impoverished and backward. This also constitutes the principal obstacle to our nation's democratization, industrialization, independence, unification and prosperity. Unless we change this situation, the victory of the Chinese people's revolution cannot be consolidated, the productive forces in the rural areas cannot be set free, the industrialization of New China cannot be realized and the people cannot enjoy the fundamental gains of the victory of the revolution. . . .

This basic reason for and the aim of agrarian reform are different from the view that agrarian reform is only designed to relieve the poor people. The Communist Party has always been fighting for the interests of the laboring poor, but the viewpoints of Communists have always been different from those of the philanthropists. The results of agrarian reform are beneficial to the impoverished laboring peasants, helping the peasants partly solve their problem of poverty. But the basic aim of agrarian reform is not purely one of relieving the impoverished peasants. It is designed to set free the rural productive forces from the shackles of the feudal land ownership system of the landlord class in order to develop agricultural production and thus pave the way for New China's industrialization. The problem of poverty among the peasants can be finally solved only if agricultural production can be greatly developed, if the industrialization of New China can be realized, and if China can embark upon the road to Socialism. The mere carrying out of agrarian reform can only solve part, but not the whole, of the problem of the peasants' poverty.

The basic reason for and the basic aim of agrarian reform are intended for production. Hence, every step in agrarian reform should in a practical way take into consideration and be closely coordinated with the development of rural production. Precisely because of this basic reason and aim, the Central Committee of the Communist Party of China has proposed that rich peasant economy be preserved and be free from infringement in future agrarian reform. This is advantageous to the development of the people's economy in our country. It is, therefore, also beneficial to the broad peasant masses. . . .

If the people's government pursues a policy of preserving the rich peasant economy, the rich peasants generally can be won over to a neutral attitude [politically]. Better protection can then be given to the middle peasants, thus dispelling certain unnecessary misgivings of the peasants during the development of production. Therefore, in the present situation, the adoption of a policy to preserve the rich peasant economy in the coming agrarian reform is necessary both politically and economically. . . .

The policy adopted by us of preserving a rich peasant economy is of course not temporary, but a long term policy. That is to say, a rich peasant economy will be preserved throughout the whole stage of New Democracy. Only when the conditions are ripe for the extensive application of mechanized farming, for the organization of collective farms, and for the socialist reform of the rural areas, will the need for a rich peasant economy cease, and this will take a somewhat long time to achieve. . . .

Agrarian reform is a systematic and fierce struggle. Our general line to be followed in future agrarian reform is that reliance should be placed on the poor peasants and farm laborers, while uniting with the middle peasants and neutralizing the rich peasants, in order to eliminate the feudal exploitation system gradually and with discrimination, and to develop agricultural production.

85. A VILLAGE REVOLUTION
[From Ting Ling, *The Sun Shines over the Sangkan River*, 1948]

For thousands of years the local despots had had power. They had oppressed generation after generation of peasants, and the peasants had bowed their necks under their yoke. Now abruptly they were confronted with this power standing before them with bound hands, and they felt bewildered, at a loss. Some who were particularly intimidated by [Schemer Chien's] malevolent look recalled the days when they could only submit, and now, exposed to this blast, wavered again. So for the time being they were silent.

All this time Schemer Chien, standing on the stage gnawing his lips, was glancing round, wanting to quell these yokels, unwilling to admit defeat. For a moment he really had the mastery. He and his many years of power had become so firmly established in the village it was difficult for anyone to dislodge him. The peasants hated him, and had just been cursing him; but now that he stood before them they held their breath and faltered. . . . The longer the silence lasted, the greater Chien's power became, until it looked as if he were going to win.

At this point a man suddenly leapt out from the crowd. . . . Rushing up to Schemer Chien he cursed him: "You murderer! You trampled our village under your feet! You killed people from behind the scenes for money. Today we're going to settle all old scores, and do a thorough job of it. Do you hear that? Do you still want to frighten people? It's no use. . . . Kneel down! Kneel to all the villagers!" He pushed Chien hard, while the crowd echoed: "Kneel down! Kneel down!" The militiamen forced him to kneel down properly.

Then the masses' rage flared up, they tasted power and stirred indignantly. A child's voice was heard: "Put on the hat! Make him wear the hat!"

Young Kuo jumped forward and asked: "Who'll put it on? Whoever'll put it on, come up here!"

While the crowd was shouting, "Make him wear the hat! Put on the hat!" a boy of thirteen or fourteen jumped up, lifted the hat and set it on Schemer Chien's head, at the same time spitting at him and cursing. . . .

By now Chien had lowered his head completely, his malevolent eyes could no longer sweep their faces. The tall paper hat made him look like a clown. Bent basely from the waist, screwing up his eyes, he had lost all his power, had become the people's prisoner, a criminal against the masses.

The man who had cursed Chien turned now to face the crowd, and they all saw that it was Young Cheng, the chairman of the peasants' association. "Friends!" said Young Cheng. "Look at him and look at me! See how soft and delicate he is: it's not cold yet but he's wearing a lined gown. Then look at me, look at yourselves. Do we look like human beings? Hah, when our mothers bore us, we were all alike! We've poured our blood and sweat to feed him. He's been living on our blood and sweat, oppressing us all these years; but today we want him to give back money for money, life for life, isn't that right?"

"Right! Give back money for money, life for life!" . . .

"All peasants are brothers!" "Support Chairman Mao!" "Follow Chairman Mao to the end!" Shouts sounded from the stage and from the crowd.

Then people rushed up on the stage, stumbling over each other to confront Schemer Chien. Mrs. Chien stood with tear-stained cheeks behind her husband, pleading with them all: "Good people, have pity on my old man! Good people!" . . .

She was like a female clown in the theater, making a fine couple with her husband. She had echoed him all her life, and now she still clung to him, unwilling to separate their fates.

One accusation was brought after another. . . . Some peasants were so carried away that they climbed onto the stage and struck at Schemer Chien as they questioned him, while the crowd backed them up: "Beat him, beat him to death!" . . .

Peasants surged up onto the stage, shouting wildly: "Kill him! A life for our lives!"

A group of villagers rushed to beat him. It was not clear who started, but one struck the first blow and others fought to get at him, while those behind who could not reach him shouted: "Throw him down! Throw him down! Let's all beat him!"

One feeling animated them all—vegeance! They wanted vengeance! They wanted to give vent to their hatred, the sufferings of the oppressed since their ancestors' times, the hatred of thousands of years; all this resentment they directed against him. They would have liked to tear him with their teeth.

The cadres could not stop everyone jumping onto the stage. With blows and curses the crowd succeeded in dragging him down from the stage and then more people swarmed towards him. Some crawled over across the heads and shoulders of those in front.

Schemer Chien's silk gown was torn. His shoes had fallen off, the white paper hat had been trampled to pieces underfoot. All semblance of order was gone and it looked as though he was going to be beaten to death. [The village Communist Party chairman stops the crowd, telling them that all executions must have the approval of the county court. The crowd then discusses what next to do with Schemer Chien, and decides to make him write a confession.]

Schemer Chien crawled to his feet again and kneeled to kowtow to the crowd. His right eye was swollen after his beating so that the eye looked even smaller. His lip was split and mud was mixed with the blood. . . .

He was a wretched sight, and as he thanked the villagers his voice was no longer clear and strong, but he stammered out: "Good people! I'm kowtowing to you good folks. I was quite wrong in the past. Thank you for your mercy ———.''

A group of children softly aped his voice: "Good people! . . ."

Then he was dragged over to write a statement. He took the brush in his trembling hand and wrote line by line. When the chairman started reading the statement the crowd grew tense again, and shouted, "Let him read it himself!"

Chien knelt in the middle of the stage, his lined gown hanging in shreds, shoeless, not daring to meet anyone's eyes. He read: "In the past I committed crimes in the village, oppressing good people———!"

"That won't do! Just to write 'I' won't do! Write 'local despot, Chien.' "

"Yes, write 'I, local despot, Chien.' "

"Start again!"

Schemer Chien started reading again: "I, Chien, a local despot, committed crimes in the village, oppressing good people, and I deserve to die a hundred times over; but my good friends are merciful———."

"Who the devil are you calling good friends?" An old man rushed forward and spat at him.

"Go on reading! Just say all the people of the village."

"No, why should he call us his people."

"Say all the gentlemen."

"Say all the poor gentlemen. We don't want to be rich gentlemen! Only the rich are called gentlemen."

Chien had to continue: "Thanks to the mercy of all the poor gentlemen in the village———."

"That's no good. Don't say poor gentlemen; today we poor people have stood up. Say 'the liberated gentlemen,' and it can't be wrong."

"Yes, liberated gentlemen."

Someone chuckled. "Today we're liberated gentlemen!"

"Thanks to the mercy of the liberated gentlemen, my unworthy life has been spared———."

"What? I don't understand." Another voice from the crowd interrupted Chien. "We liberated gentlemen aren't going to pass all this literary stuff. Just put it briefly: say your dog's life has been spared."

"Yes, spare your dog's life!" the rest agreed.

Chien had to go on: "Spare my dog's life. In the future I must change my former evil ways completely. If I transgress in the slightest or oppose the masses, I shall be put to death. This statement is made by the local despot Chien, and signed in the presence of the masses. August 3."

The presidium asked the crowd to discuss it, but very few further amendments were proposed, although a few people still felt he was getting off too lightly and they ought to beat him some more.

Schemer Chien was allowed to go back [home]. . . . All his property apart from his land was to be sealed up immediately by the peasants' association. As to the question of how much should be left him, that was left to the land assessment committee to decide. . . .

By now land reform here could be considered as well under way. Although the peasants still had certain reservations, at least they had passed one large hurdle, and overthrown their greatest enemy. They intended to continue the struggle against the bad powers in the village, settling accounts with each in turn. They meant to stand up properly. They had the strength, as the events of the day made them realize. Their confidence had increased. . . . As the meeting broke up they shouted for joy, a roar like thunder going up into the air. This was an end; it was also a beginning.

86. THE BENEFITS OF COOPERATIVE AGRICULTURE
[From Mao Tse-tung, *The Question of Agricultural Cooperation*, July 31, 1955]

Throughout the Chinese countryside a new upsurge in the socialist mass movement is in sight. But some of our comrades are tottering along like a woman with bound feet, always complaining that others are going too fast. They imagine that by picking on trifles, grumbling unnecessarily, worrying continuously and putting up countless taboos and commandments they are guiding the socialist mass movement in the rural areas on sound lines.

No, this is not the right way at all; it is wrong.

The tide of social reform in the countryside—in the shape of cooperation —has already reached some places. Soon it will sweep the whole country. This is a huge socialist revolutionary movement, which involves a rural population more than five hundred million strong, one which has very great world significance. We should guide this movement vigorously, warmly and systematically and not act as a drag on it in various ways. In such a movement some deviations are inevitable. That stands to reason, but it is not difficult to straighten them out. Weaknesses or mistakes found among cadres and peasants can be done away with if we actively assist them. Guided by the Party the cadres and peasants are going forward; the movement is fundamentally healthy.

In some places they have made certain mistakes in the work, for example, barring poor peasants from the cooperatives and ignoring their difficulties, and at the same time forcing the well-to-do middle peasants into the cooperatives and interfering with their interests. But these errors have to be corrected by education, not just by reprimands. Mere reprimands solve no problems. We must guide the movement boldly, not act like one fearing the dragon in front and the tiger behind. Both cadres and peasants will change of themselves as they learn from their own experience in the struggle. Get them into action themselves: they will learn while doing, become more capable, and large numbers of excellent people will come forward. This "fearing the dragon in front and the tiger behind" attitude will not produce cadres. It is necessary to send large groups of cadres with short-term training into the countryside to guide and assist the agricultural cooperative movement; but the cadres sent down from above also have to learn how to work from the movement itself. Going in for training courses and hearing dozens of rules explained in lectures does not necessarily mean one knows how to work.

In short, leadership should never lag behind the mass movement. As things stand today, however, the mass movement is in advance of the leadership, which fails to keep pace with the movement. This state of affairs must be changed. . . .

Needless say, neither socialist industrialization nor socialist transformation is easy. A host of difficulties are bound to crop up as some 110 million peasant households turn from individual to collective management and go ahead with technical reforms in agriculture. But we should have confidence that our Party is capable of leading the masses to overcome such difficulties.

As far as agriculture cooperation is concerned, I think we should believe: first, that the poor peasants, and the low-middle peasants among both the new and old middle peasants,[1] are disposed to choose the socialist road and energetically respond to our Party's call for cooperation—the poor peasants because of their economic difficulties and the lower-middle peasants because their economic conditions, though better than before liberation, are still not too good. Particularly active are those among them who have a deeper understanding.

Second, I think we should have confidence that our Party is capable of leading the people of the country to socialism. Our Party has led a great people's democratic revolution to victory and established a people's democratic dictatorship headed by the working class, and it can certainly lead our people to carry out, in the main, socialist industrialization and the socialist transformation of agriculture, handicrafts and capitalist industry and commerce, in the course of roughly three five-year plans. In agriculture, as in other fields, we have powerful and convincing proof of this—witness the first group of 300 cooperatives in [in 1951], the second of 13,700 [between 1951 and 1953], and the third of 86,000 [in 1954]—100,000 all told—all of which were established before the autumn of 1954 and all of which have been consolidated. Why, then, should not the fourth group of 550,000 cooperatives formed in 1954–55 and the fifth group (our provisional target) to be established in 1955–56 be consolidated too?

We must believe in the masses; we must believe in our Party: these are two cardinal principles. If we doubt these principles, we can do nothing. . . .

Members of agricultural producers' cooperatives must obtain higher yields than individual peasants and those working in mutual-aid teams. Output certainly cannot be allowed to remain at the level reached by individual peasants or mutual-aid teams: that would mean failure. What would be the use

[1]Old middle peasants are those who were middle peasants before the land reform. New middle peasants are those who have risen to the status of middle peasants since land reform. (Tr.)

of having cooperatives at all? Still less can yields be allowed to fall. Over 80 percent of the 650,000 existing agricultural producers' cooperatives did increase their yields. That is a cheerful picture, showing that members of the cooperatives are taking greater initiative in production and that cooperatives are superior to mutual-aid teams, and far superior to individual farming.

Certain things are essential in order to increase yields: first, insistence on the principles of voluntariness and mutual benefit; secondly, improvement of management (planning and administration of production, organization of labor, etc.); thirdly, improvement of farming technique (deep ploughing and intensive cultivation, close planting, increasing the acreage of land which is cropped more than once a year, selection of seed, popularization of improved farm implements, the fight against plant diseases and pests, etc.); and fourthly, an increase in the means of production (including land, fertilizer, water conservancy works, draught animals, farm implements, etc.). These are necessary conditions for consolidating the cooperatives and ensuring increased production. . . .

I shall now deal with the question of the composition of the cooperative membership. I think that, in the next year or two, in all areas where cooperatives are starting to grow or have only recently started to get going, that is, in most areas at present, we should first get the active elements of the following sections of the people organized: (1) the poor peasants, (2) the lower new middle peasants and (3) the lower old middle peasants. People in these sections who for the time being are not active must not be dragged in against their will. Wait till their understanding grows and they are interested in cooperatives, then draw them in group by group. These sections of people are fairly close to each other in their economic position. They either still have difficulties (in the case of the poor peasants who have been given land and are much better off than in pre-liberation days but still have difficulties owing to insufficient manpower, draught animals and farm implements), or are still not well off (in the case of the lower-middle peasants). Therefore, they all have an active desire to organize cooperatives. Even so, for various reasons, the degree of their keenness varies: some are very keen, some are, for the time being, not very keen, while others prefer to wait and see. So we should continue to educate for a while those who for the time being are reluctant to join cooperatives, even if they are poor or lower-middle peasants, we should continue to educate for a time and wait patiently till their understanding grows; what we must not do is to go against the voluntary principle and drag them in against their will.

As for the upper middle peasants among the new and old middle peasants —that is, the middle peasants who are economically better off—except for those who have already become conscious that they must choose the socialist road and are really willing to join—who can be admitted—none of the rest are to be drawn in for the time being, certainly not dragged in reluctantly. That is because they have not yet become conscious that they must choose the socialist road, and they will make up their minds to join the cooperatives only after the majority of people in the rural areas have joined, or when the yield per *mou* of the cooperatives equals or surpasses that of the land of well-to-do middle peasants, and then they realize that they stand to gain nothing by going on working on their own, and that it is rather more profitable to join. . . .

In the next few years we shall definitely not, in areas where the majority of the population have not joined in cooperation, take former landlords and rich peasants into the cooperatives. In areas where the majority of people have joined in cooperation, those cooperatives which are firmly established may, on conditions, at different times, take in group by group people who were formerly landlords and rich peasants but who have long given up exploitation, who are now engaged in labor and abide by law, letting them take part in collective labor and continue to reform themselves in the process.

On the question of growth, the problem that calls for criticism at present is not rashness. It is wrong to say that the present pace of development of the agricultural producers' cooperatives has "gone beyond practical possibilities" or "gone beyond the consciousness of the masses." The situation in China is like this: its population is enormous, there is a shortage of cultivated land (only three *mou* of land per head taking the country as a whole; in many parts of the southern provinces the average is only one *mou* or less), natural calamities take place from time to time—every year large numbers of farms suffer more or less from flood, drought, gales, frost, hail or insect pests—and methods of farming are backward. As a result, many peasants are still having difficulties or are not well off. The well-off ones are comparatively few, although since land reform the standard of living of the peasants as a whole has improved to a greater or lesser extent. For all these reasons there is an active desire among most peasants to take the socialist road. Our country's socialist industrialization and its achievements are constantly intensifying it. For them socialism is the only solution. Such peasants amount to 60 to 70 percent of the entire rural population. That is to say, most of the peasants, if they are to throw off poverty, improve their standard of living and withstand natural calamities, cannot but unite and go forward to socialism. . . .

But some of our comrades ignore these facts and think that the several hundred thousand small semi-socialist agricultural producers' cooperatives that have sprung into being have "gone beyond practical possibilities" or "gone beyond the understanding of the masses." . . . This is the first wrong-headed idea.

These comrades also underrate the leading role which the Communist Party plays in the countryside and the wholehearted support which the peasant masses give it. They imagine our Party is already finding it difficult to consolidate the several hundred thousand small cooperatives, and that any great growth of cooperative farming is certainly inconceivable. They paint a pessimistic picture of the present situation in the Party's work in guiding agricultural cooperation and think that it "has gone beyond the level of the cadres' experience." It's quite true, the socialist revolution is a new revolution. In the past we only had experience of bourgeois-democratic revolution; we had no experience of socialist revolution. How can we get such experience: by sitting back and waiting for it, or by throwing ourselves into the struggle for the socialist revolution and learning in the process? . . . Clearly the idea that the present state of development reached by the agricultural producers' cooperatives has "gone beyond the level of cadres' experience" shows faulty thinking. This is the second wrong-headed idea.

The way these comrades look at things is wrong. They fail to grasp the essential, main aspects and instead exaggerate non-essential, minor aspects. I am not saying that these non-essential, minor aspects should be overlooked; they have to be dealt with properly one by one. But if we are to avoid confusion about the direction in which to proceed, we should not regard them as the essential, main aspects.

We must be convinced: first, that the peasant masses are willing, led by the Party, gradually to follow the socialist road; second, that the Party is able to guide the peasants to take this road. These two points are the essence, the crux of the matter. . . .

The Soviet Union's great historical experience in building socialism inspires our people and gives them full confidence that they can build socialism in their country. . . . Some comrades disapprove of the Party Central Committee's policy of keeping agricultural cooperation in step with socialist industrialization, the policy which proved correct in the Soviet Union. . . . These comrades do not understand that socialist industrialization is not something that can be carried out in isolation, separate from agricultural cooperation. In the first place, as everyone knows, the level of production of marketable grain and industrial raw materials in our country today is very low, whereas the state's demands for these items grow year by year. Therein lies a sharp contradiction. If, in a period of roughly three five-year plans, we cannot fundamentally solve the problem of agricultural cooperation, if we cannot jump from small-scale farming with animal-drawn farm implements to large-scale farming with machinery—which includes state-sponsored land reclamation carried out on a large scale by settlers using machinery (the plan being to bring under cultivation 400–500 million *mou* of virgin land in the course of three five-year plans), we shall fail to resolve the contradiction between the ever-increasing demand for marketable grain and industrial raw materials and the present generally poor yield of staple crops. In that case our socialist industrialization will run into formidable difficulties: we shall not be able to complete socialist industrialization. The Soviet Union once faced this problem in the course of building socialism. It solved it by systematically guiding and expanding agricultural cooperation. We too solve this problem only by using the same method.

In the second place, some of our comrades do not think of linking up the following two factors: heavy industry which is the most important branch in the work of socialist industrialization and produces the tractors and other agricultural machinery, the chemical fertilizers, modern means of transport, oil, electric power for the needs of agriculture and so on, and the fact that all these can find a use or can be used on a big scale only on the basis of large-scale, cooperative farming. We are carrying out a revolution not only in the social system, changing from private ownership to common ownership, but also in technology, changing from handicraft production to mass production with up-to-date machinery. These two revolutions interlink. In agriculture, under the conditions prevailing in our country, cooperation must precede the use of big machinery. . . . What is more, there are two other things which some of our comrades do not think of linking up: the large funds which are needed to complete both national industrialization and the technical reconstruction of agriculture and the fact that a considerable part of these funds is derived from agriculture. Apart from the direct agricultural tax, accumulation of funds comes about by way of developing the production of light industry, which produces large quantities of consumer goods needed by the peasants. The peasants exchange their marketable grain and industrial raw materials for these goods. That satisfies the material demands of both the peasants and the state. It also accumulates funds for the state. But any large-scale expansion of light industry requires the development not only of heavy industry but of agriculture too. The reason for this is that you cannot bring about any great expansion of a light industry founded simply on a small-peasant economy; but only one based on large-scale farming which, in the case of our country, means socialist cooperative agriculture. Only that type of agriculture can give the peasants much greater purchasing power than they have now. We again have the experience of the Soviet Union to draw on, but some of our comrades take no notice of it. They usually take the standpoint of the bourgeoisie and the rich peasants or that of the well-to-do middle peasants who have a spontaneous tendency to take the capitalist road. They think in terms of the few, rather than take the standpoint of the working class and think in terms of the whole country and people. . . .

The first step in the countryside is to call on the peasants, in accordance with the same principles of voluntariness and mutual benefit, to organize agricultural producers' mutual-aid teams. Such teams contain only the rudiments of socialism. Each one draws in a few households, though some have ten or more. The second step is to call on the peasants, on the basis of these mutual-aid teams and still in accordance with the principles of voluntariness and mutual benefit, to organize small agricultural producers' cooperatives, semi-socialist in nature, characterized by the pooling of land as shares and by single management. Not until we take the third step will the peasants be called upon, on the basis of these small semi-socialist cooperatives and in accordance with the same principles of voluntariness and mutual benefit, to unite on a larger scale and organize large agricultural producers' cooperatives completely socialist in nature. These steps are designed to steadily raise the socialist consciousness of the peasants through their personal experience, to change their mode of life step by step and so minimize any feeling that their mode of life is being changed all of a sudden. Steps such as these can in the main avoid any drop in yields over a period of, say, the first year or two. More than that, these steps must ensure a year by year increase. And this can be done. Roughly 80 percent of the existing 650,000 agricultural producers' cooperatives have increased output. Just over 10 percent of them have shown neither an increase nor a decline. The output of the remainder has dropped. The state of affairs in both these latter categories is bad, and particularly so in the case of cooperatives where production has fallen. A great effort must be made to check over such cooperatives. Since about 80 percent of all cooperatives increased output (by anything from 10 to 30 percent), and since just over 10 percent in their first year showed neither an increase nor a decline, it must be quite possible for them, in their second year, after checking, to show an increase; and, finally, since it is feasible for the remainder that have shown a decline in output to increase it in the second year, after checking, or at least to reach the stage of neither increasing nor reducing production, our progress in cooperation is on the whole healthy, and can in the main ensure that production does not fall, but rises. The taking of these steps is, moreover, a splendid school for training cadres. Through such steps administrative and technical personnel for the cooperatives are gradually trained in large numbers. . . .

As everybody knows, we already have a worker-peasant alliance based on a bourgeois-democratic revolution against imperialism and feudalism, which took land from the landlords and distributed it to the peasants so as to free them from the bondage of feudal ownership. Now this revolution is a thing of the past and feudal ownership has been done away with. What still lingers in the countryside is capitalist ownership by the rich peasants and individual peasant ownership—an ocean of it. Everyone has noticed that in recent years there has been a spontaneous and constant growth of capitalist elements in the countryside and that new rich peasants have sprung up everywhere. Many well-to-do middle peasants are striving to become rich ones. Many poor peasants, lacking sufficient means of production, are still not free from the toils of poverty; some are in debt, others selling or renting their land. If this tendency goes unchecked, the separation into two extremes in the countryside will get worse day by day. Peasants who have lost their land and who are still having difficulties will complain that we do nothing to save them when we see they are up against it, nothing to help them overcome difficulties. And the well-to-do middle peasants who tend towards capitalism will also find fault with us, for they will never be satisfied because we have no intention of taking the capitalist path. If that is how circumstances stand, can the worker-peasant alliance stand fast? Obviously not. The problem is one that can be solved only on a new basis. That basis is, simultaneously, gradually, to bring about, on the one hand, socialist industrialization, the socialist transformation of handicraft industry and capitalist industry and commerce, and, on the other, the socialist transformation of agriculture as a whole through cooperation. In that way we shall put an end to the systems of rich-peasant economy and individual economy in the countryside and so let all people in the rural areas enjoy a common prosperity. Only in this way, we hold, can the worker-peasant alliance be consolidated. If we fail to act in this way, that alliance will really be in danger of breaking up.

87. THE ROLE OF POLITICAL LEADERSHIP
[From Mao Tse-tung's Preface to "A Serious Lesson," 1955]

Political work is the life-blood of all economic work. This is particularly true at a time when the economic system of a society is undergoing a fundamental change. The agricultural cooperative movement, from the very beginning, has been a severe ideological and political struggle. Before a brand-new social system can be built on the site of the old, the site must first be swept clean.

Old ideas reflecting the old system invariably remain in people's minds for a long time. They do not easily give way.

After a co-op is formed it must go through many more struggles before it becomes strong. Even then, the moment it relaxes its efforts, it may collapse. . . .

Opposition to selfish, capitalistic spontaneous tendencies, and promotion of the essence of socialism—that is, making the principle of linking the collective interests with the interests of the individual the standard by which all words and deeds are judged—these then are the ideological and political guarantees that the scattered, small-peasant economy will gradually be transformed into a large-scale cooperative economy.

Ideological and political education is an arduous task. It must be based on the life and experience of the peasants and be conducted in a very practical manner, with careful attention to detail. Neither bluster nor over-simplification will do. It should be conducted not in isolation from our economic measures, but in conjunction with them.

88. PROBLEMS IN THE COOPERATIVES

[From Teng Tzu-hui, "On Contradictions in APCs and Democratic Management of APCs," People's Daily, May 7, 1957]

Class contradiction long existed between the landlords and peasants in the rural areas. This contradiction was solved after liberation and the agrarian reform. After the agrarian reform, another contradiction arose as reflected in the question of whether the Chinese peasantry would take the road to capitalism or to socialism. This contradiction has also been solved after years of hard struggle and work and after the overwhelming majority of the peasants joined APCs last year. Are there any contradictions at present? There are. The new contradictions are contradictions within the ranks of the people as pointed out by Chairman Mao. From our experience in APC reorganization, it would appear that the contradictions that manifest themselves in the APCs may be divided into six categories:

First, contradictions between the state and the APCs. Such contradictions may be involved when agricultural productions plans are mapped out, when farm produce is procured and marketed under centralized plans, when the prices of farm produce and manufactured goods are fixed, when processing of farm produce is organized or when the tax rates and collection of agricultural and secondary products are determined. . . .

Second, contradictions between the APCs and their members, i.e., between the collective interests and personal interests of members. Such contradictions are reflected in the question of whether "to deduct less [of the harvest for the APC] and divide more [among members]" or "to deduct more and divide less." When the summer harvest was distributed last year, the Center instructed all areas to adhere to the "deduct less and divide more" principle, to distribute 60–70 percent of the total income of APCs among their members and to strive for a higher income for 90 percent of APC members. This guiding principle, it now appears, is a correct one for solving the contradictions between the APCs and their members and must be continually carried out hereafter. There were of course some APCs which mechanically carried out this guiding principle, not setting aside income and not making deductions from income as they should, as a result of which production was adversely affected this year. Such mechanical approaches should be avoided.

The contradictions between APCs and their members are also reflected in the question of whether side occupations should be concentrated in the hands of APCs or scattered among members. The guiding principle laid down by the Center is: "where collective operation is essential, side occupations must be undertaken by APCs; where scattered operation is desirable, members should be encouraged and helped as far as possible to undertake side occupations themselves." This directive corrects the deviation of concentrating side occupations in the APCs and restraining members from undertaking side occupations. It is an important measure to solve the contradictions between APCs and members. . . .

Third, contradictions between APCs and production teams. This is a contradiction that calls for urgent solution at the moment. Generally speaking, the power of APCs was over-concentrated in the hands of the administrative committees last year; production plans, technical measures, work norms and fiscal work were subjected to too minute and rigid control, and the production teams, lacking maneuvering power, could not act with expediency according to time and locality and, consequently the activism of production teams and members could not be brought into play. The system of "appropriate division of power between APCs and teams" and "centralized operation and divided control" introduced in various parts of the country provides the main way of solving these contradictions.

Fourth, contradictions among APC members, reflected mainly in the contradictions between the middle peasants and the poor peasants. For instance, the prices fixed for draft animals, carts, trees and fruit trees [contributed by the owners when entering an APC] are too low and payment is not made when due: these questions cause discontent among the upper-middle peasants and, if not properly handled, will also cause discontent among the poor peasants. . . . To deal with these questions, we should, on the basis of strengthening the predominance of the poor peasants, educate both sides by methods of persuasion, and economically make the necessary concessions to the upper-middle peasants and see to is that their interests are not encroached upon. For instance, the prices for draft animals and carts, if they are too low compared with the prices prevailing at the time they were turned over to the APCs, should be appropriately readjusted; draft animals and carts used for doing transport business may be placed under the charge of original owners for doing transport business, and appropriate help may be given to the original owners as regards work points. . . .

The contradictions between APC members also manifest themselves between strong labor power and weak labor power, between a higher technical
level and a lower technical level, between agricultural labor and non-agricultural labor (handicraftsmen, small merchants and peddlers, etc.) . . . These
contradictions should mainly be solved by arranging the jobs for APC members who are physically weak and are non-agricultural laborers . . . in such a
way that each may display his special skill, find his proper position and earn
more income. Those who have a higher technical standard should be given
proper consideration as regards work points. . . . APCs must mainly follow the
"to each according to his work" principle but they should take appropriate
care of those physically unfit or weak and those indigent households on a
mutual-aid and mutual-relief basis.

Fifth, contradictions between teams, mainly between poor villages and rich
villages (that is, between poor teams and rich teams). By rich villages and rich
teams are meant those villages and teams possessing better land, getting a
higher output or owning more trees and fruit trees. Their riches are due to
better natural conditions and the results of years of work and were not acquired through exploitation. Some APCs distribute income on an equal basis
without giving special consideration to the rich villages; as a result, rich
villages and rich teams suffer a loss, causing them to be discontent and even
giving rise to contrasts between villages and between teams, thus aggravating
the contradictions. This is not a proper thing to do. These contradictions may
be handled in such a way that rich villages and rich teams are properly taken
care of in connection with guarantee of production and are ensured against loss
or much loss, thereby alleviating such contradictions and facilitating unity.
Poor villages and poor teams should be given help as regards production so
that they can gradually step up their output and catch up with the rich villages
and rich teams in a certain period of time.

Sixth, contradictions between cadres and the masses. The overwhelming
majority of our primary cadres are of good quality and are bound up with the
broad masses of the peasants, but there are also numbers of cadres who are
undemocratic, not consulting with the masses, not seeking the advice of veteran peasants and not calling general meetings of APC members. [Such] APC
cadres are simply answerable to higher levels and obedient to higher levels, not
knowing that they should also be responsible to the masses and listen to the
opinions of the masses. . . . Some APC cadres still resort to methods of compulsion; they take no part in production, get too much allowance in the form
of compensatory work points, keep the accounts to themselves and even commit embezzlement and misdeeds. Because of this, APC members are not
satisfied with cadres; the problem is more serious in the case of those APCs
whose output has dropped. The accumulation of such discontent has set APC
members against cadres and even caused agitation for withdrawal from the
APCs. Obviously such contradictions, if not well solved, will weaken the
position of the poor peasants and cut the ground from under the cooperatives.
The methods set forth in the notification on democratic management of APCs
issued by the Center in April of this year provide timely solutions to these
contradictions. Recently, cadres have been transferred to lower levels, APC

cadres take part in production, veteran peasants are shown respect, accounts are made public: there are new phenomena in the countryside and the basic causes behind the gradual normalization of relations between cadres and the masses. . . .

How are these contradictions within the ranks of the people to be solved? By carrying out the guiding principle laid down by Chairman Mao and the Party Center, that is, by arousing the masses to distinguish right from wrong, persist in the right, correct the wrong through criticism and education, and achieve new solidarity. In a word, the policy of democratic management of APCs must be seriously carried out. . . . Success in agricultural production calls for close cooperation between two sides: it depends on the APC members and on the cadres, both on the enthusiasm of members and on the correct leadership of the higher level, both on the practical experience of the peasants and on the scientific knowledge of technical persons. . . . [L]eadership must be combined with the masses, centralism with democracy and theory with practice. In other words, the leadership following the mass line should be followed. As we know, the reason why our Party was able to win victory in the Chinese revolution and why leadership work is successful is because we follow one fundamental line, i.e., the mass line. . . . Chairman Mao gave us clear-cut instructions long ago: "We should gather the opinions (scattered and unsystematic opinions) of the masses and, after (studying and transforming them into concentrated and systematic opinions), propagate and explain them to the masses through cadres and transform them into the opinions of the masses. Let the masses adhere to these opinions and manifest them in action. Test the correctness of these opinions through the actions of the masses and see whether there are new problems and new opinions; then again gather the opinions of the masses and let the masses adhere to them. In this endless process the opinions will be made more correct, more impressive and richer each time." . . . It follows that the decisions of leaders are not based on the subjective imagination of leading cadres sitting at home but are made by cadres who go amidst the masses, consult with the masses, hear the opinions of the masses, collect opinions from all sides and from the masses of all strata, analyze, compare, select and sum them up into comprehensive opinions to be transformed into the opinions of the masses through a meeting and to be adhered to by the masses under the leadership of cadres. . . . [O]ver such questions as production plans, technical measures, division of teams, guarantee of work and production, work norms, absorption of investments and distribution of products, the APC cadres should consult with APC members and seek the advice of veteran peasants before making decisions through the administrative committees and representative conferences and before letting APC members carry them out. True, the state plans and the directives of higher levels should be carried out but they should be carried out flexibly in the light of specific conditions prevailing at the time and in the locality and according to possibilities and must not be carried out mechanically.

89. COMMUNES AND COMMUNISM

[From "Hold High the Red Flag of People's Communes and March On," *People's Daily* editorial, September 3, 1958]

People's communes, which mark a new stage in the socialist movement in China's rural areas, are now being set up and developed in many places at a rapid rate. . . .

The people's commune is characterized by its bigger size and more socialist nature. With big membership and huge expanse of land the communes can carry out production and construction of a comprehensive nature and on a large scale. They not only carry out an all-round management of agriculture, forestry, animal husbandry, side-occupations and fishery, but merge industry (the worker), agriculture (the peasant), exchange (the trader), culture and education (the student), and military affairs (the militiaman) into one.

People's communes so far established usually have a membership of 10,000 people each, in some cases 10,000 households. A commune generally corresponds to a township. If a township is too small, then several townships may be combined to form a commune.

Being big, they can do many things hitherto impossible to the agricultural producers' cooperatives, such as building medium-sized water-conservancy works, setting up factories and mines requiring complicated technique, carrying out big projects of road and housing construction, establishing secondary schools and schools of higher learning, etc. As a matter of fact, many of these undertakings are being carried out by the large communes and the matter of manpower shortage also becomes easier to tackle.

The people's commune represents a much higher degree of socialist development and collectivization than the agricultural producers' cooperative. Its massive scale of production requires organization with a higher efficiency and greater maneuverability of labor as well as the participation of all the women in production. Consequently more and more community mess halls, nurseries, sewing groups and other kinds of establishments are being set up, and the last remnants of individual ownership of the means of production retained in the agricultural producers' cooperatives are being eliminated. In many places, for instance, the reserved plots, livestock, orchards and major items of production tools owned by individual peasants have been transferred to the people's communes in the course of their organization. . . .

As the people's commune has for its membership workers, peasants, merchants, students and militiamen it is no longer a solely economic organization —it combines economic, cultural, political and military affairs into one entity. There is, therefore, no longer any need for the separate existence of township governments. The management committees of the people's communes are in fact the people's councils of the townships. There is also a tendency for the federation of people's communes in a county to become one with the people's council of that county. This facilitates unified leadership, closely combines the collective economy of the agricultural producers' cooperatives with the state economy of the townships and counties and helps the transition from collective ownership to ownership by the whole people.

For this reason the people's commune is the most appropriate organizational form in China for accelerating socialist construction and the transition to communism. It will become the basic social unit in the future communist society. . . .

China has now some 700,000 agricultural producers' cooperatives, mostly set up during the upsurge of socialism in 1955 and later gradually transformed into advanced cooperatives. They are undoubtedly far superior to individual farming, mutual-aid teams, and even the elementary agricultural producers' cooperatives, and have contributed enormously to the steady increase of China's farm output in the past few years. With the growth of agricultural production, especially the great leap forward in agriculture since the last winter, these cooperatives have, however, gradually become inadequate to meet the needs of the day. The reason is as follows. These cooperatives are comparatively small in size. Averaging less than one hundred households in membership, they have but a small amount of manpower. The amount of their public reserve funds is small and the rate of accumulation slow. With these handicaps it is difficult for them to engage in many kinds of production.

To achieve a high-speed advance in agriculture, enable the countryside to assume a new aspect at an early date, and improve the peasants' living standards as quickly as possible, as facts show, it is necessary to carry out large-scale capital construction that will fundamentally change the natural conditions; to apply new farming techniques; to develop forestry, animal husbandry, side-occupations and fishery side by side with agriculture; to build industries that serve agriculture and the needs of the peasants as well as big industries; gradually to carry out mechanization and electrification; to improve transport, communications and housing conditions in rural areas; and set up educational, health and cultural establishments—to do all this is beyond the power of an agricultural producers' cooperative consisting of a few dozens or hundreds of households. . . .

Some people's communes may have gone farther than others, but generally speaking, the transformation of collective ownership into ownership by the whole people is a process that will take three or four years, even five or six years, to complete in the rural areas. Then, after a number of years, production will be greatly increased. The people's communist consciousness and morality will be highly improved. Education will be made universal and elevated among the people. Differences between the workers and peasants, urban and rural areas, mental and manual labor—left over from the old society and inevitably existing in the socialist society—as well as the remnants of unequal bourgeois rights which are the reflection of these differences, will gradually vanish, the function of the state will be limited to protecting the country from external aggression; it will play no role in domestic affairs. By that time Chinese society will enter the era of communism, the era when the principle "from each according to his ability, to each according to his needs" will be realized.

Now the development of the people's communes is growing into a mass movement more gigantic than the cooperative movement of 1955. The Party committees of various places must work out appropriate plans and give active guidance to the development according to local conditions. The development of people's communes will doubtlessly be different in time, scale, pace, and method in different places. Uniformity should not be imposed. People's communes must be set up on the basis of full discussion by the people concerned and it must be a matter of the people's own choice. No rash, impetuous, or domineering attitude should be taken, especially on the question concerning change in the ownership of the means of production.

At present, work in the autumn fields allows for no delay while preparations must be made for the farm work of the coming winter and the next spring. We must give first priority to work related to production in all places, regardless of the condition whether people's communes have or have not been established.

90. REVOLUTIONIZING WAGES AND PRODUCTION
[From an Editorial in Shanghai *Liberation Daily*, September 20, 1958]

Recently, many factory workers who earn piece wages have put forward demands for reforming the existing piece wage system. . . . A number of workers hold that, at a time when all people of our country are performing selfless labor to build socialism and communism, continuation of the piece wage system is no longer in keeping with the present situation of a great leap forward. Some workers say: "Our production has doubled, is up ten times and many tens of times. This is the result of a great leap forward in industry and agriculture throughout the country. Can it be said that our wages must be doubled, raised ten times or many tens of times?" Others remark: "A technological revolution is in progress everywhere. Popularization of one advanced experience may instantly raise production efficiency several times. This is the result of collective labor. It would be unreasonable for piece-wage workers to receive a bonus for extra output." Some make sharp comments: "We work for socialism and not for money. Should politics or money assume command?"

These demands fully reflect the unprecedented heightening of communist awakening among the masses who have gone through the great rectification campaign. They understand that we work not for earning a few *yuan* more for ourselves, but for accelerating socialist construction, building a brilliant communist society, bringing happiness to everyone. To achieve this great objective, they will dedicate everything, including their energy and wisdom, instead of trying to earn a few more *yuan*. Lenin said in his *A Great Beginning,* "Communism begins when the rank-and-file workers begin to display a self-sacrificing concern that is undaunted by arduous toil for increasing productivity of labor, for husbanding every pound of grain, coal, iron and other products, which do not accrue to the workers personally or to their 'close' kith and kin, but to their 'distant' kith and kin, i.e., to society as a whole." The workers of the Chiangnan Dockyard and some factories, in the interests of production and society as a whole, have voluntarily given up and reformed the piece wage system and introduced a more rational wage system. This selfless action to subordinate personal interests to the interests of the state is precisely an expression of the communist style and is worthy of great promotion. . . .

In connection with wage work, some localities one-sidedly stressed material incentives and neglected political work in the past. In the course of the present reform of piece wages, communist education should be deliberately conducted among the masses, so that the masses can approach the wage problem in a communist way and so that communist thinking will show its great brilliance and give an impetus to the great leap forward in production.

91. NEW WAYS OF SUPPLYING GOODS AND SERVICES
[From a Report in *People's Daily*, September 29, 1958]

The people's communes in Honan are introducing a method of distribution —partial supply of the means of subsistence plus wages—in place of the former APC system of distribution purely based on working days. This important reform of the distribution system marks an unprecedented heightening of the peasants' communist thinking and awakening.

According to figures from the rural work department of the CCP Honan Provincial Committee, by the end of August 942 communes or 70 percent of the total in Honan have introduced various forms of supply system. In the majority of cases, a system of grain supply is enforced. Some communes enforce a food supply system and some a system of supplying essential needs. These three kinds of supply system have the following features: Under the grain supply system, free grain rations for all members are supplied to the commune, according to the grain supply standard set by the state. Under the food supply system, the commune undertakes to provide all its members with food expenses and members can eat in public mess halls without paying for rice, vegetables, condiments, and fuel. Under the system of supplying essential needs, the limits of supply are defined according to the economic conditions of the commune and the consumption standard of its members. For instance, some communes provide "seven things"—food, clothing, housing, maternity care, education, medical care, and wedding and funeral services. Besides these, some communes provide for "ten things" such as haircuts, baths, theater and cinema, heating, etc., or issue allowances in lieu thereof.

Simultaneous with the enforcement of the above supply systems, the communes generally introduced the distribution method of paying basic wages plus bonuses according to classification of laborers. Thus the income earned by members consists of two parts: (1) that distributed according to the "to each according to his need" supply system; (2) that distributed according to the "to each according to his work" principle and through payment of wages and bonuses. According to what the Rural Work Department of the CCP Honan Committee understands of the situation, supply generally accounts for 50 percent of members' income in the case of those communes which enforce the grain supply system; supply accounts for 60 percent and wages 40 percent of members' income in the case of those communes which enforce the food supply system; supply accounts for generally 80 percent of members' income while their wages are in fact turned into living "allowances" in the case of those communes which enforce the system of supplying the essential needs. But wages still make up a good proportion of members' income in the case of a few communes whose economic foundations are particularly good. . . .

The great leap forward achieved in agriculture since last winter has laid a strong material foundation for the new systems of distribution. The unprecedented bumper harvest this year has provided ample grain stocks for introducing the grain supply system; what is more important, with the basic elimination of flooding and drought as a result of the completion of the irrigation construction program and with new production measures such as deep-plowing and close-planting widely adopted, a stable foundation has been laid for achieving a rapid increase in agricultural production in the future. . . .

A review of the results of enforcing this new system of distribution shows four great advantages as follows: (1) The new system can better eliminate the factors that cause inequality between the rich and the poor, and can ensure rising prosperity in common. Surveys indicate that, when income was distributed according to work days in the past, about 10 percent of those families which had more population and less laborers did not earn a stable livelihood. The new system of distribution can pull out the roots of "poverty". (2) With peasants transformed into agricultural laborers, members' income is placed on a fixed basis. After introducing this new system of distribution, about 5 percent of those families with particularly strong labor power and small population earn less than in the past. However, when debates were held and particularly when they recalled the past situation in which "the harvest depended upon the Mandate of Heaven" and livelihood was not guaranteed, the vast majority of them voiced sincere support for the new system of distribution as they came to realize that the new system would guarantee their living standard. (3) The new system can overcome the incongruities in the former method of management—reviewing jobs and recording work points—and ensure the all-round development of the communes' agriculture, forestry, animal husbandry, side occupations, and fisheries and the integration of workers, peasants, merchants, students and soldiers. . . . (4) It can better enlarge and increase common accumulation. According to surveys, consumption generally accounts for only 30 percent of total income this year. In the case of Ch'iliying people's commune, for instance, consumption by members is 50 percent higher than last year, but accounts for only 20.6 percent of the total income; reserve and welfare funds make up 45.7 percent of total income, nearly a 30 percent increase over last year. After introducing the grain supply system and wage system, the Weihsing people's commune in Suip'ing *hsien* has increased common accumulations four times over last year, to 69.4 percent of total income while income distributed among members is 70 percent higher than last year.

92. COMMUNAL MESS HALLS
[From an Article in the Tientsin *Hopei Daily*, September 7, 1958]

Question: What are public mess halls?

Answer: There are many kinds of public mess halls—workers' mess halls, street mess halls, rural mess halls, and mess halls operated for profit. The first three named mess halls directly serve workers in factories, cadres of government organs, residents on streets, and members of agricultural cooperatives, and do not operate for profit. The last named category also serves the masses, but they make a profit out of their operations. The rural mess hall is a kind of mass organization for collective living, organized on the basis of the living needs of the broad masses of the people. It changes the old way of individual living when each household had its own kitchen, to the new way of collective living. It is another penetrating and extensive socialist revolution in the living habits of the masses following the collectivization of agriculture. It embodies communist factors and so has immense vitality. . . .

Question: What superior features does a public mess hall have?

Answer: A public mess hall has many superior features. They may be summed up in the following points:

1. A large force of manpower is released, particularly woman manpower, for the further development of production. In Peifeipi village in Pingshan *hsien,* there are 162 households, and in the past, one person in each household had to undertake the preparation of means. After the establishment of the mess hall, only 24 persons are used in preparing meals. After the establishment of mess halls in Hsushui *hsien,* the rate of participation in productive labor by women rose from 50 percent to 100 percent. . . .

2. Economy of supplies and improvement of living standards are achieved. With the mess halls undertaking collective preparation of meals, the phenomenon of the waste of fuel because of too many ovens, and the waste of rice because of too many pots has been overcome. In Shihkuochuang village in Antzu *hsien,* there are 131 households. After the opening of the mess hall, in June and July alone more than 4000 catties of grain were saved. . . .

3. Collective ideology and living habits have been established, and the conception of private ownership has been greatly weakened. After the opening of mess halls, people have further realized that, in order to make

their living conditions better, not only must a good job be made of collective production, but a good job must also be made of collective daily living. And so both in production and in daily living, the ideology of further reliance on the collective body has been greatly strengthened. . . .

4. All tasks in the rural areas have been facilitated. First, there is no more need for every family and every household to line up for the purchase of grain, and the work volume of the grain supply centers has been greatly reduced, while the state is in a better position to control the target of the quantity of grain to be supplied. Second, the distribution of grain in an agricultural cooperative does not have to be carried out on a house to house basis. . . .

For these reasons, after the opening of the mess halls, the relations between man and man, between cadres and the masses, have been brought closer. Harmony has been promoted between mothers-in-law and daughters-in-law, and among sisters-in-law. There have emerged more and more new-type families united in production. Social morals have been transformed. Members of cooperatives mutually respect and love one another and are happy at heart.

93. EQUALITY THROUGH HOMOGENEITY
[From an Article in *People's Daily*, October 1, 1958]

Since the nation-wide great leap forward on all fronts of industrial and agricultural production, production has been leaping forward by increasing its rate many times or even many scores of times, and the labor production rate has also been leaping forward by many times, or many hundred, many thousand times. This vigorously expanding productivity is a result of the liberation of people's minds, and at the same time it is the motive force that promotes the genesis and growth of the new relationship. So far as the progress of our socialist construction is concerned, it marks the entry of our socialist construction into a new stage of accelerated development, foreshadowing a more vigorous expansion of our industrial and agricultural production; while at the same time it enables the 600,000,000 people of our country to determine definitely the direction to take for further development and to find out a concrete road to a brilliant communist society.

The superiority and the essential characteristics of a people's commune as compared with an agricultural cooperative consist of "first, largeness; and second, community [of interests: *kung*]," which are what satisfy the objective requirements for continuously developing productivity. "Largeness" means larger size of population, larger area, greater strength, and greater variety of operations. "Largeness" may therefore be said to be a quantitative change. "Community" means greater collectivization and socialization, and may be said to be a qualitative change. The people's commune is the best organizational form for speeding up the building of socialism, and also the best form of transition toward a completely "selfless" communist society. The seeds of communism contained in a people's commune are the general tendency toward increasing "selflessness." . . .

Some preliminary inquiries may be made into the following aspects of the germs of communism that have already appeared in our actual life.

First, under the socialist system there exist two socialist systems of ownership, namely, the system of collective ownership and the system of national ownership of the means of production. Socialist collective economy is a necessary phase through which we must pass on our way from an individual economy to an economy of the whole people. It is only a transitional economic form. It is incomparably superior to the former individual economy, but as the agricultural cooperatives are generally formed on a small scale and the scope of their operations is generally limited, they are increasingly unable to cope with our new demands with the expansion of production by leaps and bounds. The merging of agricultural cooperatives into larger cooperatives and their transformation into people's communes not only overcomes the contradictions of the agricultural cooperatives, but also closely unites the collective economy of the people's communes with the *hsiang* and *hsien* state-owned economy, so that the boundary between the two socialist systems of ownership begins to break down. . . . The trends of the development of the people's communes show that in about three or four to five or six years, the system of ownership by all the people will be established in all parts of the country generally. The transition from a collective economy to an economy of the whole people is a further step toward "selflessness," one of the basic tasks of the transition of communism from its primary to a higher stage. This new economic form means a beginning of the utter elimination of class distinctions. . . .

Second, to effect the transition toward communism, it will be necessary to further eliminate the "old-fashioned division of labor" of the past several thousand years left by the old society. With regard to the realization of a communist society, Engels once said, "The old modes of production should be thoroughly changed, and the old-style division of labor in particular should be eliminated." (*Anti-Dühring*) The destruction of the old modes of production is a task of the socialist revolution. The "old-style division of labor" is that kind of old social division of labor which is characterized by the division between industry and agriculture, rural and urban areas, and mental labor and physical labor. The victory of our socialist revolution has removed the antagonism between these, but has perforce retained important differences between them. The existence of these differences is the fundamental reason why vestiges of the "inequalities" of mankind can continue to remain in a socialist society. Therefore, further elimination of the "old-style division of labor" that is characterized by these differences and the complete removal of these differences will be one of the most basic tasks of the transition toward communism.

With regard to the narrowing of the gap between industrial and agricultural workers and between rural and urban areas in our country, this process has begun to accelerate ever since the launching of the Party's general line for socialist construction and implementation of the policy of "three simultaneous developments." . . . The unique effort by our 500,000,000 peasants to set up industries in the countryside on a large scale is rapidly changing the backward aspect of the rural areas and will soon reduce the difference between the advanced industrial urban areas and the backward agricultural rural areas. With regard to the narrowing of the gap between mental labor and physical labor, a new, wholesome climate of communism has come to stay since the Party proposed the policy of operation of education by all the people and began to carry out a policy of combination of education with labor and of participation in manual labor by cadres. Middle school education is being universally developed in all rural areas, and "red and expert" universities, which completely combine technological education and scientific research with industrial and agricultural production, are being set up everywhere. Meanwhile, a movement has been launched in which everyone tries his hand at discovery and the working of miracles, in which artisans write books, peasants make literary efforts and "study the abstract," and in which workers, peasants and everyone else study philosophy. In addition, there is a movement of setting up industrial factories in schools and schools in industrial factories. . . . All these will gradually erase the boundaries between workers, intellectuals and cadres. They are a new trend toward communism and germinations of communism. All these forms of development have become consolidated and well established organizationally with the establishment of people's communes. In these people's communes the principle of combining "worker, peasant, merchant, scholar and soldier into one" is carried out, so that "when one is in the fields one is a peasant, but when one is in a factory, one is a worker" and "the worker and peasant masses have knowledge, while the intellectuals do manual labor." People are trained to be at once laborers and intellectuals. With the industrialization of the rural areas, the boundary between urban and rural areas will gradually be eliminated. That is the concrete way to eliminate the "old-style division of labor." The elimination of this "old-style division of labor" will be the most profound revolution, the final liberation of mankind and the destruction of the last roots of the "inequalities" of mankind.

94. A MASS CAMPAIGN

[From Yin Tse-ming, "The Strength of the Masses Is Limitless," 1958]

Iron smelting and steel making in the Shaoyang Special Administrative Region, Hunan Province, are rapidly developing on a mass scale. In a short period in the autumn of 1958, 12,378 local blast furnaces were built in this area. Of these, 4,816 went into immediate operation, with a daily output of more than 2,400 tons. The highest daily output has reached the 2,438-ton mark, which is an average of half a ton a day for each local furnace in operation. In the first ten days of September, 1958, daily output of iron more than trebled (the daily output on September 1 was 595 tons). Now this region has already produced 50,000 tons of iron. Not only is there a "bumper harvest" in many places but the Chinhua Iron Works in Shaotung County, "king" of local blast furnaces, has produced the remarkable record of almost three tons (5,836 catties) a day.

At present, people in many districts are working with increasing enthusiasm to produce iron and steel, and as more and more effective measures are taken, it is anticipated that there will be even greater achievement in steel and iron production in the near future.

The main reason for this remarkable progress in iron and steel production in such short time in Shaoyang region is the fact that this region has fully carried out the Communist Party's directive to let the whole Party and all the people work in iron and steel production, in keeping with the Party's general line of socialist construction.

Iron and steel production is not simply a technical job; it is also a political task that has an important bearing on all other activities. Therefore, the first condition for the rapid development of production is for the Party secretaries to take the lead and have the entire Party membership mobilized. The Party committees of Shaoyang region are all clearly convinced of the importance of the guiding principle of making steel production the first task, in order to hasten the progress of industry and agriculture and they gave iron and steel production priority. The first secretaries of different Party committees all took personal charge, leading more than ten thousand government functionaries and nearly one million workers in this battle for iron and steel. Many government functionaries organized experimental units in the factories and workshops and they all took part in actual production. By joining the movement first the leaders not only set an example for the masses and hastened its progress, but they also learned much and became experienced workers. By the beginning of September, 1958, government functionaries in this region had set up a total of 2,352 experimental blast furnaces and 500 experimental coal pits. In Lienyuan County 15 members of the county Party committee and 29 township Party secretaries have already mastered the technique of smelting iron.

In Lunghui County, deputy secretary of the county Party committee, Hsieh Kuo, set up experimental furnaces at Shihmen, but failed to produce iron in 22 unsuccessful attempts. He persisted, studying and trying again and again and finally he produced iron in all the five local furnaces. In Shaotung County, the head of Niumasze Township, Chao Lin-fu, stayed by the furnace, sleeping and eating on the spot. After 21 experiments he finally increased the daily output of each furnace from 300 to 2,250 catties. Leaders of co-ops, peasants, men and women of all ages, workers, government officials, and soldiers are all trying their skill with experimental furnaces. Many peasants want to be capable of running agricultural co-ops and factories, capable of farming as well as smelting iron.

When they first began to work in iron and steel production, many people wanted to have big "foreign" blast furnaces. They were not interested in these small native furnaces. They thought it necessary to wait for elaborate equipment. Actually that line of thinking would result in producing less, slower, more expensively, and not so well; and it would not lead to production on a mass basis. Under the timely guidance of the Central Committee and the provincial committee of the Communist Party, that policy was firmly rejected and the policy of putting iron and steel production on a mass basis, of mobilizing all the Party members, and letting politics take the lead was carried out. From the beginning, Shaoyang region initiated a gigantic propaganda campaign. All the people were encouraged to voice their opinions in a general debate on such subjects as the following: Why must iron and steel production be developed? How can it be done? What is the relationship between the production of iron and steel and agriculture? Through voicing different opinions and public debates the masses achieved a clearer understanding and became convinced; thus their enthusiasm was aroused. Within a few days more than half a million written pledges were sent to the Party in support of the campaign. The people felt elated and stimulated; millions of hearts had only one wish—to fight hard to achieve and surpass the goal of producing 300,000 tons of iron in 1958.

The strength of the masses is tremendous. All the problems of funds, raw materials, equipment, fuel, and geological survey of resources, which seemed hard to solve in the past, disappeared before the resourcefulness of the people. In honor of the anniversary of the Communist Party (July 1), 67,000 people in Hsinhua County worked for three days and nights on end and built 1,025 blast furnaces. Many people hearing the news came from as far as 100 *li* away to join in the work, carrying timber and bamboo and their food and clothes. In Szetun Township, 53 couples came to put their names down offering to help in industrial production. Within a few days this county collected a fund of more than 1.6 million yuan. There was a 50-year-old woman who voluntarily contributed more than 200 yuan, her savings of many years, for the local industry. The people contributed 1,280 pigs, more than 700,000 catties of vegetables, and 180,000 pairs of straw sandals for the people who were taking part in this industrial construction project. To solve the housing problem, the people of Tienping Township, in one morning, spontaneously vacated more than 500 rooms. The contributions from the masses became a mighty torrent, and the blast furnaces were set up very quickly. The people composed a song describing this event:

> The Communist Party is really wonderful.
> In three days more than a thousand furnaces were built.
> The masses' strength is really tremendous.
> The American imperialists will run off, tails between their legs.
> The East wind will always prevail over the West wind.

Since the supply of resources was uncertain, the people went to the hills to look for mines. In Hsianghsiang County nearly 80,000 people went prospecting and digging coal. Some made discouraging remarks, saying that such effort was in vain, "like a dog trying to catch rats," but they were answered: "Even if we have to dig through the earth, we shall find coal." As a result of this mass movement, many big iron and coal mines were discovered. Hsinhua County alone discovered 14 big iron mines of more than five million tons each and eight big coal mines of more than four million tons each. Tungshang County, which was thought to be lacking in coal and iron, was found to be extremely rich in these resources.

There were very few technicians in this region, but the rapid growth of blast furnaces made the shortage of trained workers even more acute. The usual methods of training apprentices would have taken three years. Should production be stopped for three years or should these methods be given up and the wisdom of the masses developed to the full in order to solve this problem quickly? Shaoyang's answer was to apply the mass line. First the interest and enthusiasm of the masses were aroused and then a movement was launched for people to volunteer to become experts. Many young peasants came forward, and some of them vowed to study well and practice hard so that they would learn the entire technique of iron smelting in five days, and within ten days train another ten apprentices each. During study the old workers were helped with their ideology, so that they would be willing to teach all they knew and not withhold any professional secrets. At the same time experienced workshops were encouraged to help the new workshops, old hands to help newcomers, one teaching ten, ten teaching a hundred. Then the method of "people changing trades" was adopted. The skills of the welder, the coppersmith and the blacksmith are somewhat similar to that of the iron and steel workers, so apart from a few craftsmen who remained in the villages to serve the needs of the people, all who could be spared were urged to help in smelting iron and making steel. On-the-spot meetings were held to exchange experiences and classes were organized to train large numbers of technicians. In this way the number of iron and steel workers grew like rolling snowballs. Within a few months they grew from about 300 to 26,743. . . .

As production expanded, the supply of fuel presented a serious problem, causing many furnaces to carry on from hand to mouth. To cope with this situation, the various Party committees took steps to immediately put due emphasis on fuel supply. The coal miners cooperated fully, working the mines in three shifts round the clock, improving their technique and adopting all measures that were necessary to increase production. At the same time, the people were mobilized to open small coal mines. Recently 500 such small coal mines were started in Shaoyang, with a daily increase in output of 9,000 tons. Apart from increasing the coal production, there was much coke produced by native methods. In only one month kilns for producing coke by native methods increased from 495 to 700, with a daily output that rose from 4,000 tons to 5,600 tons. . . .

In the drive to economize on fuel, all sorts of local substitutes were successfully used, thereby debunking the myth that only coke and charcoal can be used to smelt iron. Workers of the Chinchikeng Iron Works in Lienyuan County invented the method of using coal dust to smelt iron; in Wukang County they used hard coal to smelt iron and the output was high. Other places used a mixture of hard coal and inferior charcoal or a small amount of coke and charcoal to smelt iron, with very good results. . . .

Another problem that became apparent after the local furnaces started production was the uneven distribution of resources, labor and technical forces. Some places have iron but no coal, some have coal but no iron, while other places have natural resources but lack labor. Counties and townships had to forget boundaries and help each other in the spirit of all for one, one for all. This spirit of communist cooperation has already blossomed and borne fruit. The large-scale cooperation in Hsinhua County is a very good example. Among the 52 townships where furnaces were set up, 23 have iron but no coal, four have coal but no iron, one has neither iron nor coal but has adequate labor power and 24 have coal and iron but are short of workers. As a result, many furnaces could not start production. A country-wide debate was held on the subject of communist cooperation and all selfish ideas were thoroughly swept away. The county was divided into 12 areas and the labor force, raw materials and fuel were redistributed in a unified way, thus satisfactorily solving many problems. . . .

The development of iron and steel production is a political task for the entire Party and people. Different departments in the region helped in every way. The machine-building industry made equipment, commercial organizations took care of purchases, transport organizations mobilized 90 percent of the vehicles and boats to transport iron ore and fuel, and health organizations sent doctors and nurses to care for the workers.

95. THEORY OF THE MASS CAMPAIGN
[From an Article by Teng Hsiao-p'ing in *People's Daily*, October 2, 1959]

The role of the mass movements in our socialist construction is being felt more and more clearly. The fact that hundreds of millions of working people have gone all out, aimed high, stepped up their enthusiasm for labor to the maximum, and developed the mass movements for technical innovation and technical revolution on a large scale, has guaranteed the continuous leap forward of our economy. We can say for sure that our technical revolution will be many times faster than the former industrial revolution of the capitalist countries. On the basis of giving priority to heavy industry, we simultaneously develop industry and agriculture, heavy and light industry; while strengthening the centralized leadership of the Central People's Government in economic construction, we also see to it that the initiative of the local authorities at various levels is encouraged; we also see to it that the development of large enterprises goes hand in hand with medium and small-sized enterprises; while developing modern methods of production, we see to it that indigenous methods are not ignored. The operation of the policy of "simultaneous development" serves to mobilize the masses on the broadest scale, and to bring into motion various positive factors so as to push forward our socialist construction most effectively and speedily. In steel making, in 1958, we launched a mass movement in the large enterprises and those using modern methods of production as well as in medium- and small-sized enterprises and those using indigenous methods. As a result, tens of millions of people jubilantly joined the movement and displayed boundless enthusiasm for socialist construction. All this led to the enormous leap forward in steel making and laid the basis for a rational distribution of the steel industry in our country, thus creating the important conditions for a speedy development of the steel industry in the future. . . . Clearly, it is only by relying on large-scale mass movements in our socialist construction that it will be possible to overcome our economic backwardness in a comparatively short period of time.

In our ranks some people cannot see the socialist initiative of the masses and therefore entertain doubts about the mass movements. They always think that the masses are not conscious enough and that the mass movements are unreliable. The fact is, however, that the broad masses in China have very great initiative for socialist revolution and socialist construction. It is not the masses who lag behind, but those who entertain doubts of the masses that are lagging behind the masses. Of course, in keeping with the progress of socialism, it is necessary for the masses to educate themselves in order to raise their consciousness continuously. The broad mass movements led by the Party have played a significant role in promoting the cause of socialism because through these movements the socialist initiative of the masses is fully developed and they serve as the best schools for the self-education of the masses. It is through a series of mass movements in the socialist revolution and construction that the Chinese people have received a profound socialist education which has rapidly raised their socialist consciousness.

In our own ranks some people consider mass movements necessary in the revolution but maintain that it is a different matter in construction. This view is also wrong. Certainly the forms of mass movements should be different in times of revolution and construction, in political struggles and economic work. But obviously our economic construction cannot be divorced from political work, and politics should be the soul and should be in command. To do economic work well, we must observe objective economic laws. The aim of large-scale mass movements is precisely the full application of objective economic laws by bringing into full play man's subjective activity. Those who deny the role of mass movements in construction view political work and economic work as absolute opposites and therefore fail to see the very important part played by the socialist initiative of the broad masses in construction. They also view as absolute opposites two things in economic construction—reliance on the masses and reliance on technical personnel; they do not understand the vital significance of the practical experience of the masses in production for the development of science and technology. At present, there are not enough technical personnel as yet in our socialist construction, and a group of top-level, outstanding scientists, inventors and other technical experts are urgently needed. To develop their ability and the role they play, however, the experts have to work in close harmony with the masses and continuously absorb new experiences from the practical work of the masses. The view that in construction it is enough to have the management of the enterprises and a few technical experts issue orders, that the masses are negative or passive factors and that mass movements are not wanted, is obviously wrong. . . .

It is inevitable, under any circumstances, that certain isolated, local and temporary shortcomings will crop up in great, new undertakings in which several hundreds of millions of people take part. But we cannot, as the saying goes, "refuse to take food because we fear choking," and we must not negate the mass movement because we fear these shortcomings. Our mass movement is conducted under the centralized leadership of the Party, with the leaders moving ahead along with the masses and learning together with them from practical experience; therefore, when defects crop up, they are easily detected and overcome. The handful of right opportunists within our Party do not see the great achievements made in the great leap forward movement and in the movement for people's communes since 1958; they spare no efforts to exaggerate certain shortcomings in the mass movements which have already been overcome so as to oppose the Party's general line for building socialism. The positive effect of the mass movement for more iron and steel on the rapid development of our national economy is becoming more and more evident in real life; but the right opportunists think that this movement can only play a destructive role. The people's communes, after summing up the experiences gained in the initial stage, are becoming more mature and sounder; but the right opportunists think that the people's communes are "moving backwards" and that the only way out is to dissolve them. The masses of the people look upon the leap forward in our national economy as something extremely good, but the right opportunists think it is all "in an awful mess." This right opportunist viewpoint is obviously nothing but a reflection within our Party of the reactionary viewpoint of the bourgeoisie which fears the masses and is antagonistic to the mass movement. Unlike the political parties of the bourgeoisie, the Marxist-Leninist Party of the proletariat dares to bring into full play the creative power of the masses; it is forever in the van of the mass movement; it continuously shows the masses the correct path to take, puts forward in time new tasks for which they should struggle, and leads them from victory to victory. That is what our Party has been doing. . . . The Chinese Communist Party has become the core of the great unity of the Chinese people in long years of struggle. This great unity is the fundamental factor that accounts for the victories we have already won and victories we shall continue to win in the cause of socialism in our country.

CHAPTER THIRTEEN
Adjustments

From almost the beginning of the Great Leap, party leaders were sensitive to the possibility that the mass movement might get out of control, but they were divided over whether or not the benefits of excessive stimulation outweighed the possible costs, and what restraints, if any, should be applied. When it became apparent that there were severe shortages and dislocations, that most of the impressive production figures, so triumphantly proclaimed, were vastly exaggerated, and when there were several years of poor harvests, which some people attributed to the Great Leap, the mass campaign was discredited. Yet some innovations survived, in altered form. The communes were too large and unwieldly; they were reduced in size but not disbanded. Meals were again eaten at home, but some mess halls were retained because in limited ways they did provide convenient services. Though the steel produced in the backyard furnaces was found to be useless for modern industrial purposes, it could be used to manufacture simple agricultural implements, and so, though most of the commune furnaces were abandoned, many continued small-scale operations.

Nevertheless, the Great Leap was not an economic success, and as a spiritual experience it was disillusioning. In the early 1960s, revolutionary zeal was replaced by retreat, retrenchment, and adjustment, and primacy was given to production. Within each rural commune the lower-level units —the production brigades and the production teams—were given greater autonomy. A small amount of land was returned to individual peasant households to cultivate as private plots, and free markets were established in which peasants could sell the produce from these plots for personal profit. In industry and education, too, less emphasis was placed on ideology and more on technical skills, all the more important after the withdrawal of Russian technical advisors in 1960 as the Sino-Soviet split widened.

"Be Realistic and Practical" (Selection 96) conveys the temper of the early 1960s. Although the Great Leap is not mentioned, it is obviously the target of the disparaging metaphors and the allusions to "empty talk," falsification, exaggeration, and oversimplification. In some respects, the analysis has a closer affinity to Hu Shih's pragmatism than to Marxist wholism. However, by encompassing the new mode of "realism" and "practicality" within the domain of Marxism-Leninism (the name of Mao-Tse-tung, so closely associated with the Great Leap, is not mentioned), the author is able to argue that the new policies are the best means to achieve the objectives of the revolution. Since by implication totalistic mass movements are detrimental to production, the more evolutionary method of increasing production step by step is the way to create the good society. This was the position of many important party leaders.

Although life was to some extent depoliticized, the framework of Communist Party leadership, collectivized agriculture, and socialized industry and commerce remained. Discussions in the early 1960s were about adjusting the new institutions, and adjusting to them, not about replacing them. The question was how they might best contribute to solving China's problems, not whether or not they could at all.

"Love the Collective, but Love the State More," is about how one model production brigade resolved its difficulties. (Selection 97) The subject is not building an ideal society but sharing the benefits of collectivized agriculture. Compulsory deliveries and sales to the state are justified in terms of the benefits members of the collective derive from the commune and the state. The new national economic strategy of reducing investment in heavy industry in favor of more balanced growth in agriculture, consumers' goods, and heavy industry, announced in early 1961, is presented as evidence that there is an equitable distribution of burdens and rewards. This concession to peasant demand for consumers' goods was a significant departure from Stalinist concentration on heavy industry as the path to rapid modernization. Political controls remain an integral part of the system, and the author devotes considerable space to the vital role played by the party in checking the pursuit of immediate personal gain at the expense of the public.

Selection 98 illustrates two other concessions made to the peasants. The first, private raising of pigs, like private cultivation of family plots, was a reversion to conditions under the lower-stage APCs. The second practice was the making of agreements between the collective and individual households, whereby a household would contract to produce a fixed quantity of a product at a specified cost. For this work, the household would be given a stipulated number of work points, the unit of accounting used in determining the amount of collective labor for which compensation would be given at the harvest or other prearranged times. In this case, the commodity is pigs. More usually it was grain, raised on collective fields farmed out to individual households or small groups. Both of these practices were purely economic arrangements, based on private initiative and material incentives. As described here, politics still plays an important, but subsidiary role—preventing further incursions by the private sector into the collective economy, and assisting poorer peasants.

Different attitudes toward the collective and collective labor can be seen in the letter of a young commune member to the journal of the Communist Youth League. (Selection 99) Her brief account of her experiences shows the small interest in collective work, which was the most important reason for private plots and other concessions to individual enterprise. It also illustrates the sociological functions of an ideological education. Much along the lines of older Confucian morality tales, the model behavior of an upright person eventually sways those with smaller minds to behave properly. But in a very un-Confucian manner, parental authority yields to the ideals of the new morality.

The young woman's apprehensions about offending people remind us of the importance of getting along with others in traditional China. The conflict between two sets of values, between the traditional virtue of interpersonal harmony and the new ethics of loyalty to the larger common interests and struggling for their realization is the theme of Selection 100, another letter from a Youth League member.

As these letters indicate, neither family nor associates were reliable guides for youth. New models were needed. Throughout its history, the CCP had publicized the deeds of revolutionary heroes and martyrs. In the 1960s, the media disseminated stories of up-to-date model youths to meet the contemporary needs of socialist construction. Of the many such new heroes, Lei Feng (1940–62), a young PLA soldier and party member from a poor peasant background, became the most famous. In his diary, published after his death in an accident, Lei Feng appears as the embodiment of numerous communist virtues, not a few of which could also be found in Confucian exemplary tales: selfless devotion to duty, respect for authority, sincerity, humility, loyalty, diligence, frugality, introspective self-criticism, service to the people. (Selection 101)

Lei Feng represented an ideal. At the other end of the spectrum was corruption. Selection 102, an editorial commentary on several reports of cadre malfeasance, shows the persistence of two salient characteristics of officials in the past—aversion to physical labor and use of office for personal gain. As in Confucianism, the main objection is not economic but moral and political, the setting of a bad example. The new regime did not eliminate corruption, so long a part of the Chinese political system, but indications are that it was reduced to comparatively minor proportions. It was significant enough, however, to lead to a purge of lower-level cadres in the countryside in 1964.

In the more relaxed atmosphere of the early 1960s, there was greater tolerance of divergent opinions, and issues raised by the Great Leap and by other aspects of the new society were publicly discussed. Newspapers and journals provided forums for readers' views on a wide range of subjects. Was happiness the enjoyment of a comfortable standard of living or selfless devotion to revolution? (Selection 103) If it was impossible to combine professional expertise and ideological mastery, to be both red and expert, what was the worth of each? (Selection 104) What attitude should peasants, and urban youth working in the communes, take toward their work? (Selection 105) What was the role of women in the new society? (Selection 106) The red-and-expert debate was particularly vital, for it concerned the attitudes of educated youth, the successor generation to the aging party leadership. Through these various letters and articles run several persistent questions. Now that the new institutions have been established, what are the main tasks ahead, and what kind of person is best qualified to accomplish them? Do some people make a greater contribution to society, and if so, are they entitled to higher rewards? Do material incentives strengthen or sap "revolutionary will"? In answering these questions, the contributors tend to group themselves into two sides, divided over the definitions of such fundamental issues as equality and public and private interests. One can also see the persistence of deep-rooted traditional attitudes on both sides—the ideas that education provides a dividing line in social status, that the principal qualification for leadership is moral character, and that self-interest is the motive of short-sighted, bad men (called the bourgeoisie, not "small men"). Assertions about the class character of some antiegalitarian attitudes were not without substance. There is evidence that in the early 1960s the percentage of students from worker-peasant families decreased in at least some institutions of higher learning, where, as one might expect, academic definitions of ability tended to work to the advantage of children from urban backgrounds and from the former elite, brought up in an atmosphere more conductive to formal education. This was to become a major issue in the Cultural Revolution.

The value of these letters transcends their time, for in them one can see points of view also held in earlier and later periods, when there was less freedom to express them. Already one can see the greater stress given to the primacy of politics in later contributions. The re-emergence of private enterprise (legal and illegal), laxness and corruption among cadres, ideological softening and other tendencies revealed in the letters led to campaigns to increase political and ideological discipline. These were to be the preludes to the rejection of the policies of the 1960s in the Great Proletarian Cultural Revolution.

96. REALISM AND RESULTS

["Be Realistic and Practical," Canton *Southern Daily*, February 14, 1962]

Fancy kicking and fisting [as in *t'ai-chi-ch'üan*] is pleasing to the eye at an exhibition but is no match for hard blows and firm footwork in an actual fight. A silvery spearhead made of wax looks good but is of no practical use. Walls of plastered bamboo mattings are beautiful to look at but, cannot stand the blasts of wind or the beating of rain. Their common weaknesses are showiness instead of utility, superficiality instead of depth, and fragility instead of sturdiness. In a word, they are impractical.

To wage a revolution or to undertake construction is practical business. It permits not the slightest pretense. Fancy kicking and fisting is useless, however much of it may be done. Results can only be achieved with hard blows and firm footwork. Revolutionaries are honest people and know full well that without a realistic attitude it is basically impossible to accomplish anything in this world. That is why we always despise fancy kicking and fisting and favor hard blows and firm footwork in tackling actual work realistically. In other words, we call on every comrade to have a realistic style of work to be able to develop every kind of work realistically and achieve practical results.

This realistic style of work is the Marxist-Leninist style of work. It is also a fine tradition of our party. It stands in opposition to the style of work of empty talkers who "make resolutions only in speech, formulate plans only on paper, and take action only at meetings." It is different in principle from the style of work of routinists who bury themselves only in trifles for lack of ambition, foresight, and perspicacity. It is a manifestation of the combination of a revolutionary's lofty ambition with his spirit of seeking truth from facts and of the combination of his revolutionary fervor with his scientific attitude. The reason is that only people with ambition, foresight, and perspicacity will not lose their sense of direction while marching forward and will realize the truth of "heading for big targets but starting with small ones" (in Lenin's words). Thus, by integrating foresight with current practical struggle, they will do practical work realistically, solve practical problems effectively, and push their work forward toward distant, big goals with hard blows and firm footwork. Also, only people with the scientific attitude of seeking truth from facts will probe objective laws realistically, plant the roots of ambition into the foundation of reality and, realistically according to objective laws, adopt methods and measures to bring their ambitions to fruition.

This realistic style of work of combining lofty ambition with the spirit of seeking truth from facts is most valuable at all times. At present, while implementing the policy of "adjustment, consolidation, reinforcement, and improvement," we must, like eating one mouthful of rice at a time, swallow difficulties one by one and, like ascending a flight of stairs, push the national economy forward to a new upsurge step by step. This makes it all the more necessary to popularize the realistic style of work. However, some comrades, confronted by difficulties, talk vainly of ambition in hopes of winning by sheer luck. They are unwilling to work realistically as if difficulties could be blown away more easily than ash. There are also other comrades who, having done some work realistically, achieved relatively good results, and brought about a highly satisfactory situation in their localities, are drifting away from reality as a result of their initial success. In the course of work, they are fond of empty talk without going for practical results. They are in hot pursuit of only figures to the neglect of quality in their work. Their enthusiasm is for size, for show and not for skill or refinement. They are content with issuing general calls without paying attention to solving concrete problems individually. They look upon any complex problem as one of extreme simplicity which can be success-fully solved by holding a meeting, issuing a call, and setting a target. All these styles of work should be regarded as "fancy kicking and fisting" and not as hard blows and firm footwork. They run counter to the realistic style of work. In this context, the four words "be realistic and practical" need further expla-nation.

To be realistic and practical, the basic requirement is to be honest, to do practical work, to speak realistically, and to seek practical results. Concretely speaking, it means standing on solid ground, penetrating into reality, going deep among the masses, and doing practical work assiduously with reality as the starting point. Under any condition, work, whatever it may be, should be pursued realistically and in proper order. No attempt should be made to win by luck and no hope should be entertained for a "short cut" to the sky in one jump. Emphasis should be laid on practical work and not on empty talk. The object should be to seek practical results and not names of vanity. Only actual conditions, without falsification, coloring, or exaggeration, should be reflected.

In order to be realistic and practical, we must do thorough and careful work among the masses in an honest and earnest manner. The masses can be likened to land. Without land we shall have no place to plant the roots of reality. If no account is taken of the masses, we shall be like duckweed, drifting hither and thither with no roots firmly planted in the ground. . . . When performing a task, we must rely closely on the masses and consult with them. We must rely on them to think of methods of performing it and must organize them to put the methods into operation. That is to say, we must realistically tread the mass line, pass on the party's guidelines, policies and tasks to the masses, do careful ideological work among them, raise their consciousness, and turn the intentions and plans of the leadership into their conscious action. Only when this stage is reached can roots be planted in the fertile soil of the masses and can we develop our work realistically and achieve practical results. Is there any necessity for reiterating the truth of the mass line and for adding the words "realistic and practical" to the manner of treading the line? The answer is that some people know only one phase and not both phases of the problem. They know only the spectacular phase and not the practical phase and even stand the two in opposition to each other. They are unwilling to penetrate earnestly into the masses to do careful work, much less to use the method of opening a lock with its special key to do the hard work of ideological mobilization among persons and households individually. They are content with issuing general calls, holding meetings to do a little mobilization, and announcing a few policies. Their reason is that when there are policies, targets, plans, and measures for implementation, everything will be ready. But they do not realize that although everything is ready, nothing can be called complete without the "East Wind" which is the finishing touch. A realistic style of work is precisely the indispensable "East Wind." As a result of their failure to do thorough, careful mass work in a realistic manner, correct guidelines and policies cannot take root or can take root only among a small number of progressive elements and not among the broad masses. The roots of the best plans are seen only at suddenly called meetings and do not find their way into each family and each household. The roots of effective methods and measures do not extend into the conscious action of the masses. In this way, with roots lacking in length and failing to penetrate deeply, extensively, and firmly, how can we start talking about developing work realistically? Where can the practical results in work come from?

To be realistic and practical calls for seeking truth from facts and for concretely analyzing concrete conditions and concrete problems. The reason is that in a situation in which socialist construction undertakings are expanding at lightening speed, new conditions and new problems keep cropping up from time to time. If we make decisions by relying on subjective imagination and limited experience or on subjective guesswork on the strength of one-sided and superficial data instead of by conducting thorough investigation and research and making a concrete analysis of the things around us, the roots of work will inevitably be planted in the hollow mist of subjectivism. It is only by having a detailed knowledge of the conditions in various fields and at various periods and by making concrete scientific analysis to find the objective laws of things and grasp the particularity of the contradictions among various things that we can, from the concrete conditions of different historical factors in different localities as the starting point, set current tasks for certain localities to find methods of solving the concrete contradictions. It is only then that we can find effective, feasible concrete measure, methods, and plans to implement party policies and fulfill party tasks. It is only then that we can become adept in doing work in the order of importance and urgency, by stages, in batches, and in a planned and systematic manner. It is only then that we can adapt our subjective knowledge to objective conditions and thereby push our work forward realistically.

To be realistic and practical also calls for effectively solving concrete problems one by one. A task of any kind includes many small links and a large number of problems. The process of work is a process of solving these problems one by one. This is a general law of work. The fulfillment of a task or the solution of a major problem is invariably the result of the effective solution of many concrete problems. Is there any exception to this law? Rice must be eaten one mouthful by one mouthful; several dishes of meat and vegetables and several bowls of rice cannot be swallowed at one gulp. A peasant has to plow his fields piecemeal. If the problem of a chain is to be solved, the first thing to do is to solve the problem of its links. The solution of the first link creates conditions for the solution of the next link and ultimately for the solution of the whole chain. Actually this truth is quite obvious, but it is not so easy to apply it to revolutionary work. The reason is that the effective solution of concrete problems one by one looks trifling and troublesome on the surface but requires tenacity and flexibility. People without the qualities of tenacity and flexibility and people who are showy and not practical, rough and not refined, and superficial and not solid are naturally unwilling to act in this way. They look at many concrete problems without paying attention to them or dealing with them. They often attempt, in violation of the general law of work, to solve concrete problems by doing a little fancy kicking and fisting and by employing the method of chopping with a big axe instead of carving with a small chisel.

They are unwilling to proceed step by step; they want to reach the sky in one stride. As for people who are content with issuing general calls to the neglect of giving concrete guidance and who are content with exercising so-called "leadership in principle" without willingness to do practical, thoroughgoing work and to pay attention to solving concrete problems, they often disdain tackling one by one concrete problems which they regard as trifles on the pretext that they are out to "handle big problems" and "do big things." As a result, small problems are left alone but big problems are beyond their ability; small things are left undone, but confidence is lacking in doing big things. Their unwillingness to solve concrete problems one by one leads to the accumulation of big problems. Thus, work cannot be developed realistically nor can practical results be achieved.

97. THE BENEFITS OF MUTUAL COOPERATION

[From an Editorial, "Love the Collective, but Love the State More," in *People's Daily*, May 29, 1963]

Liuchuang brigade [Ch'iliying commune, Hsinhsiang *hsien*, Honan] is an economically prosperous collective as well as a brigade sparkling with the socialist spirit. In this collective, from cadres to commune members, all regard the collective as their family, devoting themselves whole-heartedly to safe-guarding the collective interests, and each contributing his best possible efforts to the collective. In this collective, cadres and commune members unite closely with one another, caring for and helping one another with one heart and one purpose, and exerting every effort toward the consolidation and development of the collective economy. The noble socialist spirit of this brigade has not only found expression in their warm love for the collective, but also has been reflected in their greater love for the state, an example of consistency in the correct handling of the relations between the collective and the state. Every year, they produce a large amount of cotton in accordance with the state plans, besides exercising great care in field management and in the study of planting techniques. As a result, the average per-*mou* yield in approximately 1,000 *mou* in cotton field has for six successive years exceeded as much as 100 catties. In addition, they surrender enthusiastically every year their yields to the state in accordance with the provisions laid down by the state, in support of socialist construction in the country. In the past five years, they have surrendered to the state 765,000 catties of ginned cotton, averaging 153,000 catties each year. Having surrendered the original quota of cotton to the state in 1962, this brigade again sold to the state over 20,000 catties of their surplus yields.

In recognition of the large cotton contribution made every year by Liu-chuang brigade toward economic construction in the country, the state has also given considerable support to this brigade. Inhabitants of Liuchuang have often reminisced about the changes from poverty to prosperity that have occurred in their village and have used vivid historical experiences to stimulate their patriotism. Before liberation, Liuchuang was so poor and backward that not a single spraying device was available for eradicating insect pests injurious to the cotton plant, not to mention agricultural machines. What is the situation now? The state has provided them with tractors for plowing cotton fields, supplying them with a large amount of chemical fertilizers and agricultural insecticides every year, besides turning over for their use a large number of vehicles fitted with rubber tires, as well as other means of production. Through the support given by the state, Liuchuang has been able to improve steadily its production conditions, introduce improved cotton-growing techniques, and expand production in firm steps, thereby making it possible for the collective economy to attain steady consolidation and growth day after day, and for commune members to live better and receive increased income. As members of Liuchuang brigade cherish a warm love for the collective, the collective economy has been substantially consolidated. They love the state more, always placing the interests of the state in the primary position. The state has also given them as much support as possible, thus further consolidating and developing the collective economy. What does this fact show? It shows that the interests of the broad masses of commune members are closely linked with the interests of the state. This is the personal observation of the cadres and members of Liuchuang brigade.

The worker-peasant alliance in our country is built on the foundation of mutual aid between urban and rural areas, and of giving support to each other between industry and agriculture. To put the development of agriculture in the primary position is our basic guideline for the development of the national economy. But agriculture cannot be developed without the strong support given by industry. In order to achieve, step by step, the great task of agricultural modernization at the present stage, industrial departments of the state are making energetic efforts to give stronger support to agricultural development in the way of the technical reform of agriculture, exerting every possible effort to provide the countryside with an ever increasing quantity of agricultural machines, means of transport, chemical fertilizers, agricultural insecticides, and other means of production. Other departments of the state have also been engaged in the work of giving support to agriculture from different fields of endeavor. It is very obvious that without the strong support given by the state, it will be impossible to achieve any progress in the technical reform of agriculture and the uniform expansion of agricultural production. This is one aspect of the picture. On the other hand, industrial construction undertaken by the state also requires agriculture to give it great support. Without the vigorous support given by agriculture, the progress of national construction will be hindered. As a consequence, the state will find it impossible to give strong support to agricultural production, and to the technical reform of agriculture. In this context, when peasants give support to industrial construction, they do so, in the final analysis, for the good of agricultural development and for the good of the peasants themselves. By giving support to each other, industry and agriculture provide a strong force for continuously promoting the progress of socialist construction.

Speaking from the aspect of developing light industry, it is all the more necessary for agriculture and industry to support each other. Since the countryside provides the biggest market for our industry, light industry must make every possible effort to render service to the peasants first. Denied the peasants' support, light industry likewise cannot achieve rapid development. This is because the bulk of raw materials needed in light industry are provided by agriculture. For this reason, when making energetic efforts to increase the output of food-grain, various production brigades and production teams of rural people's communes should try every means to boost the production of various types of economic crops, livestock products, forestry products, marine products, as well as other subsidiary products, in order to provide the state with more industrial raw materials. The more industrial raw materials are supplied to the state by the peasants, the better will light industry achieve development. With the expansion of light industry, the state will have the necessary conditions for providing the countryside with more industrial products of fine quality at low prices. . . .

Of course, considerable work has to be done when handling correctly the relations between the collective and the state among organizations at various levels in rural people's communes. First of all, we must periodically and in a penetrating manner carry out ideological and political work. To get this task done, we must first of all urge Party branches in the rural areas to step up their fighting power. Then we must call upon the broad masses of basic-level cadres in the countryside to raise their ideological consciousness and policy levels, and establish a strong concept of the whole and a concept of the state. Although a great many basic-level cadres work and live in their native villages and in their native areas, they should take the long view of the whole country and give consideration to problems [in the perspective] of the whole. Accordingly, those of broad vision can perceive long-range interests and the interests of the state, instead of confining themselves to immediate interests and those of their own units. Only by doing so will it be possible to convince, educate and influence the masses, besides raising continuously the collectivist and patriotic awareness of the masses. The experience of Liuchuang brigade has vividly proved this point.

One of the very important reasons why Liuchuang brigade has been able to handle correctly the relations between the collective and the state is that this brigade has a strong Party branch and a force of staunch and reliable cadres. All the cadres here are identified by their firm stand and their fine work style of making close contact with the masses. They pay constant attention to ideological and political work, knowing well how to keep a firm grip on ideological problems found in practical life, and how to conduct in a down-to-earth manner patriotic and collectivist education among the masses, to the extent of raising the awakening of the broad masses of commune members to the policy level of the Party and the state. From news dispatches, it can be noted that not all of the commune members in Liuchuang realized very clearly at the very beginning the problem concerning the relations between the interests of the collective and those of the state. A number of commune members there, for instance, in the face of certain temporary difficulties, advocated growing less cotton, while certain commune members also appeared hesitant on the question of whether or not surplus cotton yields should be all sold to the state. The Party branch and leading cadres of Liuchuang brigade, however, stood firm and consistently adhered to principle. When carrying out ideological education among commune members, they were able to convince skeptical commune members by patient persuasion, sound reasoning, and seeking truth from facts.

98. PROFIT AND PRODUCTION
[From a Report in *Agriculture and Forestry Work Bulletin*, June 9, 1964]

In Kaochou *hsien*, Kwangtung province, following the wide implementation of the guideline of "undertaking public raising of pigs simultaneously, with emphasis laid on private raising," an over-all development has been made in pig-raising in the past two years, and the number of pigs raised publicly and privately has increased unceasingly. At the end of 1963, there were more than 223,000 hogs in the whole *hsien*, exceeding the number of hogs in the record year of 1957 by 23.3 percent. Reckoning on the basis of the total number of peasant families in the whole *hsien*, every household had an average of 1.23 pigs. Collective raising of pigs has developed in more than 6,650 of the 11,078 production teams in the whole *hsien*, representing 60 percent of the total number of production teams, and the collective raised altogether more than 52,000 hogs, representing 23.6 percent of the total number of hogs in the whole *hsien*.

The great development in pig-raising has forcefully promoted agriculture and sideline production. Although 1963 witnessed a serious drought, the like of which was rarely seen in the past century, the total grain output in the whole *hsien* increased by 11.4 percent as compared with that in 1962. In 5,587 production teams in the whole *hsien* where diversified undertakings and sideline production were formerly non-existent, the collective raising of pigs started the diversified undertakings and sideline production, and further consolidated and developed the collective economy of production teams.

The following several points are the chief experiences in developing pig-raising rapidly in Kaochou *hsien*:

1. While implementing in an over-all manner the guideline of "undertaking public raising and private raising of pigs simultaneously, with emphasis laid on private raising," the *hsien* leadership paid close attention to changing the one-sided viewpoint cherished by some cadres and commune members. Some cadres and commune members held that it was easy to undertake private raising of pigs, but difficult to undertake public raising of pigs. As a result of this one-sided viewpoint, private raising of pigs developed rapidly, while public raising of pigs did not follow up correspondingly. This not only hindered the over-all implementation of the Party's guideline for pig raising, but also caused phenomena of imbalance in private raising of pigs. Some commune members raised many pigs, others raised very few, and still some others could not afford to raise any. For the sake of changing this one-sided viewpoint, and making

it possible to implement the guideline for pig raising in an over-all manner and to develop pig raising evenly and rapidly, the CCP Kaochou *Hsien* Committee and the Party organizations of communes and production teams did a great deal of political and ideological work. Meanwhile, they also summed up good experiences acquired by some production teams in collective raising of pigs, quoted typical examples to educate the commune members, increased the commune members' understanding on the development of collective raising of pigs, and cited facts to refute the rich and middle peasants' opinion that "collective raising of pigs was a losing business." . . . In various communes in the whole *hsien*, close attention was paid to implementing in an over-all manner the guidelines for pig raising, and while effort was made to conduct private raising of pigs well, the production teams were actively led to develop their collective raising of pigs. As a result, pig raising developed in an over-all manner and rapidly, and the collective economy was also further consolidated and reinforced.

2. The state policy of purchase was seriously enforced. In Kaochou *hsien,* the leading departments concerned assigned to the production teams the tasks of delivering pigs to the state every year, and having fulfilled their quotas, the production teams and members placed the rest at their own disposal. Production teams and commune members who had overfulfilled their assignments were to be rewarded according to regulations. In 1962, 5,024 production teams in the whole *hsien* (representing 45 percent of the total number of production teams in the whole *hsien*) overfulfilled their assignments. They were respectively rewarded. This greatly stimulated the activism of production teams and commune members in raising pigs.

3. The class line was firmly followed and, while active effort was made to conduct collective raising of pigs well, vigorous help was given the poor and lower-middle commune peasants in raising pigs. Besides allotting some hogs and loans to help needy production teams and needy families of poor and lower-middle peasants solve their actual difficulties in respect of capital for pig raising, many production teams also adopted the form of "privately raising pigs for the collective" for helping needy households of poor and lower-middle peasants in raising pigs. The work method was that the production team gave the commune members the money for buying hogs (or gave them young pigs) and fodder, and drew specifications in respect of a time limit for raising the pig, the weight of the pig upon delivery, work points for feeding the pig, and reward for overfulfillment. In this way, it was possible not only to help needy families of poor and lower-middle peasants in raising pigs, but also to increase the income of the production team, so that both the collective and the individual could be benefited. This method was adopted by the T'ien-hua production team, Hsint'ung brigade, Hsint'ung commune. In this production team, every needy family of poor and lower-middle peasants was allotted one young pig, 120 catties of rice, 300 catties of potatoes, 200 catties of potato leaves, was given ten months to raise the pig to weigh 80 catties (reward was to be given for overfulfillment) and was remunerated with 900 work points (the hay for preparing fodder was a problem to be solved by the individual). In this way, the commune members were willing to raise pigs, and the eight needy families

of poor and lower-middle peasants in this production team had pigs to rear. In 1963 the collective of the production team raised 49 pigs instead of 17 in the past, and more that 220 were raised in the whole production team, i.e., each family raised an average of more than five pigs. Given pigs to raise, the needy families of poor and lower-middle peasants generally earned more work points in addition to the rewards for overfulfillment. Each of them earned more income at the year-end distribution. In some production teams, young pigs were sold at low prices and on credit to the needy families of poor and lower-middle peasants so as to help them get pigs to raise. In the past two years, more than 22,800 needy families of poor and lower-middle peasants in the whole *hsien* were given help in this way in getting pigs to raise.

99. TWO KINDS OF COOPERATION
[From a Letter to the Editor of *Chinese Youth*, February 1, 1965]

I returned to the countryside after graduating from upper primary school in 1962. After returning, my revolutionary enthusiasm was high and I worked actively. At that time, I dared to intervene in any actions or words harmful to the collective interests, no matter who was involved. Once, I was working with the commune members in the white cabbage fields; right next to me was a young person who was hoeing very indifferently. She was not paying attention to quality at all. At that time, I went straight up to her and gave her my opinion: "Watch your hoeing! How will things grow if you hoe like this?" She lowered her eyes, made a face, and yelled at me: "Know-it-all! You've been here just a few days and you're already directing people." Another time, we were working in the cotton fields; some persons were doing things the easy way, so that in passing by, they would either lose part of the cotton bolls or would leave "eyelashes" behind. I criticized a girl, saying: "If you don't pick cleanly and leave some behind, the rain will destroy them. In the long run, who will not be harmed by this? Even you will be." Unexpectedly, she started to argue with me: "The team chief and the squad chief have said nothing about this; what do you matter?"

After running afoul of people like this for a few times, I began to vacillate: if things are handled as they should be, I will contantly "offend people"; how can this be done. If I don't concern myself and the crops don't grow well, the collective economy will be harmed, and what's to be done then? At this time, I recalled Chairman Mao's instruction on studying the completely selfless spirit of comrade Pai Ch'iu-en [the Canadian physician Norman Bethune, who died while operating a field hospital for the Red Army during the war against Japan]. I looked through my old notebook and I read four phrases which I had written on [Mao's] essay "In Commemoration of Pai Ch'iu-en." These were: "In studying Pai Ch'iu-en, we must be willing to shoulder heavy burdens, not count the cost of carrying on the revolution, and must whole-heartedly serve the people." Why was I afraid of "offending people"? Wasn't this worrying about individual gain and loss? If I was not selfish and had a firm standpoint, what would there be to fear? I wasn't a team cadre, but I was a commune member, and I ought to protect the collective interest.

In upholding revolutionary principles and protecting collective interests, we will at times meet with obstacles and there will be struggles. Since some people have been affected by old thoughts and are selfish, they are bound to be somewhat sarcastic when they see us worry about all sorts of things. But we must put up with these things and not lose our morale when we meet with set-backs. Once, in harvesting the white cabbage, I saw a person not working very hard; I expressed my opinion to him and he started to argue against me, saying that I "loved to cause trouble," and that although I was neither the team chief nor the squad chief, I still wanted a hand in everything. . . . Afterwards, he complained to my mother, and without her distinguishing right from wrong, she criticized me: "Hereafter, don't poke your nose into other people's affairs; everyone is saying that you're no good. . . . "I was startled when I first heard this, but then I though it over cooly: "If one's body is straight, one needn't fear that one's shadow will be crooked." How is it causing trouble to criticize poor quality in working and to struggle against people taking advantage of the collective interests? . . .

Of course, in upholding revolutionary principles, we must criticize words and deeds harmful to the collective; but in order for this criticism to achieve its goal, we must pay attention to our methods. This is especially true with regard to problems among the poor and lower-middle peasants; there we must all the more use patient persuasion, and not be haughty to others just because we think that we are acting correctly. I didn't pay much attention to this in the past and at times my attitude was inflexible. Later the Communist Youth League organization awakened me and I corrected myself. Once, I was in the fields along with more than ten other commune members working on cotton sprouts when an old person, who was watching the melon fields, saw that we were sweating profusely. Smiling slyly, he came over and asked if we liked sweet melons. He said: "Why don't you young people taste these and then go back to work? If the team chief asks, I'll say it was me!" Some persons said happily: "Let's go eat some sweet melons." My mind started to work: "Sweet melons are good all right, but this is the mutual wealth of the team; can we do such a thing?" I then said to everyone: "We can't eat these; if everyone of us ate one, we would consume more than ten. And we would probably go back a second time . If we can eat them, then so can the other commune members, and it would be awful if we all ate them up." A young woman didn't agree with my opinion; she said: "If anyone else eats them, I'm going to also, and I'm not going to eat them secretly. I don't want other people's good intentions to cover up for me." At this point, Shih Tso-yin, a member of the [Communist Youth] League branch committee and company commander of the militia, supported me. He stood up and said: "I agree with Chin-chin's ideas; we are all in the militia and should guard well the collective economy. How would it be if we ate everything when we came to the fields?" With that, we carefully declined the old fellow's offer. He was then very happy and praised us repeatedly. Thereafter, our team's 20 *mou* of sweet melons suffered no damage from the time they were ripe until they were all sold.

To support revolutionary principles, one must also set a personal example, ardently love the collective, and serve a model leading role in protecting collective interests. . . .

Having been back in the rural areas for more than two years, I believe that the things I've met with have been rather trivial, but that they are concerned with the collective interests. And I should concern myself with them. In so doing, I've been supported by the poor and lower-middle peasants. They have agreed with my actions and have selected me as a "five-good commune member."

100. HARMONY OR STRUGGLE?
[From an Article in *Chinese Youth Daily*, December 17, 1964]

In the countryside, we sometimes come upon the following things. Some people try to undermine the collective system or take advantage of the collective. Others do things that violate law or break discipline. . . . Some people although aware of these things, just do not care a bit, or if they do care, do not do so in a thoroughgoing way. Others try not to bother themselves with these things as much as possible whenever they come upon them, fearing that they may offend some people. The masses call those who cherish this idea persons who try to be "amicable."

Those who favor the idea of trying to be amicable in every possible way follow this approach to the problem of dealing with people and things in general. They simply do not care at all whether the wolf has devoured the sheep or vice versa. They open one eye and close the other, trying not to be a busybody. As a matter of fact, in doing so, they aid and abet in no small measure misdeeds and wrongdoing that undermine collective interests, thus bringing losses to the state and the collective. . . .

In order to get along peacefully with those who are likely to make mistakes, people who cherish the idea of trying to be amicable are even willing to give up their stand on matters of principle, so that their concessions may win other people's good will. When collective interests are impaired, they do not stand on the side of the collective and struggle against bad people and bad deeds, but instead compromise with bad people and bad deeds by adopting the attitude of "bringing losses to the public rather than to themselves." They say, "It is not easy to win the friendship of a single person, but it takes only a few words to offend someone."

Those who cherish the idea of trying to be amicable often are against understanding problems in terms of their principles. They always regard wrongdoing as "mere trifles not worth bothering about" and as "things that are excusable if done occasionally." . . . They hope to bring wrongdoers back to their senses through their "guilty conscience" and the passage of time. Such well-intentioned illusions, however, are always beyond realization.

101. A MODEL YOUTH
[Excerpts from Lei Feng's Diary, 1963]

November 2, 1959

After studying the works of Chairman Mao, I have gained much knowledge, I see an especially bright light in my heart, and the more I work, the greater vigor I have, which seems to be forever inexhaustible.

After doing something which I should have done for the masses, the Party has conferred on me a very great honor. Last year I was given the distinction of an advanced producer, and I attended the mass meeting of young activists for construction in An-shan. This is entirely the result of the Party's training, the unlimited strength Chairman Mao's thought has given me, and the support of the broad masses. I must always remember:

Only when a drop of water is put into a big sea can it never dry.

And only when a person combines himself with the collective work can he have strength.

Strength comes from unity, wisdom from labor,

Action from thought, and honor from collective.

I must permanently rid myself of pride and impetuousness, and advance uninterruptedly.

January 8, 1960

This is a day which I can never forget. I wore a military uniform and gloriously joined the People's Liberation Army, the fullfillment of a wish which I have had for a long time. . . . It was the greatest happiness I have ever had in my life.

January 12, 1960

Today I read an article dealing at length with how to struggle with difficulty. I quote the following:

"The struggle is hardest when victory is at hand; that is when vacillation is easiest. Therefore, so far as each individual is concerned, this is an important "obstacle." If the test is met and this obstacle is overcome, then he becomes a glorious revolutionary soldier. On the other hand, if the test is not met and this obstacle is not overcome, he becomes a disgraceful deserter. Whether you will become a glorious revolutionary soldier or a disgraceful deserter depends on whether you can have unshakable faith in the face of difficulty." . . .

These words have a deep educational effect on me. In the midst of difficulty, I must become a glorious revolutionary warrior, and absolutely not a disgraceful deserter. I must be a pine or cedar in a storm rather than a weak sprout in a warm room.

March 10, 1960

Today I saw in the movies the brilliant figure of the heroic revolutionary warrior Tung Ts'un-jui. He gave his life for the work of the Party and the people and for the liberation of mankind. This noble spirit is worthy of our emulation forever.

August 20, 1960

The People's Commune of Wang-hua *ch'ü*, Fu-shun Municipality, has been established. I supported it with 100 *yüan* I had saved up. When there was a flood in Liao-yang Municipality, I contributed to its people 100 *yüan* I had saved by living frugally. Some people say I am a "fool," but they are wrong. I want to do worthwhile things for the people and the country. If that is foolish, I am willing to be a fool. The revolution needs such fools, and construction needs such fools. I have but one thought, and that is that my whole heart is turned toward the Party, toward socialism, toward communism.

November 8, 1960

This is a day I shall never forget, the day on which I gloriously joined the great Chinese Communist Party, the fulfillment of my loftiest ideal.

My excited heart could not calm down for a single moment. Our great Party! Our wise Chairman Mao! Only when we have you can we have a new life. When I struggled for my life in the abyss of fire, I hoped for enlightenment. It was you who saved me, who gave me what I eat and what I wear, who sent me to school, who trained me to be worthy of the red emblem, to join the glorious Communist Youth League, to occupy a post in the industrial construction of the fatherland and now in the struggle for the defense of the fatherland. . . . I must wholeheartedly serve the people and permanently remain a loyal servant of the masses. For the Party's work, for the freedom, liberation, and happiness of all mankind, I would willingly enter a sea of fire or a mountain of swords. Even if my head were broken and my bones crushed, my red body and heart will never change!

May 3, 1961

Through the study of Chairman Mao's writings and my own practical experience, I deeply appreciate that his thinking is the basic guarantee for all work. Hereafter I must study Chairman Mao's works better and let them fortify my mind and guide all my actions, so that I can become someone beneficial to the people.

October 20, 1961

While a person's life is limited, serving the people is unlimited. I must give my limited life to unlimited service to the people.

February 27, 1962

Lei Feng, Lei Feng! I must warn you: Remember that you should never under any circumstances feel proud and arrogant. You must never forget that the Party saved you from the tiger's mouth and has given you all you have. . . . Anything you can do is your duty. What little you accomplish, whatever progress you make, you owe to the Party. . . .

March 4, 1962

So far as the revolution is concerned, the role a person plays is like that of a screw in a machine. Only when a machine is firmly held together by many, many screws can it be strong, operate smoothly, and acquire great working capacity. Though it is small, a screw's role is incalculable. I am willing to be a screw forever. Screws must constantly be kept in good condition and cleaned, so that they won't rust. So must men's thinking be regularly checked so as not to deteriorate.

August 6, 1962

Today I heard one comrade say to another: "A man lives to eat." I felt that was wrong, because we eat to live and not vice versa. I live to serve the people with all my heart and to struggle for the liberation of mankind and the realization of communism.

102. CADRE CORRUPTION
[From a Commentary in *People's Daily*, December 11, 1964]

This year,the broad masses of rural cadres have positively participated in collective productive labor. In the course of labor, they have received an education and have come to realize that they can lead production only when they take part in production as ordinary laborers. Now, the time has come for the distribution of the fruit of one year's labor. Some cadres, under the supervision of poor and lower-middle peasants, have begun to check their work points to see that they will not receive more work points than they are entitled to. They recognize that whether they take part in collective production or not is a question of whether they take part in the revolution or not, and that whether they receive work points on the same basis as ordinary commune members in the course of participating in collective production is also a question of whether they participate in the revolution or not.

From the several letters published here today, it can be seen that the calculation of work points involves a violent struggle and a major action aimed at raising our socialist consciousness. We must make it clear to the cadres that to receive more work points than one should is wrong ideologically, politically, and economically. Work points represent the quantity and quality of the work done by the commune members in collective productive labor; they form the basis of the distribution of income carried out by the basic accounting units of rural people's communes. According to the socialist principle of distribution, he who works poorly shall receive less work points; and he who has labor capacity but takes no part in labor shall receive none. If those who have labor power receive more work points than they should, then they steal the fruit of labor of others. Work points that one receives for nothing represent that part of income which one obtains without working for it. If this is not an act of exploitation, what is it?

In our socialist society, it is unlawful to receive more work points than one should.

Some people said that when some individual cadres received more work points than they were entitled to, they merely obtained some extra benefit economically. Such an idea is wrong. If a cadre fails to record his work points correctly, it first of all shows that his political thinking is not correct and his class stand is wrong. The duty of cadres is to serve the people, to protect the interests of the masses of the people. They have no right to encroach upon the interests of the masses. Taking the fruit of labor of the masses is a political question, a question of whom the cadres serve. Getting more work points than he should places a cadre in a position antagonistic to that of the laborers, turns him from a revolutionary into a non-revolutionary, and even makes him a bourgeois element who gratifies his private ends at the expense of others.

103. THE MEANING OF HAPPINESS
[From a Letter to Canton *Southern Daily*, November 17, 1963]

Some people say that "labor is happiness" and "to struggle for the liberation of mankind is happiness." I think that such a so-called happiness is only a kind of spiritual consolation. If a person has only spiritual consolation, but no material enjoyment of life, he cannot be considered as completely and really happy. When we have done our hard labor to make other people enjoy the fruits of our own labor, we shall certainly be happy at heart. But this is only an abstract happiness . . . for instance, a wounded soldier has become an invalid from the war. What is the use if he gets a few more medals? Other people make themselves very happy by strolling in the streets, but he has to support himself by a stick. Those who do not know the reason will even call him a "cripple." What kind of happiness is this? Therefore, I say that it is certainly good to have spiritual consolation, but it is even better to have material enjoyment. . . .

—Ch'un Yen, from Hsinhui *hsien*

**[From a Letter to Canton *Southern Daily,*
December 5, 1963]**

I think a man is happy if he lives well. A man must live, and, to live well, he of course has to rely on material comforts of life, and not on empty ideas and strange talk. Accordingly, the conditions for having access to the material comforts of life must include food, clothes, housing, transportation and amusement. . . . Not a single person in the world can survive on empty words, without eating anything. Whoever denies this point has lost his human nature and is worse than grass. Since good material conditions or otherwise have a vital bearing on the question of whether or not a man can stay alive and can live well, a man must fight for these conditions. Without doubt, these conditions have become the mark of happiness, that is, the substance of happiness. Happiness must be of tangible substance, for empty happiness is meaningless and non-existent as well.

A communist society does not appeal to the public by its empty and highly attractive name. Rather, by the time such a society is attained, science will reach such a high stage of development, and material wealth will be so very abundant that food, clothes, housing, transportation and amusement can completely satisfy public needs. It is precisely this rich substance of material life that stimulates people to build a communist society and call it a happy paradise. This shows that happiness basically consists of enjoying the material comforts of life. It can therefore be asserted that happiness is enjoyment. . . . Since an improvement in the living level of the people must rely on the accumulation of material wealth, gradual increases in material wealth will make it possible for the people to enjoy more of the pleasures of life. Material wealth is not to be kept in a magnificent mansion for display purpose only, but should be placed at the disposal of the people. That is why I say that happiness can only mean enjoyment of the material comforts of life.

—Ch'en Ting, from Lungmen *hsien*

**[From a Letter to Canton *Southern Daily*,
December 5, 1963]**

It is a strange logic to equate hardship with happiness, and the enjoyment of creature comforts with bourgeois thoughts. . . .

None can deny that labor and struggle is only the means of obtaining a happy life and changing people's spiritual outlook, not the goal; just as farming is for the harvest and not for the sake of farming alone. A revolutionary should have lofty ideals and noble sentiments, but he absolutely cannot ignore this point: material force can in turn increase people's revolutionary will and make them all the more confident in striving to obtain an even better future. . . . Some comrades say that labor itself is a kind of happiness; they also say that to be completely unselfish and altruistic is happiness. This spirit of self-sacrifice really deserves sincere admiration from us. But I cannot help doubting that, if all of us never care about ourselves and always try to benefit others, then who will be benefitted? If all of us think that it will be infinitely happy for us just to lay an additional brick and tile onto the great mansion of communism, then what is the use of the mansion on its completion? Just to satisfy people's desire for sightseeing? . . . The goal of our creating material wealth, in addition to being for the future, should aim at raising our standard of living. We should not regard wealth as something only for display at exhibitions, with a view to showing off the happiness of our hardship!

Our road of socialism is one of common labor and common prosperity. But common prosperity does not mean egalitarianism. As people are different in the ability to work, the contributions they make, the rewards they get, and the living they enjoy will be different. It is just because of this that we admit our differences. But some comrades say that a revolutionary can raise his material standard of living only after all the others have become well-off and that it is a bourgeois idea to demand personal enjoyment and livelihood when everyone else still leads a hard life. These comrades also say that the pursuit of material enjoyment will make people lose their ambitions. It is true that pursuit of material enjoyment will make people lose their ambitions. But is demanding a slight improvement in living enjoyment to be considered as "being obsessed" with "material things"? Can we put on an equal footing our present enjoyment of life and the extremely indulgent life of the ancient ruling classes? If this be the case, then people living in the communist society will have become people "obsessed with material things" and without any ambition, because people in the communist society will enjoy an excellent material life. We should realistically see that there are now no longer people who obtain things without labor and who get the fruits of other people's labor; at the same time, there are also no people who hope to build their happiness on the pains of other people. Most citizens in our country have become self-supporting laborers. Generally speaking, those people who can enjoy a better material life (such as professors, scholars, engineers, and so forth) are people who receive higher wages for their greater contributions; there are now thousands of such people in our country. Can we say that these people are small men without ambitions? Is it true that only those who lead a hard life and who live in the wilderness are people with great revolutionary ambitions? . . .

I am of the opinion that whether a person has revolutionary aspirations or not cannot be judged from his enjoyment of life; but it should be measured according to the ratio between his ability and his actual contributions.

—Yeh Ch'ui-ti, from Ch'engman *hsien*

[From an Article in *Chinese Youth Daily*, December 22, 1964]

The abilities of individuals vary, the contributions they are able to make and the work they do will also vary. However, as long as a person is able to serve the people whole-heartedly, and contribute his all, he will always be able to realize the greatest happiness. A revolutionary's happiness is always intimately linked to the collective and to the struggle.

Everything is either for the collective, or it is for the individual. Happiness is either complete devotion to the revolutionary struggle and serving people whole-heartedly, or it is the individual enjoyment of peace and material belongings. This is where the basic difference lies with respect to the proletarian and bourgeois concepts of happiness. . . .

The greatest happiness for us revolutionaries is to serve the people wholeheartedly. However, everyone has his own personal life. He wants to eat, have clothes to wear, a place to live and have his own family. . . . But what exactly is the correct way of regarding these things? What kind of basic approach and attitude should we have?

First, what we must strive for is the collective, we must strive to enable all the working people to have a good life, and not to strive simply for the individual. . . . A good life for the individual must be part of the good life of the collective and cannot be placed above that of the collective.

Second, a good life for the collective workers is only possible of attainment through bitter struggle. We must struggle against the class enemies, we must struggle against the natural world, and we must struggle against all kinds of difficulties. Chairman Mao said: "We want all of our young people to understand that our country is now a very poor country. Moreover, this situation cannot be basically changed in a short period of time. We rely wholly on our youth and our workers' collectives to unite in struggle and during the next several decades to create with their own hands a rich and strong nation. The establishment of a socialist system opens up for us a road to this ideal, but we must rely upon our own hard work to arrive at this ideal." Comrade Liu Shao-ch'i also once said: In a communist society "material and spiritual production expands rapidly and is able to meet all the needs of the members of that society." However, "the victory of communism will come only after a long and difficult struggle. Without this kind of struggle there can be no communist victory." To talk only of peace and enjoyment, and not to engage in bitter struggle, to be unwilling to pay the price of blood and sweat, and even to forget the enemy, to forget the class struggle, seeking after "peace and no war," will not only make it impossible to have a good life, but it will enable the imperialists, bureaucrats, and landlords to subjugate us again, with the result that we may all again lead an existence worse than that of cattle or horses.

Third, as a result of struggle and work, the living standards of all the workers will be raised, and improved: "If the river level is high, the streams will be full." The living standards of the individual will naturally rise and improve correspondingly. However, at no time should revolutionaries have a higher standard of living than the masses. Moreover, at times when the collective interest requires the carrying out of revolution, they must be able to lead a much more difficult life happily and willingly than the general masses, and feel happy doing so.

Fourth, regardless of the times, even when material production is relatively high and conditions are relatively good, we must all pay attention to being industrious and frugal and maintaining a proper attitude toward a life of arduous struggle. This is our revolutionary heritage, it is the highest virtue expected of us revolutionaries. This is the revolutionary will which we will eternally maintain, and is the important guarantee that we will always be a revolutionary group. How to handle the problem of the enjoyment of life is not as simple as some people think, for herein exists the class struggle. This is often where the attacks of bourgeois ideology break through, where "sugar-coated bullets" often find their easiest marks. For a revolutionary to pursue enjoyment can only have a debilitating effect on him politically, and he will be unable to be a true and thorough revolutionary. In the revolutionary forces, haven't there been some who started at this point and gradually became infected, changed character, and ultimately became rotten?

In short, regardless of the times, we must consider the personal enjoyment of material life as a secondary thing, and the interests of the revolution and the people as the primary thing.

—Yang Sung-shih, Yü Wan-sung, and Ch'en Shih-jen

[From an Article in *Chinese Youth,* February 1, 1965]

It is extremely important today to recognize the reactionary, decadent nature of the bourgeois view of happiness. In socialist society, is not the bourgeoisie everywhere trying to entice people into thinking of nothing but eating, dressing well, playing, and enjoying themselves? Their criminal goal is to open up gaps in the people's thinking by means of these temptations in life, to deceive the people into pursuing pure enjoyment, to turn them into disciples of a drunken, befuddled life, and thus bring about a restoration of capitalism. . . . If we do not critize this way of thinking, it will cause our youths to lose gradually their revolutionary will, their great revolutionary ideals. Detesting labor and seeking material enjoyment, they will further develop [the habit of] harming others to help themselves and exploiting others. Leading a decadent, backward life, they will begin to vacillate politically, and finally will follow the dangerous path of betraying the revolution. . . .

Comrade Lei Feng has said: "Eating is for the purpose of living; living is not for the purpose of eating." This simple phrase penetratingly expresses the view of a proletarian revolutionary towards the material life. . . .

The young people of this age live under socialist conditions. We have not been building socialism for long. We are still far behind our goal of communism. There are still extremely difficult revolutionary tasks before us. We must still undertake long-term striving, even more develop the productive forces of society, before we can realize the great ideal of communism. Therefore, the young people of this age must continue to uphold and develop the revolutionary spirit of bitter struggle, and completely eradicate the ideological influence of the bourgeois view of happiness—material enjoyment.

—Kao Tse-hung

104. SELECTIONS ON RED AND EXPERT

[From a Forum on the Question of Being Red and
Expert, *Chinese Youth Daily,* December 24, 1964]

Chinese Youth Daily Editor's Note:

The problem reflected in the [following] letter of Comrade Ch'in Jung-hsiu
of Peking Iron and Steel College is very important. An explicit discussion of
this problem will be of great significance to the revolutionization of young
intellectuals.

In conjunction with studying and implementing the spirit of the 9th National Congress of the Communist Youth League, young intellectuals in many
places are presently developing an enthusiastic discussion on the problem of
being red and expert. This discussion fires the ardor of the broad masses of the
young intellectuals to advance on the road of being both red and expert.

Some youths have, nevertheless, voiced their understanding and view in a
different way. The more popular one is the so-called idea of "politically passable, professionally proficient and living well." It is found not only among a
portion of university professors and students but also among young scientists
and technicians, young literary and art workers and other young intellectuals.
Therefore, this newspaper accepts Comrade Ch'in Jung-hsiu's recommendation, and begins to launch today a forum on "how to deal with the so-called
idea of 'politically passable, professionally proficient and living well.' "

The topics for discussion are:

1. Under the socialist conditions of our country today, should revolutionary
youth set a strict political demand for themselves? Should they strengthen
ideological remolding and realize proletarian revolutionization? If they are
satisfied by merely refraining from taking an anti-Party and anti-socialist
stand, can they be "politically passable" in the stormy class struggle?

2. Under the socialist conditions of our country today, what is the relationship between politics and professional work? What does our technical and
professional knowledge serve? If we do not remold ourselves politically, can
our technical and professional knowledge be really sound enough for the cause
of revolution and construction?

3. Under the socialist conditions of our country today, what should be the
aim of life for a revolutionary youth? Should he serve the interests of the
overwhelming majority of the people or just pursue a good life for the individual?

4. What is the ideological essence of "politically passable, professionally
proficient and living well"? How does it endanger the revolutionization of the
young intellectuals? Why must young intellectuals advance along the road of
being both red and expert?

We hope that the young intellectuals on various fronts will use Mao Tse-
tung's thought as their weapon and enthusiastically participate in this discussion in the spirit of submitting facts and reasons. Each contributor should
grasp one or two problems and concretely analyze and describe the actual

situation of his department, unit, or himself. We also welcome readers to raise other red and expert problems for discussion.

Letter from Comrade Ch'in Jung-hsiu

Comrade Editor:

Some teachers and students of our school recently held a discussion on how to understand and handle the relation between revolution and construction, and the relation between politics and professional work. This is an important problem bearing on how intellectuals should be oriented and which road they should follow. In this discussion, the understanding of certain teachers and students could be generalized by the popular idea of "politically passable, professionally proficient and living well." In place of being both red and expert, they considered this philosophy to be the most practical and effective avenue for intellectuals.

The reasons are:

1. The present era is different from the past. In the past, there was the war and the revolution, and it was necessary to set rigid political requirements. Although we are still required to carry out the revolution now, yet the principal work is to carry out construction. The exploiting class has been overthrown. Although there are still some remnants, they can do no great harm. With the times changed, the tasks are changed too.

Our current main task is to make a success of socialist construction. The principal task for us technical and professional men in particular is to carry out construction and not revolution. Hence, there is no need to make the political requirements too strict, and it will do if we are passable politically. What is called "passable" means that we must support the Party and socialism, or it can be said that we must not take the anti-Party and anti-socialist stand.

2. Politics is empty, but professional work is solid. Redness is abstract, but expertness is concrete. Only professional work can make contributions to socialist construction and directly and truly serve socialism. There must be something concrete to demonstrate whether we are red or not. To us professional men, expertness is a demonstration of redness. We are principally concerned with professional work and serving the people with our professional work. We must be professionally proficient and make a success of professional work before we can make a success of the revolution. Professional work and the revolution cannot be separated.

As a matter of fact, it is difficult to require professional work to be good both politically and professionally. This is difficult to put into practice. Redness and expertness are opposites in most cases and are seldom unified. It is only possible to be either more expert and less red, or less expert and more red. Therefore, the weight of political work and professional work should vary with persons. There must be division of labor, and the two, following different paths, lead to the same destination. As far as a scientific, technical or professional youth is concerned, the principal problem of revolutionization at present is to be professionally proficient.

3. When you are professionally proficient and make contributions, it goes without saying that the state and the people will take account of you and pay you well. This is only reasonable. Today we still adopt the system of "distribution according to work." Is it not just because they are professionally sound that some experts and specialists are held in high esteem, stand high in society, and lead a good life? It is therefore said that as long as one is professionally proficient, the question of "leading a good life"—to which the intellectuals aspire—is also solved.

How should this problem be dealt with? Is the idea of "politically passable, professionally proficient and living well" the path which the intellectuals should follow? Under the situation that there are still classes and class struggle in society, is it practical to replace the avenue of being both red and expert with this philosophy? What danger is there, if any, in following this path? I believe clarification of this problem is of significance. I suggest therefore that it should be discussed in the newspapers so that it may be correctly understood.

—Ch'in Jung-hsiu
Pressure Processing Department
Peking Iron and Steel College

[From a Letter to *Chinese Youth Daily*, December 26, 1964]

Now with our country ushered into a period of all-round socialist construction, the state is in need of large numbers of engineers, specialists and research personnel. Under these conditions, we must implement necessary division of labor. For persons handling social sciences and persons specializing in political work the demand for "redness" must be high. For persons handling natural sciences the demand for expertness must be high, and the demand for redness may be somewhat lower.

I do not say that persons handling natural sciences may entirely forsake redness. I only hold that the degree of being red should vary. . . .

According to what I know, none of the great natural scientists in history was well versed in Marxism-Leninism. It is my opinion, therefore, that different persons should be dealt with according to their conditions.

Man's time is limited and his energy is also limited. A metallurgical engineer could hardly be expected to know history and biology as well. By the same token, it is practically impossible to expect persons engaging in scientific and engineering work to be both red and expert—to have good knowledge of Marxism-Leninism as well as specialized knowledge. If the demand for redness is set too high, one's knowledge in his specialized field would definitely be affected. In this manner, it would be disadvantageous to socialist construction.

The above is my opinion on the problem of being red and expert. I welcome criticism and correction from everyone on any inappropriate points that I may have made.

—T'ien Ho-shui, student, Peking Iron and Steel College

**[From an Article in *Reconstruction,*
January 20, 1965]**

The Party requires intellectuals to be "both red and expert." Redness refers to politics. It means that intellectuals must listen to the words of the Party and Chairman Mao, assume a revolutionary character, and assume a laboring character. They are required to study Marxism and the thought of Mao Tse-tung properly, go into the midst of workers, peasants and soldiers over a long period, and take part in class struggle, production struggle, and scientific experiment. They are required to serve wholeheartedly the political ends of the proletariat and the work of socialist construction, to be able to stand firm in the struggle against imperialism, the struggle against modern revisionism, and the domestic struggle between the two roads, and to enforce the Party's directives and policies firmly in work.

Expertness refers to professional work. It means that intellectuals must study science and techniques properly, master the knowledge and theories connected with their professional work, master the skills of serving the people, and make more and better contributions toward the work of socialist revolution and socialist construction.

One who is expert but not red will go astray, embark on the wrong path, and fall into the quagmire of the bourgeoisie or revisionism. One who is red but not expert lacks professional knowledge and professional skills and will not be able to serve socialism well. In the relationship between redness and expertness, the former is the soul and the commander-in-chief. Expertness which is preceded by redness and which serves the proletariat and socialism is what we want. At the same time, redness may advance expertness. Those who have a high sense of responsibility toward the revolution are certain to study hard, study their professsional work actively, and exert effort to become expert. . . .

There are two basic ways in which intellectuals can remold their thought and change their world outlook. One is to study Marxism-Leninism and the thought of Mao Tse-tung seriously, study them flexibly and apply them flexibly, combine study with application, and equip their heads with the thought of Mao Tse-tung. The other is to plunge themselves actively into the revolutionary movements of class struggle, production struggle, and scientific experiment, unite with the masses of the workers and peasants over a long period, mix as one with them in thought and sentiment, and assume a revolutionary character and a laboring character.

—Han Fu

**[From an Editorial in *Chinese Youth Daily,*
July 24, 1965]**

How to deal with the question of redness and expertness involves the major issue of what kind of persons our younger generation will ultimately become. In more than ten thousand articles contributed by our readers, an overwhelming majority voice disagreement with the "three passable" idea and agreement with the idea of becoming both politically red and professionally sound. By presenting facts and reasoning, they penetratingly analyze the harm of the "three passable" idea. In an eloquent manner they contend that the road of both redness and expertness is the only correct path for our young people in various pursuits to take. . . .

The reason why the problem of redness and expertness has promoted repeated discussion is that it has its roots in the matter of cognition. What is more important is its class roots. What we have discussed so far has enabled us to comprehend this problem: as long as other differences are present, people will always put up this or that reason to oppose both redness and expertness and advocate expertness without redness. In this way, discussions on the question of redness and expertness will go on over and over again.

How can our young people remain firm and unshaken, steadfastly taking the road of redness and expertness, without being misled by erroneous views? The fundamental question is to equip themselves with the thought of Mao Tse-tung and become thoroughgoing revolutionaries. In this way they will establish the idea of wholeheartedly serving the greatest number of people.

In the course of discussing the question of redness and expertness, all participants have deeply realized this point: If an individual thinks more of revolutionary interests, giving little or no consideration to the matter of personal gain or loss, he will truly be able to be responsible for the revolutionary undertaking in the course of work. He will then cherish lofty ambitions, defying difficulties, advancing doggedly and unswervingly, and making his greatest contributions to the people.

On the other hand, if he always proceeds from personal considerations, doing everything around his ego, he will inevitably become narrow-minded and short-sighted. Under these circumstances, it will be impossible for him to truly implement Party policies and guidelines. Nor will he be able to do his work well. He may even bring considerable losses to the revolutionary undertaking. Therefore, only by abandoning his ego can he advance bravely along the road of redness and expertness.

105. THE MEANING OF WORK

[From Notes on a Discussion Meeting of a Communist Youth League Branch, *Chinese Youth*, November 1, 1965]

After *Chinese Youth* brought up the question of "what are we tilling land for?" we have organized League members and youths to hold several discussion meetings. The most keenly discussed subject is: Why is it wrong to till land for our own sake?

At the beginning, some youths said: There is nothing wrong if we labor well in order to have a good life. For, if everybody labors well for a good life, this will benefit not only himself but the collective and the state as well. If every one of us works well, earns more work points, sells more surplus grain, delivers more public grain, and saves more for communal accumulation, then he is directly aiding national construction and consolidating the collective economy. Furthermore, if everybody has a higher income and keeps his family adequately fed and clad, he will not need the help of the state and this will lighten the state's burden. In this way, "when small rivers have water, the big river is full," and the state will become rich and strong.

Many comrades do not agree with this view. They believe that if one does not establish the idea of tilling land for the revolution but works for himself, he will not be interested in collective production and will not work energetically in order to consolidate and develop the collective economy. This is because his aim is a better life and more work points for himself. Therefore, he will be interested only in work that benefits himself and enables him to get more work points; otherwise he will not be interested.

In the course of collective labor, he will only chase after quantity to the neglect of quality. He wants fast but not good results and even falsifies reports and records. He will definitely not take the initiative to concern himself with the big affairs of the collective and the state, nor will he consciously do good deeds for the collective. . . .

After studying Chairman Mao's works, Comrade Ch'en Nai-ying raised her ideological consciousness. Seeing that her team was short of manure, she broke the old custom of allowing no women to collect manure, and took the lead in collecting manure, carrying a basket on her back. Influenced by her, all the young people of the team collected a total of several tens of thousands of catties. This produced a very great effort on insuring increased output this year. When the team wanted to give them work points, they refused to take them, saying: "We want no work points. We work only for the revolution."

If everyone works for the collective in the same way as she does, our collective production will surely develop rapidly.

The following view is held by many comrades: Only by tilling land for revolution's sake will we stand high and see far and forever preserve the spirit of uninterrupted revolution. We shall be content with the status quo and cease to advance if we work for ourselves and for good food and clothing. There are some people in our team whose life is already quite good. But, when the team wants to further develop the collective economy and organizes every one to go to the swamp area, they become unresponsive and passive.

Some comrades say: On the surface, some people who work for a better life for themselves work with equal enthusiasm like everbody else. However, when the time for distribution comes, they always agitate for distributing more to themselves, reserving less for the collective, selling less to the state but requesting more assistance from the state. Moreover, they will seize any opportunity to take advantage of the collective and the state, thereby going the wrong way. If everybody behaves in this way, how can the collective be consolidated? How can our country become rich and strong? How can we say that "when small rivers have water, the big river is full"?

After several discussions, it was unanimously agreed that it is imperative to make a fruitful study of Chairman Mao's works, overcome individualism resolutely, and set up the idea of tilling land for the revolution.

—Peipait'a Production Brigade Changyi *hsien,* Shantung

[From a Letter to *Chinese Youth*, November 1, 1965]

In 1962, when I first returned to the countryside, I knew nothing at all about farming being for the sake of revolution. What I always thought about was personal interest. I participated in productive labor because I wanted to earn more work points, more cash, more oil, grain, and cotton. Swayed by individualistic thinking, I chose light work and shunned heavy. I always jumped at any opportunity to benefit myself at the expense of others, and sometimes I even submitted false reports. . . .

Three years of labor practice have led me to the profound realization that the aim of our tilling the land is principally decided by what our heads contain —by what we think. If we have in mind only personal interests, our families, rice coupons, work points . . . then we feel that tilling land does not give one a bright future. One will have no enthusiasm and be in low spirits; one will meet with setbacks everywhere and accomplish nothing at all.

But if we have in mind the collective cause, the socialist construction of the mother country and the world revolution, we feel that tilling land has a great prospect and we will be in high spirits. However hard the conditions may be, we will always be filled with vigor and fighting spirit.

—Chang K'o-min, Secretary, League Branch Powang Production
Brigade Hochin *hsien,* Shansi

106. ROLES FOR WOMEN
[From Letters to the Editor of *Chinese Women*, August 1963]

Chang Li-ying [in an earlier letter to the editor] said, "A woman lives not only for the sake of the revolution but also for her husband and children. As for revolutionary work and housekeeping, we should not point out which is first." I believe this view is incorrect. Matters are not as simple as that. In handling revolutionary work and housekeeping chores, we must separate them into primary and secondary matters. We must place the former in the primary position, and not treat it lightly. We should do our housekeeping chores only after we have done our work and we should not delay our work on account of housekeeping.

—Hui Min, from Chekiang

I do not agree with Chang Li-ying's view. Can we say that the revolution and the home can be treated on an equal basis? I believe those who hold this view have not yet liberated the individual from the small sphere of the family. The liberated women of China have the right to participate in the various kinds of social labor. We must value this right and with our utmost effort successfully carry out our revolutionary work first.

—Li Ch'ing, from Mian

We women have a special physical structure, which determines our natural sacred obligation to society, that is, to raise the next generation. Accordingly, no matter what kind of work a woman does, she cannot get away from this natural duty. Today, our superior social system has arranged a promising future for our children; thus, it has now created favorable conditions for women to raise their children. We should not worry about the future of our children, but we should be proud of the fact that we have raised the next generation with our own hands. From such a life, we can attain the warmth and the countless pleasures of family. At the same time, we can say without shame that we have performed our duty well.

—Hsiu Feng, from Shansi

I believe that if a woman can marry a city worker, live in a modernized industrial city, do some light social work and together with her husband enjoy the rich urban life, this is the greatest happiness and the most pleasant and interesting thing.

—Ts'ai Ying, from Heilungkiang

Comrade Ai Chuan said [in a previous issue], "When a woman can marry a husband with high position and a rich material livelihood, this is her happiness." I do not agree with this view. I believe that in their common life, a husband and a wife should be mutually affectionate and mutually helping to each other, so that their family enjoys a sweet and peaceful home. This is real happiness.

—Wang Shih-ying, from Tientsin

CHAPTER FOURTEEN
The Cultural Revolution

The Great Proletarian Cultural Revolution was the most dramatic sequence of events in the short history of the People's Republic. It was many things, interrelated, though not originating from any single source. It began in the cultural field, but was from the beginning essentially political. Perhaps of greatest immediate significance was the struggle for power within the top ranks of the CCP, the temporary weakening of party authority, and the ascent of the PLA. More spectacular were the activities of Red Guard students and other radicals. Important policy issues were also involved, which brought changes in some institutions.

Under Lin Piao (1907–71), the Minister of Defense, the PLA's role in political and economic life had steadily grown in the early 1960s, and the army was to play an even greater part in the Cultural Revolution. Selection 107, from the PLA newspaper, provides a useful perspective on some of the problems of the early 1960s and a foreglimpse of some future problems. Like Fei Hsiao-t'ung, the editorial points out that "public" is a relative term, and like Liu Shao-ch'i, that loyalties focused on local units can be detrimental to the whole. This tendency had been fostered by the transfer of authority downward in the communes, and also in industry. The conflict between the interests of lower-level units and the general public interest is seen as the product not of economic classes, but administrative organization, and hence endemic even in the new social order. It can only be overcome by politically induced identification with the whole, embodied in Chairman Mao. The reader may ask, however, whether adequate criteria are offered for determining the true interests of the whole. Is the problem of subjectivity solved, or is the answer dependent, as so frequently in previous writings, on Mao or his thought?

Divisions in society are also the concern of Mao's famous May 7 Directive, which suggests that they be broken down by a process intended to increase social homogeneity. (Selection 108) Although initially addressed to Lin Piao for use in the army, the directive was later widely applied to workers, peasants, students, and cadres as well, and has been especially influential in education.

Ideological education through practical experience became a major theme in the Cultural Revolution. The open letter to Chairman Mao from students in a Peking secondary school succinctly presents the central criticism of the educational system: The schools have been fostering a professional elite through competitive entrance examinations and by encouraging book-learning and careerism. (Selection 109) No explanation is offered for the anomaly of this moral condemnation by those who, if their own accusations are correct, are supposed to be career oriented. The assumption would seem to be that bad institutions tend to distort naturally good predispositions; hence the need to create new ones that will encourage inherent natural goodness. Following the publication of this and other similar letters that appeared at the same time, schools were immediately suspended, turning students free to participate in the mass movement soon to begin.

The famous Sixteen Point Decision of the CCP Central Committee officially sanctioned the Cultural Revolution and outlined its goals. (Selection 110) The problem is identified as the survival of the subversive legacy of the past, supported by "persons in authority in the Party taking the capitalist road," and the solution is an ideological mass campaign to eradicate these pernicious influences, which, however, are not detailed. The thought of Mao Tse-tung is stated to be the guide to action. Soon, the millions of "Little Red Books" containing Mao's sayings, which were to become the symbol of the Cultural Revolution, began to appear. While the general tenor of the document is that the Party is to lead the movement, the Party is obviously tainted by the presence of a small number of "anti-Party anti-socialist Rightists," while, on the other hand, the masses and the undefined "left" are said to be trustworthy and reliable. The critical attacks the Party had refused to tolerate from the "right" in 1957 were now virtually invited from the "left."

Red Guards started to appear in the streets of Peking in May and June and during the summer rapidly proliferated throughout urban China, eventually becoming a key force in the struggle for power. The report of representative early Red Guard activities in Selection 111 shows the great zeal that was to typify them, but gives no indication of well-defined specific goals at this stage.

The "left" propelled the Cultural Revolution into its radical phase in early 1967 with the "January Storm" in Shanghai, the center of radical power. Selection 112 proclaims the radicals' action as a seizure of power from the bourgeoisie and its agents within the Party by revolutionary masses, and announces Mao's approval and his call for the PLA to support the revolutionaries in their struggle against "rightists." This clearly implies the granting of authority to self-designated leftists to pass judgment on Party members, though other articles and editorials admonished the masses against taking precipitous action. Similar power seizures followed in other areas.

The first Revolutionary Committees, the new organs of power and administration, were formed in January 1967. Selection 113 explains the composition and functions of these committees, which by August 1968 were to be established in every province. The broader participation of non-Party people and the rising importance of the army are both evident. Warnings against the extreme "left" hint at problems caused by mass political activity—the subjectivity of the participants, the diffusion of decision making, and the weakening of party authority. Attacks by "leftists" on those they perceived as enemies and factionalism among "leftist" groups were leading to violent confrontations, disorders, and bloodshed. Army intervention was eventually necessary to restore order.

The theoretical reason for the Cultural Revolution was that there were two lines, and that the wrong one, the capitalist line, had been followed in recent years. Selection 114 is a good summation of the official explanation of the differences between the two policies. "Putting profits in command"—determining the success or failure of an enterprise by whether or not the value of its finished product exceeded the costs of producing it— is seen as generating self-centered competition for scarce resources, which disrupts the unified national economic plan. The administration of the existing economic structure by purely economic methods therefore leads to the reappearance of a market economy, an administrative elite, and concommitant social divisions. Selfishness, in short, is divisive. Hence the need to give primacy to politics to prevent this from happening and to bring unity through ideology. "China's Khrushchev" had by this time been identified as Liu Shao-ch'i. The tacit assumption that calling a person by the name of the head of the Communist Party of the Soviet Union is the worst form of vilification is indicative of how far Sino-Soviet relations had deteriorated since Stalin's time.

Since the ultimate theoretical goal was a revolution in men's thinking, some of the most important changes occurred in education. They were in the main aimed at preventing divisions in society, and especially against the development of elitist attitudes, as can be seen in the two reforms illustrated here. The May 7 Cadre Schools, named after Mao's May 7 Directive, were established for the re-education of administrative cadres. As the account of one May 7 School in Selection 115 reveals, cadres at these schools were not completely integrated with the peasants, though they did have regular contacts with them. Cadre feelings of superiority are indicated by some of their comments. The allegation that Red Guards might have been at least partly (and subconsciously) motivated by a desire to become officials again raises the question of subjectivity of professions of selfless concern for the public good, and suggests that egalitarianism could serve as an ideological justification for personal ambition.

The use of political means to check the development of elitist tendencies is also seen in the report on a model brigade elementary school in

Selection 116. Children from the former elite are said to have possessed improper advantages here as well as in the cities, and again the schools are blamed for perpetuating traditional attitudes, in this case disdain for manual labor. As in many documents from the Cultural Revolution, there is a propensity to exaggerate, even distort, earlier tendencies and practices. Great progress had been made in the first seventeen years of the People's Republic in spreading literacy.

The egalitarian trend is seen also in industry. The superiority of redness and practical experience is the theme of Selection 117, and this theory is illustrated in the anecdote in Selection 118, one of innumerable such stories published during these years. Rigid hierarchy is seen as stifling imagination and initiative. Again, an attack on the Party establishment is related to disgruntlement at being denied admission.

The ultimate logical extension in the complex relationship between public interest and private interest is demonstrated in the final document in this chapter. (Selection 119) In denouncing the "theory of merging public and private interest," the author seems to imply that appealing to even long-range self-interest has an insidious effect on the mind. As we have seen, the merging of public and private interest had for many years been a central explanation of the superiority of many new institutions, and was, like many other sins for which Liu Shao-ch'i was condemned, not a policy advocated only by Liu and a small handful of colleagues. The story used to illustrate the ideal of selfless service to the people ends with the only conclusive evidence of altruism—the hero cannot possibly gain in any material way from his deed because he loses his life in the act of doing it. Such self-sacrificing heroes and heroines appear frequently in the news media, in literature, and in the dramatic arts.

By late 1968 the Cultural Revolution was coming to an end, though it never was officially terminated. Radical elements were accused of anarchism, "ultra-democracy," and individualism, Red Guard organizations were suppressed by the army, and students were sent to the countryside to learn from the poor and lower-middle peasants. In October Liu Shao-ch'i, who, like many others, had been demoted, was expelled from the CCP. The following year a new Party constitution was adopted at the first Party congress in over a decade, and the process of rebuilding the Party and reasserting its vanguard status got under way.

107. PUBLIC AND PRIVATE IN SOCIALIST SOCIETY
[From an Editorial, "Put the Emphasis on 'Public,' " in *Liberation Army Daily,* February 9, 1966]

Chairman Mao has taught: "At no time or place should Communist Party members put personal interests in first place; personal interests should be subordinated to national and mass interests. Therefore, selfishness, a negative slowing down of work, corruption, and a desire for credit are to be despised. It is only working for public interests, positive efforts, the spirit of putting one's nose to the grindstone, that are praiseworthy."

With the brilliance of the thought of Mao Tse-tung, in the great practice of socialist revolution and construction, the spiritual world of China's people has thrown off the bonds of thousands of years of old thinking and old customs, and has undergone an unprecedentedly great change. The lofty virtues of not seeking fame or profit, of not fearing hardship or death, of not benefitting oneself but only the people, and of giving one's all for the revolution and the people are beginning to constitute the general social climate of our country. The Communist warrior Lei Feng, Wang Chieh, the proletarian struggler Mai Hsien-te, Hsien Committee Secretary Chiao Yu-lu, who wears himself out in the service of the people,[1] the Ta-ch'ing people, the Ta-chai people, the Good Eighth Company, the Hard-Bone Sixth Company,[2] and all the tens of thousands of advanced persons and collective groups—all these are proletarian heroes and representatives of the spirit of the era. In the final analysis, the essence of their thinking is centered on the concept of "public."

The issue at present is whether we are for public or private interests. This is a question which can be encountered at any time and any place in our socialist era, a question which must be answered. If one is not for the public, then one is for the private; to see which way one leans is a test for everyone. This question is very important, very universal. It involves men and women, young and old, simply everyone. For example, are the water buffalos of the production teams to be used to farm the collective fields or the private plots? Is a bucket of fertilizer to be put on the large fields, or on the private plots? Consider the workers: will they work more for more money and less for less money? or will they consciously work, forgetting about themselves? Consider the comrades in our military forces: in fighting will they advance bravely, or will they hold back fearing for their lives? As regards assignments, will we take up the heavy ones or the light ones? In general, for any person, in any job, in any situation in life, or in studying, there is always the question of public and private. This is all the more prominent in an environment of hardship or in a life-and-death struggle. These two approaches are always contending with one another in a person's mind. This struggle engulfs everyone; no one can avoid it.

When we stress politics, we are advocating the concept of "public," advocating the ideology of leaning towards the public, the revolution, and the people. Politics is the struggle of one class against another; it is a public affair, a major class affair; it is the affair of the Party, of the state, of the world. The bourgeoisie has bourgeois politics, and the proletariat has proletarian politics. When any class discusses politics, it always starts out from its own class interests, and is concerned with its own public affairs. For the bourgeoisie and all exploiting classes, the word "public" is nothing more than the private interests of the class or of the minority; it is a petty thing, a phoney thing. Only the "public" of the proletariat, the public matters of the proletariat, represent the interests

[1]Model individual Party members.
[2]Model industrial, agricultural, and military units.

of all the working peoples; this is the only true public, the great public. In our political work, we must educate people to be consciously concerned with the public matters of the proletariat; we must let the proletarian "public" take root in the minds of the people. . . .

In a socialist society why do we particularly want to advocate the idea of "public"?

The difference between socialist and capitalist society is that the means of production in the former are public. The economic base has changed, so such things as politics and ideology, which make up the superstructure, must keep up. How would it do to have us physically enter into socialism, but to lag behind in capitalism mentally? The system of public ownership demands that we have a concept of public. If everyone were to have a sense of public responsibility, public-minded morality, a concern for public matters, a love of public interests, a looking out for public wealth, then the mansion of socialism could be erected, and the state would be firmly anchored. If we only heed our own petty affairs but not the great collective matters, if we only see what is before our nose but do not see the 650 million people of the fatherland or the three billion people in the world, or if we are filled with individualism or the selfishness of the bourgeoisie, then not only will we not be able to build socialism or make the transition to communism, but there will also be the danger of a capitalist restoration. For example with regard to the public wealth, if we are selfish, if you take a little, and he grabs a bit, then how can we talk about developing production! How can we talk about building socialism! Little streamlets converge into mighty rivers; anthills can form a thousand *li* of embankments. Are we for the public, or for the private? The relationship is very important. If we are for the public, we will place bricks on the edifice of socialism; if we are for the private, we will dig away at the foundation of socialism.

"There must be meat in the stove before there is meat in the dish." "Only when there is water in the large rivers will the little streams not run dry." When we undertake work on the socialist economy, we are following the path of public prosperity; we are creating wealth for the collective and the state. If we depart from the collective and the state and try to get rich personally, then bourgeois and revisionist elements will surely emerge. In a class society no one is outside of class; all are inside and related to a certain class. With regard to our working people, had there been no social liberation and class liberation, there would have been no individual liberation. An individual cannot undertake individualism; a region or a unit cannot undertake departmentalism [*pen-wei-chu-yi*]. To undertake departmentalism, to consider only the small public but not the large public, is in actuality to expand individualism. Similarly, in a socialist state there cannot simply be consideration of oneself but not others; this might even harm others or result in a chauvinistic benefitting of oneself. If we do these things, the results will be that there will be no guaranteeing of individual interests, local interests, or state interests. Without the collective, there will be nothing of the individual. Without the victory of the whole, there can be no true victory for the part. Without the success of the world revolution, there can be no complete success for a national revolution. If we are for the public aspect, if our hearts are fixed on the collective, on the whole, on socialism, on world revolution, if individual interests are fused into collective interests, if the interests of the part are fused into the interests of the whole, if the Chinese revolution and the world revolution are tightly united, then we will be able to win everything, to win complete victory.

In building socialism and communism, we must not only destroy all old systems of man exploiting man and man suppressing man, but we must also destroy all old concepts produced by, and serving, these old systems, as well as old customs. This is a severe, complex, long-term class struggle taking place in the realm of thought. This will be more difficult than destroying the exploiting class economically. In people's thinking, if the concept of "public" is not to the fore, then the concept of "private" will be. If socialist ideology doesn't occupy the high ground, then bourgeois ideology will. There can be no merging of the public and the private in one's mind; there can be no "peaceful coexistence between socialism and capitalism." Public affairs and private affairs, small matters and big matters, collective matters and individual matters—there is always a mutual struggle between the two sides. If one thing is not predominant, then another thing will be. The Ta-ch'ing people have put it well: "The more I leave my 'ego' behind me, the greater becomes my enthusiasm. If I could completely forget my 'ego,' I would be able to walk on a mountain of knives and a sea of fire." Such are the laws of things. When we advocate the "public" and oppose the "private," when we promote proletarian thinking and destroy bourgeois thinking, it is in order to destroy finally all remnants of the exploiting class and system.

It is particularly important in the era of socialist revolution and construction to advocate service to the public, to the revolution, to the people. This is a question of direction in our political work. All the work of our armed forces, all construction for revolutionization and modernization are inseparable from promotion of the public and destruction of the private, and the struggle to promote the proletariat and destroy the bourgeoisie. We must hold all the higher the great red banner of the thought of Mao Tse-tung; . . . we must use the thought of Mao Tse-tung to arm our cadres and soldiers, so as to raise proletarian consciousness, to elevate the viewpoint of struggling for the interests of the proletariat and for the cause of communism; we must increase the viewpoint of hostility towards the enemy and of being constantly prepared to fight; we must increase concern for public affairs and for the collective; we must oppose selfishness and individualism and all the influences of bourgeois thinking. In a word, we must develop a communist world view of having our hearts fixed on the public side.

108. BREAKING DOWN THE DIVISION OF LABOR
[Mao Tse-tung's May 7 Directive, May 7, 1966]

So long as there is no world war, the armed forces should be a great school. . . . In this great school our armymen should learn politics, military affairs and agriculture. They can also engage in agricultural production and side occupations, run some medium and small factories and manufacture a number of products to meet their own needs or exchange with the state at equal values. They can also do mass work and take part in the socialist education movement in the factories and villages. After the socialist education movement, they can always find mass work to do, in order to insure that the army is always as one with the masses. They should also participate in each struggle of the cultural revolution as it occurs to criticize the bourgeoisie. In this way, the army can concurrently study, engage in agriculture, run factories and do mass work. Of course, these tasks should be properly coordinated, and a difference should be made between the primary and secondary tasks. Each army unit should engage in one or two of the three tasks of agriculture, industry and mass work, but not in all three at the same time. In this way, our army of several million will be able to play a very great role indeed.

While the main task of the workers is in industry, they should also study military affairs, politics and culture. They, too, should take part in the socialist education movement and in the criticizing of the bourgeoisie. Where conditions permit, they should also engage in agricultural production and side occupations, as is done at the Ta-ch'ing oilfield.

While the main task of the peasants in the communes is agriculture (including forestry, animal husbandry, side occupations and fishery), they should at the same time study military affairs, politics and culture. Where conditions permit, they should collectively run small plants. They should also criticize the bourgeoisie.

This holds good for students too. While their main task is to study, they should, in addition to their studies, learn other things, that is, industrial work, farming and military affairs. They should also criticize the bourgeoisie. The school term should be shortened, education should be revolutionized, and the domination of our schools by bourgeois intellectuals should not be allowed to continue.

Where conditions permit those working in commerce, in the service trades and in Party and government organizations should do the same.

109. NEW SCHOOLING FOR A NEW SOCIETY
[From a Letter to Chairman Mao from the Fourth Class of the Senior Third Grade at Peking No. 1 Girl's Middle School, June 6, 1966]

We hold that the existing system of admittance to higher schools is a continuation of the old feudal examination system dating back thousands of years. It is a most backward and reactionary educational system. It runs counter to the educational policy laid down by Chairman Mao. **Chairman Mao says that education must serve the politics of the proletariat and be integrated with productive labor. "Our educational policy must enable everyone who gets** an education to develop morally, intellectually and physically and become a cultured, socialist-minded worker." But the existing educational system is not set up in accordance with this directive of Chairman Mao. In fact it is extending and prolonging the three major differences—between manual and mental labor, between worker and peasant and between town and country. Concretely, we make the following charges against it:

1. Many young people are led not to study for the revolution but to immerse themselves in books for the university entrance examination and to pay no heed to politics. Quite a number of students have been indoctrinated with such gravely reactionary ideas of the exploiting classes as that "book learning stands above all else," of "achieving fame," "becoming experts," "making one's own way," "taking the road of becoming bourgeois specialists," and so on. The present examination system helps the spread of these ideas.

2. It makes many schools chase one-sidedly after a high rate in the number of their students who will be admitted to higher schools and as a result many become "special" and "major" schools which specially enroll "outstanding students." These schools have opened the gates wide to those who completely immerse themselves in books and pay no attention to politics and have shut out large numbers of outstanding children of workers, peasants, and revolutionary cadres.

3. It seriously hampers students from developing morally, intellectually and physically and particularly morally. This system fundamentally ignores the ideological revolutionization of youth. It is, in essence, exactly what is preached by the sinister Teng T'o[1] gang: "teaching one in accordance with his ability."

Therefore, this system of admittance to higher schools serves a capitalist restoration; it is a tool for cultivating new bourgeois elements and revisionists. . . .

Respected and beloved Chairman Mao, you have repeatedly taught us that "we should support whatever the enemy opposes and oppose whatever the enemy supports." As the enemy claps his hands and applauds the old system so desperately, can we allow it to continue to exist? No! Not for a single day! Today, in this great and unprecedented cultural revolution, we must join the workers, peasants and soldiers in smashing it thoroughly. We suggest in concrete terms that:

1. Beginning this year, we abolish the old system of enrolling students in the higher schools.

2. Graduates from senior middle schools should go straight into the midst of the workers, peasants and soldiers and integrate themselves with the masses.

We think that at a time when their world outlook is being formed, young people of seventeen or eighteen years old should be tempered and nurtured in the storms of the three great revolutionary movements.[2] They should first of all get "ideological diplomas" from the working class and the poor and lower-middle peasants. The Party will select the best from among the fine sons and

---

[1] A leading journalist, one of the first men to be attacked in the Cultural Revolution.

[2] Of class struggle, the struggle for production, and scientific experiment.

daughters of the proletariat, young people who truly serve the broad masses of workers, peasants and soldiers, and send them on to higher schools.

110. THE PROGRAM FOR THE CULTURAL REVOLUTION

[Decision of the Central Committee of the Chinese Communist Party Concerning the Great Proletarian Cultural Revolution, August 8, 1966]

A New Stage in the Socialist Revolution

The great proletarian cultural revolution now unfolding is a great revolution that touches people to their very souls and constitutes a new stage in the development of the socialist revolution in our country, a stage which is both broader and deeper.

At the Tenth Plenary Session of the Eighth Central Committee of the Party, Comrade Mao Tse-tung said: To overthrow a political power, it is always necessary first of all to create public opinion, to do work in the ideological sphere. This is true for the revolutionary class as well as for the counter-revolutionary class. This thesis of Comrade Mao Tse-tung's has been proved entirely correct in practice.

Although the bourgeoisie has been overthrown, it is still trying to use the old ideas, culture, customs, and habits of the exploiting classes to corrupt the masses, capture their minds and endeavor to stage a come-back. The proletariat must do the exact opposite: it must meet head-on every challenge of the bourgeoisie in the ideological field and use the new ideas, culture, customs and habits of the proletariat to change the mental outlook of the whole of society. At present, our objective is to struggle against and overthrow these persons in authority who are taking the capitalist road, to criticize and repudiate the reactionary bourgeoisie and all other exploiting classes and to transform education, literature and art and all other parts of the superstructure not in correspondence with the socialist economic base, so as to facilitate the consolidation and development of the socialist system.

The Main Current and the Twists and Turns

The masses of the workers, peasants, soldiers, revolutionary intellectuals and revolutionary cadres form the main force in this great cultural revolution. Large numbers of revolutionary young people, previously unknown, have become courageous and daring pathbreakers. They are vigorous in action and intelligent. Through the media of big-character posters and great debates, they argue things out, expose and criticize thoroughly, and launch resolute attacks on the open and hidden representatives of the bourgeoisie. In such a great revolutionary movement, it is hardly avoidable that they should show short-

CHANGING CHINA

comings of one kind or another; however, their general revolutionary orientation has been correct from the beginning. This is the main current in the great proletarian cultural revolution. It is the general direction along which this revolution continues to advance.

Since the cultural revolution is a revolution, it inevitably meets with resistance. This resistance comes chiefly from those in authority who have wormed their way into the Party and are taking the capitalist road. It also comes from the force of habits from the old society. At present, this resistance is still fairly strong and stubborn. But after all, the great proletarian cultural revolution is an irresistible general trend. There is abundant evidence that such resistance will be quickly broken down once the masses become fully aroused.

Because the resistance is fairly strong, there will be reversals and even repeated reversals in this struggle. There is no harm in this. It tempers the proletariat and other working people, and especially the younger generation, teaches them lessons and gives them experience, and helps them to understand that the revolutionary road zigzags and does not run smoothly.

Put Daring above Everything Else and Boldly Arouse the Masses

The outcome of this great cultural revolution will be determined by whether or not the Party leadership dares boldly to arouse the masses.

Currently there are four different situations with regard to the leadership being given to the movement of cultural revolution by Party organizations at various levels:

1. There is the situation in which the persons in charge of Party organizations stand in the van of the movement and dare to arouse the masses boldly. They put daring above everything else, they are dauntless communist fighters and good pupils of Chairman Mao. They advocate the big-character posters and great debates. They encourage the masses to expose every kind of ghost and monster and also to criticize the shortcomings and errors in the work of the persons in charge. This correct kind of leadership is the result of putting proletarian politics in the forefront and Mao Tse-tung's thought in the lead.

2. In many units, the persons in charge have a very poor understanding of the task of leadership in this great struggle, their leadership is far from being conscientious and effective, and they accordingly find themselves incompetent and in a weak position. They put fear above everything else, stick to outmoded ways and regulations, and are unwilling to break away from conventional practices and move ahead. They have been taken unawares by the new order of things, the revolutionary order of the masses, with the result that their leadership lags behind the situation, lags behind the masses.

3. In some units, the persons in charge, who made mistakes of one kind or another in the past, are even more prone to put fear above everything else, being afraid that the masses will catch them out. Actually, if they make serious self-criticism and accept the criticism of the masses, the Party and the masses will make allowances for their mistakes. But if the persons in charge don't, they will continue to make mistakes and become obstacles to the mass movement.

4. Some units are controlled by those who have wormed their way into the Party and are taking the capitalist road. Such persons in authority are extremely afraid of being exposed by the masses and therefore seek every possible pretext to suppress the mass movement. They resort to such tactics as shifting the targets for attack and turning black into white in an attempt to lead the movement astray. When they find themselves very isolated and no longer able to carry on as before, they resort still more to intrigues, stabbing people in the back, spreading rumors, and blurring the distinction between revolution and counter-revolution as much as they can, all for the purpose of attacking the revolutionaries.

What the Central Committee of the Party demands of the Party committees at all levels is that they persevere in giving correct leadership, but daring above everything else, boldly arouse the masses, change the state of weakness and incompetence where it exists, encourage those comrades who have made mistakes but are willing to correct them to cast off their mental burdens and join in the struggle, and dismiss from their leading posts all those in authority who are taking the capitalist road and so make possible the recapture of the leadership for the proletarian revolutionaries.

Let the Masses Educate Themselves in the Movement

In the great proletarian cultural revolution, the only method is for the masses to liberate themselves, and any method of doing things in their stead must not be used.

Trust the masses, rely on them and respect their initiative. Cast out fear. Don't be afraid of disturbances. Chairman Mao has often told us that revolution cannot be so very refined, so gentle, so temperate, kind, courteous, restrained and magnanimous. Let the masses educate themselves in this great revolutionary movement and learn to distinguish between right and wrong and between correct and incorrect ways of doing things.

Make the fullest use of big-character posters and great debates to argue matters out, so that the masses can clarify the correct views, criticize the wrong views and expose all the ghosts and monsters. In this way the masses will be able to raise their political consciousness in the course of the struggle, enhance their abilities and talents, distinguish right from wrong and draw a clear line between ourselves and the enemy.

Firmly Apply the Class Line of the Party

Who are the enemies? Who are our friends? This is a question of the first importance for the revolution and it is likewise a question of the first importance for the great cultural revolution.

Party leadership should be good at discovering the Left and developing and strengthening the ranks of the Left; it should firmly rely on the revolutionary Left. During the movement this is the only way to isolate the most reactionary

Rightists thoroughly, win over the middle and unite with the great majority so that by the end of the movement we shall achieve the unity of more than 95 percent of the cadres and more than 95 percent of the masses.

Concentrate all forces to strike at the handful of ultrareactionary bourgeois Rightists and counter-revolutionary revisionists, and expose and criticize to the full their crimes against the Party, against socialism and against Mao Tse-tung's thought so as to isolate them to the maximum.

The main target of the present movement is those within the Party who are in authority and are taking the capitalist road.

The strictest care should be taken to distinguish between the anti-Party, anti-socialist Rightists and those who support the Party and socialism but have said or done something wrong or have written some bad articles or other works.

The strictest care should be taken to distinguish between the reactionary bourgeois scholar despots and "authorities" on the one hand and people who have the ordinary bourgeois academic ideas on the other.

Correctly Handle Contradictions among the People

A strict distinction must be made between the two different types of contradictions: those among the people and those between ourselves and the enemy. Contradictions among the people must not be made into contradictions between ourselves and the enemy; nor must contradictions between ourselves and the enemy be regarded as contradictions among the people.

It is normal for the masses to hold different views. Contention between different views is unavoidable, necessary and beneficial. In the course of normal and full debate, the masses will affirm what is right, correct what is wrong and gradually reach unanimity.

The method to be used in debates is to present the facts, reason things out, and persuade through reasoning. Any method of forcing a minority holding different views to submit is impermissible. The minority should be protected, because sometimes the truth is with the minority. Even if the minority are wrong, they should still be allowed to argue their case and reserve their views.

When there is a debate, it should be conducted by reasoning, not by coercion or force.

In the course of debate, every revolutionary should be good at thinking things out for himself and should develop the communist spirit of daring to think, daring to speak and daring to act. On the premise that they have the same general orientation, revolutionary comrades should, for the sake of strengthening unity, avoid endless debate over side issues.

Be on Guard against Those Who Brand the Revolutionary Masses as "Counter-Revolutionaries"

In certain schools, units, and work teams of the cultural revolution, some of the persons in charge have organized counter-attacks against the masses who put up big-character posters criticizing them. These people have even advanced such slogans as: opposition to the leaders of a unit or a work team means opposition to the Central Committee of the Party, means opposition to the Party and socialism, means counter-revolution. In this way it is inevitable that their blows will fall on some really revolutionary activists. This is an error on matters of orientation, an error of line, and is absolutely impermissible.

A number of persons who suffer from serious ideological errors, and particularly some of the anti-Party and anti-socialist Rightists, are taking advantage of certain shortcomings and mistakes in the mass movement to spread rumors and gossip, and engage in agitation, deliberately branding some of the masses as "counter-revolutionaries." It is necessary to beware of such "pickpockets" and expose their tricks in good time.

In the course of the movement, with the exception of cases of active counter-revolutionaries where there is clear evidence of crimes such as murder, arson, poisoning, sabotage or theft of state secrets, which should be handled in accordance with the law, no measures should be taken against students because of problems that arise in the movement. To prevent the struggle from being diverted from its main target, it is not allowed, under whatever pretext, to incite the masses or the students to struggle against each other. Even proven Rightists should be dealt with on the merits of each case at a later stage of the movement.

The Question of Cadres

The cadres fall roughly into the following four categories:

1. good
2. comparatively good
3. those who have made serious mistakes but have not become anti-Party, anti-socialist Rightists
4. the small number of anti-Party, anti-socialist Rightists

In ordinary situations, the first two categories (good and comparatively good) are the great majority.

The anti-Party, anti-socialist Rightists must be fully exposed, refuted, overthrown and completely discredited and their influence eliminated. At the same time, they should be given a chance to turn over a new leaf.

Cultural Revolutionary Groups, Committees, and Congresses

Many new things have begun to emerge in the great proletarian cultural revolution. The cultural revolutionary groups, committees and other organizational forms created by the masses in many schools and units are something new and of great historic importance.

These cultural revolutionary groups, committees and congresses are excellent new forms of organization whereby the masses educate themselves under the leadership of the Communist Party. They are an excellent bridge to keep our Party in close contact with the masses. They are organs of power of the proletarian cultural revolution.

The struggle of the proletariat against the old ideas, culture, customs and habits left over by all the exploiting classes over thousands of years will necessarily take a very, very long time. Therefore, the cultural revolutionary groups, committees and congresses should not be temporary organizations but permanent, standing mass organizations. They are suitable not only for colleges, schools and government and other organizations, but generally also for factories, mines, other enterprises, urban districts and villages.

It is necessary to institute a system of general elections, like that of the Paris Commune, for electing members to the cultural revolutionary groups and committees and delegates to the cultural revolutionary congresses. The lists of candidates should be put forward by the revolutionary masses after full discussion, and the elections should be held after the masses have discussed the lists over and over again.

The masses are entitled at any time to criticize members of the cultural revolutionary groups and committees and delegates elected to the cultural revolutionary congresses. If these members or delegates prove incompetent, they can be replaced through election or recalled by the masses after discussion.

The cultural revolutionary groups, committees and congresses in colleges and schools should consist mainly of representatives of the revolutionary students. At the same time, they should have a certain number of representatives of the revolutionary teaching and administrative staff and workers.

Educational Reform

In the great proletarian cultural revolution a most important task is to transform the old educational system and the old principles and methods of teaching.

In this great cultural revolution, the phenomenon of our schools being dominated by bourgeois intellectuals must be completely changed.

In every kind of school we must apply thoroughly the policy advanced by Comrade Mao Tse-tung of education serving proletarian politics and education being combined with productive labor, so as to enable those receiving an education to develop morally, intellectually and physically and to become laborers with socialist consciousness and culture.

The period of schooling should be shortened. Courses should be fewer and better. The teaching material should be thoroughly transformed, in some cases beginning with simplifying complicated material. While their main task is to study, students should also learn other things. That is to say, in addition to their studies they should also learn industrial work, farming and military affairs, and take part in the struggles of the cultural revolution to criticize the bourgeoisie as these struggles occur.

The Question of Criticizing by Name in the Press

In the course of the mass movement of the cultural revolution, the criticism of bourgeois and feudal ideology should be well combined with the dissemination of the proletarian world outlook and of Marxism-Leninism Mao Tse-tung thought.

Criticism should be organized of typical bourgeois representatives who have wormed their way into the Party and typical reactionary bourgeois "authorities," and this should include criticism of various kinds of reactionary views in philosophy, history, political economy and education, in works and theories of literature and art, in theories of natural science, and in other fields.

Criticism of anyone by name in the press should be decided after discussion by the Party committee at the same level, and in some cases submitted to the Party committee at a higher level for approval.

Policy toward Scientists, Technicians, and Ordinary Members of Working Staffs

As regards scientists, technicians and ordinary members of working staffs, as long as they are patriotic, work energetically, are not against the Party and socialism, and maintain no illicit relations with any foreign country, we should in the present movement continue to apply the policy of "unity, criticism, unity." Special care should be taken of those scientists and scientific personnel who have made contributions. Efforts should be made to help them gradually transform their world outlook and their style of work.

The Question of Arrangements for Integration with the Socialist Education Movement in City and Countryside

The cultural and educational units and leading organs of the Party and government in the large and medium cities are the points of concentration of the present proletarian cultural revolution.

The great cultural revolution has enriched the socialist education movement in both city and countryside and raised it to a higher level. Efforts should be made to conduct these two movements in close combination. Arrangements to this effect may be made by various regions and departments in the light of the specific conditions.

The socialist education movement now going on in the countryside and in enterprises in the cities should not be upset where the original arrangements are appropriate and the movement is going well, but should continue in accordance with the original arrangements. However, the questions that are arising in the present great proletarian cultural revolution should be put to the masses for discussion at the proper time, so as to further foster vigorously proletarian ideology and eradicate bourgeois ideology.

In some places, the great proletarian cultural revolution is being used as the focus in order to add momentum to the socialist education movement and clean things up in the fields of politics, ideology, organization and economy. This may be done where the local Party committee thinks it appropriate.

Take Firm Hold of the Revolution and Stimulate Production

The aim of the great proletarian cultural revolution is to revolutionize people's ideology and as a consequence to achieve greater, faster, better and more economical results in all fields of work. If the masses are fully aroused and proper arrangements are made, it is possible to carry on both the cultural revolution and production without one hampering the other, while guaranteeing high quality in all our work.

The great proletarian cultural revolution is a powerful motive force for the development of the social productive forces in our country. Any idea of counterposing the great cultural revolution to the development of production is incorrect.

The Armed Forces

In the armed forces, the cultural revolution and the socialist education movement should be carried out in accordance with the instructions of the Military Commission of the Central Committee of the Party and the General Political Department of the People's Liberation Army.

Mao Tse-tung's Thought Is the Guide to Action in the Great Proletarian Cultural Revolution

In the great proletarian cultural revolution, it is imperative to hold aloft the great red banner of Mao Tse-tung's thought and put proletarian politics in command. The movement for the creative study and application of Chairman Mao Tse-tung's works should be carried forward among the masses of the workers, peasants and soldiers, the cadres and the intellectuals, and Mao Tse-tung's thought should be taken as the guide to action in the cultural revolution.

In this complex great cultural revolution, Party committees at all levels must study and apply Chairman Mao's works all the more conscientiously and in a creative way. In particular, they must study over and over again Chairman Mao's writings on the cultural revolution and on the Party's methods of leadership, such as *On New Democracy, Talks at the Yenan Forum on Literature and Art, On the Correct Handling of Contradictions Among the People, Speech at the Chinese Communist Party's National Conference on Propaganda Work, Some Questions Concerning Methods of Leadership,* and *Methods of Work of Party Committees.*

Party committees at all levels must abide by the directions given by Chairman Mao over the years, namely that they should thoroughly apply the mass line of "from the masses, to the masses" and that they should be pupils before they become teachers. They should try to avoid being one-sided or narrow.

They should foster materialistic dialectics and oppose metaphysics and scholasticism.

The great proletarian cultural revolution is bound to achieve brilliant victory under the leadership of the Central Committee of the Party headed by Comrade Mao Tse-tung.

111. RED GUARDS ATTACK THE "FOUR OLDS"
[From "Red Guards Destroy the Old and Establish the New," *Peking Review,* September 2, 1966]

Since August 20, the young Red Guards of Peking, detachments of students, have taken to the streets. With the revolutionary rebel spirit of the proletariat, they have launched a furious offensive to sweep away reactionary, decadent bourgeois and feudal influences, and all old ideas, culture, customs, and habits. This mounting revolutionary storm is sweeping the cities of the entire nation. "Let Mao Tse-tung's thought occupy all positions; use it to transform the mental outlook of the whole of society; sweep away all ghosts and monsters; brush aside all stumbling-blocks and resolutely carry the great proletarian cultural revolution through to the end!" This is the militant aim of the young revolutionary fighters. Their revolutionary actions have everywhere received the enthusiastic support of the revolutionary masses.

IN PEKING.   During the past week and more Red Guards have scored victory after victory as they pressed home their attack against the decadent customs and habits of the exploiting classes. Beating drums and singing revolutionary songs, detachments of Red Guards are out in the streets doing propaganda work, holding aloft big portraits of Chairman Mao, extracts from Chairman Mao's works, and great banners with the words: "We are the critics of the old world; we are the builders of the new world." They have held street meetings, put up big-character posters and distributed leaflets in their attack against all the old ideas and habits of the exploiting classes. As a result of the proposals of the Red Guards and with the support of the revolutionary masses, shop signs which spread odious feudal and bourgeois ideas have been removed, and the names of many streets, lanes, parks, buildings and schools tainted with feudalism, capitalism or revisionism or which had no revolutionary significance have been replaced by revolutionary names. The service trades have thrown out obsolete rules and regulations.

Support for the revolutionary actions of the Red Guards has been expressed in countless big-character posters which the masses of revolutionary workers and staff have put up in the newly renamed major thoroughfares of the capital. They have also expressed their support with street demonstrations.

Draping the many-storied front of the newly renamed Peking Department Store are gigantic banners with the words: "Resolute support for the revolu-

352

CHANGING CHINA

tionary students' revolutionary actions!" and "Salute to the young revolutionary fighters!" Workers of the Peking Steel Plant, encouraged by the actions of the revolutionary students, have launched vigorous attacks on old ideas, styles of work, methods and systems that hamper the revolution and production in their plant. They have put forward many revolutionary proposals and already begun reforms. Workers at the Peking No. 2 Cotton Textile Mill are emulating the revolutionary rebel spirit of the Red Guards and are attacking all old influences. The workers hold that everyone has the right to sweep away the influences of the old, not only outside in the streets, but also in the factories and all other enterprises and in government offices. In this way, by sweeping together, the great proletarian cultural revolution will be carried through to complete victory. . . .

IN SHANGHAI.   . . . The show windows of the Wing On Co., one of the biggest department stores in [this] city, are plastered with big-character posters put up by the Red Guards and workers and staff of the store, proposing that "Wing On" (Eternal Peace) should be changed into "Yong Hong" (Red Forever) or "Yong Dou" (Struggle Forever). The posters point out that in the old society the boss of the store chose the name "Wing On" because he wanted to be left in peace forever to exploit the working people. "For a long time now the store has been in the hands of the people and we are certainly not going to tolerate this odious name a day longer," say the posters.

In "The Great World," the biggest amusement center of Shanghai, workers and staff together with the Red Guards took down the old name sign which was several meters long. When the last character of the sign was brought down, thousands of revolutionary people in the streets and in the windows of neighboring buildings applauded and cheered: "Long live Chairman Mao!" and "Long live the great proletarian cultural revolution." . . .

The revolutionary workers and staff of Shanghai barber shops have adopted revolutionary measures in response to the proposals of the Red Guards: they no longer cut and set hair in the grotesque fashions indulged in by a small minority of people; they cut out those services specially worked out for the bourgeoisie such as manicuring, beauty treatments and so on. In those shops which sold only goods catering to the needs of a small minority of people, workers and staff have taken the revolutionary decision to start supplying the people at large with good popular commodities at low prices.

112. REVOLUTIONARIES SEIZE POWER
[From "On the Proletarian Revolutionaries' Struggle to Seize Power," Red Flag, February 1967]

Proletarian revolutionaries are uniting to seize power from the handful of persons within the Party who are in authority and taking the capitalist road.

This is the strategic task for the new stage of the great proletarian cultural revolution. It is the decisive battle between the proletariat and the masses of the working people on the one hand and the bourgeoisie and its agents in the Party on the other.

This mighty revolutionary storm started in Shanghai. The revolutionary masses in Shanghai have called it the great "January Revolution." Our great leader Chairman Mao immediately gave it resolute support. He called on the workers, peasants, revolutionary students, revolutionary intellectuals and revolutionary cadres to study the experience of the revolutionary rebels of Shanghai and called on the People's Liberation Army actively to support and assist the proletarian revolutionaries in their struggle to seize power. . . .

The current seizure of power from the handful of persons within the Party who are in authority and taking the capitalist road is not effected by dismissal and reorganization from above, but by the mass movement from below, a movement called for and supported by Chairman Mao himself. Only in this way can the leading organizations of our Party and state, enterprises and undertakings, cultural organizations and schools be regenerated and the old bourgeois practices be thoroughly eradicated.

Experience proves that in the course of the struggle for the seizure of power, it is necessary, through exchange of views and consultations among leading members of revolutionary mass organizations, leading members of local People's Liberation Army units and revolutionary leading cadres of Party and government organizations, to establish provisional organs of power to take up the responsibility of leading this struggle. These provisional organs of power must **"take firm hold of the revolution and promote production,"** keep the system of production going as usual, direct the existing set-ups in administrative and professional work (they should be adjusted where necessary) to carry on with their tasks, and organize the revolutionary masses to supervise these set-ups. These provisional organs of power must also shoulder the task of giving unified direction in suppressing counter-revolutionary organizations and counter-revolutionaries. To set up such provisional organs of power is justified, necessary and extremely important. Through a period of transition, the wisdom of the broad masses will be brought into full play and a completely new organizational form of political power better suited to the socialist economic base will be created.

A number of units, where a handful of Party people in authority and taking the capitalist road have long entrenched themselves, have become rotten. There, these persons have been exercising bourgeois dictatorship, not proletarian dictatorship. The Marxist principle of smashing the existing state machine must be put into practice in the struggle for the seizure of power in these units. . . .

The great mass movement to seize power from the handful of Party people in authority and taking the capitalist road has begun to create and will continue to create new organizational forms for the state organs of the proletarian dictatorship. Here, we must respect the initiative of the masses and boldly adopt the new vital forms that emerge in the mass movement to replace the old practices of the exploiting classes and in fact to replace all old practices that do not correspond to the socialist economic base. It is absolutely impermissible to merely take over power while letting things remain the same and operating according to old rules. . . .

As a result of arousing hundreds of millions of people from below to seize power from the handful of Party people in authority and taking the capitalist road, smashing the old practices and creating new forms, a new era has been opened up in the international history of proletarian revolution and of the dictatorship of the proletariat. This will greatly enrich and develop what we have learned from the experience of the Paris Commune, and the experience of the Soviets, and greatly enrich and develop Marxism-Leninism. . . .

Chairman Mao has called on the People's Liberation Army to actively support and assist the genuine proletarian revolutionaries and to oppose the Rightists resolutely. The great People's Liberation Army created by Chairman Mao himself has heartily responded to his call. It is making new, great contributions to the cause of socialism during the great proletarian cultural revolution. This is the glorious task of the People's Liberation Army.

113. THE REVOLUTIONARY COMMITTEES
[From "Revolutionary Committees Are Fine," *People's Daily,* March 30, 1968]

The spring breeze of Mao Tse-tung's thought has reached every corner of our motherland. The revolutionary committees which have come into being one after another stand like red flags flying in the wind. To date, revolutionary committees have been established in seventeen provinces and municipalities and in one autonomous region. More are in the preparatory stage in other areas. Vast numbers of units at the grass-root levels have set up their own revolutionary committees. This is a significant indication of the fact that the situation in the great proletarian cultural revolution is excellent and is getting even better. This is a magnificent act in the struggle for all-round victory in this revolution.

When the newborn revolutionary committees appeared on the eastern horizon a year ago, our revered and beloved leader Chairman Mao, with his great proletarian revolutionary genius, pointed out with foresight: "**In every place or unit where power must be seized, it is necessary to carry out the policy of the revolutionary 'three-in-one' combination in establishing a provisional organ of power which is revolutionary and representative and enjoys proletarian authority. This organ of power should preferably be called the Revolutionary Committee.**"

Our great leader Chairman Mao again recently pointed out: "**The basic experience of revolutionary committees is this—they are threefold: they have representatives of revolutionary cadres, representatives of the armed forces and representatives of the revolutionary masses. This forms a revolutionary 'three-in-one' combination. The revolutionary committee should exercise uni-**

fied leadership, do away with redundant or overlapping administrative struc-
tures, have 'better troops and simpler administration' and organize a
revolutionized leading group which is linked with the masses." Chairman
Mao's brilliant directive sums up the experience of revolutionary committees
at all levels and gives the basic orientation for building revolutionary committees.

The "three-in-one" revolutionary committee is a creation of the working
class and the masses in the current great cultural revolution. Chairman Mao
teaches: "We must have faith in and rely on the masses, the People's Liberation Army and the majority of the cadres." The "three-in-one" revolutionary
committee is the organ which organizationally knits closely together the three
sides pointed out by Chairman Mao after having summed up the experience
of the masses, so as more effectively to meet the needs of the socialist economic
base and the needs of consolidating the dictatorship of the proletariat and
preventing the restoration of capitalism. . . .

This "three-in-one" organ of power enables our proletarian political power
to strike deep roots among the masses. Chairman Mao points out: "The most
fundamental principle in the reform of state organs is that they must keep in
contact with the masses." The representatives of the revolutionary masses,
particularly the representatives of the working people—the workers and peasants—who have come forward en masse in the course of the great proletarian
cultural revolution, are revolutionary fighters with practical experience. Representing the interests of the revolutionary masses, they participate in the leading
groups at various levels. This provides the revolutionary committees at these
levels with a broad mass foundation. Direct participation by the revolutionary
masses in the running of the country and the enforcement of revolutionary
supervision from below over the organs of political power at various levels play
a very important role in ensuring that our leading groups at all levels always
adhere to the mass line, maintain the closest relations with the masses, represent their interests at all times and serve the people heart and soul.

This "three-in-one" organ of power strengthens the dictatorship of the
proletariat. "If the army and the people are united as one, who in the world
can match them?" The great Chinese People's Liberation Army is the main
pillar of the dictatorship of the proletariat and a Great Wall of steel defending
the socialist motherland. The revolutionary "three-in-one" combination carries our army-civilian unity to a completely new stage. In its work of helping
the Left, helping industry and agriculture, exercising military control and
giving military and political training, the People's Liberation Army has made
big contributions over the past year and more and has been well steeled in the
process. As a result of the direct participation of PLA representatives in the
work of the provisional organs of power at all levels, our dictatorship of the
proletariat is better able to withstand storm and stress, better able to smash
the intrigues by the enemy, whether domestic or foreign, and play a more
powerful role in the cause of socialist revolution and socialist construction.

Revolutionary leading cadres are the backbone of the "three-in-one" organs
of power. They have rich experience in class struggle and are a valuable asset
to the Party and people. By going through the severe test of the great proletar-

ian cultural revolution and receiving education and help from the masses, they were touched to the soul and remolded their world outlook further. The combination of the revolutionary leading cadres and representatives of the PLA and of the revolutionary masses in the revolutionary committees makes them better able to carry out Chairman Mao's proletarian revolutionary line, grasp and implement the Party's policies, and correctly organize and lead the masses forward. At the same time, veteran cadres and young new cadres work together in the revolutionary committees, learn from each other and help each other so that, as Chairman Mao teaches, **the veterans are not divorced from the masses and the young people are tempered**. Organizationally, this guarantees the work of training successors to the proletarian revolutionary cause.

This "three-in-one" organ of power has absolutely nothing in common with the overstaffed bureaucratic apparatus of the exploiting classes in the old days. It has an entirely new and revolutionary style of work of its own and it functions in a way which is beneficial to the people. The "three-in-one" revolutionary leading body brings together the PLA "three-eight" working style,[1] the laboring people's hard-working spirit and our Party's fine tradition of maintaining close contact with the masses. **"Remain one of the common people while serving as an official."** Maintain **"better troops and simpler administration,"** and drastically reform old methods of office and administrative work. Have a small leading body and a small staff, as certain revolutionary committees have begun doing, so that there is no overlapping or redundancy in the organization and no overstaffing, so that bureaucracy can be prevented. In this way, the style of hard work, plain living and economy is fostered, corrosion by bourgeois ideology is precluded; and the revolutionary committee becomes a compact and powerful fighting headquarters which puts proletarian politics to the fore and is full of revolutionary enthusiasm and capable of taking prompt and resolute action. . . .

Of all the good things characterizing the revolutionary committees, the most fundamental is the creative study and application of the thought of Mao Tse-tung and the doing of this well. Revolutionary committee members are outstanding PLA commanders and fighters, revolutionary leading cadres and representatives of the revolutionary masses who have been assessed and selected by the broad masses in the course of the struggle. The highest demand which they put upon themselves is to be loyal to Chairman Mao, to the thought of Mao Tse-tung and to Chairman Mao's proletarian revolutionary line. We hope that all the leading members of the revolutionary committees will continue to regard studying, carrying out, spreading and defending Chairman Mao's instructions as their most sacred duty. The revolutionary committees should see to it that Chairman Mao's instructions are transmitted most promptly and accurately so that the masses of workers, peasants and soldiers are imbued with the thought of Mao Tse-tung, and so that it is translated into

[1]The Chinese People's Liberation Army, under the leadership of Chairman Mao, has fostered a fine tradition. This fine tradition is summed up by Chairman Mao in three phrases and eight additional characters, meaning firm, correct political orientation; a plain, hard-working style; flexibility in strategy and tactics; and unity, alertness, earnestness and liveliness.

the conscious action of the masses and becomes an inexhaustible source of strength in transforming the world.

The revolutionary committee is something new which has emerged in the course of the revolutionary mass movement and it is continuing to develop. It should be cherished and supported by all revolutionary comrades. As for the shortcomings and mistakes which are inevitable in the course of its growth, we should make well-intentioned criticism so as to help it keep on making progress and improving. It is necessary to be on guard against and expose plots by the class enemy to shake and subvert the revolutionary committees either from the Right or the extreme "Left." All personnel of the revolutionary committees should resolutely implement Chairman Mao's proletarian revolutionary line, carry out his latest instructions in an exemplary way, make strict demands on themselves, have a correct attitude to themselves and to the masses, conduct constant criticism and self-criticism and pay the closest attention to wiping out any vestige of being divorced from the masses.

114. THE TWO LINES

[From an Article, "Two Diametrically Opposed Lines in Building the Economy," *People's Daily*, August 25, 1967]

There are two diametrically opposed lines in building up a country after the proletariat has gained political power.

One is the Soviet modern revisionist line, which stresses only the material —machinery and mechanization—and goes in for material incentives. It opposes giving priority to proletarian politics, ignores class struggle and negates the dictatorship of the proletariat. It leads to capitalism, not to socialism. The Soviet Khrushchev renegade clique and its successors are fanatical advocates of this line. In tune with the Khrushchev of the Soviet Union, the Khrushchev of China also vehemently pushed this line in China for the purpose of restoring capitalism. . . .

Our most respected and beloved leader Chairman Mao resolutely criticized and repudiated this revisionist line and set forth the correct Marxist-Leninist line. . . .

Ever since New China was founded, there has always been a sharp struggle between the two lines on the economic front. The crucial point at issue is whether or not to put proletarian politics in command, to build up the country in accordance with the great thought of Mao Tse-tung. In essence, it is a struggle over the question of whether China should build a socialist or a capitalist economy, whether it should take the socialist or the capitalist road.

In leading us in building a socialist state Chairman Mao has always given priority to revolutionizing people's thinking. He teaches: **"Political work is the life-blood of all economic work"; "not to have a correct political point of view is like having no soul."** Among the innumerable ways of expanding socialist production, carrying out a political and ideological revolution is cardinal. If this is done well, there will be an all-round increase in the production of grain, cotton, oil, iron and steel and coal. Otherwise, production will not rise in any field. The fundamental guarantee for the success of our socialist construction lies in instilling Mao Tse-tung's thought in the minds of the masses.

China's Khrushchev does exactly the opposite. He opposes putting proletarian politics in command and spreads the lie that we are using "ultra-economic methods" to guide the country's economic construction. He advocates "using economic methods to run the economy." Shaking his finger he said fiercely: "Why must we run the economy by administrative methods instead of by economic methods?" There has never been an economy independent of politics. No part of a class society exists in a political vacuum. If proletarian politics is not in command in any department or any field, then bourgeois politics must be in command; if Marxism-Leninism Mao Tse-tung thought is not in command, then revisionism, bourgeois ideology, must be in command. By opposing putting proletarian politics in command and by putting bourgeois politics in command instead, China's Khrushchev seeks to restore capitalism.

His so-called using economics to run the economy is in fact putting profits in command. He openly declared: "A factory must make money. Otherwise, it must close down and stop paying wages to the workers." In other words, in order to make money, one is allowed to ignore the unified state plan and the overall interests and engage in all sorts of selfish, speculative activities detrimental to the socialist economy.

This is nothing but that notorious "material incentive." In capitalist fashion, China's Khrushchev said: "Give him a good reward if he works honestly"; "if you don't give him more money, there'll be no incentives, and he won't do a good job for you." He attempted to corrupt the masses by instilling bourgeois egoism, diverting people's attention from politics, widening the income gap and creating a privileged stratum. . . .

This also means shamelessly glorifying capitalism. China's Khrushchev said brazenly: "Capitalist economy is flexible and varied"; "We should learn from the experience of capitalism in running enterprises, and especially from the experience of monopoly enterprises." He told our cadres to "seriously learn" from the capitalists, saying that the latter's "ability in management far surpasses that of our Party members." In his eyes, money-grubbing capitalists are a hundred times wiser than Communists.

In the last analysis, "using economic methods to run the economy" means letting the capitalist law of value reign supreme, developing free competition, undermining the socialist economy and bringing about the restoration of capitalism. . . .

The opposition of China's Khrushchev to putting politics in command also manifests itself in his opposition to the large-scale mass movement. The socialist cause is the revolutionary cause of the millions of the masses. We must fully arouse the masses and rely on their revolutionary initiative to build a socialist economy. Whether or not one launches an energetic mass movement is an important gauge of whether or not one carries out the principle of putting proletarian politics in command; it is also an important aspect of the fundamental antagonism between the two lines in economic construction.

Our great leader Chairman Mao trusts the masses, relies on them and thoroughly respects their initiative. He has taught us: **"Of all things in the world, the people are the most precious. Under the leadership of the Communist Party, as long as there are people, every kind of miracle can be performed";** and **"the mass movement is necessary for all work. It cannot progress without the mass movement."** It is because we persevered in both putting politics in command and vigorously launching a mass movement that we achieved the momentous great leap forward and advanced rapidly in industry, agriculture, national defense, science and culture.

With his reactionary bourgeois standpoint, China's Khrushchev bitterly hated the revolutionary mass movement and did his utmost to boost the one-man-leadership system and the reactionary line of relying on experts. . . .

According to China's Khrushchev, in economic construction we can rely only on a few "experts," "rely on directors, engineers and technicians" who give orders while the revolutionary masses are only "manpower" and "ignorant rabble" "rising up in a furor," who can only obediently carry out other people's orders. In order to exercise a bourgeois dictatorship over the workers, he and his followers racked their brains to work out a series of revisionist regulations that hold the workers' initiative in check and put them in a strait jacket. In doing this they not only dampened the socialist initiative of the masses and obstructed the development of socialist economic construction, but also placed the cadres, administrative personnel and technicians, who are only a handful of people, in a position of antagonism to the workers, turning them into bureaucrats and new bourgeois elements who rode roughshod over the masses, thus gradually changing the nature of socialist enterprises.

Marxism tells us that **politics is the concentrated expression of economics.** The degeneration of the socialist economic base inevitably leads to a restoration of capitalism in politics. The whole set of lines, principles, policies and measures advocated by China's Khrushchev for so many years were aimed at fostering capitalist forces in both urban and rural areas and undermining the socialist economic base so as to cause the socialist economy to degenerate into a capitalist economy. Once the economy degenerated, our Party and the state would inevitably change color step by step and capitalism would be restored throughout the country. The struggle between the two lines in economic construction is, therefore, a struggle between two political lines, two roads and two destinies for China. . . .

The facts of the struggle between the two lines on the economic front have taught us that we should never forget Chairman Mao's teachings, never forget to put politics in first place.

Chairman Mao has taught us: **"While we recognize that in the general development of history the material determines the mental, and social being determines social consciousness, we also—and indeed must—recognize the reaction of mental on material things, of social consciousness on social being and of the superstructure on the economic base."**

The most powerful moral strength of our time is the invincible thought of
Mao Tse-tung and the strongest fighting power is the people armed with Mao
Tse-tung's thought. . . . We Chinese Communists firmly believe that the people
are the creators of history and that once they grasp Mao Tse-tung's thought,
they will become infinitely wise and brave and display inexhaustible strength.

The current Great Proletarian Cultural Revolution, started and led by
Chairman Mao, is the best school for studying and applying Mao Tse-tung's
thought in a living way, a great moving force for the development of our
country's social productive forces. Through this revolution, the bourgeois
reactionary line of China's Khrushchev on economic construction will be
eradicated, and, with the continuous consolidation and strengthening of proletarian state power, a huge new upsurge will make its appearance in our socialist
construction. **"The Chinese people have lofty aspirations and abilities. They
will certainly catch up with and surpass advanced world levels in the not too
distant future."** There is no doubt that all imperialist and revisionist countries
will be left far behind us!

115. RE-EDUCATING CADRES

[From an Article about a May 7 Cadre School in Heilungkiang, in *People's Daily,* October 5, 1968]

The "May 7" Cadre School is a school for tempering people. All its activities
center around the question of remolding its students' world outlook. The
productive labor, studies, military training and everyday life of the students
are closely linked up with the implementation of Chairman Mao's May 7
Directive and the fostering of boundless loyalty to Chairman Mao. In productive labor and other activities, they make a constant effort to remold their
ideology conscientiously by carrying out on-the-spot rectification campaigns,
holding forums in the fields to exchange experience in creatively studying and
applying Mao Tse-tung's thought, and organizing meetings to assess merits
and shortcomings, and carrying on mass criticism and repudiation. After
several months' tempering, the students became still more diligent in their
study of Chairman Mao's works, their proletarian feelings for Chairman Mao
were deeper, and their desire to remold their world outlook grew stronger. . . .

In remolding one's world outlook, it is essential to get a firm grip on the key
issue. The core of the bourgeois world outlook is self-interest. It finds its most
concentrated and glaring expression in a cadre's desire to become an official.
In the past, some cadres, urged on by self-interest, sought after official posts
and finally became revisionists. So the desire to become an official is the key
issue. In order to solve the question of world outlook among cadres, a vigorous
effort to eradicate this desire is essential.

Set up as it is in the front line of the three great revolutionary movements,
the "May 7" Cadre School provides conditions and an environment that are

very favorable for cadres to remold their world outlook and wipe out their desire to become officials. The students have come to this gully from the big cities; they have moved from their multi-storied buildings into huts; from being "officials," they have become ordinary people—all these changes have not failed to touch everyone to the depths of his being and have greatly shaken their old world outlook. Students have said, "Here in the 'May 7' Cadre School, no matter how high your official post is, once you take up a sickle or hoe, most of your official airs go." The problem, however, lies not merely in getting rid of official airs. What is more important is to wipe out the ideas of becoming an official and overlord.

In order to enhance the cadres' consciousness in remolding their world outlook, the school organizes study classes for its students to creatively study and apply Mao Tse-tung's thought and to analyze their own world outlook. At the same time, constant efforts are made to guide them to dig out the problems arising from the struggle between the two lines and trace these to the roots in their world outlook. Some cadres who in the past had assumed very high and mighty official airs were sharply criticized by the masses during the great cultural revolution. Their official airs turned into a bellyful of grumbling complaints. Through the revolutionary mass criticism and repudiation, they lost all the "laurels" that they prided themselves on, and, complaining turning into throwing in the sponge, they simply lay down on their jobs. After entering the "May 7" Cadre School, however, they have enhanced their consciousness in remolding their world outlook and discovered in their old world outlook the causes of the mistakes they committed. As a result, their complaints and despondent mood have been replaced by courage to correct their mistakes and vigor to continue making revolution.

Some young revolutionary rebels looked upon themselves solely as a part of the motive force of the revolution. They did not think of themselves as being at the same time targets of the revolution. But after entering the "May 7" Cadre School, they discovered that they, too, in the depths of their being, harbored the rotten idea of wanting to become officials. This discovery strengthened their resolve to consciously remold their world outlook.

To enable the students to remold themselves effectively, the school frequently sends them to be tested and tempered in storm and stress. They have been assigned to do many things which some thought impossible of fulfillment, and besides they had to do these things well. These included reclaiming outlying wasteland, damming rivers, living in simple huts, eating wild vegetables, climbing mountains and crossing marshes. In this life of hard work, many occasions demanded the making of quick decisions; at the critical moment they had to decide whether to dash forward or retreat. If they dashed forward, the public interest got the upper hand; if they retreated, self-interest came out on top. Here was a sharp conflict between the public interest and self-interest, and a "hand-to-hand fight" between the two world outlooks. Because the students strongly desire to remold themselves, they achieve rapid results in revolutionizing their thinking. . . .

. . . On joining the school, the students work in groups which include the more than 100 workers and poor and lower-middle peasants originally belonging to the farm. This has created very favorable conditions for integration with the workers and peasants. But some students looked down on the worker and peasant masses either because their prolonged separation from the working people had gradually corroded their thinking and feelings or because they had been affected by the old education. As a result, these students put on airs in the school and lacked a common language with the workers and peasants. Some even asked: "Should they educate us? Or should we educate them?"

This shows that simply being among the workers and peasants does not of itself mean that one has integrated oneself with them. To really achieve such integration, one has to undergo protracted and even painful tempering. . . .

The school has two ways of bringing the students into wide contact with the workers, peasants and soldiers so that they can better receive re-education from them. One is to ask some of the workers, poor and lower-middle peasants and PLA commanders and fighters to come to the school to tell the students about their experiences in creatively studying and applying Mao Tse-tung's thought and to give them lessons on class struggle and the struggle for production. The other way is to have the students go to the industrial and mining enterprises and rural production teams in a planned way to carry out social investigations and do mass work. In the past five months, they have invited 16 persons to come to the school on successive occasions to re-educate the students and sent out 6 study teams to make studies outside the school.

116. REFORMS IN RURAL EDUCATION
[From a New China News Agency Story about a Model Brigade School in Liaoning, October 1968]

Why are the masses of poor and lower-middle peasants dissatisfied with the old educational system? Why are there so few children of the poor and lower-middle peasants in school? Why did so many of them have to repeat courses or leave school before finishing the courses? The poor and lower-middle peasants have clear-cut answers.

"In the past," said one poor peasant, "it was said that our children were not as clever as those of the landlords and rich peasants.[1] That's nonsense. A landlord told his son when he came back from school: 'Just bury yourself in your books. I have no hope in this society because our family's class origin is not good. I hope that you study well so that you'll become an official and have a bright future.' This was how he told his son to carry on the landlord class! But when my second son got back from school, I would tell him before he put down his school bag: 'Go and do something. After six hours of going through books, you ought to do some manual work.' . . ."

One wants his son to be an official, the other wants his son to be a laboring person with both socialist consciousness and culture. Here are two entirely

---

[1]Class nomenclature in this article refers to former class status.

different demands put forth, from two entirely different stands on the question of how to bring up their children, by two classes. The old poor peasant had good reason to be angry when he said: "But the educational system laid down by China's Khrushchev favors the bookworms and the schools kept their doors wide open for such persons and make it easy for them to have more schooling and seek officialdom. See which class this system serves!"

Another poor peasant added: "What's more, our children were driven out of the school on the pretext that they were frivolous and disobedient. The hell with that! Who should obey whom? It is good to be obedient to Chairman Mao's teachings. Our children could not put up with bourgeois rules, so they rebelled. But the old educational system won the hearts of the sons and daughters of the landlords and rich peasants. . . ."

One young man who returned to his village after graduating said, "Aside from restricting children of the poor and lower-middle peasants, the schools forced the few who got into the schools to do nothing but dig into their books. They were given no chance to link their study with production and reality. I learned many useless things and not much that is useful. After 12 years of schooling, I returned to find my home too dirty and the field work too tiring. Though I have a knowledge of algebra and geometry, I can't do bookkeeping and can't even figure out a formula for terracing hillsides. I have learnt chemistry and physics, but I can't tell insecticide from fertilizer. I wouldn't even dare to put in a light bulb. My father cursed me for having become good-for-nothing after attending school."

A poor peasant added: "We couldn't make out why children of poor and lower-middle peasants would forget their class origin after going to school in the new society. When my son graduated, he considered himself superior to those around him. He even thought that I was dirty and he'd walk past me with his head high. Now that Chairman Mao has sent the poor and lower-middle peasants to manage the schools, I have come to see that our schools are still dominated by the bourgeoisie and that there are landlords, rich peasants, counter-revolutionaries, bad elements and rightists among the teachers. . . . It would be strange if our children did not turn bad since they were taught by such bad fellows. I'm full of anger at the very mention of such an educational system."

Some persons doubt the ability of the poor and lower-middle peasants to carry out the educational revolution since they are "uncultured persons who can't even read a single character." But the fact is that, armed with Mao Tse-tung's thought, the poor and lower-middle peasants know the old educational system most clearly and hate it most bitterly, and their repudiation of the revisionist line on education is most forceful and to the point. . . .

What orientation should the rural schools persist in after the old educational system is renounced? The poor and lower-middle peasants say: we must firmly carry out Chairman Mao's latest instruction that "In the countryside, schools and colleges should be managed by the poor and lower-middle peasants—the most reliable ally of the working class. We must keep tight hold on educational power and exercise political leadership in the schools. We must use Mao Tse-tung's thought to occupy the schools and bring up successors to the proletarian revolutionary cause." . . .

In 1964, the poor and lower-middle peasants in the Sungshu production brigade, southern Liaoning, established a primary school run on a part-time farming and part-time study basis with teachers selected from among the educated people who returned to their village after finishing their studies. Lacking money and a school building, the school relied on the poor and lower-middle peasants and has grown, having an enrollment now of 155 students as against 14 when it started. . . .

An old livestock keeper commented: "Our school has not spent a cent of the state's. The students pay no tuition fees. We poor and lower-middle peasants never spend a cent on it either. The school is mainly supported by the teachers and students themselves who participate in collective labor and earn work points. The teachers are just like us peasants, they earn work points by giving lessons. They are of one heart with us. From the very beginning, the students learn to work and foster devotion to the collective. Whenever Chairman Mao or the Party Central Committee or the Cultural Revolution Group under it issue new instructions, the teachers promptly explain them to the students who then disseminate them at home. Generally we learn of important domestic and international affairs from our children. In this way, the school teaches adults as well as the children." . . .

Teacher Hsu Ching-fang, who is the daughter of a poor peasant and has won the hearts of the poor and lower-middle peasants in the production brigade, said: "Running this school involved a struggle. With nothing to its name, our school was looked down on by those above in the county and the commune. But, we have the most favorable condition, all-out support from the poor and lower-middle peasants. We invite old poor peasants to lecture on class struggle. Livestock keepers lecture on stock breeding, cart drivers on carts, and poor and lower-middle peasants on farming. I only give lessons in reading and writing and do some organization work. . . ."

. . . The orientation of the school in the Sungshu production brigade is precisely that indicated by Chairman Mao. With the poor and lower-middle peasants in power, such schools truly serve them and are closely linked with them. . . . Such schools are simple and run with industry, linked with reality and productive labor; they are truly training and bringing up workers with both socialist consciousness and culture.

117. THE RELIABILITY OF THE MASSES
["Refuting the Theory that 'The Masses Are Backward,' " Peking Review, December 20, 1968]

Chairman Mao recently pointed out: **"Direct reliance on the revolutionary masses is a basic principle of the Communist Party."**

Chairman Mao has the greatest faith in the masses, places reliance on them and respects their initiative. In the current great proletarian cultural revolution movement, Chairman Mao pays great attention to bringing into play the role of our working class and has instructed that the advanced elements from among us workers should be admitted into the Party. This is an expression of Chairman Mao's deepest concern for and greatest faith in us revolutionary workers.

The arch scab Liu Shao-ch'i, however, looked on the masses as a "mob" and as "ignorant and incapable." He wildly clamored for a "struggle against the backward ideas and backward phenomena among the masses." Using the theory that "the masses are backward," he and the handful of his agents kept out of the Party large numbers of outstanding workers with proletarian revolutionary spirit, and imposed on them a bourgeois dictatorship. What happened to Comrade Tien Wen-liang, a revolutionary worker of our printing house, is a typical instance.

Comrade Tien Wen-liang as a child grew up in the misery of the old society. Three generations from his grandfather down to himself had been workers. His father toiled for a capitalist throughout his life. When he fell ill he was kicked out of the factory by the capitalist and died from cold in the street. When Tien Wen-liang was seven years old, he began begging with his mother from door to door and suffered from the bullying and insults of the capitalists. He cherishes wholehearted love for Chairman Mao and profound gratitude to the Communist Party because it is the Communist Party and Chairman Mao that have led the poor people in liberating themselves. That is why he does his work well.

Nurtured on Mao Tse-tung's thought, he has been constantly raising his level of political consciousness. He is determined to follow Chairman Mao in making revolution. With sincere feelings of ardent love for Chairman Mao, he has on three occasions written and sent in applications eagerly asking to be admitted into the Party. But contrary to his expectations, the handful of capitalist roaders in the printing house slandered him as a "backward element" and his applications one after another were shelved. On the other hand, they opened the door of the Party wide to a handful of renegades, enemy agents and capitalists, glorifying them as "good comrades" and admitting them into the Party. A capitalist, for instance, was admitted by them into the Party and promoted to be deputy director of the printing house. When the workers learned about this, they were deeply angered.

Personally initiated and led by Chairman Mao, the great proletarian cultural revolution started. Then the masses of revolutionary workers came to understand more fully that Liu Shao-ch'i was the chief behind-the-scene backer of the handful of capitalist roaders in the printing house.

It was precisely the theory that "the masses are backward" advocated by this arch scab that had for a long time kept many outstanding workers out of the Party and exercised a bourgeois dictatorship over them. Fired with deep hatred for the bourgeois reactionary line, and fighting heroically in defense of Chairman Mao's revolutionary line, Comrade Tien Wen-liang rose in rebellion against the handful of capitalist roaders in the Party in our printing house.

Comrade Tien Wen-liang displayed the valuable proletarian revolutionary spirit of a worker with a high level of consciousness. This was noted by everyone and he who had once been regarded as a "backward element" by the capitalist roaders was elected a worker representative of the printing house to attend the National Day celebrations.

By loudly advocating the theory that "the masses are backward," Liu Shao-ch'i vainly attempted to separate the Party from the masses and thereby undermine their close relations, to prevent the Party from taking in fresh blood and thus cause the Party to lose its revolutionary vitality and step by step to degenerate. This was a vain attempt by him to turn the great, glorious and correct Communist Party of China into a tool for restoring capitalism. We must hold high the great red banner of Mao Tse-tung's thought, smash Liu Shao-ch'i's theory that "the masses are backward," and constantly take in fresh blood so as to build our Party into a vigorous vanguard organization of the proletariat.

118. THE CREATIVE SPIRIT OF THE MASSES
[From "The Lowly Are Most Intelligent; the Elite Are Most Ignorant," *Peking Review,* November 22, 1968]

The Peking No. 1 General Machinery Works was dominated by the counter-revolutionary revisionist line of the arch renegade Liu Shao-ch'i in the past. The designs for many products were irrational and quality was below standard. One nine-cubic-meter air compressor shaft broke after 50 hours of use. Highly indignant, the workers gathered around the machine with the broken shaft, shouting "Bring the capitalist roaders and the bourgeois technical 'authorities' here!" A criticism and repudiation meeting began. . . .

Full of hatred, the workers repudiated them, saying: "In the past you all sat in big buildings and became officials and lords. Even on the rare occasions you entered the workshops, you pulled up your trousers for fear the grease might stain them. The road you took was the capitalist one. You ran the plant in accordance with Liu Shao-ch'i's revisionist line, and it could only go from bad to worse. This wasteful machine with the broken shaft is the evidence of your crimes."

"The workers must be relied on to run the plant!" Pointing to two clutches on display, the workers said: "The clutch is an important part of an air compressor. Look at the junk the bourgeois technical 'authorities' designed in the past! There are too many parts and it was hard to operate. The clutch we workers designed is splendid! It is simple and also easy to operate!" Hardly was this said than the crowd was astir, shouting: "Make these scoundrels count the parts! How many are there in the clutch you designed? And how many are there in the one the workers designed? Which is better?" Looking at the clutches, they stammered: "The clutch we designed has more than 90 parts. The workers' has only 16. It is constructed simply and it is practical."

In the face of iron-clad facts, the handful of capitalist roaders and reactionary technical "authorities" were completely deflated, while the workers' morale was high. Fully justified, the workers at the meeting made this denunciation: "The arch renegade Liu Shao-ch'i and his agents only trusted 'experts' and 'authorities'; they trampled on the workers. Let them see what we, the working class, can do! Now that Chairman Mao has called on the working class to exercise leadership in everything, we, the working class, must be sure to wield power in the plant."

This brief but forceful criticism and repudiation meeting ended in triumph amid the shouting of the slogan "Down with Liu Shao-ch'i."

119. TWO KINDS OF MOTIVATION

["The Theory of 'Merging Private and Public Interests' Is Poison Corrupting the Souls of Party Members," *Peking Review,* December 20, 1968]

What kind of world outlook should a Communist have? In one of his talks Liu Shao-ch'i smugly said: "Under the conditions of socialism, anyone who works solely for his personal interests will not secure them. Serving the people with one mind will satisfy personal interests in return." "The benefits come later and this is a question of world outlook."

"The benefits come later," though only a few words, vividly portrays the rotten soul of Liu Shao-ch'i, the No. 1 capitalist roader in the Party, and his malicious intentions to poison Communists.

Chairman Mao teaches us: **"In the matter of world outlook, however, today there are basically only two schools, the proletarian and the bourgeois. It is one or the other, either the proletarian or the bourgeois world outlook."** Every one of us Communists must have a thoroughgoing proletarian world outlook.

The core of the proletarian world outlook is **"to serve the people wholeheartedly," "utter devotion to others without any thought of self,"** that is, devotion to the public interests. The core of the bourgeois world outlook is to fight for personal fame, gain and power, that is, self-interest. The essence of "the benefits come later" is the theory of "merging private and public interests" advocated by Liu Shao-ch'i, it is the bourgeois world outlook of working entirely for self-interest.

What are "benefits"? Different classes have different views.

Chairman Mao teaches us to **"proceed in all cases from the interests of the people"** and to become persons **"very useful to the people."** Armed with the invincible thought of Mao Tse-tung, proletarian vanguard fighters regard as the greatest benefit the complete liberation of the Chinese people and all the people of the world and the realization of the grand ideal of communism. They look upon the hard struggles and heroic sacrifices involved in achieving this lofty goal as their greatest glory and happiness. This is precisely the reason why Comrade Li Wen-chung, Model in Helping the Left and Cherishing the People, had no fear of death when saving the young Red Guard fighters in the turbulent Kankiang River. In the last moment of his life, his only thought was of Chairman Mao and Chairman Mao's Red Guards and he uttered the resounding words: "Don't worry about me!"

What are the so-called "benefits" Liu Shao-ch'i talked about? They are "personal interests," that is, the enjoyment of "position and fortune throughout one's life," "excelling others," "becoming the No. 1 or No. 2 person" in China, and so on, all of which he has sought after and talked so much about all his life. In short, they are personal fame, gain, and power. This is clearly a replica of the exploiting-classes' philosophy of life—"If one does not work for oneself, then one is doomed." Is there the slightest inkling of a proletarian idea here!

But, sometimes Liu Shao-ch'i also pretended to talk about "serving the people." Why did Liu Shao-ch'i, who devotes himself to seeking his personal "benefit," talk so much about "serving the people"? He himself answered: "Serving the people with one mind will satisfy personal interests in return." It reveals that working for the public interest is only a false front and the real thing is to work for one's self-interest; "serving the people" is the means and securing "personal interests" is the aim.

Why did he put "personal interests" at a "later" stage? He said: "Under the conditions of socialism, anyone who works solely for his personal interests will not secure them." This proves that to put "personal interests" at an "earlier" stage exposes everything to the light and so one may get nothing. Only when personal interests are put at a "later" stage, can one get them. Despite all his efforts to disguise himself, Liu Shao-ch'i cannot cover up his true face of ultra-selfishness. To put self-interest at an "earlier" stage means working for oneself; so does putting it at a "later" stage. The latter method is more despicable and scheming.

We Communists will make it our only purpose **"to serve the people wholeheartedly"** according to the great leader Chairman Mao's teachings. We must creatively study and apply Chairman Mao's works, thoroughly wipe out all the pernicious influence of Liu Shao-ch'i, strive hard to remold our world outlook, replace self-interest with devotion to the public interest, follow Chairman Mao to make revolution throughout our lives, and become vigorous communist fighters worthy of the name.

CHAPTER FIFTEEN

Reconstruction and Discord

The years following the Cultural Revolution have seen striking changes in China and in China's position in the world. The admission of the People's Republic into the United Nations and President Nixon's visit signaled the recognition of the new China as a major power in international affairs. Lin Piao's death after an apparent attempt to assassinate Mao Tse-tung again opened the question of the succession to the aging Chairman, which was still further unsettled by the death of the masterful Chou En-lai in early 1976, and the fall of his apparent successor, Teng Hsiao-p'ing, shortly thereafter. As Mao's health deteriorated, a struggle for power took place between one group of party leaders, who had risen to prominence as proponents of radical policies during the Cultural Revolution, and more moderate leaders associated with Chou and Teng. Mao's death in September was rapidly followed by the purge of the radicals in October, the appointment of Hua Kuo-feng to succeed Mao as party chairman, and indications that important policy changes would be made in 1977.

Although these events were of momentous significance, the documents in this chapter do not center on the political rivalries within the party leadership. Rather, they have been chosen to illustrate underlying issues and to offer a review of some of the most salient features and continuing problems of the People's Republic as they manifested themselves in the 1970s.

The CCP remains the ruling elite. The rebuilding of the party and reassertion of its authority after the upheavals of the late 1960s are the subjects of Selection 120. The Cultural Revolution is not repudiated, and its effects are said to have been healthy, as evidenced by the infusion of fresh blood into the Party. In the assertion that the struggle between the two lines continues, even within the Party, there is an implied admission that the Cultural Revolution's stated goal has not been attained. Admonitions to Party members to be modest, prudent, and tolerant are oblique allusions to some of the excesses of the recent past. The main point is the reaffirmation of the necessity of CCP leadership.

A problem of another, less consequential, sort in the aftermath of the Cultural Revolution can be seen in a discussion among members of a commune brigade. They attempt to draw a distinction between material incentives, in disrepute because associated with Liu Shao-ch'i, and giving greater compensation for more and better work. It is difficult to tell whether they perceive the issue as saying the right thing or doing the right thing, whether in this instance the impact of the Cultural Revolution has been semantic or substantive. (Selection 121)

The rapid incorporation of current political themes into literature is illustrated in a review of novels of the early 1970s. (Selection 122) Similar examples might also be cited from other artistic media. Although the fall of the radicals in late 1976 was followed by intimations of more freedom and diversity in the arts, the essentially utilitarian view of literature seems likely to continue.

Education was a central issue in the Cultural Revolution, and educational reforms, particularly in higher education, have been among the most enduring of the changes made during the late 1960s. The principal reforms are described in Selection 123, and recent disputes over their effects are discussed in Selection 124. The issue is not merely education, but the preparation and hence the character of the future national leadership, and the shape of the society it should be prepared to lead. The position of university authorities who object to the reforms has not been published in full, but even from the fragmentary passages quoted within the polemical context of Selection 124, it can be fairly well reconstructed. In brief, professional training requires maintaining high academic standards. Insofar as there is an educational philosophy in this essentially political essay, the author would seem to believe that there can be no equality of opportunity without egalitarian standards of judgment, and that in the long run egalitarian standards will ultimately bring about a general elevation of overall quality. In addition, without egalitarian standards, divisive selfishness will be encouraged. Egalitarianism, social homogeneity, selfless service to the common interest, and unity are once again conjoined and juxtaposed to hierarchy, selfishness, and divisiveness.

The issue of the stability of the new institutions, of long-range economic growth within an ordered framework vs. continuing social transformation, is asserted to be the heart of the political struggle described in Selection 125. Teng Hsiao-p'ing, who had been disgraced along with Liu Shao-ch'i, reappeared in 1973 and rapidly rose to high positions. By late 1975, Teng appeared to be in line to succeed the ailing Chou En-lai as premier, the position Chou had held since the founding of the People's Republic in 1949. But soon after Chou's death from cancer in January 1976, Teng was attacked and removed from office. It is worth noting that although the author accuses Teng of advocating policies associated with the capitalist road, he does not suggest that material incentives be abolished, nor does he call for a mass movement against other incipient capitalists within the party. Are the differences between the two lines absolute, or merely a question of emphasis? Is Teng being criticized for doing something wrong, or are his words being used against him for other political purposes?

These same questions are also relevant to Selection 126, an important policy statement by Hua Kuo-feng, the new party chairman. The policies for which Teng Hsiao-p'ing was attacked in Selection 125 are defended, and the criterion used to determine who are the bourgeois enemies of the party is not social and economic policy, but personal political ambition. Hua stresses the familiar themes of the necessity of Communist Party leadership, the need for discipline and unity within the party to make party leadership effective, and the need for ideological education and rectification campaigns to ensure correct ideology. The defense of the "theory of productive forces," the importance ascribed to professional expertise, the statement of the need to "systematize rational rules and regulations and improve and strengthen socialist management," and the promise of higher living standards, all point toward a policy of orderly economic development within the framework of existing institutions, using material incentives along with political campaigns. Note that, like Tseng Kuo-fan in his Proclamation on the Taipings, Hua distinguishes between a small group of top leaders guilty of unpardonable crimes and their deluded followers, to whom amnesty is offered.

It seems unlikely that factional strife, so long endemic in Chinese politics, will disappear. And China still faces many difficult social and economic problems. Yet Hua's definition of the problems and his proposed solutions may serve as a kind of concluding summation of how much China has changed since its doors were opened to the outside world more than a century ago.

120. REBUILDING THE PARTY
[From "Our Party Is Advancing Vigorously," Editorial in *People's Daily,* August 27, 1971]

Under the close concern of the Party Central Committee with Chairman Mao as its leader and Vice-Chairman Lin as its deputy leader, the Party congresses of the country's provinces, municipalities and autonomous regions (except Taiwan Province) have been formally held one after another and new provincial, municipal or autonomous regional committees of the Party have been elected. This is a most important guarantee for further strengthening Party leadership and doing a better job of continuing to fulfill the fighting tasks set forth by the Party's Ninth National Congress and the First and Second Plenary Sessions of the Ninth Party Central Committee. This is a great event in the political life of the comrades of the whole Party and the people of the whole country, a magnificent result of the Great Proletarian Cultural Revolution and a great victory for Chairman Mao's proletarian line on Party building. . . .

The Great Proletarian Cultural Revolution is the broadest and most deep-going movement to consolidate our Party in its history. During this revolution, our great leader Chairman Mao has issued a series of very important instructions on Party consolidation and Party building, guiding us in constantly making criticism of the renegade, hidden traitor and scab Liu Shao-ch'i's counter-revolutionary line on Party building, in adhering to the Marxist-Leninist principles of Party building and in stepping up Party building ideologically and organizationally. Through the movement of Party consolidation and Party building, our Party has rallied all the more closely around the Party Central Committee with Chairman Mao as its leader and Vice-Chairman Lin as its deputy leader. . . .

A few revolutionary committees at the provincial level were first set up in 1967. This put the question of consolidating the Party organizations on the agenda. The criterion upon which our Party is to be consolidated and built is a matter of principle of vital importance. Chairman Mao has pointed out: **"The Party organization should be composed of the advanced elements of the proletariat; it should be a vigorous vanguard organization capable of leading the proletariat and the revolutionary masses in the fight against the class enemy."** This set the political orientation for our Party consolidation and Party building. The whole Party has kept to this orientation and steadily eliminated the remaining pernicious revisionist influence of [Liu Shao-ch'i's] sinister book *How to Be a Good Communist* and the six sinister "theories" (the theory of "the dying out of class struggle," the theory of "docile tools," the theory of "the masses are backward," the theory of "joining the Party in order to get ahead," the theory of "inner-Party peace," and the theory of "merging private and public interests"), and combated the erroneous tendencies to lower the level of our Party or to obscure the character of our Party. The Party members have strengthened their proletarian Party spirit and overcome bourgeois factionalism. . . .

Chairman Mao has also pointed out: **"Every Party branch must reconsolidate itself in the midst of the masses. This must be done with the participation of the masses and not merely of a few Party members; it is necessary to have the masses outside the Party take part in the meetings and give their comments."** In line with this very important instruction of Chairman Mao's, Party organizations in various places have opposed the closed-door tendency and persisted in the mass line. They have carried out an open-door Party consolidation, in which the masses helped and supervised the consolidation and building of every Party branch and the education and examination of every Party member. . . .

. . . During the First Plenary Session of the Ninth Party Central Committee, Chairman Mao warned members of the whole Party, particularly the senior cadres of the Party, that they must be prudent and careful and must not forget themselves in moments of excitement. Speaking of some comrades from grass-roots units who were elected to the Party Central Committee for the first time,

Chairman Mao said: **"See to it that they do not divorce themselves from the masses or from productive labor while performing their duties."** Chairman Mao once again sounded a warning to the whole Party at a time of victory. We should firmly bear in mind Chairman Mao's teachings and be modest and prudent, and guard against arrogance and rashness. . . .

. . . Reviewing the process of Party consolidation and Party building, we understand more deeply that only by carrying out Chairman Mao's proletarian line on Party building, and adhering to the character of the Party as the vanguard organization of the proletariat, to the dialectics of inner-Party contradiction, to the Party's mass line and to education in ideology and political line, can interference from both "Left" and Right be fought off and a further step taken in building our Party into a revolutionary Party armed with Marxist-Leninist revolutionary theory and style of work.

This Party consolidation is a most important Marxist-Leninist education movement. . . . A handful of proven renegades, enemy agents, absolutely unrepentant persons in power taking the capitalist road, degenerates and alien-class elements have been cleared out of the Party. Advanced elements of the proletariat who have come to the fore from among the masses of workers, poor and lower-middle peasants, revolutionary armymen, revolutionary cadres and revolutionary intellectuals have joined the ranks of the Party. The principle of the three-in-one combination of old, middle-aged and young people is carried out in leading bodies of the Party at all levels; this means the inclusion in these bodies of both proletarian revolutionaries of the older generation and fine Party members who are middle-aged or of the younger generation and the inclusion of new blood from workers and peasants and cadres at the grass-roots level. Our Party has improved its quality and expanded its ranks, and is purer and more powerful and has a greater fighting capacity than ever. . . .

Chairman Mao teaches: **"Ours is a great Party, a glorious Party, a correct Party. This must be affirmed as a fact. But we still have shortcomings, and this, too, must be affirmed as a fact."** It must not be assumed that contradictions and the struggle between the two lines will no longer exist within the Party after the Party consolidation and the establishment of new Party committees. Opposition and struggle between the two lines within the Party are the reflection inside the Party of contradictions between classes and between the new and the old in society; they will exist for a long time. In accordance with the requirements set in the new [1969] Party Constitution, we must take the ideological and organizational building of our Party as a long-term task and take hold of it constantly, repeatedly and seriously so that our Party will give better play to its role as the core of leadership, as the vanguard organization of the proletariat leading the people of the whole country in the great struggles for socialist revolution and socialist construction.

The Chinese Communist Party is the core of leadership of the whole Chinese people. Without this core, the cause of socialism cannot be victorious. Once established, the new Party committees at all levels must effectively strengthen centralized leadership by the Party. The new Party Constitution stipulates: "The organs of state power of the dictatorship of the proletariat, the People's Liberation Army, and the Communist Youth League and other revolutionary mass organizations, such as those of the workers, the poor and lower-middle peasants and the Red Guards, must all accept the leadership of the Party." On many occasions, Chairman Mao has stressed this as an important organizational principle of the Party. All Party members and all departments must enhance their concept of the Party, place themselves under the absolute leadership of the Party and reject the reactionary theory of many centers, that is, of no center. The Party committees must bring into full play the role of the revolutionary committees, strengthen Party leadership over economic work and over consolidating and building the Communist Youth League, and step up the Party work in consolidating and leading revolutionary mass organizations, such as those of the workers, the poor and lower-middle peasants and the Red Guards. . . . All of this is for one purpose, that is, the consolidation of the dictatorship of the proletariat must be achieved fully in every primary unit. . . .

To strengthen centralized leadership by the Party, it is imperative to conscientiously carry out the Party's democratic centralism. The Party committees at all levels must practice "letting all people have their say" and oppose "my word is final." Any issue of major importance must be discussed by the collective and different opinions must be given a serious hearing. It is necessary to continue opposing conceit and complacency, fostering modesty and prudence and strengthening the unity of the Party. Chief leading cadres must have the largeness of mind of the proletariat, **"be good at uniting in our work not only with comrades who hold the same views as we but also with those who hold different views."** It is necessary to help veteran revolutionary cadres give play to their backbone role and to train new forces with enthusiasm so that successors to the revolutionary cause of the proletariat can mature faster and better. Towards comrades who have committed errors, it is necessary to adopt a "watch-and-help" attitude, allow them to overcome errors and encourage them to atone for past mistakes. All the new and old cadres must learn from, respect, cooperate with and support each other and persist in using Mao Tse-tung Thought to achieve **unity in thinking, policy, plan, command and action.**

121. MATERIAL INCENTIVES OR REWARDS FOR LABOR?

[From a Report on Discussion Held in a Production Brigade in Shensi, in *People's Daily,* October 1972]

Secretary of the Brigade Party Branch: Recently, in the firm implementation of the policy "from each according to his ability and to each according to his labor," various teams showed no unity of understanding and followed different approaches where the problem of labor remuneration was concerned. Some teams subjected part of the farm work to a flexible basic-point assessment and part to a fixed workpoint assessment. In both cases, the assessment was based on the quality and amount of labor. Some people thought that as the basis of remuneration assessment, ideological performance should be added and that only in this way could proletarian politics be put in command in fixing labor remuneration. After all, what is the best approach? Let everyone give his views.

Political Instructor of No. 8 Production Team: The socialist principle of distribution is: "From each according to his ability and to each according to his labor." For commune members participating in collective labor, we should take the quality and amount of labor as a basis of assessment for remuneration. Some commune members did not have a high consciousness and must be given patient help and given strengthened education. . . .

Political Instructor of No. 10 Production Team: To solve ideological problems by awarding more or less workpoints looks like an act of attaching importance to ideological consciousness but in reality this has a weakening effect on ideological-political work.

Workpoint Recorder of No. 9 Production Team: After our team recorded workpoints on the basis of the quality and amount of labor, some commune members were awarded more workpoints than others for high work efficiency and good work quality. What's the difference between this and "putting workpoints in command"?

Political Instructor of No. 13 Production Team: Some time ago, the commune members of our brigade went uphill to cut weeds. Some started out early and returned late. For work exceeding the fixed quota, they were awarded more workpoints according to the provisions. Some got fewer workpoints for not having met the quota. We think that this means more remuneration for more labor and less remuneration for less labor, and that it is a practice which fits in with the Party policy and which cannot be called "putting workpoints in command."

Female head of No. 7 Production Team and Representative of the poor and lower-middle peasants: More remuneration for more labor is in essence different from "putting workpoints in command." "Putting workpoints in command" is prompted by bourgeois self-interest. Commune members are induced to grab at immediate personal material interests by every possible means and are thus led astray. This is revisionist sinister stuff. More remuneration for more labor, on the other hand, encourages people in working energetically and creating wealth for socialism, under conditions of unrelenting ideological education. Just as there is a difference in the quality and amount of labor, so there is a difference in remuneration. This is the very way to carry out firmly the Party's policy of distribution according to labor and arouse and maintain commune members' socialist activism. It cannot be criticized as "putting workpoints in command."

122. THE NEW LITERATURE
["New Novels," from *China Reconstructs*, May 1975]

More than thirty new novels have appeared in China over the last three years. They cover a wide range of subjects: the revolutionary wars, life and struggle on the industrial front during the socialist period, great changes collectivization has brought to the countryside, men of the armed forces defending the country, and the cultural revolution. The new works have been quickly and widely acclaimed by the workers, peasants and soldiers. Many have been made into plays, films, picture-story books and are narrated by storytellers.

The Content

While portraying the different facets of life with different methods of treatment, the new novels have a striking characteristic in common. They all reveal the essential truth that during the period of the democratic revolution, and in particular the period of the socialist revolution and construction, there is always a struggle between the proletariat and the bourgeoisie, between the Marxist line and the revisionist line.

Following his immensely popular *Bright Sunny Skies,* the well-known writer Hao Jan produced *The Bright Road,* a story of the fierce struggle between the two classes and the two lines in the countryside during the early 1950s. The novel, set in a north China village, raises a vital question at the outset: After the proletariat has won political power and land reform has given the peasants the land they have long yearned for, which road for the Chinese countryside—the capitalist road which would bring prosperity to a small number of individuals, or the socialist road which would bring collective well-being? The story's answer: only the socialist road is the bright road.

Wave upon Wave by Pi Wan and Chung Tao is set in the northeast countryside just before and during the cultural revolution. The Tiehling production brigade, led by Party secretary Hung Chang-ling and young army veteran Fang Liang, follows Chairman Mao's teachings and works to mechanize its farming with its own efforts.

Deputy county Party secretary Kuo Huai, on the other hand, a representative of the bourgeoisie who has wormed his way into the Party, is against the peasants getting their own machines, claiming they would not know how to operate them, that they should wait their turn for the state to give them big modern machines. When Hung opposes him, he dismisses Hung from his post. Backed by the county Party secretary, Hung stands up to the blow. In the cultural revolution which has just begun, he defeats the revisionist line and wins the struggle. Having deepened their understanding of class struggle and the two-line struggle during the cultural revolution, the people of Tiehling brigade move toward a new phase in the socialist revolution and construction. *Wave upon Wave* vividly shows that the cultural revolution was "absolutely necessary and most timely."

The Seething Mountains by Li Yun-teh re-creates the complex struggle of the workers of the Kuyingling Iron Mines in northeast China, liberated in 1948, to get them into production while the War of Liberation is still going on in the rest of the country. Should it be done by relying on the working class and their own efforts or by depending on a small number of specialists and imported equipment? This is the focus of the struggle between the proletariat and the bourgeoisie in industrial construction. The mine Party leadership, believing in the policy of self-reliance, leads the workers in a two-pronged struggle: against remnants of the Kuomintang armed forces and hidden enemy agents on the one hand, against the bourgeois line in construction, conservative thinking and the backward force of habit on the other. Surmounting barrier after barrier, the miners restore production in less than a year.

Morning Sun on the River, a 470,000-word novel that has gone through seven printings in two years, portrays with rich flowing language the indefatigable spirit of Chen Hua, a veteran of revolutionary wars who still carries bullet scars on his body. In his new job as Party secretary of a production team on a state farm, he makes a deep study of Marxism-Leninism-Mao Tse-tung Thought and boldly fights revisionist tendencies, the idea of private ownership and outdated traditional views.

The Heroes

The new novels have created a gallery of heroes active in China's socialist revolution and construction.

Sung Tieh-pao in *Spring Comes in with Whirling Snow*, by Chou Liang-szu, is a representative of the industrial workers. A young leader of a tunnelling team in an iron mine, he is a fine example of the new generation of the working class with a deep awareness of class struggle and the two-line struggle.

Chung Wei-hua in *The Long Trek*, by Kuo Hsien-hung, is a middle school graduate from Shanghai who has been steeled and tempered in the cultural revolution. When Chairman Mao says, "It is highly necessary for young people with education to go to the countryside to be re-educated by the poor and lower-middle peasants," Chung goes and settles down in a production brigade in the border province of Heilungkiang. Helped by the peasants, he matures in the three great revolutionary movements of class struggle, the struggle for production and scientific experiment.

Once Chung Wei-hua joins in a fight to protect a bridge during a flash flood. He sticks to his post on a scaffolding and drives down the last pile. As the scaffolding is about to be swept away by the flood, he unbuckles his life belt and gives it to a comrade. Battling in the roaring current, the thought of his vow to dedicate his life to the revolution gives him strength. Saved, he continues on the long trek of the revolution and matures into an able successor to carry on the cause of the proletariat. Millions of young readers, moved by Chung's ideology and deeds, have come to look upon him as an example to follow.

Author Cheng Chih in *The Battle at Nameless River* creates a hero of the Chinese People's Volunteers aiding Korea and fighting U. S. aggression—Kuo Tieh, a company commander in the railway corps. The U. S. imperialists try to destroy the Nameless River Bridge with heavy bombing. It is a strategic communications link on the Korean battlefield, and Kuo Tieh and his men, braving death, repair the bridge again and again to keep it open for military transport.

Out inspecting the rail line before the passage of 18 military freight trains, Kuo discovers that an enemy agent has removed the bolts on a rail joint plate in the middle of the bridge. Replacing two bolts with the only spares he has, he thrusts the pointed handle of his big wrench into the third bolt hole, and, clinging to the bridge structure, keeps the plate in place as the 18 trains speed over his head.

Kuo Tieh draws the strength for his selfless heroism from his proletarian internationalist spirit, his love for the Communist Party, Chairman Mao and the socialist motherland, and his deep understanding of Chairman Mao's revolutionary line.

Portraying representative workers, peasants and soldiers as they continue the revolution under the dictatorship of the proletariat is a basic task of proletarian literature. The new novels have done well in this task. There are Chung Wei-hua and Kuo Tieh described above. There is Kao Ta-chuan, a grass-roots cadre in *The Bright Road*. There is Chiao Kun in *The Seething Mountains,* who combats the bourgeois line, sticks to self-reliance and launches mass movements in industrial construction. These and the heroes in the other works all have their own clear-cut personalities, yet they also share some common essential characteristics: a deep awareness of the two-line struggle, a revolutionary spirit of going against the tide, and a firm determination to continue the revolution.

The Authors

The authors of the new novels come from different walks of life. Some are professional writers who have spent their lives among the workers, peasants or soldiers. Some are workers, peasants or soldiers with a world of practical experience, who with fresh language and subject matter have given China's literature a new militancy. In China the workers, peasants and soldiers are both the masters and the creators of literature.

Hao Jan, author of *The Bright Road,* comes from a peasant family in north China. He took part in the land reform and the struggle at every stage of agricultural cooperation. Later he was a rural cadre at the grass-roots for a long time and then a rural reporter. Now a professional writer, he still goes to a production brigade regularly and works in the fields with the peasants, keeping in close touch with the people and production. He also goes to factories, other rural areas and army units where he brings his study of Marxism-Leninism and Chairman Mao's works to bear on learning from society. This is a fruitful source for his writing.

Li Yun-teh, a worker who wrote *The Seething Mountains,* fought in the War of Liberation and after demobilization made his home in a mining town.

Before writing *The Long Trek,* Kuo Hsien-hung, once a bench worker, went to the Heilungkiang countryside and lived and worked with the Shanghai middle school graduates there.

Two factory workers, Li Liang-chieh and Hu Yun-chuan, are the authors of *The Contest,* a novel about the life and struggle in industry.

Chou Liang-szu, the author of *Spring Comes with the Whirling Snow,* is a worker in the Meishan Iron Mines in Kiangsu province. While writing the novel he got help and advice from a member of the mine leading group, a young technician and four veteran miners. After finishing each chapter, he read it to miners to collect their comments and criticism.

The Heroes of Tungpo is the story of how a brother and sister are reunited after long separation, told against the background of a PLA unit's battle to liberate the Tungpo area in east China. It is a collective work by people who took part in the struggle the novel is based on. Told over the radio in serial form, it was very popular with young listeners.

Wang Lei, a young man who went to the countryside after graduation from middle school, has written the story of such a group of graduates in *Waves of the Sword River.*

Hungnan's Fighting History, about the struggle between the two lines in the movement for agricultural cooperation in the countryside around Shanghai, is the product of three-way cooperation. It was written by a group of peasants with help from a commune Party leader and an editor from a publishing house. Such cooperation in novel writing, which appeared during the cultural revolution, has proved a good way to put Chairman Mao's revolutionary line in literature and art into practice. While a new book is being written, new writers are being trained. It is a correct orientation in developing socialist literature.

Never has Chinese literature been so close to the real life of the working people, never have there been so many workers, peasants and soldiers writing, never have novels been printed in such large editions. A number of the books were first issued in a trial edition distributed among workers, peasants and soldiers. Their comments and criticism were collected through forums to help the authors revise and improve their works. Press reviews give warm support to these new novels, encourage the authors to portray real-life struggle more intensely, point out shortcomings and raise questions for deeper study.

123. REVOLUTIONIZING HIGHER EDUCATION
[From "Educational Revolution in Tsinghua University," *China Pictorial,* April 1976]

Since the Great Proletarian Cultural Revolution, a vigorous revolutionary situation has emerged on China's educational front. In the past seven years of educational revolution since the working class took the university's leadership in 1968, Tsinghua University has undergone profound changes.

Tsinghua is a university of science and engineering with a history of 65 years. Before Liberation, under the control of imperialists and Kuomintang reactionaries, its teaching system, curricula, and teaching materials and methods were copied from the imperialist countries. After Liberation, Liu Shao-ch'i and his followers usurped power in educational circles and frenziedly pushed a counter-revolutionary revisionist line in education.

In the 17 years before the Cultural Revolution, the university's leadership was monopolized by bourgeois intellectuals. It was dominated by feudal, bourgeois and revisionist forces. Workers, peasants and soldiers were barred from the university. It carried out an educational system divorced from proletarian politics, from productive labor and from the workers and peasants. Under the evil influence of the old educational system, many young people were not concerned with the future of their motherland and mankind but only sought personal fame and gain and longed to become experts. Engineering students of the old Tsinghua did not know how to operate and repair machines; those who studied natural sciences were confined to classroom lectures. Some feared hardship and death and were unwilling to take the posts assigned to them by the Party and the state; some even degenerated into bourgeois Rightists.

During the Great Proletarian Cultural Revolution in response to Chairman Mao's call **"Education should be revolutionized,"** hundreds of millions launched a great movement unprecedented in the history of education. Chairman Mao pointed out: **"The working class must exercise leadership in everything."** Acting on this instruction, a Mao Tse-tung Thought Propaganda Team composed of Peking workers and PLA soldiers entered Tsinghua University on July 27, 1968. From then on the rule of the university by bourgeois intellectuals ended and the working class really took hold of the leadership.

As soon as the propaganda team moved into the university, they firmly implemented Chairman Mao's proletarian revolutionary line, armed the faculty members, students and workers with Marxism-Leninism-Mao Tse-tung Thought and led them in criticizing the revisionist line in education and waging the proletarian educational revolution. **"The leading role of the proletariat is realized through the leadership of the Communist Party."** In line with Chairman Mao's instructions on educational revolution Tsinghua University's Party committee in the past few years, taking class struggle as the key link and adhering to the Party's basic line, has made important reforms in the system of enrollment, the way of schooling and other aspects in order to bring up worthy successors to the revolutionary cause of the proletariat, and turn the university into an instrument of the dictatorship of the proletariat.

In accordance with Chairman Mao's directive that **"Students should be selected from among workers and peasants with practical experience,"** the university Party committee began enrolling students from the workers, peasants and soldiers in 1970. These are outstanding activists in the three great revolutionary movements of class struggle, the struggle for production and scientific experiment. They attend and manage the university with the spirit of masters and transform it with Marxism-Leninism-Mao Tse-tung Thought.

In line with Chairman Mao's teaching: **"In all of its work the school should aim at transforming the students' ideology,"** the university Party committee has given proper guidance to the students in taking class struggle as the main course and put emphasis on the ideological and political work among them. It organized the student body to systematically study basic Marxist concepts in close connection with important political struggles at home and abroad, and the Party's main tasks. Students take part in various political movements in factories, people's communes and PLA units, learning from the workers, peasants and soldiers. They take part in the class struggle on the educational front and carry out class education in various forms and organize education in revolutionary traditions and communist ideals so as to temper themselves in the struggle of combating and preventing revisionism.

"Education must serve proletarian politics and be combined with productive labor." In implementing this instruction of Chairman Mao, the university Party committee has in recent years led the faculty and student body in carrying out an open-door education program which links the university with factories, in running its own plants, in having the factories guide the school specialties, and in establishing a new "three-in-one" system which combines teaching, scientific research and production. The purpose is to develop new-type educated workers with socialist consciousness.

Open-door education is a fundamental transformation thoroughly breaking the domination of the schools by bourgeois intellectuals. In the past few years, large numbers of teachers and students of the university have gone to more than 100 factories, worksites, rural communes and PLA units, whole-heartedly relying on the working class in running educational institutions. They have striven to integrate themselves with the workers and peasants, take part in productive labor, and link theory with practice. In the course of open-door schooling, workers, peasants and soldiers have taken part in the leadership of the educational revolution and of key teaching links. Their direct participation is making education truly a matter of concern for all society. The teachers and students modestly learn good thinking and style and rich practical experience from the workers, peasants and PLA fighters. According to the needs of socialist revolution and construction they are transforming the old teaching system and establishing a new one.

Combining study with work proves an effective measure for integrating teachers and students with the workers and peasants, and mental with manual labor. In the past few years the university has made efforts to transform and build its own factories and laboratories. The students have taken part in this work. While **"The students' main task is to study, they should also learn other things."** In implementing this principle, their work is assigned according to the specialities they learn. The students do work-shifts fulfilling production quotas while taking specialized courses in connection with production. The workers work, take a study program and participate in the revolution in education. Some of them have quickly become worker-teachers. Teaching while working, the teachers have enhanced their ideological remolding and raised their professional level.

Open-door schooling and work-study programs have promoted a new "three-in-one" combination of teaching, scientific research and production. It links teaching and learning with typical and concrete projects. This enables the students to attain theoretical knowledge and practical experience and contribute their share to socialism. In the past few years the teachers and students of Tsinghua University have completed nearly 1000 items of production, scientific research problems and major technical innovations.

Teachers and students led by the university Party committee have also set up branches in the rural areas, help run workers' colleges in factories, and give various kinds of short-term training classes. The varied forms of schooling help bring greater, faster, better and more economical results in developing the proletarian cause of education, and closely combine study by the students with the mastery of knowledge by the working people.

Under the guidance of Chairman Mao's revolutionary line, the worker-peasant-soldier graduates are determined to go to the countryside and places where conditions are the harshest and the Party and the people need them most. Two groups of worker-peasant-soldier students graduated from Tsinghua University in 1974 and 1975 respectively. In their pre-graduation field-work they completed 564 items of research, production tasks and major technical innovations. One third of them reached advanced national standards or filled gaps in China's technology. The worker-peasant-soldier students' revolutionary outlook of a new generation and their accomplishments in pre-graduation fieldwork are infinitely superior to those of the Tsinghua graduates before the Cultural Revolution.

Last summer, a Right deviationist wind rose in the society. Its source was from that unrepentant capitalist roader in the Party [i.e., Teng Hsiao-p'ing]. A few persons in Tsinghua who clung to the revisionist line, echoing the absurd views of revisionism, attacked the educational revolution's orientation, claiming "it still has not been properly resolved." They wanted to reinstate the old system of the 17 years before the Cultural Revolution. This evil wind was aimed not only at nullifying the educational revolution but also the Cultural Revolution. It clamored for a change of the Party's basic line and the restoration of capitalism. With the concern of Chairman Mao and the Party Central Committee, the Tsinghua Party committee led the faculty, students and workers in waging a mass debate on educational revolution, mounting effective counter-attacks. They are determined to crush this evil wind and unswervingly carry the proletarian revolution in education through to the end along the path indicated by Chairman Mao.

124. HIGHER EDUCATION AND THE NEEDS OF SOCIETY
[From an Article in *People's Daily,* March 15, 1976][1]

How do [the critics of current educational policies] look at the situation of the educational revolution in the past few years? They say that since the great cultural revolution, the orientation of the educational revolution "has never been properly solved," that "the level of college education is even lower than that of the secondary technical schools in the past," and that "college students are far from being true college students." They vituperate that things are in a complete mess, with "metaphysics running wild on the educational front"

[1]Liang Hsiao, the pseudonymous author (or authors) of this article and a leading spokesman for the radical faction, was purged in late 1976.

and say that it is necessary for them to come out to "reverse" the situation and rectify the "deviation." . . .

What should be the fundamental nature of a school and what kind of people should it train? They openly forbid anyone to turn the school into a tool of the dictatorship of the proletariat and they tamper with Chairman Mao's educational policy. They disallow the criticism of such revisionist fallacies as "intellectual culture above all else," "private ownership of knowledge" and "studying in order to become officials," and are opposed to training workers with both socialist consciousness and culture. They say: "Why should one be afraid of a little bit of white expertise? We should cherish and praise such people." In their eyes, college students cannot be on an equal footing with workers and should become worker-aristocrats. They want to once again turn the school into a place for training bourgeois intellectual aristocrats or tools for restoring capitalism.

What is their attitude toward socialist new things on the educational front? They criticize and try their utmost to oppose the enrollment of students from among workers, peasants and soldiers with practical experience, and babble about "selecting and sending good middle school students directly to college." They attack the attendance, the management and the transformation of universities by worker-peasant-soldier students, and claim that "this has been overdone." They slander open-door education as "only creating a labor force." . . .

Who should lead the school after all? They criticize that leadership over educational work in the past few years leaves much to be desired, and advocate that "there must be laymen who are enthusiasts for science to exercise leadership." They vainly attempt to negate the political leadership of the working class and to enable the bourgeoisie to usurp once again leadership in educational departments.

What is the main danger on the educational front at present? They deny that revisionism is still the main danger today and advocate time and again that "in recent years the greatest crisis is that students don't study," in a vain attempt to use the "vocational typhoon" to sweep away the key link of class struggle and abolish the important fighting task of combating and guarding against revisionism on the educational front. . . .

The great proletarian revolution and the revolution in education initiated and led by Chairman Mao himself have, with the force of a thunderbolt, **"turned the world upside down"** in the educational battlefield dominated by the exploiting classes generation after generation. In this great revolution, a new proletarian educational system is being established step by step through various experiments. Socialist new things have emerged in an endless stream on the educational front. Never before have the proletarians, the makers of history, charted with their own heavily callused hands, the course for the training of the younger generation. School doors are open to the workers and peasants. Education is closely linked with the practice of the three great revolutionary movements. Filled with revolutionary pride, group after group of graduates from colleges and middle schools have gone to the countryside and frontierlands to places where life is hardest and to fighting posts where they are needed by the Party and the people to resolutely take the road of

integration with the workers and peasants. What an inspiring scene this
is! . . .

Millions of workers, peasants, soldiers and revolutionary teachers and students are greatly elated over this excellent situation, but those who whipped
up the Right-deviation wind to reverse verdicts rampantly attack it as wrong
in every respect. They babble that "the quality of education has been lowered"
and that "the four modernizations are held back." . . .

The great cultural revolution put an end to the domination of our school
by bourgeois intellectuals, and with the working class occupying the school
and beginning to exercise all-round dictatorship over the bourgeoisie in the
field of education, the thorough implementation of Chairman Mao's revolutionary line is effectively guaranteed. Shouldering the great trust of the class,
the worker-peasant-soldier students attend and manage universities and transform the universities with Marxism-Leninism-Mao Tse-tung Thought, thus
becoming a new political force of the proletariat on the educational front.
Open-door education puts the teachers and students as well as all kinds of
work in school under the supervision and solicitude of the broad masses of
workers, peasants and soldiers, thus greatly increasing the strength of the
proletariat in transforming the educational battlefront. Under the leadership
of the working class, and re-educated by the workers, peasants and soldiers,
the faculties have raised their consciousness in transforming their world outlook. In the struggle to criticize the bourgeoisie, profound changes are made
in teaching materials, teaching methods and school systems. The balance of
class forces on the educational battlefield has also undergone a great change
in favor of the proletariat. . . .

The proletariat is charged with the unprecedented task of transforming the
old world, and is required to eliminate all class differences and **"create conditions which made it impossible for the bourgeoisie to exist or to emerge again."**
This can only be accomplished by relying on the people of many generations
to persist in continuing the revolution under the dictatorship of the proletariat
for a long period. In order to transform the world, the most important thing
is to transform and educate people, because the transformation of the world
depends on people. Therefore the proletariat must occupy the educational
battlefield, take it as an important aspect in exercising dictatorship over the
bourgeoisie, and use it to disseminate the proletarian world outlook, criticize
the bourgeois and revisionist ideologies, and train generation after generation
of revolutionary successors who can persist in fighting for the dictatorship of
the proletariat and the realization of communism. . . .

The concoctors of the absurd arguments in educational circles allege that
we have not all-sidedly implemented the Party's educational principles as
though they are the most "all-sided." This is only the use of the tactic of
eclectic sophistry to deceive people. They tamper with the Party's educational
policies, are opposed to putting socialist awareness in the first place and to
training common laborers, consider "having culture" as the main thing, and
wildly advocate "putting intellectual culture above all else." . . .

They criticize that proletarian education "does not emphasize the study of
culture," which actually means that present-day students do not study as many

books as in the old schools. In their opinion, studying Marxist revolutionary theory, doing well in the main course of class struggle, criticizing and transforming the old-style schools, conducting open-door education and linking the learning of culture and scientific knowledge useful to the socialist revolution and construction with reality are not counted as studying culture, but are "excessive impositions" and "not devoting oneself to one's proper vocation." . . .

They hold that the task of a university is only to train cadres and scientists, and allege that since the universities at present "train workers and peasants only, they can be dispensed with." They openly oppose criticism of "studying in order to become officials" and training of ordinary workers. This reveals . . . that the so-called "cadres" and "scientists" they want to train are none other than those bourgeois spiritual aristocrats who take "knowledge" as capital to lord it over the workers and peasants. . . .

A mass debate on the revolution in education is being vigorously carried out throughout the country. No progress can be made in the revolution in education unless we resolutely hit back at the rabid attacks launched by the unrepentant capitalist roaders within the Party against Chairman Mao's revolutionary line. So long as there is still class struggle, the bourgeoisie and its representatives within the Party will still make use of this educational battlefield to serve their purpose of restoring capitalism. . . .

125. TWO DEFINITIONS OF THE PROBLEMS OF CHINESE SOCIETY
[From "Teng Hsiao-p'ing's Total Betrayal of Marxism," Red Flag, May 1976]

The theory of the dictatorship of the proletariat is the quintessence of Marxism and the most important content of scientific socialism. To uphold or to oppose the dictatorship of the proletariat has always been the focus of the struggle between Marxism and revisionism.

Teng Hsiao-p'ing is a renegade to the dictatorship of the proletariat. He denied class struggle in socialist society, opposed the proletariat exercising all-round dictatorship over the bourgeoisie, and vainly attempted to subvert the dictatorship of the proletariat and restore capitalism. Thus he completely betrayed the Marxist theory of the dictatorship of the proletariat. . . .

. . . As far back as 1949, Chairman Mao pointed out that after the seizure of political power throughout the country, the principal contradiction at home was one between the proletariat and the bourgeoisie. After the socialist transformation of the ownership of the means of production was in the main completed, Chairman Mao has, in a series of works and instructions, repeatedly set forth the views: Throughout the historical period of socialism, there are still classes, class contradictions and class struggle, and the principal contradiction is that between the proletariat and the bourgeoisie. He has also

formulated the basic line of our Party to persist in the dictatorship of the
proletariat and prevent the restoration of capitalism. . . . Recently, he further
pointed out: **"You are making the socialist revolution, and yet don't know
where the bourgeoisie is. It is right in the Communist Party—those in power
taking the capitalist road. The capitalist-roaders are still on the capitalist
road."** . . .

Revisionists invariably allege that after the basic completion of the socialist
transformation of the ownership of the means of production, the revolution in
the relations of production and in the superstructure is also accomplished and
that, after this transformation, the primary and even the only task is to develop
the productive forces. Teng Hsiao-p'ing is a stubborn trumpeter of this theory
of productive forces. As early as 1956, he and Liu Shao-ch'i advocated that
the principal contradiction at home was "the contradiction between the advanced socialist system and the backward social productive forces," that "the
future task is construction as the task of revolution has in the main been
completed." Last year, Teng Hsiao-p'ing once again trotted out the theory of
productive forces to serve as the theoretical basis of his revisionist line. . . . His
real aim was to sweep away the movement for the study of the theory of the
dictatorship of the proletariat in order to protect bourgeois right and safeguard
the economic base on which the bourgeoisie and especially the bourgeoisie
within the Party rely for existence.

The theory of productive forces denies in a fundamental way that in socialist
society there are still contradictions between the relations of production and
the productive forces and between the superstructure and the economic base,
that among the various factors of productive forces, it is people, not things,
that are decisive. Therefore, it denies that the only way to develop the productive forces is to take class struggle as the key link, persist in putting proletarian
politics in command, deepen the socialist revolution and persevere in mobilizing and relying on the masses. It turns a blind eye to the fact that there are
still birthmarks of capitalism in the socialist relations of production, that there
are two possibilities for the development of the socialist relations of production, namely, if the proletariat does not persevere in continuing the revolution
and does not restrict bourgeois right nor struggle against the bourgeoisie, then
not only will socialism be unable to move on to communism but it will
degenerate into capitalism. It is therefore clear that if Teng Hsiao-p'ing's
theory of productive forces were followed, the already established socialist
relations of production would surely be wrecked and those things in the
relations of production which differ very little from those of the old society
would be retained forever and continuously expanded. In this way, capitalism
and new bourgeois elements would emerge at a more rapid pace from the soil
of bourgeois right, laying the social base for capitalist restoration.

One of Teng Hsiao-p'ing's favorite remarks was: "It doesn't matter whether
it is a white cat or a black cat, any cat that catches mice is a good cat." This
serves better than many long articles to reveal more clearly the revisionist
nature of the theory of productive forces. In criticizing Teng Hsiao-p'ing,
Chairman Mao has pointed out: **"This person does not grasp class struggle;
he has never referred to this key link. His theme still is 'white cat, black cat,'
making no distinction between imperialism and Marxism."** Teng Hsiao-p'ing

regarded revisionist and imperialist trash as treasures. In his eyes, material incentives, putting profits in command, servility to things foreign, the doctrine of trailing behind others at a snail's pace were things which he could not part with for a moment. If his revisionist line were followed, it would be impossible to develop socialist production. Only socialism and only Marxism-Leninism-Mao Tse-tung Thought can save China. This has been proven by history and reality. . . .

Teng Hsiao-p'ing's aim in advocating material incentives was to further strengthen and expand bourgeois right. The theory of material incentives is an important viewpoint of revisionist political economy. The Soviet revisionist clique has always used it to protect their special privileges and legalize their wanton appropriation and exploitation of the Soviet proletariat's fruits of labor; at the same time, it inculcates decadent ideas of bourgeois selfishness in the minds of the laboring people so as to blunt their revolutionary will and make them willingly submit themselves to oppression and exploitation. . . . In socialist society, the class basis and economic conditions for engendering revisionism still exist. In advocating material incentives, Teng Hsiao-p'ing was safeguarding and expanding the economic conditions for engendering revisionism. This is diametrically opposed to the interests of the workers, peasants, revolutionary cadres and revolutionary intellectuals. Chairman Mao has said: **Politics is the commander, the soul. "Political work is the life-blood of all economic work."** Our experience in the past two decades and more has proven that only by adhering to the principle of putting proletarian politics in command can the socialist enthusiasm of the masses be really aroused, and only in this way can they be guided to advance along the socialist road. Going in for material incentives will only lead to the expansion of bourgeois right and foster the concept of private ownership, and the result would be departing further and further from socialism and going nearer and nearer to capitalism. The reality in the Soviet Union is a mirror. In that country, material incentives are all pervasive, resulting in the enrichment of a handful of bureaucrat-monopoly capitalists and the increasing poverty of the laboring people. Isn't it crystal clear which class benefits and which class suffers from material incentives, and whether it is Marxism or revisionism? Teng Hsiao-p'ing's clinging to material incentives shows precisely that he is a revisionist who has betrayed Marxism.

126. OUTLINE FOR A NEW FUTURE

[From Hua Kuo-feng's Speech at the Second National Conference on Learning from Tachai in Agriculture, December 25, 1976]

Comrades!

Nineteen seventy-six will soon be over and 1977 is fast approaching. Comrades are all interested in the situation of the country and the tasks ahead. Here

I would like to review briefly the fighting course we have traversed in 1976 and outline our fighting tasks for 1977.

Nineteen seventy-six has been a most extraordinary year in the history of our Party and of the dictatorship of the proletariat in China. It has been a year in which the whole Party, the whole Army, and the people of all nationalities throughout the country have stood rigorous tests, a year in which we have won a great historic victory. This year the proletariat has waged a fierce, momentous struggle against the bourgeoisie and crushed the anti-Party "Gang of Four" of Wang Hung-wen, Chang Ch'un-ch'iao, Chiang Ch'ing, and Yao Wen-yüan. As a result, a major retrogression and split has been averted in China and we can continue to push the proletarian revolutionary cause forward in the direction pointed out by Chairman Mao. . . .

This year saw the passing of our most esteemed and beloved Great Leader and Teacher, Chairman Mao Tse-tung, the great founder of our Party, our Army, and our People's Republic, who had led our Party and people in valiant struggles for more than half a century; and the passing of Chairman Mao's long-tested and close comrades-in-arms, our esteemed and beloved Premier, Chou En-lai, and Chairman Chu Teh of the Standing Committee of the National People's Congress. Vice-Chairman of the Party Central Committee, K'ang Sheng, and Vice-Chairman of the N. P. C. Standing Committee, Tung Pi-wu, also died last year.

The successive passing in so short a time of so many great proletarian revolutionaries, who enjoyed high prestige among the people, undoubtedly brought enormous difficulties to the leadership of our Party Central Committee. The death of Chairman Mao in particular is an immeasurable loss to the whole Party, the whole Army, and the people of all our nationalities, and our grief defies description. . . .

It was at this time that the "Gang of Four," the Wang-Chang-Chiang-Yao anti-Party clique, perversely exploited the grave difficulty confronting the Party and the people and tried to usurp the supreme Party and state leadership, which was their long-cherished ambition. Before Chairman Mao's death, they went against a series of directives issued by Chairman Mao and the Party Central Committee, played their own game in the criticism of Teng Hsiao-p'ing, and thus caused great ideological and political confusion and enormous economic losses. After Chairman Mao's death, thinking their chance had come, they quickened the pace of their move to usurp the supreme Party and state leadership and mounted unprecedented wild attacks in an attempt to knock down the Party and the people. If their scheme had succeeded, it would have led to a great retrogression and split in our Party and country and touched off a major civil war; they would have directly capitulated to imperialism and social-imperialism, relying on the aggressors' bayonets to prop up their puppet throne, and there would have been both internal strife and foreign aggression. At that time we were faced with the very immediate danger of a capitalist restoration, a danger of our Party turning revisionist and our country changing its political color. For a time the skies over China were filled with tumultuous dark clouds. Such a grave situation had never arisen since the founding of our People's Republic and has rarely been seen in the history of our Party.

At that time class enemies at home and abroad were jubilant while our people, our comrades, and our foreign friends and comrades were gnawed by deep anxiety and concern over the destiny of our Party and state. Everybody was saying to himself: In the past, with Chairman Mao at the helm, we defied whatever difficulty or hazard was before us. Now that Chairman Mao has passed away, are we able to withstand the frenzied attacks of the Wang-Chang-Chiang-Yao Gang? What will become of China's future? Such anxiety and concern were fully understandable. However, the people are the makers of history and they have answered the question. In the acute and complex struggle between the two lines in 1976, particularly the decisive battle in October, our Party Central Committee adopted resolute measures and smashed with one blow the plot of the "Gang of Four" to usurp Party and state power. Under the leadership of the Party, our heroic people, our heroic Army, and the vast numbers of Party members and cadres displayed a high level of political consciousness and firm unity in this great struggle. As soon as the Party Central Committee gave the order, the broad masses rose in response and swung into action, and the issue was settled without firing a single shot or shedding a drop of blood. Armymen and people throughout the country were overjoyed and the situation was very stable. . . .

The struggle of our Party against the Wang-Chang-Chiang-Yao anti-Party clique is another major struggle between the two lines in the annals of our Party. The Wang-Chang-Chiang-Yao anti-Party clique is a bunch of ultra-rightists, and their counterrevolutionary revisionist line is an ultra-right line. They are ultra-rightists because they practice revisionism, create splits, and engage in intrigues and conspiracies under the cloak of Marxism, trying by hook or by crook to usurp the supreme leadership of the Party and the state, subvert the dictatorship of the proletariat, and restore capitalism. On the question of who are our enemies and who are our friends—which is of the first importance for the revolution—they have deliberately turned things upside down as to the relations between ourselves and the enemy in the historical period of socialism, decking themselves out as "Leftist" and "Revolutionaries" while regarding as the targets of the "revolution" the revolutionary leading cadres of the Party, government, and Army at all levels who uphold Marxism. They have thus adulterated the very essence of Chairman Mao's great theory of continuing the revolution under the dictatorship of the proletariat.

The Great Leader Chairman Mao summed up the positive and the negative experience of our country as well as of the international communist movement and, by using the Marxist-Leninist theory of the unity of opposites, made a penetrating analysis of class relations in the period of socialism and put forward the great theory of continuing the revolution under the dictatorship of the proletariat. For the first time in the history of the development of Marxism, he pointed out in clear-cut terms that, after the socialist transformation of the ownership of the means of production has in the main been completed and in the entire historical period of socialist society, there are still classes, class contradictions, and class struggle; there is the struggle between the socialist road and the capitalist road; and there is the danger of capitalist restoration. It is therefore essential to continue the revolution. Chairman Mao taught us: **You are making the socialist revolution and yet don't know where the bourgeoisie is. It is right in the Communist Party——those in power taking the capitalist road. The capitalist-roaders are still on the capitalist road. He also put forward the basic principles of Practice Marxism, and not revisionism; unite, and don't split; be open and aboveboard, and don't intrigue and conspire,**[1] which are our fundamental criteria for identifying capitalist-roaders in the Party. . . .

Comrades!

We have won a great historic victory in 1976. But we must not be complacent amidst the cheers of victory. We should continue to press forward. Our tasks ahead are both glorious and arduous. There will be all sorts of difficulties on our road of advance, particularly those resulting from prolonged interference and sabotage by the "Gang of Four" in the political, ideological, organizational, economic, and other spheres. Nevertheless we are fully confident that we can surmount them all. We must unswervingly follow Chairman Mao's proletarian revolutionary line and his various principles and policies, **remain modest, prudent and free from arrogance and rashness,** and in the coming year grasp class struggle as the key link and exert ourselves to win still greater victories.

What are the main fighting tasks for the whole Party, the whole Army, and the people of all nationalities throughout the country in 1977?

First, Deepen the Great Mass Movement to Expose and Criticize the "Gang of Four." This Is the Central Task for 1977.

To expose and criticize the "Gang of Four" is a great political revolution. In the past two months and more, there has been an upsurge in this mass movement, which has unfolded itself in all parts of the country. We should do still better next year. . . .

For a long time, with the mass media under their control, the "Gang of Four" spread a host of revisionist fallacies, trampled on the fundamental principles of Marxism, and tampered with and distorted Chairman Mao's proletarian revolutionary line and his principles and policies. Metaphysics ran wild and idealism went rampant. The gang represented many correct things as incorrect and vice versa, reversed right and wrong, confounded black and white, and caused confusion in people's thinking. It is imperative in the course of struggle to study Marxism-Leninism–Mao Tse-tung Thought conscientiously and let the masses themselves distinguish Marxism from revisionism and the correct line from the incorrect line. In industry, agriculture, commerce, education, military affairs, government and Party, it is essential to take the Party's basic line formulated by Chairman Mao as the guide; sum up

[1]These are the "Three Dos and Three Don'ts" to which Hua refers later in the speech.

through earnest investigations and study the positive and negative experience in the past as well as in the Great Proletarian Cultural Revolution; get clear about the specific line of work and specific principles, policies, and methods in each field; and constantly improve and perfect them in the course of practice so that the work in all these fields can advance faster along Chairman Mao's revolutionary line. It is essential to defend and develop the victories of the Great Proletarian Cultural Revolution; continue to do a good job in the revolution in the fields of education, literature and art, public health, and science and technology; do our work well for the educated youth going to the countryside; encourage new socialist things; restrict bourgeois right; and make sure that the task of consolidating the dictatorship of the proletariat is carried out in grassroots units.

In the struggle to expose and criticize the "Gang of Four," it is necessary to draw a strict distinction between the two types of contradictions of differing nature and to handle them correctly and carry out Party policy in earnest. Our contradiction with the "Gang of Four" is one between ourselves and the enemy. We must have a clear understanding of this. Those who followed the "Gang of Four" and made mistakes must be treated on the merit of each case. Among them only a few participated in their conspiracy, while the great majority erred because they had come under the ideological influence of the gang. Even those who participated in the conspiracy did so to varying extents. Whatever the extent, they are welcome once they make a clean breast of their part in the conspiracy before the Party and the people and draw a clear line between themselves and the "Gang of Four." The target of attack should be confined to the "Gang of Four" and the handful of their unrepentant sworn followers. As for those who erred under the gang's ideological influence, it is all the more necessary to stress the need to educate them, to help them distinguish between the correct and incorrect lines, and to recognize the contents, harmful consequences, and causes of their errors and the ways of rectifying them. . . . We must unite with all those that can be united, including those who wrongly opposed us, to fight together against the enemy.

Second, Strengthen Party Building. It Is Necessary to Carry out a Movement in Education in Marxist Ideology throughout the Party, Centering on Strengthening the Party's Unified Leadership and Democratic Centralism and the Promotion of tis Fine Style of Work, so as to Build up our Party Well.

The Party is the core force that leads everything. In complete betrayal of the basic principles of the "Three Dos and Three Don'ts," the "Gang of Four" practiced revisionism, created splits and engaged in intrigues and conspiracies to undermine and disintegrate the Party, and ganged up to pursue their selfish interests [chieh-pang ying-ssu] and usurp Party power. In the few places and units where they maintained tight control and did much damage, unified Party leadership was impaired, all principles of Party life were trampled underfoot, and the Party's fine style of work was sabotaged. New Party members were recruited in violation of the provisions in the Party Constitution, cadres were promoted in disregard of the five requirements put forward by Chairman Mao, and even bad elements were drawn into the Party and smuggled into leading bodies. Under the protection of the "Gang of Four," some brazenly asked for leading positions and grabbed power at every opportunity. They would stoop to anything for the selfish interests of themselves or their gang. This evil bourgeois trend was highly corrosive to our Party's organism and corruptive of the minds of our Party members. It was most harmful to the Party's fighting power and its relations with the masses. We must carry out extensive education among Party members so that they will truly realize the seriousness of the harm caused by the "Gang of Four" on the question of Party building. They will understand the fundamental principle that the Party is founded for the public interest [*li-tang wei-kung*], that the interests of the Party and the people are above everything else, and that ganging up to pursue selfish interests is not allowed. They will understand the Party rule that forbids the formation of any faction or secret group within the Party. They will understand the importance of unified Party leadership and Party discipline and the harm of anarchism. They will understand that Party members must uphold the proletarian Party spirit and oppose bourgeois factionalism. They will understand that Party cadres are all servants of the people and must in no case ask the Party and the people for higher posts and power. . . .

In drawing the lesson from Chang Kuo-t'ao's attempt to split the Party [in the mid-1930s], Chairman Mao pointed out: **"We must affirm anew the discipline of the Party, namely: (1) the individual is subordinate to the organization; (2) the minority is subordinate to the majority; (3) the lower level is subordinate to the higher level; and (4) the entire membership is subordinate to the Central Committee."** Today, in drawing the lesson from the attempt by the "Gang of Four" to usurp Party power by forming a small clique, we, too, must affirm the four democratic centralist principles of organization and discipline and ask all Party organizations and every Party member to strictly observe these principles in their actions and wage resolute struggles against all words and deeds that run counter to these principles. . . . We must improve democratic life within the Party and among the people in accordance with democratic centralist principles, let people air their views, let people criticize, allow the minority to reserve their differing views, and strive to create a political situation in which there are both centralism and democracy, both discipline and freedom, both unity of will and personal ease of mind and liveliness. . . .

It is highly necessary to carry out a Marxist ideological education movement throughout the Party in the struggle to criticize the "Gang of Four." Plans have been made at this conference for Party consolidation and rectification in the countryside. The Central Committee is going to launch a movement of Party consolidation and rectification throughout the Party at an opportune time next year. . . .

While strengthening Party building, we should strengthen the building of revolutionary committees at various levels in keeping with the developing situation. At an appropriate time next year, people's congresses should be held in the provinces, municipalities, and autonomous regions and, after full discussion and democratic consultation, comrades who meet the five requirements for worthy successors set forth by Chairman Mao, maintain close links with the masses, and have their genuine support should be elected into revolutionary committees, leading bodies composed of the old, the middle-aged, and the young, which should be enabled to play a more active role under the centralized leadership of the Party.

Third, Deepen the Mass Movements of "In Agriculture, Learn from Tachai" and "In Industry, Learn from Taching," and Strive to Push the National Economy Forward.

Revolution means liberating the productive forces. The great revolution that has smashed the "Gang of Four" has done away with a bane that disrupted the productive forces and obstructed their growth. The revolutionary enthusiasm of the worker and peasant masses long suppressed by the "Gang of Four" is bursting forth. And prospects are very bright for a rapid development of our national economy. We must implement in real earnest the strategic concept **"Be prepared against war, be prepared against natural disasters, and do everything for the people,"** and the principle **"Take agriculture as the foundation and industry as the leading factor,"** bring into full play the initiative of both central and local authorities, mobilize the masses, make determined and maximum efforts first to run agriculture well and also to run light industry well and organize the market well. Meanwhile, we must do a good job in transport and communications and in heavy industries that produce fuel, electricity, petro-chemicals, iron and steel, and other raw and semifinished materials, so as to ensure the smooth operation of industry as a whole. We must launch a major drive to increase production and practice economy, step up technical innovations, tap production potential, lower costs, improve the quality of products, raise labor productivity, increase accumulation, give full scope to the production capacity of existing enterprises, and bring about an upsurge in grasping revolution and promoting production. . . .

The tasks of learning from Tachai in agriculture and building more Tachai-type counties and of agricultural mechanization have been discussed and set at the present conference, and the whole Party must make serious efforts to fulfill them. . . . Chairman Mao held up Tachai and Taching as two red banners, but the "Gang of Four" vainly attempted to cut them down. We must hold them high. Learning from Tachai and Taching means persevering in taking class struggle as the key link and thoroughly exposing and repudiating the "Gang of Four." It means implementing Chairman Mao's instruction that **management itself is a matter of socialist education,** building leading bodies that adhere to Chairman Mao's revolutionary line and maintain a militant unity so that leadership is truly in the hands of the Marxists and the workers and the poor and lower-middle peasants. It means doing ideological and political work conscientiously and effectively, strengthening the revolutionary unity of the working class and the poor and lower-middle peasants and revolutionizing our ranks. It means launching mass movements energetically, bringing into full play the enthusiasm, wisdom, and creativeness of the cadres and masses, unfolding socialist-emulation campaigns, and building socialism in a big way. Whether in industry or in agriculture, or in any other economic undertakings, we must follow the policy of building our country, running all our enterprises diligently and thriftily, relying on the masses, systematizing rational rules and regulations, and improving and strengthening socialist economic management. We should encourage people to raise their cultural and technical levels for the sake of the revolution and to acquire proficiency in their work so as to be both red and expert. Leading comrades at all levels must persistently take part in collective productive labor, and eat, live, and work together with workers and peasants. We must pay attention to the well-being of the masses and raise the living standard of the people step by step on the basis of increased production.

It is one of the fundamental tasks for the dictatorship of the proletariat to develop the socialist economy energetically. On condition that the socialist orientation is adhered to and proletarian politics is put in command, the more and the faster production develops, the better. By labeling this as the "theory of productive forces," the "Gang of Four" distorted Marxism and vilified the workers, peasants, and other working people. As early as 1957 Chairman Mao pointed out that only when the social productive forces were fairly adequately developed could our socialist economic and political system be considered to have acquired its own fairly adequate material foundation. In his report on government work to the Fourth National People's Congress in 1975, Premier Chou En-lai reiterated the grand plan Chairman Mao mapped out for our country to accomplish the comprehensive modernization of agriculture, industry, national defense, and science and technology and to bring our national economy to the front ranks in the world before the end of the century, and pointed out that the decade between 1976 and 1985 would be decisive for the realization of this plan. Now a year has passed. It is chiefly owing to interference and disruption by the "Gang of Four" that the achievements of our national economy this year are not as great as they should have been. . . . The work in 1977 has a vital bearing on the situation of the subsequent eight years. We must exert ourselves, **maintain independence, keep the initiative in our own hands, and rely on our own efforts,** and strive to make outstanding achievements in all fields.

Fourth, Make Further Efforts to Bring about a New High Tide in the Mass Movement to Study the Works of Marx, Engels, Lenin, and Stalin and Chairman Mao's Works.

"We need Marxism in our struggle." Whether in thoroughly exposing and criticizing the "Gang of Four," or in successfully building the Party, or in pushing the national economy forward, we must study conscientiously and well the works of Marx, Engels, Lenin, and Stalin and Chairman Mao's works and the theory of the dictatorship of the proletariat, and use Marxism-Leninism–Mao Tse-tung Thought to guide our struggle and command our work. . . .

In the course of conscientiously studying the works of Marx, Engels, Lenin, and Stalin and Chairman Mao's works and penetratingly criticizing the "Gang of Four," our whole Party, from the Central Committee down to local Party organizations, from departments in charge of ideological work to all other departments, must effectively grasp theoretical work. In order to guide such complex struggles, a Party as large as ours must grasp theoretical work well. For the present, too, we must do theoretical work well in order to clear up the political and ideological confusion caused by the "Gang of Four." . . .

Comrades!

The internal situation at present is excellent. Our great leader and teacher Chairman Mao said: **"Great disorder across the land leads to great order."** By disorder Chairman Mao meant disorder among the enemy. What the "Gang of Four" did was to create disorder in the Party, in the Army, and among the people. Now that we have thrown the "Gang of Four" into disorder and toppled them in revolution, we will certainly be able, in the course of the acute struggle between the two classes, to achieve **stability and unity** in our country, consolidate the dictatorship of the proletariat, and bring about great order across the land. . . .

We are determined to carry out Chairman Mao's behests, to take upon our shoulders the cause of proletarian revolution bequeathed to us by him, and to carry it through to the end.

We are determined to win victory. We can certainly win victory. Let us, the 800 million people and the more than 30 million Party members, unite and wage a common struggle to win still greater victories!

Sources

CHAPTER ONE

1. E. Backhouse and J. O. P. Bland, *Annals and Memoirs of the Court of Peking* (London: Heinemann, 1914), pp. 322–34.
2. Harley Farnsworth MacNair, ed., *Modern Chinese History: Selected Readings* (Shanghai: Commercial Press, 1923), pp. 175–78.
3. Ibid., pp. 182–83, 187.
4. Thomas Taylor Meadows, *Desultory Notes on the Government and People of China and on the Chinese Language* (London: Wm. H. Allen & Co., 1847), pp. 228–35.
5. Ssu-yü Teng and John K. Fairbank, eds., *China's Response to the West* (Cambridge, Mass.: Harvard University Press, 1954), p. 28.
6. MacNair, op. cit., pp. 16–17.
7. Hosea Ballou Morse, *The International Relations of the Chinese Empire* (London: Longmans Green, 1910–18), III, 670–73.
8. Ibid., III, 684–85.

CHAPTER TWO

9. Franz Michael, in collaboration with Chung-li Chang, eds., *The Taiping Rebellion: History and Documents* (Seattle: University of Washington Press, 1966–71), II, 144–49.
10. Ibid., II, 370–73.
11. Ibid., II, 312–20.
12. Ibid., II, 388–91.
13. Ibid., II, 163–67.
14. Tseng Kuo-fan, *Tseng Wen-cheng kung ch'üan-chi* (Taipei: Shih-chieh shu-chü, 1952), VIII, 147–49.

CHAPTER THREE

15. Feng Kuei-fen, *Chiao-pin lu k'ang-yi*, 1897 ed., pp. 67a–69b.
16. Ibid., pp. 58a–62b.
17. Li Hung-chang, *Li Wen-chung kung ch'üan-chi* (Taipei: Wen-hai ch'u-pan-she, 1965), I, 110–11.
18. *Ch'ou-pan yi-wu shih-mo: T'ung-chih*, 25:4–10.
19. Li, *op. cit.*, V, 11.
20. Hsüeh Fu-ch'eng, *Yung-an ch'üan-chi*, 1888 ed., 12:46b–49a.

CHAPTER FOUR

21. Chou Chen-fu, ed., *Yen Fu shih-wen-chi* (Peking: Jen-min wen-hsueh ch'u-pan-she, 1959), pp. 14, 26, 31–32.
22. Wm. Theodore de Bary, ed., *Sources of Chinese Tradition* (New York: Columbia University Press, 1960), pp. 733–35.
23. Chien Po-tsan et al., eds., *Wu-hsü pien-fa* (Shanghai: Jen-min ch'u-pan-she, 1957), III, 33–34.
24. Ibid., III, 321–22.
25. Ibid., III, 111–13.
26. Ibid., III, 160.
27. Su Yü, ed., *Yi-chiao ts'ung-pien*, 1898, 5:3b.
28. Wang Hsien-ch'ien, *Hsü-shou-t'ang shu-cha*, 1907 ed., 2:73–74.
29. de Bary, op. cit., pp. 750–53.
30. Li Yu-ning and Chang Yü-fa, eds., *Chin-tai Chung-kuo nü-ch'üan yün-tung shih-liao* (Taipei: Chuan-chi wen-hsüeh she, 1975), I, 562–66.
31. de Bary, op. cit., pp. 744–49.

CHAPTER FIVE

32. Justus Doolittle, *Social Life of the Chinese* (New York: Harper and Brothers, 1865), I, 299–300, and J. Macgowan, *Sidelights on Chinese Life* (London: Kegan Paul, Trench, Trübner and Co., 1970), pp. 185–88.
33. Edward Alsworth Ross, *The Changing Chinese* (New York: The Century Co., 1911), p. 133.
34. Macgowan, op. cit., pp. 272–84, 295, and Doolittle, op. cit., I, 321–22.
35. Ross, op. cit., pp. 120–22.
36. M. Huc, *The Chinese Empire* (London: Longman, Brown, Green, and Longmans, 1855), I, 96–97.
37. Arthur H. Smith, *Chinese Characteristics*, 2nd ed. (New York: Fleming H. Revell Co., 1894), pp. 113–14.
38. Arthur H. Smith, *Village Life in China* (New York: Fleming H. Revell Co., 1899), pp. 39–42.
39. R. F. Johnston, *Lion and Dragon in Northern China* (New York: E. P. Dutton and Co., 1910), pp. 135–48.
40. Ross, op. cit., pp. 90–91, 127–28.
41. Huc, op. cit., I, 248–52; II, 233–34, 347–48.

42. Ibid., II, 283–85.

CHAPTER SIX

43. Huang Chi-lu, ed., *Ko-ming jen-wu-chih* (Taipei, 1968), IV, 483.
44. Chang Yü-fa, ed., *Wan-Ch'ing ko-ming wen-hsüeh* (Taipei: Hsin-chih tsa-chih, 1972), pp. 3, 7–8, 46–48.
45. Tsou Jung, *Ko-ming Chün* (Shanghai: Chung-hua shu-chü, 1958), pp. 1–2, 29–32, 36–37.
46. Teng and Fairbank, op. cit., pp. 227–29.
47. *Chung-kuo pai-hua-pao*, No. 1 (Kuang-hsü 29/11/1).
48. Liang Ch'i-ch'ao, *Yin-ping-shih ch'üan-chi* (Taipei: Wen-hua t'u-shu kung-ssu, 1967), pp. 1, 6–7, 12–16.
49. Ibid., pp. 270–74.

CHAPTER SEVEN

50. Louis Magrath King, *China in Turmoil: Studies in Personality* (London: Heath Cranton, Ltd., 1927), pp. 15–24.
51. Nora Waln, *The House of Exile* (Boston: Little, Brown and Co., 1933), pp. 25–28.
52. Shen Ts'ung-wen, *Ts'ung-wen tzu-chuan* (Hong Kong: Wen-li ch'u-pan-she, 1960), pp. 72–81.
53. Paul S. Reinsch, *An American Diplomat in China* (New York: Doubleday Page and Co., 1922), pp. 347–48.
54. Mary Ninde Gamewell, *The Gateway to China: Pictures of Shanghai* (New York: Fleming H. Revell Co., 1916), pp. 161–70.
55. Ibid., pp. 223–25.

CHAPTER EIGHT

56. Ch'en Tu-hsiu, *Tu-hsiu wen-ts'un* (Hong Kong: Yüan-tung t'u-shu kung-ssu, 1965), I, 49–62.
57. de Bary, op. cit., pp. 815–18.
58. *Hsin Ch'ing-nien*, December 1919.
59. Teng and Fairbank, op. cit., pp. 252–55.
60. Sun Ch'ang-wei, ed., *Ts'ai Yüan-p'ei hsien-sheng ch'üan-chi* (Taipei: Shang-wu yin-shu-kuan, 1968), pp. 638–39.
61. Ibid., pp. 208–9.
62. Hu Shih, *Hu Shih hsüan-chi* yen-shuo (Taipei: wen-hsing shu-tien, 1966), pp. 37–40.
63. Li Ta-chao, *Li Ta-chao hsüan-chi* (Peking: Jen-min ch'u-pan-she, 1962), p. 463.
64. Yang Hsien-yi and Gladys Yang, trans., *Selected Stories of Lu Hsun* (Peking: Foreign Languages Press, 1960), pp. 1–5.
65. Ch'ü Ch'iu-pai, *Ch'ü Ch'iu-pai wen chi* (Peking: Jen-min wen-hsüeh-she, 1954), I, 164–66.
66. Lao She, *Lao She hsiao-shuo-hsüan* (Hong Kong: Ta-t'ung shu-chü, 1961), pp. 26–28.

67. Chu Tzu-ch'ing, *Chu Tzu-ch'ing ch'üan-chi* (Tainan: Ta-tung shu-chü, n. d.), pp. 127–29.

CHAPTER NINE

68. Li Chien-nung, *The Political History of China, 1840–1928*, trans. by Ssu-yü Teng and Jeremy Ingalls (Princeton, N. J.: D. Van Nostrand Co., 1956), pp. 450–56.
69. Ch'en T'ien-hsi, ed., *Tai Chi-t'ao hsien-sheng wen-ts'un tsai-hsü-pien* (Taipei: Shang-wu yin-shu-kuan, 1968), II, 437–40.
70. Ibid., II, 481–82.
71. C. M. Chang, "A New Government for Rural China: The Political Aspect of Rural Reconstruction," *Nankai Social and Economic Quarterly*, Vol. 9, no. 2 (July 1936), pp. 266–94.
72. H. D. Fong, *Cotton Industry and Trade in China* (Tientsin: Nankai Institute of Economics, 1932), Industry Series, Bulletin No. 4, II, 317–20.
73. Fei Hsiao-t'ung, *Hsiang-t'u Chung-kuo* (Shanghai: Kuan-ch'a-she, 1948), pp. 22–31.

CHAPTER TEN

74. Mao Tse-tung, *Selected Works of Mao Tse-tung* (Peking: Foreign Languages Press, 1967), I, 23–33, 44–46.
75. Liu Shao-ch'i, *How to Be a Good Communist* (Peking: Foreign Languages Press, 1951).
76. *China Reconstructs*, Vol. 24, no. 8 (August 1975), p. 18.
77. James Bertram, *Unconquered: Journal of a Year's Adventures among the Fighting Peasants of North China* (New York: John Day, 1939), pp. 138–39.
78. Mao Tse-tung, *Mao Tse-tung on Literature and Art* (Peking: Foreign Languages Press, 1960), pp. 85–111.

CHAPTER ELEVEN

Note: The following abbreviations are used for Part III:

CB—Current Background (U. S. Consulate General, Hong Kong)
FLP—Foreign Languages Press (Peking)
JPRS—U. S. Joint Publications Research Service
NCNA—New China News Agency
PR—Peking Review
SCMM—Survey of China Mainland Magazines (U. S. Consulate General, Hong Kong)
SCMP—Survey of China Mainland Press (U. S. Consulate General, Hong Kong)
SPRCP—Survey of People's Republic of China Press (U. S. Consulate General, Hong Kong)

79. Mao Tse-tung, op. cit., IV, 411–22.
80. Mao Tse-tung, *On the Correct Handling of Contradictions Among the People* (Peking: FLP, 1959).
81. SCMP no. 1550, June 14, 1957, p. 12; SCMP no. 1575, July 23, 1957, pp. 8–9; SCMP no. 1574, July 22, 1957, pp. 8–10; CB no. 470, July 26, 1957, pp. 48–51; SCMP no. 1581, July 31, 1957, p. 1.
82. JPRS no. 7273, January 19. 1961, pp. 27–30, 34–43, 61–62, 117–18.

CHAPTER TWELVE

83. *The Marriage Law of the People's Republic of China* (Peking: FLP, 1959), pp. 1–10.
84. *The Agrarian Reform Law of the People's Republic of China Together with Other Relevant Documents* (Peking: FLP, 1950), pp. 79–97.
85. Ting Ling, *The Sun Shines over the Sangkan River*, trans. by Yang Hsien-yi and Gladys Yang (Peking: FLP, 1954), pp. 285–94.
86. Mao Tse-tung, *The Question of Agricultural Cooperation* (Peking: FLP, 1956).
87. *Socialist Upsurge in China's Countryside* (Peking: FLP, 1957), pp. 302–3.
88. SCMP no. 1531, May 16, 1957, pp. 2–7.
89. *People's Communes in China* (Peking: FLP, 1958), pp. 18–25.
90. SCMP no. 1875, October 15, 1958, pp. 32–33.
91. Ibid., pp. 28–30.
92. CB no. 538, December 12, 1958, pp. 12–13.
93. SCMP no. 1887, November 3, 1958, pp. 9–13.
94. *600 Million Build Industry* (Peking: FLP, 1958), pp. 91–100.
95. CB no. 595, October 5, 1959, pp. 19–21.

CHAPTER THIRTEEN

96. SCMP no 2699, March 16, 1962, pp. 3–5.
97. SCMP no. 3001, June 18, 1963, pp. 8–12.
98. SCMM no. 429, August 10, 1964, pp. 30–31.
99. JPRS no. 28,987, March 3, 1965, pp. 10–13.
100. JPRS no. 29,480, April 7, 1965, pp. 81–82; also in SCMP no. 3374, January 11, 1965, pp. 17–18.
101. JPRS no. 18,344, March 25, 1963, pp. 12–23; *Lei Feng jih-chi* (Peking: Chieh-fang-chün wen-yi she, 1963).
102. SCMP no. 3370, January 5, 1965, pp. 23–24.
103. SCMP no. 3185, March 24, 1964, p. 14; SCMP no. 3145, January 23, 1964, p. 16; SCMP no. 3185, March 24, 1964, pp. 15–16; SCMP no. 3383, January 22, 1965, pp. 15–16; SCMM no. 460, March 15, 1965, pp. 26–28.
104. CB no. 757, March 10, 1965, pp. 1–6; SCMM no. 458, March 1, 1965, pp. 16–18; SCMP no. 3517, March 13, 1965, pp. 1–6.
105. SCMM no. 504, December 28, 1965, pp. 15–17.
106. JPRS no. 21,645, October 29, 1963, pp. 22–26.

CHAPTER FOURTEEN

107. JPRS no. 34,372, March 3, 1966, pp. 12–16.
108. CB no. 891, October 8, 1969, pp. 56–57.
109. PR, June 24, 1966, pp. 18–19.
110. *Decision of the Central Committee of the Chinese Communist Party Concerning the Great Proletarian Cultural Revolution* (Peking: FLP, 1966).
111. PR, September 2, 1966, pp. 17–18.
112. *On the Proletarian Revolutionaries' Struggle to Seize Power* (Peking: FLP, 1968), pp. 1–13.
113. PR, April 5, 1968, pp. 6–7.
114. NCNA release, August 26, 1967, pp. 18–20.
115. PR, November 8, 1968, pp. 9–11.
116. SCMP no. 4290, November 1, 1968, pp. 17–21.
117. PR, December 20, 1968, pp. 12–13.
118. PR, November 22, 1968, p. 12.
119. PR, December 20, 1968, p. 15.

CHAPTER FIFTEEN

120. PR, September 3, 1971, pp. 4–7.
121. SCMP, no. 5250, November 7, 1972, pp. 69–71.
122. *China Reconstructs*, Vol. 24, no. 5 (May 1975), pp. 27–29.
123. *China Pictorial*, no. 334, (April 1976), pp. 4–9.
124. SPRCP no. 6063, March 26, 1976, pp. 218–26.
125. PR, June 4, 1976, pp. 13–18.
126. Hsinhua News Agency, Peking, December 27, 1976.

Selected
Bibliography

A brief list of some of the more useful general books on modern China, with emphasis on broad surveys and documentary collections.

Boorman, Howard L., ed. *Biographical Dictionary of Republican China.* 4 vols. New York: Columbia University Press, 1967–71.

*Bianco, Lucien. *Origins of the Chinese Revolution, 1915–1949.* Trans. Muriel Bell. Stanford: Stanford University Press, 1971.

*Brandt, Conrad, Benjamin Schwartz, and John K. Fairbank, eds. *A Documentary History of Chinese Communism.* Cambridge: Harvard University Press, 1952. Atheneum paperback, 1966.

*Chow, Tse-tsung. *The May Fourth Movement: Intellectual Revolution in Modern China.* Cambridge: Harvard University Press, 1960. Stanford paperback, 1967.

*Clubb, O. Edmund. *Twentieth Century China.* Second ed. New York: Columbia University Press, 1972.

*de Bary, Wm. T., et al., eds. *Sources of Chinese Tradition.* New York: Columbia University Press, 1960.

*Fairbank, John King. *The United States and China.* Third ed. Cambridge: Harvard University Press, 1971.

———, Edwin O. Reischauer, and Albert M. Craig. *East Asia: The Modern Transformation.* Boston: Houghton Mifflin, 1965.

*Gasster, Michael. *China's Struggle to Modernize.* New York: Knopf, 1972.

*Harrison, James Pinckney. *The Long March to Power: A History of the Chinese Communist Party, 1921–1972.* New York: Praeger, 1972.

*Hinton, William. *Fanshen.* New York: Monthly Review Press, 1966. Vintage paperback, 1968.

Ho, Kan-chih. *A History of the Modern Chinese Revolution.* Peking: Foreign Languages Press, 1959.

*Available in paperback, from same publisher unless otherwise noted.

*Houn, Franklin W. *A Short History of Chinese Communism.* Second ed. Englewood Cliffs, N. J.: Prentice-Hall, 1973.

Hsü, Immanuel C. Y. *The Rise of Modern China.* Second ed. New York: Oxford University Press, 1975.

*Hsüeh, Chün-tu, ed. *Revolutionary Leaders of Modern China.* New York: Oxford University Press, 1971.

Hummel, Arthur W., ed. *Eminent Chinese of the Ch'ing Period.* 2 vols. Washington: U. S. Government Printing Office, 1943.

Jen, Yu-wen. *The Taiping Revolutionary Movement.* New Haven: Yale University Press, 1973.

Klein, Donald W. and Anne B. Clark. *Biographic Dictionary of Chinese Communism, 1921–1965.* 2 vols. Cambridge: Harvard University Press, 1971.

*Li, Dun J., ed. and trans. *China in Transition: 1517–1911.* New York: Van Nostrand Reinhold, 1970.

*———. *The Road to Communism: China Since 1912.* New York: Van Nostrand Reinhold, 1969.

MacNair, Harley Farnsworth, ed. *Modern Chinese History: Selected Readings.* Shanghai: Commercial Press, 1923. Paragon reprint, 1967.

Michael, Franz and George E. Taylor. *The Far East in the Modern World.* Third ed. Hinsdale, Ill.: The Dryden Press, 1975.

*Pellisier, Roger, ed. *The Awakening of China, 1793–1949.* Ed. and trans. Martin Kieffer. New York: G. P. Putnam's Sons, 1967.

*Pruitt, Ida. *A Daughter of Han: The Autobiography of a Chinese Working Woman.* New Haven: Yale University Press, 1945. Reissued by Stanford University Press, 1967.

*Schram, Stuart. *Mao Tse-tung.* Baltimore: Penguin, 1967.

*Schurmann, Franz and Orville Schell, eds. *The China Reader.* Vols. I–III. New York: Random House, 1967.

*Schurmann, Franz, David Milton, and Nancy Milton, eds. *The China Reader.* Vol. IV. New York: Random House, 1974.

*Seymour, James D. *China: The Politics of Revolutionary Reintegration.* New York: Thomas Y. Crowell, 1976.

Sheridan, James E. *China in Disintegration: The Republican Era in Chinese History, 1912–1949.* New York: The Free Press, 1975.

*Teng, Ssu-yü and John K. Fairbank, eds. *China's Response to the West: A Documentary Survey, 1839–1923.* Cambridge: Harvard University Press, 1954. Atheneum paperback, 1963.

*Townsend, James R. *Politics in China.* Boston: Little, Brown, 1974.

Wakeman, Frederic Jr. *The Fall of Imperial China.* New York: The Free Press, 1975.

Wilbur, C. Martin. *Sun Yat-sen: Frustrated Patriot.* New York: Columbia University Press, 1976.

*Wright, Mary C., ed. *China in Revolution: The First Phase, 1900–1913.* New Haven: Yale University Press, 1968.

Wu, Yuan-li, ed. *China: A Handbook.* New York: Praeger, 1973.